ALSO BY DAVID E. CAMPBELL

Why We Vote: How Schools and Communities Shape Our Civic Life

A Matter of Faith: Religion in the 2004 Presidential Election (editor)

Charters, Vouchers, and Public Education
(editor, with Paul E. Peterson)

72-73 generational change
80 argument in brief re worship attendance
ch. 3. generational, life cycle, social change
232-33 This book is about religious people –
individuals – not about religious
organizations.

ALSO BY ROBERT D. PUTNAM

Better Together: Restoring the American Community
(with Lewis M. Feldstein)

*Democracies in Flux: The Evolution of Social Capital
in Contemporary Society* (editor)

Bowling Alone: The Collapse and Revival of American Community

Disaffected Democracies: What's Troubling the Trilateral Countries?
(edited with Susan J. Pharr)

Making Democracy Work: Civic Traditions in Modern Italy
(with Robert Leonardi and Raffaella Y. Nanetti)

Double-Edged Diplomacy: International Bargaining and Domestic Politics
(edited with Peter B. Evans and Harold K. Jacobson)

Hanging Together: Conflict and Cooperation in the Seven-Power Summits
(with Nicholas Bayne)

Bureaucrats and Politicians in Western Democracies
(with Joel D. Aberbach and Bert A. Rockman)

The Comparative Study of Political Elites

*The Beliefs of Politicians: Ideology, Conflict,
and Democracy in Britain and Italy*

AMERICAN GRACE

How Religion Divides and Unites Us

❖

Robert D. Putnam
David E. Campbell

with the assistance of
Shaylyn Romney Garrett

Simon & Schuster
NEW YORK • LONDON • TORONTO • SYDNEY

Simon & Schuster
1230 Avenue of the Americas
New York, NY 10020

First Simon & Schuster hardcover edition October 2010

SIMON & SCHUSTER and colophon are registered trademarks
of Simon & Schuster, Inc.

For information about special discounts for bulk purchases,
please contact Simon & Schuster Special Sales at
1-866-506-1949 or business@simonandschuster.com.

The Simon & Schuster Speakers Bureau can bring authors
to your live event. For more information or to book an event,
contact the Simon & Schuster Speakers Bureau at
1-866-248-3049 or visit our website at www.simonspeakers.com.

Text designed by Paul Dippolito

Manufactured in the United States of America

1   3   5   7   9   10   8   6   4   2

Library of Congress Cataloging-in-Publication Data

Putnam, Robert D.
American grace : how religion divides and unites us /
by Robert D. Putnam and David E. Campbell
p.   cm.
Includes bibliographical references (p.   ) and index.
1. United States—Religion—1960–   2. Religion and sociology—
United States.   I. Campbell, David E., 1971–   II. Title.
BL2525.P88   2010
201'.7097309045—dc22   2010027838
ISBN 978-1-4165-6671-7
ISBN 978-1-4165-6688-5 (ebook)

To Kirsten, Katie, and Soren and
To Miriam, Gray, Gabriel, Noah, Alonso, and Gideon
Who grace our lives with their love

CONTENTS

AMERICAN
GRACE

CHAPTER 1

RELIGIOUS POLARIZATION
AND PLURALISM
IN AMERICA

In the 1950s, the Fraternal Order of Eagles teamed up with movie director Cecil B. DeMille for a unique promotion of the epic movie *The Ten Commandments*. In a form of reverse product placement, the Eagles and DeMille donated monuments of the biblical Ten Commandments to communities all around the country. Rather than putting a product in the movie, the primary symbol of the movie was instead placed in prominent locations—in public parks, in front of courthouses, and in the case of Texas on the grounds of the state capitol. These monuments reflected the zeitgeist, as the 1950s brought public, even government-sanctioned, expression of religion to the fore in many ways. This was also the decade in which "In God We Trust" was added to American currency, and the Pledge of Allegiance was amended to include the words "under God."

Those monuments stood for decades without causing a fuss. In recent years, however, they have led to court battles over whether their location on publicly owned land violates the constitutional prohibition on a government establishment of religion. In other words, fifty years ago these displays were so noncontroversial that they could safely be used as a marketing ploy for a big-budget Hol-

1

lywood movie. Now they are the subject of litigation all the way to the Supreme Court.[1]

Something has changed.

In 1960, presidential candidate John F. Kennedy had to reassure Protestants that they could safely vote for a Catholic. (At the time 30 percent of Americans freely told pollsters that they would not vote for a Catholic as president.) At the same time, Kennedy won *Daddy* overwhelming support from his fellow Catholics, even though he explicitly disagreed with his church on a number of public issues. In 2004, America had another Catholic presidential candidate—also a Democratic senator from Massachusetts, also a highly decorated veteran, and also with the initials JFK. Like Kennedy, John (Forbes) Kerry also publicly disagreed with his church on at least one prominent issue—in this case, abortion. But unlike Kennedy, Kerry split the Catholic vote with his Republican opponent, and lost handily among Catholics who frequently attend church. Kennedy would likely have found it inexplicable that Kerry not only lost to a Protestant, but in George W. Bush, an evangelical Protestant at that. Writing about the religious tensions manifested in the 1960 campaign, political scientist Philip Converse described the election as a "flash of lightning which illuminated, but only momentarily, a darkened landscape."[2] Kerry's candidacy was another flash of lightning, but the landscape it revealed had changed significantly. In 1960, religion's role in politics was mostly a matter of something akin to tribal loyalty—Catholics and Protestants each supported their own. In order to win, Kennedy had to shatter the stained glass ceiling that had kept Catholics out of national elective office in a Protestant-majority nation. By the 2000s, how religious a person is had become more important as a political dividing line than which denomination he or she belonged to. Church-attending evangelicals and Catholics (and other religious groups too) have found common political cause. Voters who are not religious have also found common cause with one another, but on the opposite end of the political spectrum.

Again, something has changed.

This book is about what has changed in American religion over the past half century. Perhaps the most noticeable shift is how Americans have become polarized along religious lines. Americans are increasingly concentrated at opposite ends of the religious spectrum—the highly religious at one pole, and the avowedly secular at the other. The moderate religious middle is shrinking. Contrast today's religious landscape with America in the decades following the Second World War, when moderate—or mainline—religion was booming. In the past, there were religious tensions, but they were largely between religions (Catholic vs. Protestant most notably), rather than between the religious and irreligious. Today, America remains, on average, a highly religious nation, but that average obscures a growing secular swath of the population.

[*margin annotation:* We *(religious left)* don't even register on this spectrum.]

The nation's religious polarization has not been an inexorable process of smoothly unfolding change. Rather, it has resulted from three seismic societal shocks, the first of which was the sexually libertine 1960s. This tumultuous period then produced a prudish aftershock of growth in conservative religion, especially evangelicalism, and an even more pronounced cultural presence for American evangelicals, most noticeably in the political arena. As theological and political conservatism began to converge, religiously inflected issues emerged on the national political agenda, and "religion" became increasingly associated with the Republican Party. The first aftershock was followed by an opposite reaction, a second aftershock, which is still reverberating. A growing number of Americans, especially young people, have come to disavow religion. For many, their aversion to religion is rooted in unease with the association between religion and conservative politics. If religion equals Republican, then they have decided that religion is not for them.

Religious polarization has consequences beyond the religious realm, because being at one pole or the other correlates strongly with one's worldview, especially attitudes relating to such intimate matters as sex and the family. Given that American politics often centers on sex and family issues, this religious polarization has been especially visible in partisan politics. A "coalition of the religious" tends to vote one way, while Americans who are not religious vote another.

The current state of religious polarization has led social commentators to use heated, even hyperbolic, language to describe the state of American society. The bestseller lists are full of books highly critical of religion, countered by pundits whose rhetoric decries a public square made "naked" by religion's absence.[3] In an overused metaphor, America is supposedly in the midst of a war over our culture.[4]

And yet, when one ignores these venomous exchanges, and looks instead at how Americans of different religious backgrounds interact, the United States hardly seems like a house divided against itself. America peacefully combines a high degree of religious devotion with tremendous religious diversity—including growing ranks of the nonreligious. Americans have a high degree of tolerance for those of (most) other religions, including those without any religion in their lives.

Religion's role in America thus poses a puzzle. *How can religious pluralism coexist with religious polarization?*

The answer lies in the fact that, in America, religion is highly fluid. The conditions producing that fluidity are a signal feature of the nation's constitutional infrastructure. The very first words of the Bill of Rights guarantee that Congress—later interpreted to mean any level of government—will favor no particular religion, while ensuring that Americans can freely exercise their religious beliefs. In the legal arena, debates over such matters as whether the Ten Commandments can be displayed on public property hinge on the interpretation of the Constitution's words. More broadly, the absence of a state-run religious monopoly combined with a wide sphere of religious liberty has produced an ideal environment for a thriving religious ecosystem. Religions compete, adapt, and evolve as individual Americans freely move from one congregation to another, and even from one religion to another. In the United States, it seems perfectly natural to refer to one's religion as a "preference" instead of as a fixed characteristic.

This state of flux has actually contributed to religious polarization. A fluid religious environment enables people seeking something different to leave one religion for another, to find religion for the first time, or to leave religion altogether. This churn means that people gradually, but continually, sort themselves into like-minded clusters—their commonality defined not only by religion, but also by the social and political beliefs that go along with their religion.

The malleable nature of American religion, however, means that these clusters are not bunkers. Instead, the same fluidity that contributes to religious polarization means that nearly all Americans are acquainted with people of a different religious background. Even if you personally have never gone through a religious change, you likely know someone who has. Furthermore, that someone is likely to be more than a passing acquaintance, but rather a co-worker, a close friend, a spouse, or a child. All of this religious churn produces a jumble of relationships among people of varying religious backgrounds, often within extended families and even households, which keeps religious polarization from pulling the nation apart.

The contrast between John F. Kennedy in 1960 and John Kerry in 2004 is thus doubly revealing. It not only highlights the new ways that religion divides American society but, more subtly, it also reminds us that old divisions are largely forgotten. In 1960, Kennedy faced overt hostility to his Catholicism, even in polite company. We find it no coincidence that this was also a time when there were many social barriers to relationships between Catholics and Protestants. John Kerry ran in a different world. By 2004 his Catholicism presented no problems for Protestants. We again find it hardly coincidental that in the years between Kennedy and Kerry, Americans of many different religious backgrounds increasingly came to connect with one another—as neighbors, friends, and spouses. That electoral flash of lightning in 2004 thus illuminated more than the changed political topography; it also exposed an altered social landscape. Interreligious personal connections have resulted in a social web interwoven with different religions and people with no religion at all—with implications far beyond presidential politics.

Over the last fifty years, American religion has thus experienced two countervailing transformations. The first is the emergence of a new religious fault line in American society. Left on its own, such a fault line could split open and tear the nation apart. The second change, however, is precisely why the fault line has not become a gaping chasm. Polarization has not been accompanied by religious segregation—either literally or even metaphorically. To the contrary, rather than cocooning into isolated religious communities, Americans have become increasingly likely to work with, live alongside, and marry people of other religions—or people with no religion at all. In doing so, they have come to accept people with a religious background different from theirs. It is difficult to demonize the religion, or lack of religion, of people you know and, especially, those you love. Indeed, interreligious relationships are so common that most Americans probably pay them little mind, and consider them unremarkable. But their very commonness makes them remarkable indeed.

Polarization and pluralism are the principal themes in the recent history of American religion, but they hardly exhaust all that has changed, is changing, and will change in the nation's religious environment. The sheer vitality of religion in America means that it is ever evolving, although that evolution takes place against a backdrop of some constants too. We begin by asking how and why American religion became polarized, and close by asking—and answering— how polarization and pluralism can coexist. But to get from polarization to peaceful pluralism, we consider a number of other questions along the way:

To what extent do Americans engage in religious mixing and matching?

Which religions win, and which lose, in the religious marketplace? Historically, who have been the winners, and who the losers?

What keeps people in their congregations, and why do they switch from one to another? How have religious entrepreneurs

*responded to the second aftershock, which is pushing people—
young people especially—away from religion?*

*How has religion engaged three major trends in American society:
the revolution in women's rights, rising income inequality, and
growing ethnic and racial diversity?*

*What happened to cause religious devotion to be so strongly asso-
ciated with partisan politics, and what will the future likely hold
for the connections between religion and politics?*

*How does politics happen, or not, inside a congregation? How
can religiosity be so closely associated with partisan politics when
overt politicking from the pulpit is rare?*

*Who is right: those who make the case for the positive contri-
bution of religion to civil society, or those who make the case
against?*

BACKDROP

Any discussion of religion in America must begin with the incontro-
vertible fact that Americans are a highly religious people. One can
quibble over just how religion, and religiosity, should be gauged, but,
by any standard, the United States (as a whole) is a religious nation.
In general, Americans have high rates of religious *belonging, behaving,*
and *believing*—what social scientists call the three Bs of religiosity.[5]
Eighty-three percent of Americans report belonging to a religion;
40 percent report attending religious services nearly every week or
more;[6] 59 percent pray at least weekly; a third report reading scripture with this same frequency. Many Americans also have firm religious beliefs. Eighty percent are absolutely sure that there is a God.
Sixty percent are absolutely sure that there is a heaven, although
fewer (52 percent) have this level of certainty about life after death.
Slightly fewer, 49 percent, are certain that there is a hell.

Yet it is also important to note that not every American is so religious, or religious at all. After all, 15 percent *never* attend religious services, 17 percent do *not* identify with a religion, 20 percent are *not* certain about the existence of God, 40 percent are *not* sure there is a heaven, and 48 percent are *not* certain there is life after death.

When we put these basic facts together, a picture of religion in America comes into focus. Americans overwhelmingly, albeit not universally, identify with a religion. Identity, however, does not necessarily translate into religious activity because not all who identify with a religion frequently attend religious services, or engage in other religious behavior. The vast majority of Americans also believe in God, but Americans are less sure about life beyond the grave. Ever an optimistic people, Americans are more likely to envision heaven than hell. In fact, more Americans are certain about heaven than are certain about life after death. When we probe further, we find that Americans believe in a God who is loving and not very judgmental. Sixty-two percent say they "very often" feel God's *love* in their life, while only 39 percent say that they feel God's *judgment* this frequently. Americans' God is more avuncular than angry, and it turns out (as we shall see in Chapter 13) that this sort of everyday theology has real implications for the ways in which Americans get along with one another. This is merely one example among many that we shall discuss in which Americans' religiosity and community connections are closely tied together.

By any objective standard, this profile shows the reasonably high religiosity of the United States. That profile appears even stronger when the United States is compared to the rest of the planet, especially other industrialized, democratic nations. The United States ranks far ahead of virtually all other developed nations in terms of all three Bs of religiosity. To take just one example, Figure 1.1 displays how the United States compares to the rest of the world in a measure of religious behavior, namely the weekly attendance of religious services. Indeed, in this global ranking of religious observance America edges out even the Iran of the ayatollahs.

The United States also has an equally high degree of belonging and believing. For instance, 38 percent of Americans report being an

Figure 1.1

COMPARED TO OTHER INDUSTRIALIZED NATIONS, THE U.S. HAS A HIGH RATE OF WEEKLY ATTENDANCE AT RELIGIOUS SERVICES

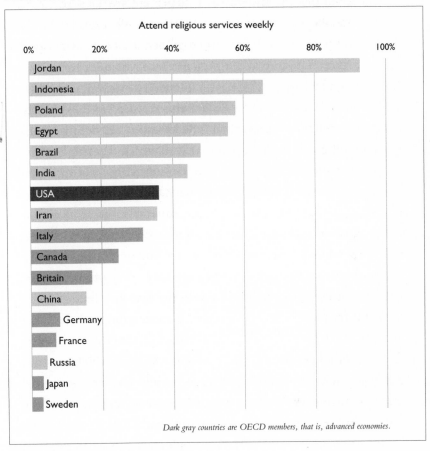

Dark gray countries are OECD members, that is, advanced economies.

SOURCE: WORLD VALUES SURVEY, 2005–2007.

active member of a church or religious organization, compared to only 16 percent of Australians, 9 percent of Italians, and 4 percent of the French. Likewise, while nearly half, 47 percent, of Americans affirm that religion is "very important" in their lives, only 17 percent of the Swiss, 12 percent of the Dutch, and 9 percent of Swedes say the same.[7]

Americans' high religiosity is thrown into especially sharp relief with a comparison to our close cultural cousins, the British. While 54 percent of the British say they never pray, only 18 percent of

Americans say the same. A third of Americans believe that scripture is the actual word of God, compared to only 9 percent of the British.[8]

One measure of Americans' religiosity illustrates particularly nicely how religion permeates the lives of many but is absent from those of others. Almost half (more precisely, 44 percent) of the American population reports saying grace or a blessing before meals at least daily, while almost precisely the same percentage (46 percent) says grace occasionally, or never.[9] (In this context, we use the Christian term "grace" as a shorthand for all prayers said before meals, in whatever religious tradition.) We are hard-pressed to think of many other behaviors that are so common among one half of the population and rare among the other half—maybe carrying a purse.

We single out grace saying because it turns out to be an excellent indicator of overall religiosity that, in turn, predicts many other attitudes and behaviors. For example, grace saying reappears in Chapter 11, where we show that the frequency of saying blessings before meals has a strong connection to one's partisan politics.

The Faith Matters Surveys

We can tell you about grace saying and many other aspects of religiosity in the United States because we have conducted extensive surveys of Americans in which we asked a wide-ranging set of questions about their religious lives, as well as their civic involvement, social relationships, political beliefs, economic situation, and demographic profile. The first survey was administered to a randomly selected, nationally representative sample of 3,108 Americans in the summer of 2006, and then followed up with a second, separate survey with as many of the same people as we could find (1,909, to be precise) in the spring and summer of 2007. Known as the Faith Matters surveys, together they constitute one of the most detailed examinations ever undertaken of Americans' religious and civic lives. As will become apparent, interviewing people more than once has turned out to be extremely valuable in understanding religious change. Because of the dynamism in American religion, even the short period of time that elapsed between the first and second interviews provides insights into small but significant shifts in various aspects of Americans' religious lives.[10] Throughout this book, we make repeated reference to the data collected in the two Faith Matters surveys. Usually we report on results from the 2006 survey, since it has a larger and more representative sample, and also included a more extensive set of questions. Whenever it is appropriate, however, we report results from the 2007 survey. In either case, we always identify the survey to which we are referring.

Throughout this book, we rely on the Faith Matters surveys heavily but not exclusively. The coin of our realm is convergent validation—that is, testing interpretations against as many sources of data as possible—so whenever possible, our key claims have been confirmed with the General Social Survey, the National Election Studies, the Pew Religion and Public Life surveys, and other comparable, publicly available sources of data. We have listened carefully to what the data have to say; the data are loudest when they speak in harmony.

Religious Traditions

Anyone who wishes to describe and then analyze the state of religion in America has to grapple with the fact that there are an enormous number of religious faiths, and myriad denominations and other subgroupings within those faiths. The aforementioned religious fluidity has meant schisms, mergers, the founding of new faiths, and the arrival of faiths from other nations. Take, for example, Lutheranism, an important group within Protestantism. Lutheranism is not monolithic. There are the Evangelical Lutheran Church in America (ELCA), the Missouri Synod Lutherans, the Wisconsin Synod Lutherans, and still other Lutheran denominations. While these denominations share common Lutheran DNA, as they all have Martin Luther as a progenitor, they nonetheless exhibit significant differences in worship, practice, and theology. And that is just the many varieties of Lutheranism. Multiply the same phenomenon across Presbyterians, Methodists, Baptists, Pentecostals, Jews, and so on and you begin to see the complexity of trying to discuss each denomination separately. Further complicating matters, there is also a growing trend toward Christian churches with no denominational label at all.

The situation, though, is not hopeless, as American religion can be usefully analyzed using a taxonomic system that, to paraphrase Albert Einstein, is as simple as possible, but no simpler. The huge array of denominations can be grouped into a more manageable number of *religious traditions*. To use a biological metaphor, religious traditions are like a genus, while the individual denominations are like species.

Evangelical, Mainline, and Black Protestants

Protestantism presents the greatest challenge to any system of religious morphology, as no other category better illustrates the mutability of religion in America. To return to biological taxonomy: If a religious tradition is a genus, then Protestantism is analogous to a religious family. Within that family there are three significant genera: evangelical, mainline, and Black Protestant.

Evangelical Protestants comprise one of the most significant religious traditions in America—particularly for understanding change in American religion. Historian Mark Noll notes that evangelicalism dates as far back as the early eighteenth century, when a movement began within Protestantism to find a "true religion of the heart." [11] Evangelicalism was the dominant strain within American Protestantism through most of the nineteenth century. Then, in the late 1800s and early 1900s, Protestants split over a debate between fundamentalists and modernists, a split that still echoes today. For our purposes, an evangelical Protestant is someone who, knowingly or not, has taken the fundamentalists' side in that debate. During this period, writes sociologist Christian Smith, Protestant churches increasingly adopted "liberal theology, biblical higher criticism, and an increased skepticism about supernaturalism." [12] The result was a parting of the ways between these questioning modernists and the fundamentalists, who held fast to a more traditional, and thus conservative, interpretation of scripture.

bib.
literalism?

While the fundamentalist–modernist debate raged within religious denominations, it also spilled over into American society more generally. One important rallying cry for the fundamentalists was a rejection of evolution as an explanation for the origin of man. The issue came to a head in 1925 with the famous Scopes Monkey Trial, over the question of whether evolution could be taught in the public schools of Tennessee. Few today remember that the fundamentalists won the battle in the courtroom, as the state's anti-evolution statute was upheld. Better remembered is that they lost the war of public opinion beyond the courtroom, as their beliefs were subjected to national ridicule. In the wake of this derision fundamentalists largely retreated from engagement with wider American society.

Fundamentalists began to reemerge from their self-imposed exile with the founding of the neo-evangelical movement in the wake of the Second World War. With Billy Graham as their most public face, the neo-evangelicals were moderates within the fundamentalist wing of Protestantism who sought to soften the hard edge of fundamentalism and reengage with American society. They maintained orthodox Protestant beliefs, but shed the anti-intellectualism and insularity that had come to characterize fundamentalists in the wake of their post-Scopes withdrawal. This new style of conservative Protestantism has become the norm, such that in public parlance the "neo" came to be dropped from their name. The term "evangelicalism" now encompasses all theologically conservative Protestants (except Black Protestantism, as explained below), whether they be Billy Graham–like neo-evangelicals, members of "seeker-sensitive" megachurches, traditional fundamentalists, or Pentecostals.[13]

Because they are an amorphous group defined by admittedly blurry boundaries, one can debate just who counts as an evangelical. The label is not necessarily one that people willingly adopt for themselves, even if their belonging, believing, and behaving all align with the standard scholarly usage of the term. This was brought home to us when we interviewed members of the Saddleback megachurch (see Chapter 2). We asked a number of people at this high-profile church, widely identified as quintessentially evangelical, how they described their religious affiliation. Overwhelmingly, they said "Christian," not "evangelical." Similarly, many people reasonably identify themselves as belonging to a specific denomination, like the Missouri Synod Lutherans, rather than a nebulous movement like evangelicalism.

The solution to this definitional ambiguity is to identify evangelicals by their congregation's denominational affiliation (or, as the case may be, the absence of such an affiliation).[14] Therefore, when we refer to "evangelicals," we mean people who report identifying with one of a large number of denominations that generally endorse the tenets of evangelicalism.[15] For our purposes, evangelicals also include people who attend a nondenominational church, since, in recent years, a large number of nondenominational churches are evangelically inclined (e.g., the typical megachurch is both evangelical and nondenominational).[16]

While evangelicals are the heirs to the fundamentalists, mainline Protestants are descendants of the modernists. Loosely speaking, mainline Protestant denominations are more liberal theologically than their evangelical counterparts. Importantly, they are more likely to emphasize the Social Gospel—that is, the belief that a Christian's priority should be the reform of social institutions—than personal piety. As described by political scientists Kenneth Wald and Allison Calhoun-Brown:

> Stressing Jesus's role as a prophet of social justice, the mainline tradition sanctifies altruism and regards selfishness as the cardinal sin. In this tradition, which extends membership to all and understands religious duty in terms of sharing abundance, the Bible is treated as a book with deep truths that have to be discerned amidst myth and archaic stories.[17]

The term "mainline" connotes that these are the denominations that have historically been the closest thing to establishment churches in America: the Episcopalians (the American branch of the Anglican Communion), for example, and the Congregationalists (successors to the Puritans).[18] By the 1950s, when our story opens, mainline Protestant denominations—Methodist, Lutheran, Presbyterian, Episcopalian, Congregationalist, and a few others—represented the dominant religious tradition in America, but as we shall see, that dominance would change dramatically in the ensuing half century.

While the split between evangelical and mainline Protestants centers on theology, Black Protestantism—the third tradition within the Protestant family—is instead defined by race. Black Protestantism is a legacy of racial segregation. As detailed in Chapter 9, the Black Church (the term used to refer to all historically African American congregations and denominations) has a long and distinctive history in the United States. Black Protestants generally blend an evangelical focus on personal piety with a strong dose of Social Gospel. Just as importantly, the Black Church is an inherently racialized institution—race is integral to Black Protestants' theology, iconography, and worship. The result is a unique religious tradition.[19]

Catholics, Jews, and Mormons

Of course, Protestantism does not exhaust the many varieties of religion in the United States. Catholics are also a major share of the religious population, but they are more easily recognized through self-identification, since their denomination, religious tradition, and self-identity are all one and the same. Catholics thus use the same label to describe themselves as do academics and other observers. You might say that Catholics know who they are.

Jews and Mormons[20] can also be easily recognized through self-identification. While they are each a much smaller share of the population than Protestants or Catholics, both are highly distinctive traditions that, because of their size, are often neglected in analyses of the American religious environment.[21]

"Other Faiths"

The sheer variety of American religious traditions means that, even after classifying most Americans into these religious traditions, there are still a small number of people spread across a wide array of different religions. These include Sikhs, Hindus, Buddhists, Muslims, and many more. Many of these other faiths are a growing presence on the American religious scene, having grown from roughly one percent in the 1970s to between 2 and 3 percent today. But being, at most, 3 percent of the population still means they collectively comprise a small proportion of the national population, with each individual group being smaller still. Since the Faith Matters survey was administered to a randomly selected representative sample of the United States, it contains the correct proportion of each group. . But the absolute number of these other faiths is too small to permit reliable analysis.[22] We are thus limited in what we can report about these disparate faiths.

No Religion / The "Nones"

The final category consists of people who report no religious affiliation, those who have come to be called the "nones."[23] That is, when asked to identify with a religion, they indicate that they are "nothing in particular." These nones are not necessarily hard-core secularists, as we shall discuss in Chapter 4. This category, though, does include that small fraction of the American population who describe themselves as either atheists or agnostics, although these labels turn out to have little common usage.[24] While atheism has recently gained prominence, particularly on the bestseller lists, self-identified atheists and agnostics comprise a vanishingly small proportion of the U.S. population. For instance, in the 2006 Faith Matters survey precisely five people out of 3,108 chose either label.

Figure 1.2 displays the percentage of the American population in each religious tradition, sorted from largest to smallest. The largest group are evangelicals, with roughly 30 percent of the U.S. population fitting that classification. While evangelicals grew in the 1970s and 1980s, their proportion of the population has been slowly declining since about 1990.

The single largest denomination is the Roman Catholic Church. Catholics comprise about a quarter of the U.S. population, a proportion that has remained steady for decades. However, as we dis-

Figure 1.2

RELIGIOUS TRADITIONS IN THE UNITED STATES

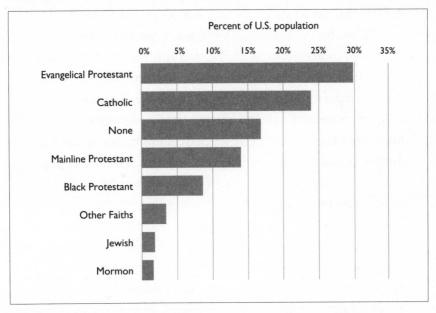

SOURCE: FAITH MATTERS SURVEY, 2006.

cuss in Chapter 9, Catholics' steady share of the population obscures a dramatic change within American Catholicism. Over the last few decades, large numbers of "Anglo"—that is, non-Latino—Catholics have been dropping out of or disengaging with the Catholic Church, without being replaced by other Anglo converts. During the same period, however, the number of Latino Catholics has grown tremendously. Given current trends, this demographic transformation means that the American Catholic Church is on its way to becoming a majority-Latino institution, as we discuss in Chapter 4.

The third largest "religious" group in the United States is actually defined by the absence of a religious affiliation—the "nones." There are more nones (17 percent) than mainline Protestants (14 percent), a striking fact given that the mainline wing of Protestantism once represented the heart and soul of American religion and society. Significantly, the ranks of the nones have been growing, while the mainline Protestants' share of the population has been shrinking.

Note also that Jews, one of the oldest religious traditions, rank right alongside Mormons, one of the newest (both are roughly 2 percent of the population).

Religiosity

Divvying up the population into religious traditions is only one way to make sense of the American religious landscape. Think of religious traditions as being like the "flavor" of one's religion. And just as flavors come in varying levels of intensity, so can religion. Religious intensity can also be referred to as "religiosity," and measured with a series of questions that tap into different ways of being religious, including both behaving and believing. In the next few pages we describe the way we measure religiosity in detail. Our discussion gets into statistical matters that some readers would probably prefer to skip over and this can be done without a loss of continuity. We provide this level of detail for the practical reason that religiosity is a recurring matter in the pages to follow. However, it also speaks to a fundamental question that goes right to the heart of any study of religion: What does it mean to be religious?

The specific questions we use to measure religiosity include the following:

- How frequently do you attend religious services?
- How frequently do you pray outside of religious services?
- How important is religion in your daily life?
- How important is your religion to your sense of who you are?
- Are you a strong believer in your religion?
- How strong is your belief in God?

Taken together, these questions run the gamut of ways that a person might be religious. They include the public activity of attending religious services, the (typically) more private activity of praying outside of religious services, the salience of religion in one's life, and how strongly someone believes in God.

We have combined these questions into a single measure called the "religiosity index," because when analyzing an overall concept they are more illuminating in combination than individually. Any single measure of religiosity, no matter how good, will inevitably misclassify a few people. Church attendance is, for example, an excellent measure of religious commitment in most cases, but for the elderly or infirm it can be misleading. Strength of belief in God is usually a good indicator, to take another example, but there are some exceptions. As St. Augustine said, "Doubt is but another element of faith," so for some deeply religious people, the absence of doubt is not the best measure of religious commitment. Combining multiple indicators, assuming that each of them is fairly accurate, produces an even more reliable overall measure, for the same reason that diversification improves the performance of a stock portfolio. In loose terms, the religiosity index is a weighted average of responses to these questions. Those that contribute more to the common thread holding them all together—in this case, religiosity—receive more weight. (For our statistically savvy readers: We have created a factor score of these six items.[25])

Since the nature of what it means to be religious is inevitably fraught with ambiguity and controversy, it is important to keep a few things in mind about this method of measuring religiosity. First, some readers may wonder whether, say, frequency of attendance at worship services (a public activity) really taps into the same concept as frequency of prayer (often done in private), and whether these two types of behaving really align with measures of belief like the existence of God. It is true that these index items are logically distinct, but in practice they are tightly bound together. Nearly all people (99 percent) who say that religion is very important in their lives are also "absolutely certain" that they believe in God; most people (79 percent) who attend religious services also pray at least once per day. And so on.

Second, keep in mind that this index does not rest on the inclusion or exclusion of any one particular item. For example, excluding how frequently someone prays does not change the substantive results contained herein one whit (likewise for any other individual item in the index). The fact that religiosity does not hinge on a single measure underscores that together these different questions are tapping into a common underlying concept.

Third, readers may wonder whether these particular questions favor one religious tradition over another. This is a common concern when social scientists study religion, as religiosity is sometimes measured with questions that are normative within Protestantism, specifically for evangelicals. Some such indices include items that ask whether the Bible is inerrant, or whether the respondent has ever been "born again." Such questions are as distinctively Protestant as keeping kosher is distinctively Jewish. Our religiosity index avoids the problem of parochialism by including only items that could apply to all religious traditions. Still, we acknowledge the concern that perhaps this particular religiosity index is inadvertently biased toward evangelical Protestantism, or some other religious tradition.

There is, however, a conundrum in trying to determine whether this, or any other, method of measuring religiosity favors one religious tradition. How would we tell whether it is biased toward one tradition? Because people in that tradition score more highly on it. But do members of that tradition show up as highly religious because of the idiosyncrasies of the index, or because—no matter the measure—they truly are more religious? We will see that evangelicals, Black Protestants, and Mormons all rank high on the religiosity index. Is that because the index is somehow rigged to pick up the particular ways that members of these three traditions live their religions? In this case, the validity of our religiosity index as a general purpose gauge is bolstered by the fact that the same index, with questions worded identically, shows Muslims in Britain to have an extremely high level of religiosity.[26] An index that is allegedly biased toward evangelical Protestants, Black Protestants, and Mormons in the United States could hardly also be biased toward Muslims in Britain.

A less formal but perhaps just as convincing test of this, or any other, way of empirically measuring religiosity is to ask whether it matches our intuitive sense of what it means to describe someone as religious. If you know someone who attends religious services frequently, prays often, has a strong belief in God, holds religion to be important, believes that religion defines her identity, and says that she strongly believes in her religion, would you not describe her as highly religious? And, likewise, would you describe someone who does *not* do or believe these same things as *not* being religious? That, perhaps, is the most convincing test of all.

While not the only possible way of measuring a concept as multifaceted as religiosity, the index is an empirically tractable, conceptually coherent, and intuitively compelling method of doing so. One important question that will recur in the following pages is this: Which matters more, the flavor of a person's religion or the intensity? Does a highly devout Catholic have more in common with, say, a lapsed Catholic or a devout Jew? The answer will vary, of course, but for some matters we will see that intensity actually matters more than flavor. In that sense religiosity itself (as distinct from membership in a particular denomination or sect) turns out to be increasingly important in contemporary America.

Comparing the Most and Least Religious Americans

Consider the religiosity index to be a measurement tool, like a thermometer. Using it enables comparisons between Americans of varying levels of religiosity. Putting the most religious Americans (those in the top 20 percent) next to the least religious (bottom 20 percent) reveals that, on some matters, they differ dramatically. On others, there are few differences at all.

The most and least religious Americans differ, for example, on how "spiritual" they consider themselves to be. While 4 percent of the least religious describe themselves as very spiritual, 80 percent of the most religious do. Among rank-and-file Americans spirituality and religiosity go hand in hand. Americans' attitudes on evolution are also sharply divided by religiosity. Less than 2 percent of the most religious Americans believe that "human beings have developed over millions of years from less advanced forms of life but God had no part in this process," compared to 45 percent of the least religious. Over three quarters of the most religious reject evolution altogether, and believe instead that God created human beings less than ten thousand years ago. Interestingly, this position is also held by 16 percent of the least religious.[27]

The most and least religious also differ on ways to spend their leisure time. Both casinos and R-rated movies are apparently more likely to be frequented by secular, not religious, Americans. Sixty-one percent of those at the top of the religiosity index say that gambling is always wrong, compared to only 10 percent of those at the bottom of the index. Roughly the same percentages also believe that it is always wrong to watch movies with "a lot of violence, profanity, or sexuality."[28] But this is not to say that religious and not-so-religious Americans could never find something to do together. Both are equally likely to participate in the two great American pastimes of watching sports and eating out.[29] And even if they stay in, they are about equally likely to watch television.[30]

When it comes to leisure activity of another sort, more and less religious Americans disagree sharply on the propriety of premarital sex. While 4 percent of the least religious portion of the population say that premarital sex is *always* wrong, only 3 percent of those in the top 20 percent of religiosity say that sex before marriage is *never* wrong.

Similarly, opinions on abortion vary substantially according to religiosity. Sixty-five percent of the least religious Americans believe in a woman's unfettered right to choose when it comes to abortion, a position held by only 13 percent of the most religious. Attitudes toward homosexuality differ dramatically as well. Nearly nine out of ten highly religious people say that homosexual activity is always wrong, in contrast with two out of ten of secular Americans. In Chapter 11, we shall see that both abortion and homosexuality have come to be especially salient in contemporary politics, which in turn has led to a religious divide at the ballot box.

Abortion and homosexuality have an unusually strong connection to religiosity. Smaller differences are seen on other matters. While just 6 percent of secular Americans believe that divorce is always wrong, 24 percent of the highly religious believe the same.

That is surely a nontrivial gap, but it also means that three quarters of religious Americans approve of divorce in at least some circumstances.

When it comes to the public policy question of how the government spends tax money, religious and nonreligious Americans are more alike than different. Majorities of both want to spend more on conservative issues like fighting crime and protecting the border, but majorities of both also support the liberal position of more spending to help the poor.[31]

AMERICANS' RELIGIOUS PROFILE

When we compare the religiosity of Americans to one another, interesting patterns appear. Take, for example, what happens when you map the flavor of religion (religious tradition) against intensity. Just as some flavors are more likely to be intense than others, so are members of some religious traditions more likely to be religiously intense than others. Figure 1.3 shows both flavor and intensity. The more intense flavors—the traditions that are more highly religious—are to the right of the line, while those that are less intense are to the left. The line itself represents the national average of religiosity.

Which religious tradition has the average level of intensity? Catholics, with mainline Protestants coming close. Not surprisingly, nones are the least religious group in the population. Jews are next, yet even though they fall below the average, they still score well above the nones. (Non-Jews may be surprised to find, as our synagogue visit described in Chapter 10 illustrates, that half of all self-identified Jews are not so sure they believe in God.) On the other side of the spectrum, the three most religious groups in America are Mormons, Black Protestants, and evangelicals, in that order. Their shared level of religious intensity means that members of these three traditions have much in common, although we shall see that they do not see eye-to-eye on everything.

Comparisons across religious traditions are merely one way to describe the religious landscape in America. In addition to asking

AMERICAN GRACE

Figure 1.3

MORMONS, BLACK PROTESTANTS, AND EVANGELICALS ARE THE MOST RELIGIOUSLY OBSERVANT GROUPS IN AMERICA
Religiosity is standardized with a mean of 0 and a standard deviation of 1

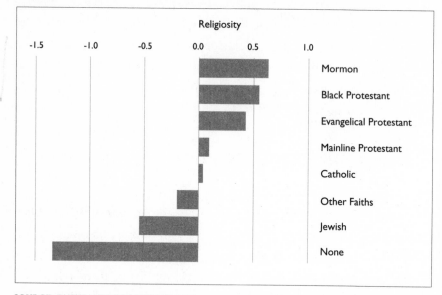

SOURCE: FAITH MATTERS SURVEY, 2006.

which religious traditions are most, and least, religious, it is also informative—and perhaps illusion-shattering—to see the types of individuals who are, and are not, religious. We describe these comparisons below; you can see them in Figure 1.4.

First, women are modestly but consistently more religious than men. According to the 2006 Faith Matters survey, women are more likely to say that they consider themselves to be spiritual and to report having experienced the presence of God. And this is only the beginning. More women than men say that right and wrong should be based on God's laws rather than the views of society; women are more likely to believe that God created the world less than ten thousand years ago. Women more frequently say that there are clear guidelines to good and evil. More women than men believe that the world will end soon, that scripture is the literal word of God, and that everyone will answer for their sins. Women read scripture, talk about religion, and read religious books more than men. You get

Figure 1.4

RELIGIOSITY VARIES A LOT BY RACE AND AGE, AND A LITTLE BY GENDER, TYPE OF COMMUNITY, AND INCOME

Vertical axis is religiosity, standardized with a mean of 0 and a standard deviation of 1

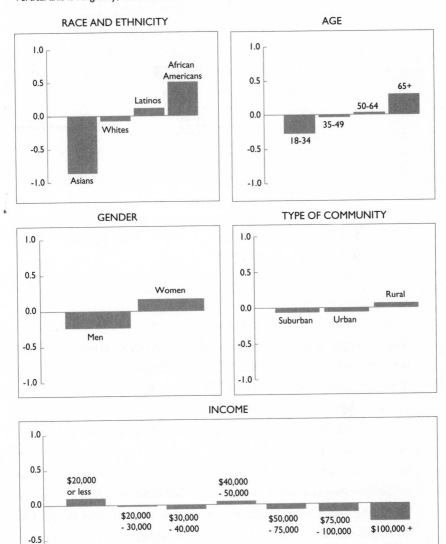

SOURCE: FAITH MATTERS SURVEY, 2006.

the point. No matter the specific yardstick, women exhibit a greater commitment to, involvement with, and belief in religion.[32]

Second, African Americans are far more religious than whites, or any other ethnic or racial group in America. Nearly 60 percent of blacks report attending religious services "nearly every week," compared to 39 percent of whites; 84 percent of blacks say that religion is very or extremely important to them, while 56 percent of whites do. Seven in ten African Americans report that their religion is very important to them when making personal decisions, twice the level for whites (35 percent). Eighty-two percent of blacks in America report saying grace at least daily, compared to 38 percent of whites. As with comparing men and women, we could go on, but the pattern is clear. Religion infuses the lives of African Americans in a way it does not for most whites. By nearly every indicator, Latinos are also more religious than whites. Yet lest one think that religiosity is simply equated with minority status, Asian Americans are less religious than whites. We shall have more to say about race, ethnicity, and religion in Chapter 9.

Age matters a lot too, as the old are more religious than the young. There can be different reasons for such variation by age, including natural variation in the life cycle—people who are closer to the grave tend to be more religious—as well as generational differences that are frozen in place as people age. The explanations for these differences are treated in more detail in Chapter 3, but for now note that, as a descriptive matter, being older means a higher likelihood of being religious.

Religiosity also varies by the size of the community in which one lives. John Mellencamp sings that he "was taught the fear of Jesus in a small town" and it appears he is not alone. People who live in rural communities are more religious than city folk, although the difference is modest.

Furthermore, Southerners are more religious than the rest of the country.[33] As can be seen in Figure 1.5, Arkansas, Louisiana, Mississippi, and Alabama are the most religious states in the union, with

Figure 1.5

THE DEEP SOUTH, UTAH, AND THE MISSISSIPPI VALLEY ARE THE MOST RELIGIOUS REGIONS

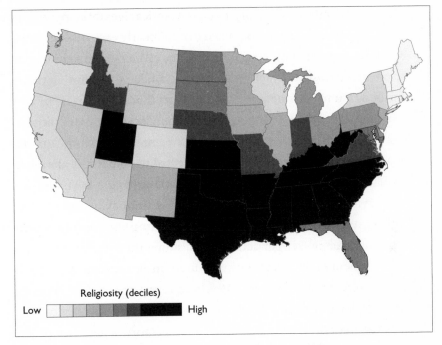

Religiosity (deciles)

Low ░░░░░░░ High

SOURCE: RELIGIOUS LANDSCAPE SURVEY, PEW RESEARCH CENTER.

the bordering states just slightly less so. Utah is also a highly religious state, nearly matching the Bible Belt for religiosity. The patchwork nature of America's religious quilt is underscored by the fact that Utah is bordered by Colorado, one of the least religious states. Colorado's secularism, though, is less than that of the states of the Far West and the Northeast, which have the lowest religiosity of all.

Income has a _more complex relationship_ to religiosity. At the extremes, the very poor are somewhat religious while the very rich are somewhat secular. But those right in the middle of the income scale (earning between $40,000 and $50,000 per year) are about as religious as the very poor. Further complicating matters, attendance at religious services is not related to income. No matter their income, roughly two out of five Americans report attending religious services weekly. And when it comes to education, another measure of social class, having more education corresponds to a higher level of attendance at religious services.

Comparisons across subgroups within a population are always tricky to interpret, because one characteristic can actually be standing in for another. Consider the claim that iPhone users have a low level of religiosity (which may or may not be true, but works as an illustration). Is it because they own an iPhone? Or is it because iPhone owners tend to be young, and young people are (on average) less religious than their elders? The latter seems more likely. Likewise, is the South more religious than (most of) the rest of the country because more African Americans live there than in the rest of the country? Or because more Southerners live in small towns?

The answer to such questions lies in testing the impact of many characteristics—age, gender, income, and so forth—on religiosity simultaneously using the statistical method of multiple regression, which will reemerge often in the subsequent chapters. For the statistical novice, this type of analysis enables us to see whether each of these demographic characteristics continues to be a predictor of religiosity, even when accounting for all of the other characteristics at the same time. That way, if one characteristic is really just standing in for another—if the South is serving as a proxy for living in a small town, say—its statistical connection to religiosity will disappear. It will have been revealed as a substitute for something else. Such a statistical analysis reveals that gender, age, race/ethnicity, size of community, and region all have an independent connection to religiosity. Income, however, does not.

Given all this, who personifies the most religious type of American? An older African American woman who lives in a Southern small town. And the least religious? A younger Asian American man who lives in a large Northeastern city.

While there is every reason to think that race, age, and geography have long been related to religiosity, the religious changes we describe later on highlight that all three have become more strongly predictive of religiosity in recent years. Chapter 4 details a general drop-off in religiosity, but it is concentrated among whites. Accordingly, over the last thirty years, the gap between black and white religious observance has widened. Furthermore, that drop-off in whites' religiosity is also more pronounced among young people and Northerners. And while there is no overall trend for gender, the demographic slice of the population that is most rapidly turning away from religion is young men. In short, the most religious social categories in America are becoming even more religious, and the least religious are becoming even less religious.

CONGREGATIONS MATTER TOO

While individuals' religious involvement and commitment are obviously a vital component of the American religious landscape, neither are they the whole story. Americans generally do not worship alone, but instead gather in congregations. The importance of the congregation is made clear by the extent of congregational involvement within the American population. As shown in Figure 1.6, more Americans are involved in a religious congregation than in any other type of association, group, or club. The 2006 Faith Matters survey asked respondents to indicate whether they belong to a wide array of groups: from hobby groups to professional associations to self-help programs. Three in five Americans (62 percent) have a particular place of worship where they attend services. The next most popular group is the extremely broad category of "hobby, sports, arts, music, or other leisure activity"; about half of all Americans are involved in a group of this type.

Many Americans have a level of involvement in their congregation that exceeds mere membership. Thirty-six percent of the total population report participating in either Sunday School or another form of religious education, while a quarter participate in prayer or other small groups associated with their congregation (13 percent do so monthly or more frequently). Fourteen percent of all Americans have served as an officer or committee member within a congregation.[34] A lot of Americans apparently like their congregation enough

Figure 1.6

CONGREGATIONS ARE THE MOST COMMON FORM OF ASSOCIATION IN AMERICA

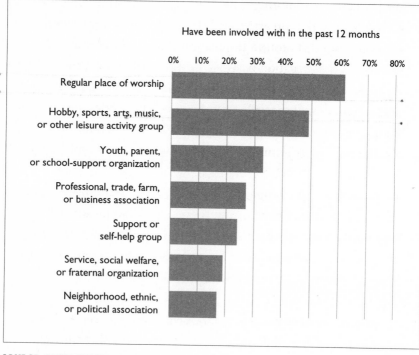

SOURCE: FAITH MATTERS SURVEY, 2006.

to invite others to attend it as well. Over half of all churchgoers, 55 percent, have invited someone to visit their congregation.[35]

To Americans reading this book, an emphasis on congregations as the primary organizational locus for religion undoubtedly seems familiar, as this is the most prevalent form of religious organization within the United States. Indeed, many Americans have probably never thought much about the alternative organizational forms for religion found in other societies. However, the congregation as an all-purpose association with members who choose it, belong to it, and make contributions to it is actually a very Protestant model of religious organization.[36] This form and function of the typical American congregation—of whatever religious tradition—is thus a consequence of America's Protestant heritage. The United States may not be a Protestant nation in law, but its Protestant legacy shapes the contours of the religious landscape.[37]

The centrality of the congregation, and its Protestant influence, can be seen in how immigrants' religions adapt to the American religious ecosystem upon arriving in the United States. Even faiths that are not organized around the congregation in other nations come to adopt a congregation-based structure here in the United States. From there, it is a small step to adopting many of the same practices as American, especially Protestant, congregations. For example, Islamic mosques in the U.S. often hold Sunday school, or provide a social hall for community events—not what they typically do in other nations. In the U.S., imams are frequently called upon to serve as counselors and to engage in public relations, responsibilities outside the purview of imams elsewhere, but common for many congregational leaders in the United States. Alan Wolfe, a keen observer of religion in America, describes the contrast between mosques in America versus those in Muslim-majority nations:

> Without intermediaries that stand between the believer and God, Islam has not traditionally had churches in the way Christians understand that term. Rather than a congregation with a fixed membership, mosques in Muslim societies were—and continue to be—convenient places into which one steps in order to pray, depending on where one is in the course of the day. . . . But in the United States, mosques inevitably come to resemble churches.[38]

Congregationalization is not limited to Muslims. For example, Hindu temples in the United States also have a churchlike feel to them, even though Hinduism, like Islam, is not typically organized around a local congregation. Nor is this a new phenomenon. Writing back in 1948 a sociologist described American Buddhist communities as having "congregational bodies analogous to those which appear in contemporary Christian, and particularly, Protestant churches." Furthermore, these individual congregations were "in no way reminiscent of the temple structure of the Japanese homeland."[39]

With congregations as the dominant mode of religious organization, religious communities are a common nexus for friendships—whether because one becomes a member of a congregation and finds friends there, or one makes friends and then joins their congregation. A majority of Americans, 56 percent to be precise, have at least one close friend in their religious congregation.

The prevalence of friends made at one's place of worship serves to illustrate the social significance of America's congregations. Faith-based social networks tend to keep people from switching congregations, foster good citizenship—generosity and civic engagement—and strengthen the connections voters make between their religion and their politics (see Chapters 5, 11, 12, and 13).

CONGREGATIONAL VIGNETTES

It is because the congregation is the focal point of American religion that, in addition to our statistical data, we provide a series of vignettes about different congregations from across the United States. These vignettes complement the statistical story by bringing to bear much greater richness than is possible with the abstractions of aggregated responses to a survey, providing an opportunity to see how real people live their religions. Without these portraits of individual congregations—and the people who belong to them—you would get only half, and probably less, of religion's story. In reading them you will experience a wide variety of congregations, representing each of America's largest religious traditions and located all around the United States. They are based on many hours of attending worship services, prayer groups, picnics, as well as scores of interviews with both clergy and laity. The prose of the vignettes has been written by Shaylyn Romney Garrett, who also conducted the bulk of the interviews on which the vignettes are based. In writing these vignettes, we have used pseudonyms for people who are not acting in an official capacity for their congregation. In each case, we secured permission from congregational leaders before beginning our research and ensured that the people we observed and interviewed knew that we were writing a book that would draw on what we saw and heard.[40]

These vignettes are reportorial rather than analytical, as their primary purpose is to describe what goes on inside many different types of congregations. These "views from the pews" have influenced our statistical analyses in many ways, but their purpose here is not to confirm or contradict broad generalizations. They are not case studies in the sense that most academics would use the term, but something more akin to bringing a video camera inside. We have taken these congregants and clergy at their word, enabling you to experience their religion as they see it. So as not to interrupt the narrative flow of the stories these chapters tell, we do not stop to flag when a particular experience or quotation resonates with our statistical analysis. While the congregational close-ups are introduced with brief descriptions of how we think they connect to the analytical themes in the remainder of the book, the reader is largely left to discover how the voices from these vignettes speak to the arguments and observations we make elsewhere.

ROADMAP

We aim to offer an even-handed description of American religion. Some of our findings will irk the deeply religious reader, while others will disconcert the deeply secular. Each side in the so-called culture wars is likely to be offended by something we say. We Americans genuinely differ on religious matters, but mutual misperceptions have added confusion to the national conversation. For example, we shall see that most secular Americans are more sympathetic to religious values than most religious Americans realize. Meanwhile, most religious Americans are more tolerant of their adversaries and more supportive of the constitutional separation of church and state than most secular Americans fear. Against the din of grinding axes in the background, our objective in this book is to use the best available empirical evidence to explain the facts about religion's changing role in the contemporary United States, and to note where uncertainty remains.

Our journey begins with vignettes that illustrate both the old and the new in American religion. We describe three Boston-area parishes of the Episcopal Church, one of the most venerable of all denominations in America, and then take you inside Southern California's Saddleback megachurch, an archetype of contemporary seeker-sensitive evangelicalism. The contrast between these two forms of religion sets the stage for the first four analytical chapters of the book (Chapters 3–6). Chapters 3 and 4 cover the broad historical changes over the last fifty or so years that have produced the current state of religious polarization—the shock and two aftershocks mentioned earlier. Chapter 5 shifts our focus from broad patterns of national change to patterns of religious change at the individual level, highlighting the precise patterns of religious mixing, matching, and switching that have shaped the religious landscape. Chapter 6 offers yet another perspective on religious change by examining what leads people to leave their current congregation for a new one, and speculating about what the future of religious innovation may hold. How and why has religion in America changed over the last half century, and how might it change in coming decades—that is the broad set of questions addressed in the first section of the book.

The second section of the book (Chapters 7, 8, and 9) applies a different way of asking about change in religion. How has religion been changed, or not, by social currents that have transformed so much else in American society? Conversely, has religion resisted or deflected those currents? These include the revolution in women's rights, growing income inequality, and increasing ethno-racial diversity. The section begins with the vignettes of Chapter 7, which include a very conservative Lutheran church in Houston, where traditional gender roles are taught and enforced. This particular congregation— which is like a "little Germany" in the midst of Houston, Texas— also shows how ethnicity and religion are often tightly linked. These vignettes include other examples of congregations where ethnicity and religion are mutually reinforcing: a prominent black church in Baltimore, and a group of Catholic parishes in Chicago where Latinos have a large presence. The subsequent two chapters then examine the issue in a more systematic way, tracing how religion has neither slowed nor hastened the women's revolution and the rise of class inequality, but has been touched by America's changing ethnic and racial composition.

The third section (Chapters 10, 11, and 12) narrows in on politics, and thus returns to the theme of polarization. How is it that America has arrived at a historically anomalous point, in which religious devotion has largely replaced religious denomination as a salient political dividing line? And where might the nation's politics be headed? Again, the section begins with vignettes, in this case of three congregations where politics plays out in very different ways. One is a conservative evangelical megachurch in Minneapolis, where religion and partisan politics are sometimes mixed overtly. Another is a synagogue in suburban Chicago, where liberal political views are widely shared and discussed, even if partisan politicking is rare. The third is a Mormon ward (congregation) in suburban Salt Lake City in which a few liberals—rare among Mormons—are swimming against the powerful tide of political conservatism among Latter-day Saints. The two analytic chapters in this section ask first how, at the national level, politics and religion have become intertwined, and then how individuals make the link between their faith and their politics.

The fourth and final section specifically examines how religion affects society. It begins with Chapter 13, which tests whether religious Americans are better, or worse, citizens than those who are not religious—and why. Chapter 14 then examines the potential for religion to divide American society, by describing the areas of disagreement between religious and secular Americans, and among members of different religious traditions. The final chapter then brings our story full circle, by asking—and answering—how the United States can combine religious diversity, religious commitment, and religious tolerance, especially in a period of religious polarization. Truly, the United States presents a puzzle of religious pluralism.

The solution to the puzzle lies in the same feature of the American religious landscape which enables polarization—religious fluidity. The high rate of religious switching results in a lot of religious mixing, even within the most intimate of our relationships. Indeed, your authors' own families illustrate the social and familial networks that knit together people of many different religions. Neither of our stories, however, is unusual.

One of us (Campbell) is a Mormon. He is the product of what was initially an interfaith marriage—as his Mormon mother married his mainline Protestant father. Eventually, his father converted to Mormonism. His mother too had been a convert years before. As a child she left Catholicism to become a Mormon, along with her parents but only some of her siblings. Consequently, a reunion on either side of the family brings together a multi-religious mix.

The family tree of your other author (Putnam) also encapsulates the religious churn that is so common in America. He and his sister were raised as observant Methodists in the 1950s. He converted to Judaism at marriage; he and his wife raised their two children as Jews. One child married a practicing Catholic, who has since left the church and is now secular. The other child married someone with no clear religious affiliation but who subsequently converted to Judaism. Meanwhile, Putnam's sister married a Catholic and converted to Catholicism. Her three children became devout, active evangelicals of several different varieties. So this homogeneous Methodist household in midcentury America has given rise to an array of religious affiliations (and nonaffiliations) that reflects the full gamut of American religious diversity. It would be hard to rouse anti-Jewish or anti-evangelical or anti-Catholic or anti-Methodist or even anti-secular fervor in this group.

Our own families exemplify how religious pluralism is not merely an abstraction; pluralism is often personal. And that personal pluralism means that America is graced with religious harmony.

CHAPTER 2

VIGNETTES:
THE OLD AND THE NEW

We begin with vignettes from two wings of American Protestantism: Episcopalians and evangelicals. As the American version of Anglicanism—that is, the Church of England—Episcopalians are steeped in tradition. And while evangelicalism has deep roots as well, the particular type of congregation represented here—the megachurch—represents a decidedly nontraditional approach to worship. These examples of the old and the new exemplify both constancy and change within American religion.

A TALE OF TWO TRINITIES

It's 10:00 in the morning on the third Sunday of Advent, and cars line both sides of Elm Street in historic Concord, Massachusetts, as parishioners gather for worship at Trinity Episcopal Church. Latecoming families park their Volvos and luxury wagons two blocks away and brace themselves against the icy wind as they hurry across an old stone bridge that straddles the narrow Sudbury River. Trinity's original Gothic chapel, built in 1886, stands on the corner of the church's small lot, flanked by sloping lawns and a low hedge. Founded as a haven of Anglicanism in the theological shadow of Ralph Waldo Emerson's Unitarian Church, Trinity gradually gained a foothold in Concord and soon became an important part of the town's civic and religious landscape. With its rough-hewn stone walls and arched, stained glass windows, the tiny church is the picture of New England charm.

All is quiet on the parish grounds as the last two or three families make their way up the stone steps to the main sanctuary, a large worship space built onto the back of Trinity's original chapel as the congregation swelled in the early 1960s. Protruding awkwardly above the much older buildings, the huge, prismlike shingled roof of the modern church overhangs a concrete patio bearing a seven-foot wooden cross.

Girls in dresses with matching striped tights and boys in corduroy pants and oxford shirts run ahead of their parents down to the basement where they attend Church School during the first half of worship. In the space known as the undercroft, classrooms equipped with low plastic banquet tables and tiny chairs are littered with toys, crayons, and construction paper, as volunteer teachers prepare activities and lessons for their two- to twelve-year-old charges.

One of 194 Episcopal[1] parishes in the Massachusetts diocese, Trinity claims some nine hundred baptized members, but the parish draws barely more than a quarter that many attendees across two services on a given Sunday during the "program year," which spans September through May. Turnout during the summer months drops to a mere one hundred worshippers a week. "Things here are incredibly stable," says The Rev. Tony Buquor, Trinity's current rector. "There is very little growth, and over the last decade the congregation has even declined a bit." Declined a bit more, that is, than it already had since the 1950s, when seeing five hundred parishioners per Sunday was the norm. While a handful of young suburbanite families from neighboring towns have found a home at Trinity, Buquor says that the core of the church's attendees are older, wealthy members of the Boston intelligentsia, most of whom have a long family history in Concord.

Heading back up the stairs, parents stop to search for their pin-on nametags, alphabetized on a large board in the hallway off the sanctuary. In the main sanctuary's shadowy narthex two elderly white men serving as volunteer ushers offer a whispered welcome and a program containing the ten-page order of service. Making their way past the slat-wood screen at the back of the church and down the green-carpeted center aisle, middle-aged couples join the widowed retirees standing in the pews as the triumphal, organ-accompanied processional hymn concludes. "Blessed be God: Father, Son, and Holy Spirit," the celebrant declares in dramatic cadence. "And blessed be God's kingdom, now and for ever. Amen," responds his congregation. Worn copies of the 1979 Book of Common Prayer rest in the pew backs, and the worshippers keep up with the flow of the Mass by juggling a hymnal, the printed order of service, and its one-page liturgical insert, which contains the canonical readings of the day. The sanctuary at Trinity Concord is cathedral-shaped with two sections of pews facing a marble altar and a huge suspended metal cross—two transepts a few rows deep on either side. Though built to seat 650, it is rarely more than halfway filled. Stalls for the thirty-eight-member choir face the congregation, and vaulted ceilings culminate in a magnificent triangular stained glass window—the only artwork in sight. Though the morning sun illuminates its colorful shards of glass, the window admits only fractured light, leaving the worship space dim and chilly, a feeling compounded by the concrete floor and iron-braced pews.

"May your word only be spoken, may your word only be heard," proclaims Nicholas Morris-Kliment, Trinity's associate rector, before climbing to the raised wooden pulpit to deliver his sermon. The Rev. Morris-Kliment is a soft-spoken man with graying, bowl-cut hair, round glasses, and a dark gray beard. He wears a purple stole over his belted white vestments, and raises his hands to both sides in a symbolic embrace as he addresses his congregation.

"The Anglican tradition," Morris-Kliment sermonizes, "teaches the idea that all of life is deeply sacramental." He pauses to define "sacrament" for his hearers: "We do have a catechism in the Episcopal Church—it's in the back of your Prayer Book," he jokes, drawing laughter from the congregation. He urges them to see the sacramental in the everyday. "Seeing God's unmerited, unearned, consoling, strengthening power at work," he continues in a solemn yet soothing tone, allows us each to "get help, and find the presence of God in our lives right now." As he concludes and steps down from the pulpit, the congregation follows the program's directive of *Silence*, the hush broken only by the rustling of pages echoing hollowly off the stone walls.

While Episcopal services generally adhere to a standard liturgical structure as laid out in the Book of Common Prayer, the experience of worship can vary significantly from church to church and even from service to service within a parish. Trinity Concord is a place where people come to find "more traditional worship," Buquor explains, and as a result the parish is "often thought of as being a bit more stuffy." Audrey Windsor, a longtime parishioner, agrees: "Trinity is stiff in liturgy and seems more formal," she says, which is attractive to her. She admits, however, that to many people "Trinity's worship is not appealing because it's more disciplined, not charismatic, and doesn't have that 'good feeling' stuff."

The Episcopal Church is often considered to be a "middle way" between Roman Catholicism and Protestantism. Though maintaining liturgical practice as the core of worship, the denomination affords a significant amount of autonomy to individual congregations, which hire their own priests and are governed by lay committees called vestries. While possessed of a canonical, Bible-based theology, Episcopalianism places equal emphasis on the roles of reason and experience in the evolution of church belief and practice, and this is nowhere more evident than at Trinity Concord. "I've never seen so many Ph.D.'s teaching church school," says Buquor, noting that to the faithful of Trinity Concord, "education and the mind are very important." One congregant describes the parish as "a highly educated, reasonable church, filled with thinking people."

"We believe in one God, the Father, the Almighty, maker of heaven and earth, of all that is, seen and unseen . . ." The service picks up again as the faithful stand to recite the Nicene Creed, which is followed by the Prayers of the People. "For George our president, and Deval our governor, let us pray to the Lord," the celebrant states fervently. "Come, O Lord, and save us," the audience responds in mumbled unison. "Most merciful God, we confess that we have sinned against you in thought, word, and deed, by what we have done, and by what we have left undone . . ." the parishioners then recite the confession, and their collective voice reverberates as the waves of sound drift up into the airy chancel.

Hospitality Training

About fifty adults linger in Trinity's Parish Hall after the service concludes, hovering around two tables filled with boxed donuts, plates of banana bread, and bowls of carrot sticks. A few children run gleefully among the clusters of chatting parishioners who hastily sip a cup of coffee before rounding up coats, hats, and gloves and heading home. "Many people think of Trinity Concord as not particularly open or friendly," says Buquor. "It just doesn't do a lot of fellowshipping," agrees Audrey Windsor, echoing a refrain heard nearly every time parish leadership solicits feedback from members. Lack of outreach is also a common reason other local Episcopalians give for choosing to attend neighboring parishes over Trinity Concord. At staff meetings this failure of community comes up frequently, and is a growing concern as the parish struggles to maintain its membership.

According to The Rev. Buquor, his parishioners "often live out of the head as opposed to the heart," making things like community, fellowship, and group life something of a challenge—and it isn't just visitors and new members who struggle to connect. "Trinity members are not that friendly to each other," reports Regina Walton, the Church School director. "Some will have attended Coffee Hour for fifteen years but still don't know one another. I'm amazed at the number of times I'll mention someone's name to a parishioner, and they don't know who it is."

Always looking for new strategies to address the lack of community cohesiveness, parish leadership has introduced the use of nametags at worship, created picture directories each year, and set up a Welcome Table in the narthex staffed by a volunteer wearing a fluorescent pink "Ask Me!" button. They've even thought of offering hospitality training for willing parishioners, but these efforts have met with limited, if any, success. Most recently the clergy tried dividing the church into neighborhood groups, encouraging them to gather for cocktail parties and informal gatherings to facilitate fellowship. Parishioners resisted, however, arguing that "their social circle was separate from who they lived near," Buquor explains. "So the program didn't work, and people simply didn't come back." A follow-up proposal has been the creation of "virtual neighborhoods"—this time around affinity rather than geography. Buquor is "hoping we can develop leaders of these groups, and that the groups will develop intentionality."

By "intentionality," the rector means friendship, support giving, and spiritual growth, but he admits these are lofty goals. When the parish's Church School director recently circulated an informal written survey to parents, one of the questions asked was, "Are you interested in connecting with other families?" Of twenty-five families surveyed, only five responded affirmatively. "We're not creating any expectations for these social gatherings," Buquor explains, "but we're hoping it will be used for communication." Because there is no strong social network tying the parish together, often the clergy "doesn't even find out about the needs of parishioners and what's going on in people's lives," Buquor says. Ministering to his flock is a challenge when he sees people only once a week—offering a greeting and a handshake as they file out of Mass.

Outside of worship and Church School the most active program at Trinity is the adult choir, followed by the rector's midweek Bible study class, which consists of about fourteen retirees. A handicrafts group meets weekly to knit together, and the Office Guild convenes every Thursday to assemble the programs for worship, but neither gathering draws anyone beyond a handful of elderly women. On a given weekday evening one or two rooms might be filled at Trinity's parish house, but more often than not it's with a local chamber music society or cancer support group to whom the church lends its meeting space. In recent years an annual lock-in—a sleepover in the church—for youth has been canceled due to lack of interest, and when the clergy arranged for the parish to host a day-long antiracism conference taught by the diocese, only eight parishioners signed up.

Since the 1940s, Trinity Concord has been organized into seven volunteer "Commissions" that oversee different aspects of ministry such as Worship, Education, and Stewardship. While the original goal of this system was to involve parishioners in all aspects of congregational life, Buquor notes that "it's always the same few people running the church, and giving their time." He feels that the parish needs "a fruit-basket upset, to allow some space for new members to get involved." Buquor would like to see Trinity "move toward a more organic understanding of parish life. We need something more life-giving," he says. Shortly after taking the helm as rector in 2003, he introduced an initiative called Planning for Ministry. "We're really asking ourselves who we are today, and what we are called to *today*," he says, alluding to Trinity's strong tendency to allow tradition and history to outweigh innovation and growth. The goal of Planning for Ministry has been to get parishioners to take ownership over the parish's future and also to head up new exploratory "action groups" around areas such as Small Groups and Spiritual Growth. One of the 150 parishioners who attended the initial meeting observed that "people enjoyed it but people's lives are very, very full." Because many of the ideas brought to the table would require lay leadership and parishioner volunteerism—something that hasn't been forthcoming in the recent past—there's little hope for a dramatic renaissance of parish life.

Episcopalianism has long been one of America's largest Protestant denominations, and the church flourished throughout most of the twentieth century. However, recent decades have brought a slow decline in adherents, leaving parish communities such as Trinity Concord struggling to thrive and facing an uncertain future. The Rev. Buquor recognizes the success other denominations have had attracting members by offering "a smorgasbord of things people can graze on." And he worries about the "competition" that neighboring churches pose. "We have lost our identity," he says of his parish, "we have no 'brand.'" Many families at Trinity attend Episcopal

Mass, but send their kids to the youth group at the United Church of Christ down the road. "The local UCC church is booming because kids like going there," explains a Trinity parishioner. Yet Fr. Buquor isn't convinced that programs and social activities are what church is supposed to be. "If your understanding of church is that it's there to offer interesting things and a variety of self-help offerings, that's great," he explains, but he feels church should "lead people to the cross, to be self-giving and sacrificial." "So how do we do that in a way that doesn't completely disconnect with the culture?" he wonders.[2]

A Corporate Parish

On a cold Monday morning twenty miles to the east of Concord, the parish leadership at Trinity Episcopal Church in the city of Boston gathers for a Program and Ministry meeting, where they will coordinate the weekly goings-on at one of the largest Episcopal parishes in the country. Situated in the middle of downtown's busy Copley Square, Trinity Boston dwarfs its Concord counterpart. As a "regional church," this Trinity draws its congregants from all over the greater Boston area, some 64 percent commuting into the city from the suburbs for one of seven weekly worship services. Claiming nearly 1,200 "pledging units"—a measure of membership based on the number of households making an annual financial commitment—the church counts four thousand individual members, about a quarter of whom are regular attendees. On an average Sunday, Trinity will welcome around 1,350 worshippers.

Trinity Boston stands out as a community focal point because of its prominent place in the historical, religious, and physical landscape of the city. Dedicated in 1877, for over a hundred years the turreted sandstone and granite church has been named one of the nation's top ten most architecturally significant buildings, and draws over 100,000 visitors annually. Many view Trinity as simply a tourist destination, but behind the La Farge stained glass and exemplary Romanesque Revival architecture dwells a healthy, 275-year-old congregation.

The largest Episcopal community in the Massachusetts diocese, Trinity Boston is what most Episcopalians would characterize as a "corporate parish."[3] It is where large diocesan gatherings are held, where other faith communities in Boston meet the Episcopal Church, and where parishioners come to participate in the over sixty programs operated under the Trinity umbrella. Keeping up with both worship and parish life requires the full-time attention of a rector, a vicar, three associate rectors, one assistant rector, and three lay associates, as well as an additional thirty-three full-time and eleven part-time staff members. Of the church's $7 million annual operating budget, almost half is spent on salaries and benefits for employees, the majority of whom keep their offices on two rented floors of a high-rise building across the street.

For all its bustling activity, Trinity Boston faces many of the same challenges as Trinity Concord. The question of how to keep membership growing and community thriving occupies much of the time and energy of this parish's professional staff. From outreach ministries, to lecture series, to youth groups, in the past two decades Trinity has ramped up its nonworship programming significantly as a way to stay relevant in a changing religious landscape. "We're not too far from a megachurch in terms of offering a full-service Christian opportunity," admits The Rev. Michael Dangelo, associate rector for congregational growth. He feels that increasing program offerings is a growing trend among mainline Protestant churches, many of whom are looking for ways to bolster shrinking congregations. "If you're going to get people involved, you have to have a program that has attractiveness on its own," he explains. Yet Fr. Dangelo says that while many of Trinity's programs "were created to keep people," despite making huge investments in those programs—and more than doubling its paid staff in order to run them—the parish today sees about the same number of active parishioners as it did twenty years ago.

"I didn't get into this to become an events coordinator," one priest confesses, noting the disconnect he often feels between his calling and the daily reality of running a large, program-oriented parish. According to Trinity's most recent Parish Profile—an exten-

what is 'attractiveness on its own?'

sive, survey-based document assembled by a search committee as
a way of taking stock of parish life in preparation for a change in
rectors—many Trinity members "believe the clergy have too much
on their plate to spend a lot of one-on-one time with parishioners.
People say, 'Don't bother the clergy; they are too busy.' But some
parishioners say they are hurting for pastoral attention."[4] Joy Fallon,
a lay program head, agrees. "The yearning in the church is enormous," she says. "People want a priest to know them by name,"
which is something that only a very few seem to experience at this
urban megaparish.

The danger in offering so many programs and activities is creating a congregation that "gathers as consumers, not as community,"
says Dangelo. "What we need to do is break down the walls of the
transactional relationship that . . . creates." To this end, the church
has launched Trinity Connections, a program consisting of several
affinity groups such as a Nigerian Bible study, a Hardy Perennials ("a
youth group for those over sixty"), and a Gay and Lesbian Fellowship. But results have been mixed.

Upon joining the church a few years ago, Linda Lowe quickly
realized that Trinity is a place where "you can take what you want
and leave, but you can't really make connections." So she joined
CommonGround, the 20s and 30s Fellowship, and started attending social activities and the occasional brunch after Sunday services.
Yet she felt the group was "very fluid," and she ultimately stopped
attending because in her view it offered "no sense of deeper connection between participants." "It doesn't work as well as we'd like it
to," Dangelo admits of the parish's attempt at creating community
through fellowship groups. Other efforts have been more successful.
A recently created parish softball team—part of a league formed with
a local Congregational church—has a roster of twenty-five players,
and about twelve show up per game. "Their lifestyles are prevent-
ing them from making a weekly commitment," says Dangelo, who
heads up the team, referring to the young professionals who participate, and whose job demands run high. Nevertheless, he's proud of
the camaraderie that has formed among the players, who often go

out for dinner or a drink after practice. One team member says that playing softball "has opened a lot of doors at Trinity," and "makes [her] feel more comfortable" going to worship or attending events at the church.

"The First Experience of Community"

A dozen worshippers surround the altar on a rainy Thursday evening as The Reverend William Rich—an elaborate purple chasuble over his white alb—administers the 6:00 P.M. Holy Eucharist. "The Body of Christ," he says to each communicant—some in business attire on their way home from work, some wearing coats and scarves to guard against the cold in the low-lit, drafty hall. The priest's voice can barely be heard from the back of the vast, 1,400-seat sanctuary, which stands entirely empty except for the tiny group tucked intimately into the gilded chancel. As the service concludes, Rich makes the long walk down the center aisle, and stands waiting to bid farewell to each member of his tiny flock as they file out into the darkness of Copley Square.

Downstairs, a group of twenty-four newcomers to Trinity gathers for dinner before the final session of the Inquirers' Class—"a crash course in the Episcopal Church." Held twice each year, the Inquirers' Class is a two-month course designed to introduce basic organizational and theological concepts to individuals who wish to learn more about Trinity. Having concluded the Eucharist and hung up his vestments, Rich comes downstairs and gives a "five minute warning" for the start of the lecture, set to begin at 6:30. A jumble of coats, handbags, and umbrellas lines the bench around the perimeter of the room, which contains five round tables, each with a printed sign bearing the name of a biblical city. The members of the "Bethlehem" group get up one by one to throw out their paper plates and refill their water glasses, then take out pens, paper, and matching white binders containing class materials.

According to Rich, senior associate rector for Christian Formation, the Inquirers' Class appeals to a few different demographics: individuals raised in the Episcopal Church whose activity lapsed in their teens or twenties; Christians from other faith traditions who enjoy "the Episcopal/Anglican flavor"; people who were not raised in any faith—often young parents; and interreligious married couples who are looking for a "compromise religion." Many participants will attend the church for a year or more before venturing into the class, which is held in the fall and spring.

Tonight's lecture is the last in the eight-session series and covers the topic of Stewardship. "Time, Talents, and Treasure," Rich writes in black marker on a large flip pad set up on an easel at the front of the room. "Treasure is the polite word for our money," he explains, "and is usually referred to in the church by the jargon word 'tithe.'" He explains the Old Testament doctrine of giving 10 percent of all income to the church, but adds that "then Jesus comes along and says that's not enough—that *everything* belongs to God. These are two impossible standards, but historically, that's how Jews and Christians have thought about the stewarding of money," he goes on, encouraging the new members to view their relationship to the collection plate not as a mathematical formula, but as privately determined, and as a symbol of their relationship to God. "Frankly, it's something—like giving to NPR—where if there is no one there to remind you it's a priority, you don't do it," comments a young woman at the "Jerusalem" table. "Making a pledge is a scary commitment," adds a middle-aged man sitting next to her, "but it has helped me to take a look at how I spend my time and my money. It's been a good reality check for me." After the lecture, each of the four Pilgrim Groups fans out into different rooms in the church to discuss what they've learned.

One group finds their way to the Angel Room, a small carpeted space in the Parish Hall lined with bags of canned food that have been collected at Mass over the past few weeks. As soon as everyone settles in around the table, the group's volunteer facilitator asks for reactions to the presentation, and reflections on the course as a whole. Kevin, a thirty-something man in a black coat and black slacks, ventures a comment: "From the beginning of the class to now I definitely feel different, but I still have a lot of reservations—about baptism, about commitment. I've been coming to Trinity for about a year, and at first it was forced, but now every week there's something about Trinity in my life," he says. "I grew up very lonely—we never had family gatherings, I never had a lot of friends, and then the whole gay thing too. I tended to push people away. But this is the first place I've felt it's okay to be liked—that I won't be judged. This is the first experience of community I remember truly feeling in my life. I know it's just a couple of hours a week, but it makes a difference."

Though the group is friendly and clearly knows one another well, everyone struggles to follow Kevin's heartfelt comments. "I don't want to make you sit in silence . . ." the facilitator, a middle-aged woman named Lindsey, offers up timidly. "Maybe if we all just share something we've gotten out of the class," Kevin ventures. "I already did," he says, chuckling self-consciously, which makes the whole group erupt in laughter, finally breaking the ice. Each person then shares a thought or two. Celeste admits that "deciding how much of a priority it is to come on Sunday" is consistently tough for her. "But once I get here I'm so glad I came," she says, to a chorus of agreement. "I don't think I'd be interested in doing any of these ministries before this class," says young, smartly dressed Jim, who is now considering joining a prison tutoring program at Kevin's urging.

· The Rev. Rich feels strongly that in order to experience the element of life changing that is the goal of Christian Formation, "parishioners need to get to know one another in trusting ways so they can depend on one another and form a small community." While Sunday discussion forums and lecture series are also part of Rich's program, he recognizes that "formation happens not through the head only, but through sharing life stories . . . and finding the Christ in each other." Which is why the parish's smaller gatherings like the Inquirers' Class, and its follow-up series called DOCC (Disciples of Christ in Community), have provided a way to break through the anonymity that many congregants experience at Trinity Boston.

Back together with the rest of the Inquirers' Class, Rich thanks his students for a wonderful semester, and reminds them that he is always available to help as they continue their spiritual journey at

Trinity. He places a stack of orange forms on a table at the back of the room and encourages anyone who is "ready for confirmation or baptism" to fill one out and return it to initiate further discussion and preparation. While the Inquirers' Class will draw anywhere from forty to eighty participants each year, the parish averages only about five adult baptisms annually. Rather than a conversion tool, the class serves to open up newcomers to the possibility of community and of a "deeper, richer life in Christ" in this "big, busy church."[5]

You Can Believe in Dinosaurs

Hundreds of congregants spill out of the sanctuary to the sound of a spirited organ recessional as the second Sunday worship service at Trinity Boston comes to an end. Many worshippers make their way down to the undercroft, where Coffee Hour and a weekly lecture forum are set to begin. The church's imposing cornerstones protrude into a cozy, carpeted area complete with a glass-walled gift shop and a multipurpose meeting room lined with polished wooden benches and comfortable but functional chairs.

Women in pants suits and designer shoes, and men donning tweed jackets and Burberry scarves greet friends with polite hugs and then find a place among the hundred or so chairs that have been laid out for the forum. As the meeting begins, Fr. Rich welcomes his parishioners, and proceeds to read a meditation from the Book of Common Prayer. About half of the group bow their heads and close their eyes, while the other half look forward thoughtfully, grasping their paper cups filled with fair-trade coffee and tea. By the end of the prayer, the event is standing room only, as a wave of younger congregants stream in from a separate CommonGround Coffee Hour, held in the upstairs Parish Hall.

Speaking at the forum today is The Rev. Anne Berry Bonnyman, recently installed as the rector of Trinity Boston. Having surrendered their previous rector to an appointment at the National Cathedral, the congregation undertook a year-long search that resulted in the hiring of The Rev. Bonnyman to lead its "spiritual journey" into the future. As part of her initiation into parish life, the Rector has been asked to share insights from her personal spiritual journey, which began as a child in a Roman Catholic parish in Appalachia. Speaking with a Southern drawl that seems tempered by a Northern education, Bonnyman recalls growing up in "a fundamentalist culture," but notes that her parents did their best to "bring reason into the situation." "Which made me prime material for an Episcopalian," she adds, drawing laughter and applause from the audience. Bonnyman goes on to expound upon her feeling that "life's task is to blend our faith with our reason," and describes the difficult quest she faced in changing faiths, and feeling called to the ministry. The Episcopal Church had recently voted to allow the ordination of women, and church members were adjusting, some slowly and reluctantly, to the change.

As the Q&A portion of the meeting draws to a close, a tall, gray-haired man stands and asks Rev. Bonnyman what she reads in her personal time. Rather than a book of scripture, or a work of Christian scholarship, she speaks of mystery novels and a fictional account of life in India. "But honestly when you're in the midst of moving," she says, "there's no time for anything but the newspaper and *The New Yorker*." Her audience chuckles in approval, and a final prayer is read before the meeting concludes.

At the entrance to the gift shop, a table filled with featured books and the latest CD recordings by the Trinity choir also displays a fabric torso model wearing a navy blue T-shirt proclaiming "The Top Ten Reasons to Be an Episcopalian." From number nine, "You can believe in dinosaurs," to number seven, "You don't have to check your brain at the door," the list, though clearly lighthearted, epitomizes what Episcopalians at Trinity Boston seem to find most attractive about their chosen faith—its ability to blend scripture and tradition with reason and experience. The parish prides itself on providing a "big tent" where Christian believers of all stripes may feel at home. One priest describes the Episcopal Church as "made up of people who are willing to walk a faith journey—asking questions and not necessarily finding answers," and Trinity Boston seeks to be a safe haven for the spiritually ambivalent. According to its Parish Profile, less than 6 percent of the church's congregants regard the Bible as either "strongly" or "somewhat" literally true, and nearly half feel that circumstances, rather than absolutes, should be the main source of guidance on ethical questions.[6] "At Trinity, there is a lot of space for believing, doubting, working your way through," says one parishioner. "It's okay to be a seeker on that path. Trinity offers space to question and opportunities for these explorations."

Reason number three on the Episcopal top ten: "All of the pageantry, none of the guilt." A surprising number of congregants at Trinity Boston have found their way to Episcopalianism by way of other, often more orthodox, religions. "I like the Episcopal faith because I can embrace all of its beliefs. It expresses Christian traditions without being judgmental or exclusive," says one former Catholic who now attends Trinity Boston. The Episcopal Church is a church with "no guilt," says another. "It's a compromise church. It's not too Catholic, and it's not too Protestant," explains The Rev. Gale Davis-Morris, rector of Church of the Good Shepherd in Acton, Massachusetts, who estimates that nearly half of her congregants are former Catholics. "I'm a cradle Episcopalian," agrees Steve Adams, one of Good Shepherd's parishioners, "which is almost an anomaly in the church these days. If it weren't for people leaving the Catholic Church, the Episcopal Church would have died a long time ago in America."

"A Moment of Theological Crisis"

While "refugees" from stricter faiths relish the more liberal theology that parishes like Trinity Boston espouse, this is only part of the story for the denomination as a whole. "I go to clergy meetings and I feel like I'm practicing a different religion," says Fr. Jurgen Liias, rector of Christ Church, the Episcopal Church in Hamilton, Massachusetts. Fr. Liias argues that while reason and experience have long been revered as interpretive tools in the Anglican tradition, scripture has nonetheless been regarded as sacred; and that the faith has never embraced as much moral ambiguity as some Episcopalians would now like to claim. "The Church is in real crisis," says Fr. Liias. "The soft center has fallen out, and the two ends find themselves some-what polarized." As to the future of the denomination, his faith lies in the "rebuilding" of "orthodox Anglicanism." "People will follow orthodoxy and certainty," he says. "There is a need for, and a useful-ness to, a religion that says *this is how it is.*"

"How it is" for Fr. Liias is a reading of scripture that places him and his congregation far to the theological right of Trinity Boston and Trinity Concord. Liias famously spoke out against the practice of blessing homosexual unions as well as the proposed election of Gene Robinson, a homosexual priest, as bishop. Nevertheless, the diocese sent Liias as a delegate to the 2003 Episcopal General Convention where the ordination issue was to be debated and voted upon, and where he represented the only dissenting voice from Massachusetts. He describes his being appointed a delegate as "a miracle in itself." Indeed, conservative voices such as Liias were outnumbered, and the convention delegates voted to confirm Bishop Robinson.

According to Fr. Liias, when the resolutions passed, "an enor-mous amount of people were really upset with what the church had done." A conference was organized a few months later in Plano, Texas, that brought together two thousand Episcopal lead-ers and parishioners who were opposed to the outcome, and twenty members of Liias's Christ Church attended. Out of this confer-ence emerged the Anglican Communion Network, an organiza-tion of parishes that opposes the theological "drift" of the Episcopal Church. The Network has since grown into the 100,000-member Anglican Church in North America (ACNA), a new denomination established in June 2009, which has sought a direct relationship to the worldwide Anglican Communion, circumventing the author-ity of the American Episcopal Church. These historic moves toward schism have hit home in Liias's Christ Church, which has split into two separate congregations—one loyal to the denomination, one joining the ACNA. Liias now plans to resign leadership of the Epis-copal parish and take the helm of the ACNA parish, a group drawn from his former congregation and still meeting under its same roof.

"The church is experiencing a moment of theological crisis right now," explains Fr. Mike Dangelo of Trinity Boston, admitting that, "in a time of conservatism, we've declined in membership because we simply can't offer certainty. Our greatest strength is that we don't come down hard on a lot of issues. But it's also our greatest weakness," he admits. As a minister in a denomination now wrestling with schism, one wonders if Fr. Dangelo—the youngest member of Trinity Boston's clergy—ever feels he has stepped onto a sinking ship. "Sinking? Well, I think she's taking on water, and it's going to be hard," he says. "But the truth is that there is no purpose-driven life. There are no seven steps to a highly effective spiritual life. You are who God made you to be. I proclaim I believe the Nicene Creed— I can offer that. I can offer Jesus Christ alive, dead, and risen," he explains. "Sometimes I feel like the Statue of Liberty, and that's what gives me hope in the Episcopal Church."

COME ONE, COME ALL TWENTY THOUSAND

It's 11:00 on Sunday morning, and the traffic in the left turn lane on Portola Parkway is backed up a quarter of a mile, as a line of cars waits to turn onto Saddleback Parkway, the private road that winds its way onto the 120-acre campus of Saddleback Church in Orange County, California. Drivers inching their way toward the parking lot are sure to notice the bumper stickers on the cars ahead: "1 Cross + 3 Nails = 4Given," "You Matter to God—Saddleback Church." Once around the bend, an army of "traffic ministry" volunteers in red T-shirts directs each car into one of the 2,460 on-campus parking spaces. Longtime Saddleback members are encouraged to make the sacrifice of parking in one of the 1,250 off-campus spaces—serviced by a fleet of twelve buses—so that first-timers can park within walking distance.

Saddleback is part of a growing number of city-sized Christian congregations known as megachurches. Founded in 1980 when Pastor Rick Warren and his wife, Kay, held a seven-person Bible study in their living room, Saddleback has grown to become the fourth largest church in the nation, with over 100,000 names on its membership rolls, and an average weekend attendance of 22,000.

Families and couples dressed in jeans, shorts, Hawaiian shirts, flip-flops, and sunglasses get out of their cars and make their way through the lot toward the Worship Center. There to greet them stands a perky volunteer, a white woman in her mid-forties who dutifully shakes the hand of every person. At the top of the stairs sits Tent #2, which seats 750 and houses singles worship on Saturday nights as well as Overdrive, a hard-rock worship service, and Epic, a hip, intimate service held on Sundays. In an attempt to meet the varying tastes of its members, Saddleback offers different styles of worship in different "venues." Each venue is led by a staff pastor, who welcomes the congregation, introduces the musical performers, and sees that the simulcast of Warren's sermon (live in the Worship Center up the hill) comes through properly on the JumboTrons in each tent. This way everyone's diverse needs are met, but "the quality of teaching is assured," explains Pastor David Chrzan, Saddleback's chief of staff. Also on offer every weekend are services in Spanish, a gospel choir service, and even a Polynesian-style service complete with mumu-clad dancers and a lei-wearing pastor. And if none of the "venues" appeal, visitors may find their way to the Terrace Café, an outdoor snack bar where they can sit at plastic tables and chairs, sip lattés, and anonymously watch the sermon on overhead television screens. Here, one pastor explains, is where the church tries to provide an entry point for even the most hesitant newcomers.

Many megachurches—including Saddleback—use words like "seeker-sensitive" to describe their goal of attracting unchurched Christians by making worship a more "inviting" experience. The demand for a modern take on traditional Christianity became obvious to Rick Warren as he went knocking on doors in Orange County twenty-eight years ago, asking his neighbors what they wanted in a church. As he often explains when sharing his rags-to-riches story, many told the newly minted pastor that they were believers, but didn't like the stuffy, legalistic religions in which they grew up. Their preferences ultimately shaped the place of worship that Warren built, and the result of that consumer-driven approach to creating Saddleback is a deliberately contemporary, highly professionalized operation with a carefully orchestrated feel-good atmosphere.

Directed by volunteers across Saddleback Parkway, congregants encounter Tents #1 and #3, where the high school and junior high ministries hold services. Kids quickly part ways with their parents—drawn by the loud Christian rock spilling out of the tents and the crowds of teens chatting and flirting before the start of the service. Outside the junior high tent is a Beach Café, where before and after services the kids can buy hamburgers and sodas, and sit at grass-hut-like picnic tables while watching a pickup game of beach volleyball. The feel in the lot surrounding the venue tents is something like that of an outdoor music festival, as hip, goateed pastors wearing trendy jeans and T-shirts try to "reach" their flock of young worshippers.

As the crowd continues up the perfectly manicured walkway toward the main Worship Center, each visitor is greeted by three more hand-shaking volunteers. To the left is the Children's Ministry Center, complete with two multimedia worship auditoriums, two Bible-themed playgrounds, forty classrooms, live lizards, an aquarium, and scores of televisions with video game equipment ("Xboxes on the left, Nintendo GameCubes on the right," a staff member points out during a tour). On any given weekend, the volunteer baby-sitters and Sunday School teachers will service 3,500 children, each of whom is checked in electronically with a bar-coded key fob given to parents at registration.

Finding unique ways to present a gospel message is one of Saddleback's main techniques for making church more "accessible." Hence, the entire Saddleback campus is Bible-themed, and is intended to be a living lesson in Christianity. "What we find is that most adults are biblically illiterate," says Pastor David Chrzan, "and the campus is used to teach them." He estimates that there are forty to fifty Bible stories told by the landscaping and playground equipment. The technological wonders include a tomb with a removable stone door, a miniature Golgotha atop a grassy hill, and a stream outfitted with a remote-controlled demonstration of the parting of the Red Sea. "We're not trying to be a theme park," Chrzan is quick to emphasize. "Theme parks are about happiness, which is temporary. We're about changed lives, and we're simply trying to reach the people God has given us to reach," he says. Such ready explanations for the church's user-friendly brand of religion are common at Saddleback, whose leaders often seem to anticipate criticism even as they tout their success at spreading the gospel.

At 11:15, congregants are greeted at the door of the Worship Center by yet another volunteer, who offers a program and a pen. It is in this 3,100-seat venue—perched at the top of the campus—where Warren, known to his congregation as "Pastor Rick," plays to a live audience. Each sermon at Saddleback is accompanied by a shiny, multicolored bulletin containing a hole-punched outline, which is designed so that listeners can fill in the blanks as Pastor Rick hits his most important points. As worshippers take their seats, a full choir and band perform contemporary jazz and soft-rock Christian music, including such songs as "Trading My Sorrows" and "Only a God like You." The lyrics to the songs flash on the five television screens suspended above the stage, and the entire congregation is on its feet—many singing along with eyes closed and arms stretched toward heaven. To the left of the stage stands an understated wooden cross—the only Christian icon in view—and the title of the sermon is projected in colored lights on the back wall.

At 11:30, Pastor Rick takes the stage, dressed in a loose, short-sleeved button-down shirt and black cotton chinos. His hair is receding, and he wears it gel-spiked, with a goatee and mustache. While there is no ritual component to worship at Saddleback, anyone who happens to attend twice in one weekend will notice total continuity across services—Pastor Rick wears the same outfit both Saturday and Sunday, and gives a virtually identical sermon emphasizing the same catchphrases, using the same anecdotes, and telling the same carefully timed and regionally appropriate jokes. In case anyone should need to use the restroom, get some air, or check on a child during the service, the campus is fitted with a series of speakers atop twenty-foot poles so the sermon can be heard anywhere. A live feed of Pastor Rick's voice echoes across the campus six times every weekend.

Today's sermon is the second in a four-week series entitled "Use It or Lose It," and centers on how to use talents and time in a way that maximizes one's ability to live a happy, fulfilled Christian life. As he speaks, Pastor Rick pleads like a concerned father for his congregation to take his message to heart, occasionally saying things like "Would you write this down?" Warren carries a thin Bible as he moves to and from the podium, but never opens it during the sermon, which feels very much like a self-help seminar. At the conclusion of the message, Jesus is held up as a "model for time management," and Pastor Rick implores those who have not yet accepted Christ to offer a prayer in their heart: "Be the CEO of my life, Jesus." "Let me pray for you," he says, and the congregation bow their heads as Rick offers up his pastoral supplication to "Father God."

As soon as the final "Amen" is said, the electric guitarists, drummers, and saxophone players spring into action. Ushers pass collection baskets during the closing song and people begin to file out onto the plaza. Some linger to chat with friends and family, and some head to the pavilion to purchase a copy of today's sermon, already recorded on CDs and DVDs, or to pick up curriculum materials for their small group. Most retrieve their children, head directly to their cars, and make their way back home to one of the ninety-five Orange County cities that Saddleback serves. By about 1:00, the plaza is deserted, awaiting the next flood of worshippers.

"The R&D Department of Christianity"[7]

It's 4:00 P.M. on a Monday afternoon—the first day of Volunteer Appreciation Week at Saddleback—and the staff has rolled out the red carpet in honor of the over five thousand volunteers who help run the church's four hundred–plus ministries. Past the waterfall and palm trees that decorate the front entrance to the church's Ministry Center, visitors enter through automatic sliding glass doors, and are greeted with a display of helium balloons and signs declaring "Thanks for Volunteering, You Changed Lives Today!" and "Thanks for Making an Eternal Difference." Just inside, the Saddleback reception desk is equipped with a computer, two flat screen monitors, and a switchboard. Under the desk's glass top are displayed various flyers, registration packets, and pamphlets advertising a summer camp for preteens, high school ministry activities, a seniors luncheon, small groups for kids, Woman to Woman Mentoring, career coaching and counseling, single adult ministries, and Celebrate Recovery, Saddleback's Christ-centered addiction recovery program. According to Pastor Scott Hitzel, in any given month, Saddleback will host some three thousand separate events—including everything from the nineteen multimedia worship services, to tiny gatherings of believers whose quirky common interests bring them together. "There's a program called Gig," he says, "which is basically just a few guys who like to get together on campus and play the guitar."

The woman sitting at the front desk is middle-aged and white; plump, well manicured, and conservatively but casually dressed. She greets everyone with a sweet grandmotherly smile. Between answering the phone through her telemarketer-style headset ("Thank you for calling Saddleback, how may I direct your call?") she invites each in a steady stream of visitors to sign in and out. The activities of the Ministry Center alone require the work of one hundred full-time employees, 150 part-time employees, and four thousand volunteer hours per month.

Just to the left of the entrance is a room that serves as a Resource Center, where one can purchase everything from Bibles to "Saddleback—25 Years of Purpose" baseball caps. The center is primarily an outlet for curriculum materials used by the church's small groups, and the media on offer include videos and DVDs of sermons and special events, workbooks and journals, gift books and pocket-sized copies of *The Purpose Driven Life*, the bestselling guide to Christian living that put Saddleback on the map and made Rick Warren the celebrity he is today. The book is now printed in sixty languages, and sales are approaching 35 million copies worldwide.

The 51,000-square-foot, state-of-the-art Saddleback Ministry Center has an airy architectural style complete with skylights and wall-to-wall windows. Aside from subtle scriptural references on the posters, and the contemporary Christian music playing behind the reception desk, an unwitting visitor might be hard-pressed to identify the building as a church. A sign keeps "walk-in" parishioners at bay, noting that staff pastors are available "by appointment only." Once past the reception desk, the Ministry Center takes on a casually corporate look and feel. Small offices line the hallways, each with beveled glass doors displaying the names of the ministers and employees who occupy them, as well as snippets of the church-meets-modern-management jargon that pervades the organization. Rested casually on one cabinet top is a huge corrugated plastic sign in the shape of an arrow that reads, "BAPTISM TODAY."

A large Conference Room and the Office of the Pastor take up the bulk of the second floor and have the feel of the executive suites of a corporate headquarters. Two smiling female administrative assistants guard the open doors to the offices of Pastor Rick Warren and Pastor David Chrzan, Warren's right-hand man. These offices are spacious and well lit, furnished with overstuffed leather furniture, and filled with family portraits, Christian artwork, gifts of state, oddities collected from the four corners of the earth, and bookshelves lined with Bibles, Christian classics, and management tomes by Peter Drucker and others. It is here where Rick Warren advises a network of more than 37,000 Purpose Driven churches worldwide, formulates plans for Saddleback's hurtle into the future, and prays over his burgeoning flock.

"Contemporary Without Compromising the Truth"

For all the church's consumer-driven variety, many attendees agree that the message taught at Saddleback is the main attraction for them. One couple who have attended Saddleback for five years say they chose the church because "Pastor Rick is very simple and his sermons are easy to apply. He teaches you *how* to love your neighbor, and challenges you to do it in the coming week." Though often criticized as offering a "watered-down" version of Christianity, Warren dismisses this critique. In *The Purpose Driven Church* (a how-to book for pastors that preceded *The Purpose Driven Life*), he explains that his way of introducing the gospel to the unchurched is, simply, effective—and, he argues, inspired by Christ himself. "Jesus never lowered his standards," he writes, "but he always started where people were. He was contemporary without compromising the truth."[8]

In CLASS 101, a crash course in "Discovering Church Membership," new and prospective members hear all about what it means to believe and belong at Saddleback. Pastor Steve Gladen pumps up the crowd by telling them that when joining Saddleback "you're not just joining a church, you're joining a movement." Discussion of this "movement" dominates the first session of the CLASS—a two-hour presentation about Saddleback's history and organizational philosophy, followed by a thirty-minute overview of its basic beliefs.

The religion taught at this megachurch is more about lifestyle than laws or liturgy, and though the theology it espouses is biblically literalist and straitlaced evangelical, this fact is emphasized to varying degrees, depending on the context. Saddleback is officially a member of the Southern Baptist Convention, but most congregants admit not having realized this until taking CLASS 101. In fact, many Saddleback members seem uncomfortable classifying themselves any further than simply as "Christians."

CLASS 101 attendees are taught that there is a hierarchy of belief at Saddleback—some things are viewed as "essential beliefs," or teach- *adiaphora* ings that one must accept in order to join the church. These include things like the doctrine of the Trinity, the divinity of Jesus, the reality of heaven and hell, the preeminent role of grace in salvation, and the inerrancy of the Bible. Beyond this list, parishioners have "liberty" to believe what they want. Doctrine as such is rarely discussed in sermons, but is explored in the curricula the church develops for use in small group Bible studies, giving participants the option to pursue the "truth" at whatever length and depth suits them. This approach is certainly "contemporary," but Warren's evangelical peers often reject his assertion that it isn't "compromising."

Saddleback curricula come primarily in the form of DVD presentations to be shown at in-home small group meetings. Topics center on the concepts in *The Purpose Driven Life*, but also cover a variety of other subjects—everything from how to evangelize members of other religions, to a verse-by-verse exploration of the Beatitudes. In a 2005 meeting in which the discussion questions for a video on the Sermon on the Mount were being written, none of the pastors or staff members present had a Bible open in front of them—the questions they came up with were almost entirely about application, not exegesis. And in a discussion of how to help small group hosts answer doctrinal questions that surface at in-home discussions, one pastor explained to area leaders that Saddleback is currently developing an online FAQ, but added that, "for all the basic questions, we of course just direct people to allaboutgod.com."

Not everyone is satisfied with Saddleback's approach to theology. For example, June Hendersen, a former Saddleback congregant, was raised as a Methodist in the South, but became a member of Warren's church later in life. She attended happily for many years, but eventually left because she "was looking for something with a little more meat" in the areas of theology and doctrine. In her opinion Saddleback is ultimately a church for the seekers, and delving deeper into scripture and spirituality is better done elsewhere.

Though Warren doesn't feel he is teaching Christianity Lite, many of the worshippers who have found their way to Saddleback definitely seem pleased to have found a religious experience that liberates them from specific, strict, or proscriptive theology, and that primarily centers on self-help and self-improvement. What Bill Monson, who attends worship every Sunday and participates in a weekly men's Bible study, likes about the church is that "Pastor Rick really emphasizes the relationship with God" rather than "religion." To Monson, "religion is just all about rules." Congregant Peter Allen finds the worship experience to be "very therapeutic." "I go for the message," he says. "Every week I pick up a pearl that I can use as a self-improvement tool."

After attending CLASS 101, visitors may join the church by agreeing to a "Membership Covenant," and filling out an application on which they check a box to certify that they have "Committed [their] life to Jesus Christ and trusted Him for [their] salvation," "been baptized by immersion *after* [they] committed [their] life to Christ," and "have completed Discovering Church Membership 101." The covenant also includes commitments to move toward joining a small group, volunteering in the church, and tithing. At the June 2005 membership class, Pastor Steve Gladen surveyed attendees, and over half of the audience admitted to having attended Saddleback for three or more years before taking the membership course. One woman had attended Saddleback for over twenty years, had participated in every other aspect of the church, but had never actually become a member until that day. Saddleback's CLASS 101 literature encourages attendees to join the church by noting, "we live in an age where very few want to be committed to anything. . . . This attitude has even produced a generation of 'church shoppers and hoppers.' Membership swims against the current of America's 'consumer religion.'" This is a surprising assertion for a church that prides itself on offering consumer-driven worship experiences, and a customizable theology.

At the break in the three-hour CLASS 101, Gladen told his flock, "There are sandwiches and drinks under the tents outside—we'll meet back here in ten minutes to continue with the class."

"Oh, and if you've committed your life to Christ," he added casually, "go and see Dave at the back and get your free Bible."

• *Created for Community*

Though its ability to draw a crowd is Saddleback's most conspicuous characteristic, its leadership feels that what truly defines the church is its orientation toward small group fellowship. In a 2007 interview for the nationally syndicated radio show *Speaking of Faith*, Warren explained worship services at Saddleback this way: "The Sunday morning service is simply a funnel. It's the most visible, but it is honestly the least significant part of the church." Most significant, Warren emphasizes, is what happens when members take the step from anonymously attending a service to joining the church, and then joining a small group. "We're constantly turning up the commitment."[9]

Usually consisting of ten or fewer adults, small groups are miniature Christian communities that are member-led and meet weekly (usually in homes) to study the Bible, offer friendship and encouragement, and serve as a forum for discussing Pastor Rick's weekly sermons. Though numbers fluctuate, Saddleback counts over 3,300 small groups located in ninety-five Southern California cities. DB Tran, a Vietnamese woman who had a born again experience in a Christian church after coming to the United States as a refugee, is now one of Saddleback's most enthusiastic proponents, a member of two small groups, and a lay program head. She feels small groups are a key to the church's success because they utilize the talents and enthusiasm of the church's laity, and compel people to relate to and depend upon one another. "That's why Saddleback small groups work—it's real people without theology and training. It's about relating. The message of Christ becomes a message of love and care and sharing," she says. "When you do this and go to their house every week, it's powerful." Small groups also function as an easy point of entry for seekers who might otherwise be turned off by the megachurch worship format. "I can't invite a non-Christian friend to Saddleback [worship services] but I can always invite them to my small group," DB explains.

Pastor Steve Gladen, minister for small groups, says that groups formed around affinity or some shared demographic interest or identity have the highest "stick value," but small groups can also be geographic, or assembled more randomly. Gladen says that small groups are the lifeblood of Saddleback, and the church invests heavily in their promotion, organization, and management. Doing so has yielded members like the Ricardo family, who say they were looking to live "more of a Christian lifestyle," and decided to try Saddleback after having moved to Lake Forest. Such a large church was "a different concept" for them, and they believe that had weekend worship been their only point of contact, they might not have kept attending. Yet once they got involved in small groups, and Joan Ricardo started attending women's meetings, they "felt more grounded" and started "participating in every way." The Ricardos say they are now so attached to Saddleback that they've passed up the opportunity to move to a better neighborhood because they wanted to stay "close to campus."

As David Chrzan explains, "People tolerate a big church, but they don't like it because they don't feel their needs are being met. At Saddleback we keep breaking it down in an effort to hide the church's size." But what began as an organizational imperative—"how to make a big church feel small"—has evolved into a normative way of life. "You find your meaning in community," Warren declares as he sermonizes on small groups. "We were created for community." Attending a service gives any visitor the clear message that in order to get the full Saddleback experience—indeed the full Christian experience—one *must* join a small group.

Though the church's "Group Is Life" maxim is embraced by many congregants, some find it off-putting. Mark Weston resents the church's constant insistence that he join a small group. Religion, he thinks, is about his personal relationship with God, not his membership in a social club. From Pastor Gladen's point of view, that outlook reflects someone who has trouble "downloading the paradigm." "There are churches *with* small groups and churches *of* small groups," he explains, and, to his mind, Saddleback is decidedly the latter.

Prayer Requests

At 6:30 A.M. on Thursday a Saddleback small group of business professionals is gathering for their weekly Bible study at Coco's restaurant in Lake Forest. The majority of the group's ten members are seated around a large, long table in the front of the restaurant, and the waitress brings coffee and takes her regulars' usual orders.

Each small group at Saddleback is led by a "host," a leader who initiates the group and either opens his or her home for weekly meetings, or coordinates if the group is held at another location. Small group hosts are given support and training by community leaders (CLs), who are in most cases part-time paid employees of the church who have other full-time professions, but are serious about devoting a portion of their week to ministry. Of the small group convening today, Ted Romeo is simply a member, but also happens to serve as the group's CL. A soft-spoken man with a friendly demeanor, Ted guides the gathering with a soft touch, quietly adding comments here or there as each member speaks. Ted is a lawyer, but as he gives a personal update to the group, he mentions that he has just completed a seminary degree, and is in the process of interviewing for a ministry position at Saddleback. His friends express surprise that he is considering such an abrupt change of profession, and he asks for their prayers as he considers his options.

Ted explains that the group's official host is Christina Firth, a tall, slender thirty-something with an earnest, sober manner. She also is an attorney, but as she takes her turn to speak, she too alludes to a recent job change. Christina had been a top associate at a major law firm, but says she had become uncomfortable with the demanding hours she had to put in, and the consequent strain on her marriage. Through serious discussions with the members of her small group, she was encouraged to quit her job without any idea of where she would go. She took the "leap of faith," and shortly thereafter was invited to join a former partner in starting a new venture, which, she says, has turned out to be a perfect fit professionally, as well as allowing her to work half the hours of her previous job. She attributes the events to God and to her small group. "They really have been my support system," she says, "and I've also met a number of different people whom I never would meet any other way. Now they're my good friends," she adds, looking around the table thoughtfully.

Ted explains that the group's "leader of the day" is Jin, an environmental engineer from China. This distribution of leadership roles is typical of Saddleback's small groups, and is a feature of the system, which is designed to continually "raise up" new leaders who Pastor Gladen hopes will eventually branch out of their existing groups, spawning new ones. Jin has the appearance of a scientist, and has been a member of Saddleback for several years, but has been a Christian for exactly seven years, and has attended this small group for two and a half.

The other members of the group include Cynthia and James Grover, and Denise and Bob Carter. The Carters own a contracting business and have attended Saddleback for fifteen years. They are a clean-cut, happy-looking couple in their fifties who are decidedly less buttoned-down than the other professionals in the group. Bob is not terribly well spoken and has an awkward manner, but seems to fit in comfortably nonetheless. His wife is cheerful and friendly and has a warm, inviting smile. The couple has attended this small group for two years, and in describing what the fellowship has meant to them, Bob states, "It has been really, really special to us—we can open our hearts, really open up, and not be judged." Later in the meeting Bob demonstrates his newfound openness by asking the group to pray that he'll develop patience, admitting that he often gets out of control in staff meetings when "things just aren't getting done right." He says that Saddleback's Celebrate Recovery anger management classes have changed his life, but that he still needs the ongoing support of his small group.

As the group sips coffee and ice water, three more members trickle in: Joan, a quiet, petite middle-aged Chinese woman; Ethan, an inventor whose latest product is scripture-bearing custom decals for golf clubs; and Greg Matthews, a wisecracking, fifty-something lawyer—the only person at the table dressed in a suit and tie. After everyone is served their orders of oatmeal, omelets, and French toast, Christina explains that the group often begins their meeting with a brief reading or study of a biblical passage. Ted mentions that often the subject of conversation is a particular business issue that a group member faces, which they discuss in order to provide advice and support. Christina points out that this group tends to be most focused on "prayer requests," which consist of each group member discussing in turn the struggles and successes of their personal lives, and asking the other members to include them in their daily prayers. As they prepare to begin this portion of their meeting, almost everyone pulls out a notebook and a pen to write down what the others say.

As the requests come out, they include everything from "a big case I have coming up, which is important to my family financially," to a son whose final exams are around the corner, to the family of a cousin who recently committed suicide. There are requests for prayers for wisdom and guidance on major life decisions, and pleas for healing of ailments as simple as a common cold, or as weighty as a mother who is suffering from dementia and deteriorating rapidly. Each of the updates and requests is peppered with questions from the other group members. "How is your sister doing these days?" "How has it been going sharing Christ with your brother?" "Have you had any success with the product you've been trying to market?" In addition to requests for prayer and help, the group rejoices collectively when a member shares a success in their life, such as Ethan, who just this week has hired his first employee—"you've just doubled the size of your company!" remarks Jin.

By the time they have circled the table, each person has a page-long list of things to pray for in the coming week. Christina then offers to close with a prayer, and everyone instinctively bows their head and closes their eyes. For the next ten minutes, and amid the din of the restaurant's breakfast crowd, Christina offers a thorough and impassioned prayer, "laying before the Lord" exactly what each group member has brought up. Though cell phones ring intrusively at adjacent tables, pop music plays overhead, and the wait staff breeze back and forth, none of these professionals seems to feel the slightest bit uncomfortable with praying so openly. As they close with a collective "Amen," those who have to make it to work say their goodbyes and get up to leave, while the others linger around the table as the waitress comes to clear the empty plates.

"It's the Changed Lives"

With its user-friendly form of worship, flexible theology, multi-leveled membership commitments, and diverse family of small groups, Saddleback Church seems to have found a way to be all

things to all people, which may be one explanation for its stagger-
ing growth. Yet the most powerful connection many members claim
to Pastor Rick's megachurch is the transformative effect they feel it
has on their lives. People at Saddleback commonly share stories of
having been changed by their membership there, and Warren and
his staff say they work to create a "culture of transformation." As
men's pastor Kenny Luck explains, "the biblical Christ said 'Hungry?
Feed. Naked? Clothe.' This church is very much like that. It's about
meeting felt needs. You take an alcoholic and help him beat alco-
holism, and he'll say to you, 'What's next?' There are thousands of
people in this world who have never experienced that, and the fact is
that if you're helped in a felt-need way, you're incredibly loyal." Pastor Scott Hitzel agrees, adding, "We invest in the things that really
change us." Investment—temporal, financial, and spiritual—is certainly something that abounds at Saddleback, and Rick Warren's bet
is that the returns will only grow as his Purpose Driven network of
churches expands.

CHAPTER 3

RELIGIOSITY IN AMERICA: THE HISTORICAL BACKDROP

T rinity Episcopal Church in Boston (founded 1733) and Saddleback Church in Orange County (founded 1980) stand at opposite corners of America. Although they have much in common as sites of worship and fellowship, Trinity Boston and Saddleback represent different phases in the centuries-long development of American religion. This chapter and the next aim to provide a succinct interpretive summary of religion in America in the decades since the end of World War II.[1] Writing contemporary history is hazardous, because our understanding of the past, especially the recent past, inevitably changes as the future unfolds. Peaks, valleys, and landmarks dwindle as we move forward and then reappear in a new perspective as our path winds on. Reinterpretation of the past never ceases. Nevertheless, some sense of how we got here is crucial to describing and assessing where we are today.

The theme of Chapters 3 and 4 is change. Yet we begin by emphasizing that some things never change or at any rate change so slowly as to be virtually imperceptible. The most important fact about religion in America is that we are now—and have been since the Founding—a relatively pious and observant people, as we saw in Chapter 1. Scholars hotly debate exactly whether and how attendance at religious services has changed in the United States in recent decades, and we shall shortly join that debate, but most agree that church attendance has been relatively high in America throughout our history. Indeed, many argue that church attendance was higher in the twentieth century than in previous eras.[2]

Closer to our focus on the postwar era, when national surveys began to provide firmer evidence about Americans' religious beliefs and practices, one survey in 1948 found that 73 percent of Americans believed in the afterlife.[3] Six tumultuous decades later our 2006 Faith Matters survey found a statistically indistinguishable 70 percent. In 1937 an early Gallup Poll reported that 73 percent of Americans were members of a church or synagogue, and as late as 1999, despite some ups and downs, that figure was still 70 percent.[4]

In terms of private religious behavior one finds virtually the same rock-steady levels of religiosity. Polls covering the four decades between 1948 and 1990 found that nine out of ten Americans pray at least occasionally, a fraction that did not vary more than a few percentage points over these decades. The wording of a similar question in the General Social Survey between 1983 and 2008 differs slightly, but three quarters of Americans say they pray at least once a week, also a figure that has not varied more than a few percentage points from year to year throughout the last quarter century. The General Social Survey also suggests that the fraction of Americans with a self-described "strong" religious affiliation has held steady at just over one third (35–40 percent) since 1974.[5] In sum, while this chapter and the next will focus on some important changes in American religion over the last half century, we begin with the bedrock fact that America is now and always has been an unusually religious country.

Another enduring feature of American religion helps explain that relative stability: American religions, compared to religions in many other countries, have shown a remarkable ability to adapt to changing circumstances.[6] This chapter and the next, focusing on change, paradoxically confirm that enduring adaptability.

SLOW, STEADY, AND BARELY PERCEPTIBLE CHANGE

Most people's religious views and habits are formed fairly early in life. All of us then tend to evolve in fairly predictable ways as we age, following what social scientists call life cycle patterns. Most people become somewhat more observant religiously as they move through their thirties, marry, have children, and settle down. Then as we retire and approach the end of our lives, we often experience another phase of increased religiosity—"nearer my God to thee," perhaps.[7] These patterns produce a kind of life cycle escalator toward greater religiosity as an individual ages. However, people born and raised in different eras get onto that escalator at different levels. People raised in a less religious era may never become as observant as people raised in a more observant time, even though compared to their own earlier selves they may have become more observant. Such a difference between people born and raised in different eras is termed by social scientists a generational effect.

Both generational and life cycle patterns involve change, but in pure form they produce very different patterns of change. In pure life cycle patterns, individuals change, but society does *not* change.[8] Conversely, in pure generational change, individuals do *not* change, but society *does* change, as different generations enter and leave the population. However—and this point is crucial to understanding this chapter and the next—social change embodied in generational change is slow and gradual, because at any given time the population includes people from many different generations, and thus society-wide figures represent a kind of moving average. For example, the generation formed by the experiences of World War II was born in the 1920s, entered the adult population in the 1940s, became numerically dominant in the 1950s and 1960s, and began to disappear from the population in the 1980s and 1990s. Thus, their impact on aggregate American attitudes and behaviors was still being felt sixty to seventy years after their birth.

Generationally based change is thus much slower than other

forms of social change. If people of all ages experience simultaneous change in a particular period—what social scientists term a "period effect"—then like a school of fish the whole society can change direction very quickly, and can also reverse course just as quickly. But if only the youngest cohort in society changes (and then persists in that new direction throughout their own life cycle), society as a whole changes inexorably but almost imperceptibly, like a massive supertanker changing course.

Over time, therefore, generational change is especially important, mandating special attention to differences among successive cohorts of young people. Society-wide measures of religious behavior muffle portentous change that may be occurring at the younger edge of the population, so social prognosticators (just like commercial advertisers) focus on trends among young adults, trying to discern which aspects of behavior are what they are because the youths are *young*, and which aspects are what they are because of *when* they are young.

All three sorts of change—life cycle, generational, and period—can occur simultaneously, and thus we are likely to misperceive the slow but inexorable effects of generational change. Similarly, the ups and downs of daily weather patterns can easily obscure the slower but inexorable effects of climate change, as we are tempted to say, "What global warming? This has been an awfully cold winter." Careful measurement is needed to detect long-term climate change amidst the ups and downs of the daily weather report, and so too we will need careful measurement to detect generationally based change in religious behavior.

One final caution: If the differences between one generation and the next are small, then generationally based social change will be real (and significant) but very slow—perhaps taking many decades to become substantial. However, if for some reason a younger generation deviates substantially from its predecessors, then the aggregate social change may be quicker—significant over a few decades, for example, though still slower than period effects that produce substantial change over a few years.

To sum up, *period effects* that simultaneously affect people of all ages produce social change measurable over a few years; *large generational differences* produce social change measurable over a few decades; *small generational differences* produce social change measurable only over many decades; and pure *life cycle effects* produce no social change at all. As we shall now see, American religious life over the last half century offers excellent examples of all varieties of change. We begin with an important example of real but very slow change, driven by real but modest intergenerational differences.

The clearest and possibly the most important instance of slow generational change involves religious observance, as measured (for example) by attendance at religious services. Figure 3.1 provides a visual image of how generational change has influenced religious attendance over the last forty years.[9]

Each line in the graph traces the religious trajectory of people born in a given decade, from those who came of age before 1940 to

Figure 3.1

TRENDS IN RELIGIOUS ATTENDANCE
BY DECADE IN WHICH RESPONDENT REACHED ADULTHOOD (1972–2008)

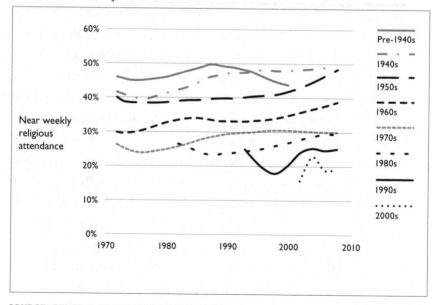

SOURCE: GENERAL SOCIAL SURVEY; DATA LOESS-SMOOTHED.

those who came of age in the twenty-first century. The slight rise in each line reflects the life cycle effect of gradually increasing observance as a given group aged. (The final downturn in church attendance among those who came of age before 1940 at the top of the chart probably reflects the impact of infirmities, as that cohort aged through their eighties.) The vertical displacement between each successive line reflects generational differences where each successive cohort began its ascent up the life cycle escalator, or in other words, the gradual generational decline in religious observance. For example, as people entered adulthood in the 1970s, roughly 25 percent of them attended church weekly, but as their own children came of age in the 2000s, roughly 20 percent of them attended church that often.[10]

If we focus on individuals (or birth cohorts) as they age, they become slowly more religiously observant. However, if we focus on social change—accounting for differences between those entering the population and those leaving the population—society became slowly *less* observant over this period. That society-wide trend is shown in Figure 3.2.

Some complicated statistical manipulation is needed to pull apart the effects of individual aging and cohort replacement (and to distinguish them from possible period effects), but that sort of calculation suggests that in round numbers each decade in an individual's life adds one more week of church attendance to his or her annual average. Conversely, people born in each successive decade have attended church about one week fewer per year than people born a decade earlier. People born in the 1950s and now in their fifties, for example, attend church about one week fewer per year than people born in the 1940s when *they* were in *their* fifties.[11]

These specific numbers should not be taken too seriously, of course, since we are simplifying the religious ups and downs of millions of Americans over half a century. We cite them merely to illustrate how slowly generationally driven changes in church attendance accumulate. In round numbers, our calculations suggest, at this rate it would take a *century* of this same slow generational change to

Figure 3.2

AGGREGATE TREND IN RELIGIOUS ATTENDANCE IN AMERICA
(1972–2008)

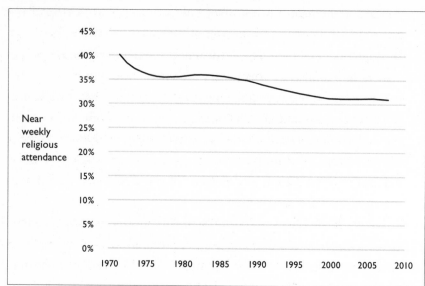

SOURCE: GENERAL SOCIAL SURVEY; DATA LOESS-SMOOTHED.

lower average American church attendance from (say) thirty times a year to twenty times a year. People sometimes speak of a process of "secularization" in America that will bring church attendance to the current levels of Western Europe, but this sort of calculation suggests that if we are witnessing such a process in the United States, at this rate it will take a couple of centuries to reduce American religious observance to the current European levels. It would be a foolhardy historian indeed to predict what will happen to U.S. religion over a period of centuries, and thus, while recognizing the slow generational decline in American religiosity over the last half century, we are skeptical about bold assertions of secularization in America.[12]

• Closer examination of the differences among the cohorts in Figure 3.1 reveals that the pace of the decline in religious attendance from generation to generation is not constant. In particular, the pace of the decline accelerated significantly as the baby boomers (born 1946–1964) came of age from the mid-1960s to the mid-1980s. Precisely that same acceleration appears in a comparable analysis (not presented here) of data from the National Election Studies. Consider the aggregate implication of that timing. From the mid-1960s to the mid-1980s, the relatively less observant baby boomers swarmed into adulthood in massive numbers, just as their much more observant grandparents departed the scene. In round numbers, about 25 percent of the arriving boomers were regular churchgoers, whereas 45 percent of those departing had been that observant. To be sure, like their parents and grandparents, the boomers gradually became more observant as they aged. But the boomers would never catch up with the levels of observance of previous generations, and over the long run that process of generational succession put very slow, but steady, downward pressure on national rates of church attendance.[13]

One way of zooming in on the religious observance of different generations of American youth is to consult evidence from a long-running study of successive cohorts of college freshmen nationwide, conducted annually by researchers at UCLA ever since 1966.[14] Every year this massive sample of young people has been asked if they attended religious services at least occasionally in the previous year—that is, their senior year in high school. Figure 3.3 gives a snapshot of how adolescent religious observance has fared over the last four decades. Note that because we are examining people of the same age over this entire period, we are, in effect, excluding any possible life cycle change.

First, adolescent attendance at religious services seems to have become steadily less common over this period.[15] Of college freshmen in 1968, barely 8 percent had attended *no* religious services in the previous year, but by 2009 that entirely unobservant fraction of young people had more than tripled to 25 percent. (This specific question embodies a very low threshold of observance, but related evidence from the General Social Survey suggests that more demanding questions would have shown a parallel decline.) That decline from cohort to cohort underlies the patterns shown in Figures 3.1 and 3.2.

Second, however, the chart hints at two periods when youthful disaffection accelerated—the 1960s (only the latter part of which is

Figure 3.3

DECLINE OF ADOLESCENT RELIGIOUS OBSERVANCE (1968–2009)

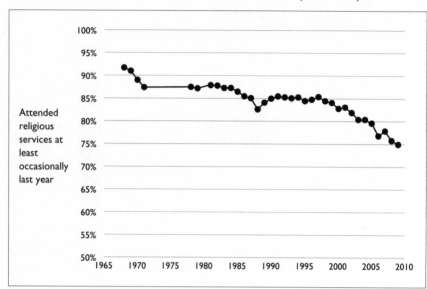

SOURCE: THE AMERICAN FRESHMAN ANNUAL SURVEYS.

visible through this window) and the 1990s and early 2000s, separated by more than a quarter century of relatively little change between 1971 (13 percent nonobservance) and 1997 (15 percent nonobservance). In the next chapter both those periods of concentrated change, along with the intervening period of stability, will get more attention.

One final bit of evidence regarding long-term trends in religious observance in America comes from simply asking Americans "How often did your family attend religious services when you were growing up, if at all?" and comparing the answers to their own religious attendance today. In our 2006 Faith Matters survey, 46 percent say they attend church less often than their family did when they were growing up, 34 percent say the same, and 20 percent say they attend more frequently now than their family did.[16]

As Figure 3.4 shows, Americans who came of age in the twenty-first century are much more likely than Americans who came of age in the twentieth century to report lower church attendance than

Figure 3.4

RECENT COHORTS REPORT A BIGGER DROP-OFF FROM THEIR
PARENTS' RELIGIOUS ATTENDANCE

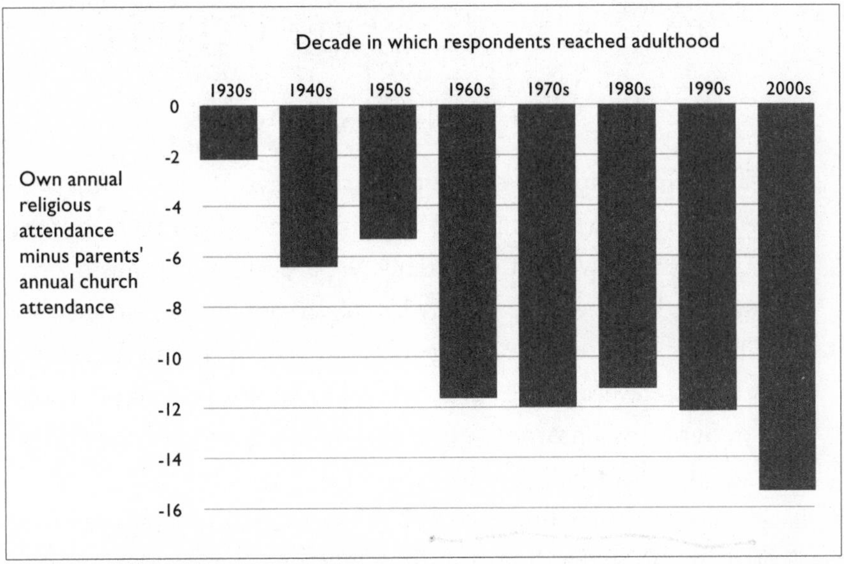

SOURCE: FAITH MATTERS SURVEY, 2006.

was true of their families when they were growing up, a pattern
that confirms our conclusion that generational replacement is producing a slow but steady decline in religious observance. On closer
examination, Figure 3.4 suggests most of the change from cohort
to cohort seems to have occurred in two specific periods—with the
advent of the boomers, who reached adulthood from the mid-1960s
to the mid-1980s, and then with the advent of the millennial generation, who reached adulthood in the 2000s. That specific timing—that
generationally based declines in religious observance sped up in the
1960s, stabilized from the 1970s to the 1990s, and then accelerated
again toward the turn of the century—is consistent with the evidence in Figure 3.3. We shall return to that issue of timing in the
next chapter.

To sum up, independent streams of evidence suggest that Americans have become somewhat less observant religiously over the last
half century, mostly because of slight but cumulative declines from

generation to generation, especially with the coming of age of the boomers in the 1960s and of the millennials at the end of the century.

FAST, UNEVEN, PERCEPTIBLE CHANGE—A SHOCK AND TWO AFTERSHOCKS

So far in this chapter we have discussed ways in which American religious behavior has changed very little, and ways in which it has changed very slowly but inexorably. We are still a religious people, though we have become slightly less observant and (as we shall see in Chapter 5) much less stringent about religious boundaries. We now turn to several more abrupt and momentous periods of change and even reversal in Americans' religious beliefs, practices, and identities over the last half century.

Our argument in brief is this: While change and adaptability have long been the hallmark of American religion, over the last half century the direction and pace of change have shifted and accelerated in three seismic phases. Since the 1950s one major shock and two major aftershocks have shaken and cleaved the American religious landscape, successively thrusting a large portion of one generation of Americans in a secular direction, then in reaction thrusting a different group of the population in a conservative religious direction, and finally in counterreaction to that first aftershock, sending yet another generation of Americans in a more secular direction. Just as an earthquake and its aftershocks can leave a deep fissure in physical terrain, so too this religious quake and its pair of aftershocks have left a deep rift in the political and religious topography of America.

We begin this discussion with a survey of the American religious countryside in the 1950s, in retrospect a relatively placid period of pervasive but diffuse religiosity. We then in Chapter 4 observe how a temblor of social, sexual, and political turmoil in what historians call "the long Sixties" coincided with the alienation of a large part of the Baby Boom generation from conventional religion and conventional morality. ("The long Sixties" refers to the fact that much of what is commonly referred to as "the Sixties" lasted through the early 1970s.) This seismic upheaval (the first of our three metaphorical shocks) was so widely felt and discussed that this part of our story will mainly be a reminder of just how swiftly religious and moral beliefs and practices shifted in those years.

Slightly less well known is the fact that just as the political and social movements of the Sixties provoked a political reaction in the form of what Richard Nixon called "the Silent Majority," so too a significant number of Americans, some young and some older, were appalled by what they saw as the moral and spiritual decay of that era. This counterreaction was spurred by many aspects of the Sixties, but standards of personal sexual morality (or immorality) were an important part of the story. In denominational and organizational terms these impulses led many concerned Americans toward evangelical and conservative churches, and eventually into what became known as the Religious Right. As we shall see, during the 1970s and 1980s this part of the American religious spectrum attracted attention, energy, adherents, and eventually political prominence. Thus, the rise of evangelicals and then of the Religious Right constituted the first aftershock to the tumult of the 1960s.

Certainly not all evangelicals were (or are) deeply conservative or members of the Religious Right. Most of them are in church for the religion, not the politics, as we shall see later in this book. But beginning in the 1980s and continuing into the first decade of the new century, conservative politics became the most visible aspect of religion in America. While that development encouraged a certain kind of triumphalism among some leaders of the Religious Right, it deeply troubled many other Americans, especially those whose attachment to organized religion was weak, in part because they were just coming of age. For many Americans raised in the 1980s and 1990s, religion as they saw it around them seemed to be mostly about conservative politics and especially about traditional positions on issues of sexual morality, like homosexuality. In effect, many of these Americans, who might have been religiously inclined, but were liberal on moral issues, said "if that's what religion is all about, then it's not for me." Thus, the second aftershock, during the 1990s and 2000s, thrust a substantial number of Americans, especially young Americans, in a decidedly nonreligious direction.

We disavow any single causal interpretation of historical trends—too many different things are going on in modern society for any simple story to be explanatory. Many factors contributed to each shock and aftershock in this half century of American religious history. That said, one common theme throughout the period, we shall argue, is the significance of personal sexual morality. In unacademically vivid language, intended for clarity's sake, but at the risk of oversimplification, we argue that throughout these last five decades *libertines* and *prudes* have successively provoked one another: Liberal sexual morality provoked some Americans to assert conservative religious beliefs and affiliations, and then conservative sexual morality provoked other Americans to assert secular beliefs and affiliations.

With each seismic expansion of the fissure over this half century, fewer and fewer Americans remained in the center of the religious spectrum, and those at each growing pole became more hostile and suspicious toward their opponents at the opposite extreme. Moreover, this religious dimension became steadily more aligned with the conventional left–right (or Democrat–Republican) spectrum in American politics, producing the so-called God gap. At midcentury, religiosity and politics had been barely correlated: Liberals were common in the pews of the 1960s, and they were matched by plenty of unchurched conservatives. By the end of the century both groups had become rare. Political and religious divides now reinforce one another, rather than cutting across and thus attenuating the divisions. This historical sequence forged the sociological undergirding for the much discussed culture wars of our time.

• THE 1950s: THE HIGH TIDE OF CIVIC RELIGION

Since flux is a constant in American religion, there is no "normal" period in our religious history, and certainly not the 1950s. The years after World War II witnessed an unusual surge in public religiosity, so much so that some observers classified it as another of the Great Awakenings of evangelical fervor that have punctuated American religious history, helping to produce such epochal events as the American Revolution, the abolition movement, and the Progressive Era. That labeling of the 1950s was in retrospect misleading, because unlike the ecstatic enthusiasms of earlier awakenings, the postwar surge was channeled primarily through conventional and even establishment institutions, portending no great revolution, either civil or religious. For our story the postwar period is important primarily as the backdrop for the momentous religious changes of the ensuing half century.

The anxieties of World War II seem to have revived American interest in religion that had flagged in the 1920s and 1930s—"no atheists in foxholes," it was said—though elsewhere wars have often been associated with a decline of religion.[17] Postwar affluence, social mobility, and the onset of the Cold War and its attendant nuclear standoff encouraged a paradoxical mixture of optimism and anxiety and a renewed appreciation for traditional values, including both patriotism and religion. Most important, the returning veterans and their wives began producing what would soon be called the baby boom. Then, as now, getting married, settling down, and raising children were associated with more regular churchgoing.

The resulting surge in religious involvement during the 1950s was truly massive, even compared to the seismic events later in the century. Figure 3.5 outlines the ups and downs of religious attendance in America over the last seventy years. The level of religious attendance reported in the Gallup surveys probably exaggerates the reality, especially in recent decades, when most other surveys show a gradual decline.[18] Virtually all experts agree, however, that the period from the late 1940s to the early 1960s was one of exceptional religious observance in America.

The upsurge was heavily concentrated among twenty-somethings. Figure 3.6 pulls together evidence from scores of Gallup surveys to illustrate that, while all generations participated in this

Figure 3.5

RELIGIOUS ATTENDANCE IN AMERICA: THE 1950s BOOM (1939–2008)

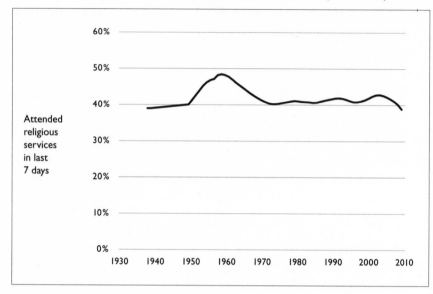

SOURCE: GALLUP POLL REPORTS; DATA LOESS-SMOOTHED.

postwar upsurge, it was especially marked among young adults in their twenties in the 1950s. In that group, weekly church attendance skyrocketed from 31 percent in February 1950 to an all-time record for young adults of 51 percent in April 1957, an astonishing rate of change in seven years, implying millions of new churchgoers every year.

Further analysis (this time of the National Election Studies archives) shows that the surge was somewhat greater among whites[19] and among college-educated men. Of white men aged twenty-one to thirty-four, weekly churchgoing rose from 28 percent in 1952 to 44 percent in 1964.

Who were these unusually pious young men? Of all American men born in the 1920s, 80 percent had served in the military during World War II, and after the war many took advantage of the GI Bill to become the first college-educated persons in their families. It was this GI generation who as young husbands and fathers, together with their wives, led the surge to church in the late 1940s and 1950s.

ure 3.6

ENDS IN RELIGIOUS ATTENDANCE BY AGE BRACKET (1950–2008)

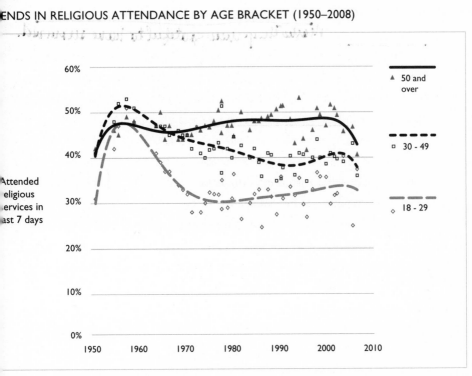

SOURCE: GALLUP POLL REPORTS; DATA LOESS-SMOOTHED.

We saw earlier (in Figures 3.1 and 3.4) that this cohort would remain unusually observant for the rest of their lives. Throughout all the shocks and aftershocks of the ensuing half century and even into the next millennium the GIs and their wives and widows would form the bedrock of American religious institutions (and of civic institutions as well).[20]

This surge had no partisan political cast. Republicans and Democrats, liberals and conservatives were equally represented among those thronging the pews. Rather, the distinguishing features of the men now accompanying their wives to church were that they were mostly young fathers, mostly veterans, and mostly college-educated. The postwar boom in churchgoing was fueled above all by men who had survived the Great Depression as teenagers and World War II as grunts, and were now ready at last to settle into a normal life, with a steady job, a growing family, a new house and car, and respectable middle-class status. Churchgoing was an important emblem of that respectability.   *Maybe they were grateful to have survived.*

Singling out the sociological center of the surge should not obscure how widespread religious engagement was during this period, visible in nearly all segments of society. In fact, the returning GIs were merely narrowing the gap in church attendance with women, blacks, and older Americans, who had always been (and remained) more observant than young white men, so the GIs deserve pride of place in our account only on the theological principle that the newly saved merit special praise.

Though most visible in mainline Protestant and Catholic churches, the surge was felt in all religious traditions. Sketching this period against the backdrop of more than three centuries of American religious history, Sydney Ahlstrom summarized:

> American religious communities of nearly every type (Protestant, Catholic, and Jewish; churches, sects, and cults) were favored during the postwar decade and a half by an increase of commitment and a remarkable popular desire for institutional participation.[21]

As Ahlstrom observed, religious vitality was marked not merely by increasing attendance, but by the institutional commitment embodied in church membership that burgeoned from 49 percent of the adult population in 1940 to 69 percent in 1960. Church building set new records to accommodate all those new worshippers. Historian Patrick Allitt noted that "huge numbers of the young families living in the new suburbs decided to join their local churches. Their plentiful children, the baby boom, needed not only sanctuaries but also playgrounds, youth groups, and Sunday schools."[22] In inflation-adjusted dollars, church construction rose from $26 million in 1945 to $304 million in 1950 and then to $615 million in 1960.[23] Bibles were printed at an ever-increasing rate, and polling (in its infancy) suggested that those Bibles were actually being read and believed.[24]

More and more clergy were called to minister to larger and larger flocks, so seminary enrollments surged.[25] The now oversized main sanctuary of Trinity Episcopal Church in Concord, Massachusetts, that we visited in the previous chapter, built in 1963, is a monument to the expansive (and as it turned out, unrealistic) expectations for church growth characteristic of postwar America.

In their beliefs, as in their behavior, Americans in the 1950s seemed exceptionally religious. In 1952, 75 percent of Americans told Gallup pollsters that religion was "very important" in their lives, an all-time record. In 1957, given a choice that Gallup has posed for more than half a century—whether religion "can answer today's problems" or is "old-fashioned and out-of-date"—81 percent said religion was relevant to today's world, another all-time high.[26]

• It was not just private fervor that brought people to church in postwar America. At least as important was social pressure. In 1948 a national sample of Americans was asked "why do you go to church?" The single most common answer (32 percent) reflected a spiritual motivation: "the need or desire for some sort of inspiration or uplift." However, virtually all the other commonly cited reasons for churchgoing were more social than theological. In declining order of frequency they were "obedience to convention or duty," "habit," "to hear the sermon," "to set a good example," "to hear the music," and "to see people."[27]

For many of the families now packing the pews, religious attendance was less an act of piety than an act of civic duty, like joining the PTA or Rotary, organizations whose membership rolls, not coincidentally, were also exploding in these same years.[28] George Gallup Jr. and Jim Castelli report that "a remarkable 24 percent of American adults said that at some time in 1957 they had called on people to ask them to attend or join their church. And as many as 60 percent said they had been called upon to attend or join a church."[29] Churchgoing was the thing to do.

It was so, in part, because in the era of the Cold War against "atheistic communism," religion represented patriotism, a central, unifying theme of national purpose, or what sociologist Robert

Bellah would later term "civil religion."[30] "Being a church member and speaking favorably of religion became a means of affirming the 'American way of life,'" reported Ahlstrom.[31] It was no accident that "under God" was added to the Pledge of Allegiance in 1954 and "In God we trust" stamped onto our coins as the national motto in 1956. As Ahlstrom wryly observed, these civic embodiments of religious sentiment "were not forced upon an unresponsive people by a few pious political leaders. Given the temper of the electorate, it is more likely that even impious congressmen found it expedient to vote for God."[32]

Ahlstrom aptly summed up the civic dimension of the 1950s religious boom:

> Religion and Americanism were brought together to an unusual degree. This was especially true of the 1950s, when President Dwight D. Eisenhower served for eight years as a prestigious symbol of generalized religiosity and Americans' self-satisfied patriotic moralism. The president even provided a classic justification for the new religious outlook. "Our government," he said in 1954, "makes no sense unless it is founded on a deeply felt religious faith—and I don't care what it is."[33]

To which one critic at the time sniffed, "President Eisenhower, like many Americans, is a very fervent believer in a very vague religion."[34] Eisenhower was not alone in disregarding fine theological distinctions, however; according to historians Maurice Isserman and Michael Kazin, "The more citizens dutifully attended a church or synagogue, the less the traditional content of their faith seemed to matter to them."[35]

A sense of shared generic (or "Judeo-Christian," a term invented in this period) values began to emerge, and in institutional terms the ecumenical movement gathered steam. Mainline (or what was sometimes called liberal) Protestantism, which had long dominated American society, was at floodtide. Catholicism, while still a target of some prejudice and discrimination as an "immigrant" religion, was moving toward the mainstream as second-generation immigrants moved into middle-class suburbia. Evangelical Protestantism was expanding beyond its early-twentieth-century fundamentalist isolation in the rural South, and sawdust revivalist Billy Sunday was replaced by "pastor to presidents" Billy Graham as the public symbol of evangelicalism. There was talk of moderate neo-evangelicalism, as the older theological debates between modernists and fundamentalists receded into the past.[36]

As historian Uta Andrea Balbier points out, neo-evangelicalism took from its fundamentalist roots "its concentration on a literal reading of the Bible, its belief in the Second Coming of Christ, and its emphasis on Victorian family ideas. But neo-evangelicalism discarded one important aspect of its fundamentalist roots: It no longer relegated religious conviction to the private sphere but let it cross over into the public realm."[37] That would be an important factor in enabling this religious tradition to flourish in the coming decades.

Demarcations among the major religious traditions still dominated American maps of organized religion. Will Herberg argued in his 1955 classic book *Protestant—Catholic—Jew* that religion was as much about identity as about faith, with denominations linked to specific immigrant flows. Assimilation, he argued, occurred not in a single national melting pot, but in three separate melting pots (Protestant/Catholic/Jew), and religious tradition was replacing national origin as the basis of Americans' identity. In 1961, sociologist Gerhard Lenski emphasized the persistence of religious segregation and foresaw rising rates of church attendance and ever deeper communal division among America's separate religious groups.[38] In fact, however, although American religious culture in this period was "informed by" denominational divisions, as sociologist Robert Wuthnow would later argue, American religion was on the verge of realignment, as those traditional divisions were supplanted by a polarizing distinction between religious liberals and religious conservatives.[39]

Whatever the balance between denominational separatism and ecumenical togetherness, between theological rigor and theological vacuity, America was clearly a very religious place in the 1950s. Most Americans expected that trend to continue. In 1957, 69 percent of Americans told Gallup pollsters that "religion is increasing its influence on American life." Within barely a decade, those expectations would be utterly overturned, as the first of our three seismic shocks rumbled through the land.

CHAPTER 4

RELIGIOSITY IN AMERICA: SHOCK AND TWO AFTERSHOCKS

1960s: THE SHOCK: SEX, DRUGS, ROCK 'N' ROLL AND "GOD IS DEAD"

The comfortable era of civic calm for many Americans continued into the first few years of the 1960s. However, President Kennedy's shocking assassination in 1963, followed by racial upheaval, more tragic assassinations, and the growing controversy about the Vietnam War signaled the arrival of the long Sixties by mid-decade. America's ensuing cultural revolution proved less lethal than Mao's, but more enduring.

The Sixties represented a perfect storm for American institutions of all sorts—political, social, sexual, and religious. In retrospect we can discern a mélange of contributing factors: the bulge in the youngest age cohorts as the boomers moved through adolescence and into college, the combination of unprecedented affluence and the rapid expansion of higher education, "the Pill," the abating of Cold War anxieties, Vatican II, the assassinations, the Vietnam War, Watergate, pot and LSD, the civil rights movement and the other movements that followed in its wake—the antiwar movement, the women's liberation movement, and later the environmental and gay rights movements. This is not the place to sort out the importance of those and other factors, still less to render historical judgment on any of them. The crucial points for our story are, first, that hardly any institution or sector of society was immune from attack, especially youthful attack, and second, that virtually every major theme in the Sixties' controversies would divide Americans for the rest of the century, setting the fuse for the so-called culture wars.

Writing just as this era was ending, Sydney Ahlstrom aptly summarized this period in the long sweep of American religious history:

> The decade of the Sixties was a time, in short, when the old foundations of national confidence, patriotic idealism, moral traditionalism, and even of historic Judaeo-Christian theism, were awash. Presuppositions that had held firm for centuries—even millennia—were being widely questioned. Some sensational manifestations came and went (as fads and fashions will), but the existence of a basic shift of mood rooted in deep social and institutional dislocations was anything but ephemeral. . . . [I]t was perfectly clear to any reasonably observant American that the postwar revival of the Eisenhower years had completely sputtered out, and that the nation was experiencing a *crise de conscience* of unprecedented depth.[1]

One facet of the tumult would be especially important for subsequent phases of our story—the explosive emergence of the "sex, drugs, and rock 'n' roll" youth counterculture. Even in retrospect it is hard to appreciate just how rapidly traditional sexual norms were overturned, especially among American youth. Not surprisingly, we lack detailed statistical evidence on when and how sexual behavior itself changed, but sociologists David Harding and Christopher Jencks have painstakingly pieced together survey data from a variety of sources on when and how norms changed, and specifically on the question of whether premarital sex was right or wrong.[2]

The best evidence is that the fraction of all Americans believing that premarital sex was "not wrong" doubled from 24 percent to 47 percent in the four years between 1969 and 1973 and then drifted upward through the 1970s to 62 percent in 1982. Relevant surveys prior to 1969 are even rarer—silent testimony to how uncontested the norm of premarital chastity was in the 1950s—but scattered evidence suggests that virtually all the change in the norm came in one burst of liberation in the late 1960s and early 1970s.

• Not surprisingly, older people, socialized in the first half of the century, were less likely to change their views, though they did become slightly more liberal in later years. For the most part, however, this is a classic case of generational change, since the cohorts who came of age in the 1960s—that is, the boomers—were exceptionally more liberal about premarital sex—with upward of 80 percent saying that premarital sex was "only sometimes wrong" or "not at all wrong." Similarly, in 1970 nearly half of all Americans reported that they were more liberal than their parents on premarital sex.[3] As they aged, boomers would become somewhat more conservative on sexual issues, but they remained (and remain today) much more accepting of premarital sex than their elders ever were.

The post-boomer generations who arrived on the scene in the 1980s were more conservative than the boomers on many political, social, and religious topics, but they did not revert to traditional norms that proscribed premarital sex. On the other hand, neither did they push beyond the boomers on this issue. Although the steady rhythm of cohort replacement gradually shifted nationwide norms in a slightly more liberal direction after the 1970s, none of that was new change, but instead reflected the long-term effects of that extraordinary moment of massive generational change in the late 1960s and early 1970s.

We focus on premarital sex because rigorous evidence over time on this specific norm allows us to be precise about the pace and contours of change. That norm represents merely a single indicator (though a potent one, as we shall shortly see) of a broader set of attitudes regarding sexual morality, pornography, and the like. Attitudes toward extramarital sex and homosexuality followed different paths, and in neither case did the Sixties have the same transformative power.[4] Nevertheless, the norm regarding premarital sex does encapsulate an astonishingly rapid change in intimate mores, as a well-defined cohort of young people, four fifths of whom accepted sex before marriage, charged into a population of their elders, four fifths of whom rejected that principle—literally a revolution in traditional moral views, at a pace almost certainly unprecedented in American history. As we shall see, the reverberations from that quake continue to shape American society, including American religion.[5]

Against a backdrop of such widespread, rapid, multifaceted change—in sexual morality, in politics, and in every other sphere of society—religion could hardly remain unchanged. Maurice Isserman and Michael Kazin, the preeminent chroniclers of the Sixties, conclude that "Nothing changed so profoundly in the United States during the 1960s as American religion."[6]

First, alongside most other major institutions, religious institutions suffered a dramatic loss of confidence and self-confidence. During the 1950s, as we have seen, religious institutions had been among the most authoritative in the country. The youth movements of the Sixties followed the widespread bumper-sticker advice to "Question Authority," however, and survey after survey in the 1970s and 1980s reported steadily declining confidence in all institutions, including organized religion.[7]

"As questions of justice, equality, war and peace, rights and responsibilities burst onto the stage of national attention," observed Robert Wuthnow, "religious leaders found it impossible to sit quietly on the sidelines."[8] Mainline or liberal Protestant churches, accustomed to more than a century of social dominance, were especially struck by inspiration or demoralization or both. Some liberal clerics, Catholics as well as Protestants, such as William Sloane Coffin (antiwar chaplain at Yale) and Fathers Daniel and Philip Berrigan (forceful antiwar activists), became prominent in the movements of the era. Perhaps the most widely discussed theological book of the 1960s was Harvey Cox's *The Secular City* (1965), arguing that the church should be in the forefront of social change.

Some radical theologians espoused post-Christian ideas in the so-called death of God movement. Indeed, so dramatic was the change from the placidly religious and conservative 1950s that in 1966 this theology made it to the cover of *Time* magazine (see Figure 4.1). Despite or because of (opinions differed drastically, of course) theological, liturgical, and political experimentation, liberal churches began to hemorrhage members.

· Only a few years after seminaries had been crammed with applicants, many denominations found that large numbers of clergy had lost their calling or lost their way. A nationwide survey of clergy in 1971 found that 40 percent of those under forty had seriously considered leaving the clergy. Another subtle seismic signal: Sales of reli-

Figure 4.1
IS GOD DEAD?

gious publications as a percentage of all books and pamphlets sold in the United States dropped by one third between 1954 and 1972.[9]

The Catholic Church was severely affected not merely by events in America, but also by decisions in Rome. Vatican II, a major Catholic reform council held from 1962 to 1965, triggered far-reaching changes in liturgy (for example, Latin replaced by vernacular English in the U.S.), practices (for example, the virtual disappearance of confession), ecumenism (for example, papal recognition of the legitimacy of other religions), and the structure of the church (for example, the role of the laity)—changes that were on the whole welcome to church liberals, but anathema to conservatives. On the other hand, the church's insistent opposition to birth control was opposed by two thirds of American Catholics, and while some of them simply ignored *Humanae Vitae* (the papal encyclical of July 1968 prohibiting contraception), many others stopped going to church.[10] The number of self-identified Catholics did not decline much, but attendance at Mass among American Catholics (especially young Catholics) fell so dramatically that Catholics alone accounted for much of the aggregate decline in religious attendance during the long Sixties.[11] "No denomination underwent more rapid or wrenching change," concluded Isserman and Kazin.[12]

As we shall see in more detail later, the process of disaffection was not identical among Catholics and mainline Protestants. Catholics deserted Mass, but often continued calling themselves Catholic, whereas disaffected mainline Protestants tended to stop calling themselves Methodist or Presbyterian or whatever, so that ironically attendance levels among those who remained identified with mainline Protestant faiths did not fall much. Focusing on attendance made it look as though Catholics were in more trouble than mainline Protestants, whereas focusing on formal identification made it look as though mainline Protestants were in more trouble, when in fact both were in trouble, and those troubles would continue in the decades ahead.

The long Sixties also saw unprecedented religious experimentation outside traditional denominational channels.[13] Some boomers, interested in what they called the "spiritual," but disdaining conventional religion, were soon dubbed "seekers," looking for new *what sea?* spiritual homes. "Personalism," "situational ethics," and "multiple truths" became hot topics in theological debates. Much less highfalutin but more evocative was the emergence of "Sheilaism," named after a woman quoted by Robert Bellah and his colleagues in their bestseller *Habits of the Heart*:

> "I believe in God. I am not a fanatic. I can't remember the last time I went to church. My faith has carried me a long way. It's Sheilaism. Just my own little voice . . . My own Sheilaism . . . is just try to love yourself and be gentle with yourself. You know, I guess, take care of each other." [14]

In this climate of opinion, emphasizing personal truths, writes historian Amanda Porterfield, "religious certainty begins to erode and a certain degree of religious relativism is inevitable." [15] In pop culture, this was the Age of Aquarius and Jesus freaks, Scientology and *Jesus Christ Superstar*, Zen Buddhism and *est*, Transcendental Meditation and the Unification Church (or "Moonies").

Meanwhile, as religious liberals let a thousand flowers bloom, conservative evangelicals quietly marshaled their forces, and laid the groundwork for their counterattack, as marked, for example, by the expansion of the Campus Crusade for Christ staff from 109 employees in 1960 to 6,500 in the mid-1970s. [16] With the notable exception of evangelical initiatives, few of the religious innovations of the 1960s would survive as significant elements on the American religious scene, but the very diversity of the spiritual menu laid before the seekers was symptomatic of the disarray in conventional American religion. *Variety itself survives.*

In the end, however, the most substantial indication of the breadth of change wrought by the Sixties' earthquake was the rapid decline in religious observance itself. The fraction of all Americans who said that religion was "very important" to them personally fell from 75 percent in 1952 and 70 percent as late as 1965 to 52 percent in 1978, while the fraction who said that "religion can answer today's problems" dropped from 81 percent in 1957 to 62 percent in 1974. According to the Gallup Poll, weekly church attendance nationwide plummeted from 49 percent in 1958 to 42 percent in 1969, by far the largest decline on this measure ever recorded in such a brief period.[17]

Such nationwide averages, moreover, drastically understated the rate of change among young people. Among twenty-somethings, the rate of decline in church attendance was more than twice the national average. Indeed, among those over fifty (as Figure 3.6 showed) there was virtually no decline at all, while among those aged eighteen to twenty-nine, weekly religious attendance was cut nearly in half, from 51 percent in April 1957 to 28 percent in December 1971.[18] This youthful disengagement affected virtually all segments of society, black Americans (long the most observant ethnic group in the nation) even more than whites.[19] Just as the religious surge in the postwar period had been led by the college-educated GI generation, so too the decline of the long Sixties was somewhat more rapid among college-educated young people, though it affected all levels of the socioeconomic hierarchy.[20]

It is hard to imagine a more clearly defined generational phenomenon. Although later in life boomers would move up the conventional life cycle toward somewhat greater religious observance, they would always remain much less observant than their parents had been at an equivalent age. Throughout their lives boomers would attend religious services about 25–30 percent less often than their parents had done at the same stage of life. For example, when the birth cohort of the 1920s (broadly speaking, the boomers' parents) were in their fifties, they averaged 42 percent weekly or near-weekly church attendance; when the boomers were in their fifties, they averaged 32 percent weekly or near-weekly church attendance.[21] Just as the boomers' parents had been largely responsible for the postwar surge in religiosity, the boomers themselves were largely responsible for the collapse in religiosity two decades later.

Perhaps the most sensitive seismometer recording this religious temblor was provided by the American people themselves. Recall that as late as 1957, 69 percent of Americans had observed that "the influence of religion in America is growing." Barely five years later that number had fallen to 45 percent, and it continued to fall to 33 percent in 1965, 23 percent in 1967, and 18 percent in 1968, finally bottoming out at 14 percent in 1969 and 1970, before recovering to 30–40 percent in the late 1970s. This measure too showed a substantial generation gap, as young people in the 1960s were far more inclined than their elders to believe that religion was losing influence.[22]

The timing and the generational location of the dramatic change in sexual mores that we discussed earlier and the timing and generational location of this dramatic change in religious observance were strikingly similar. Moreover, the two affected the very same people— the young people who adopted liberal views on sexual morality were mostly the same young people who skipped church. So it is natural to wonder whether sexual liberation led to religious apostasy or the reverse, or whether (perhaps more plausibly) both were the result of some third factor, like the boomers' rejection of traditional authority. For better or worse, however, it is impossible at this date to make any firm judgments about that issue. All we can sensibly conclude is that the rapid change in religious observance in the long Sixties and the rapid change in understandings of sexual morality in those same years were closely intertwined.

When Americans were asked in 1986 to explain the decline in religious observance that they had seen around them, they offered a diagnosis that even in hindsight seems reasonable. Their replies, according to the Gallup Poll:

1. Young people were losing interest in formal religion, finding it not "relevant."
2. The increase in immorality, crime, and violence.
3. Materialistic distractions.
4. The church was not playing its proper role in society—equal numbers said the church was not keeping up with the times, and that it was too involved in current social and political issues.[23]

Almost overnight, it seemed, America had turned from God's country to a godless one.

1970s AND 1980s:
FIRST AFTERSHOCK:
THE RISE OF RELIGIOUS
CONSERVATISM

Many Americans were deeply unhappy about the direction the country had taken during the long Sixties, and they expressed themselves both religiously and politically over the next several decades. History's current rarely runs straight, and in the mid-1970s trend lines in American religiosity began to level off and edge back upward. By 1976, as America elected its first avowedly born again president, 44 percent of Americans said that the influence of religion was once again rising. (Recall that only six years earlier that figure had stood at 14 percent.) It was a seismic warning sign that America's religious landscape was beginning to shift again, this time in a more religious (and conservative) direction. Most of America's presidents into the twenty-first century would claim that they too had experienced religious rebirth, seemingly a new token of readiness for national leadership.

Church attendance nationwide stabilized in the 1970s and 1980s and on some evidence may even have risen slightly, but recall that generational patterns are muffled when we look only at national averages. To detect change (or its absence) it is more important to look at the newer cohorts arriving at adulthood in the late 1970s and 1980s. Figures 3.1, 3.3, and 3.6 have already shown that these cohorts did not follow the example of declining religious observance set by their boomer predecessors, so that youthful church attendance leveled off in the 1980s and even began to rise again in some places.

Just as the 1950s religious boom and the 1960s religious crash had been signaled by changes among college-educated young people, our first aftershock—the upturn in conservative religiosity in the 1970s and 1980s—was most visible in that same demographic niche.[24] "Student radicalism peaked between 1968 and 1970, and by 1971 observers were noting a new quietism on college campuses," wrote Dean Hoge and his colleagues in their wide-ranging survey of trends in college student values between the 1950s and the 1980s. With the important exception of sexual liberalization, which persisted, they concluded that the 1970s on campus was in good measure "a return of the fifties."[25] As this first aftershock shifted youthful attitudes, the long Sixties began to seem a mere interlude between the conservative Eisenhower years and the conservative Reagan years, at least for college students. Only on issues of sexual morality did the earthquake of the Sixties continue to rumble.

The effects of the first aftershock in boosting religious observance among college kids were unmistakable. Figure 4.2 shows that the fraction of college freshmen who rejected all religious identification, which had more than doubled in five years between 1966 and 1971, plunged back almost as rapidly in the ensuing decade.

Figure 4.2

YOUTHFUL REJECTION OF RELIGIOUS IDENTITY (1966–2008)

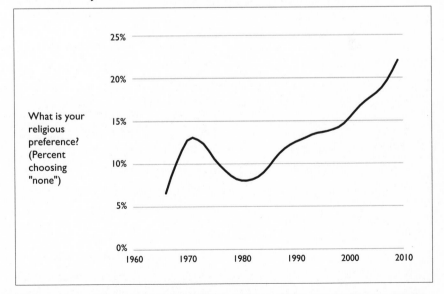

What is your religious preference? (Percent choosing "none")

SOURCE: THE AMERICAN FRESHMAN ANNUAL SURVEYS (UCLA); DATA LOESS-SMOOTHED.

Figure 4.3 summarizes evidence from the General Social Survey on trends in youthful church attendance. The GSS evidence shows that college-educated young people reconnected with organized religion in the 1970s and 1980s, though less educated young people did not. Between the early 1970s and the mid-1980s, weekly (or near-weekly) church attendance among young people with some college education rose from about 24 percent to about 32 percent, an increase of one third, while among their peers who had not attended college regular attendance fell from about 28 percent to about 21 percent, a decrease of one quarter. The middle-class edge in church attendance then somewhat narrowed, but persists to this day.

The first aftershock in American religion during the 1970s and 1980s, however, was not best measured by how often people went to church, but by which church they went to. Just as in politics, many Americans of all ages were deeply troubled by the moral and religious developments of the Sixties. For the next two decades, these people—conservative in both religion and politics—swelled the

Figure 4.3

RELIGIOUS ATTENDANCE AMONG YOUTH, 18–29, BY EDUCATION (1973–2008)

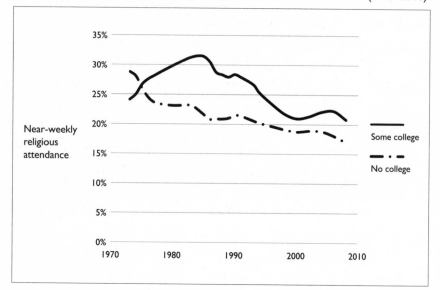

SOURCE: GENERAL SOCIAL SURVEY, 1973–2008; DATA LOESS-SMOOTHED.

ranks both of evangelical Protestant denominations and of the rapidly growing evangelical megachurches that disavowed denominations and termed themselves simply "Christian."

Whether the evangelical portion of the American religious spectrum actually grew during the 1970s and 1980s, and if so, by how much, depends to some extent on how you look at it. Let's begin with religious identification—that is, how people describe their religious affiliation. As described in Chapter 1, in this book we follow the conventional typology of religious traditions worked out by scholars of religion, which includes evangelical Protestants as one category.

This classification is straightforward enough for groups like Baptists or Pentecostals or even Missouri Synod Lutherans (an evangelical branch of the mostly mainline Lutheran family), but it is more difficult to place the rapidly growing number of nondenominational churches that call themselves simply "Christian" or "evangelical." Prior to the 1970s, such churches had been uncommon and mostly ecumenical or even liberal, but since the 1980s such churches have proliferated, and now serve roughly 7 percent of all Americans. That makes the nondenominational category larger than the largest of the mainline Protestant denominations (Methodists at 6 percent) and by far the fastest growing group on the U.S. religious spectrum. Moreover, since the 1980s the theology and liturgy of these nondenominational Christian churches and the views of their members have become virtually indistinguishable from denominational evangelicals. For that reason, we (like many experts in the field) have classified the churchgoers among them as "evangelical." [26]

Against that backdrop, Figure 4.4 shows how Americans have divided themselves among the various religious traditions over the last thirty-five years. While deciphering the chart may seem daunting at first, it will repay a bit of effort. The width of each band represents the fraction of Americans who in any given year identified with a given religious tradition. So, for example, the bottom band refers to evangelical Protestants, who constituted 23 percent of all Americans in the early 1970s, increased to 28 percent by the mid-1990s, and thereafter slumped to 24 percent. The next band up represents main-line Protestants, whose share of the American religious marketplace plummeted steadily from 28–29 percent in the early 1970s to 13 per-cent by 2008. The fraction (that is, the band width) for Black Protes-tants, Catholics, and Jews did not change much during this period, although we shall shortly see that that impression is deceptive in the case of Catholics. The bands corresponding to other Christians (such as Christian Scientists, Mormons, Eastern Orthodox, and so on) and other faiths grew significantly over this period, although that is slightly misleading in the case of "other Christians," since that band includes a growing number of people who say that they are "Chris-tian," but who rarely if ever attend church. Finally, the band at the top of the chart corresponds to the fraction of Americans who (in response to a standard question about their religious affiliation) say they have none. We discuss these nones in more detail later in this chapter, but it is important to keep in mind that the category sim-ply refers to the absence of affiliation or identification with any reli-gious tradition. It does not necessarily imply anything about beliefs or church attendance; many nones say they believe in God and even attend religious services occasionally. As discussed in Chapter 1, van-ishingly few Americans identify themselves as "atheists" or "agnos-tic," terms only five people (0.2 percent) in our Faith Matters sample of 3,108 Americans in 2006 offered as a self-description, so these nones, though religiously unaffiliated, do not think of themselves as "atheists," and in the 2006 Faith Matters survey, nearly half of them (47 percent) say they are "absolutely sure" of God's existence. As Figure 4.4 shows, the fraction of religiously unaffiliated nones was a steady 7 percent until the early 1990s, when (in the second aftershock of our chapter) this category suddenly began to increase.

Several things are worth noting about Figure 4.4.

First, we can see here the dimensions of the rise of evangelical-ism in the 1970s and 1980s. The rise was real and statistically signifi-cant, but it amounted to adding roughly one American in twenty to the ranks of evangelicals. Despite the mountains of books and news-paper articles about the rise of the evangelicals, in absolute terms the

Figure 4.4

TRENDS IN RELIGIOUS IDENTITY (1973–2008)

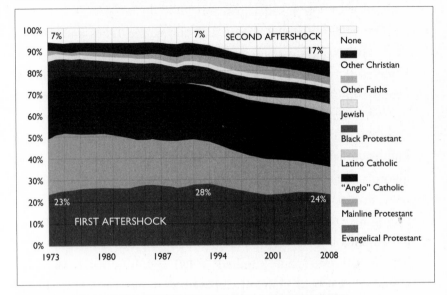

SOURCE: GENERAL SOCIAL SURVEY, 1973–2008; DATA LOESS-SMOOTHED.

change was hardly massive, except by comparison to the collapsing mainline Protestant denominations.

Second, we can see that this evangelical rise ended by the early 1990s, and over the last two decades the number of evangelical adherents has actually slumped. Indeed, if we had restricted our definition to the standard denominational evangelicals (Baptists and the like), the post-1993 decline in evangelical Protestants would have appeared sharper, but that recent loss among denominational evangelicals has been partly offset by the rise of nondenominational evangelical churches. Since this fact is not widely understood, it is worth reemphasizing—*the evangelical boom that began in the 1970s was over by the early 1990s, nearly two decades ago.* In twenty-first century America expansive evangelicalism is a feature of the past, not the present.

Third, we can see how the rise of evangelicals at the most conservative end of the religious spectrum, followed after 1990 by the rise of the nones at the most liberal end of the spectrum, has in effect polarized the spectrum as a whole by squeezing down the more moderate portions of the spectrum. In 1973 evangelicals plus nones comprised 30 percent of the American population, but by 2008 these two extremes comprised 41 percent.[27]

The evidence so far shows that during the 1970s and 1980s a modestly increasing share of Americans identified as evangelical Protestants, while a sharply declining share identified as mainline Protestants, but Figure 4.4 leaves the impression that the Catholic Church emerged from this period relatively unscathed. That impression, though sometimes endorsed by the church itself, is fundamentally misleading, because the numbers we've examined thus far ignore how active people are in the churches with which they nominally identify.

Figure 4.5 addresses that issue by exploring the ups and downs of religious attendance in each of these religious traditions. Here we ask: Of every one hundred Americans, how many of them attend what sort of church in an average week? The figure shows, for example, that in the early 1970s about 12 percent of all Ameri-

Figure 4.5

HOW MANY AMERICANS ATTEND WHICH TYPE OF RELIGIOUS SERVICE IN AN AVERAGE WEEK? (PER 100 ADULTS)

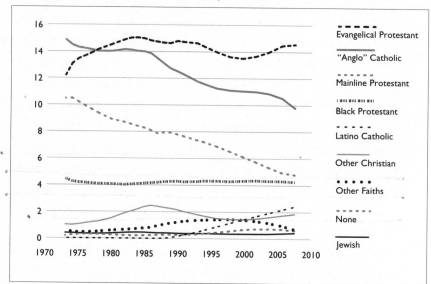

SOURCE: GENERAL SOCIAL SURVEY, 1973–2008; DATA LOESS-SMOOTHED.

cans were regular evangelical church-goers, a figure that had risen to about 15 percent by the mid-1980s. The chart thus takes into account simultaneously how many adherents a given religious tradition had in a given year and how often those adherents actually attended religious services. Several striking patterns appear in Figure 4.5.

First, because evangelical adherents are much more likely to show up on Sunday, their fraction of people in American pews is higher than their fraction of nominal members. Moreover, the post-1990 slump that appeared in Figure 4.4 is minimized when we take account of attendance. In short, what the evangelical churches have lost in adherents over the last two decades has mostly been made up for by the evangelicals' zeal.

Second, we see here that while the numbers of nominal Catholics did not decline much over this entire period, the number at Mass on Sunday has fallen substantially and steadily. In terms of people in pews, the Catholic Church has lost roughly one quarter of its strength over the last thirty-five years. In Chapter 9 we will examine yet another wrinkle in Catholicism over the last several decades that appears in Figures 4.5 and 4.6—the sharp rise in the number of observant Latino Catholics. In recent decades as large numbers of white ethnic Catholics (the grandchildren of an earlier wave of immigrants) were slipping out one door of the church (mostly to vanish into the category of lapsed Catholics), a large number of Latino immigrants have rushed in through another door. Figures 4.4, 4.5, and 4.6 take these new Catholics into account.[28] Without the timely arrival of these new immigrants, the collapse of attendance at Mass would have been even steeper.

Third, Figure 4.5 shows that previous accounts of stable attendance among liberal Protestants are misleading, since those attendance figures are based only on the rapidly diminishing numbers of people who still claim adherence to one of the mainline denominations.[29] In effect, observers who claim that the fraction of observant mainline Protestants has not changed overlook the fact that the mainline losses have come mostly in the denominator (members), not the numerator (attenders).

What is implied in Figure 4.5, but not easily visible, is that the total volume of church attendance in America—the number of people sitting in pews somewhere in an average week—has fallen fairly significantly since the early 1990s. Figure 4.6 presents the same information as Figure 4.5, but in a form that shows this aggregate trend more clearly. Each band represents the number of people (per one hundred Americans) who are sitting in the pews of each religious tradition in an average week.[30] It shows that the relatively stable attendance of evangelical churches (both black and white) over this period (along with stable though modest attendance at miscellaneous "other" houses of worship) has been more than offset by major declines in Catholic and mainline Protestant churches, especially since the early 1990s.[31] In a moment, we shall examine this post-1990 inflection in more detail.

But first, what have we learned about religion in America during the late 1970s and 1980s?

Figure 4.6

VOLUME OF RELIGIOUS ATTENDANCE BY RELIGIOUS TRADITION (1973–2008)(PER 100 ADULTS)

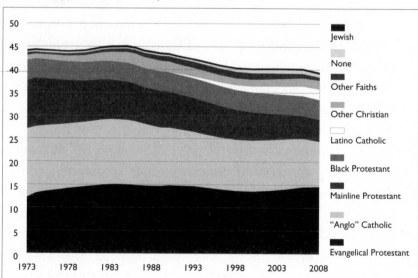

SOURCE: GENERAL SOCIAL SURVEY, 1973–2008; DATA LOESS-SMOOTHED.

First, the hemorrhage of religious observance characteristic of the long Sixties was stanched and to some extent reversed, at least among better educated young people. Since older Americans' religious practices had been much less affected by the events of the 1960s, the net effect was to stem the aggregate losses in the 1970s and 1980s. The fraction of Americans telling Gallup pollsters that religion was "very important" in their personal lives began to edge upward in the early 1980s, as did the numbers who said that "religion can answer today's problems."

Americans seemed to be getting back in touch with God, and that is what Americans themselves reported to those same Gallup pollsters. The "gaining influence"/"losing influence" ratio, which had stood at 69:14 in 1957 and had plummeted to 14:75 in 1970, recovered to 44:45 by 1976 and to 48:39 in 1985. Americans did not think we were yet back in the 1950s, religiously speaking, but we seemed headed there.

That impression was strengthened because evangelical Protestantism gained adherents and worshippers during this period, certainly in comparison to America's other major religious traditions, but also (though modestly) in absolute terms. Coupled with the scattered evidence of a nationwide religious recovery, the new fervor, both public and private, of the evangelicals had the hallmarks of an aftershock, though less powerful than the initial shock of the Sixties. The tectonic movements of the 1970s and 1980s were, in short, most visible in the conservative half of the American religious landscape.

What could explain this first aftershock sociologically? To be sure, evangelical churches probably had been growing since at least the 1950s, so this was not, strictly speaking, a revival.[32] On the other hand, Catholic and mainline Protestant denominations also had been increasing in the 1950s, as we have seen, so the important question is this: Why did evangelicals attend church in increasing numbers in the 1970s and 1980s when other houses of worship were increasingly deserted?[33]

Rather than evangelical faith and fervor, the dominant explanation among sociologists of religion today, most clearly articulated by

Michael Hout and his colleagues, emphasizes purely demographic factors.[34] Simply put, for most of the twentieth-century evangelical parents had more children than other parents. Moreover, after the 1960s evangelicals did a better job of keeping their offspring in the family's religious tradition. (See Chapter 5 for more discussion of religious inheritance.) More kids, more of whom stay in the faith, must mean more people of that faith in the next generation.

This is an important part of the story. Hout and his colleagues offer persuasive evidence of the higher birth rate among evangelicals, and our own Faith Matters surveys confirm their view that evangelicals care more about keeping their children within the faith than do most other Americans. This demographic story implies that evangelical churches were probably growing faster even before the 1960s, and although rigorous evidence on that point is sparse, we believe it is true.

For several reasons, however, we doubt that demographics alone can explain the rise and subsequent slump in evangelicalism over the last four decades. First, evangelical churches have also gained significantly from converts in recent decades, both from other religious traditions and from the previously unchurched. Roughly one third of evangelicals today were not raised as evangelicals, and as evangelical churches grew during the first aftershock, the fraction of converts in them also grew. Ever since the 1970s evangelicalism has gotten much more than its fair share of converts, no matter how we calculate "fair share." [35] In short, a significant share of evangelical growth came from new converts.

Second, although in recent decades evangelicals suffered fewer intergenerational losses than most other religious traditions, evangelical offspring were not always so loyal. As late as the 1960s, as evangelical children moved up the social hierarchy, they tended to shift from evangelical to mainline denominations—moving from the Baptist chapel to the Episcopal church, along with trading in your Chevy for a Buick, was the classic mark of middle-class respectability. In the 1970s and 1980s, however, most educated evangelical young people stayed in their original faith, thus swelling evangelical churches, while at the same time moving evangelicalism as a whole up the social scale. In other words, the loyalty of evangelical children rose simultaneously with the first aftershock. That increased loyalty is an important part of the story of growth, but itself needs explanation. It seems plausible that whatever drew nonevangelicals to the evangelical banner during the first aftershock might also explain the increased loyalty of evangelical offspring in that same period.[36]

Finally, the generational profile of evangelicals is not entirely consistent with the demographic explanation. If birth rates alone explained the difference, then evangelicals as a group should have been younger than the rest of the population, but that was not the case. Moreover, if birth rates were the whole story, then evangelical growth should have been visible between successive birth cohorts, not within them, but that is also not the case.[37] Finally, the long-term inertia of demographic arithmetic should have continued to push up the evangelical share of the population for at least several decades more, even after the evangelical birth rate converged to the nonevangelical birth rate. That this increase did not happen implies that something besides demography was influencing evangelical adherence. This issue is admittedly subtle and no one has all the evidence needed to resolve it fully. But it is important to ask what else (beyond their familial origins) characterized evangelicals, as their numbers grew during the first aftershock.

We can, perhaps surprisingly, rule out the possibility of a nationwide theological shift to the right. To be sure, evangelicals as a group are much more likely than others to believe in the inerrancy of the Bible, for example, the very bedrock of evangelical theology. However, in recent decades, support for the classical tenets of Protestant fundamentalism—a belief in the Bible as the literal word of God, for example—has not risen. On the contrary, as Figure 4.7 (drawing on Gallup Poll data) shows, biblical literalism has steadily slumped for almost half a century. Evidence from the General Social Survey is wholly consistent and further shows that although the *level* of literalism is twice as high among evangelicals as among other Americans (roughly 60 percent as compared to roughly 30 percent), the *trends*

DECLINING BIBLICAL LITERALISM (1963–2008)

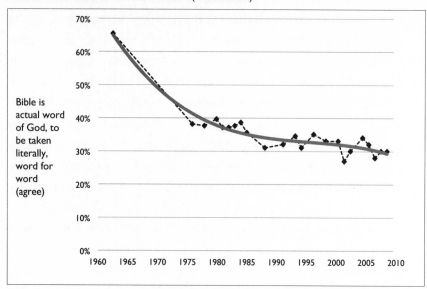

SOURCE: VARIOUS GALLUP POLL PUBLICATIONS.

in literalism among evangelicals and nonevangelicals are identical— indeed, belief in the literal truth of scripture is on the decline in all Christian traditions in America. Moreover, the explanation is identical in all these cases: younger generations are better educated, and better educated people are (whatever their religious tradition) less literal in their interpretation of the Bible, so the slow but steady process of generational turnover is moving all American denominations in a less literal direction. Moreover, the growth in evangelical adherence during the 1970s and 1980s was actually concentrated among better educated Americans. So the fervor and growth of evangelical churches in the 1970s and 1980s does not seem to be based on some major conversion to "old-time religion."[38] The first aftershock of our story, though real, was not driven by theological revivalism.

So demography is part of the background to the rise of evangelicalism in the 1970s and 1980s, but not the whole story. Theological conversion seems not to be the explanation for the nationwide shift, however important it might have been for individual worshippers. A third broad explanation is harder to quantify, but probably important—the greater organizational energy and inventiveness of evangelical religious leaders in those years. As we will discuss in more detail in Chapter 6, American evangelicals have always been innovative entrepreneurs as they reach out to save souls, and that was surely true in this period. The vignettes of Chapter 2 illustrate some of the innovations—contemporary music and contemporary liturgy, a widespread use of small groups, building new sanctuaries in places to which Americans were moving, applying techniques of modern marketing to the task of making church attractive to a new generation of Americans.[39] To be sure, other religious traditions—mainline Protestants, Catholics, and so forth—could have followed that marketing strategy and in time, as they saw the effectiveness of the new techniques, they would, as we noted in our visit to Trinity Episcopal Church in Boston in Chapter 2. In 1984, Joseph Cardinal Bernardin founded the first Catholic megachurch, Holy Family Catholic Community, in suburban Chicago as "an evangelical church in the Roman Catholic tradition," explicitly modeled on and competing with Willow Creek Community Church, three miles away, the first of the major U.S. evangelical megachurches.[40] However, like Sears belatedly mimicking Walmart, they were playing catch-up.

But none of these common explanations—demography, theology, marketing—seems to us sufficient to explain the first aftershock. The single most crucial element in the success of the evangelical movement after the long Sixties, we believe, was captured in St. Paul's exhortation to the Corinthians to stand firmly for their faith, "for if the trumpet give an uncertain sound, who shall prepare himself to the battle?"[41] This was an age of turmoil that many Americans found deeply repugnant to their fundamental moral and religious views. Other trumpets might be uncertain, but evangelical trumpets were not. Evangelicals were prepared to heed Paul's advice and stand up for their values.

Evangelicals' distinctive moral outlook, inherited from their fundamentalist forebears, is dark and somewhat puritanical (or Victorian). They share a view of the world as sinful and of God as a harsh judge. For them, heaven, hell, and judgment day are realities, not metaphors, and moral issues are framed in absolute, black-and-white terms.[42] In our 2006 Faith Matters survey, three quarters of evangelicals said that "there are absolutely clear guidelines as to what is good and evil," while a majority of nonevangelicals said instead "there can never be absolutely clear guidelines as to what is good and evil." The evangelical stance was perfectly suited to Americans deeply alienated from the culture of the Sixties. Some of these people had evangelical roots and thus were inclined (unlike their counterparts in other traditions) to renew their religious involvement, while others were drawn into evangelical circles for the first time.

Even as late as 2006, after a quarter century of rising national prominence and power,[43] more than two thirds of evangelical Protestants in our Faith Matters survey said that they felt that their values were "seriously" or "moderately threatened in America today," a sense of embattlement greater than in any other major religious tradition. If something about the Sixties threatened conservative values and heightened the appeal of conservative evangelicalism, what might that something have been? Here are some possibilities, beginning with those for which, in fact, we find little empirical support:

- *Great Society liberalism.* This topic motivated many political conservatives, some of whom were also evangelicals, but it was never a major theme of evangelical religious leaders, and there is no evidence that it played a role in the first aftershock. The General Social Survey shows those most skeptical about government welfare policies were hardly more likely to be found in evangelical churches.
- *The civil rights movement.* The heartland of evangelicalism in the smaller towns of the South was also the heart of Dixie's massive resistance to racial reform. Desegregation shifted many Southern conservative Democrats into the Republican camp. The efforts of the Carter administration in the late 1970s to remove the religious tax exemption from "white academies" helped trigger the creation of the Religious Right. So it is plausible a racist backlash might have played a role in the rise of evangelical churches. We

shall see, however, that while evangelicals were readier to defend racial segregation than nonevangelicals, in part because of where they lived, their distinctiveness on this dimension declined as evangelicalism grew. The gap between evangelicals and nonevangelicals on issues like racial intermarriage or a possible black president narrowed in the 1970s and 1980s, suggesting either that the newly recruited evangelicals were less racist than average to begin with or that exposure to evangelical teachings, at least in this period, reduced support for segregation. Thus, we conclude that racism and support for segregation were not, in fact, major elements in the rise of evangelicalism.

- *Changing gender roles.* The 1970s witnessed a dramatic change in gender norms and gender roles in America, and while many Americans welcomed those changes, a significant minority (among both men and women) did not. Fundamentalists had long espoused more traditional gender roles—"the woman's place is in the home." However, as we shall discuss in more detail in Chapter 8, even though such views remain frequent among a minority of very fundamentalist evangelicals, they are—in all religious traditions, including evangelicalism as a whole—much less common now than a generation ago. Precisely during the years of evangelical expansion, views among evangelicals on gender roles were moving sharply in a progressive direction. Traditional gender norms, so offended by the "bra burners," "women's libbers," and Equal Rights Amendment advocates of the 1960s and 1970s, were at most a modest and fading factor in the rise of evangelicalism.[44]

- *Supreme Court decisions that widened the separation of Church and State.* The key decisions—*Engel v. Vitale* in 1962, which forbade state-sponsored prayer in schools, and *Abington v. Schempp* in 1963, which banned mandatory Bible reading—inspired much disapproval, with evangelicals among the loudest in protest. Efforts to amend the Constitution to allow prayer in school foundered as supporters bickered over what kind of prayer should be allowed and over provisions for students to opt out. Were views about school prayer and religion in the public square part of the story of the first aftershock? We will offer evidence that views about school prayer and religion in the public square part were, at most, a modest contributor to evangelical growth.

- *Moral decadence and sexual permissiveness.* We have already seen how dramatically sexual norms changed during a few years at the end of the 1960s and beginning of the 1970s. These interconnected issues involving nonmarital sex, homosexuality, pornography, and abortion had become white-hot during the long Sixties. While national norms shifted in a liberal direction in that era, that shift itself was felt as a fundamental moral challenge to conservative Americans of all ages. Americans not swept up in the cultural revolution sought support for their resistance to that revolution (and what they feared would be its social and moral consequences) in a more conservative religious tradition. We shall shortly see that concern about sexual morality (or immorality) was closely associated with the rise of evangelicalism.

How important were each of these issues in the first aftershock and the rise of evangelicalism in the 1970s and 1980s? There is no single perfect way to answer that question empirically. However, we can get some clues by examining how the views of evangelicals differed from nonevangelicals on these issues, especially during the period of maximum evangelical expansion between the early 1970s and the early 1990s.

If that growth was linked to the stance of evangelical churches on the moral issues arising out of the 1960s, then the gap between evangelicals' and others' views should be substantial and stable or growing. On the other hand, if the views of comparable evangelicals and other Americans tended to converge during the evangelical expansion, then it is reasonable to conclude that these issues were not a significant part of the first aftershock.

Recall, by way of background, the dramatic changes in sexual mores that we earlier described during the long Sixties. While many boomers experienced that set of changes as "sexual liberation," many other Americans of all ages were appalled by the new "licentiousness." On homosexuality, abortion, and marijuana, as the Sixties receded in the rearview mirror, views among younger Americans in the 1970s and 1980s actually moved in a conservative direction. Among eighteen to twenty-nine-year-olds the view that homosexuality was "always wrong" rose from 62 percent in 1974 to 79 percent in 1987, and opposition to legalization of marijuana rose from 50 percent in 1976 to 80 percent in 1990. It is reasonable, therefore, to speak of a backlash—not universal and not uniform, but significant—against many of the lifestyle changes brought by the Sixties. (This backlash did not encompass gender roles and the women's movement nor fundamental issues of segregation, such as racial intermarriage, where opinion continued to shift in a liberal direction.) These youthful swings were damped in the population as a whole, but the overall mood of the country nonetheless became more conservative on social and moral issues.

Against that backdrop, Figure 4.8 compares the levels and trends in opinion on six relevant issues among evangelicals and other Americans. The gap was widest and growing on premarital sex, followed by homosexuality, abortion, and prayer in school. The gap on racial integration was wide, but mostly because of the concentration of evangelicals in the South, and that gap narrowed as the number of evangelicals grew. The gap on gender roles, though real, as we shall discuss in Chapter 8, was more contained, especially on the issue of women working outside the home, which was accepted as a reality by evangelicals and nonevangelicals alike during the 1970s and 1980s.

During the first aftershock, as evangelicals flourished while other religious traditions faded, evangelicals were distinguished primarily by their views on personal sexual morality (of which premarital sex was a key marker), along with the Church–State issue of school prayer. The first aftershock was caused by many things, to be sure, but a central theme was concern over collapsing sexual morality.

We have explored in greater statistical detail the question of which of these issues most divided evangelicals and other Americans over this period, controlling for demographic differences as well as views on all these issues simultaneously.[45] Comparing two statis-

AMERICAN GRACE

Figure 4.8

EVANGELICAL AFFILIATION AND MORAL-SOCIAL VIEWS (1973–2008)

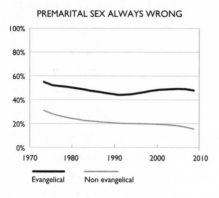

PREMARITAL SEX ALWAYS WRONG

Evangelical   Non evangelical

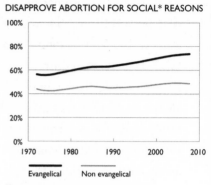

DISAPPROVE ABORTION FOR SOCIAL* REASONS

Evangelical   Non evangelical

Social = abortion in cases of single mother, poor family, and/or mother wants no more children

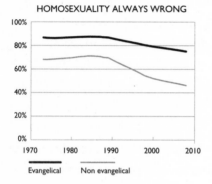

HOMOSEXUALITY ALWAYS WRONG

Evangelical   Non evangelical

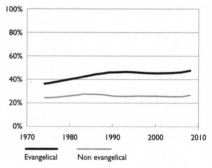

SUPPORT PRAYER IN SCHOOL

Evangelical   Non evangelical

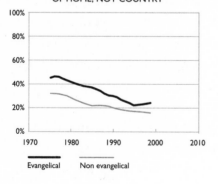

WOMEN SHOULD TAKE CARE OF HOME, NOT COUNTRY

Evangelical   Non evangelical

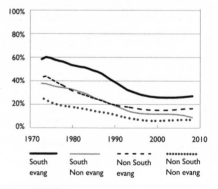

RACIAL INTERMARRIAGE SHOULD BE ILLEGAL

South evang   South Non evang   Non South evang   Non South Non evang

SOURCE: GENERAL SOCIAL SURVEY; DATA LOESS-SMOOTHED.

tical twins in this sense, the one who judged premarital sex to be "always wrong" was nearly twice as likely to be an evangelical as the one who judged premarital sex "sometimes" or "always" acceptable. Also important by this test are homosexuality, feminism, abortion, and pornography, though none was so powerful as premarital sex. With these added controls, views on school prayer appear less powerful in distinguishing between evangelicals and nonevangelicals. In all our analyses, views on premarital sex (rather than on abortion or homosexuality) are the most robustly associated with evangelicalism, suggesting that what sparked the growth of evangelicalism was less hot-button politics than deeply personal moral concerns.

In the absence of experimental evidence (in which we would artificially induce matched subjects to have different views on premarital sex and then see whether they became evangelicals, or randomly assign some people to become evangelicals, and see how that affected their sexual views) we cannot sort out cause and effect here. Did people move to evangelical churches because they were upset about declining sexual morality, or did they move there for some other reason and then acquire their conservative views on sex? Or (more likely) did concern about changes in the world of the long Sixties simultaneously move them in a more conservative direction on these issues and move them to active involvement in the religious tradition in which those concerns were most fervently emphasized? The evidence available to us won't let us resolve those questions. But we can say that many Americans became deeply concerned about public and private morality in the long Sixties, and that a disproportionate number of those people ended up in evangelical pews in the 1970s and 1980s.

In Chapter 11 on the emergence of the God gap in American politics we discuss how leaders such as Jerry Falwell and Pat Robertson, simultaneously men of the cloth and politically astute strategists, drew on this new combination of religious, moral, and political conservatism to create the Religious Right. The leaders of the Religious Right did not cause the rise of evangelical religion during the first aftershock, but they responded to it in ways that were, initially at least, highly effective. Religiosity and conservative politics became increasingly aligned, and abortion and gay rights became emblematic of the emergent culture wars. For our immediate purposes, the most important result of this aftershock was that religion itself and conservatism (theological, social, moral, and political) became increasingly symbiotic and identified, especially in the public eye, as the Religious Right. To many religious Americans, this alignment of religion and politics represented a long-sought consummation, an appropriate retort to the excesses of the Sixties. Many other Americans were not so sure.

1990s AND 2000s:
SECOND AFTERSHOCK:
YOUTH DISAFFECTION
FROM RELIGION

As the 1990s opened, many Americans were increasingly unhappy about the growing public presence of conservative Christians. In 1980 in the midst of the first aftershock, with Jimmy Carter, a progressive evangelical, on the ballot, of all voters who said that it made a difference to them if a presidential candidate was an avowed evangelical, twice as many said that it would make them more likely to vote for that candidate as said it would make them less likely. By 1988, however, after nearly a decade of publicity about the Religious Right, in response to the same question, a solid majority of those who said it would make a difference said they would be *less* likely to vote for such a candidate. The terms "Religious Right" and "Christian Right" were becoming pejoratives in most Americans' view, representing a noxious mixture of religion and political ideology.[46]

As early as 1984, according to Gallup polling, most Americans opposed the idea of religious groups campaigning against specific candidates, although most agreed that religious leaders should speak out on the moral implications of public issues, a practice with an honored pedigree in American history. Symbols of the Religious Right, such as the Moral Majority and Jerry Falwell, were viewed unfavorably by most voters. Political scientists Louis Bolce and Gerald De Maio show that after 1990 "Christian fundamentalists" were increasingly identified in the public mind not merely with controversial causes, but with ideological intervention in politics, binding evangelicals to the Republican party.[47] After 1991, increasing numbers of Americans of all ages expressed deep concern that religious leaders should not try to influence either people's votes or government decisions. Figure 4.9 summarizes this evidence. Similarly, Gallup Polls showed a nationwide growth in the view that organized religion should have less influence from 22 percent in 2001 to 34 percent in 2008.[48]

This change was visible in all parts of the religious spectrum, though least strongly among evangelicals and most strongly among the growing number of nones, those who rejected all religious identification. Young Americans came to view religion, according to one survey, as judgmental, homophobic, hypocritical, and too political.[49] All these were premonitory signs that a second major aftershock was about to roil the American religious landscape. But it was the rise of

Figure 4.9

GROWING OBJECTIONS TO INFLUENCE OF RELIGIOUS LEADERS (1991–2008)

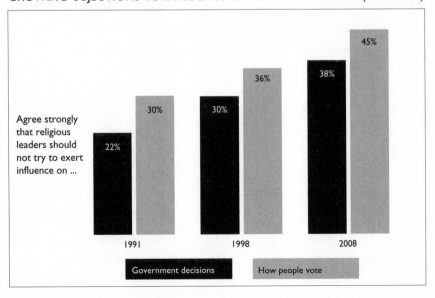

SOURCE: GENERAL SOCIAL SURVEY.

the nones after 1990 that marked unmistakably the beginning of this third temblor.

Historically, whatever their degree of religiosity, almost all Americans have identified with one religion or another.[50] In response to standard questions in the 1950s about "what is your religious preference?" roughly 95–97 percent responded either with a specific denomination (Methodist, Baptist, and so forth) or with a religious tradition (Christian, Jewish, etc.). Only a very small fraction responded by saying "none" or "nothing in particular."[51] The shock of the long Sixties had increased the national incidence of nones from about 5 percent to about 7 percent, and it remained virtually unchanged until the early 1990s.

At that point, however, the fraction of Americans who said they were "none" suddenly began to rise, and at virtually the same time the fraction of people who said that they "never" attend church also began to rise, as is shown in Figure 4.10. This figure captures the essence and timing of what we are calling the second aftershock.

Figure 4.10

EMPTYING PEWS AND INCREASING NONES (1973–2008)

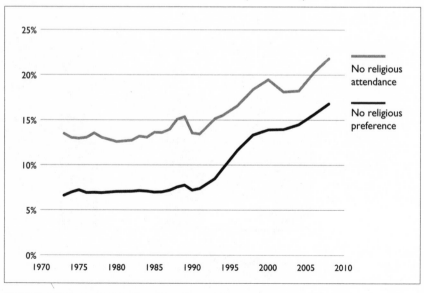

SOURCE: GENERAL SOCIAL SURVEY; DATA LOESS-SMOOTHED.

Just like the earlier turning points we have discussed, the rise of the nones in the 1990s was heavily driven by generational factors. As Figure 4.11 shows, the incidence of nones was about 5–7 percent in the pre-boomer generations who reached adulthood before 1960, doubled to about 10–15 percent among the boomers (who came of age in the 1960s, 1970s, and 1980s), and after 2000 doubled again to about 20–30 percent among the post-boomers (who came of age in the 1990s and 2000s).[52] Nor is there any evidence in this figure that as the younger generations age, they are becoming more attached to organized religion—quite the contrary! Since 2000 generational succession has meant that cohorts of whom barely 5 percent say they have no religious affiliation are being replaced by cohorts of whom roughly 25 percent say they have no religion, massively increasing the nationwide incidence of nones.

As in the earlier shock and aftershock, Americans themselves noticed the second aftershock. Recall that the "gaining influence/

Figure 4.11

THE RISE OF THE NONES

BY DECADE IN WHICH RESPONDENT REACHED ADULTHOOD (1972–2008)

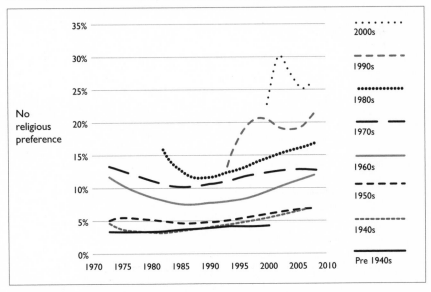

SOURCE: GENERAL SOCIAL SURVEY; DATA LOESS-SMOOTHED.

losing influence" ratio in response to the standard Gallup query
about religion in America plummeted from 69:14 in 1957 to 14:75
in 1970, as Americans registered the shock of the Sixties. During the
first decade of the twenty-first century that ratio dropped from 55:39
in 2001 to 25:70 in 2009, as Americans again sensed the ground moving.[53] The Richter rating of this second aftershock is greater than
that of the first aftershock and rivals that of the powerful original
quake of the Sixties.

Once again, this latest shock is most visible among the youngest
generation, as is apparent in Figures 4.12 and 4.13, which summarize evidence from the annual survey of college freshmen and the
General Social Survey.[54] The freshmen data suggest that the increase
in irreligion among college students began in the mid-1980s, accelerated in the mid-1990s, and affected both religious attendance and
religious identification. The GSS evidence shows, first, the modest
but real impact of the first aftershock on young people, as the fraction of evangelicals among eighteen- to twenty-nine-year-olds edged

Figure 4.12

ESTRANGEMENT FROM RELIGION AMONG COLLEGE FRESHMEN (1965–2009)

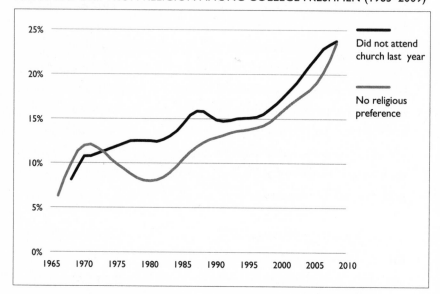

SOURCE: THE AMERICAN FRESHMAN ANNUAL SURVEYS; DATA LOESS-SMOOTHED.

Figure 4.13

EVANGELICALS AND "NONES" AMONG AMERICAN YOUTH (18–29), 1973–2008

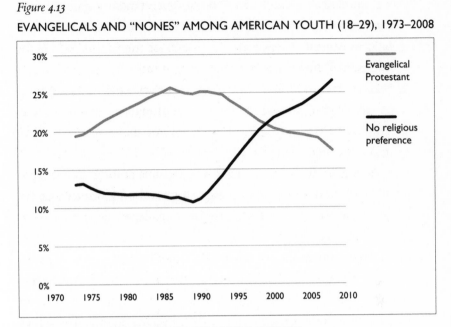

SOURCE: GENERAL SOCIAL SURVEY; DATA LOESS-SMOOTHED.

up from less than 20 percent in the early 1970s to more than 25 percent in the mid-1980s. More obviously, Figure 4.13 also confirms the
sharp rise of the nones among young adults, beginning around 1990,
along with a mirroring decline in the number of young evangelicals
at about the same time. In the mid-1980s, evangelicals had outnumbered nones among American twenty-somethings by more than 2:1,
but by 2008 those proportions were almost completely overturned,
as young nones outnumbered young evangelicals by better than
1.5:1. These data do not prove—and in fact we do not believe—that
individual young people were shifting directly from evangelical faith
to a complete lack of religious identity. But the timing does suggest that both indicators might have been moved by some common
change in the religious marketplace.

Who are these new nones, who have appeared so suddenly in
the last two decades? Although the development was unexpected,
as seismic events almost always are, scholars have already begun to
investigate,[55] and there is broad agreement on certain facts:

1. Except that they are heavily drawn from post-boomer cohorts, the new nones do not differ much from the rest of the U.S. population in terms of education or social standing, and even racial and gender differences are modest.

2. Men, whites, and non-Southerners are modestly more likely to be nones than women, nonwhites, and Southerners. However, since as we saw in Chapter 1, men, whites, and non-Southerners in America have long been less attached to religion than women, nonwhites, and Southerners, it is not clear that these specific gender and racial imbalances are significant, beyond the fact that the new nones are drawn from groups traditionally less predisposed to religious commitment.

3. The new nones are not uniformly unbelievers, and few of them claim to be atheists or agnostics. Indeed, most of them express some belief in God and even in the afterlife, and many of them say that religion is important in their lives. While the new nones are, by definition, less attached to organized religion than other Americans, they do not seem to have discarded all religious beliefs or predilections.[56] While observers sometimes describe them as "spiritual, not religious," they themselves generally do not use that language. They reject conventional religious affiliations, while not entirely giving up their religious feelings.

4. The nones were disproportionately raised in nonreligious backgrounds, so some of them are the children of boomers who had discarded formal religious affiliations a generation ago. As Hout and Fischer put it, "being raised with no religion fueled cohort change." On the other hand, the rise of nones is apparent even among young people whose parents were religiously observant. The 2007 Pew survey of the American religious landscape found that 16 percent of American adults say they are currently unaffiliated with any particular religion, compared with only 7 percent who were raised unaffiliated, so most of the nones must have been raised as "somethings."[57] Of all nones in the 2006 Faith Matters survey, 74 percent report that their parents had been religiously affiliated, 56 percent report that their family attended

religious services nearly every week when they were growing up, and 51 percent say that they attended Sunday school or religious education classes "very often." Since these figures of religious upbringing are only modestly lower than the comparable figures for all Americans of the relevant generation, inheritance clearly accounts for only a fraction of the recent increase in nones.

5. Because the rise of the new nones was so abrupt, this increase seems unlikely to reflect secularization in any ordinary sense, since theories of secularization refer to developments that transpire over decades or even centuries, not just a few years.

6. The new nones are heavily drawn from the center and left of the political spectrum. Hout and Fischer have shown that the rise of the new nones closely corresponds (with a lag of about half a decade) to the visibility of the Religious Right in the public media, suggesting that the rise of the nones might be some sort of backlash against religious conservatism.[58] Our Faith Matters surveys confirm that few of the new nones come from the right half of the political spectrum.

So far, researchers have not devoted much attention to the social and moral beliefs of the new nones, but some highly suggestive evidence appears in trend lines measuring attitudes on certain sex- and drug-related issues over this same period. On issues like homosexuality and marijuana, the 1970s and 1980s had witnessed a distinct conservative turn, especially among young Americans, as we noted in the previous section. Around 1990, however, the climate of opinion in America, especially (but not only) among the youngest cohort, took a sharp turn toward liberal views on marijuana and especially homosexuality. As it happens, the timing of that inflection point is virtually identical to the timing of the rise of the new nones. Figure 4.14 offers some of the evidence.

Precisely this same sharp left turn on both homosexuality and marijuana appears in the annual survey of college freshman at the end of the 1980s, as shown in Figure 4.15, so it is no statistical fluke. This rapid, massive reversal of attitudes toward gays has

Figure 4.14

VIEWS ON SEX, DRUGS, AND RELIGION AMONG
AMERICAN YOUTH, 18–29 (1973–2008)

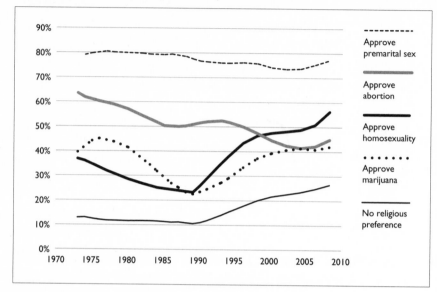

SOURCE: GENERAL SOCIAL SURVEY; DATA LOESS-SMOOTHED.

been noticed by other researchers; indeed, Judith Treas compares it to the revolution in attitudes toward premarital sex at the end of the 1960s. The most common (but probably incomplete) explanations are (a) that over time the AIDS crisis made gays seem more sympathetic, (b) that as more gays came out, more straights felt that gays were normal, and (c) that TV and the movies normalized homosexuality during this period.[59] We have found no comparable discussion of the simultaneous reversal on marijuana, and it is not easy to see how the explanations regarding homosexuality would work for marijuana as well, so we remain agnostic about the origins of this inflection point.

There was no similar liberal shift in young people's views about premarital sex (approved by roughly four fifths ever since the shock of the late 1960s). Moreover, young people's views about abortion continued to move in a conservative direction during the 1990s and 2000s, as we discuss in more detail in Chapter 11. But the simultane-

Figure 4.15

VIEWS ON HOMOSEXUALITY AND MARIJUANA AMONG
COLLEGE FRESHMEN (1965–2009)

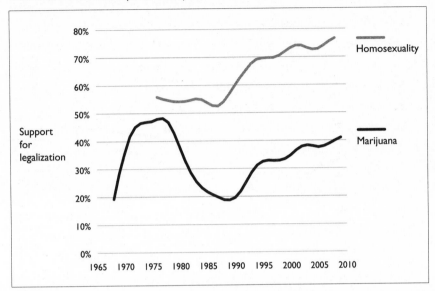

SOURCE: THE AMERICAN FRESHMAN ANNUAL SURVEYS; DATA LOESS-SMOOTHED.

ity of the shifts on two important moral or lifestyle norms, and the rise of the new nones, seems unlikely to be coincidental.[60]

Furthermore, the young people whose views on these issues (especially on homosexuality) were more liberal were the very same people now disclaiming any religious identity. Taking both demographic factors and social and political attitudes into account, what distinguishes the new nones among the millennials after 1991 is, above all, their liberal stance on homosexuality.[61] Those millennials whose views on homosexuality are more tolerant are more than twice as likely to be religious nones as their statistically similar peers who are conservative on homosexuality. Views on marijuana and school prayer also have some predictive power. Although abortion has been the most hotly contested issue in the culture wars, once we take into account views on other moral issues, views on abortion itself are not a powerful predictor of being a none among this younger generation.

In sum, Americans who reached adulthood after 1990 had markedly more liberal views on homosexuality and marijuana than the generation only a few years older than them. Something had caused this younger generation to be more liberal on these moral issues, and those very same young people increasingly rejected organized religion, forming the lion's share of the new nones. Moreover, when we look closely at the individuals who reduced their religious engagement between our interviews with them in 2006 and 2007—becoming nones (instead of "somethings") and reporting lower church attendance—we find that their attitudes on moral issues were strong predictors of who would change, even holding other factors constant, including their level of religiosity in 2006. This pattern provides some modest additional evidence that liberal views on sexual morality contributed to their disaffection from religion.[62]

We make no strong claims about causation here, and we do not believe that it was simply differences over public policy that weakened the ties of this generation to organized religion. Rather, we suggest, the dramatic contrast between a young generation increasingly liberal on certain moral and lifestyle issues (though still potentially open to religious feelings and ideals) and an older generation of religious leaders who seemed to them consumed by the political fight against gay marriage was one important source of the second aftershock.

As we have seen, during the 1990s Americans of all ages became increasingly uneasy about mixing religion and politics. It is not surprising that younger Americans, still forming religious attachments, translated that uneasiness into a rejection of religion entirely. This group of young people came of age when "religion" was identified publicly with the Religious Right, and exactly at the time when the leaders of that movement put homosexuality and gay marriage at the top of their agenda. And yet this is the very generation in which the new tolerance of homosexuality has grown most rapidly. In short, just as the youngest cohort of Americans was zigging in one direction, many highly visible religious leaders zagged in the other.

Given these patterns, it is not at all surprising that when the Pew

Forum on Religion & Public Life asked a large national sample of nones why they rejected religious identification, their objections were not theological or scientific. Instead the new nones reported that "they became unaffiliated, at least in part, because they think of religious people as hypocritical, judgmental or insincere. Large numbers also say they became unaffiliated because they think that religious organizations focus too much on rules and not enough on spirituality."[63] It is also unsurprising that the increasing opposition to religious influence in politics and government registered in Figure 4.9 is heavily concentrated among the new nones.

Many devout religious people would have preferred to (and did) sit out the culture wars, and some liberal Protestant groups have tried hard to keep up with the evolving views of young people on issues of sexual (and homosexual) morality. It is very hard, however, for a religious "brand" forged in the fires of the Reformation four centuries ago to "rebrand" itself overnight. Moreover, this youthful generation seems unwilling or unable to distinguish the stance of the most visible, most political, and most conservative religious leaders from organized religion in general.

• From our analysis thus far, it might appear that Christian conservatives have lost the culture wars by fighting too hard. Before jumping to that conclusion, however, we need to glance at the evolution of views among evangelicals in the pews. During the first aftershock of the 1970s and 1980s American views on sexual morality moved in a broadly conservative direction, and evangelical churches attracted a growing share of that growing pool. During the second aftershock of the 1990s and 2000s, by contrast, American views on sexual morality, especially homosexuality, moved in a liberal direction, and evangelical churches were left with a growing share of a shrinking pool. Consequently, the gap between evangelicals and other Americans on sexual morality has steadily grown since 1990, as is clear in Figure 4.8.

In effect, the reach of evangelicalism is increasingly defined by the desire to convert conservative sexual morality into public policy. (Ironically, abortion is not likely to be the determining issue, since millennials are actually more skeptical about abortion than their parents.) Within the pool of true believers, evangelicals are doing as well as ever—perhaps better than ever. Evangelicals have been hit less hard by the rise of the new nones than other religious traditions. However, if the broader appeal of conservative sexual morality emblazoned on the evangelical banner continues to wane (as it is likely to do because of generational succession), the evangelical movement may face a dilemma familiar to American evangelicals a century ago, a dilemma encapsulated in the differences between fundamentalism and neo-evangelicalism over how much to accommodate religious views to modernity. Continuing to sound the public trumpet of conservative personal morality may be the right thing to do from a theological point of view, but it may mean saving fewer souls now than it did a generation ago.

CONCLUSION

As we noted at the outset of this chapter, in important ways the landscape of American religion has remained remarkably stable through this turbulent half century. Tens of millions of Americans go to religious services each week, just as their parents and grandparents did. Yet the three successive shocks whose seismographic records we have traced in this chapter have gradually polarized the American religious scene, as people (especially young people) have increasingly sorted themselves out religiously according to their moral and political views, leaving both the liberal, secular pole and the conservative, evangelical pole strengthened and the moderate religious middle seriously weakened. Religious polarization has increasingly aligned Americans' religious affiliations with their political inclinations.

Many forces have produced this result. We have highlighted the linkages between sexual norms and religious affiliations, deriving from the cultural revolution of the Sixties and its complicated aftermath in which libertines and prudes seem to have provoked an increasing polarization along the religious spectrum. However, we would be misunderstood if this chapter seemed to argue that religion is "just about sex." People are drawn to (or repelled by) religion for many reasons—some spiritual, some intellectual, some emotional, some transcendent, some sociological, some liturgical, and some political and moral. In the chapters that follow we explore how those diverse motivations play out in contemporary America.

We close this chronicle with an important caution. History never ends, especially the history of religion in pluralist, entrepreneurial America. In a religious cafeteria in which rapidly growing numbers of young Americans are manifestly unhappy with a menu that is too political or hypocritical for their taste, religious entrepreneurs have a powerful incentive to concoct more palatable offerings. To these entrepreneurs the rapidly proliferating nones are an under-served niche, or in more appropriate language, souls waiting to be saved. We could be misled if we considered the rise of the nones simply a symptom of ineluctable secularization. In Chapter 6 we shall consult the history of religious entrepreneurship in America and consider how that characteristic of American religion might produce yet more twists and turns in the evolving history of religion in America.

CHAPTER 5

SWITCHING, MATCHING, AND MIXING

INHERITING VERSUS CHOOSING RELIGION

"From generation to generation," God commanded Moses from the burning bush, His name should be passed down to Moses' descendants.[1] In accord with this ancient precept we often assume that religion is a fixed, inherited trait. Compared to other aspects of our selves—our attitudes, values, identities, habits—our religious outlooks are, in fact, highly stable. The unprecedented Faith Matters panel surveys (in which we interviewed the same people in 2006 and again in 2007) allow us to confirm that Americans' religious beliefs and practices are remarkably stable over the course of a year—far from the haphazard, near-random patterns that social scientists typically find when studying social attitudes and habits. For example, asked how often they went to religious services, 58 percent of our respondents gave the identical reply in 2006 and 2007 (and 86 percent gave virtually the same reply in the two years[2]), while only 33 percent gave the identical response in both years to a comparable question about how often they "had friends over to your home."[3] From year to year, most Americans have firm, stable commitments on religious topics. Even on esoteric tenets of theology, such as whether "the path to salvation lies in our faith and beliefs, or through our actions and deeds," our views are as stable as our views on widely debated public questions, such as whether government spending on environmental protection should be increased or decreased. That stability is itself evidence of how important religion is to most Americans.

On the other hand, "highly stable from year to year" does not mean "perfectly stable." Over the course of a lifetime, individual change in religious outlook turns out to be important. This chapter tells the story of how religious identity in America has become less inherited and fixed and more chosen and changeable.

The previous chapter examined stability and change at the aggregate level—how American religion has evolved over the last half century—but aggregate stability can conceal individual instability. For example, our panel survey found that although the aggregate proportion of nones (that is, people who claim to have no religious affiliation) was virtually identical in the two years (15.9 percent in 2006 and 16.5 percent in 2007), those responses were relatively unstable at the individual level. Of all those who claimed no religious affiliation in 2006, only 70 percent repeated that response in 2007, while the 30 percent of former nones who claimed some substantive religious tradition in 2007 were replaced by an equal number of people who had been something in 2006 but now described themselves as none.

Surprisingly, very few of these people who seemed to have discarded or acquired a religious affiliation between 2006 and 2007 experienced any other significant change in religious belief or practice. In response to an explicit question about recent change in their "religious beliefs or practices," slightly *fewer* of them (9 percent) reported change than did people whose religious affiliation remained unchanged (10 percent). They prayed as often in both years, they believed in God just as fervently (or just as tentatively), they went to church virtually as often.[4] So they are not really converts in any ordinary sense. The only thing that changed was how they described their religious identity.

These folks seem to be standing at the edge of a religious tradition, half in and half out. Sometimes we catch them thinking of themselves as a "something" (Baptist or Catholic or whatever), and other times they think of themselves as a "none." We have come to call these people, who seem to be standing on the threshold of a religious tradition, betwixt and between, "liminals," from the Latin word for "threshold."[5]

These religious liminals are distributed around each of the major religious traditions in roughly the same proportion, so that each tradition (and each denomination) seems to be surrounded by a penumbra of roughly 10 percent who are liminal members, neither entirely in nor entirely out. Our discovery of liminals is fully consistent with a report from the Pew Forum on Religion & Public Life that (aside from weddings, funerals, and trips) 24 percent of all Americans regularly or occasionally attend services of faiths other than their own.[6] In the real world, entirely apart from genuine conversion or apostasy, American religious identities are fuzzy around the edges.

Most Americans share the same religious identity as their parents, and in that sense religion appears to be inherited.[7] In round numbers nearly three quarters[8] of all Americans currently espouse the religious tradition in which they were raised. However, that figure is slightly misleading because:

1. For children of religiously mixed marriages, "parents' religion" is ambiguous.[9]
2. According to our 2007 Faith Matters survey nearly 20 percent of Americans were raised in a religion different from their parents' religion, *even when the parents shared a single religion*, so there is obviously additional slippage between their "original" religion and their parents' religion.
3. A significant number of those who are currently in the religion of their parents—10 percent in both our 2006 Faith Matters survey and the Pew Religious Landscape Survey—had switched away for a while, before returning to their original faith.
4. Another significant fraction of Protestants, while still in their original religious tradition, such as mainline Protestant, have switched to a different denomination (say, from Presbyterian to Methodist).

If we take all these qualifications into account, then less than two thirds of all Americans simply inherited their parents' religion. Moreover, fidelity to one's parents' religion is twice as high among blacks and Latinos (for whom, as we shall discuss in Chapter 9, religious identity is closely bound up with ethnic identity) as among whites and Asian Americans, so all things considered, roughly 35–40 percent of all Americans and 40–45 percent of white Americans have switched at some point away from their parents' religion.[10] In short, it is misleading to think of religious identity in contemporary America as an inherited and stable characteristic.

Yet a further qualification to the image of religion as transmitted faithfully from generation to generation arises when we take into account not only what religious affiliation a person claims, but also whether he or she is religiously observant. In Chapter 4 we saw that if we take into account the fact that the affiliation of a lapsed Catholic (or Methodist or Jew) is merely nominal, that discount can significantly alter our assessment of changes in average religiosity nationwide. Precisely the same point is true at the level of the individual. Figure 5.1 summarizes the incidence of switching and lapsing among white Americans across major religious traditions. (Operationally, "lapsed" refers to self-identified members of a religious tradition who attend services no more than several times a year.)

While more than half of the adult children of Mormons and of evangelical Protestants in America today remain observant members of their parents' faith, the same is true of fewer than half of "Anglo" Catholics and mainline Protestants and only about one fifth of Jews and other non-Christians, though the figures for lapsing non-Christians are exaggerated, since attendance at weekly religious services is less common in those faiths, even among observant members. To be sure, even among Christians, some of those we are calling lapsed are themselves the children of lapsed parents, but lapsing (that is, nonattendance) has risen very sharply across the generations. Of our 2006 Faith Matters respondents, 42 percent told us that they attended religious services no more than several times a year, but when we asked about their family's attendance when they were

Figure 5.1

SWITCHING AND LAPSING BY RELIGIOUS TRADITION (WHITES ONLY)

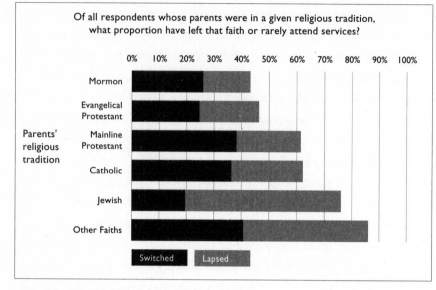

SOURCE: FAITH MATTERS SURVEY, 2006.

growing up, the comparable figure was only 12 percent. Most of the lapsing in Figure 5.1 represents real intergenerational change.

So while inherited religion is commonplace in America, it is far from universal. Has the rate of inheritance changed much over the course of the twentieth century? The best available evidence on that important issue comes from comparing inheritance rates among different birth cohorts in the General Social Survey. That is, of people in that survey archive who were born in the 1890s (or the 1980s), how many of them reported that at the time of being interviewed they were in the same religious tradition as they had been raised in? In round numbers, these data suggest that the rate of switching rose slowly over the century from about 19 percent among those Americans born at the beginning of the twentieth century to about 27 percent among those born at the end of the century, for an increase of almost 50 percent in the rate of switching over this century.[11] (Keep in mind that these figures do not include the various upward adjustments in switching that might be made for lapsing, "out and back" switching, and denominational switches.) All things considered we Americans seem less firmly anchored in our various religious heritages than we were a generation or two ago.

We can get further insights into patterns of religious inheritance by tracing trends separately for the major religious traditions: Catholics, mainline Protestants, evangelical Protestants, and nones.[12] This evidence is displayed in Figure 5.2.

• The most striking change in religious inheritance over the twentieth century was the dramatic increase in the fraction of people raised without a religious affiliation who *stayed* that way as adults. Throughout most of the century, "none" parents were likely to have "something" children, so that intergenerationally, the category of "no religion" was highly unstable.[13] As we saw in the previous chapter, the fraction of all Americans who claimed no religion was quite small (roughly 5–10 percent) until the 1990s; it rose sharply after 1990 among the millennial generation. Now, however, we see

Figure 5.2

RETENTION RATE BY RELIGIOUS TRADITION AND GENERATION (WHITES ONLY)

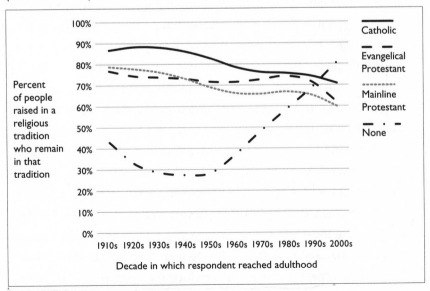

SOURCE: GENERAL SOCIAL SURVEY, 1973–2008; DATA LOESS-SMOOTHED.

that the retention rate of nones rose steadily during the second half of the twentieth century, beginning with the baby boomers, until by the cohort of people who came of age during the first decade of the twenty-first century the retention rate of nones is actually higher than that of the major religious traditions. This is yet another symptom of what we described in Chapter 4 as the second after-shock, which has made many youth (regardless of their religious background) conclude that religion is not for them.[14]

The dramatic increase in retention rates among the nones in Figure 5.2 dwarfs the changes in the three principal religious traditions, but the magnitude of those changes over the century is far from trivial. Retention rates of each of those traditions tended to fall throughout the twentieth century. Looked at more closely, the retention rate was very high for Catholics born during the first third of the century, reaching nearly 90 percent among young people coming of age in the 1920s and 1930s. Those young adults were mostly second-generation immigrants, born to Catholic parents who had themselves come to America in the massive immigration wave of 1890–1914. For this generation, being Catholic was simply part of what it meant to be Polish American, or Italian American, or Irish American. (We explore this connection between ethnic identity and religious identity in more detail in Chapter 9.) As ethnic assimilation progressed during the middle of the century, however, Catholic loyalty tended to fade, until by the end of the twentieth century, the retention rate among "Anglo" Catholics was hardly higher than in any other religious tradition.[15] Two additional points must be added to fill out this picture:

- First, as we saw in Figure 5.1, almost as many people raised as Catholics are now lapsed Catholics or have actually left the church, but those lapsed Catholics are still shown as loyal Catholics in Figure 5.2. In that sense, Figure 5.2 seriously underestimates the downward trend in "Anglo" Catholic fealty over the twentieth century. All things considered, roughly 60 percent of all Americans today who were raised in America as Catholics are no longer practicing Catholics, half of them having left the church entirely and half remaining nominally Catholic, but rarely, if ever, taking any part in the life of the church.[16]

- Second, however, Figure 5.2 entirely omits Latino Catholics. (Until very recently the General Social Survey was conducted only in English and thus omitted Spanish-only speakers, so it is a poor source of information about trends among Latino Catholics.) Our 2006 Faith Matters survey, however, shows that the defection rate among "Anglo" Catholics is twice as high as among Latino Catholics, so in that way Figure 5.2 exaggerates the decline in Catholic fealty in the recent decades.[17]

One implication of these two points taken together is that the Latinoization of the U.S. Catholic Church (described in more detail in Chapter 9) will certainly accelerate in the years ahead, as older cohorts of "Anglo" Catholics are replaced by young, more faithful Latinos.

For mainline Protestants the retention rate fell fairly sharply among people who came of age between roughly 1920 and 1960, and thereafter remained at a relatively low plateau of 60–65 percent, the lowest among any major religious tradition. In other words, for the last half century roughly one third of people raised in one of the mainline Protestant denominations have left that faith, mostly to become either evangelical or none. Keep in mind as well, as Figure 5.1 showed, that another 20 percent of mainline offspring have stopped coming to church, while remaining nominally in the faith. So in round numbers mainline Protestants, like "Anglo" Catholics, have lost more than half their children over the last half century.[18]

Until recently the story among evangelical Protestants was somewhat different. For most of the twentieth century, Figure 5.2 shows, evangelical Protestantism kept about three quarters of its children in the faith. Moreover, among the evangelical cohorts who reached adulthood in the 1970s and 1980s the evangelical retention rate actually rose, at the same time that the retention rate of Catholics and mainline Protestants was falling. Not coincidentally, this was the heyday of neo-evangelicalism—what we called in the previous chapter the first aftershock. However, at least according to the General Social Survey, the retention rate of evangelical young adults plunged among the cohort who came of age at the turn of the twenty-first century, falling from 75 percent among those who came of age in the 1980s to 62 percent among those who reached adulthood in the 2000s. It is probably not a coincidence that this cohort of less steadfast evangelical offspring was coming of age in the midst of the second aftershock, and this factor helps explain the youthful evangelical downtrend shown in Figure 4.13.

The fate of a religion in numerical terms depends not merely on its losses, but also on its gains, in terms of recruiting converts. We shall turn in a moment to this double-entry bookkeeping, as we ask about winners and losers among the major American religious traditions. First, however, we should pause to ask, apart from the ups and downs of particular religious brands, *what explains who remains faithful to the religion of their parents and who leaves?*

Apart from ethnicity, ordinary demographic factors, such as gender and education, make very little difference in retention rates. Women are no likelier to remain faithful to the religion of their parents than men, college grads no more than high school dropouts, and so forth. Religious socialization plays a bigger role.[19]

The most important factor predicting religious retention is whether a person's family of origin was religiously homogeneous and observant, or not. Children of mixed marriages are much more likely to leave the faith within which they were raised, regardless of whether we assign that family's faith to the father or the mother or to whichever faith the child was raised in. Moreover, children of mixed marriages are more likely to become nones or to attend religious services rarely, even if they remain nominally affiliated with a religion. Conversely, people who were involved as children in religious activities, such as Sunday school, are significantly less likely to leave their parents' faith as adults.[20] No doubt part of this pattern is attributable to theological conviction, on the "as the twig is bent" theory. Another important part of the story, however, is surely social and familial pressure, since more religiously engaged parents are more likely to care about whether their children stay within the faith,[21] and in particular are (as we shall see momentarily) more likely to care whether their children marry inside the faith.

Marrying someone of another faith, not surprisingly, increases the likelihood of leaving one's original religion. In the Bible's most poetic treatment of intermarriage, Ruth declares "Wherever you go, I will go; and wherever you lodge, I will lodge. Your people shall be my people, and your God, my God."[22] Ruth was the exception that proves the rule. In recent years, however, about 60 percent of switching from one's religious tradition of origin seems to have been unrelated to marriage—that is, either the switcher was unmarried or the switch was to a religion different from the spouse's current religion. Roughly 25 percent of switching was probably directly related to marriage, because the switch was to the spouse's religion, and another 15 percent of switching involved both spouses switching to some third, shared religion. To be sure, some conversions in these latter two categories could have been nonmarital in origin, but that seems unlikely. Figure 5.3 shows that as a fraction of all switching, nonmarital switching has grown over the last three decades, even though both switching and (as we shall shortly see) intermarriage have grown, presumably factors that boosted marital switching.[23] So switching is up, and nonmarital switching is up even more. The implication: More and more Americans are choosing their religion independently of *both* their family of origin *and* their current family.

Finally, in light of the previous chapter's discussion of shocks and aftershocks, we should say a word here about religious switching and politics. As we saw in Chapter 4 (and will discuss in more detail in Chapters 11 and 12), a half century ago political ideology and religiosity were essentially uncorrelated in America, with lots of liberals in church pews and many unchurched conservatives. Even today, among those who have inherited their religious affiliation (that is, nonswitchers) the correlation between religion and politics is much more muted than among those who have chosen their religious affiliation (that is, switchers).[24] In other words, people

Figure 5.3

RELIGIOUS SWITCHING FOR MARITAL AND NONMARITAL REASONS
(1973–1994)

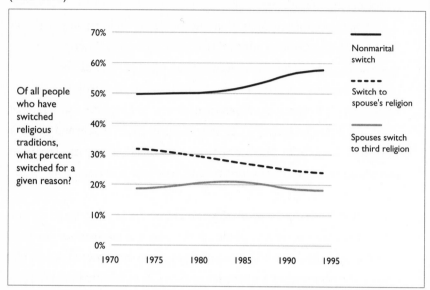

SOURCE: GENERAL SOCIAL SURVEY, 1973–1994; DATA LOESS-SMOOTHED.

who have left their parents' religion have switched in ways that have tended to move political liberals toward the secular end of the religious spectrum and political conservatives toward the devout end of the religious spectrum. Political conservatives who were raised as evangelicals tended to stay evangelical, and political conservatives who were raised as something else tended to become evangelical. Conversely, political liberals who were raised as evangelicals tended to switch their religious affiliation, and political liberals who were raised in some other religious tradition tended to switch their religious affiliation to none.[25]

Since there are more of these switchers among more recent cohorts, the correlation between politics and religion is stronger among those younger cohorts. Among people born in the 1930s and 1940s there are still many churched liberals and unchurched conservatives, but among people born in the 1970s and 1980s there are fewer such "misfits." As long as the older generation is still with us, its members tend to dampen the alignment of religion and politics, but as they pass from the scene generational replacement tends to heighten that alignment.

Somewhat surprisingly, this pattern of switching suggests that people whose religious and political affiliations are "inconsistent" as judged by today's partisan alignments—that is, liberal churchgoers and unchurched conservatives—are more likely to resolve the inconsistency by changing their religion than by changing their politics. We were initially skeptical of this finding, since it seemed implausible that people would hazard the fate of their eternal soul over mundane political controversies. But as we probed the evidence, the case seemed stronger.

Even within the brief time span of our Faith Matters panel survey (2006–2007) we found evidence of growing consistency between political ideology and religiosity, as liberals moved toward the secular end of the continuum and conservatives moved toward the religious pole.[26] Not many people changed their religious affiliation in that short span of time, but those who did continued the decades-long sorting out of political liberals into the secular camp and political conservatives into the highly religious camp. When religion and politics were initially inconsistent, religious commitment, not political commitment, was more likely to change. Even with these panel data (analyzed as described in Appendix 2) it is impossible to be absolutely certain whether politics is driving religious conversion, or religion is prompting political conversion, but the available evidence strongly suggests the former. It is likely that both are happening, and we don't claim that in all eras politics would be in the driver's seat, but in this era it seems to be. The net result, in any event, is clear: heightened religious/political polarization, as the growing numbers of religious switchers increasingly sort themselves out politically.

Given what we have learned about religious departures and arrivals, what can we conclude about winners and losers among the various religious traditions in contemporary America, recognizing (as we saw clearly in Chapter 4) that past performance is no guarantee of future performance?

- Catholics: Catholicism, as we have seen both in this chapter and in the previous one, suffered serious losses, both to conversion and to lapsing. Conversely, conversions to Catholicism have been dwarfed by these losses.[27] More portentously, the average age of Catholic converts today is about sixty-five, suggesting that conversion to Catholicism was largely a phenomenon of the 1950s and 1960s, when non-Catholics marrying Catholics were expected to convert. The combination of high losses among Catholic young people and low gains from conversion has been only partly offset by a higher birth rate among Catholics than among the general population. Except for the timely arrival of large numbers of Latino immigrants, the future of the American Catholic Church might appear bleak. In any event, the transformation of the church from a largely white ethnic organization (led by a predominantly Irish American hierarchy) to a largely Latino organization is inexorable, as we discuss in more detail in Chapter 9.

- Mainline Protestants: As we saw in Figure 5.1, the outflow of the young from mainline Protestant denominations has been virtually as great as the comparable outflow from the Catholic Church, and in both cases the losses have been due partly to conversion and partly to religious apathy. Like Catholics, mainline Protestants have recruited few recent converts to offset those losses, but unlike Catholics, mainline Protestant denominations lack the offsetting benefits of high fertility and high immigration. In a purely arithmetical sense, this combination of high losses and low gains has produced the near-catastrophic falls in mainline Protestant adherence that we described in the previous chapter.

- Evangelical Protestants: At least during the second half of the twentieth century, evangelical churches benefited from a retention edge among their offspring compared to Catholics and mainline Protestants—not massively higher, but coupled with somewhat higher birth rates during that period, enough to help raise their share of the American religious spectrum, as we discussed in Chapter 4. Again until recently, evangelicals also gained many more converts than either the Catholic Church or mainline

Protestant denominations, mostly (as we have seen) from the conservative half of the political spectrum. It appears, however, that the demographic advantages of a higher birth rate and a higher retention rate among evangelicals ended in the 1990s, coinciding with a leveling off and even slumping of the evangelical share of the religious marketplace. Whether those recent trends will continue is impossible to predict.

• Nones: Until recently, secular parents were much more likely than religious parents to lose their children, and those large losses kept the number of nones nationwide relatively small, even with a steady inflow of apostates from other religious traditions. However, as we have seen, during the second half of the twentieth century this disadvantage steadily diminished, and by the early twenty-first it seems to have disappeared. As the hole in the bottom of the bucket was slowly plugged, and as the flow into the top of the bucket significantly increased, especially after 1990, the volume of nones has risen sharply, especially among the youngest cohorts of adults.

Because of the historically high rate of churn among nones, most nonreligious Americans were raised in religiously active homes, and that is still true today. As we noted in Chapter 4, three quarters of the nones in the 2006 Faith Matters survey had religiously engaged parents, and more than half had religious education as children themselves. Moreover, of nones who are married nearly half have religiously identified partners. In short, most secular Americans are much more intimately familiar with religious beliefs and practices than their secular counterparts in Europe. They may have rejected religion, but it is not alien to them. In America, even nones who no longer attend religious services are likely to know the Lord's Prayer or the Kaddish by heart, and as we shall see in Chapter 15, that cultural familiarity has important implications for religious comity in America. On the other hand, if our analysis of generational gains and losses is accurate and (more conjecturally) if these trends continue unabated into the future, the personal basis for that comity will be weaker a generation from now, since increasing numbers of Americans will never have experienced religion firsthand, even as children.

More could be said about the complicated flows of Americans from one religion (or nonreligion) to another, but we close this section by noting one final implication of what we have learned. Many Americans—at least one third and rising—nowadays choose their religion rather than simply inheriting it. And a significant fraction of those who remain in the religion of their parents must surely have contemplated leaving it, and they too may be reasonably said to have chosen and not simply inherited that religious affiliation. Religion in America is increasingly a domain of choice, churn, and surprisingly low brand loyalty. That is the demand side of the religious marketplace. On the supply side, we would expect successful "firms" (denominations and congregations) in such a fickle market to be especially entrepreneurial in "marketing" their product, a prominent feature of American religious life on which historians have recently commented.[28] We turn to religious innovation and entrepreneurship in the next chapter.

RELIGIOUS INTERMARRIAGE

In Chapter 3 we noted a slow, steady, long-term decline in religious observance underneath the shorter-term upheavals of recent decades. A second such glacially slow development, perhaps even more momentous, has been a lowering of interfaith barriers, marked most notably by gradually increasing rates (and acceptance) of religious intermarriage. Evidence on this topic is less abundant than evidence on attendance at religious services, but the available data point unambiguously toward a gradual but inexorable softening of the once impermeable social and cultural boundaries among America's various religious traditions.

The best evidence suggests that roughly *half* of all married Americans today are married to someone who came originally from a different religious tradition (as defined in the introductory chapter), and a bit fewer than *one third* of all marriages remain mixed today.

(The difference between these two figures is accounted for by the roughly 20 percent of all marriages in which one spouse has converted to the other's faith, or both have converted to a third faith.)

If we count marriages between two different mainline Protestant denominations (say Methodists and Lutherans) or two different evangelical denominations as mixed, then the intermarriage rates are roughly 10 percentage points higher—40 percent currently mixed and 60 percent originally mixed.[29]

This high rate of intermarriage has important implications that we shall discuss throughout this book. For now, we ask not about the consequences of intermarriage (and more generally, of interfaith ties), but about how America today stands on this measure of interfaith social integration, in both comparative and historical perspective. Since the vast majority of Americans today live in religiously integrated settings, we may not fully appreciate how unusual such a society is. Take, for example, Northern Ireland, one of the few places in the Western world today similar to America in terms of religious observance. As the twenty-first century opened, roughly 10 percent of all marriages in Northern Ireland were currently mixed, about one third of the contemporary U.S. rate.[30]

American intermarriage rates a century ago, however, were much more similar to those in violently strife-torn, religiously divided Northern Ireland. Our most reliable evidence on U.S. intermarriage rates in the first decade of the twentieth century suggests that about 12 percent of couples married in that decade remained in separate faiths (as compared to the above-mentioned 10 percent in Northern Ireland today). In round numbers, the U.S. rate of religious intermarriage more than doubled over the course of the last century, moving us far away from the Northern Ireland model of a religiously segregated society.

Our best estimates of the detailed trend line come from marriage cohort data, comparing the rate of mixing within marriages formed in different decades.[31] Figure 5.4 summarizes this evidence, showing that the reduction of interfaith barriers was slow, but steady across the twentieth century.[32] The upper line refers to marriages in which the spouses came originally from different religious traditions, and the lower line refers to marriages in which the spouses worship currently in different religious traditions. The difference between the two lines is, generally speaking, attributable to the convergent conversion of one or both spouses.

Figure 5.4 clearly shows the increasing permeability of the boundaries around religious traditions. Though not visible in that figure, the same applies to the religion/no-religion line; that is, the frequency of marriages between people with some religious identity and people who disclaim any religious identity. To be sure, in the oldest cohorts nones (that is, the religiously unaffiliated) were very rare, so very few marriages could cross that line, but as the number of people without a religious identity rose in more recent cohorts, so too the likelihood of a marriage between a none and a something rose. In our Faith Matters survey of 2006, nearly half of all married nones have a something spouse.

Since religious diversity has increased over this period, one might ask whether increasing intermarriage might simply reflect a more religiously diverse pool of potential partners. We have carefully calculated, however, the changing odds of random intermarriage, and that factor plays at most a supporting role in the trend shown in Figure 5.4.[33]

Evidence of lowered interfaith barriers also comes from questions in Gallup Polls and in our 2006 Faith Matters survey, asking how people feel about religious intermarriage. By 2006, 57 percent of our respondents said calmly that it was "not very important" or "not important at all" that their children marry someone of their own faith, and only 22 percent insisted it was "very important." Not surprisingly, those for whom marrying inside the faith remains "very important" are heavily drawn from the most religious fraction of the U.S. population and are deeply embedded in religiously homogeneous social networks, but by 2006 they represent less than one American in four. Most Americans, even in their personal lives, live comfortably in a religiously diverse world, as we shall explain in more detail in Chapter 15.

Figure 5.4

INTERMARRIAGE BECAME MORE COMMON THROUGHOUT
THE 20TH CENTURY

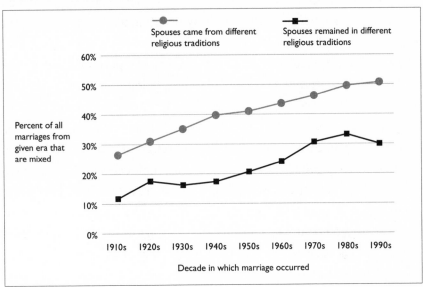

SOURCE: GENERAL SOCIAL SURVEY, 1972–2008.

When did the change toward tolerance of intermarriage occur? A first clue comes from a pair of older Gallup Poll questions about whether people approved or not of marriage between a Catholic and a Protestant or between a Jew and a non-Jew. Figure 5.5 shows that approval of these forms of religious intermarriage was already around 60 percent when these questions were first asked in 1968, and that approval continued to rise to nearly 80 percent by 1982, when the question stopped being asked.

The Gallup archives also contain bits of evidence that social norms regarding intermarriage must have been changing in the decades after World War II, since as late as 1951, 54 percent of Americans had told Gallup that "two young people in love who are of different religious faiths—Protestant, Catholic, or Jewish—should *not* get married."

Even clearer evidence of a long-term generational shift in favor of religious intermarriage comes from a pair of surveys in 1982 and

Figure 5.5

APPROVAL OF RELIGIOUS INTERMARRIAGE ROSE BETWEEN
1968 AND 1982

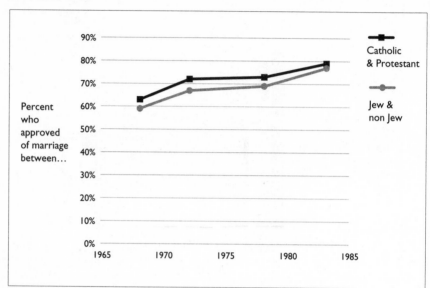

SOURCE: GALLUP POLL REPORTS.

1990 (summarized in Figure 5.6) that asked "how important are shared religious beliefs to a successful marriage?"[34] Among Americans who had reached adulthood before 1930 a substantial majority said that shared religion was "very important," suggesting that marriage inside the faith was a widely shared norm in the first part of the twentieth century. That fraction, however, steadily shrank as interfaith openness increased throughout the century, so that among Americans coming of age in the 1990s only 24 percent endorsed that norm.

Thus, the best available evidence on both the "is" and the "ought" of religious intermarriage strongly suggests that the liberalizing trends were slow and steady throughout the twentieth century. To be sure, specific public episodes punctuated this long trend, such as the 1971 ruling of the National Conference of Catholic Bishops that the conscience of a non-Catholic spouse was to be respected; but in the lives and the values of ordinary Americans, beneath the

Figure 5.6
YOUNGER GENERATIONS ARE MORE OPEN TO RELIGIOUS INTERMARRIAGE

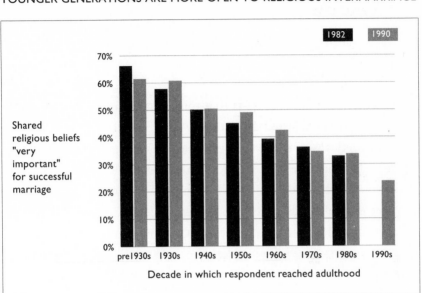

SOURCE: WORLD VALUES SURVEYS, 1982 AND 1990.

official veneer, interfaith boundaries had softened gradually but inexorably throughout the entire century.

In short, during the twentieth century both the norms governing religious intermarriage and actual marriage patterns moved toward greater interfaith openness and integration, as religiously insular generations were succeeded by their more open-minded children.[35] Less detailed evidence on interfaith friendships is available, but such evidence as we have suggests that they too became slowly but steadily more prevalent, at least over the last two decades of the twentieth century.[36]

Two decades ago Robert Wuthnow, reflecting on "society and faith since World War II," first called attention to the decline of denominational boundaries in American religion:

A larger number of people move across religious boundaries to visit, to join, or even marry someone from another faith. And attitudes toward other faiths show a considerably higher degree of acceptance. In these ways, denominationalism has become less significant as a basis for social and cultural tensions and divisions . . . As the population has become better educated, denominational barriers have ceased to function as hermetic categories of religious identification.[37]

Our new evidence suggests that this trend characterized all educational levels and lasted the entire twentieth century.

Americans continue to be unusually devout, as we noted in Chapter 1, but the once stark sociological boundaries among our religions have steadily faded over the last century. Indeed, a close comparison of the trends in religious attendance in Chapter 3 and these trends in intermarriage suggests that Americans have become religiously open faster than we have become religiously less observant. We are much more open to crossing religious boundaries than our grandparents were, but we are only modestly less observant than they were. In other words, our best estimate is that the fraction of Americans who are both religiously observant and religiously open has grown over the last century. As we shall see in Chapter 15, that fact has powerful implications for the role of religion in contemporary American life.

WHO INTERMARRIES?

In exploring differences in religious in-marriage by religious tradition, we must take into account the size of the group, since it is easier to find a mate of the same religion in a large religious group than in a small one. If a large group and a small group have identical observed rates of intermarriage, that implies a greater preference for in-marriage in the smaller group, who have had to look harder for a suitable mate of their own religion, or perhaps that the larger group is especially resistant to marriage into the smaller one.[38] We begin with a glance at how norms regarding intermarriage vary across the major religious traditions in America today, and then we explore how actual mating patterns differ.

Figure 5.7 shows that Mormons, Jews, evangelicals, Black Protestants, and Latino Catholics remain more insistent on their children marrying inside the faith than other Americans. As we have seen before, ethnic minorities are more concerned about their children "keeping the faith," as are evangelicals.[39]

Turning next to evidence on actual intermarriage rates, Figure 5.8 (which does *not* control for opportunity and includes all American adults in 2006) and Figure 5.9 (which *does* control for opportunity and compares successive birth cohorts) provide relevant evidence.[40] Figure 5.8 shows separate bars for marriages between people who are *currently* in different religious traditions and for marriages in which the spouses came *originally* from different religious traditions, with the difference between the two representing conversion by one or both partners.[41]

As Figure 5.8 shows, intermarriage is rarer among Latino Catholics, Black Protestants, and Mormons, but intermarriage is common in all other religious traditions. (Interfaith marriage was rare among

Figure 5.7

OPPOSITION TO INTERMARRIAGE BY RELIGIOUS TRADITION

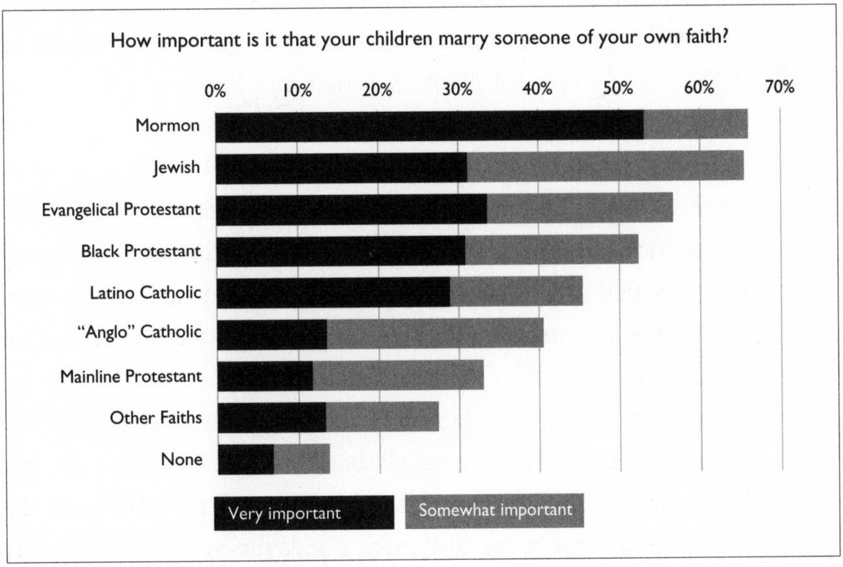

SOURCE: FAITH MATTERS SURVEY, 2006.

AMERICAN GRACE

Figure 5.8

INTERMARRIAGE RATES BY RELIGIOUS TRADITION

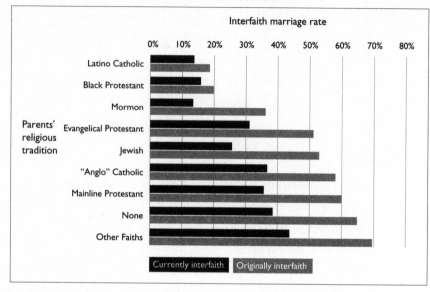

SOURCE: FAITH MATTERS SURVEY, 2006.

Jews born before 1950, but not afterward.) Even among evangelical offspring—whose parents, as we have just seen, care a good deal about their children marrying inside the faith—nearly half chose spouses who came originally from nonevangelical backgrounds. Note that nearly two thirds of the children of nones (that is, parents who had no religious tradition) married someone from a religious background. Moreover, of married nones (that is, people who say they currently have no religious identity), almost half have religiously identified spouses, and those spouses are distributed proportionally across the various religious traditions, yet further evidence that secular America is, in fact, intimately integrated with religious America.

Figure 5.9 shows the odds of marriage within a given religious tradition, adjusting for the size of that group. If the odds are 1:1, members of that tradition are no more likely to marry within the faith than would happen randomly, given the size of the group; the more lopsided the odds, the more that a given group tends to

Figure 5.9

PROPENSITY FOR IN-MARRIAGE, BY RELIGIOUS TRADITION AND
GENERATION (WHITES ONLY)

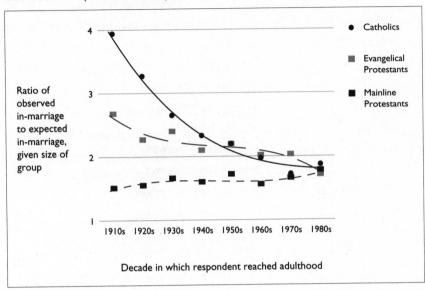

SOURCE: GENERAL SOCIAL SURVEY, 1973–1994.

marry within the faith. For example, the figure shows that, taking
into account the size of their group, Catholics who came of age in
the 1910s were about four times more likely to marry another Catholic than we would have expected by chance, given the number of
Catholics in America, but Catholics who came of age in the 1980s
were less than twice as likely to marry another Catholic than we
would have expected randomly. (Keep in mind that we are unable
to include Latino Catholics in this analysis, since Spanish speakers were excluded from the surveys throughout the period shown
in Figure 5.9.) In other words, controlling for the opportunity for
in-marriage given by the number of Catholics, the Catholic propensity for in-marriage used to be very pronounced, but among more
recent generations Catholics are no more likely to marry within
their faith than Protestants are to marry within their faiths, taking
the size of the various religious traditions into account.

    Similarly, among Americans born early in the twentieth century
the propensity for in-marriage among evangelicals was nearly twice

as high as among mainline Protestants, but in more recent cohorts the two are not very different. Controlling for opportunity flattens the apparent mainline Protestant decline in in-marriage. In other words, the reason for lower in-marriage among liberal Protestants today is simply that there are fewer liberal Protestants to mate. Conversely, there are now more evangelicals to marry, but taking that fact into account, in-marriage among evangelicals is significantly lower now than it was in the past. In short, among young people coming of age at the end of the twentieth century, every religious tradition had a modest propensity to marry within the faith, and that propensity did not vary much across the major traditions.

What (apart from religious tradition) predicts rates of religious intermarriage? [42]

- Religiosity and religious socialization: The propensity for marriage within the faith is much higher among more religious people—not surprisingly. We can't say for sure whether low religious commitment is a cause or a consequence of intermarriage—or more likely, both cause and consequence—but intermarriage is strongly associated with lower religious observance. Intermarriage is higher among people who were raised less religiously, who come from less religious families, and who come from families that were themselves religiously heterogeneous. In that sense, a propensity for religious intermarriage might be said to be socially inherited. Similarly, both normative acceptance of intermarriage and actual intermarriage are much higher among people with religiously diverse social networks (friends and neighbors), although it is impossible to tell which is cause and which effect in that strong relationship. In any event, the data strongly suggest that intermarriage rates are a reasonable proxy for interfaith integration in other spheres. Those of us who crossed religious boundaries to find our mate are very likely to have crossed those same boundaries to find our friends.
- Ethnic minorities have a stronger preference for in-group marriage, in part because they have more religiously homogeneous

social networks, but also because ethnic identification itself discourages religious intermarriage. The religious intermarriage rate for whites is substantially (20 percentage points) higher than for blacks and Latinos. Even within a given ethnic group (that is, *among* whites or *among* blacks), the more strongly a person identifies with his or her ethnic group, the less likely he or she is (a) to switch religions, (b) to intermarry, and (c) to be open to intermarriage for the next generation. This linkage between ethnic identification and religious identification is even stronger among Catholics than among Protestants. These patterns confirm that religion and ethnicity are closely bound up together in America, as we explore in more detail in Chapter 9.

In sum, the well-tossed religious salad bowl created by Americans' high level of switching and intermarriage is quite unlike the strictly defined religious pillars (or closed communities) characteristic of other deeply religious societies. Moreover, both switching and intermarriage have risen significantly over the last century. That feature of American religious life has powerful implications for religious tolerance and pluralism in America, as we discuss in greater detail in our concluding chapter.

SUMMING UP

What have we learned in this chapter about religious change and religious intermarriage?

First, although religious commitments are more stable than many other aspects of our outlook on society and politics, they are not perfectly stable, especially in the long run. While most of us still tend to follow our parents' religious commitments, at least if their commitments were clear and consistent, a substantial number of Americans now choose their religious affiliations and beliefs, rather than inheriting them. Roughly half of white Americans have departed from their parents' religious stance, either through switching to a different religious tradition or through lapsing into religious indifference. Both intermarriage and defection from family religious tradition are lower among ethnic minorities, as well as among the most devoutly religious families. For most of the twentieth century that latter group was disproportionately drawn from evangelical Protestants, although the evangelical edge has diminished and virtually vanished in recent cohorts. Meanwhile, religious intermarriage rose steadily throughout the twentieth century to the point that today roughly half of all married Americans chose a partner from a different religious tradition.

For virtually all religious traditions the rate of religious inheritance declined and the rate of intermarriage rose over the course of the twentieth century, especially for Catholics. The Catholic fraction of the U.S. population has held steady only because the departing grandchildren of white ethnic immigrants of the first decades of the twentieth century have been roughly balanced by arriving Latino Catholics. Evangelical Protestants gained more adherents from inheritance and conversion than they lost through defection for most of the twentieth century, while nones remained a small fraction of the population because of their low rate of inheritance. In the last decade or two, however, the balance of trade has turned neutral for evangelicals and strongly positive for nones. Meanwhile, mainline Protestants suffered from the near-fatal combination of high defection and low in-conversion.

One result of all these changes is that individual choice has become virtually as important as inheritance in explaining Americans' religious affiliations, raising the stakes for religious marketing and innovation, which we discuss in the next chapter. A second implication, perhaps less obvious, but more important, is that Americans now live in a more religiously integrated society, the consequences of which will become clearer in subsequent chapters.

CHAPTER 6

INNOVATIONS IN RELIGION

In the nineteenth century, the American frontier presented a problem for religious leaders. People, especially young people, were spread out in far-flung communities, many of which were too new to have churches. And so both Protestant ministers and Catholic priests came up with an ingenious solution—the chapel car. Clergy would use these train cars repurposed into mini-chapels to travel from town to town, holding services for the otherwise unchurched settlers on the frontier. They are largely forgotten today, but in their day chapel cars represented the state of the art in bringing religion to remote areas.[1]

The chapel car is merely one small example of the innovation that has always characterized American religion. As another example, consider the chapel car of our day, online church. Chapel cars physically brought worship to the people: Internet churches deliver a virtual worship experience to anyone with an Internet connection. An exemplar of online religion can be found at the Web site of LifeChurch.tv, a pioneer in offering worship on the Web. While LifeChurch also has physical locations, it provides an innovative platform for Internet users to "go to church" without leaving home. The entire online experience of "attending" LifeChurch is designed to be interactive. While watching a service streamed online, viewers can respond to altar calls with a link that appears on their screen; they can make a contribution to the virtual collection plate; they can even chat online with other people watching the service.[2]

Both the chapel car and online religion are examples of using technology to spread the gospel. Such technological innovation, though, only scratches the surface of the inventiveness within the American style of religion. Far from always being a bulwark against change, many religions have historically incorporated change—even faiths with conservative sensibilities. Alan Wolfe, a careful observer of religion in America, comments, "The United States has conservatives aplenty, but it lacks traditionalists, if for no other reason than so many religious conservatives are the inventors of new forms of religious practice."[3]

This chapter continues the discussion about religious switching. In Chapter 5 we saw the fluidity of American religion as we examined the long-term trends in gains and losses within the major religious traditions. That discussion of religious switching is like viewing the landscape from 30,000 feet. You can make out broad contours but miss most of the movement and, therefore, detail. In this chapter, we zoom in for a closer look at religious switching, by focusing on movement from congregation to congregation. When it comes to religious switching, the action is in the congregations—the primary point of contact most Americans have with their religion.

Religious switching, or congregation shopping, would be for naught if every religion, and every congregation, was basically the same. If necessity is the mother of invention, religious fluidity is the mother of innovation. Or, perhaps, innovation is the mother of fluidity. Either way, Americans have a wide array of religious choices, as religious entrepreneurs—a term we do not use pejoratively—constantly refine and reinvent both the substance and the presentation of religion in the United States. The result is a dynamic religious landscape, so much so that one of the most frequently used metaphors to describe it is a marketplace.[4] To understand switching and shopping, therefore, requires understanding the constant stream of innovation within American religion. Therefore, this chapter begins with a sketch of the many different types of religious innovation.

It is against this backdrop of religious innovation that we then turn our attention squarely on America's congregations. We present new data on why Americans have chosen the congregations they attend, and what predicts a switch from one congregation to another.

The chapter culminates by extrapolating from the past prevalence of religious innovation to speculate on what the future may hold. Given the rise of religious nones, it would seem that there is a potential constituency for a new form of religion within the contemporary United States. We thus speculate that religious entrepreneurs will increasingly seek to reach this untapped pool—and offer examples of innovators who appear to be trying to do so already.

INNOVATIONS

In order to offer informed speculation about future religious innovations, we first should consider past innovations. We note that while our focus is on the United States, innovation in religion is hardly confined to the U.S. However, the United States clearly has an enormous volume of religious innovation. So common have been changes in the American religious landscape that the history of religion in the United States could be written as a history of religious innovations. Innovations, though, come in different types.

Some innovations consist of an old message presented through a new medium. The chapel car and LifeChurch are two examples, but so are methods used by revivalists like George Whitefield in the mid-1700s, Dwight Moody in the late 1800s, and Billy Graham in the mid-1900s. Each one regularly spoke to massive crowds, but each also pioneered ways of using the communications media of his day to bring his message to still more people. Whitefield used newspapers, including the newspaper network of Benjamin Franklin, to publish his sermons and publicize his revivals. Moody also used the press to turn his revivals into newsworthy events. Like Whitefield and Moody, Graham spoke to many thousands in halls, auditoriums, and stadiums, but expanded his reach further by broadcasting his revivals on radio and television. Today, the Internet is the new frontier in

communication, and as expected from the past embrace of innovation, religious entrepreneurs have taken their message online.[5]

Sometimes an innovation is less a new medium and more a
new form of religious organization. The Methodists, for example,
invented circuit riding as a way to bring ministers to the masses. In
the age before railroads, itinerant preachers would ride long, often
arduous, circuits to visit far-flung communities, winning many converts to Methodism as they did so. This was a far cry from an organizational model in which the local minister put down roots within
his community. Today, the megachurch arguably consists of a new
organizational model. In a typical megachurch, worship services
bring together many thousands, in numbers that resemble revivals
more than a traditional church service. At the same time, the proliferation of small groups—the cells of the megachurch congregation—
provide members with a small-scale sense of community.[6]

Other religious innovations are better described not as a new
medium but as a new message, sometimes resulting in a new religion
altogether. America is the birthplace of myriad new faiths, some of
which flourish and some of which flounder. Examples abound, but
include Pentecostalism, Seventh-day Adventists, the Christian Scientists, and the Mormons. In other cases, new religions were born
abroad but found a receptive audience in America, like the Methodists, the Shakers, and even the Unification Church.

In still other cases, innovations consist of adopting new practices
within an existing faith. Sometimes, those innovations are sweeping
and apply across an entire religious tradition, spanning the globe.
Arguably most sweeping of all is the Second Vatican Council of the
Catholic Church—Vatican II—which led to widespread change in
Catholic practices. No longer was the Mass said only in Latin, but
in the language of the parishioners; no longer did priests turn away
from the congregation during the Mass, but rather turned toward
them in a sign of inclusion. This period was also marked by local
reforms in many dioceses. For example, in many areas the prohibition on eating meat on Fridays outside of Lent was lifted.[7] Similarly
sweeping was the decision within many mainline Protestant denom-

now changed back (handwritten marginal note)

inations to ordain women, and now the decision within a smaller but growing number of Protestant faiths to ordain homosexuals.[8] The Mormons have also changed their practices, most notably in the 1890s, when the LDS church ended its practice of polygamy and, in the 1970s, when it ceased denying black males entry into the church's lay priesthood. Within Judaism, Reform synagogues have long been innovators. In the nineteenth century, many incorporated organ music into their services—common within Christianity, but not in Judaism—and also adopted mixed-gender seating.

In some cases, innovation consists not of anything new but rather maintaining what is old in the face of change. Some denominations—and within denominations, some congregations— thrive by offering a traditional style of worship, and a traditionalist worldview. Our Savior Lutheran, the conservative Lutheran church we highlight in Chapter 7, fits this profile. As do Catholic parishes that have returned to the pre–Vatican II Latin Mass, and Jewish synagogues in the Orthodox tradition—with no organs, and separate seating for men and women.[9]

Of course, not all innovations succeed. Some fail to catch on and thus are not remembered at all. Other innovations lead to rapid growth only to fade out. The Shakers were prominent in the early 1800s, but today have dwindled to fewer than ten members (perhaps inevitably, given that they teach celibacy for all their members). In the 1840s, William Miller attracted many followers as he taught that the world was to end in 1844. Millerism lost some luster when the end did not come on the designated day, but it did not fizzle out entirely. In a telling example of the dynamism within American religion, some of those Millerites became Seventh-day Adventists, a thriving denomination that endures today.

We could fill a book with the innovations that run through religion, specifically in its American variants. Those that are most likely to be remembered in the history books are large-scale changes, particularly the creation of new faiths altogether. Any list of American religious innovators is sure to include Joseph Smith (founder of Mormonism) and Mary Baker Eddy (founder of Christian Science). However, dramatic breaks with current religious practice are actually not the norm in religious innovation. Rather, as described by sociologist Mark Chaves, innovation is more typically introduced incrementally. "Religious movements and religious entrepreneurs partly innovate, but they also partly seek continuity with major existing traditions in their cultural field." [10]

For every innovation on the scale of founding an entirely new denomination, a relatively rare event, there are many thousands more small, incremental innovations being tried by unsung pastors within their local congregations. In subtle ways, congregational leaders from virtually all faiths are often trying out new initiatives and ideas, either to attract new members or hold on to their current ones, or both. As these efforts succeed and fail, congregations shrink and grow—they even come and go. [11] In the course of our research, we experienced firsthand how an individual congregation can be reinvigorated. Since we first visited it near the beginning of our research, Trinity Concord, featured in Chapter 2, has undergone a resurgence, having increased its attendance at Sunday services and, when compared to 2003, tripling the attendance at its church school.

CONGREGATIONS

Many—undoubtedly most—religious innovations, therefore, happen at the congregational level. In reading the vignettes of the congregations we have highlighted, one cannot help but be struck by their sheer variety and inventiveness. Our Savior Lutheran in Houston emphasizes its German heritage, even replicating the architecture of chapels in Germany; Beth Emet synagogue in Evanston, Illinois, hosts a wide variety of classes (some on Judaism, others not); St. Frances of Rome Catholic parish in Cicero, Illinois, has been holding Mass on the street, conducted in both English and Spanish. And so on. For most Americans their congregation is how they experience their religion. We suspect that few members of Rick Warren's Saddleback Church specifically went looking for a Southern Baptist congregation, the official denominational affiliation of this most mega of megachurches. Rather, they found a congregation they like, which also happens to have a Southern Baptist affiliation.

When Americans switch from one congregation to another, they often move too from one religion to another. When we focus only on switching from one religious tradition to another, we risk missing where the real action is found: congregations. Recall that switching to a new congregation but not a new religious tradition (e.g., a United Methodist attending a Presbyterian church) does not count as a switch under the system used in Chapter 5. Looking only at switches across the borders of religious traditions, therefore, *undercounts* the extent to which American religion is in flux. Consider the story of a friend of one of your authors. He and his family recently moved to a new community, and began looking for a church. They attended a Catholic parish, a United Methodist megachurch, a Lutheran church (of the mainline denomination), and an Episcopal parish. In the end, they chose to attend the Episcopal parish—a mainline Protestant church. But they could have ended up at the Catholic parish, which would have meant they would be sorted into a different religious tradition altogether. Like many Americans, they chose their church on the basis of the local congregation they attended—what they heard over the pulpit, the programs it offers, the friendliness of the congregants, and so forth.

CONGREGATIONAL CHOICE

Does the prevalence of congregation shopping mean that most churchgoers are restless consumers, constantly scanning the horizon for new and different options? Or does the fact that most congregations are local mean that most Americans have found a congregation they like and are sticking with it?

American churchgoers are mostly satisfied with their congregations. Finding deep dissatisfaction, in fact, would actually call into question the whole notion of high religious fluidity. If people are so dissatisfied with their congregation, why not leave? Thus, it is not surprising that only 2 percent told our interviewers that they are "not at all satisfied," while another 7 percent indicated only a slight level of satisfaction (see Figure 6.1). However, clergy should not be complacent and assume that they need not worry about losing their flocks. While most churchgoers told us that they are satisfied with their congregation, the intensity of that satisfaction seems to leave open the possibility of considering other options. Fifty-eight percent said they are "very satisfied" with their current congregation, but one third of Americans say they are just "moderately" satisfied. Someone who is moderately satisfied sounds to us like someone who is willing to shop around. As we will see, we do in fact find that people who are not perfectly satisfied with their congregation are the most likely to seek out another one.

Many Americans have shopped around for a new congregation. Roughly half (47 percent) of all Americans indicate that they have

Figure 6.1

WHILE OVER HALF OF CHURCHGOERS ARE VERY SATISFIED WITH THEIR CONGREGATION, A THIRD ARE ONLY MODERATELY SATISFIED

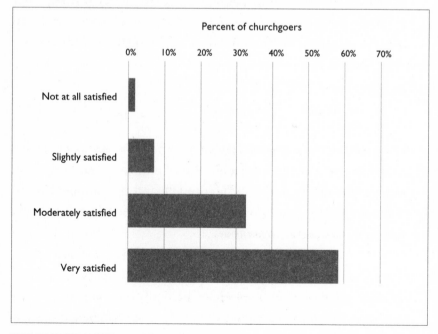

SOURCE: FAITH MATTERS SURVEY, 2006.

searched for a new place of worship at least once, while a third say that they have done so at least a "few times." For about half of these church shoppers, their latest search for a new congregation was triggered by a move, which leaves roughly one quarter of all Americans who have searched for their current congregation for a reason other than a change of location.[12] Americans are inveterate shoppers, and religion is no exception.[13]

As an indication of how church shopping is ingrained within the American religious landscape, we even find congregation shopping among nearly one third of Catholics, when Catholic parishes are generally defined in terms of territory rather than personal choice.[14] While Catholics engage in less congregation shopping than Protestants, there is still a sizable number who do.

As we shall discuss in Chapter 9, the system of territorial boundaries has implications for increasing the ethnic diversity of Catholic parishes, but as also revealed in our case study of parishes in Chicago, many Catholics are as willing to vote with their feet as Protestants when deciding where to worship.

We should note that while many Americans do at some point in their lives shop for a congregation, few switch congregations frequently. Shopping for a congregation is more like buying a house than picking a restaurant—a decision made for the long, or at least medium, term.[15]

When Americans shop for a new congregation, what do they look for? To find out, we asked those Faith Matters respondents who currently have a congregation why they have chosen it. We offered a wide menu of options and did not require people to choose one reason over the others. All could be equally important or unimportant.

As displayed in Figure 6.2, the most common criterion selected as a "very important" reason for selecting one's current congregation is "theology or religious beliefs," which suggests a calibration between what is taught at church and what the individual believes. This presumably provides some consolation to those critics who worry that American religion is all sizzle and no steak, as churchgoers are saying that what is actually taught at their church matters to them. (We

Figure 6.2

WHY DID YOU CHOOSE YOUR CURRENT CONGREGATION?

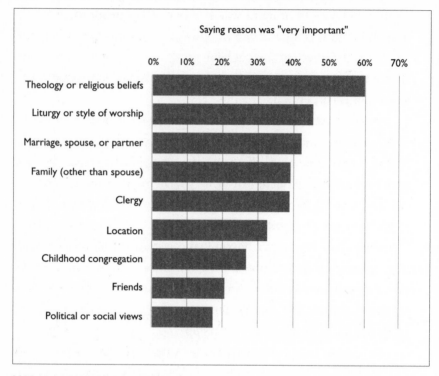

SOURCE: FAITH MATTERS SURVEY, 2006.

concede, however, that this does not address concerns over the *content* of what is taught, which we leave for the theologians.) Likewise, the second most important criterion is the liturgy or style of worship. Interestingly, clergy is further down the list. While a still substantial 39 percent of churchgoers say that their clergy is a very important reason that they attend their current congregation, this percentage is lower than theology (60 percent) or worship style (45 percent).

The next two most important criteria go together, as they refer either to a spouse or to other family members. In both of these cases, roughly equal proportions (40 percent) say that either it is very important or not important at all. A still smaller, but hardly negligible, percentage (27 percent) indicate that "the fact that this was your childhood congregation" is a very important reason for choosing it (or, in this case, choosing to stay within it). This proportion should be kept in mind in light of our discussion of America's religious fluidity. For all the religious switching and congregation shopping that we see, over one quarter of churchgoers say that they are now in the same congregation as during their childhood.

At or near the bottom of the list are factors that do not pertain to religion or family. Location is near the bottom (32 percent say it is very important), while the two least important reasons are one's friends and "political or social views." The fact that friends rank so low suggests that it is more common to *become* friends with members of their congregation than to be pulled into a congregation *because* of one's friends. Finally, the limited importance of politics and social views foreshadows Chapter 12, where we will discuss how most churches in America feature little to no *overt* politicking (which, as we will explain, is different from saying that nothing of political relevance happens at church).

This seems like a leap.

We pause to note what may appear to be a discrepancy between the reasons reported for switching congregations and the bird's-eye view on switching between religious traditions discussed in Chapter 5. There, you will recall, we suggested that views on sexuality and politics have shaped the religious landscape. And yet here we find that political or social views are an infrequent explanation for shifting congregations.

Really, though, there is no inconsistency. First, remember that it is the nones who are most likely to have *left* religion, and thus a congregation, over political matters. Since nones do not have a congregation, they do not show up when we ask churchgoers why they chose their current place of worship. Second, we have also suggested that many Americans gravitated toward evangelical churches because of a perceived decay in morals, exemplified by attitudes toward premarital sex. To choose a church because of its teachings on sexual morality would seem consistent with choosing it because of theology and religious beliefs. Recall that attitudes toward premarital sex best predict who is an evangelical, more than attitudes on more overtly partisan issues (even including abortion).

WHY DO PEOPLE MOVE FROM ONE CONGREGATION TO ANOTHER?

Asking people why they are in their current congregation is one way to understand congregational choice. Asking people to explain why they have done something, however, is fraught with ambiguities. People often have trouble articulating their motivation for anything they do. Last night at dinner, why did I order fish instead of steak? Was it because the fish was cheaper? Because the fish was more healthful? Because I like fish more than steak? Because, as a child, I was socialized to have a positive attitude toward fish? Because my wife ordered the steak, and I prefer not to order the same thing she does? Could it be all, or none, of the above?

Because of the ambiguity in asking about motivations, it is informative to take a different perspective, and simply observe the kind of people who stay in their congregation versus those who move to a new one. Since we conducted a follow-up to our original Faith Matters survey with the same people roughly one year later, we have a unique opportunity to watch congregation shopping as it happens. While most of our respondents did not change congregations within a year, roughly 8 percent did.[16] Although 8 percent may not sound like much, when multiplied over many years it actually reflects a remarkably fluid religious environment.

When we look at congregation shopping across different religious traditions, we find very few differences. Evangelicals are as likely to switch as are mainline Protestants, who in turn are as likely to do so as Catholics, and so on. The one exception is people who indicated that they have no formal religious affiliation but nonetheless attend a particular congregation. Roughly 15 percent of these nonaffiliators-but-attenders—that is, approximately twice as many as the population in general—found a new congregation over the course of a year.[17] It makes sense that this would be the group most likely to find a new congregation, as they were presumably not well invested in their first congregation. At least, they were not invested enough to report a formal affiliation with that congregation.

The importance of what we might call *congregational investment* for keeping people in their current congregation shows up in many different ways. For example, we have looked at who switches congregations, while accounting for a host of individuals' characteristics, including their age, gender, marital status, whether they have kids at home, their race, their education level, how long they have lived in their community, whether they own their own home, and whether they are satisfied with their life or economic situation. So as to focus on those who did not have external factors leading to a choice of new congregation, we limited our analysis to people who did not move to a new community in the intervening year.

Only a few of these many characteristics we tested show up as having any impact on whether one finds a new place to worship. One is marital status, as married people are slightly more likely to have switched congregations. This comports with our earlier observation that one's spouse is a common reason for choosing one's congregation. The only other factor that matters in a statistical sense is owning a home. Owners are less likely to switch congregations than renters. We suspect the reason is that, just as owners are literally more invested in their community, they are also more invested in their congregations.[18]

Not surprisingly, another factor that correlates with finding a new congregation is dissatisfaction with the old one. As we saw above, most Americans are happy with their current congregation. But those who are not are the most likely to find a new one. However, congregational dissatisfaction is not the whole story, as connections within a congregation also matter.[19] Having more friends within a congregation means a lower likelihood of switching to a new one.

Still another factor keeping people in their congregations is inertia. The longer you are in your congregation, the less likely you are to leave it. Time spent in a congregation actually explains the impact of both congregational satisfaction and the number of friends one has within the congregation. By this, we mean that when we account for the number of years within one's congregation, the statistical effects of both satisfaction and number of friends evaporate. This is as expected; we would expect those who like their congregation to stick with it, and to have made many friends within it.

With such a tangle of closely related factors, we are hesitant to conclude that one matters above all. Does having friends in a congregation lead to someone staying within it? Or does staying within it naturally lead to having more friends? Likewise, does congregational satisfaction drive longevity, or the other way around? Whatever the precise causal relationships, it is clear that social connections within a congregation are an important part of the story. There is an interesting contrast between the reasons people give for choosing their current congregation, and what we observe among those who have just chosen a new one. Americans may select their congregations primarily because of theology and worship, but the social investment made within that congregation appears to be what keeps them there.

The contrast between why people select a congregation— theology / worship—versus stick with a congregation—friendships— suggests what religious entrepreneurs must do to create a thriving congregation. On the one hand, they must provide resonant teachings and worship to bring people in the door, but once in the door those people must find ways to connect with one another if they are to keep coming back. We suspect that the importance of congregational community will come as no surprise to clergy or laity. In our many vignettes of congregations, we see the common theme of pastors and lay leaders working to foster social connections among congregants—from the myriad small groups organized by Saddleback and Living Word Christian Center to the efforts at forming neighborhood groups at Trinity Concord to the many classes offered at Beth Emet.

THE FUTURE OF
AMERICAN RELIGION?

Thus far, our discussion of congregation shopping and switching has dealt only with people who start in one congregation and move to another. Intercongregational moves of this sort conjure up an image of dueling pastors squaring off against each other in a competition to win converts. Other churches, however, are hardly the only—or even the primary—source for new members in a given congregation. If we think in terms of competition, churches are just as likely to compete against secular activities as against other congregations. The entertainment industry provides a good example of what we mean. NBC is not only looking to win over viewers from CBS and ABC; it also has to worry about attracting people away from movie theaters, video games, even books. Likewise, while some congregational innovations may be designed to attract people who would otherwise attend another church, others are designed to attract people who would not otherwise attend church at all. In many respects, the jump from none to some religion is an even bigger change than moving from one religion to another.

In Chapter 4, we laid out the evidence for the rising proportion of the American population who have turned away from organized religion, or at least are unwilling to say they have a formal religious affiliation. With this change unfolding, the history of religious innovation in America suggests a logical consequence. We should expect religious entrepreneurs to craft new ways of reaching this untapped pool, and thus fill a niche in the religious ecosystem. This was the motivation for the chapel car, with which we began this chapter. The frontier was populated by a lot of people without religion in their lives, and so the chapel car was invented to bring religion to them.

A similar reaction to an untapped market, you will recall, is what drove the first aftershock to the libertine Sixties. Innovative religious leaders, particularly within the evangelical tradition, found new ways to deliver a moral message that resonated with Americans unsettled by the changing mores of the time. Evangelical entrepreneurs like Rick Warren reinvented the congregational experience, and the megachurch was born.

Today, we have argued, the new nones have been turned off from religion by its political overtones. Is it feasible that these nones might be wooed back to religion? It seems so, since many of them are not actually ardent secularists. A large proportion of those who demur from indicating a formal religious affiliation believe religion is important, pray regularly, and even attend a given congregation on occasion. Sociologists Michael Hout and Claude Fischer refer to them as "unchurched believers."[20] They are the liminals we described in Chapter 5, people who flit back and forth between reporting a religious affiliation or not. Liminals, especially young liminals, should represent an inviting target for religious entrepreneurs. In biblical terms, Jesus told his disciples to be fishers of men, and this is a group where there are plenty of fish to be caught.

What sort of religion might appeal to the new nones? If we are right that a major factor pushing them away from religion is an aversion to what they see as the merger of religion and politics—specifically because of an emphasis on sex and family issues by evangelicals allied with the Republican Party—then they would be pulled toward religion that deemphasizes such politically resonant matters for other priorities.

We see evidence that none other than Rick Warren, a highly successful religious entrepreneur, is aware of the potential for an evangelical gospel stripped of an emphasis on sex and family issues. In 2009 he was invited by the nonpartisan Pew Forum on Religion & Public Life to speak to a group of national journalists about the association many Americans make between evangelicals and politics. In his remarks, he listed his church's signature issues. They are: leadership training for pastors, a Bible-based addiction recovery program, an AIDS initiative, a global effort to provide humanitarian aid in the developing world, an initiative to foster civil public dialogue, care for orphans, and a program to oppose religious persecution. Note that this list does not include any mention of abortion, gay marriage, or any of the sex and family issues that have defined evangelical religion over the last generation. Warren himself is certainly a social conservative, as he publicly opposes both abortion and same-sex marriage, but those are not the issues he puts front and center.[21]

Perhaps the new nones will be wooed back to religion by mainline Protestant congregations, which are generally not associated with the conservative politics of their evangelical counterparts. As an example of such an effort, consider an ad campaign by the United Church of Christ (UCC) of a few years ago. In one television spot, people walking up the steps to a church are met by bouncers manning a rope line, as though they are standing guard outside a nightclub. The bouncers tell two men, holding hands, to "step aside," while admitting a well-heeled heterosexual white couple with two children. Two dark-complexioned people are also turned away, as is a man in a wheelchair. The tag line for the ad, and the whole campaign, is "Jesus didn't turn people away. Neither do we." This ad generated controversy when it was created in 2004, as the NBC and CBS television networks declined to air it.[22]

We don't know whether this campaign produced a surge in membership for the UCC, controversy and all, but such re-branding efforts take time. Over time, the new nones may be won over by an emphasis on inclusiveness. However, given their poor track record in maintaining, let alone growing, their market share, it seems unlikely that mainline Protestant congregations such as the UCC will stanch the flow of young people out of religion. But unlikely does not mean impossible.

Perhaps the new nones will be won over by a new type of religion specifically targeted to them. One potential example is a movement known as the "emerging church." We describe the emerging church at some length, not as an endorsement but simply to provide a contemporary example of the perpetual innovation within American religion. The emerging church is a loose confederation of congregations bent on attracting twenty- and thirty-somethings. In keeping with our theme of congregational diversity, it is appropriate that there is wide variety among congregations that might be described as within the emerging church movement, although even the term "movement" implies more cohesion than is actually the case.

Congregations of emerging churches are often urban, and blend traditional religious symbolism with modern technology. In his book *The Emerging Church*, Dan Kimball describes how the modern church took out stained glass and replaced it with video screens; in the emerging church, stained glass was brought back in *on* video screens. In his words, in the modern church, "crosses and other symbols [were] removed from the meeting place to avoid looking too religious," while in the emerging church, "crosses and other symbols [were] brought back into meeting places to promote a sense of spiritual reverence."[23] At the same time, emerging church services are typically punctuated with loud contemporary music and irreverent banter more akin to a late night talk show than your typical Sunday morning sermon. While not describing the emerging church per se, sociologist Robert Wuthnow perfectly captures the sentiment behind this mishmash of styles when he describes young adults as comfortable "tinkering" with religion and spirituality.[24]

Leaders within the emerging church movement, however, say that it is not the style of worship that distinguishes congregations of the emerging church from your typical megachurch, many of which also have unconventional aspects to their worship. Rather, they describe a difference in the substance of what they teach. Emerging church leaders speak of "missional living," by which they mean an emphasis on what people do rather than the specific doctrines they believe. Indeed, the literature of the emerging church makes frequent allusions to theirs being a postmodern approach to religion.[25] And, as we would expect given our earlier discussion of social connections as an anchor holding people in place, the emerging church places a lot of emphasis on building community within their congregations.

From the perspective of market differentiation, perhaps the most significant aspect of the emerging church is its avoidance of sex and family issues like abortion and homosexuality. In a sense, the emerging church appears to be precisely the sort of religion we would

have predicted to emerge to reach the new nones—evangelically fla-
vored, but without the connections to right-wing politics. The niche
occupied by the emerging church was brought home to us when in
a private conversation a very conservative evangelical megachurch
pastor in Florida specifically cited the emerging church as a threat
to his style of evangelicalism, especially among the young, because
it avoids the politics that has kept many young people out of his
church, and evangelical churches more generally.

Rick Warren recognizes the potential of the emerging church
movement to be the new thing in American religion. In reference to
Dan Kimball, one of the founders of the movement, Warren writes
that Kimball describes "what a purpose-driven church can look like in
a postmodern world. . . . You need to pay attention to him because
the times are changing." [26] Perhaps Warren is right, and a generation
from now we will speak of the emerging church as we now speak of
the megachurch, a form of religious organization that has reshaped
the American landscape.

Or it could be that the emerging church is another religious flash
in the pan. Maybe online worship will be the innovation that woos
the nones back to religion. Or maybe both the emerging church and
Web worship will end up as forgotten innovations, like the chapel
car. If so, the consistent pattern of religious entrepreneurship in
America leaves us confident that more innovations will emerge.
Such changes will be mostly incremental, mostly within local congregations, but always inventive.

CHAPTER 7

Vignettes:
Ethnicity, Gender,
and Religion

The vignettes to follow include a Lutheran congregation in Houston, a predominantly African American congregation in Baltimore, and a group of Catholic parishes in Chicago. Each illustrates the different ways in which ethnicity and religion are intertwined—Our Savior Lutheran celebrates its German heritage, Bethel AME exemplifies how racial and religious identities are mutually reinforcing within the Black Church, and the Chicago-area Catholic parishes illustrate the growing presence of Latinos in the Catholic Church. In the case of Our Savior Lutheran, we also see how the theological conservatism of this congregation extends to a very conservative perspective on gender roles—both inside and outside the church.

THE BURNING OF THE BULL

It's Reformation Sunday at Our Savior Lutheran Church in Houston, Texas, and around 9:00 A.M. a handful of cars begin to turn off Tidwell Road and onto Martin Luther Lane, which winds its way toward the sanctuary. Two large black gates and a white stone gatehouse mark the entrance to the church grounds, lending an air of exclusivity to the forty-two-acre campus, not visible from the road. Set atop a hill overlooking the northwest suburbs of Houston, OSL, as the church is known to its membership, is home to a congregation of 1,500—about 535 of whom will gather for worship this morning. With its meandering walkways, shaded lawns, and duck-filled pond, OSL's grounds have the feel of a retreat center—quiet, protected, and set apart from the low-rent apartment complexes, strip malls, and tract housing of the surrounding neighborhood.

Originally "a mission outreach church," OSL was started in 1944 by Immanuel Lutheran parish in an effort to lay the groundwork for ministry in Houston's burgeoning suburbs. One lifelong congregant remembers that OSL began "literally with twenty families," and the original white wood-frame chapel was built "out in the country on a gravel road leading out of Houston." By 1960, suburban development had caught up with the church, and the resultant congregational growth had moved the parish into a new, modern sanctuary. Having opened a school whose needs eventually outstripped even what this new facility had to offer, in 1992 the congregation voted to purchase a large tract of land some five miles further west, and began construction on a campus envisioned to be tailor-made for the educational, worship, and social life of the church.

Over the course of the subsequent eight years, church leaders conducted extensive research—including several trips to Germany—in order to design and build a sanctuary that would stand as a monument to Lutheranism and its German roots. The sanctuary is a replica of a chapel in Seiffen, Germany, which itself is modeled after the Frauenkirche, a Lutheran cathedral in Dresden. According to Dr. Lawrence White, pastor of OSL since 1980, the new chapel represents "a distinctively Lutheran approach to church architecture." As in its German counterparts, every detail of Our Savior Lutheran's worship space is designed to direct visitors' minds to Christ's teachings—a full explication of the symbolism found throughout the church fills a sixty-seven-page book written by Pastor White upon the building's dedication. "Every church you build embodies some theology," he explains. Of megachurches, he says, "you're providing a stage for your performance." In Catholic churches, "worshippers don't have to be close or involved." And in Lutheranism, says Pastor White, "churches were configured to cluster people around the architectural representations of the means of grace."

Rounding the corner toward the parking lots, a visitor sees the beautiful three-story octagonal sanctuary—its bronze tower and stainless steel steeple gleaming atop a crisp white stone exterior. Multigenerational families pull their minivans up to the covered driveway at the chapel's main door, dropping off aged grandparents and eager children who make their way inside, welcomed at the large iron doors by two elderly white men dressed in matching blue blazers. The greeters acknowledge their fellow parishioners by name, handing them a thirty-six-page, eight-and-a-half-by-eleven order of service, whose cover bears a painted depiction of Martin Luther's "burning of the bull," the papal edict that called for his excommunication from the Catholic Church in 1520. This event marked the birth of Lutheranism. Though Pastor White estimates that the majority of the congregation was raised in other Christian traditions, OSL's denominational identity is incredibly strong. The parish is part of the conservative, biblically literalist Missouri Synod Lutheran Church (LCMS), the eighth largest Protestant denomination in the United States. In constructing their new worship space, the congregation has taken every opportunity to pay homage to Lutheranism's sixteenth-century history and the American denomination's German immigrant roots. Hundreds of photographs, postcards, and paintings of the Seiffen and Frauenkirche chapels line the hallways in OSL's basement, and the narthex contains German mementos of every imaginable variety—from tourist-quality dolls dressed in lederhosen to antique Bibles and handcrafted nutcrackers. Much of the artwork throughout the sanctuary was specially ordered from workshops in Europe—many pieces are exact replicas of statues and reliefs found in German Lutheran churches. An outer wall of the sanctuary bears a famous bronze relief of Martin Luther at the Diet of Worms, but includes Pastor White's unmistakable image cast amid the crowd of robed onlookers, lending this otherwise staid work of art an oddly whimsical air.

The liturgical color of Reformation Day is red, and red suits, hats, ties, and sweaters dot the congregation in the now full sanctuary as the 9:30 service begins. One of the church's five choirs, dressed in green robes, processes in as a live brass quintet plays a prelude of classical selections. The choir takes their places in the lofted stalls, some thirty feet above the floor of the sanctuary, giving them a distant, angelic quality that complements the gilded sword-and-trumpet-bearing cherubim scattered throughout the room. Stained glass windows, lifelike statues of saints, painted banners, and gilded candlesticks create the space's elaborate ornamentation, which is set against the backdrop of a gleaming Neoclassical pipe organ. The sanctuary mirrors the octagonal shape of the building itself, and five sections of pews, each five to eight rows deep, face the center, where an octagonal altar stands beneath an enormous suspended crucifix.

As the processional hymn is sung, Pastor White, dressed in a white robe with an embroidered stole and a gold rope around his waist, looks out over the floor of the sanctuary and up into the two balconies, observing the typically large congregation that has gathered by 9:45. The service is highly structured and fervently celebratory, and all follow along in the program—standing, sitting, and standing again—as the Prayer of Invocation is read, the Canticle is sung, and the various other liturgical elements unfold, setting the stage for Pastor White's sermon. "My fellow redeemed," he begins, standing at a raised octagonal pulpit. Pastor White is fifty-something with receding brown hair that he combs straight back, and wears large bifocal glasses that cover half his bearded face. He has a self-assured manner that borders on smugness, and his deep voice fills the sanctuary authoritatively as he emphatically delivers his sermon. "Through faith in Jesus Christ we already have full and complete salvation," he proclaims. "Like Luther, you and I can come to know a God who sent his only Son to die for each and every one of our transgressions." His congregants gaze forward in reverent assent, as children rustle anxiously in the pews, some scribbling on the back of the printed bulletin. "Though hurricanes howl, banks fail, and the economy slumps, we will not fear, for the God of Jacob is our refuge."

"Traditional Substance"

During Pastor White's almost thirty-year tenure, Our Savior has more than doubled in membership. Though it started out as a neighborhood church, now members are scattered across the northwest quadrant of Houston and beyond. Pastor White says he is "not necessarily focused on growing the church," but rather is "quite deliberate about the theology" at OSL, which, he feels, is what has attracted so many new members. Essentially, the church has become a regional magnet for Lutherans seeking a particularly conservative incarnation of their faith. One congregant goes so far as to call OSL "the most conservative church in the world." One way in which the parish's conservatism manifests itself is in its strict interpretation of the LCMS doctrine of Closed Communion. An explanation of this practice appears in the parish's printed program, the weekly bulletin, and on the pew cards, and is carefully and tactfully explained to any self-identified visitors, who are given a green welcome ribbon to pin on as they enter the sanctuary. "Those who commune together at this altar . . . declare their personal allegiance to the doctrinal position of this Lutheran congregation," the explanation reads. "Therefore, participation in Communion is normally limited to members of this congregation or of sister congregations within the confessional fellowship of the Lutheran Church—Missouri Synod." This reading of Closed Communion is indicative of how seriously the parish takes its beliefs. "If you take Communion in the wrong way," explains Assistant Pastor Thomas Glammeyer, "you are asking God's punishment." Though other Missouri Synod congregations do open the practice to more than just LCMS members (in line with what is arguably the denomination's official stance on the issue),[1] OSL's resistance to this trend epitomizes the church's overall unapologetic, uncompromising commitment to its highly conservative identity. As Pastor White puts it, "We're not called to be popular, we're called to be faithful."

One of the main ways in which OSL seeks to be faithful is by providing a Christian education through the Our Savior Lutheran

School, which was started one year after the church's founding as "a mission outreach to the community" and an alternative to the increasingly secularized public school system. What attracts parents to the school, White says, is "the quality of education, the security, and the spiritual component." Such parochial schools are common at LCMS churches, and White explains that OSL's school is central to parish life: "We built the school first [and] worshipped in the school cafeteria for four years," he says. "The school has always been the core component of this church's ministry." Indeed, many congregants at OSL describe having first come to worship at the church after enrolling their children in the school, and White describes it as "the largest source of newcomers" to OSL. Enrollment hovers around 225 students, from pre-K to eighth grade. Lance Gerard, the school's principal, estimates that all but twenty of the children in the congregation are enrolled, and students are taught the doctrines of Missouri Synod Lutheranism. "Most kids attending the school are Baptist, and they come because it's close to the freeway and to downtown, and it's an excellent education."

"One of the things we're trying to move away from is being a school that just has a religion class," Gerard says, stating that in so doing OSL wouldn't be "much different than a public school." Both the church and the school's leadership felt the teachers "needed to do a better job in integrating the faith across the curriculum," and therefore decided to introduce a "classical education" model. Gerard explains this approach as putting Christianity and history into relationship by asking questions such as, "What does the Apostle Paul have to do with the Caesars of Rome?" With classical education, the school is able to "teach everything from a biblical worldview," and under the new plan history will be taught continuously from second to eighth grade, starting with creation and moving toward the present. The curriculum also focuses on the Ten Commandments, and while not explicitly teaching abstinence, does not include any sex education. "Mostly I think that's the responsibility of the parent," Gerard says. At the end of the eighth grade students are required to complete a Confirmation Class, taught by Pastor White, who teaches "the differences between men and women" and "the role of the man and the role of the woman in the household."

Describing the OSL school, Pastor White says it offers "a curriculum specifically geared to biblical family values" that "comes from the Word" and is an "alternative to the dominant culture." "People have the sense that many of our churches are simply going with the flow, giving people what they want," he explains. Pastor White's approach, he says, is different: "We maintain the traditional substance without going through the same old motions in the same old way. You don't have to give people what they want if you're giving them what they need, presented in a way that is relevant." Pastor White clearly sets the ideological tone for his congregation, a major component of which is the belief that modern secular culture is corrupting individuals, churches, and society. The conservatism of Our Savior Lutheran is a deliberate "counter-cultural" stand. White sees "a window of opportunity that is closing" as he looks at churches' influence in modern society. "If we're going to move, we've got to move quickly."

Lutherans for Life

Perhaps the single largest indicator that American culture is on the wrong track, explains Pastor White, is the national abortion rate—"Fifty million dead in the last thirty-three years," as he describes it—and it is this disturbing trend that he and his congregants feel most passionate about curbing. Pastor White is a nationally known pro-life activist who travels to churches across the country trying to convince fellow Christians to take up the cause. "The discussion in the culture has shifted toward the defining questions of human identity," he says, explaining his belief that "politics has moved into the church, the church hasn't moved into politics."[2]

It's 12:00 on Sunday afternoon as about twenty-five people, mostly retirees, gather in a basement classroom at OSL for a meeting of Houston Lutherans for Life. Though Pastor White is not in attendance, he has sent his second-in-command, Thomas Glammeyer, a slim man with a serious demeanor and a white mustache, who has recently celebrated his fiftieth year as a Lutheran minister. Pastor Glammeyer leads the group in prayer before they partake of a pot-luck lunch including fried chicken and deviled eggs. The Houston chapter of Lutherans for Life (LFL) has been meeting since 1998, and recently merged with another regional group, bringing OSL into the fold. Claiming 108 members, the chapter meets every two months at various participating parishes.

The meeting begins with another prayer and a spiritual message from James Kerry, who urges his fellow activists to "pray daily" and "ponder God's Word as it relates to the life issues." "We are at war with the darkness," he concludes, ceding the floor to Mike Jolley, the chapter's president. "I understand how busy everybody's time is," Mike says, urging his members to stay active. He remarks that "lots of times life issues are very untouchable," and that he is "proud" of what the chapter has "accomplished so far." During the announce-ments portion of the meeting, George Johnson calls the group's attention to a crisis pregnancy center in the area that closed for lack of volunteers. The center's closure is of particular concern because of its proximity to a Planned Parenthood facility. "If we had known, maybe we could have done something," George says, and the group discusses the possibility of fund-raising in order to give monthly financial support to other local crisis pregnancy centers, which coun-sel and support women with unwanted pregnancies, encouraging them to avoid abortion. The group's fund-raising committee reports on efforts to reach out to other congregations, one of which recently donated $5,000 to the chapter; and also announces plans to hold a garage sale and a car wash in the OSL parking lot to raise money.

Brian Williams, representing the chapter's Education Program, then stands to speak. He describes an idea to build a "Web site with a biblical basis" that will be a "one-stop shop for people who want to talk intelligently about life issues," which seem to include every-thing from eugenics to euthanasia to abortion. "Satan is trying to conceal God's Word from God's people," but LFL members' role is to "witness to the sanctity of life," he concludes. The meeting then opens into a discussion about ways to become active on behalf of "life issues." One man recently trained as a volunteer counselor for a crisis pregnancy center, and another is a volunteer driver, picking up supplies for a similar center. A younger woman brings up the Texas Futile Care Law, which mandates that hospitals "cut off all care . . . including food and water" if a patient's case is considered hopeless after ten days of treatment. She suggests that LFL undertake some lobbying around the issue. Finally, an older man shares that recently he "went down to Planned Parenthood" where he was shocked to find that pro-choice people "volunteer their Saturday mornings to make sure that women go in and kill their babies." He suggests the chapter "pray for our enemies." "We could all consider Planned Parenthood our enemy . . . doing the devil's work," he adds gravely.

The gathering concludes with a guest speaker from the Houston Coalition for Life, which is working to block the construction of a Planned Parenthood facility that will be dedicated to performing late-term abortions. They plan to "bombard the city with flyers," getting "media coverage" to "educate the city of Houston about Planned Parenthood." The coalition is also organizing a Forty Days for Life Campaign, in which Lutherans for Life is invited to participate. This will be a round-the-clock "prayer vigil at an abortion facility," she says, encouraging her audience to sign up for a time slot once a week. The idea is to "pray for . . . the conversion of the hearts of the moms." Just yesterday at Planned Parenthood, a girl decided not to have an abortion at the last minute, the speaker concludes. She stopped before going in and said to a pro-life demonstrator, "Can I stand with you? I decided not to kill my baby today." The chapter members are visibly moved by the story, and the meeting concludes with a recitation of the Lord's Prayer.

Women Should Be Silent

Just after worship on Sunday morning, a group of ten women gathers in the small, cozy Family Room in the basement of the church for a weekly women's Bible study—one of six classes offered during the after-service hour. Kathy, a slim middle-aged woman in a

jean jacket and skirt, joins Denise and Elsa on the couches and comfortable chairs that form a close square in the center of the room.
The meeting begins with each woman offering a brief update on her
family members—Kathy speaks of missing her young daughter, who
is visiting her father in another city. Denise shares her worries over
her sister's health problems, and Elsa describes her ongoing struggle in caring for an elderly relative. The conversation is warm and
familiar, each woman listening attentively and offering sympathetic
responses.

The discussion soon turns to the course of study the women
are working on, a book entitled *Love, Joy, Peace* by Lane Burgland.
Therese Schmidt, the group's leader, asks the women to take out
their books and Bibles and to turn to the page where they had left
off the previous week. She also reminds the class of their "first rule:
what happens in this room stays in this room." (Recall that, in fact,
all participants knew that we were present and writing about this
meeting and that we have used pseudonyms in all our vignettes.)
Therese has been teaching the women's Bible study at OSL for three
years. Having received all of her education in Lutheran schools,
toward the end of high school she decided that she wanted to go
to Concordia Teachers College. A representative of the college visited her school, looked at her transcript, and offered her a financial
aid package, which she was "so excited" to tell her family about.
But as soon as she did so, her father forbade her to go. At the time,
this was a bitter disappointment for Therese, but looking back, she
says simply, "It wasn't meant to be." She finally found her chance to
become a teacher when she took Pastor White's Bethel Bible Study.
"The purpose was for students to come out and do some teaching,"
she explains. She says that before the course she "never had the confidence" to lead a class on her own, but says the experience—and
Pastor White's "wonderful" teaching—empowered her to no longer
fear to speak or pray out loud. She now takes pride in creating in her
Bible study a safe space where women "can share things in our small
group that they would not share in Pastor White's class."

Denise reads the first paragraph on page twenty-five of *Love, Joy, Peace*:

> Paul instructs a wife to "fear" her husband (Ephesians 5:33 ASV).
> Some translations offer "respect" (like the NIV, ESV, NKJV,
> NRSV) or "reverence" (KJV). The key to understanding "fear" in
> this passage is the biblical phrase "fear of the LORD." This "fear"
> includes respect and reverence, but its central feature is saving
> faith (as is obvious in 2 Chronicles 19:9; Proverbs 14:27; 19:23;
> Isaiah 11:2–3, 33:6; Acts 10:34–35). Thus Paul advises wives to
> trust their husbands, submitting to their husbands as the church
> submits to the Lord. Paul does not mean that a wife must cower
> in the presence of her husband.

The women begin looking up and reading the biblical references
aloud, and a discussion of the meaning of Paul's teaching about
wives submitting to their husbands ensues, wherein Therese ventures to draw a contrast, rather than a parallel, between a woman's
relationship with her husband, and with the Lord. She boldly offers
her interpretation: "The word referred to in Ephesians is properly
understood as 'respect,' *not* 'fear.' When I think of fear, I think of fear
of *the Lord*. Yet the word describing the relationship between *husbands and wives* is *respect.*" The group discusses what respect between
husbands and wives means. Therese remarks that sometimes the
women's group might go a bit too far in complaining to one another
about their marriages, and that they should strive to live in a way that
is respectful, rather than critical of their husbands. When a woman
has a difficult relationship with her husband, she shouldn't complain
about him to others or put him down. "You fell in love with him in
the first place," says Therese. Another woman agrees, mentioning
that respect also means loyalty.

While not present at the women's Bible study, Pastor White has
many observations on gender roles. "When God created mankind,
at the core of that creation was gender," explains Pastor White. Gender is "a major subject of Genesis 1 and 2," which include passages

that describe "our creation as male and female," and God's decree that "what Adam needs is a helpmate fit for him," he says. "Gender identity, male and female, is of the essence of the human." Gender roles are central to the theology of Our Savior Lutheran, and represent another way in which the congregation sees itself as a bulwark against an increasingly liberal society. "Abortion is in itself the tip of the iceberg," says Pastor White, who feels that "the Judeo-Christian moral consensus that recognizes marriage as a keystone" is in rapid decline, leaving behind "promiscuous lifestyles" and "high divorce rates." One cause of this decline was "the war," which brought many women into the workplace and led to the breakdown of "the traditional view that the family includes one full-time parent, usually the woman." Many women at OSL seem to agree with the pastor's interpretation of gender, and though several have worked at some point, many of those who have had jobs outside the home still see their husbands as, in the words of one such woman, "the sole supporter," and themselves as the primary homemaker. Congregant Jim Carver echoes this view: "To say it doesn't really matter that Adam was created first" is to "forget the order and pattern of creation," adding that "as protector and provider man has all the responsibility."

Encouraging women to embrace their roles as wives and mothers is only one way in which gender enters into life at OSL. The church also prevents women from voting in the congregational assemblies that govern the parish. While some 80 percent of Missouri Synod Lutheran churches have adopted women's suffrage, OSL has stood its ground because, as Pastor White explains, "the Bible says that . . . leadership both within the family and the church" is for men. The exclusion of women from congregational voting is cited by many male members as an integral part of the church's conservative identity; and because in Pastor White's view the basis of this practice is scriptural, he finds no reason to equivocate. "If you have a problem with that, you're probably not going to be attracted to our church," he says. Dale, who has been a member of OSL since 1990, says that he joined after a careful search for a conservative church. He was "already Missouri Synod Lutheran," but says he was "disappointed in how liberal [his] church was" because "they had open Communion and women's suffrage."

Though most women at OSL seem to embrace traditional gender roles, a few find being denied the right to vote hard to swallow. "I know the Bible verses," says Gertrude Kline, a retired grandmother and longtime member of OSL, "but I do believe that we should have something to say about what goes on in the church." Yet many others accept the practice without complaint, and actually see it as a positive feature of church life. "It doesn't bother me at all," says Therese Schmidt, noting that the idea that "women should be silent" comes from the New Testament book of Ephesians. "It bothers a lot of women [but] that's just the way I grew up," she says. Sharon Middleton agrees. "Pastor White will show you exactly biblically that women aren't supposed to vote," she says, and she agrees with that policy. "The man is the head of the house," she goes on. "There may be a lot of people that will disagree but that's one good thing about Pastor White . . . you do according to what the Bible says." Denise Carver also likes the fact that women don't vote at OSL, because she feels it forces the men to take more responsibility at church, and is another way OSL is "remaining close to conservative ideas." "It's never been challenged so I guess everyone feels the same way," she concludes. Yet some who favor the practice still point out that it is wrong to disenfranchise widows and single women, who have no husbands to represent their views. "It's unfair in some ways," admits one woman. "We have so many widows, and they have nothing to say about what goes on," but, she notes, they are nevertheless asked to make financial donations to the church. In terms of making exceptions to the rule and allowing these women to vote, Therese Schmidt says "the time has come."

"We talk about OSL as a conservative church," says Norman Adams, president of the congregation, "and we believe scripture says that in the church women are not supposed to vote. I'll tell you one thing—I've been president of the church for twenty years, and we haven't done anything they didn't want us to do," he jokes, adding, "I don't think we could get the ladies to attend a voters meeting if we asked them to!" Adams says that though it hasn't come up on a congregational level recently, discussion about the possibility of instituting women's suffrage "used to take place every two years." Each time, he says, "we'd go back through it again." "We will discuss it until we're all dead," he concludes, but given Our Savior's belief in the biblical basis of the policy, its gendered voting practices are not likely to change. Adams believes that at other churches, where women have been given the vote, "the teachers just got tired of proving the point."

"An Enjoyable and Decent Life"

At the conclusion of the Reformation Day services, about half of the congregation walks across the campus to the school gymnasium where Lutherfest, an annual party celebrating the church's namesake, is set to begin. Four musicians playing a guitar, a horn, a synthesizer, and an accordion sit atop a small platform on which hangs a banner emblazoned with the group's name—Alpenfest—written in Germanic font. Billed as "the busiest German band in Texas," the group also includes four dancers dressed in lederhosen, dirndl, and knee socks. Seven children join hands and dance in a circle to the oompah-like sounds of the band, while the hungry churchgoers form a line leading into the school cafeteria. Pastor White soon enters the gym in black pants, a black shirt with a clerical collar, and black cowboy boots, and carries a foil-wrapped disposable casserole pan into the kitchen.

Volunteer members of the church Fellowship Board dish up hearty portions of sauerkraut, bratwurst, potato salad, and cooked cabbage. Also on offer are huge plastic bowls of Costco green salad, giant bottles of ranch dressing, and Texas-sized Styrofoam cups filled with iced tea and lemonade. The school cafeteria staff has cooked the Reformation Day feast, which congregants eat while chatting and catching up with one another at the twenty-odd banquet tables that have been set up in the gym—the floor carefully covered over with brown plastic tarps. Each table sports a red plastic tablecloth, a Bible, and a white rose—the symbol of Lutheranism. "It is by grace you have been saved, through faith . . . the gift of God," proclaim the printed banners decorating the tables, which are held in place by bowls of pretzels.

In the back corner of the room stands a table set up for committees advertising upcoming parish events, and two women sell tickets to the November turkey supper fund-raiser—depositing the money they receive into a large Ziploc bag stuffed with cash and checks. On the other side of the gym, a man dressed in a brown monk's costume and Birkenstock sandals stands at a table to the left of the stage, just under the huge American and Lutheran flags hanging on the wall adjacent to the electronic scoreboard. Posing as Martin Luther himself, he leads kids and parents in a blindfolded game of Pin the Theses on the Door. If they don't find success there, they can try to win one of twelve or so donated cakes in the Strudel Walk, or attempt to throw chocolate coins through a cardboard cutout of a pudgy priest in the Tetzel Toss, named for an infamous sixteenth-century seller of indulgences. When Pastor White describes OSL as "a deliberately Lutheran church," it's hard to imagine any place on earth more deserving of that description.

Though OSL cultivates its strong sense of separateness, Pastor White predicts that the future will bring a lamentable increase in "the distinction between the church and the culture in which it lives" because of America's continual abandonment of tradition and conservative values. "The plight of American society cannot be blamed on the ACLU or the feminists or the abortionists," White taught his congregation in a 2006 sermon. Instead, the moral corrosion he sees as rampant in American society is the fault of Christians who have "failed to take a strong enough stand against the dominant culture." Pastor White describes the modern era as the "eleventh hour" for America, and believes the nation may soon experience the judgment of God if Christians fail to influence its current cultural trajectory. In the 1940s there were "less material things, and church played a much more important part in people's lives," Pastor White laments. Amidst all our abundance, "is anybody happier?" he asks. "I know this sounds like nostalgia," he admits, adding that he doubts America will ever return to the state it was in culturally, socially, and religiously two generations ago. While "you can't withdraw from the culture in which you live," Pastor White says with a turn of optimism, "there is a way to live an enjoyable and decent life." And for members of Our Savior Lutheran, that life means abundant Bible study, turkey supper fund-raisers, and—at least once a year—a good old-fashioned Tetzel Toss.

THE CALL TO WORSHIP

Leaving Baltimore's city center and heading about one mile north on Paca Street visitors enter Druid Heights, one of the poorest neighborhoods in the greater Baltimore area. As one crosses over Martin Luther King Boulevard, the splendor of downtown's fancy office buildings, restaurants, and Inner Harbor quickly gives way to what is clearly an urban ghetto, where the median household income is one half the national average, and nearly 90 percent of residents are black.

At 7:45 A.M. on a chilly fall day, Bethel African Methodist Episcopal Church—Druid Heights's most prominent place of worship—is slowly filling with congregants as the praise music for the 8:00 service begins to swell. Bethel AME occupies an imposing, Gothic-style white stone building with a towering steeple that stands out amid the surrounding boarded-up brownstones, low-rise public housing, and crumbling, mostly vacant row houses. The neighborhood's only other visible institutions are schools, community outreach centers, and small storefront churches—at least one on every block. There are few signs of legal economic activity aside from a corner convenience store, a Wendy's fast food restaurant, and a hot dog vendor who occasionally parks his truck outside Bethel after services. Nearby, worn wood-and-concrete benches at a city bus stop bear faded lettering proclaiming Baltimore "The Greatest City in America."

As Baltimore's first independent black institution, and one of the first all-black churches in the United States, Bethel AME has been inextricably tied to African Americans' struggle for freedom and equality for over two hundred years. As early as 1785, free blacks in Baltimore began to leave Methodist meeting houses because of racially discriminatory practices, and what began as a prayer group of disaffected black Christians gathering in private homes grew into the Bethel Free African Society, whose earliest official meetings date back to 1787. Since then, leading abolitionists, pan-Africanists, and anti-lynching crusaders including Frederick Douglass, Marcus Garvey, and Ida B. Wells have spoken from Bethel's pulpit. The church was an important station on the Underground Railroad as well as a rallying point during the civil rights movement, when national figures including Rosa Parks and Thurgood Marshall came to speak to Bethel's faithful.

In its public documents, Bethel today claims a membership of fifteen thousand, which seems optimistic for a church that comfortably seats 1,500 and draws around three thousand across three worship services each Sunday. Although the actual size of its membership is difficult to determine, Bethel is successful at attracting new congregants. According to the pastor, someone has joined the church or given his or her life to Christ almost every single Sunday since 1975.

So early on a Sunday morning the neighborhood has a hushed, abandoned feel to it, which contrasts sharply with the joyful noise that spills fitfully out of Bethel as its doors open and close for entering worshippers. A group of middle-aged black men in overcoats and fedoras motion for drivers to roll down their windows and identify themselves as they turn onto Lanvale Avenue, one of the church's side streets. Comparing names to printed lists, they gingerly direct traffic. Regular congregants park around the back side of the church in an unpaved lot, while expected VIPs are directed to spaces marked off by orange and white cones, amid cars bearing "State Assemblyman" license plates, and the pastor's signature BMW. On weekdays, the streets adjacent to the church are usually empty of cars, but on Sunday mornings they swell like a river about to flood—filled with Mercedes, minivans, and luxury SUVs—as Baltimore's black middle class drives in from other city neighborhoods and "County" suburbs.

Entering through the side door of the church, and passing through a small foyer with a glassed-in reception desk, Bethel's more prominent members mingle and network in the Brooks Chapel before the service begins. The chapel is a multifunction room lined with plastic banquet tables where the women of the Bishop Brooks Sunshine Circle take orders for Holiday Gift Baskets, where the Outreach and Evangelism Ministry offer wallet-sized American Bible Society tracts entitled "The Lord Protects Me" and "God Loves the Unborn," and where guest preachers sell autographed copies of their books after services. Built in 1868, Bethel's building has a solid yet well-worn feel that reflects both the church's rich history and the impoverished state of the community just outside its doors.

Around 8:00, those still lingering in the chapel begin to make their way through two tiny passageways on either side of the sanctuary. Ducking through a small doorway as they enter, churchgoers are met by a rousing musical rendition of the Lord's Prayer. A middle-aged woman in a red suit adorned with a plastic button proclaiming "Jesus Loves Me!" offers a twenty-page service bulletin with a glossy purple and gold cover, and greets her fellow church members with a shouted "Welcome!" as she sways and claps to the music. The boisterous gospel-style singing and praising is overwhelming, and by 8:15 the floor of the sanctuary is nearly full, with more congregants coming down the main aisle from the front doors and taking whatever seats remain in the straight-backed wooden pews. The choir is in full song and the band plays along loudly as people clap and shout in answer to "The Call to Worship."

Bethel's sanctuary is a traditionally long rectangular hall with four forward-facing sections of pews on the floor, and a gallery-style balcony above. Small television monitors hang from the underside of the balcony, allowing congregants to get a better view of the speakers and occasionally themselves as a cameraman makes his way through the crowd, capturing up-close the jubilant scene of worship and praise that is intensifying throughout the sanctuary. All eyes are on the dais—a raised, three-tiered platform where the twenty-five-person choir provides a swaying backdrop for the imposing white pulpit, its accompanying golden cross, and a row of high-backed chairs occupied by the church's leadership.

Sun streams in through stained glass windows, casting a warm glow on the golden angels keeping watch over the dais and the sanctuary. Beneath them hang two flags—one the pan-African red, green, and black; the other bearing Bethel's signature purple and white insignia. In place of a crucifix, the wall behind the altar bears a painted multicolor tribute to what one congregant calls "the upward progress of black people throughout the world." Encircled by a row of white, marquis-style lights, green, blue, and red images of native Africans, slaves, sharecroppers, minstrels, lynching victims, ballot casters, and marching hippies entwine upward toward a liberated black man and woman at the pinnacle, embraced by a shining Christ figure and a radiating yellow cross.

The church's officers—eleven trustees and thirty-eight stewards—steadily take their places in the first three rows of the sanctuary. A virtual who's who of Baltimore's black elite, Bethel's officers are a handpicked group that includes politicians, magazine publishers, doctors, lawyers, professors, and multimillionaire businesspeople. Behind the officers sits the Altar Guild—a group of grandmotherly women in matching red outfits—next to whom stands one half-empty pew, roped off as "Reserved" seating for former mayor Kurt Schmoke, current mayor Sheila Dixon, city comptroller Joan Pratt, and other community power brokers who call Bethel their home church. At some point during the service's opening, Bethel's pastor, the Reverend Dr. Frank Madison Reid III, slips in through a door on the dais, and takes his place in a thronelike chair behind the pulpit.

"Teach Me!"

Pastor Reid, dressed in a fine black pinstriped suit, takes to the podium and welcomes his congregation: "It's good to *be* in the house of *God!*" he proclaims. Reid is a light-skinned black man whose graying hair and mustache are smartly and meticulously groomed. He has large round eyes and a narrow smile. He takes time to acknowledge those watching on television or on Streaming Faith, an online broadcast of the service, and calls out to any visitors, asking them to stand. Pastor Reid then launches into a call for prayer requests and offerings, a two-segment sermon, responsive scriptural readings, and Communion, all of which essentially constitute one long pastoral performance, which builds steadily in intensity over the service's remaining hour and culminates in the Call to the Altar, wherein Reid invites new converts to come forward and give their life to Christ. Pastor Reid is a gifted preacher whose ability to alternately command like a prophet and entreat like a parent plays off the emotion and Christian devotion of his flock with near-perfect pitch. Once he takes to the pulpit, the service ignites with passionate enthusiasm— each congregant gratefully drinking in the practical gospel message without missing a beat of the pastor's rhythmic rhetoric.

"Open your church notebook and write this down," Reid exhorts his congregation, as he begins the "Millionaire Moment, Billionaire Blessing," the first of four calls for tithes and offerings woven into the service. "Black people have been taught that the purpose of money is to spend. The purpose of money is to *reap* so that you can *sow*, and to *sow* is to *invest*," he explains. "Stop using those check-cashing services and payday loans," Reid goes on, and encourages everyone present to open a bank account, citing a *Wall Street Journal* article indicating that some 55 percent of adult blacks don't have one. "Spending," the pastor preaches, should go something like this: "Pay God, pay myself, and live off the rest. Ten percent to God, 10 percent to savings, and live off the rest," he states, gradually elevating his tone. "Tithing derides consumer Christianity, with its focus on what God can do for *you*," Reid proclaims. "God kept me from being broken and busted!" he shouts, working up a sweat. "Look at your neighbor and say, 'God *fed* me!'" Latoya Washington, a twenty-seven-year-old single woman in the second row, joins the murmurings of the congregation as she turns to a middle-aged woman at her left, makes eye contact, and says enthusiastically, "God fed me!" "It may not have been *filet mignon*, but you sure enough *ate* this week!" Reid says to a chorus of laughter, shouted agreement, and applause.

The intensity of the service grows as gold plates appear and are passed around, and nearly everyone offers either cash or envelopes. White-gloved ushers dump the plates into cloth-lined baskets and raise the offering up onto the altar, and the choir sways as the organ-accompanied song grows louder. Worshippers are standing, eyes closed, raising hands and Bibles. "We are praising His name because Jesus made this all possible!" "That's right!" shouts a woman in a sea foam green frock with a matching hat and white gloves. A man in the pews stands waving his right hand, and clasping a Bible in his left—his head is lowered and his body trembling as the drums and organ hit full volume, sending pulsating waves of sound throughout the sanctuary.

"Who says what we can't do?" Two elderly ladies in the third row nod expressively as Reid picks up steam: "When you do it in the name of *God* all things are possible, Hallelujah!" he says, growling out his appeal to the divine. "It's time to tell our God, *thank you* for taking me from nowhere to somewhere! *THANK YOU* for graduating me from college when I was the first in my family!" Half the congregation now stands and cheers like fans at a sporting event, and several men step out into the aisles to sway and swing their arms toward heaven. "Who's your master?" Reid bellows. "*Teach* me!" Latoya Washington shouts back, now on her feet.

"We were brought here as slaves, our men were castrated, our women were raped, but we're *still* here," he sings out, punctuating his phrases in time with the organ, which has chimed in to accentuate the cadence of his speech. "The *Word* becomes triumphant!" Reid hollers, taking off his jacket to reveal gray and black suspenders, and wiping the sweat from his brow. The overhead screens now show close-ups of people crying, jumping, and swaying in the pews. "I've seen losers become winners," Reid shouts, wagging his finger vigorously. "I came to Bethel and preached for twenty years and I've seen mayors elected, comptrollers who weren't *supposed* to get to office. Is there anybody here who can *testify?*" he roars out. Many from the congregation are now shouting at their preacher, approaching the pulpit and seeming to close in on him. "When Martin came around they *laughed* at him, but somewhere he heard a preacher say . . .

SOMEWHERE HE HEARD A *PREACHER* SAY . . ." Reid, moaning and shaking his head, begins to raise his arms to heaven as the organ picks up tempo. The congregation is dancing in the pews shouting, "Say it! Say it, Pastor!" to which Reid responds by collapsing on the podium, sighing deeply, and saying softly, as a father would speak to his child, "You must be saved in the blood of Jesus Christ. And you must become a member of a *revolutionary* church."

The congregation bows their heads in agreement, and breathes a collective sigh as the organ music dies down to a soothing sound. The church officers begin to position themselves to administer Communion, and the congregation joins the choir in singing, "Let us break bread together on . . . our . . . knees," accompanying the pastor's prayer over the wafers and wine. While the congregants approach the dais to receive Communion, Pastor Reid stands at the podium looking out on his flock with his chin rested on his hand. He drinks from a crystal water goblet and stares out expressively over his small, wire-framed glasses, lips pursed, eyebrows raised, and arms folded.

Chief Spiritual Officer

It is hard to exaggerate the critical role played by the pastor in black churches in America, and Bethel is no exception. Charisma and personality, combined with a rousing ability to preach and elicit cathartic spiritual responses are highly valued by black churchgoers.[3] W. E. B. Du Bois wrote that a black pastor's success depends not only upon his spiritual gifts, but on his stewardship over the church as a whole, of which his congregation is merely one part. Of critical importance, Du Bois wrote, is "his financial success, his efforts to increase church membership, and his personal popularity. The result is that the colored Methodist minister is generally a wide-awake businessman, with something of the politician in his makeup, who is sometimes an inspiring and valuable leader of men."[4] Though writing nearly a century before his time, Du Bois may as well have been describing the Reverend Dr. Frank Madison Reid III.

Dr. Reid, as he is often called, is Bethel's fifty-third pastor, and has been the church's appointed leader since 1988. As chief spiritual officer, a title he has apparently bestowed upon himself, he acts much like a steward of a large corporation, which includes the Bethel Christian School, a K–5 academy subsidized by church income; an urban outreach center offering a food pantry, clothing distribution, and emergency assistance; and a fluctuating number of thirty to forty ministries including Bible studies, choirs, youth programs, and social events. Yet for all the church's component parts, Dr. Reid himself is clearly the main attraction at Bethel. Church members, employees, and volunteers, as well as teachers at Bethel School, and even guests of Bethel's soup kitchen, unanimously and repeatedly praise Reid as "educated," "well read," "dynamic," "inspiring," "visionary," and "legit." Reid is a fifth-generation AME minister who holds degrees from Yale, Harvard, and United Theological Seminary, is the author of several books and pamphlets, and has traveled all over the world preaching and teaching. He takes care to cultivate his persona of an enlightened Christian man, and many attending Bethel cite this as their main reason for being attracted to the church. Timothy Walters joined Bethel mainly because he thought Reid was "a man's man" and that he could "grow as a man, father, and husband through his teaching." Tim also likes the fact that Dr. Reid "gets much respect in the 'hood." Artistic depictions of the beloved minister and articles and interviews outlining his achievements adorn the walls of the offices and hallways on the floors above the sanctuary. In every way Bethel is clearly *his* church.

Given the incredible assembly of talent represented by Bethel's officers, its trustees and stewards have surprisingly little involvement in both setting the agenda of the church and leading it. The Executive Board, which is scheduled to meet on the first Saturday of every month, rarely convenes. Both lay leaders and his fellow clergy agree that on almost every level Bethel's agenda is set personally by Dr. Reid, and to him it "comes straight from above." Reid is keenly aware of nearly everything of consequence that happens at Bethel, and the sense that the pastor's approval is required for even small decisions is palpable. "I'm not the one to make that call," "that's not what Pastor said," and "let me check with Lady Marlaa'" are phrases frequently on the lips of Bethel members, and Reid relies on a small inner circle—including his wife, his executive assistant, and a handful of trustees, ministers, and elders—to run a tight ship.

Lady Marlaa', Pastor Reid's wife, is known as the first lady of Bethel, and while she has no official role in the church hierarchy, she has crafted a powerful position for herself alongside her husband. Frequently praised by female members for her professional style and dynamic speaking ability, Lady Marlaa' influences many aspects of life at the church. It is well known at Bethel that many matters of church business must unofficially pass through her before receiving final approval from the pastor. The first lady frequently speaks from the floor of the church, though not the pulpit, and is often called upon to offer prayers and introductions of her husband or invited guests. Marlaa' Reid is also a nationally known motivational speaker, and plans and executes her own events, but usually does so alongside, rather than within, official church structures. Most Bethel material on the first family highlights Dr. Reid's accomplishments, but calls Marlaa' simply a "woman of God." Though clearly a leader in her own right, Bethel's first lady stands dutifully behind her husband, handing him water and taking his jacket during sermons.

In his sermons Pastor Reid often stresses obedience to the word of God, to God Himself, and to the word of the pastor. A good Christian, Reid says, "is one who knows how to fall in line behind the pastor." In his view, the church works best when everyone obeys the appropriate authority and "people aren't fighting over who's in charge." Bethel's churchgoers, leaders, and administrators seem to agree. There is a constant insistence on "following protocol" at the church, and members are always careful to do *only* their job and nothing more or less. One full section of Bethel's new member class is devoted to the importance of obedience, and cites multiple biblical passages on the subject. Yet the pastor is not just a figure to be obeyed, he is also a familiar voice and a beloved shepherd. References to Dr. Reid frequently find their way into Bethelites' casual conversation: "You know what Pastor says . . ." can often be heard as they walk the halls of the church or congregate after services, and many members can be found finishing Reid's sentences during his sermons when he calls out a familiar phrase.

Jake's Men

"All the men present, please stand," Dr. Reid says as he takes to the pulpit during a Sunday worship service. Some seventy men rise to their feet, amid claps and cheers from the congregation. "Now look at all these males. It's good to see you in the house of God," Reid says. "And all of God's leading ladies?" The sanctuary erupts as grandmothers, mothers, and single women—the vast majority of attendees—stand to be recognized. On a given Sunday at Bethel, the congregation will be composed of at least 80 percent women, and the majority of the church's ministry heads are female. For Reid, the lack of men in the pews is a problem because the church's social goals cannot be accomplished if "half the society is not present." To Pastor Reid's mind, church and religion are solutions—they change individuals' lives and help communities overcome challenges. If black men are not taking part in these solutions, then the problems plaguing black communities cannot be effectively addressed.

Jake Colbert, founder of the church's Freedom Now Ministry, is one Bethel member whose testimony is often called upon by Dr. Reid in his weekly sermons to show that God is real and that Christ can change anyone for the better. Reid often holds Jake up as a model Christian man, and his testimonial is one of the pastor's most powerful tools for attracting men to the Bethel family, and demonstrating God's power in broken-down lives.

Speaking with the patience and eloquence of someone who has told his story many times before, Brother Jake is glad to share his experience of God's saving grace. In his early sixties, he dresses plainly and speaks softly and with a slight Southern accent. Raised mostly in Baltimore in a churchgoing family, Jake says he graduated from high school but soon started "running with the wrong crowd." "I don't try to give the devil a commercial—it was my fault, it was my decisions," he explains, accounting for his start as a small-time dealer who over the years became one of the biggest drug distributors in Baltimore. Jake eventually started using his product, and after ten or fifteen years found himself addicted and willing to do almost anything to feed his habit. "I did lots of things I am not proud of," he explains, "and the devil had his grip on me and it was by the grace of God that I got out."

For a period of five to six years, Jake was in and out of jail, and while incarcerated was "a very productive member of jail society," he says, working as a cook, a counselor—whatever job he could get. But each time he was released back onto the streets, he couldn't transfer those good habits into the real world. He would quickly backslide into drugs and start stealing to pay for his habit. Eventually, he says, he "got locked up, but really got rescued."

During his final stint in jail at age forty-six, Jake saw Dr. Reid's television broadcast and, he remembers, "there was something about that man that attracted me to him." When facing a parole judge Jake finally decided to ask for help. The judge sent him to a treatment program and it was there that he met a friend who brought him to Bethel. In his early days at the church, Jake always sat in the balcony—always in the back, and it was at a Monday night Men's Bible Study that he finally decided to give his life to Christ. He visited other congregations too, but says he "didn't have that feeling at the other churches," so he decided to stick with Bethel.

Soon Pastor Reid took a personal interest in Jake and encouraged him to join a ministry. According to Jake, "Pastor had a vision" and told him, "One day you're going to be a leader of this church." After joining the Men's Choir and eventually heading it up, Jake was appointed to the Trustee Board and soon, with Reid's help, he started his own ministry. The Freedom Now and Overcomers' Ministries are both headed by Jake—one focuses on outreach and the other on recovery. Men from the program are invited to Bethel each Sunday, and the first three or four rows of seats are reserved for them at the 11:45 service.

Many of the individuals who participate in Freedom Now and Overcomers are recently released from prison and live in halfway houses, and Jake's Men (as they are called by Bethel members) all attend substance abuse counseling through the program he started. The outreach portion of the ministry is more loosely organized, consisting of "three or four brothers" who occasionally decide, at Reid's prompting, to go out into the community at night and try to minister to people buying and selling drugs. In actual numbers, Jake's outreach ministry has only five or six members who don't meet regularly, but who know each other well and can readily be activated when the need arises. Many of the ministries' participants look to Jake as an example: "He was once a junkie and now owns a home," one says. For these men, the power of Jake's testimony drew them to Bethel and Reid's extra attention keeps them coming back. Ask anyone at a worship service about the men in the front rows, and they will all say the same thing: "Those are Jake's Men."

"For Folk Out in the County"

Though addressing the social dislocation of urban blacks by way of the gospel is high on Dr. Reid's agenda, men like Jake Colbert, who come out of the neighborhood to attend church at Bethel, are a rarity. Over half of Bethel's membership drives to church from suburbs outside the city, and the church's historian estimates that of those who are city residents, most do not live in the tough neighborhoods surrounding Bethel. The contrast between its inner-city location and its middle-class, commuter congregants is striking at Bethel, and is a concern for Reid, who has suggested ideas such as "dress down Sunday" as possible strategies for "attracting the poor" to church.

Though neighborhood residents are not filling the pews, they are, however, lining up at the Bethel outreach center, where the church acts as a service provider for its impoverished community. The original Free African Societies from which Bethel was born were explicit in their blending of religion and social services. Drawing on its history of political activity, social striving, racial solidarity, and liberation theology, the modern AME Church is organized under the motto "God Our Father, Christ Our Redeemer, Man Our Brother," and takes as its mandate service to the needy as well as the saving of souls. Bethel AME's long history of meeting needs began with its ministry to newly emancipated slaves, and the church opened its first formal community center in the 1970s. Its William Smith Outreach Center, through which it currently feeds an estimated fourteen thousand people annually, was constructed in 1990 at a cost to the church of $1.2 million.

Despite the AME tradition's explicit, even doctrinal, focus on helping the needy, Bethel's congregation is surprisingly uninvolved in the projects on which their tithes and offerings are spent. At the outreach center, seeing a Bethel member serving as a volunteer is the exception not the rule. Most of the church's members limit their involvement with the neighborhood to financial support, and seem unfamiliar with the specifics of the church's outreach activities. "Where is the outreach center again . . . is it downtown still?" one congregant asks another as they walk upstairs after Sunday services. "No, I think it's still across the street," her friend replies. In fact, the center is located three blocks from the church.

Even the Bethel Christian School, which is subsidized by member donations, has only one member child enrolled. To Janice Clemens, one of the only members of the school staff who also attends Bethel, the lack of congregational involvement with the school is frustrating—Bethel's members "have so much to offer" the students, she says. Another teacher agrees, and adds that she finds members' lack of involvement to be in keeping with the generally "snotty" and "elitist" attitudes of congregants. One volunteer at the outreach center, herself a resident of Druid Heights, echoes this sentiment. She prefers to worship at one of the neighborhood's storefront churches rather than at Bethel, which she sees as being "for folk out in the County." And in a move to follow its membership, Bethel has recently purchased 257 acres of land in the suburbs to begin construction on a new worship space, with plans to convert the historic sanctuary into a multipurpose space for use by the outreach center. But whether the church will be able to sustain an even further divided ministry remains to be seen.

Though not a place where interclass mingling happens regularly,

Bethel nonetheless serves as an important agent of wealth redistribution in the black community. Many members make a point of paying exactly 10 percent of their income to the church, and contribute additional funds when called upon by Reid. Wealthy church members even use voluntary giving as a form of praise during worship services. On occasions when Pastor Reid's preaching hits a particularly high point, congregants throw crumpled twenty-dollar bills at his feet, and sometimes a member will be so moved as to walk down the aisle and slap a bill on the podium from which the gospel is being proclaimed. The various forms of giving at Bethel serve as a gathering-in from the middle class, allowing Dr. Reid and his outreach ventures to meet needs in the surrounding resource-poor community.

"Seen but Not Heard"

It is from the ranks of the clergy that many black political and intellectual leaders have been born and raised, and Pastor Reid is no exception. To say that Frank Reid is politically connected would be a dramatic understatement. A former candidate for Congress, he holds influence with many national, state, and local Democrats, and even some Republicans. Politics and the political world underlie nearly everything said and done at Bethel, and Bethel, through Dr. Reid, plays an active role in Baltimore's political world. Reid has claimed publicly that Bethel "touches the lives" of some 100,000 Baltimoreans, and city officials take notice of his apparent ability to galvanize his flock behind any chosen candidate or issue. While politicians tend to show up at worship around election time, Reid's goal is "to stay connected all year long," hosting prayer breakfasts for local leaders and holding networking lunches at an exclusive Baltimore club where businessmen and politicians often meet, and where it isn't uncommon to see a City Council member approach Reid to "pay his respects."

When discussing how politics finds its way into the church, Bethel members often use the expression "seen but not heard." Politicians enjoy the ability to stand and be recognized by the pastor during worship at Bethel, but are never allowed to speak on behalf of their cause. Endorsing candidates is left to Reid, who does what church attorney Leronia Josey calls "a dance," whereby "he never comes out and says what he means, but he makes it clear what he wants you to do." Reid will often recognize politicians in his sermon, and use their public actions to make a point, thereby expressing either approval or disapproval. But he has also been known to use less subtle tactics such as endorsing candidates at press conferences on the steps outside the church. Leronia Josey admits that her "hair is gray" because Pastor Reid is "always dancing on the line" of legality.

As far as his political agenda, Dr. Reid seems most concerned with channeling resources to the black community—in addition to taking an active role in electoral politics, Bethel lobbies state and local government, often successfully, to obtain funds for various programs at its outreach center. It is in these efforts that the ties between the church and the political world appear most entangled, as became evident in 2006 with Bethel's involvement in a controversial partnership with a private development corporation. A municipal board approved a bid by the white-owned Cordish Company to manage and redevelop Pier Six, an outdoor concert pavilion in the heart of Baltimore's Inner Harbor. Many among the city's black elite opposed the deal, arguing that minority companies should be given precedence in harbor projects. Dr. Reid, however, supported the Cordish contract, having negotiated a deal with the developer in which Cordish would donate 10 percent of its yearly Pier Six profits to Bethel, which would have no obligation to contribute to the management of the project. David Cordish, the company's head, touted the tithe as part of his religious and civic duty to reinvest in the city and its impoverished residents, and Reid saw the deal as seed money for his plan to buy and renovate residential properties in Druid Heights.

However, shortly after news of the deal broke, questions were raised about its appropriateness, given that two members of the municipal board that approved the deal—Joan Pratt and Sheila Dixon—are active Bethel members whose successful candidacy owed largely to Reid's endorsement and the volunteer mobilization of fellow church members. Though Pratt and Dixon abstained from the vote that approved the contract, further questions surfaced about the influence of Maryland's governor Martin O'Malley—a candidate Reid both endorsed and supported with thousands of dollars in campaign donations—in the approval of the deal.

Reid was incensed by these accusations of wrongdoing, and devoted much of one February 2006 sermon to refuting them. "We ought to go down there to Pier Six and show them!" he shouted to his congregation from the pulpit, his fury ultimately giving rise to a high-profile Easter Sunday event at Pier Six that same year. Reid used his ability to gather thousands of churchgoers and local VIPs to the event both to demonstrate the church's clout and to underscore the development deal's intent of redistributing profits to the inner-city black community of Baltimore. Dr. Reid performed three "miracles" during the service by giving a brand-new minivan to one member who had been in a terrible car accident, and paying off the consumer debt of two other poor but loyal church members. Reid said of the miracles that he wanted to "show that the church is willing to sow a seed just as people sow into the church," and then himself "sowed" $3,000 by writing a personal check to Bethel.

"It's Not Just About Waiting on Jesus"

Dr. Reid sums up his churchgoers' reasons for choosing Bethel as their home church in his signature alliterative style. "There are four I's of attendance," he says: "Ignorance, Inspiration, Information, and Influence." Those who attend out of "ignorance," Reid explains, are the "unreflective," who go out of habit and family tradition. Others go "to get inspired" and "fill themselves with the Word." Some others, Reid believes, attend Bethel for "information": to learn about God, Jesus, and the Bible, and to learn what's happening in their church, their community, and their nation. It is for these people that the church tries to raise awareness about issues facing the black community by, for example, offering money management training from the pulpit in the midst of a call for offerings.

Finally, Reid says, many attend church—and Bethel particularly—

because they have a sense of "influence" as a member. Whether through giving, doing, or voting, they feel they are part of an efficacious body and enjoy the sense of active citizenship and active Christianity that that affords. Shondra Dennis, a longtime congregant, agrees. "Dr. Reid's holistic ministry" is what attracted her to the church. "At Bethel," she explains, "it's not just about waiting on Jesus. Yes, we wait, but in the meantime there is a focus on acting too."

EL PADRE

It's 10:00 A.M. on a hot day in July, as Beatriz, a middle-aged Mexican woman, rounds the corner to the parish offices at St. Pius V Catholic Church in Pilsen, a heavily Latino neighborhood on Chicago's Lower West Side. St. Pius, known to its Spanish-speaking parishioners as "San Pio" occupies the corner of 19th Street and Ashland Avenue, and is a central feature of this Little Mexico, where street vendors sell *paletas* and pork rinds, and painted signs advertise *lavanderías* and *tarjetas telefónicas*. Pilsen's main public park—a wide field of scorched grass with a Latin Cultural Center on one side— is often filled with young men playing soccer, and on warm summer nights women and children sit on their front stoops laughing and gossiping as the El lumbers by overhead. Though rumor has it that this section of the city is on the cusp of gentrification, Pilsen is still largely a neighborhood of empty lots and boarded-up buildings, where gangs roam after midnight, and groups of men congregate on street corners to drink and carouse.

On the corner of Ashland and West Cullerton Street sit the St. Pius parish offices and parochial school, in a building that used to be a convent. The school serves children pre-K through grade eight, and is heavily subsidized by the archdiocese, without whose funding it would not survive. The multipurpose building—one of seven owned by the parish—is also used for catechism on Sundays, as well as other church activities including a reflection group for kids in gangs.

Beatriz tries to get into the three-story brick building without success, and decides to walk down the block to the large green-turreted brick chapel, where she finds a lone maintenance worker on his knees cleaning the floor. The worn but spit-shined sanctuary is silent this weekday morning and the life-size statues of La Virgen de Guadalupe and St. Jude, aglow in shadowy candlelight, gaze benevolently out of their gaudy, flower-bedecked encasements.

Back at the locked office doors, Beatriz explains that she has been having serious *problemas* in recent weeks, and had come to speak with *el padre* the previous day. He had promised to find her a counselor if she came to the office. "He gave me a lot of good advice. Sometimes you just feel so alone here in this place," she says in Spanish, as her eyes well up with tears. "You just have no one," she adds, explaining that her husband had recently gone off seeking work in another state, leaving her to face the difficulties of immigrant life alone. She had driven all the way from a northern suburb to seek help at St. Pius.

Finally buzzed in, Beatriz makes her way up a dark stairway to the second floor offices, where Elena Martínez, the parish receptionist, sits in a small room behind a plexiglass window with a bank teller–like hole through which to speak to visitors. The waiting room is crowded with five green vinyl chairs, a tall old drinking fountain, and a pile of shabby toys atop a Little Tykes play table. Beatriz joins the five other adults and two children who are waiting. The walls are haphazardly decorated with various flyers and posters—all in Spanish—including one advertising a street fair that took place back in May. Others proffer "The Rights of a Child," "Economic Help for Victims of Crime," and "Domestic Violence Is Everyone's Issue." The room is virtually indistinguishable from any other agency or government office in an inner-city neighborhood, and a framed "Faith Leadership Award" certificate from the mayor is the only visible hint of the office's higher purpose.

In the adjacent office, Elena buzzes in a stream of visitors and attends to the steady phone calls. *"Muy buenos días, San Pío,"* she says, in a chipper voice. Elena speaks English fairly well, but none of the callers require it. She sits behind a metal desk that holds a large printer and computer, both of which face the opposite direction and are turned off. She makes casual conversation with two elderly volunteers who have come in to rest by the window air-conditioning unit, which seems to be making no progress against the heat, despite its noisy clamor. Elena's office overlooks another block of buildings owned by St. Pius, the outward walls of which are painted with huge colorful murals that the parish has commissioned. One mural reads, *"Dejen que los niños se acerquen a mí,"* "Suffer the little children to come unto me," and portrays six smiling children running and jumping. Another features Latino faces depicted as graduates, teachers, and sports players. Still another shows the parish's pastor and figurehead, Fr. Charles Dahm, wearing white ceremonial vestments and a brightly colored Mexican stole as he holds up a Latina child in the act of ceremonial presentation.

Fr. Dahm—or Padre Carlos, as he is known by parishioners—is a graying white man whose more than twenty years pastoring St. Pius make him eligible for retirement, though his doing so anytime soon seems unlikely. Dahm has been at the parish so long that his personality and charismatic leadership have come to define it. In explaining his role at St. Pius and in Pilsen, he describes himself as "something of a gatekeeper" who brokers resources, solves problems, and builds coalitions on behalf of his parishioners. Pausing for a moment's reflection, Dahm removes his large bifocal glasses and rubs his eyes exhaustedly. On his right wrist he wears a woven bracelet made of purple and pink yarn. His navy blue Dockers and navy socks, powder blue Guayabera shirt and black leather comfort shoes make him look more like a vacationing grandfather than an inner-city parish priest. In addition to finding jobs, homes, and other assistance for his communicants, much of Fr. Dahm's time is spent as an advocate for recent immigrants who turn to him in times of crisis. Many of the people who show up at St. Pius's offices have never attended Mass at the parish, but come because of their familiarity with the Catholic Church and their knowledge that they will encounter Spanish speakers there—they know they will be received with compassion, and they know that *el padre* will be able to help.

A seemingly endless parade of families continues to come in and out of the parish offices requesting aid. Some wish to enroll in *pláticas* to prepare for their child's baptism, others want to find out where and when they can get assistance through the food pantry. One woman is waiting impatiently for an appointment she has with a counselor, who has had to attend to another client's emergency. Most of the people, like Beatriz, have come to see *Padre*, who is meeting with a family in the next room. The moment he emerges they all clamor for his attention, and he stops to talk with a young man who is waiting with his wife. The man is trying to enroll in some sort of school, but does not have *papeles*, or proper citizenship documentation, and wants Padre Carlos's help. "How am I supposed to help you?" Dahm responds in Spanish, and with impatience. "What do you think I can do for you?" The young man gets a little uncomfortable and says that he doesn't know exactly, at which point Fr. Dahm softens up a bit and tells him that the parish can write some sort of letter, but that is all he can offer. The cowed young man gratefully promises to leave his contact information, as Dahm tries to head out the door and to his office on the third floor. Three other people call timidly after him as he leaves.

Though he coordinates the parish's seventeen weekly Masses, offers Holy Communion, and performs his duties as a confessor, Fr. Dahm rarely refers to his role as a spiritual leader, or to the role prayer and worship play in his parishioners' development. He calls himself a "social activist," and sees Mass as an opportunity to educate his parishioners and empower them politically—often inviting guest speakers to address topics such as AIDS, military recruitment of minorities, and immigration laws in place of traditional scriptural homilies. Dahm also says he makes "a special effort to incorporate songs about struggle," into the parish's liturgy—with hymns such as "Give Us a Heart Willing to Fight" making regular appearances on the order of worship. Doing this creates a sense of peoplehood and collective action, Dahm says: "This is all social stuff—so they're singing as a people and not singing as individuals." While he admits that this activist tone in worship "has alienated some people," he shrugs off controversy, stating that "those who like Pius will come, and those who don't go somewhere else. That's just the way it is."

When it comes to addressing the pathologies that plague his parishioners, Father Dahm's faith lies mostly in the power of psychotherapy, and the parish spends a huge portion of its operating budget on professional counseling services and youth intervention programs, which are in short supply in Pilsen. As to whether he does much spiritual counseling, Dahm says that he is "not trained" as a counselor, and so functions as a first contact for needy parishioners because of his visibility as a priest, but he merely tries to identify areas of need and then refer parishioners to his staff of clinicians. "These days I see people going back to strict communication with God to solve their problems," Dahm says, but he has come to feel that this is not enough to bring meaningful and lasting change to the severely problematic families and relationships he encounters daily at St. Pius. "I use God with people all the time. I appeal to their faith because faith is a resource for people's growth—it's not something to be ignored. In academia social workers will be discouraged from relying on faith—they're taught to ignore it or circumvent it. But in this community religion is so important and so much a part of people's lives that you can't ignore it."

Between meetings and trips in and out of the waiting room, Fr. Dahm makes a few phone calls on behalf of Silvia, a parishioner whose husband is being held in a suburban jail after having been arrested for allegedly possessing a shotgun. Given only two minutes of phone time, Silvia's husband called and told her where he was being held, but when she had gone to the police station, the officers refused to give her any information. Afraid and not knowing where to turn, she called Padre Carlos. "I'm going to call the police station today," Fr. Dahm says. "Usually when they hear someone like me on the phone they'll respond. A lot of my day is about stuff like that," he concludes with a sigh.

A Cultural Component

St. Pius parish maintains a list of approximately 4,500 registered member families, but according to Fr. Dahm neither the list nor the numbers it reflects are very valuable, simply because there is so much turnover in the neighborhood. There are also cultural challenges to getting immigrants to identify with any parish home, and to register as members. Dahm says that in his experience Mexican Catholics "don't have the concept of being a parishioner, or a member of a particular church." Their thought process is " 'I'm baptized as a Catholic and I go to Mass wherever I want.' They don't have the sense that they have to sign up." The parish has tried to update its membership rolls in the past and has also undertaken registration drives, but those efforts haven't been successful because "when you push it, they get suspicious," Dahm explains, referring to the fact that his immigrant parishioners—many of whom are working in the United States illegally—fear to give too much personal information to an organization that, in their home countries at least, has ties to the government.

Despite the fluidity in parish membership among immigrants, a sense of Catholic identity is uncompromisingly strong. St. Pius's congregants describe their faith as familial and cultural—something inextricable from their identity. "It's who I am," says one parishioner. "Catholicism is our inheritance," explains another. "It's my roots," says Elena Martínez, and St. Pius's ability to connect spiritually and experientially to those roots is a key to its popularity. "Do you style things in order to reach people? Of course," Fr. Dahm explains. "Here the music and preaching always refer to Latin culture and things that are familiar. You can't just translate the Mass from one language to another—you have to add a cultural component. You have to include references to traditions, symbols, beliefs, places, and food that are familiar. . . . People see that here, and they don't see it in other churches." Another parishioner describes St. Pius as "a common point in the Hispanic community," and a place where the culture immigrant Mexicans have had to leave behind is nurtured and preserved: "This parish is Mexican, and it reminds you of your Spanish-speaking country."

The River of Life

On Monday night at 6:30 a group of young Latinas make their way into a building across the street from the parish offices, and up the stairs to a long green-and-gray-tiled room drenched in fluorescent light. Tonight is the first meeting of a four-session *Quinceañera* preparation class, to help these young girls get ready for their "coming out" Mass, a cultural and religious rite of passage celebrating their fifteenth year of life.

The plastic chairs lining the perimeter of the musty, airless room eventually fill as twenty-two girls and their two facilitators, one of whom is Elena Martínez, the parish receptionist, wander in. All dressed to impress, many of the girls wear tight jeans and flip-flops with painted toenails, some sporting gold jewelry and carefully coiffed hair, and others in designer basketball shoes and oversized T-shirts. Most of them sit cross-legged with arched eyebrows and a look of detached skepticism, others slump in their chairs, proudly demonstrating their annoyance at being forced by meddling parents to attend a church activity.

As Elena begins her introductions, a harried mother in a work uniform rushes in late with her daughter, who looks at the floor in embarrassment. Elena thanks the mother, and invites her to come back at 8:00. The session is strictly for the youths, and parents are not allowed. Other rules include things like "no cell phones," "no gum," and strict confidentiality. Elena explains that the classes require a $50 deposit, redeemable only if the girls come to all sessions—each Monday night for a month.

In the middle of the room sits a short, makeshift table covered with a lace tablecloth, a pink candle, an open Bible, and a stack of photocopied prayers. Overseeing the display is a small statue of a young girl with a "15" decorating her flowing dress. The class opens with a prayer read aloud as the group stands and holds hands uncomfortably. Elena instructs them to cross themselves as they pray. The girls have come from far and wide for the class—most of them don't attend the same school, and only a couple of them seem to know each other.

The activity Elena has planned for the class is something she calls "Río de la Vida," the River of Life. On an easel at the front of the room she draws a line with a marker and explains that it represents her life. She then adds waves, clouds, and sometimes confused, blackened areas that represent tragedies she has experienced. At the end she draws a sun and flowers. In a disarmingly matter-of-fact tone, she tells her life story of domestic violence, abuse, attempted rape by family members and teachers, and the resultant crushing self-loathing that haunted her until she sought help through St. Pius's counseling programs.

As she concludes her story, she invites the girls to draw their own rivers. She passes out colored markers and paper, and each girl marks her paper gingerly, glancing around the room self-consciously. Then begins the sharing time, and though they are slow to launch in, once each young girl finds her voice, their life stories tumble out amid the tears and silent sympathies of their peers: families torn apart by infidelity and divorce, apartment buildings that have burned to the ground, mothers and fathers with cancer and other life-threatening illnesses, drug use, gang violence, pregnancy, sexual abuse, domestic violence. Two hours come and go, and the self-protective defiance many of the girls had brought with them transforms into extraordinary honesty—heartache and fear laid bare.

As the confessional wends its way around the circle and begins to conclude, the girls anxiously wipe away their tears, and take up their obstinance once again as thoughts of their parents waiting outside the door begin to encroach upon the fragile intimacy of the classroom. Elena thanks the girls for their openness, and assures them that the class's purpose is to help them work through these problems—to help them overcome their anger and grief. She goes over the curriculum for the coming weeks, which includes topics such as self-esteem, anger management, and communication.

The focus of the *Quinceañera* class is like that of St. Pius

in order to?

generally—meeting the social and emotional needs of its people, and encouraging and empowering them to use the resources of the church to navigate the rapids in their rivers of life. The girls listen intently as Elena stands before them and testifies that she has overcome, and that they can too. "For whatever you're facing," she says, *"en San Pio hay la ayuda."* "There's help at St. Pius."

A Sense of Community

St. Pius's—and Fr. Dahm's—devotion to the Latino community and to immigrant Catholics has enlarged the parish's popularity beyond the bounds of the Pilsen neighborhood, and over the years it has become something of a regional church. Former parishioners who have moved up economically and fanned out into the suburbs very often still commute to attend the colorful, loud, and lively Spanish Mass in the old neighborhood. In a waiting room outside the *Quinceañera* class, three women chat as they wait for their daughters and offer volunteer child care for other parishioners attending a parenting class downstairs. One of the women, Marnita, has attended St. Pius for fifteen years, and had lived in Pilsen at first, but has now moved to a suburb near O'Hare Airport. "I miss the neighborhood," she says in Spanish, "but we wanted a house with a big yard for our kids to play in." She explains that life is different in the suburbs, and though she relishes the comforts and the "respect" she has gained as a homeowner, she misses the community in Pilsen, and tries to stay connected through St. Pius. Marnita's drive to Mass and to weekday activities takes anywhere from forty-five to ninety minutes. In the suburbs "there are priests who try to speak Spanish, but it just isn't the same," she says, explaining that the long commute takes her past many other parishes that offer worship in Spanish. Marnita says that she "doesn't feel comfortable" in churches other than St. Pius. "This is the first church that they found that welcomed them when they came [from Mexico]," Fr. Dahm explains, "and here there is a sense of community in the celebration"—of the Mass, of Latin culture, and of the upward march of a downtrodden people.

MIGRANT WORSHIPPERS

A mere fifteen minutes west on Chicago's Eisenhower Expressway, Pilsen and the West Side quickly give way to a swath of inner suburbs filled with small one- and two-story brick houses. The town of Cicero, made up of narrow tree-lined streets and aging strip malls, is a mostly working-class neighborhood with a large rail yard dominating its south side. With their concrete front stoops and tiny, chain-link-fenced yards, Cicero's houses were once home to families from Czechoslovakia, Italy, and Ireland—most of whom have now moved further from the city, making room for the vast number of Latinos who have migrated in since the 1980s, and now make up nearly 80 percent of the town's population.

St. Frances of Rome is one of seven Catholic parishes in Cicero's six square miles, and counts 972 families as members, though only a third that many attend. Fr. Mark Bartosic, the current pastor of St. Frances of Rome, has headed up the struggling congregation for seven years. He describes the heritage of the parish as a fairly glorious one: "When you look at the people who came out of this parish, it's clear that it was a really important place," he says. One former pastor went on to become an archbishop, and another became the rector of the Pontifical North American College. "Some of the real old-timers remember [St. Frances] in the 1960s and 1970s, and they will often say, 'now *that* was a great parish,'" Fr. Mark notes. Unfortunately, however, this distinguished history contrasts rather sharply with the St. Frances of today, which struggles to fill its Masses and fund its school, has no parish council, and runs only a very few lay programs. Leadership problems, congregational aging, and declining participation in the denomination as a whole have taken their toll on this once thriving religious community. Yet the greatest challenge St. Frances now faces is the rapidly growing number of Latino Catholics in Cicero who need a church home, and who are slowly displacing the former English-speaking parishioners.

Fr. Mark, who speaks fluent Spanish and is doing his best to lose his *gringo* accent, says two English Masses and two Spanish Masses every Sunday, as well as a bilingual Mass every weekday morning, in which he alternates saying different portions of the liturgy in each language. "We're trying to really push now the fact that everybody who lives within the parish boundaries has a home here," he says. In total, the Spanish Masses draw about eight hundred weekly attendees, and the English masses a mere 250—which, according to longtime parishioners, actually represents a recent uptick. The worship offerings have seemed to meet the needs of most parishioners, but Fr. Mark still entertains grievances fairly often. "It's very challenging because when parishes face the kind of demographic change we've seen they have two options," he explains. "One is to try to be all things to all people, and the other is to say, 'now I'm here just for the—fill-in-the-blank.'" Fr. Mark's approach has been to try to "hold on to the few white parishioners" he still has, while creating a welcoming, comfortable church home for the burgeoning Latino population that represents the parish's future.

Though Spanish Masses draw three times as many communicants as English services, participation in worship is only part of what St. Frances needs in order to stay viable. Much more difficult than filling the pews is getting Latinos involved as lay leaders. "The white, English speakers are the real leaders and have the real leadership skills," Fr. Mark says. Yet whites represent a shrinking percentage of the congregation, and so "finding people in the parish who are organized and have leadership skills" is one of St. Frances's biggest challenges. In Fr. Mark's experience, "Latino people very often struggle with their self-esteem, so they very often think, 'I can't do this.'" Also a problem is the fact that "often they're working very, very hard to make their living so they haven't got a lot of spare time."

In addition to the challenge of finding Latinos to lead activities, Father Mark also deals with the difficulty of loosening the Anglo grip on organizational and leadership responsibilities. "Our big events [are] all run by Anglos. Our finance council is all Anglos. The church cleaners—that's driven really by Anglos; even though it's not high-powered leadership by any means, it's still organizing. A lot of it is because they've been doing it for so long. When people become elderly they like to hold on to things, and it's hard to train new people," Fr. Mark explains. Not only that, but the older white leaders often tend to be less progressive than their pastor would hope. They're usually unenthusiastic about heading up activities that involve bridging the two communities. "Efforts at resurrecting the past when the parish was all white—that's what really gets them going," Fr. Mark admits. As a result, outside of Mass and the parish school, St. Frances has very few communal activities to offer its congregation. On weekdays the church grounds are virtually empty, and the parish offices are quiet with the exception of the occasional family trickling in to register a child for a catechism class. In a given week, St. Frances parishioners might participate in a meeting of the St. Vincent de Paul Society, attend a marriage preparation class, or rehearse with the contemporary music group—none of which draws more than a handful of members. The closest thing to a regular community gathering is the weekly bingo game, where elderly neighbors assemble every Friday night in the school auditorium, silently dabbing rows of cards in hopes of taking home the $500 grand prize.

A Meeting of the Masses

The church plant itself serves as a striking metaphor for St. Frances's embattled state, its main feature a vast, crumbling, and usually empty parking lot where the former sanctuary building—torn down in the late 1990s—used to stand. On one side of the parking lot stands the modest rectory, which houses the parish offices, and on the other sits a dilapidated Assembly Building, used by nonprofit groups for English classes and AA meetings. In the parish's heyday, an adjacent three-story 1960s-era building housed the parish middle school, and the chapel in the basement was then used for student Masses. Now the only worship space left at St. Frances, the small school chapel seems the parish's last refuge against extinction. The chapel's main door is on a quiet side street, but the entrance near the parking lot is the one most used on Sunday mornings since it provides access to the elevator—a necessity for the parish's many elderly congregants. More nimble parishioners make their way down an open staircase into a small foyer whose glass doors and windows admit the only sunlight that finds its way into the basement-level sanctuary. Two life-sized statues of Mary and Joseph stand in the linoleum-tiled entranceway, each with a kneeling rail and a few candles and flowers scattered at their feet. Between the statues, an easel displays a computer graphic of a red thermometer illustrating the parish's progress in its recent capital campaign. With the money collected, Fr. Mark has been able to make modest repairs like replacing mismatched glass paneling on the main building, and moving a large statue of St. Frances to the sidewalk outside the church entrance— an effort to address the fact that most passersby get no indication that the building houses a chapel.

The sanctuary's low ceilings and carpeted floor give it a nontraditional feel, and though it is tidy and well maintained, its folk-art decor seems to date the space considerably. The wall behind the altar is a backlit multicolored glass mosaic upon which hangs a large crucifix, and a row of small white lights illuminates the altar below. A wood-carved sculpture of the Holy Family stands to the right, gazing over the baptismal font. The dimly lit room contains two sections of long blond-wood pews, perhaps twenty rows in all, and around the walls hang framed, painted ceramic-tile renderings of the Stations of the Cross.

Preparing for the 10:30 Sunday morning Mass, Carlotta, the parish cantor, arranges sheet music on a small stand to the left of the altar, on the square platform usually used by a band or choir. Carlotta is an elderly Italian American who has lived in the parish for fifty years, and who was married in the old church before it was torn down. As she begins to sing a prelude number her feeble, high-pitched voice warbles loudly over the sound system into the half-full room. The music is slow, subdued, and uninspiring, but somehow seems appropriate for the over-sixty crowd that has gathered for the English Mass.

Fr. Mark takes to the podium and welcomes the hundred or so congregants in the pews, and then proceeds with the liturgy at a measured, methodical pace. The homily is offered by a Scalabrini missionary, invited by Father Mark to share his experiences ministering to immigrants in border towns. "There are not borders or nationalities in the church" he begins in broken English, "we are all brothers and sisters." Speaking of Jesus, the priest goes on: "He is an immigrant, and He will tell us one day, 'What did you do for me when I was an immigrant?' Our mission is to help the migrant people who are looking for a better life for themselves and their family. They should not be viewed as a stranger—because they are Jesus. Rejecting migrant people is to reject Jesus." The congregation applauds, and the lector indicates that the second collection will be designated for the Scalabrini mission. "Please be generous," he adds. Four older white men dressed in polyester suits collect the offerings in wire baskets attached to long metal poles, which soon fill with five- and ten-dollar bills.

As Fr. Mark prepares to celebrate Communion, he asks the congregation to stand and recite the Apostles' Creed as a declaration of their faith. "Let's see how we all feel about this Christian thing," he jokes. Fr. Mark is a quiet man, who tries to engage his parishioners with the occasional witticism, which, however, usually gets stifled by the humorless manner in which he speaks. He has an air of seriousness about him, and there appears to be a sort of endless sigh of frustration emanating from his body. Nevertheless, he is beloved by his parishioners, who describe him as unassuming, loving, and fully engaged in the life of the parish—apparently a welcome contrast to the pastors St. Frances has had in the recent past.

"I believe in the Holy Spirit, the Holy Catholic Church, the communion of saints, the forgiveness of sins, the resurrection of the body, and the life everlasting . . ." The congregation recites the Creed, and the Eucharist is administered by a small group, including the parish's two priests and one deacon. As the English Mass winds to a close, Fr. Mark reminds the congregation of the parish's weekly effort to knock on doors in different areas of the neighborhood to encourage fellow Catholics to attend Mass. He goes on to give a testimony about how he feels this will help the St. Frances community, and reminds the congregants to please attend the street Mass they will be hosting during the coming week.

After the recessional hymn, many parishioners stay and chat with one another for a few minutes, before slowly making their way back outside. Anglos and Latinos pass each other on the staircase as one Mass ends and another begins. The two groups of parishioners barely acknowledge one another as they brush shoulders at the entrances of the chapel.

As the Spanish Mass starts, a band complete with trumpets, guitars, and an accordion player assembles on the platform and lively Latin music fills the room. A framed portrait of the Virgen de Guadalupe is brought ceremoniously down the main aisle and placed in front of the altar. At noon the sanctuary is only half full, but by the middle of the service, it is filled to capacity. Two ushers stand at the doors, offering to seat latecomers—a task that gets more difficult as the Mass proceeds. Mothers stand in the outer aisles and rock their fussing infants, and fathers offer stern looks in response to their children's antics. The Spanish service includes almost double the number of musical interludes as the English Mass, and a small band and small choir sing upbeat, Latin-style hymns, to which most of the congregation sings along. Even though the ceiling fans are now going at full speed, the basement room becomes oppressive with all the activity.

The invited speaker gives his homily, this time a bit more confidently in his native tongue. The content of the sermon is nearly identical, but he speaks now directly to the "strangers" he was championing in the previous Mass. "We must make the community to which we come feel that we are not strangers," he urges in Spanish. "Within the church *we* must create a consciousness of the fact that the stranger is Jesus himself." The only difference in his message as he speaks to his target audience is that his tone of exhortation has turned to one of empowerment. "The presence of the Hispanic Catholic is a blessing," he says. "We enrich the church. To be Hispanic is not to be a second-class citizen. There are more than a million Hispanics in Chicago and there are not enough Masses in

Spanish," he says, telling stories of having ministered to Hispanic American Catholics who "have gone twenty years without confessing," because they could not find a Spanish-speaking priest. His words have the tenor of a visionary leading his people in a struggle for justice, although few in the pews seem visibly moved by his message. As he finishes his remarks, his audience applauds, and again the collection baskets are passed—this time by two men dressed in T-shirts and jeans, and two more in slacks and short-sleeved shirts. Parents place crumpled dollar bills in their toddlers' hands, urging them to toss them in the baskets.

As the Mass ends, the congregants file out, eager to get a breath of fresh air. On the sidewalk a young Mexican man rings a bell and sells *paletas* from a large pushcart cooler. Children beg their parents for the treat, and several families—fathers dressed in cowboy hats and boots—stand around the entrance to the church, as the sounds of Spanish fill the hot summer air.

White Flight

"I heard someone say once, or read somewhere, that people who have been part of an organization for a long, long time would rather see the whole place go down the toilet than have to give up their parking place—and there's certainly been some of that going on here," says Fr. Mark, in reference to the fact that while embracing Latino communicants has been a necessity for this foundering parish, it hasn't come without a cost. To say that offering Mass in both languages and hiring a bilingual staff meet the needs of the whole parish is to mask the reality that only the most loyal (or most sedentary) of the English-speaking parishioners have actually stuck around since Spanish has been fully introduced. Father Mark is well aware of the departure of white parishioners that has occurred at St. Frances over the years. As to why most whites have gone, he says, "a lot of people simply subscribe to the American Dream of getting a bigger house on a bigger lot in a subdivision further away from the city. So in that sense, they want to move just because that's what people do. And the added incentive of all these Mexicans around is there as well."

Indeed, not all of the flight the parish has experienced has been from physical migration. According to Fr. Mark, plenty of whites who still live in the parish boundaries no longer wish to attend St. Frances now that a substantial place has been carved out for Spanish speakers. "A lot of people actually go to Ascension, and to St. Odilo," he explains, referring to two neighboring parishes whose priests have declined to offer Spanish Masses, despite obvious—and growing—demand. "Those parishes would be the places to which people go because of the fact that we serve Hispanics here. There are other places to which they go just because something happened [at St. Frances] that they don't like. But it seems to me that the lion's share of people choose to go to a place where they don't have to deal with the Hispanics."

Susan Hess is a former member of St. Frances of Rome who hasn't attended for a couple of years, but who decided to come to a bilingual street Mass the parish was offering on her block. Standing in her front yard looking over the small crowd gathering for the event, Susan recalled how she left the parish, and why. "I *lived* at St. Frances," she says, explaining that she had served on the school board, the parish council, and many other committees in years past, and had sent two of her three children to the parish school. But once the Spanish Masses began, she started to back away. "Father Mark is great but I'm one of those people who feel like if you come to this country, you should learn English," she explains. "I don't care if you're Polish, Italian, French—it doesn't matter what language. It's not just that it's Spanish. I mean if I traveled to those countries, I would expect to have to speak *their* language." And what about attending the English Masses? "Yeah, the English ones are nice," Susan admits, "but not when they do the Mexican [Masses]." "Like just now," she goes on, referring to the bilingual street Mass. "I don't understand half of what they're saying." As more and more parish activities were being offered in Spanish, Susan felt pushed out, and resented the fact that the priest would "cater" to the Hispanics. At first unwilling to admit that she attends another parish, she eventually admits having gone to Mass at neighboring Ascension for some time. "We're not really supposed to do this," she says sheepishly. "We're *supposed* to belong to St. Frances, but we go to Ascension anyway."

Susan's neighbor Lisa, a younger white woman, shares Susan's feelings. The main reason Lisa stopped attending St. Frances, she says, was that she needed to put her kids in catechism classes on Saturdays, but Saturday classes were offered only in Spanish. "I'm a single mom," she explains, "and it's hard—I can't be taking my kids at 2:30 in the afternoon on a weekday." She says that the fact the class wasn't offered in English at a convenient time was "the last straw." Now she and her children also attend Ascension, where they "feel more at home." "We just feel like we fit in there—like we're welcomed," she says. Susan nods along, and adds, "If we're going to have a mixed congregation, then *everything* should be offered in both languages—it should be fair. If they offer catechism in Spanish on Saturday, they should also offer it in English—as well as on Wednesdays."

Despite her strong feelings about the direction St. Frances has taken, at Fr. Mark's urging Susan volunteered to bring a plate of cookies to the street Mass taking place on her block, which was being coordinated by her Latino neighbor Andrés. "When I got a little involved here with the outdoor Mass, I sort of started to miss it," she comments, looking wistfully across her lawn toward the card tables filled with soda cans, plastic cups, and bags of potato chips. "Well, I guess we should go socialize a little bit," she says, and walks over to the drink table to congratulate Andrés on a job well done. They exchange pleasantries in English and joke together for a few minutes before Susan returns to join the six or seven Anglos grouped in the middle of the street, conspicuously apart from their Latino neighbors.

Brothers and Sisters in Christ

Among those who have chosen to forge a middle ground at St. Frances rather than (for the Anglos) flee to all-white Ascension, or (for the Latinos) return to the old neighborhood and San Pio, a general feeling of mutual respect seems to prevail. Despite the losses St. Frances has sustained since introducing Spanish Masses, Fr. Mark feels that "the people who are left want to see integration happen and they're willing to put up with some of the inconveniences that might cause them," and this attitude seems to be reflected by the white parishioners who remain. Elise Carbonara, who has attended the parish for forty years, argues that ethnicity simply "doesn't make a difference." "It's still the Catholic Church," she says. "God is the same no matter where you go," agrees another elderly white parishioner, who describes himself as "very contented" at St. Frances of Rome. Though mainly based on an idea of mutual toleration rather than any form of integration, several of the white parish leaders at St. Frances have a positive take on the incoming Latinos. And the attitude among the Latino community seems to be equally positive—most feel that they are on the whole very well received at the parish. María, the religious education coordinator, feels that St. Frances "is [her] family," and notes that "the community has become more united with the passage of time." She says she "sees a good spirit of service to the parish, creating community, and forming a united church." Miguel Cárdenas, a younger Mexican who leads a charismatic worship group called *Jóvenes Católicos en Acción*, Young Catholics in Action, thinks of St. Frances "as if it were [his] own home." "We all get along very well," he adds, but as to integrating parish activities, he admits that it's "a little difficult." Benjamin, another Mexican congregant, notes that "the Americans sometimes feel more in the minority than the majority" at the parish. This fact "doesn't bother" him, however. "I'd like to see more unity, but sometimes it's impossible."

Indeed, despite mutual good feelings, the fact remains that no matter how welcoming they might like to be, St. Frances's white parishioners often simply cannot communicate meaningfully with their non-English-speaking counterparts. On the other hand, many of the Latinos who attend the parish have been in the United States for some time and do know English, but Fr. Mark says that they are often "diffident" about speaking it, strongly preferring their native tongue. Jim McKinney is an eighty-six-year-old Irishman and retired professor of sociology who speaks Spanish fluently, having learned it many years ago. McKinney has lived in Oak Park and within the St. Frances boundaries for twenty-five years. He is perhaps the only elderly white parishioner who speaks Spanish, and as such has tried to build some bridges between what he admits are two separate communities. McKinney says he has "tried to get some Spanish-speaking friends to join the council," referring to the biweekly Knights of Columbus meetings at the parish, but he hasn't had success. The parish has also tried to integrate the Holy Name Society: "We offered to hold meetings bilingually," says McKinney, "but no one comes."

Despite the most optimistic of integrated visions, the barriers to bridging are persistent. "I want the people who live within our parish boundaries to think of this as home, and of their neighbors as their brother or sister in Christ," Fr. Mark says, explaining his vision for the parish. "It's very slow, but I think little by little it's happening."

CHAPTER 8

The Women's Revolution, the Rise of Inequality, and Religion

T he remarkable evolution in the role and character of religion in America that we have described in the preceding chapters is not the only important social transformation of this country over the last half century. At least three other broad changes have had similarly far-reaching consequences:

1. The role of women in both private and public life has undergone revolutionary changes, as millions of women moved into the paid labor force and toward more equal social and economic status with men. With an eye toward earlier women's movements, this historical transition is sometimes termed "second wave feminism."

2. The social class gaps within American society have widened at an almost unprecedented rate, as the distribution of income (which had become more equal during the first two thirds of the twentieth century) suddenly shifted toward greater inequality, creating discrepancies between rich and poor seldom seen in American history, at the same time that class segregation in residential and even marital patterns increased.

3. Ethnic diversity has grown steadily and substantially, as the effects of the civil rights revolution reverberated throughout society, and

as a massive wave of immigration from Asia and Latin America increased the number and prominence of nonwhites.

All three of these dimensions of society—gender, class, ethnicity— are intimately connected with religion, not only in this country, but throughout world history. In this chapter and the next we examine how these three massive social transformations have interacted with religion in contemporary America. These social transformations coincided with the seismic shocks that reverberated through American religious life. As Americans have become more polarized in religious terms, how has that transformation interacted with evolving gender, class, and racial relations? To what extent has religion resisted each of these changes, reinforced them, redirected them, or simply adapted to them?

Historically, American religion has remained vital mostly by adjusting to large-scale social change. "American religious leaders were not brakesmen on change in the American past," says religious historian Laurence Moore. "Religion stayed lively and relevant to national life by reflecting popular taste."[1] On the other hand, in some important cases religion itself fostered social and political change, most especially (as we shall detail later in this chapter) in the periodic Great Awakenings, those moments of religious revivalism that helped to encourage the American Revolution, the emancipation movement, the temperance movement, the Progressive Era, and the civil rights movement. Even George W. Bush, a close observer of contemporary American politics and religion, mused publicly about whether we might be in the midst of another such Great Awakening, this time with conservative political consequences.[2]

In this chapter we focus first on religion and gender and then on religion and social class.[3]

We devote the next chapter to the relationship of religion and ethnicity in America. In each case we ask how religion responded to social change, exploring differences between more religious and less religious Americans and among the major religious traditions.

One caveat: In these chapters, as in much of the rest of this book, we focus on religious people and less on religious organizations per se, such as denominational hierarchies and lobbying groups. Religious institutions have had manifold effects on gender, race, and inequality. Religiously affiliated organizations lobbied for and against the Equal Rights Amendment, religious charities played a role in sheltering poor individuals from the full force of growing economic inequality at the same time that many in the Religious Right resisted any public response to this issue, and church congregations, black and white, played important roles in the civil rights movement as well as in opposition to that movement. Our view from the pews encompasses those institutional actors, but our attention is focused on the attitudes and behavior of individual Americans—those in the pews and those not.

RELIGION AND GENDER

Religion in America is disproportionately a women's sphere of activity, as we noted in Chapter 1. In the average Sabbath service women outnumber men by three to two. Women believe more fervently in God, they aver that religion is more important to their daily lives, they pray more often, they read scripture more often and interpret it more literally, they talk about religion more often—in short, by virtually every measure they are more religious. To be sure, not all women are religiously inclined, but the correlation between gender and religiosity is robust. This is just as true among Americans with graduate degrees as it is among high school dropouts, as true in the secular Northeast as in the devout Deep South, and equally true at all ages, among all races, and in all religious traditions, including those who disclaim all formal religious affiliation![4] However, just because religion is, in this sense, a *feminine* sphere does not mean that it is a *feminist* sphere. On the contrary, more religious women tend to be *less* feminist, if we use that term to refer to nontraditional views about gender roles. So how religious currents interacted with second-wave feminism in the last half of the twentieth century is an intriguing puzzle.

To sense the profound transformation in women's rights during the second half of the twentieth century, contrast June Cleaver with Sarah Palin. Cleaver, the *Leave It to Beaver* mom, epitomized the 1950s stay-at-home mom, quietly serving her husband and children, with hobbies of needlepoint and arranging tea roses. Sarah Palin, the populist former Alaskan governor who ran for vice president in 2008, is a self-described hockey mom, enjoys moose hunting from a helicopter, has written a national bestseller, is widely followed as a blogger and television commentator, and thrives on rousing large adoring crowds. Between the Age of Cleaver and the Age of Palin, women achieved a much broader role in society—in the workplace, in schools and sport, and in public life. We ask in this section how these wide-ranging shifts in gender roles played themselves out among religious and secular Americans and in houses of worship, given religion's historic endorsement of a traditional division of labor between men and women.

The women's revolution remade American secular *and religious* institutions and remade secular *and religious* women, broadening conceptions of women's role in both politics and religion, and making working women the norm rather than the exception. Men and women, religious and secular, all became significantly more "feminist" in their views over this period, although the gap between secular and highly religious Americans persisted on some aspects of gender roles, mostly because of a firmly antifeminist minority within certain fundamentalist religions.[5]

The dramatic movement of women from kitchen to office in the second half of the twentieth century arguably affected a greater portion of Americans than the move from fields to factories during the Industrial Revolution a century earlier. The percentage of women in the civilian labor force nearly doubled from 30 percent in 1950 to approximately 60 percent by 2008. Among women with children under age eighteen, more than seven in ten were working for pay by 2008.[6]

Women have moved toward greater equality in the last half century in terms of entry in occupations, of pay, and of shared responsibility for housework and child care. In the 1970s and 1980s women rapidly entered formerly male-dominated professions like wholesale/retail buying, public relations, pharmacy, financial management, computer operations, advertising, bartending, operations and system analysis, accounting/auditing, and public administration.[7] Pay gaps between men and women with comparable education have narrowed but stubbornly persisted.[8] Men have assumed responsibilities for housework and child care, but working mothers still spend roughly two extra hours a day on these tasks, even though many of these responsibilities were outsourced to day care providers, fast food delis, and cleaning services.[9] Though progress has been rapid, women remain under-represented in many professional or high-prestige occupations like physicians, lawyers, politicians, corporate CEOs, and religious leaders.[10]

What occasioned the rise of women in the workforce? Historians and sociologists do not agree on a single cause, but plausible contributors include the culture shift embodied in women's liberation; technological changes, including birth control; and economic and policy shifts.[11]

One might not have expected churches to be receptive to increased gender equality. Strict religious groups, far removed from most Americans' religious experience, such as Orthodox Jews, devout Muslims, the Amish, Mormons, and Christian fundamentalists, clearly delineate separate roles for men and women. Even within religious traditions with a larger representation among Americans, many advocate traditional perspectives on women's roles. For example, the Southern Baptist Convention, the largest Protestant denomination in America, officially espouses the view that a woman should submit to her husband.[12] Our field research in Our Savior Lutheran Church in Houston (described in the previous chapter) took us to a congregation that advocates highly traditional roles for men and women, going so far as to prohibit women from voting in church governance.[13] And while many American religions permit female clergy nowadays, there are notable exceptions across the religious spectrum, including the Catholic Church and the Mormons.[14]

Furthermore, language enshrined in scripture appears to deni-grate women's rights. Bible readers learn that God formed Eve from the rib of Adam, implying a secondary status for women. The New Testament advises women to be silent and submit to their husbands.[15] Jewish tradition excludes women from the *minyan* (the minimum of ten men required for a regular religious service), and an Ortho-dox Jewish prayer (*berakhot*) praises God "who hast not made me a woman." While such texts might be dismissed as historical rhetoric, by sanctifying traditional gender roles, religion—and especially con-servative religious institutions—might be expected to slow and per-haps even halt women's quest for equal rights and responsibilities.

The last third of the twentieth century witnessed a substantial change in traditional gender roles and norms, at the same time that religious conservatism, which had historically favored traditional gender roles, experienced a resurgence. Against that backdrop, we pose three questions about this period:

- How (if at all) did religiosity affect the pace of women's entry into the paid labor force?
- How (if at all) did religiosity affect changing norms about gender roles within the family and in the public arena?
- How (if at all) did norms and practices regarding the role of women in religious institutions themselves change?

WOMEN AT WORK, IN THE FAMILY, AND IN THE PUBLIC ARENA: DOES RELIGION MATTER?

The early 1970s were the dawn of second wave feminism. In 1973 roughly 40 percent of American women, regardless of their reli-giosity, worked outside the home.[16] Most women (and even more men, of course) endorsed traditional gender roles, but churchgo-ing women were consistently more opposed to gender equality than secular women. Sixty-one percent of women regularly attending church in 1974 thought "most men are better suited emotionally for

politics than are most women," compared to 41 percent of nonattending women. That same year, 43 percent of women churchgoers
believed that "women should take care of running their homes and
leave running the country up to men," compared to only 28 percent
of nonattending women. As late as 1977, even 50 percent of non-
observant women thought that "it is more important for a wife to
help her husband's career than to have one herself." Sixty-one percent of female churchgoers agreed with this statement. So roughly
a decade after the bra burnings and Miss America protests of the
late 1960s the view that women should have equal status was not
yet widespread among American women, and especially not among
those in the pews. And all this (as we saw in Chapter 4) just as the
1970s aftershock in American religious life was tightening the linkage between religious observance and attitudes to sexual morality.

Against the backdrop of this resistance of religious American
women to women's liberation, it is perhaps surprising that religious
and secular American women actually entered the workforce at
about the same rate. Even more surprising, as Americans became
more liberal on gender issues in the ensuing decades, religious Americans became feminist at least as fast as and sometimes even faster
than more secular Americans. Both the norms and the facts about
gender roles were transformed in virtually all parts of the American
religious spectrum. With few exceptions, American religion adapted
to the revolutionary change in gender relations with surprisingly
little dissent, an especially notable development when contrasted
with the staunch, passionate resistance of many of these same
churches and same women to the simultaneous changes in sexual
morality.

How did women's entry into the paid workforce vary by religiosity or by religious tradition? Hardly at all. From 1973 to 2008, highly
religious women (those who attend church almost every week) and
secular women (those who almost never attend) entered the workforce in increasing numbers and at virtually the identical pace (see
Figure 8.1).[17] The labor force participation rate of highly religious
women rose from 40 percent in 1973 to 56 percent in 2008, while

Figure 8.1

RELIGIOUS AND SECULAR WOMEN ENTER THE LABOR MARKET
(with birth cohort held constant)

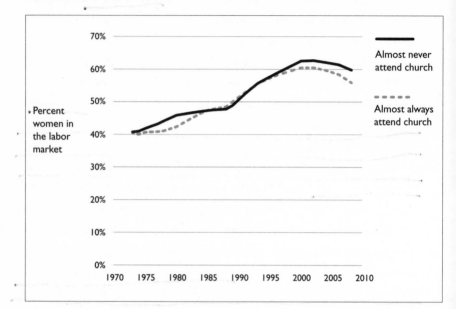

SOURCE: GENERAL SOCIAL SURVEY, 1973–2008; DATA LOESS-SMOOTHED.

the rate for highly secular women rose from 41 percent in 1973 to 60 percent in 2008.

Within every single one of the major religious traditions, as well as nones, women moved into the paid labor force between 1973 and 2008 along just about the same trajectory, rising from roughly 40–45 percent in the early 1970s to roughly 55–60 percent in the 2000s. In particular, the trends for evangelical women and for religiously unaffiliated women over these thirty-five years are virtually identical, with a gradually shrinking gap of roughly 6–8 percentage points between the two groups. In short, religious tenets and religious institutions seem to have had virtually no braking effect on the movement of women toward greater participation in the economic life of the country.

As more and more American women went off to work, attitudes toward working women changed dramatically as well. Both men and women increasingly dissented from traditional gender norms that "It is more important for a wife to help her husband's career than to have one herself" and that "It is much better for everyone involved if the man is the achiever outside the home and the woman takes care of the home and family." Conversely, Americans during these three decades became more likely to agree that "A working mother can establish just as warm and secure a relationship with her children as a mother who does not work," and "If [my] party nominated a woman for President, I would vote for her if she were qualified for the job." [18]

Most of this cultural transformation occurred in the 1970s and 1980s—that is, at the peak of the first aftershock and the rise of evangelical, conservative religion. Thus, it is all the more striking that the same "feminist" cultural transformation occurred among religious and secular women and men, and at about the same pace. Figure 8.2 shows the basic pattern, limiting our analysis to women respondents, since in most cases (it turns out) the religious/secular distinction matters more for them than for men. [19] At the beginning of the 1970s religious women were less "liberated" or more "traditional" in their attitudes to gender, but the subsequent pace of change among more religious and less religious women was remarkably parallel throughout the next four decades on virtually all measures of feminism.

Even by the end of our period religious women were roughly 5–10 percentage points more likely to endorse traditional gender roles than secular women. That difference reflects the persistence of traditional gender norms among a minority of religious conservatives, and the difference may well prove to be enduring. But to overemphasize this gap between religious and nonreligious American women in their attitudes toward gender would be to overlook the sweeping transformation in gender norms *shared* by religious and nonreligious Americans, men and women alike, over the last generation.

Intriguingly, women's views on gender roles in the home and

Figure 8.2

TRENDS IN FEMINIST VIEWS, BY CHURCH ATTENDANCE
(women only, with birth cohort held constant)

MARRIED WOMEN SHOULD NOT WORK

BETTER FOR MAN TO ACHIEVE,
WOMAN TO TEND TO HOME

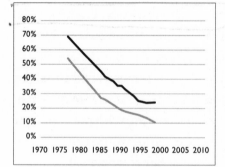

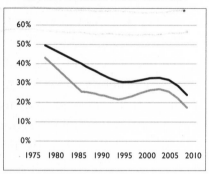

WIFE SHOULD HELP HUSBAND'S
CAREER, NOT HER OWN

MOTHER WORKING HURTS CHILDREN

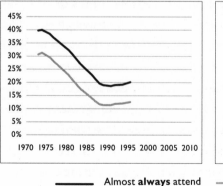

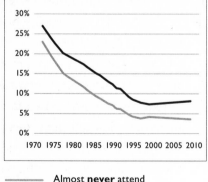

WOMEN SHOULD TAKE CARE OF
HOME, NOT COUNTRY

WOULD NOT VOTE FOR FEMALE PRESIDENT

——— Almost **always** attend   **———** Almost **never** attend

SOURCE: GENERAL SOCIAL SURVEY; DATA LOESS-SMOOTHED.

in public life are today more closely tied to their religiosity than are men's views. In other words, the difference between religious and secular women is modestly but consistently greater than the difference between religious and secular men. Alas, our surveys cannot allow us to untangle the causal pathways here. Perhaps women are more responsive than men to traditional religious teachings about gender roles. Or perhaps feminist women are more likely to have been turned off by religion than equally feminist men. Or perhaps women with traditional gender views have been more attracted to conservative churches than men with equally traditional views on gender. In any event, the evidence is not consistent with the view that it is only male chauvinists who are thronging to church over the objections of their more liberated spouses.

Men and women in the pews today remain more traditionalist about gender roles than their contemporaries who are not in the pews, but they are less traditionalist than their religious counterparts had been a generation ago. In fact, deeply religious Americans are less traditionalist in their views about gender roles than their *secular* counterparts had been a generation earlier. This is true across all measures of feminism we have examined: attitudes toward women and work, toward women and child care, toward women in public life, and toward the division of labor within marriage. In short, in both occupational and normative terms the feminist revolution of the last generation swept as rapidly through the ranks of religious men and women, including evangelicals, as it did through the ranks of secular Americans.

Compare this phenomenon to the massive and widening gap between religious and secular Americans on issues of sexual morality that we discussed in Chapter 4. Combining what we learned there and what we have just learned, we can see that a modest but growing fraction of American women are conservative on sexual morality but progressive on gender equality, and those women are disproportionately religious.[20] Religious Americans have largely accepted the gender revolution, at the same time that many of them, especially evangelicals, staunchly resist the sexual revolution.

WOMEN IN RELIGIOUS INSTITUTIONS: AN EMERGING FEMINIST CONSENSUS IN THE PEWS

By the early twenty-first century a broad consensus had formed around an increased role for women in economic and public life, despite a minority of highly religious Americans (men and women) who resisted that consensus. The same is true, perhaps more surprisingly, of the role that women should play in religious institutions themselves. Most Americans in most religious traditions believe that women should have expanded roles in church, including the pulpit. In this sense, most Americans today are religious feminists.

Women have gained rights in many congregations over time. Women in religious traditions that once required them to sit apart from men and play a subordinate role now sit with men and vote. On the other hand, entry into the pulpit (and thus positions of religious authority) has been slow. A century ago one quarter of U.S. Christian denominations gave women full clergy rights, a figure that had risen slowly to almost 50 percent as the twenty-first century opened. But as sociologist Mark Chaves has shown, denominational policies and actual practice are only loosely coupled, so that some formally progressive denominations are laggards when it comes to women in the pulpit, while some formally conservative denominations are actually more feminist in practice.[21] Women represented a paltry 8 percent of clergy in churches as recently as 2006–2007 (up from 6 percent in 1998), although women represent a third of all students in theological schools.[22] Among self-described liberal congregations, women comprised 37 percent of clergy in 2006–2007, up from 23 percent in 1998, but among self-described moderate congregations, the figure was 7 percent, and among self-described conservative congregations, only 5 percent.[23]

On the core issue of female clergy, views in the pews have been changing more rapidly than presence in the pulpit. In Figure 8.3 we compare evidence from the General Social Survey in 1986 with evidence from our Faith Matters survey in 2006. Although the questions

Figure 8.3

INCREASING MAJORITIES IN MOST RELIGIOUS TRADITIONS
FAVOR ALLOWING FEMALE CLERGY

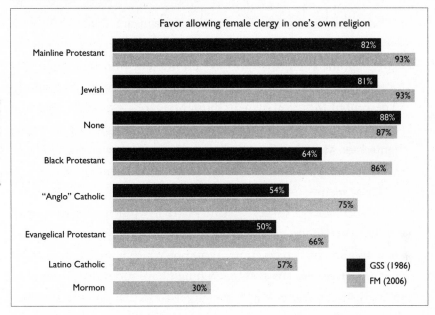

SOURCE: GENERAL SOCIAL SURVEY, 1986 AND FAITH MATTERS SURVEY, 2006.

are not identical,[24] they produce comparable results, and suggest a
roughly 15–20 percentage point increase in support for female clergy
over these twenty years in every religious tradition, with the greatest
gains coming in the more conservative religious traditions (evangelicals, Black Protestants, and Catholics). Moreover, evidence points to
generational succession as a major source of change, because in the
1986 survey opposition to female clergy was concentrated among
the oldest cohorts. Twenty years later these people (born in the first
several decades of the twentieth century) had mostly been replaced
by a younger generation who were overwhelmingly in favor of
women clergy.

By 2006 majorities of every religious tradition except Mormons
had come to favor women clergy, though the majorities were less
than overwhelming among evangelicals and Latino Catholics. Except
for Mormons and Black Protestants there are no significant differ-

ences between men and women in their support for female clergy, and in both these exceptional cases men are, if anything, more supportive of female clergy than are women. Male Black Protestants are more supportive of female clergy than are Black Protestant women, 91 percent to 82 percent. Mormon women are overwhelmingly opposed to women as (lay) priests, but Mormon men have more mixed views: 90 percent of Mormon women as compared to 52 percent of Mormon men. In short, Mormons, especially Mormon women, appear to be the only substantial holdouts against the growing and substantial consensus across the religious spectrum in favor of women playing a fuller role in church leadership.

These results are confirmed by responses to a question from the 2006 Faith Matters survey: "Some say that women have too much influence in religion, others say that women don't have enough influence in religion. Which comes closer to your views?" Nearly three quarters of Americans said that women have too little influence in religion, a view that is widely shared across virtually all religious traditions and by both men and women. (Overall, 74 percent of women want more influence for women in religion, compared to 71 percent among men.) Despite this broadly feminist consensus across the religious spectrum, however, a firmly traditionalist minority exists in certain religious traditions, particularly among Latino Catholics, Mormons, and more fundamentalist evangelicals. (We distinguish here between Latino and "Anglo" Catholics, because their responses to this question are so different.) Figure 8.4 shows how this openness to greater female influence in religious institutions varies across the major religious institutions.

Among evangelical Protestants, the one in four who cleave most fervently to fundamentalist Protestant theology (biblical inerrancy, millenarianism, justification by faith, creationism, and "one true faith") are deeply skeptical about a greater role for women in the church.[25] Of these most fundamentalist evangelicals, 52 percent object to women in the clergy, compared to only 27 percent of other evangelicals, a figure only slightly above the national average of 23 percent. Of the most fundamentalist evangelicals, only

Figure 8.4

MOST MEMBERS OF MOST RELIGIOUS TRADITIONS FAVOR A BIGGER ROLE FOR WOMEN IN CHURCH

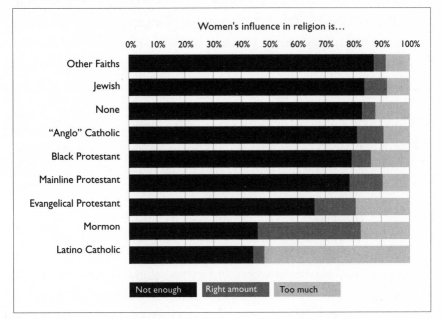

SOURCE: FAITH MATTERS SURVEY, 2006.

54 percent say that women should have more influence in church, compared to 70 percent of other evangelicals, a figure only slightly below the national average of 73 percent. In short, while evangelicals as a group are somewhat more skeptical than other Americans of what we are calling religious feminism, that difference is almost entirely concentrated among an extremely fundamentalist minority of evangelicals. We shall see more evidence in Chapter 15 of the distinctiveness of this very conservative minority within the evangelical tradition.

We are far from saying that the feminist views in the pews will prevail institutionally. The fact that a clear majority of American Catholics favor the ordination of women does not mean that female ordination will happen anytime soon, and the same is true for conservative Protestant churches. Given religion's longtime commitment to traditional gender roles, however, and given the lukewarm endorsement of women's liberation in the pews as late as the 1970s, this emergent feminist consensus was surely unforeseen. In marked contrast to the fervent and growing resistance of religious Americans to liberal sexual morality, discussed in Chapter 4, religious institutions in the end did not—or could not—obstruct the feminist revolution, in part because this revolution was sweeping through their own congregations. In sum, while religion did not create or encourage the feminist revolution of the last half century, neither did religion do much to forestall it, even among the most fervent opponents of the near-simultaneous revolution in sexual morality. Gender and sex, it appears, are not the same thing.

RELIGION AND SOCIAL CLASS

In many respects the least widely recognized of the three massive social transformations whose links with religion we are examining in this chapter and the next is the steadily widening gap between haves and have-nots in America. Because of the central role of race in American history, because class and race are so closely correlated, and because America has made significant though incomplete progress on overcoming racial divisions in recent decades, many of us have not noticed that during these same years division by socioeconomic status has grown. Sociologists Claude Fischer and Greggor Mattson have argued that while much talk about America fragmenting is overblown, "gaps by social class and educational attainment are widening among Americans by almost any measure." [26]

The gap between rich and poor in America generally narrowed during the first half of the twentieth century, and in the first two decades after World War II the distribution of income was stable and relatively egalitarian. In the 1970s, however, a long rapid increase in inequality began that persists to the present day. Figure 8.5 provides a graphic overview of how the share of national income going to the richest tenth of the population has changed since World War II. Other measures of inequality tell the same story.

Those at the bottom of the income distribution experienced a

Figure 8.5

INEQUALITY IN AMERICA: THE INCOME SHARE OF THE TOP DECILE
(1945–2007)

SOURCE: THOMAS PIKETTY AND EMMANUEL SAEZ, "INCOME INEQUALITY IN THE
UNITED STATES, 1913–1998," *QUARTERLY JOURNAL OF ECONOMICS*, 118, NO. 1 (2003):
1–39 (LONGER UPDATED VERSION PUBLISHED IN A. B. ATKINSON AND T. PIKETTY
EDS., OXFORD UNIVERSITY PRESS, 2007), TABLES AND FIGURES UPDATED TO 2007 AT
HTTP://ELSA.BERKELEY.EDU/~SAEZ/ (ACCESSED MARCH 2, 2010).

slow decrease in their share of the national pie, those in the middle
barely kept up, and those at the top (especially those at the very top)
experienced breathtaking increases.[27] So stark was the change after
1970 that economists Claudia Goldin and Lawrence Katz entitled
their summary of the twentieth-century history of American wage
inequality "A Tale of Two Half-Centuries."[28]

Virtually everyone who has examined the evidence agrees on the
significance of this sharp increase in economic inequality over the last
three to four decades, but views vary widely on the causes. Among
the chief suspects are technological changes that increased the value
of higher education; globalization that exposed the working class to
low-wage competition from abroad; changes in public policy that
gave tax breaks to the well-off, undermined minimum wage laws,

and discouraged unions; and the fading of social norms that had (in
the aftermath of the Great Depression and World War II) restrained
upper-class avarice. Whatever the tangled causal origins, the result
is that at the same time that religion in America was undergoing the
divisive aftershocks described earlier in this book, the extremes of
wealth and poverty in America were pulling apart.

Over these same decades residential segregation by income was
also increasing, with affluent gated communities at one end of the
spectrum matched by zones of concentrated poverty at the other.
While racial residential segregation was declining, class segregation increased, mainly because the affluent increasingly clustered in
specific metropolitan areas and specific municipalities within those
areas. The trend toward greater class segregation in 1970s and 1980s
was visible among both blacks and whites. The trend toward class
segregation moderated in the 1990s, as income disparities stopped
growing, but then apparently resumed after 2000. "Class segregation
and the spatial concentration of poverty at historically high levels,"
concluded demographer Douglas Massey and his colleagues, "when
juxtaposed with the growing concentration of affluence at all geographic levels, portends a divided society that runs counter to the
egalitarian ideology of the United States and its historical commitment to equality."[29]

At the very same time that physical distance increasingly separated rich and poor in America, so too the social distance between
them swelled. We saw in Chapter 5 that social integration among
religious traditions was signaled by steadily growing intermarriage
across religious lines. In the case of social class, by contrast, the trend
(as measured by education) was very nearly the reverse. Between 1940
and 1960, to be sure, couples increasingly married across class lines,
but over the ensuing half century that trend reversed, as Americans
more and more confined their marital choices to people of similar
educational level, "consistent with a growing social divide between
those with very low levels of education and those with more education," in the words of sociologists Christine Schwartz and Robert
Mare.[30] We have less systematic evidence of growing class segrega-

tion in associational life, but sociologist Theda Skocpol has made a powerful case that fraternal and civic organizations no longer bring together people from different social and economic backgrounds as once they did. Economists have found evidence that de facto segregation by education is increasing in the workplace.[31]

In short, over the last three to four decades Americans have been increasingly polarized into haves and have-nots—living increasingly segregated and unequal lives. This yawning gap, which reversed earlier decades of narrowing class cleavage, reflects arguably the most important socioeconomic change in America over the last half century. How has American religion responded to this dramatic transformation? Has religion reinforced or resisted those trends toward class divergence? Did religion stand prophetically on the side of the poor demanding social justice (as some Christians believe Jesus did), or did religion forestall social reform, providing deadening consolation for economic injustice (as Karl Marx argued in speaking of religion as the "opiate of the masses")?

That American religion might stand with the left, protesting economic inequality and social segregation, could seem incongruous to secular observers today, accustomed to thinking of religion and political conservatism as perfectly correlated. But commitment to social justice has deep scriptural roots. Proverbs 29:7 intones prophetically that "The righteous care about justice for the poor, but the wicked have no such concern." Mark 10: 17–25 describes Jesus admonishing a religiously observant rich man that he should give up everything to the poor, since "it is easier for a camel to go through the eye of a needle than for a rich man to enter the kingdom of God." Isaiah's angry God (Isaiah 3:15) thunders at the elders and rulers, gathered to face his righteous wrath: "How dare you crush my people, grinding the faces of the poor into the dust?"

Many contemporary secular progressives have forgotten that the history of religion in America is replete with powerful examples of evangelical revival promoting social reform and equality. Indeed, it is harder to identify purely secular progressive movements in American history than to find progressive movements infused with deep religious commitment and undergirded by religious institutions. The First Great Awakening, the wave of Protestant evangelical revivalism that swept from England through the colonies from about 1730 to about 1760, was thoroughly infused with egalitarian ideology and formed part of the background to the American Revolution. Revivalist ministers in this Awakening were, observed historian Gordon Wood, "eager to promote the idea of equality that became so important in the Revolution" and "became deeply involved in reform movements of the early Republic."[32]

The Second Great Awakening, in the 1830s, America's next wave of religious enthusiasm, was centered among backcountry settlers. Although historians debate the social origins of this evangelical revival, one leading historian, Nathan Hatch, argues that these religious leaders had a "passion for equality" and a vision of an America that would be fairer; and others argue that revivals were "often infused with a prophetic, egalitarian impulse," democratizing religion.[33]

Many historians link the Second Great Awakening to the birth of abolitionism; for example, regions where revival meetings were most intense tended subsequently to vote for antislavery candidates. Henry Ward Beecher, probably the most prominent clergyman of his day, raised money to buy rifles (called "Beecher's Bibles") for antislavery forces fighting in "Bloody Kansas." Charles Grandison Finney, the most influential preacher of the Second Great Awakening, was an outspoken critic of slavery, just as William Wilberforce, the most renowned and successful British advocate of abolition, had been famously motivated by profound evangelical fervor. Of course, as we emphasize in the next chapter, not all religious leaders in America were abolitionists. On the contrary, many were staunch supporters of slavery. But many pietistic religious leaders in the antebellum North were strong voices for social justice.

In the second half of the nineteenth century the Industrial Revolution brought in its train an unprecedented cleavage in American society between haves and have-nots, both urban and rural. Religious leaders were among the most vocal critics of the social injustices of this Gilded Age, giving rise to the Social Gospel movement and even to Christian Socialism.[34] Social Gospel leaders were predominantly associated with the liberal wing of the Progressive movement, and with such social reforms as settlement houses, the YMCA, and labor law reform. At the same time, working-class radicals used religious precepts and rhetoric as the moral foundation on which to rest their critique of industrial exploitation.[35]

Many radical Populists raging against inequality were fervent evangelical Protestants. Most notably, William Jennings Bryan, "The Great Commoner" and the fieriest critic of the new concentrations of wealth and power, fused fundamentalist religious fervor and political radicalism, culminating in his famous "Cross of Gold" peroration at the Democratic National Convention of 1896.[36] The phrase "What would Jesus do?" was popularized in a bestselling 1899 novel by Charles Sheldon, a Congregational minister in Topeka, Kansas, as an appeal to overturn economic inequality.

> What would Jesus do? . . . It seems to me sometimes as if the people in the big churches had good clothes and nice houses to live in, and money to spend for luxuries, and could go away on summer vacations and all that, while the people outside the churches, thousands of them, I mean, die in tenements, and walk the streets for jobs, and never have a piano or a picture in the house, and grow up in misery and drunkenness and sin.[37]

The Salvation Army (an evangelical revivalist group that arrived in America in 1880) proclaimed that the chief social evil was the unequal and unjust distribution of wealth.[38]

To be sure, many captains of industry during the Gilded Age (beginning at the pinnacle with John D. Rockefeller) were also deeply religious. Religious people stood on both sides of the barricades. American history is very far from a simple story of religious revival leading to progressive politics. Not all religious institutions or religious people favored the American Revolution or abolition or the Progressive movement. What some religious historians term the "Great Reversal" of the 1920s saw evangelical fundamentalism take a decisively more conservative stance on social and economic reform, partly in reaction against liberal Protestantism's Social Gospel.[39] Furthermore, grand reform movements had secular roots, not just religious ones. Finally, religion has often provided motivation and mobilization for conservative political movements, such as prohibition, anticommunism, and, as we discuss in more detail in Chapter 11, the contemporary Religious Right. God in American history has not been a consistent partisan of left or right.

But throughout American history periods of upheaval over social and economic and political inequality have very often been periods of religious revival aimed at redressing that inequality. Not all religiously based movements are progressive, but most American progressive movements have had powerful religious roots. The decades since 1970 have seen both growing inequality and religious revival, so it is important to ask how religious Americans have responded to the class cleavages of our time.

First, we need to ask about the correlation between religious engagement itself and social class.[40] An intriguing fact about church attendance in America over the last thirty years, amidst all the ups and downs that we saw in Chapter 4, is the slow, but unmistakable reappearance of a "class gap." In the first half of the twentieth century "the college educated participated more in the churches than did the lesser educated,"[41] but in the 1960s and 1970s, as the baby boomers came of age, the decline in church attendance was concentrated among the better educated. With the subsequent pair of aftershocks, however, religious observance tended to rise faster, or fall more slowly, among the better educated, blacks and whites. Both the General Social Survey and the National Election Studies show that since the late 1970s among whites forty-five and under, weekly church attendance has been essentially flat among the college-educated (perhaps slipping from 30 percent to 27 percent), but has dropped by about one third among those without college (from roughly 30–32 percent to roughly 20–22 percent).[42] The rise of evangelicalism in the 1970s and 1980s was concentrated among the middle and upper middle classes. In short, over the last several decades, the religious institutional ties of have-nots in America, especially men, seem to be weakening.

This trend is clearly contrary to any idea that religion is nowadays providing solace to the disinherited and dispossessed, or that higher education subverts religion. Secularization (at least in terms of organized religion) seems to be proceeding more rapidly among less educated Americans.[43] If you listen carefully, hymns in American houses of worship are sung increasingly in upper-middle-class accents.[44] In this respect, at least, religious institutions appear to be one more setting in which the class divergence over the last three to four decades is manifest.

What about personal ties of friendship and acquaintance that cross class divisions? Since most Americans are uncomfortable with the language of class, we (and some other researchers) use an indirect way of measuring cross-class ties. As a measure of upward personal ties, we ask whether our respondents have a personal friend "who owns a business" (or "who owns a vacation home"), and as a measure of downward personal ties we ask whether any of their friends "is a manual worker" (or "has been on welfare"). Since we can make a reasonable judgment about the respondent's own social standing by using a combination of income and education, we can then ask which Americans in the upper third of the socioeconomic hierarchy are most likely to have downward ties and which Americans in the lower third of the hierarchy are most likely to have upward ties. Such questions inevitably disregard important facets of the reported friendship, such as how intimate or egalitarian it actually is, but they can give us some basic measure of the strength or weakness of aggregate connections between different strata in the American socioeconomic hierarchy.

Strikingly, religiosity is correlated with greater class bridging, especially downward bridging. That is, among the American upper middle classes, those who are religiously observant are more likely to report friendship and social interaction with people on welfare or manual workers than comparably placed secular Americans. To be sure, the strongest predictor of cross-class ties is simply one's total number of friends; no doubt if we had asked about friendship with elderly Fijians or redheaded lacrosse players, one's total number of friends would also be the best predictor. But controlling for that (and many other factors, including race, age, region, civic involvement, education, gender, income, and so forth), religious Americans report more friends lower in the social hierarchy than do secular Americans. We also find some evidence that upward bridging is more common among religiously involved lower-class Americans, but that pattern is much less robust.[45]

Furthermore, this pattern seems to be driven not by generalized religiosity or theology in itself, but by involvement in religious social networks, like prayer groups and Bible study groups and (above all) having more friends in one's congregation. Just "being religious" does not seem to produce more social bridging. In short, religious social networks seem to serve as a counterweight against growing class segregation.

Significantly, these downward social bridges are not concentrated among people who volunteer, so they are not primarily a function of religious volunteers connecting with clients in a social service setting (a connection that might have paternalistic overtones). On the contrary, class-bridging ties are concentrated among people with lots of friends at church, even holding constant their total number of friends. In short, our evidence suggests—though it does not strictly prove—that the cross-class contacts occur largely within congregational activities.

Finally, this religiously based class bridging is heavily concentrated among evangelical Protestants, probably because evangelical congregations are both more diverse in class terms and highly social in terms of a proliferation of small groups, such as Bible study or prayer groups.[46] Fundamentalist theological beliefs are uncorrelated with bridging, so it seems to be the sociology, not the theology, of evangelicalism that produces the bridging. Thus, evangelical churches, because they are both socially diverse and socially active, appear to be one important exception to class segregation in America.

The available evidence does not allow us to say whether or not there are other niches in contemporary America in which interclass ties are fostered, but the three independent national surveys that we have examined confirm that evangelical congregations are one such niche.[47] On the other hand, cross-class contact does not seem to translate into more support for redistributive public policies nor into more generous philanthropic behavior. As we will see in Chapter 13, religious people are typically more generous, especially to social welfare charities, but that generosity itself does not seem to be boosted by having personal ties to people lower in the socioeconomic hierarchy.

What are the views of religious and secular Americans on issues of inequality, poverty, and government action to address inequality and poverty?

Nearly two thirds of all Americans in our 2006 Faith Matters survey said America did not have equal opportunity for all, and a clear majority supported government actions to address poverty and inequality. Support for antipoverty policy was higher among Democrats, among poorer, less educated Americans, among women, among racial minorities, and in the Northeast; and by contrast, support was lower among Republicans, Southerners, and people over sixty-five.

Against this backdrop, how were these views related to religiosity? Blacks and Latinos are highly religious and very supportive of antipoverty policy, an important but hardly surprising pattern. Among white Americans, support for egalitarian public policy is somewhat lower, especially among the most religious Americans. Figure 8.6 summarizes some of the evidence, holding constant other background factors in order to focus specifically on the impact of religiosity.[48] Most Americans, religious or not, do not believe that equality of opportunity is a reality in America. When we ask about government policies to reduce inequality and fight poverty, however, support fades a bit, especially among religious Americans. About 66 percent of the most secular Americans favor government action to reduce the gap between rich and poor compared to 57 percent of the most religious fifth of the population. Roughly two thirds of

Figure 8.6

RELIGIOSITY AND VIEWS ON POVERTY AND GOVERNMENT POLICY
(*whites only, with standard demographic characteristics held constant*)

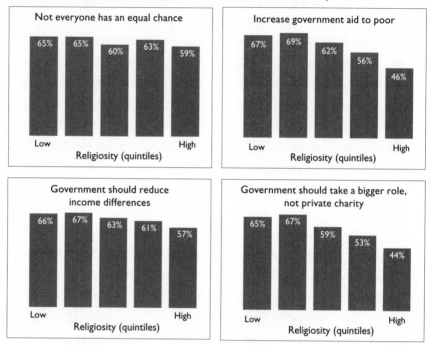

SOURCE: FAITH MATTERS SURVEY, 2006.

secular Americans favor increased government aid to poor people, compared to 46 percent among the most religious fifth of the population.

Thus religiosity in white America today is linked with more conservative views on government help for the poor, though this link is far weaker than the correlation between religiosity and views on sexual morality, like premarital sex, abortion, and homosexuality, and far weaker than the correlation between political party or ideology and views on aid to the poor. We shall return to this question in Chapter 11.

Deeply observant Americans in all religious traditions prefer to help poor individuals through private charity rather than to address the structural causes of poverty through government action.

Figure 8.7 shows how religious traditions differ on whether public policy or private charity is the proper approach for attacking poverty.[49] As we shall see in Chapter 13, deeply religious people are, in fact, more generous in terms of their own giving and volunteering for social service, so in this sense religious people seem to walk the walk.

In sum, by most measures, highly religious Americans today are somewhat less supportive than the general population of public policies to address poverty and inequality, and they prefer private provision to public action. They have not worked to stem the growth of inequality, unlike past religious people who, as we have seen, often

Figure 8.7

WHO SHOULD PRIMARILY CARE FOR THE POOR: GOVERNMENT OR PRIVATE CHARITY?

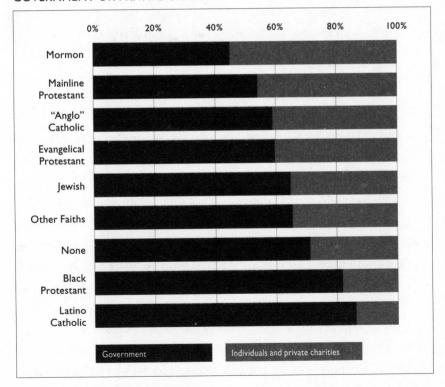

SOURCE: FAITH MATTERS SURVEY, 2006.

campaigned passionately for greater equality and social justice. On the other hand, their modestly greater giving and substantially greater volunteering, especially for social service, is consistent with their emphasis on private provision.

Reasonable people might differ about whether public or private provision is a more effective solution to growing inequality. One side holds that public provision is less paternalistic and more effective in addressing large, structural issues. The other side holds that private provision is more attentive to the situations of needy individuals and more responsive to spiritual as well as material needs.

A century ago, faced with mounting class inequality, a Salvation Army leader argued that private philanthropy was not adequate to the task of overcoming poverty and fighting injustice: "To right the social wrong by charity is like bailing the oceans with a thimble." [50] The failure of American religion (and especially evangelicals) today to mount a more vigorous campaign against class disparities could thus be seen as a sin of omission, especially compared to the struggles for social justice that people of faith mounted in comparable periods of American history.

How did American religion react to the two major social transformations discussed in this chapter—growing gender equality and diminishing socioeconomic equality? In the generally conservative era we have analyzed, the answer is not much in either case. Religious women went to work in numbers equivalent to secular women, and while a small minority of religious fundamentalists continue to resist egalitarian gender norms, the second wave of increasingly feminist views seems to have swept through the pews just about as rapidly as elsewhere in contemporary America. In the case of socioeconomic segregation, evangelical churches seem to have provided one niche for cross-class friendship, but by and large religious America has offered little support for public action to redress growing class inequities, unlike the stance of many devout Americans in earlier eras.

As in the case of the gender revolution, religious Americans have adjusted with little opposition to the growing class cleavages in our society. The striking contrast with the revolution in sexual mores, fervently opposed by so many religious Americans, makes their relatively untroubled adjustment to these other two social revolutions particularly notable.

CHAPTER 9

DIVERSITY, ETHNICITY, AND RELIGION

I n the previous chapter, we saw how American religion has adapted to two major social transformations: the growth of both women's rights and income inequality. Now we turn to a third transformation, the growth in ethnic diversity. How have American religions adapted—or not—to the rising share of the population who are minorities? In discussing the trend toward greater diversity, we use the term "minority" cautiously, since the U.S. Census Bureau projects that today's minorities will comprise a majority of the American population by 2042.[1] No matter the metric, there can be no doubt that because of both immigration—legal and illegal— and high birth rates among minority populations, the United States is becoming an increasingly diverse nation.

As we will detail in this chapter, ethnicity and religion are often mutually reinforcing. It is no coincidence that the United States is both a nation of immigrants and a nation with high religiosity. Many immigrants find refuge in religion, perhaps as a way of affirming their ethnic heritage, perhaps to find familiarity within a strange land. Similarly, in the African American population religion and racial identity have a symbiotic relationship. In the Black Church, racial and religious themes are often bound together. However—and this is a key point we hope to make in this chapter—the link between ethnicity and religion is not limited to immigrants, nor to minority groups. Instead, it is a more general phenomenon as many Americans, including many whites whose ancestors immigrated several generations ago, evince a connection between their sense of ethnic identity and various manifestations of their religiosity.

Historically, one consequence of the connections—implicit or explicit—between religion and ethnicity is, notwithstanding all of the flux in American religion, that most churchgoers attend ethnically or racially homogeneous congregations. Yet we will also see exceptions to the generalization that religion is highly segregated. We will describe two examples of religious organizations where Sunday mornings provide an opportunity for integration rather than segregation. One is Catholic parishes, given that Latino immigration has caused a demographic transformation in the American Catholic Church that is even more pronounced than in the population as a whole. The other example of racial diversity in the pews is evangelical megachurches, a small but growing niche within the largest single religious tradition.

It is tempting to conclude that, owing to the symbiosis between religion and ethnicity, religion has been a bastion of racism. Actually, it turns out that in contemporary America religiosity has very little to do with racial attitudes. Furthermore, in a pattern that resembles the changes in attitudes toward gender equality, the last thirty years have seen more religious and less religious Americans alike become more accepting of racial equality. When we look across religious traditions, we find that there has been convergence on some racial issues (like the propriety of interracial marriage), while modest differences remain on others (like laws prohibiting discrimination in housing). Where there are differences across major religious traditions, evangelicals are less likely to take a racially egalitarian position than are mainline Protestants, Catholics, and people with no religious affiliation.

TWO EXAMPLES

To underscore our point that ethnicity and religion are often tightly bound together, consider the case of Mount Olivet Lutheran Church in Minneapolis. Mount Olivet Lutheran was one of the nation's first megachurches with an average Sunday morning attendance of six thousand—large by any standard. Founded in 1920, for at least a half century it has been the nation's largest Lutheran church. Indeed, it was established long before anyone thought to attach the prefix "mega" to the word "church." It may be mega in size, but not in style. Unlike the typical evangelical megachurch, Mount Olivet is decidedly old-fashioned. There is an organ, not a band; an altar, not a stage. There is no video projection system, no coffee shop, and—certainly—no pastors in Hawaiian shirts. Here the ministers wear time-honored white robes, adorned with colorful stoles. This is a Lutheran church steeped in tradition.

And, as reflected in its architecture, Mount Olivet was once a distinctively Swedish Lutheran Church. In its merger of Swedish ethnicity and Lutheranism, Mount Olivet exemplifies much of American religion. One of Mount Olivet's ministers described for us how the early years of his ministerial career were spent in Duluth, where there was a Lutheran church "every two blocks." The Swedes, Norwegians, Danes, Finns, and Germans all had their own churches. Some congregations even held services only in the native tongue of their particular nationality.

Our Savior Lutheran in Houston, one of the congregations we describe in Chapter 7, provides still another example of how ethnicity and Lutheranism often intertwine. Not only does OSL preach a conservative brand of religion, it is also a German enclave. In fact, during our time there we heard German spoken in the hallways and classrooms of the church, even though virtually all the German origins of OSL parishioners date back more than four generations! Some OSL parishioners are undoubtedly attracted to the congregation as a means to affirm their ethnic German identity.

ETHNICITY AND RELIGION

In the last four decades America has experienced another of those massive waves of immigration that have periodically washed over our shores. As a share of the population immigrants rose from about five percent in 1970 to about thirteen percent in 2010. Though the present wave of immigration is smaller proportionally than the wave of immigration that arrived between 1870 and 1910, these millions of new Americans are, like their predecessors a century ago, striving to put down roots in their new home, while preserving the familiarity of the cultures within which they were raised. Speaking of those earlier arrivals, America's preeminent historian of immigration Oscar Handlin wrote, "Struggling against heavy odds to save something of the old ways, the immigrants directed into their faith the whole weight of their longing to be connected with the past."[2] This recurrent pattern in American history means that religion and ethnicity are intimately linked.

Religious historian Martin Marty has described race and ethnicity as the "supporting framework" of religion in America because many of America's religions have deep ethnic roots.[3] One prominent observer of the 1950s even attributed the religious upswing of that decade, described in Chapter 3, to the rediscovery of ethnic identity. In his bestselling book *Protestant—Catholic—Jew*, Will Herberg argued that the religious resurgence of that day resulted from the bond between ethnicity and religion that, having lain largely dormant for decades, resurfaced in the middle of the twentieth century. As Herberg described it, members of immigrant groups turned to religion in order to reinforce their ethnic heritage while also remaining fully American. Referring to the experience of the typical immigrant, Herberg wrote that "not only was he expected to retain his old religion, as he was not expected to retain his old language or nationality, but such was the shape of America that it was largely in and through his religion that he, or rather his children and grandchildren, found an identifiable place in American life."[4] All those ethnic groups that flowed into the country during an earlier era of widespread immigration had now established their American bona fides and thus experienced a religious awakening.

In fact, the precise pattern for immigrants' religiosity described by Herberg is observed today. People born outside the United States

(first generation) have the same frequency of religious service attendance as those whose grandparents were born abroad (third generation), while the in-between generation has a lower rate of attending
religious services. We see this pattern in both the General Social Survey and PS-ARE (the Panel Study of American Religion and Ethnicity); the fact that two sources of data agree adds to our confidence
that the pattern is real.[5]

Herberg undoubtedly overstated his case, as there were many
other reasons for the heightened religiosity of the 1950s, but we
nonetheless find it revealing that a best-selling author would look
out at the religious bull market and conclude that ethnicity was
behind the boom. Interestingly, even though the immigrants of
whom Herberg wrote came from different nations and thus had
different ethnicities than current immigration flows, the intergenerational pattern he described persists. And while there are many
explanations for the varying levels of religiosity across generations,
his fundamental insight about the often tight relationship between
race, ethnicity, and religion still echoes today.

Among that evidence is the Black Church, the only religious tradition commonly defined in terms of race. The Black Church is the
quintessential example of a fusion between ethnicity and religion
but, we hope to show, it is not unique. Instead, it illustrates the more
general phenomenon of how ethnicity and religion can reinforce
one another. Black Protestants, then, exemplify a type. We could
highlight numerous other racial and/or ethnic groups that, while
obviously not sharing precisely the same experience as African Americans, nonetheless meld ethnicity with religion. For example, in a
contemporary extension of the argument made by Herberg decades
ago about a different collection of ethnic groups, many new immigrants reinforce their ethnic identity through their participation in
religious organizations. The Korean American Christian community
is one widely noted case, as are Muslims from Middle Eastern and
South Asian nations and Sikhs with an Indian heritage.[6]

There are so many different immigrant groups where ethnicity
and religion overlap that we would need a whole book, and probably

multiple books, to cover them adequately. We instead focus on the largest such group, Latinos.[7] While Latino immigration is affecting both Catholicism and Protestantism—and to some extent Mormonism as well—it leaves the deepest imprint on the American Catholic Church.

RELIGION, ETHNICITY, AND GEOGRAPHY

One of the more subtle manifestations of the intertwining between religion and ethnicity becomes apparent when we step back from our usual focus on individual people and turn instead to the communities in which those individuals live. When we examine the demographic makeup of America's counties, for example, we often see an overlap between the presence of a particular ethnic group and members of ethnically rooted religions. These connections hold up even though many generations have passed since those ethnic groups arrived, and in spite of the fluidity that characterizes American religion. The Dutch are a case in point of how ethnicity and religion overlap, as there is a tight connection between the population of people with Dutch heritage within a county, and the proportion that belongs to Christian—more loosely, Dutch—Reform churches. That single measure of the percentage of people with Dutch ancestry has an 80 percent accuracy rate when predicting the proportion of Christian Reform adherents within a county.[8] Indeed, the link between Dutch heritage and Christian Reform adherents is the single strongest relationship between the ethnic and religious composition of American counties that we have found. However, it does not stand alone, as there are other examples of ethnic and religious overlap that differ in degree but not in kind. For example, there is also a strong connection between the percentage of a county's population who report Greek ancestry and the proportion belonging to the Greek Orthodox Church. Likewise for the connection between Scottish or Scots Irish ancestry and membership in Presbyterian churches.

Dutch Reform and Greek Orthodox are, admittedly, religions

with an overtly ethnic dimension, and so we might have expected
that they would display such a strong connection between ethnicity and religion. Even the Scots and Presbyterian connection would
likely be expected. Yet there are many other examples of ethnic and
religious overlap, some perhaps not so expected, that serve to illuminate the themes discussed further in this chapter. The overlap can be
seen most clearly when we look at maps that show the clustering of
both ethnic and religious groups. Clearest of all is the overlapping
presence of German Americans and Lutherans, as displayed in Figures 9.1 and 9.2. These maps, and those that follow, display the concentration of each ethnic or religious group in each county within
the forty-eight contiguous states.[9]

Turning to Figures 9.1 and 9.2, not only do we see a high proportion of Lutherans and German Americans in the Upper Midwest, notice the concentration of German Americans in places like
Houston (home of Our Savior Lutheran). Where there are Germans

Figure 9.1
LUTHERANS

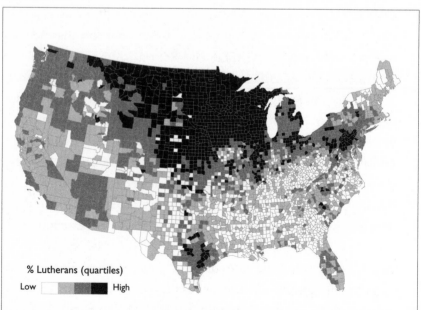

% Lutherans (quartiles)

Low [   ] High

SOURCE: ASSOCIATION OF STATISTICIANS OF AMERICAN RELIGIOUS BODIES, 2000.

Figure 9.2

PEOPLE OF GERMAN DESCENT

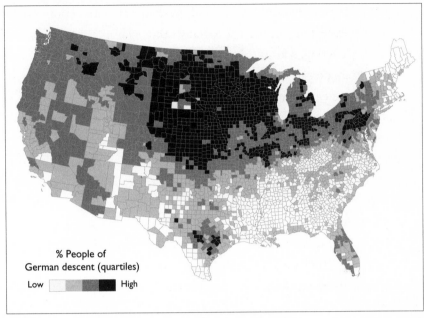

SOURCE: U.S. CENSUS, 2000.

there are Lutherans, and Houston is no exception. As seen in Figure 9.3, there is also overlap between the presence of Americans with Scandinavian ancestry and Lutherans, but less so than with the German Americans. (Many counties in the Mountain and Pacific West states have a lot of Scandinavians, but not as many Lutherans.) These maps suggest that German, and to a lesser extent Scandinavian, ethnicity is intertwined with Lutheranism. Even though Lutheranism has fractured into different denominations that vary along a liberal–conservative continuum, the common ethnic roots of the faith endure.

The primary ethnic groups that populate Lutheran churches— Germans, Swedes, Norwegians, and the like—settled in the United States many years ago, and so the overlap between religion and ethnicity has continued over generations. Catholics, however, are a different story. Or rather, there are two Catholic stories. The first story parallels that of the Lutherans, as some heavily Catholic eth-

Figure 9.3

PEOPLE OF SCANDINAVIAN DESCENT

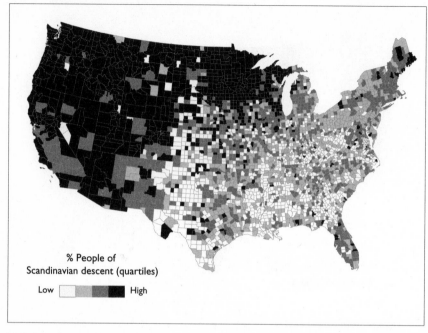

SOURCE: U.S. CENSUS, 2000.

nic groups—Irish, Poles, Italians—first put down roots well over a century ago. In recent years, however, Latinos have arrived in large numbers. As noted above, while not all Latinos are Catholics (many adhere to an evangelical brand of Protestantism), roughly two thirds are.[10] This rise in Latinos constitutes the second Catholic story. (Of course, Latinos have a much longer history in the United States and the American Catholic Church, but only in the last generation have their numbers swelled so rapidly.) Our maps tell both of American Catholicism's stories. Figure 9.4 displays a map of Catholics by county, while Figure 9.5 shows the presence of Italian Americans, the ethnic group that has the strongest statistical connection to Catholicism.[11] Italian Americans show a fair degree of overlap with the Catholic population, although nothing like the overlap of Germans and Lutherans. The greatest overlap between Italians and

Figure 9.4

CATHOLICS

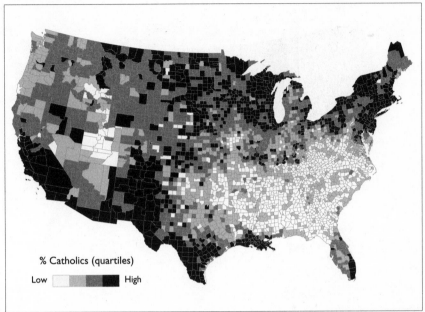

% Catholics (quartiles)

Low ▢ ▨ ▩ ▇ High

SOURCE: ASSOCIATION OF STATISTICIANS OF AMERICAN RELIGIOUS BODIES, 2000.

Catholics occurs in the Northeast, with a little in the Western states (particularly California) as well. To round out our account of Catholics' presence we must add a map of where Latinos are found across the United States. (See Figure 9.6.) Adding the Latino population to the picture fills in the Southwest, where both Catholics and Latinos are concentrated. However, that still leaves the Catholic footprint in the Upper Midwest unaccounted for; that is a function of the Germans, Poles, and other European ethnicities.[12] The fact that the proportion of German Americans overlaps with both Lutherans and Catholics reminds us that a given ethnicity need not be the exclusive province of one faith or another.

While much more could be said about the myriad ethnic groups under the Catholic umbrella, even this cursory look makes clear that Catholicism is home to a diverse collection of ethnic groups, including the expanding population of Latino Americans. We will

Figure 9.5

PEOPLE OF ITALIAN DESCENT

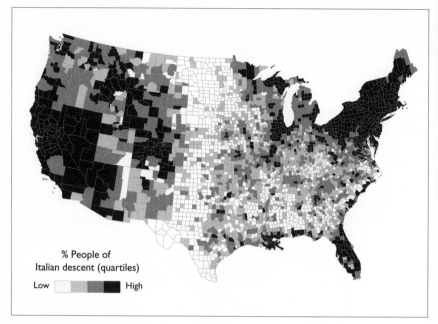

% People of
Italian descent (quartiles)

Low ▢▨▨■ High

SOURCE: U.S. CENSUS, 2000.

Figure 9.6

LATINOS

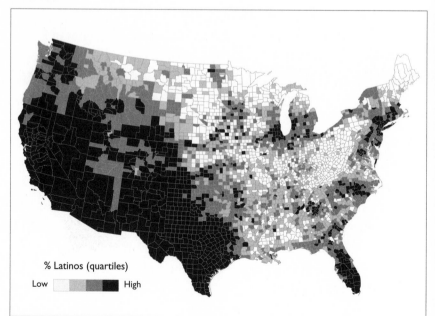

% Latinos (quartiles)

Low ▢▨▨■ High

SOURCE: U.S. CENSUS, 2000.

have more to say about the imprint left by Latinos on the American Catholic Church.

To foreshadow still another theme of the chapter, we note one other interesting overlap, in this case between religion and the *absence* of an ethnic affiliation. We measure the proportion of an ethnic group within a county from the U.S. Census, which asks people to record their ethnic ancestry. Quite a few people choose not to report an ethnicity from beyond America's borders and simply identify their ancestry as "American," or that they are from the United States—essentially, they report no long-standing ethnic heritage. Figure 9.7 maps the proportion of people within a county who reported their ethnic affiliation as American, while Figure 9.8 displays the population within a county that belongs to an evangelical denomination. There is considerable overlap between the two, which is consistent with the fact that, in the 2006 Faith Matters survey, evangelicals generally report a weak ethnic identity. Unlike Lutherans and Catholics,

Figure 9.7

PEOPLE WHO REPORT THEIR ETHNICITY AS "AMERICAN"

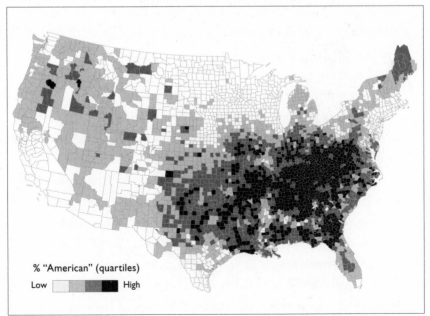

% "American" (quartiles)

Low ▢▨▨■ High

SOURCE: U.S. CENSUS, 2000.

Figure 9.8

EVANGELICALS

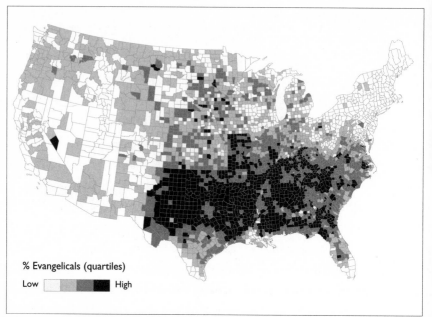

% Evangelicals (quartiles)

Low [   ] High

SOURCE: ASSOCIATION OF STATISTICIANS OF AMERICAN RELIGIOUS BODIES, 2000.

for whom ethnicity and religion have historically been in a symbiotic relationship, ethnicity and evangelicalism are not so closely intertwined.

It is important to note that the geography of demography can only suggest the ways in which ethnicity and religion are related. We must be wary of drawing inferences about individuals from data that describe only groups, which is why we have been careful to speak only of the overlap between ethnic and religious groups across the United States. Maps cannot tell us, for instance, how many Americans of German descent are Lutherans, or the other way around. We can only say that Germans and Lutherans are found in the same places. Yet this still tells us a lot, as we can see how the ethnic character of a community is interwoven with its religious composition.

Stronger evidence of the connection between ethnicity and religion can be seen when we examine data from individuals, rather than counties. As shown in Figure 9.9, people who say that religion

Figure 9.9

ETHNIC AND RELIGIOUS IDENTITY GO TOGETHER

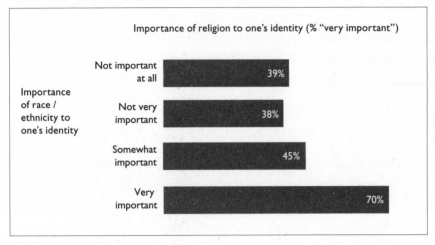

Importance of religion to one's identity (% "very important")

Importance of race / ethnicity to one's identity		
Not important at all	39%
Not very important	38%
Somewhat important	45%
Very important	70%

SOURCE: FAITH MATTERS SURVEY, 2006.

is important to their sense of who they are (i.e., their identity) are also likely to say that ethnicity is an important part of their identity.[13] Likewise, those whose religion does not inform their identity say the same about their race or ethnicity.[14]

The same pattern appears when we divide people by religious tradition. Notably, the nones (people who report no religious affiliation) rank the lowest on both measures of identity. In between fall most other religious traditions, arrayed almost as though in a straight line—the stronger the ethnic identity, the stronger the religious identity. One notable exception, as suggested by the data on counties, is evangelicals. They rank high on the importance of religion, but low on the importance of their ethnicity. Mormons are also off the line. We find it no coincidence that these are both religious traditions that specialize in proselytizing, actively and even aggressively pursuing converts from many different ethnic and even language groups. They base their appeal on religious fervor rather than ancestral ties—on beliefs instead of blood. We might call them post-ethnic religions.

A higher percentage of Black Protestants say that both their ethnicity and their religion are important to their identity than members of any other religious tradition. Black Protestantism is a clear—indeed, the clearest—example of the symbiosis between ethnicity and religion, as underscored by the fact that it is the only religious tradition explicitly defined in racial terms. To understand how race and religion can be fused, therefore, requires a close look at Black Protestantism, or the Black Church.

BLACK PROTESTANTS

Many scholars and pundits speak of *the* Black Church as a singular entity, notwithstanding the many different denominations found within Black Protestantism.[15] In doing so, they are assuming that what unites these denominations—race—supersedes the theological, stylistic, and organizational differences that might divide them.

Whether common practice or not, should Black Protestants be defined as a separate religious tradition? Social scientists have an obligation to ensure that the taxonomies we use reflect reality and do not artificially impose divisions that don't exist. In this case, does combining *Black* with *Protestant* clarify or obscure our understanding of American religion? Are Black Protestants merely "Protestants who happen to be black," or truly a distinctive branch of religion? In the provocative words of Andrew Greeley and Michael Hout, "Is not a black evangelical every bit as much an evangelical as a white evangelical?"[16]

Greeley and Hout make a persuasive case. After all, Black Protestantism has a distinctly evangelical flavor; Black Protestants share common origins with the group we have labeled evangelicals (who are mostly white). No matter the measure of religious behavior or belief, Black and evangelical Protestants rank side by side, although in most cases the Black Protestants are the more devout group. The evangelical–Black Protestant similarities are underscored when we compare them both to mainline Protestants. In doing so we are, in a rough sense, holding Protestantism constant. Whether we look at frequency of church attendance, the importance of religion in one's daily life, or the importance of religion for personal decisions, Black Protestants are, on average, a little more religious than evangelicals, and both groups are a lot more religious than the mainline Protestants (see Figure 9.10). As shown in Figure 9.11, Black Protestants and evangelicals also have similarly high rates of Bible reading, talking about religion, and personal prayer (although evangelicals are 6 percentage points more likely than Black Protestants to say that they pray daily). Black Protestants are especially likely to report saying grace. Eighty-five percent of Black Protestants report that they say grace daily, compared to 58 percent of evangelicals and 38 percent of mainline Protestants. Furthermore, Black Protestants are also more likely than evangelicals or mainline Protestants to be engaged in their congregations beyond attending services, as evi-

Figure 9.10

BLACK PROTESTANTS' LIVES ARE INFUSED WITH RELIGION,
EVEN MORE SO THAN EVANGELICALS

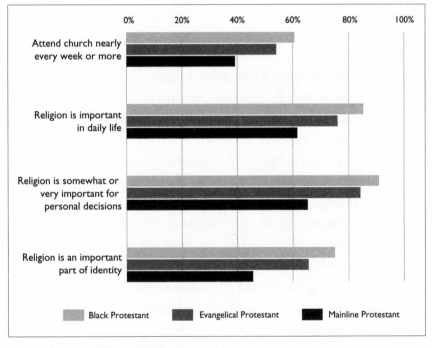

SOURCE: FAITH MATTERS SURVEY, 2006.

Figure 9.11

RELIGION, PARTICULARLY SAYING GRACE, IS A DAILY PART OF MANY
BLACK PROTESTANTS' LIVES

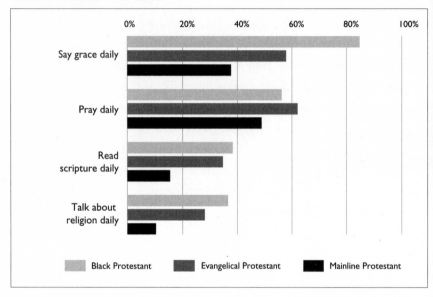

SOURCE: FAITH MATTERS SURVEY, 2006.

denced by their participation in small groups and as church officers
or on church committees. In short, religion infuses the lives of Black
Protestants to an even greater extent than it does evangelicals' lives.

In another parallel with evangelicals, churchgoing among both
groups is most common among those with a college education (see
Figure 9.12). Across the board, Black Protestants have higher church
attendance than evangelicals but in both groups college graduates
attend more frequently than those with less education. (Among
mainline Protestants, church attendance does not vary appreciably
by education level.) Of course, another way to describe that same
pattern is that evangelical and Black Protestant churches are both
less successful in mobilizing Americans of lower socioeconomic status than those who are higher on the socioeconomic ladder.

Among African Americans, in fact, religion has increasingly
become a middle-class affair. Since roughly the mid-1980s, black college graduates have become increasingly likely to attend church. At

Figure 9.12

FOR BLACK PROTESTANTS AND EVANGELICALS, CHURCHGOING IS MORE
COMMON AMONG THE COLLEGE EDUCATED

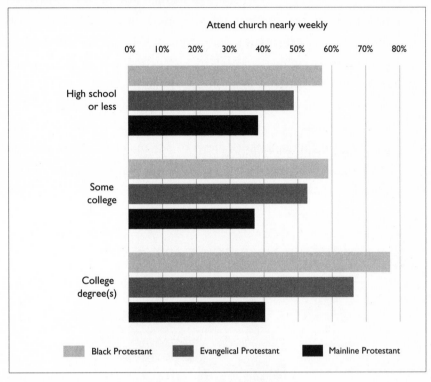

SOURCE: FAITH MATTERS SURVEY, 2006.

the same time, there has also been an increase in the percentage of
African Americans with a college degree[17]—a double boost for the
average level of Black Protestants' church attendance. As a consequence, overall levels of church attendance among African Americans have been rising. This rise has occurred over the same period
that average attendance among whites has fallen slightly, resulting in
a black–white attendance gap.

The relatively high average education level of African American
churchgoers might be expected to dampen the religious orthodoxy
of Black Protestants. After all, in general a higher level of education is associated with less orthodoxy—that is, less support for fundamentalist religious beliefs. Among Black Protestants, however,

fundamentalist beliefs are common. On questions about biblical literalism and whether the world will end soon, Black Protestants are substantially more likely to take a fundamentalist position than even evangelicals, and far more so than mainline Protestants. Black Protestants and evangelicals are about equally likely to endorse biblical creationism—roughly two thirds of each group say that God created humans in their present form in the last ten thousand years, compared to only 37 percent of mainline Protestants. (See Figure 9.13.) When taken together, the beliefs of Black Protestants show them to have the most fundamentalist views of any major religious group in America, and this racial disparity is especially marked among middle-class college graduates.

Figure 9.13

BLACK PROTESTANTS ARE RELIGIOUS TRADITIONALISTS, EVEN MORE SO THAN EVANGELICALS

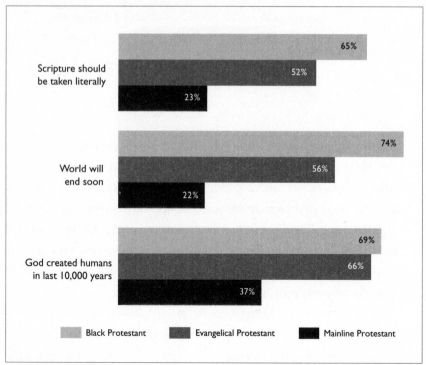

SOURCE: FAITH MATTERS SURVEY, 2006.

Whether we are talking about religious salience, behavior, or beliefs, Black Protestants demonstrate a level of religiosity and traditionalism that either ranks next to or, more typically, exceeds that of evangelicals. By these measures, Black Protestants and evangelicals stand side by side. We might even say that Black Protestants are more evangelical than the evangelicals, which, given that Black Protestantism is historically an evangelical form of religion, makes perfect sense. Indeed, if we knew nothing more than the results reported here, we would conclude that Black Protestants ought not to be treated as a unique religious group.

But we do know more, and what we know underscores why—their similarities with evangelicals notwithstanding—Black Protestants are not simply evangelical Protestants who happen to be black. Although they have a common origin, the two traditions evolved along very different paths.

The Black Church includes a constellation of denominations and independent congregations, some of which broke away from other Protestant denominations and some which were founded *ex nihilo*, as it were. Splits, schisms, upstarts—this is typical of all Protestantism, and Black Protestant churches have been no exception. Unlike divisions among other Protestants, however, those that led to the creation of black churches were primarily about race.

While early evangelicalism had egalitarian impulses, in racial matters these were often suppressed by a reification of the status quo. So while historian Nathan Hatch notes how revolutionary-era Methodists and Baptists "aligned their cause with that of the slave," [18] sociologists Michael Emerson and Christian Smith describe how George Whitefield, the leading revivalist of the pre-revolutionary period, "preached his message of radical equality in Christ, and shared the salvation message with slaves," but was also "a supporter of slavery." As the abolition movement gained momentum, evangelicals themselves split on the subject of slavery. "Although some of the more outspoken abolitionists were evangelical, most evangelicals were not outspoken abolitionists," as Emerson and Smith observe. [19]

Indeed, from the 1840s to 1860s, the question of slavery divided a number of prominent white Protestant denominations into Northern and Southern wings. As a result, the antislavery denominations were located where there were very few blacks. And, at any rate, opposition to slavery was typically not accompanied by a rejection of racial segregation. Consequently, notwithstanding their common evangelical roots, African Americans created their own array of churches that were distinct from the churches attended by white evangelicals.

As institutions created by and for African Americans, black churches have long served as a supporting pillar within African American communities. When Gunnar Myrdal wrote his classic work on blacks in America, *An American Dilemma: The Negro Problem and Modern Democracy*, he noted the unique role played by African Americans' churches:

> The Negro church is a community center *par excellence*. . . . [T]he Negro church means more to the Negro community than the white church to the white community—in its function as a giver of hope, as an emotional cathartic, as a center of community activity, as a source of leadership, and as a provider of respectability.[20]

Thus, while religion infuses the lives of individual African Americans, one misses the essence of Black Protestantism by focusing only on individualized measures of personal religiosity. Black Protestants share with their evangelical cousins an emphasis on individual salvation and piety, but they also have a strong communal element to their religion that more closely resembles the social gospel of mainline Protestantism. That communal dimension often includes the provision of social services by congregations and even extends to political activity. While, as detailed further in Chapter 12, politics is hardly a common activity in America's religious institutions, it is more common in black churches than in the houses of worship in other religious traditions (only Jews come close). Black Protestants rank high on all the measures of church-based political activity we asked about in our Faith Matters surveys. Some other religious traditions are comparatively high on one form of political activity or another, but only Black Protestants are high across the board. They are the most likely to report that their church has voter registration drives or distributes voter guides; they rank alongside Catholics, Jews, and "others" for the frequency of marches organized by their place of worship; and only Jews are more likely (slightly) to report that they hear sermons on social or political issues from the pulpit.

Black Protestants uniquely combine individualistic piety with communal identity, the two ways in which religion shapes political activism.[21] In other religious traditions, we generally see a trade-off between these two. Where there is more politics over the pulpit, the people in the pews are generally less likely to say that religion affects their personal political decisions. Black Protestants, however, stand out as a notable exception. First, they are among the most likely to use religion as a guide when making political decisions— in this respect, they are closer to evangelicals than mainline Protestants. However, they are also among the most likely to say that they participated in "political or social action" with someone from their congregation—which puts them closer to mainline Protestants than evangelicals.[22]

We find it telling that the religious tradition in which politics flows most naturally is also the tradition whose members are the most likely to report that both their religion and their race are important sources of their personal identity. Black churches have long served to reinforce African Americans' racial identity and spur black empowerment. Most famously, the civil rights movement was born and nurtured in black churches.[23]

In earlier periods, the high levels of religiosity observed among African Americans led some observers to describe African Americans' religion as encouraging a focus on the "other world" rather than making changes in this one.[24] That once may have been the case but, if so, the civil rights movement caused a sea change. Certainly, not all black clergy marched with Martin Luther King, not all black churches were involved in the civil rights movement, and not all Black Protestants actively worked for the cause of civil rights. However, the historical record makes clear that instead of passive acceptance rooted in "otherworldliness," many black clergy encouraged their parishioners to participate in the marches, protests, and sit-ins of the civil rights era. In rebutting earlier scholarship purporting to show that religion dampened political involvement for African Americans even during the era of the civil rights movement, political scientist Fredrick Harris provides convincing evidence that "rather than acting as an opiate, religion stimulated many kinds of black activism in the sixties."[25] Many individual black churches provided both the organizational resources to support, and the belief system to sustain, the often dangerous work undertaken by civil rights activists. Churches in black communities also served as the nodes for networks of black activists—venues for raising money, mustering volunteers, and planning strategies. As houses of worship, they were places of refuge for those who suffered indignities and injuries on the front lines of the battles against segregation. In addition, black churches have long been sacred space where racial and religious identities could be mutually reinforcing, providing African Americans with a repertoire of symbols, stories, and songs to console and inspire. African Americans were, and are, invigorated by worshipping with their neighbors, seeking solace in such biblical stories as the Israelites' escape from Egyptian slavery, finding strength in the communal singing of stirring Negro spirituals, and building solidarity as black clergy address the contemporary concerns of the African American community.[26]

Over many generations black churches have developed an extensive religious vocabulary with unique resonance within the African American community. No one has drawn on that symbolic reservoir more effectively than Martin Luther King Jr. His legendary speech at the March on Washington in 1963 ended with the stirring peroration, drawn from a Negro spiritual, "Free at last! Free at last! Thank

God Almighty, we are free at last!" Both blacks and whites were inspired as they heard these words. For most of the whites, it likely would have been for the first time. For many in his African American audience, however, their inspiration sprang from the deep well of familiarity. Many had stood in church, surrounded by fellow African Americans, singing those same hopeful words, which evoke a better day when, as the rest of the song goes, "Me and my Jesus going to meet and talk."

The overlap between religion and politics in black churches underscores an important point about the complex relationship between politics and religion more generally. Like evangelicals, Black Protestants are highly religious and embrace a highly traditional form of religion. Yet they support the Democratic Party and its candidates to a much greater degree than evangelicals support the Republicans. It is conventional political wisdom that African Americans are a reliable Democratic constituency. However, without looking at the numbers one cannot appreciate the deep unpopularity of the Republicans among blacks in general and among Black Protestants in particular. As shown in Figure 9.14, while 47 percent of evangelicals identify as Republicans, only 8 percent of Black Protestants do. Seventy-three percent of evangelicals voted for George W. Bush in 2004; 15 percent of Black Protestants did. In the 2006 congressional elections, 63 percent of evangelicals voted Republican, compared to a paltry 6 percent of Black Protestants—this last level of support is so low as to rival the margin of error. Even closer to the margin of error is the less than 1 percent of Black Protestants who voted for John McCain over Barack Obama in 2008, compared to 69 percent of evangelicals.[27]

Among every major religious group other than Black Protestants, highly traditional religious beliefs generally lead to political conservatism and support for the Republican Party. However, Black Protestants have the highest degree of traditionalism and the highest level of religious activity and yet are the staunchest members of the Democratic coalition. Even though African Americans' support for the Democratic Party completely contradicts the assumption that

Figure 9.14

BLACK PROTESTANTS SHARE FEW POLITICAL VIEWS WITH
EVANGELICAL AND MAINLINE PROTESTANTS

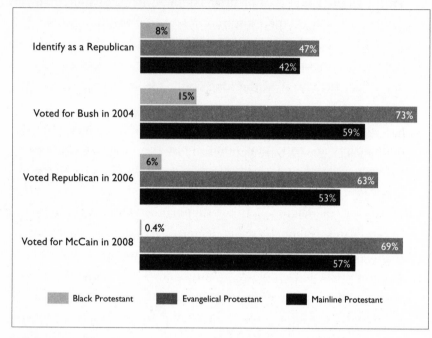

SOURCE: FAITH MATTERS SURVEYS AND NATIONAL ELECTION STUDY, 2008.

religion and conservative politics go hand in hand, it rarely receives
much attention. As Andrew Greeley and Michael Hout rightly note,
the way in which religion and politics come together among African Americans is often conveniently ignored, as "partisans and commentators alike tend to dismiss it as beside the point." [28] Rather than
being beside the point, the overlap of religion and politics among
African Americans *makes* a very important point. The intersections
between faith and politics can, and do, vary across religious traditions. As we will explain further in Chapter 11, those connections
have also varied over the course of American history.

BEYOND BLACK PROTESTANTS

The case of Black Protestants also underscores the primary point of this chapter, namely that religion and ethnicity often reinforce one another. However, given the history of slavery, one might reasonably ask whether Black Protestants are anomalous. Do other minority groups also have a high level of religiosity? The answer is that it depends on the minority group. Asian Americans, for example, have a much lower level of religiosity than whites, blacks, or Latinos. In keeping with our hypothesis that ethnic and racial identity go together, it also turns out Asian Americans have a much lower sense of ethnic identity than blacks or Latinos.[29]

Latinos, however, are a highly religious minority group. While on average they are not as religious as African Americans, they are generally higher in religious intensity than whites. This is true for both Latino Catholics (two thirds of the Latino population) and Latino Protestants (roughly 20 percent of Latinos). Figure 9.15 displays how Latinos compare to whites, or Anglos, within both Catholicism and Protestantism. Among Catholics, Latinos are between 16 and 17 percentage points more likely than Anglos to say that religion is important for personal decisions, that religion is extremely or very important in their lives, and that religion is an important part of their personal identity. Latino Protestants are almost entirely evangelicals,[30] so the most sensible comparison is with white, or Anglo, evangelical Protestants. In Figure 9.15, we see that both Latino and Anglo evangelicals are more likely than their Catholic counterparts to endorse these various ways of measuring the salience of religion in one's life. As high as Anglo evangelicals score on these measures, however, Latino evangelicals score even higher.

African Americans and Latinos are two minority groups that have a high level of religiosity. However, as has been suggested already in this chapter, even with the blurring of ethnic boundaries, there is still a connection between religion and ethnicity among white Americans.

However, the relationship between ethnic identification and reli-

Figure 9.15

LATINO CATHOLICS ARE MORE RELIGIOUS THAN "ANGLO" CATHOLICS

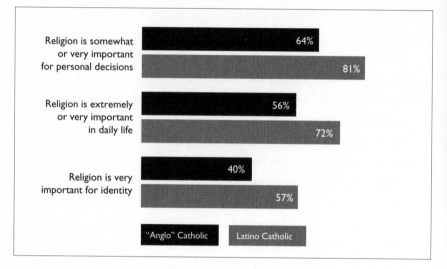

LATINO EVANGELICALS ARE MODESTLY MORE RELIGIOUS THAN ANGLO EVANGELICALS

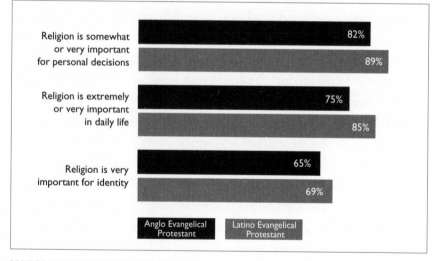

SOURCE: FAITH MATTERS SURVEY, 2006.

giosity among whites is nowhere near as strong as it is among African Americans or Latinos. While ethnicity does not matter as much for the religion of whites as it does for blacks, this hardly means it does not matter at all. Recall that above we noted that strength of ethnic identity corresponds to strength of religious identity (see Figure 9.9). That relationship, however, is not limited to blacks and Latinos. It also applies to non-Latino whites, a group for which we might not necessarily expect race or ethnicity to be highly salient. Similarly, our data suggest that a strong ethnic identity has consequences for the transmission of religious affiliation from one generation to the next, even when we account for myriad other factors that might affect religious attachment. As displayed in Figure 9.16, a stronger ethnic identification means an increased likelihood of having married within one's childhood religion, which in turn is a key predictor of remaining within the same religion. As expected, therefore, those with a strong ethnic identity are also less likely to leave the religion of their parents.[31] Admittedly, these results leave ambiguous the question of which causes which. Does the strength of ethnic identity lead to staying in one's childhood religion, or does staying in the religion of your childhood lead to a stronger sense of ethnic identity? As partial evidence that it is ethnicity which strengthens the connection to your religion (rather than the other way around), we also find that respondents with a stronger ethnic identity are more likely to say it is important that their children marry someone of the family's religion. It is difficult to see how wanting your child to marry someone of the same religion—a hypothetical scenario—could cause a greater sense of ethnic identity. Rather, it seems more plausible that either a stronger ethnic identity leads to a desire that your child marry within the family's faith, or that both ethnic identity and the connection to your religion are themselves caused by something else.

Rather than get bogged down in a debate over whether the relationship between ethnicity and religion only flows one way or both ways, we simply note the deep interweaving of ethnicity and religion over the course of American history (and even longer). As ethnic and religious identities have evolved together, many religions and many ethnicities have developed a symbiotic—and thus mutually reinforcing—relationship.

Figure 9.16

STRONGER ETHNIC IDENTITY MEANS STRONGER BELIEF IN AND
INTER-GENERATIONAL TRANSMISSION OF RELIGION
(whites only, with standard demographic characteristics, as well as religious characteristics, held constant)

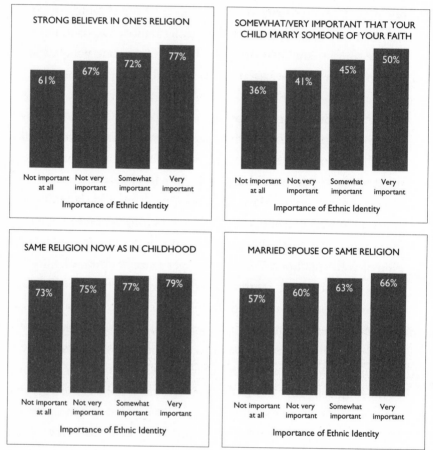

CONGREGATIONAL DIVERSITY

The symbiosis between religion and ethnicity means that, for many Americans, religion pulls together people with a common ethnic background into particular denominations and, within denominations, into particular congregations. But this symbiosis also means that, across denominations and congregations, religion has pushed apart people of different ethnicities. For most Americans, through most of American history, worship has been divided along racial lines. In writing about the ethnic channels of American religion in the 1950s, Will Herberg expressed no concern about the racial divisions that inevitably resulted. Martin Luther King, however, did. He looked at the same America as Herberg and famously lamented that "at 11:00 on Sunday morning when we stand and sing that Christ has no east or west, we stand at the most segregated hour in this nation."[32] As ethnic groups clustered together in their churches—Swedes worshipping with fellow Swedes, Norwegians with Norwegians—they replicated the racial divisions outside the church. There were not many black Swedes, nor many Norwegian members of the African Methodist Episcopal Church.

Four decades after Martin Luther King uttered his lament, does 11:00 on Sunday morning remain the nation's most segregated hour? For the most part, yes, although that has been changing. For example, between 1978 and 1994 the General Social Survey asked a representative sample of Americans about whether they attend church with people of another race (whites were asked about blacks, blacks about whites). Over that period, the overall percentage rose steadily, from 34 percent in 1978 to 48 percent in 1994. The upward trend is observed across all major religious traditions.

When discussing the ethno-racial composition of congregations, we need a measuring stick. What counts as diverse? The indicator from the General Social Survey, for instance, reflects the percentage of Americans who say that *any* people of another race attend their congregation. Respondents did not report on the overall diversity within their place of worship. Sociologist Michael Emerson, a leading expert on religion and race, has proposed that in order for a congregation to be called multiracial, or diverse, "more than 20 percent of congregation must be racially different than the largest racial group."[33] He notes that the 20 percent threshold is not arbitrary, but stems from research into diversity along different dimensions in many different contexts. Twenty percent constitutes a critical mass, as "at this percentage, the proportion is high enough to have its presence felt and filtered through a system or organization." In the Faith Matters surveys, we gave our respondents four possible responses when describing the racial composition of their congregation. They were asked the proportion of their congregation who are "of the same race or ethnicity as you: All or almost all, About three quarters, About a half, About a quarter or less."

We use "about three quarters" as the cutoff for describing a congregation as ethnically or racially diverse. Since we asked about the proportion of co-congregants who are of the *same* race or ethnicity, this threshold means that we define a diverse congregation as one in which roughly 25 percent of the members are a different race than the respondent. Lest you be concerned that our 25 percent cutoff differs substantially from Emerson's threshold of 20 percent, we note that he finds that most people "tend to overestimate the diversity in their congregation, usually by rounding to the next highest 5 percent."[34] In rough terms, a 25 percent level of diversity is probably closer to 20 percent.[35]

Before discussing our results in detail, we pause to acknowledge the imperfection of how we measure congregational diversity. It would be far more accurate to send observers to the congregations attended by our respondents to independently assess the level of diversity—far more accurate, but very expensive and thus impractical. We instead rely on the respondents to the 2006 Faith Matters survey to report on the degree of diversity within their congregations. This presents some ambiguities. For example, we have to rely on whatever respondents consider their own race or ethnicity to be—do they consider themselves to be white? Swedish? Nor were respondents asked to indicate the specific mix of ethnicities and races within their congregation. Therefore, we do not know whether a diverse congregation has just two predominant groups, or a mixture of many groups. Furthermore, when interpreting these numbers, we should keep in mind that members of majority groups have a tendency to overestimate the proportion of minorities in their surroundings (a form of misperception that presumably applies to churches), therefore inflating the degree of diversity reported by congregants.[36]

Fortunately, we can cross-check our estimates of congregational diversity with the National Congregations Study (NCS), a nationally representative study of congregations. Unlike the Faith Matters surveys, the National Congregations Study relies on clergy to report on the characteristics of their congregation, including its racial composition. Comparisons between Faith Matters and NCS cannot be made precisely, as the NCS asked about four racial groups in seriatim: What percentage of your congregation is white? Black? Latino? Asian? Recall that Faith Matters asked respondents the proportion of their congregation who share their race or ethnicity. Likewise, the NCS is a study of congregations, not individual churchgoers, and the interviews were with clergy, not laypeople. Nonetheless, the two studies are similar enough to indicate whether the Faith Matters results are way off the mark. It turns out that our numbers come very close to the NCS, giving us confidence that the results for Faith Matters are in the ballpark. According to our survey, 84 percent of Americans attend a congregation that is "about three quarters" or "all/almost all" of the same race or ethnicity. The 1998 NCS indicates that 87 percent of congregations have three quarters or more of the same race.[37] By the slightly stricter standard of the 80 percent cutoff, Emerson reports that in both the 1998 and 2007 iterations of the NCS, roughly 93 percent of all congregations are not racially diverse.

Our measure of congregational diversity confirms that most Americans attend churches right out of Martin Luther King's America, in which ethno-racial separation is the norm. However, while most Americans attend a racially homogeneous congregation, not all do. Across religious traditions, there are important differences in congregational diversity. As shown in Figure 9.17, no religious tradition leaps off the page as an ethnic or racial melting pot, but the degree of ethno-racial diversity nonetheless varies. Note that members of "other faiths" have some of the most diverse congregations

Figure 9.17

MOST AMERICANS DO NOT ATTEND A RACIALLY DIVERSE CONGREGATION, BUT DIVERSITY VARIES BY RELIGIOUS TRADITION

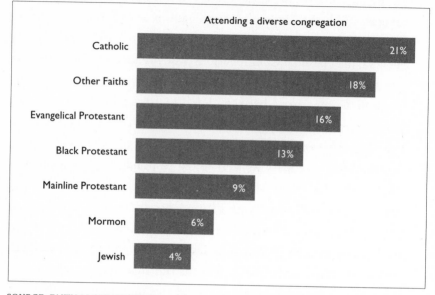

SOURCE: FAITH MATTERS SURVEY, 2006.

in America (second only to Catholics, discussed below). Recall that this category includes a grab-bag of different religious groups, each of which is too small to be analyzed on its own. These include (but are not limited to) Muslim mosques, as well as Buddhist, Sikh, and Hindu temples. Mosques, in particular, are often characterized by their ethnic diversity.[38] This is an interesting finding, suggesting that many adherents to religious traditions that in the United States have a relatively small presence worship with people of different ethnic and racial backgrounds. How much multiethnic worship affects the fusion of ethnicity and religion is a subject worthy of further study, but beyond our scope here.

Jews have the least racially or ethnically diverse congregations. Mormon and mainline Protestant congregations also score on the low end of diversity. Interestingly, these three groups have congregations that are even less diverse than Black Protestants, the religious tradition explicitly defined by race. Seeing that Black Protestants do not rank as the least diverse reminds us that race and religion are not inseparable. Thirteen percent of "blacks who are Protestants" attend racially diverse congregations, which almost certainly do not fit the mold of a black church per se.[39] The high level of racial homogeneity among Mormons comes as no surprise, as the 2006 Faith Matters survey finds that 86 percent of Mormons report that they are white. While the Mormon church is highly evangelistic, working to win converts worldwide, the demographic composition of the church's membership within the United States remains predominantly white. The proportion of Jews who are white is even higher: 97 percent.

Like Jews, mainline Protestants are overwhelmingly white (also 97 percent). This remarkably high level of racial homogeneity results from the patterns we observed earlier (in Chapter 5) regarding religious retention, defection, and conversion. Mainline Protestantism has experienced a slow but steady exodus of members and very few converts. Consequently, the current demographics of mainline Protestant churches are racially homogeneous, reflecting mainline Protestantism in its postwar heyday. As the unofficial establishment of the time, mainline Protestantism was predominantly white then, and with few conversions remains predominantly white now. It is as though the racial divisions described by Martin Luther King have been preserved in amber.

Note, however, that a congregation which appears homogeneous to today's eyes might actually have been considered diverse in times past. Take Mount Olivet, the Swedish Lutheran church that has shed nearly all vestiges, save its architecture, of its Swedish roots. One explanation for the church's size has been its decades-long effort to attract Lutherans of all ethnic backgrounds. A pamphlet produced by the church, in fact, takes pains to describe how it has been diverse from the beginning, "Although Mount Olivet was strongly influenced throughout its history by Swedish immigrants, two of the first four families who were leaders in starting the congregations were full-blooded Norwegians." While today it probably seems comical to describe the mingling of Swedes and Norwegians as diversity, this response only shows how the boundaries defining racial and ethnic groups are a product of our time, as meanings shift over time. As one of Mount Olivet's pastors indicated to us in an interview, there was once "warring between Swedes and Norwegians." He further noted that his great-grandparents met opprobrium for their "mixed marriage"—a Norwegian and a Swede.

Today we think it is safe to say that an inter-Nordic marriage would raise no eyebrows at Mount Olivet or anywhere else in America. Just as the lines dividing white ethnic groups have dissolved in American society more broadly, they have almost entirely dissolved within mainline Protestantism as well.

WHO ATTENDS DIVERSE CONGREGATIONS?

In comparing the level of congregational diversity across religious traditions, can we be sure that there are not factors above and beyond being a mainline Protestant or an evangelical, or any other religious tradition, that explain the degree of ethno-racial heterogeneity? Perhaps the differences we observe are not because of the religious tradition per se, but are owing to other characteristics of the people who belong to each of those traditions. To sort this all out, we have tested the impact of numerous characteristics describing individual churchgoers as possible predictors of attending a diverse congregation, allowing us to compare their relative impact on congregational diversity. Imagine that members of one religious tradition are more likely to attend diverse congregations because they are more likely to live in urban areas, and urban areas are themselves more diverse. If so, it would be the congregation's location, not its religious tradition, that explained its degree of diversity. By testing the impact of all the relevant factors simultaneously, we can be sure that one is not standing in for another; thus we untangle the many influences on congregational diversity.

The various predictors included in our model can be divided into characteristics of the individual, the community, and the congregation.

- Individual-level characteristics include age; gender; race-ethnicity; and education level. Of these, women, the young, and Hispanics are more likely to attend diverse congregations—education level has no relationship to the diversity of one's congregation. As shown in Figure 9.18, where we compare how gender, age, and Latino ethnicity compare as predictors of congregational diversity, the impact of each can be described as modest at best. Women are 4 percentage points more likely than men to attend a diverse congregation, twenty-year-olds are 5 percentage points more likely to do so than seventy-year-olds[40] and Latinos are 10 percentage points more likely than whites.

- Community-level factors include the region of the country in which a person lives; location in an urban, suburban, or rural area; and the racial heterogeneity of one's county. Congregations in the Western states are more diverse than those in the Northeast, South, and Midwest (Westerners are 8 points more likely to attend a diverse congregation than residents of other regions). Simply living in an urban environment does not predict attending a diverse congregation. Rather, what matters is the racial heterogeneity of one's county—moving from the least (1st percentile) to the most (99th percentile) diverse county corresponds to an 11 percentage point increase in the likelihood of attending a diverse congregation.[41]

- Congregation-level factors include the individual religious tradition and the size of the congregation. Congregation size turns out to be the most important predictor of attending a diverse congregation.[42] People attending the largest congregations (99th percentile) are 15 percentage points more likely to report worshipping with a diverse group of co-parishioners than those who attend the smallest congregations (1st percentile).

Even when simultaneously accounting for these many factors that correlate with congregational diversity, some religious traditions still come out as higher or lower on congregational diversity. As in Figure 9.18, we again see that a modestly, but significantly (in statisti-

Figure 9.18

WHAT PREDICTS ATTENDING A DIVERSE CONGREGATION?

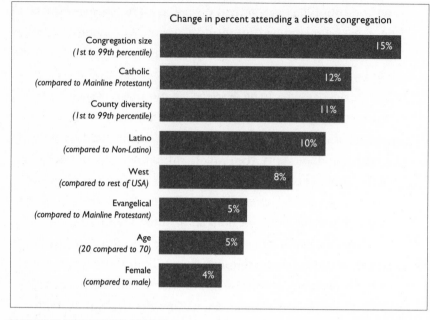

Change in percent attending a diverse congregation

Congregation size *(1st to 99th percentile)*	15%
Catholic *(compared to Mainline Protestant)*	12%
County diversity *(1st to 99th percentile)*	11%
Latino *(compared to Non-Latino)*	10%
West *(compared to rest of USA)*	8%
Evangelical *(compared to Mainline Protestant)*	5%
Age *(20 compared to 70)*	5%
Female *(compared to male)*	4%

SOURCE: FAITH MATTERS SURVEY, 2006.

cal terms), higher percentage of Catholics and evangelicals attend diverse congregations.[43]

In other words, even when we account for differences across individuals and the communities in which they live, we still find that some religious traditions are distinctively diverse. This suggests that, generally, traditions differ in how they have facilitated (or inhibited) congregational diversity in this period of increasing national diversity. For our purposes, two important examples are also America's two largest religious traditions: Catholics and evangelicals.[44]

CATHOLICS

If all we knew about Catholics was their retention rate, we would be surprised to find that they have the highest level of ethno-racial diversity within their congregations.

As discussed in Chapter 5, Catholics' religious retention rate is low, which means that, like mainline Protestants, they are hemorrhaging members. The dropouts are not replaced with new converts, as the flow out is far greater than the flow in. The comparatively low rate of retention among Catholics reflects the dissolving of Catholicism's ethnic roots. For those groups sometimes labeled white ethnics, like Poles and Italians, the ethnic dimension of the Catholic experience has diminished in significance. Many American cities were once neatly divided into Catholic parishes defined along ethnic lines, while today parishes are more often distinguished by their style of worship and/or their program offerings.[45]

The reason Catholics have more diverse congregations than mainline Protestants, or anyone else for that matter, is no secret. American Catholicism has experienced an influx of Latinos who are transforming the church in many ways, not the least of which is the mingling of Anglos and Latinos within parishes.[46]

In generations past, to be Italian (or Polish, Hungarian, Irish, and so on) was to be Catholic—an example of what it means to say that religion and ethnicity are mutually reinforcing. As these groups immigrated to America, religion flowed naturally out of their ethnic heritage, while ethnicity buttressed their religion. Catholic parishes became the way station for these huddled masses, offering them both spiritual and material support.[47] The sheer number of immigrant Catholics in the early twentieth century is impressive by any standard. One indicator of ethnic heterogeneity within Catholicism is the use of a language other than English by members of a parish, which permits us to see where non-English speakers were concentrated. According to data collected by the U.S. Census Bureau, in 1906 there were 4,711 Catholic parishes, with roughly 6.3 million members, who reported using a language other than English.[48] By 1916 that had grown to 6,076 parishes, with 7.6 million members. In percentage terms, that represented a rise in parishes using a language other than English from 54 percent of total Catholic parishes to 63 percent a decade later. In terms of members, this means that by 1916, 57 percent of all Catholics attended a parish that did not use English exclusively (compared to 43 percent in 1906).

The local parish, rooted in the neighborhood, was the primary institution for these immigrants as they adjusted to life in America. In the words of historian Joseph Casino:

> The parish, with all of its functions, did ease the process of assimilation for many immigrants, provided very practical services to the poor, the struggling, and the uneducated, and certainly gave meaning to the ordinary rites of passage through religious and community support.[49]

In some cases, the definition of parishes by ethnicity was de jure (aka "nationality parishes") while in other cases the ethnic fragmentation was de facto, based on geography, as ethnicity and neighborhood boundaries were coterminous anyway.[50] Whether de facto or de jure, the objective was to provide a linguistically and culturally comfortable niche in which members of the different ethnic groups could experience their religion, and reinforce their ethnicity. That is, these parishes were all meant to provide variations on the common theme of Catholicism, each in a different ethnic key. A symposium from 1923 on Catholics and immigration reflects that aspirational universality, using the language of the day:

> Throughout the ages the Church has displayed a remarkable ability in assimilating the most divergent races, in bringing them under the same governing head, the same rules of belief and conduct. In America today, she is but repeating the same experiment.[51]

In other words, the Catholic Church was trying to act as an agent of assimilation, although that process was not nearly as smooth nor as complete as this quotation suggests. The objective is noteworthy nonetheless.

Not only were there tensions integrating different ethnic groups into Catholicism, tension also resulted from integrating these predominantly Catholic immigrant groups into a largely Protestant

American society. Catholics' growing presence often engendered hostility among the Protestant majority, giving them further reason to band together and reinforce their ethnic traditions. But as these European ethnic groups assimilated, tensions with Protestants subsided and, as either a cause or consequence, the ties between their faith and their ethnicity began to loosen.

Today, we again are experiencing a period of high immigration, which again has triggered hostility toward the newcomers. Again that ethnic group—Latinos—is predominantly Catholic. And once more the church has become a refuge for these immigrants.

If Latinos were only a small contingent within the American Catholic community, these historical parallels would be only an interesting sociological observation, with little impact on the overall state of Catholicism in the United States. In reality, by dint of their sheer numbers, Latinos are reshaping the American Catholic Church, with every indication that their impact will only increase in years to come.

An appreciation of the Latino factor within American Catholicism begins with simple arithmetic. The relatively low retention rate of Catholics, combined with few conversions, would have to mean an inexorable decline in their share of the population—paralleling the decline of mainline Protestantism. Over the last three decades, though, the Catholic share of the U.S. population has held steady at roughly 25 percent, remaining the single largest religious denomination in the country. Such stasis in the aggregate is possible only through the influx of Catholics from another source—immigration, largely from predominantly Catholic nations in Latin America. While Latinos for centuries have been an important group within the American Catholic mosaic, in recent years they have comprised a larger and larger share of the American, and thus the Catholic, population. Without the inflow of Latinos to shore up the number of Catholics in the United States, the American Catholic population would have experienced a catastrophic collapse. According to the 2006 Faith Matters survey, 35 percent of all American Catholics today report Latino ethnicity.

The growing presence of Latinos within the Catholic Church is made clearest with a comparison of generational differences in the demographic composition of the Catholic population, as shown in Figure 9.19. Latinos comprise roughly 15 percent of Catholics age fifty and above. That percentage increases to 34 percent for those ages thirty-five to forty-nine (roughly the overall average), and then rises to 58 percent among Catholics under thirty-five. In other words, among young Catholics in today's America, six out of ten are Latinos.

Even six out of ten understates the Latino share of the young Catholic population if we consider who is actually sitting in Mass. Among older Catholics whites are more likely than Latinos to attend church weekly, but for younger Catholics that trend is reversed. Among the youngest age group of Catholics (under thirty-five), and thus the future of American Catholicism, Latinos are far more prevalent than Anglos. Nearly seven in ten (67 percent) of young Catholics who attend church regularly are Latinos.[52]

Further evidence for the growing Latino presence within the Catholic Church derives from the simple fact that, as described in Chapter 5, Latino Catholics are far more likely to stay in the faith

Figure 9.19

A MAJORITY OF YOUNG CATHOLICS ARE LATINO

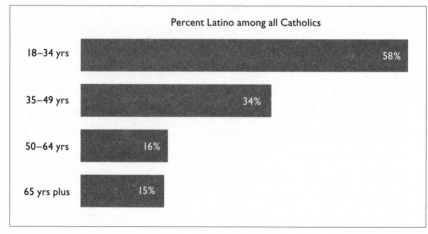

SOURCE: FAITH MATTERS SURVEY, 2006.

(or, at least, continue identifying as Catholic) than "Anglo" Catholics. Remembering our earlier observation that a strong ethnic identity enhances religious retention, this is as we expect, since Latinos report a strong ethnic identity. While the overall retention rate of Catholics is 63 percent, among Catholics there is a big gap between Anglos and Latinos: 57 percent vs. 78 percent, respectively. Should that difference in religious dropouts persist, the next generation of Catholics will have a still greater proportion of Latinos. In short, the future of the U.S. Catholic Church is largely a Latino future, because just as white ethnic Catholics have rushed out one door of the Church, they have been replaced by new Latinos rushing in the other door.

The increasing Latino presence within American Catholicism matters not only quantitatively, but qualitatively as well. Latinos differ from "Anglo" Catholics in a variety of ways, including both their behavior and their beliefs. As we saw above in Figure 9.15, in both Protestantism and Catholicism, Latinos are more religious than Anglos.

The differences between "Anglo" and Latino Catholics are especially stark when we turn to religious beliefs that are specific to Catholicism, rather than these more general measures of personal religiosity. Figure 9.20 shows us that as a group Latino Catholics consistently adopt a more orthodox perspective than their "Anglo" co-religionists, although neither group could be characterized as hewing closely to the official teachings of the Catholic Church. In fact, the low percentage of Catholics who endorse orthodox Catholic doctrine is striking.

More Latino than "Anglo" Catholics say that they have confidence in the leadership of the Catholic Church. Similarly, Latinos are more likely to hold the opinion that to be a good Catholic, one must agree with the Pope on, as the 2006 Faith Matters survey put it, "issues like birth control, abortion, or divorce." Given their greater support for the church hierarchy and their willingness to endorse church teachings, we should therefore not be surprised Latinos are also more likely to agree with the church's policy that only men

Figure 9.20

LATINO CATHOLICS HAVE MORE ORTHODOX BELIEFS THAN
"ANGLO" CATHOLICS

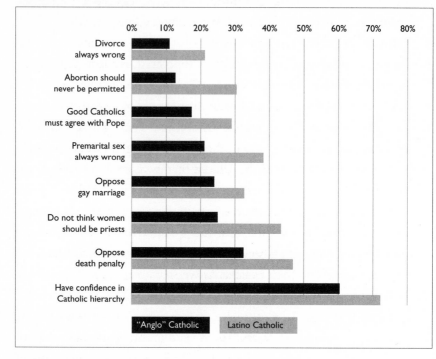

SOURCE: FAITH MATTERS SURVEY, 2006.

should be priests (though less than half of Latino Catholics hold this view). Likewise, when compared to "Anglos," more Latino Catholics say that divorce, abortion, and gay marriage are wrong. As a reminder, however, that Catholic orthodoxy does not always align with the left–right political spectrum, Latino Catholics are also more likely to oppose the death penalty—in accord with Catholic teachings, but counter to the political conservatism otherwise reflected in questions about issues pertaining to sex and the family.

In highlighting these differences between "Anglo" and Latino Catholics, it is tempting to conclude that Latinos are "better" Catholics, if only because more of them agree with official church teachings. Instead, it is more accurate to recognize that Anglos and Latinos experience their Catholicism differently. On still other measures, Anglos come out ahead of Latinos. Anglos are far more likely to report that they are officially a member of their parish, for example. And they are also more likely to report having abstained from "food, drink, or tobacco" for religious reasons, which in the Catholic context largely means the observance of Lent. There are elements of the Latino experience that explain these differences, but the differences remain nonetheless. For example, in our study of Catholic parishes in the Chicago area, priests told us that many Latinos are reluctant to register as members of a parish owing to concerns about immigration officials obtaining the records—even if they are legally within the United States, many have friends and family who are undocumented. We have also been told an instructive anecdote about Latinos and Lent by a colleague who is a Catholic priest. Raised in Chicago, years ago he spent time in Chile. While there as a young priest, he remembers teaching Chilean Catholics that they should abstain from eating meat during Lent. They would look at him quizzically and say, "Father, where the heck would we get meat?" While most Latinos in the United States are not destitute like those Chileans of years past, the story suggests that religious practices—or, in this case, the absence of a practice—evolve within a given cultural (or even economic) context. If generations of Latinos outside the United States did not observe Lent by abstaining from eating meat, we can understand why Latinos inside the United States may not either.

Latino and "Anglo" Catholics also differ in ways beyond their practice of Catholicism. We have already noted that Latinos and Anglos differ on abortion and same-sex marriage, with Latino Catholics more likely to endorse the position of the church, and thus aligning with the conservative side of the political spectrum. However, Latino Catholics are more likely to take liberal positions on economic issues. While 61 percent of "Anglo" Catholics say that the government should reduce income differences between rich and poor, 86 percent of Latino Catholics say the same. Similarly, 40 percent of "Anglo" Catholics believe the government should spend more to aid the poor, a position held by 87 percent of Latino Catholics. If these differences in opinion persist, then we would expect that American Catholic opinion will shift leftward on attitudes toward social welfare.

In short, whether it is their endorsement of traditional Catholic beliefs, their distinctive practices, or their differing political opinions, Latinos leave their stamp on American Catholicism. Not unlike, we suggest, the stamp left by other ethnic groups—the Irish, the Poles, the Italians.

For all that we have emphasized Latinos' distinctiveness within the American Catholic Church, it is fair to ask whether this means that Latino Catholics are analogous to Black Protestants and thus distinctive enough to constitute a separate religious tradition. In a word, no. Black and white evangelicals consciously went their separate ways in the 1800s, while Latino and "Anglo" (and other) Catholics have remained united within a single tradition. Indeed, as we saw in Chapter 7, they are often found within the same parish.

As we look forward to the future of American Catholicism, sheer demography indicates that the church will only see an increase in the Latino share of the Catholic population. Even if immigration were to end tomorrow, the higher retention rate—not to mention birth rate—among Latino Catholics would ensure that they become a larger slice of the Catholic pie. But with immigration from heavily Catholic nations continuing apace, the Latinoization of the American Catholic Church will only be accelerated. It remains an open question whether Latinos will change the American church, or whether the American church—or, simply, living in the United States—will change Latinos. The history of the Catholic Church having served as a refuge and gateway for immigrants suggests (but does not guarantee) a capacity for accommodating the growing number of Latinos within its fold.

While we may not know what the future holds for the increasing Latinoization of the American Catholic Church, we can speak to one implication of its growing ethnic heterogeneity here and now. Recall that Catholics report a relatively—and, we stress, relative is the operative word—high degree of diversity within their congregations. With the recognition of the large and growing presence of Latinos within the Catholic population, one reason for this diversity becomes clear. Although Catholics include nearly every racial and ethnic group, ethnic heterogeneity within Catholic parishes owes largely to the mix of whites and Latinos, of the sort we witnessed at St. Frances of Rome in Cicero.

In noting both the ethnic history of Catholics and the congregational diversity reported in the present, we do not mean to imply that Catholic parishes are a multiethnic utopia. In many cases, in fact, Anglos and Latinos do not belong to the same parishes or, if they do, they attend separate English and Spanish services, as at St. Frances. Evidence that Latinos are often separated from Anglos can be seen when we compare the reported congregational diversity of "Anglo" vs. Latino Catholics. Whites are more likely to report that they worship with a diverse group than are Latinos, suggesting that there are many parishes entirely composed of Latinos, as at San Pio.

Even if the mixing of whites and Latinos is uneven across parishes, the average level of ethno-racial diversity within Catholic congregations is still notable. There are many reasons that members of different racial groups do not often interact with one another, whether at church or in other social settings. Of course, outright racism is one. Overt racial hostility aside, though, people also have a more benign tendency toward associating with people who are like themselves—whether by conscious choice or owing to other choices (such as where they work or go to school) that produce racially uniform social networks. Birds of a feather flock together. Add to that the relatively high degree of racial segregation in housing—birds of different feathers often do not nest together—and we can further see why we should expect congregations to be racially homogeneous.

However, one feature of Catholicism can be a potentially countervailing force, bringing birds of different feathers into a single flock. Unlike Protestants, who generally choose the congregation they attend, Catholics are, at least ostensibly, assigned to a parish based on geographic location. While this policy is generally no longer enforced strictly, geographic assignment remains the norm, and means that church shopping among Catholics is less common than among Protestants.[53] As a consequence, when parish boundaries encompass both Anglos and Latinos, that situation provides the opportunity to bring the two groups together in worship, congregational activities, and perhaps even to form friendships as well.

Geographic assignment to parishes does not ensure racial mixing within Catholic congregations. Parish boundaries themselves may be drawn to reinforce ethno-racial separation, rather than ameliorate it. In the past, parish boundaries have often served to separate Catholics of different ethnicities and races—Poles and Italians, blacks and whites. Similarly, today parish boundaries also have the potential to facilitate more, or less, mixing of Anglos and Latinos.

Mixing, however, does not automatically lead to interracial social relationships. As suggested by our vignettes of Chicago parishes, the blend of whites and Latinos within a parish is typically awkward and often tense—differences in race overlap with differences in language, culture, and class, which all present their own complications. Nevertheless, many Catholic parishes are in the vanguard of finding ways to solve the challenges presented by racial diversity. All across the United States, Catholics like Fr. Bartosic of St. Frances of Rome parish are working hard to build bridges between whites and Latinos, albeit with varying success (see Chapter 7). Given the rising share of Latinos within the American Catholic population, more and more parishes will undoubtedly be engaged in this same effort—either by choice or necessity.

Over the long haul, it remains to be seen whether Catholic parishes will continue to be sites of Anglo-Latino mingling. We are likely in the second act of a three-act play. In the first act, there were relatively few Latinos in the American Catholic Church, and little parish-level mingling between Anglos and Latinos. Now, in the second act, the number of Latinos is expanding; Anglo-Latino mixing is on the increase. Will the third act see the increasing separation of Anglos and Latinos, a real possibility given the frequency of congregation shopping and switching? Whether that separation occurs or not, the American Catholic Church is on its way to becoming a majority-minority organization.

What about Latinos within evangelicalism? Should we expect a similar demographic transformation within the evangelical community? Currently, Latinos' share of the evangelical population is considerably smaller than within Catholicism. For example, roughly 10 percent of all evangelicals are Latino. Among evangelicals under thirty-five though, the proportion of Latinos is nearly twice that: 19 percent. But that still pales in comparison to Latinos' majority share of the young Catholic population. We expect to see Latinos grow as a proportion of the evangelical population, but not to predominate within evangelicalism as they likely will within Catholicism. In addition, the completely free choice of congregations within Protestantism will likely limit the amount of interethnic mixing at the congregational level.

MEGACHURCHES

In Figure 9.18, we saw that evangelicals report attending diverse congregations. In addition we also saw that arguably the biggest predictor of a racially diverse congregation is its size. Digging deeper, we find that size and evangelicalism work together to predict congregational diversity. Diversity appears to spike only when congregational size numbers in the thousands.

The racial diversity within evangelical megachurches is a new phenomenon of roughly the last decade or so. Comparing the 1998 and 2007 National Congregational Studies, sociologist Michael Emerson reports "dramatic growth" in the diversity of large, evangelical congregations. In just under a decade, the percentage of such congregations classified as ethno-racially diverse grew from 6 percent to 25 percent. He credits the increase to an effort by megachurch pastors to diversify their congregations, and even describes the new emphasis on diversity as a social movement. According to Emerson, congregational diversity is promoted through changes both symbolic (e.g., minority pastors) and pragmatic (e.g., recruitment methods). "Together, these changes are used to help racial and ethnic diversification, and then to manage the challenges of that internal diversification."[54] On the other hand, sociologist Mark Chaves points out that the growth in congregational diversity has come primarily from the least diverse congregations becoming moderately less white, rather than an upswing in deeply integrated congregations.[55]

We have witnessed the diversity within evangelical megachurches. While not every megachurch we visited was racially mixed (Saddleback's congregation, for instance, is predominantly white), many were. In Minneapolis, worshippers at the Living Word megachurch comprise a multiracial mix, with a visual scan suggesting that 15–20 percent of the worshippers are nonwhite. An even more striking example is Lakewood Church in Houston, the largest church in America. Housed in a former basketball arena, Lakewood is pastored by Joel Osteen, bestselling author and a nearly ubiquitous presence on Christian television. To many non-evangelicals, Osteen undoubtedly "looks the part" of the stereotypical white evangelical pastor. Yet the worshippers who assemble weekly at his Lakewood Church do not "look the part" of how evangelical congregations are stereotypically portrayed in the mainstream media. From our personal observation, more than half of the thousands thronging Lakewood are people of color. Furthermore, this multiethnic mix is not confined to the large worship services. We found people of different races mingling in Bible study groups, classes for married couples, and at Turbo Night—an evening designed to recruit people to join the various small groups hosted by the church.

INTERRACIAL FRIENDSHIP[56]

While sitting next to someone of a different race during worship is surely a meaningful experience, such fleeting interracial contact pales in comparison to genuine friendships with people of different races. Does attending a diverse congregation lead to more sustained social relationships between people of different races? Our 2006

Faith Matters survey sheds some light on that question. In addition to asking people about the racial composition of their congregation, we also asked them about their close friends. Are any of their close friends white? Latino? Asian? Black? Because we know the race of the person answering the question, we can create an index of inter-racial friendships—a single measure that records whether someone has at least one friend of another race (57 percent of Americans say that they do).

As the reader can see in Figure 9.21, we find a strong correlation between attending a racially diverse congregation and having at least one friend of another race. This holds even when we account for our standard bundle of demographic factors that might plausibly be related to the racial composition of one's congregation or to one's friendship network, or both—including the racial diversity of

Figure 9.21

CONGREGATIONAL RACIAL DIVERSITY CORRELATES WITH
RACIAL DIVERSITY AMONG FRIENDS
(with standard demographic characteristics, as well as geographic characteristics,
held constant)

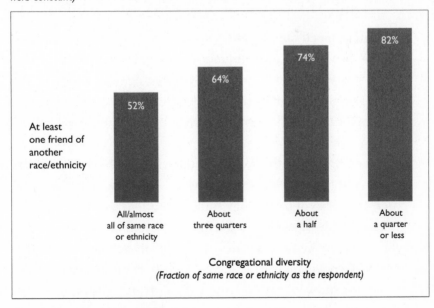

the community in which one lives and the sheer number of friends one has.[57]

We do not know whether the respondent's friend(s) also attend the same church, so we cannot be sure that interracial friendships stem from attending a diverse congregation. Yet even if we did know that the friendships were made at church, we still would not be able to infer that diverse congregations foster interracial friendships. It could very well be that some people seek out diversity, both at church and among their friends. Or perhaps having interracial friendships leads one to attend a diverse congregation. Surveys like Faith Matters can reveal only a correlation between congregational composition and friendship networks, not causation.

But correlations can still be informative. Even if diverse congregations don't cause diverse friendships but instead both are driven by the same desire for diversity—and, at this point, we cannot say one way or another—it is still important to know that the two go together.

HOW WHITES HAVE RESPONDED TO DIVERSITY

Having examined how religious institutions have adapted to diversity, we turn now to the question of how individuals—specifically, whites—have responded to diversity in the decades following the changes brought about by the civil rights era of the 1960s. Does religion fan the flames of racism? Or does religion inhibit racial intolerance?

It is common to hear the charge that among whites religion and racism go together. For example, a recent article has concluded that, based on a series of psychology studies from 1964 to 2008, "only religious agnostics [are] racially tolerant."[58] Given the tiny proportion of agnostics in the United States, this would mean that a preponderance of the population is racist. Such a claim compels a close look.

The backdrop for any discussion of trends in racial attitudes must be that over the last forty years America has undergone a dramatic transformation in opinions on race. According to the General Social Survey, since the early 1970s white Americans have become more racially tolerant on a host of matters. In 1973, for example, nearly two in every five white Americans (38 percent) said that they would favor a law forbidding a marriage between someone who is black and someone who is white. By 2002, that percentage had fallen to 11 percent. In 1973, only one third (34 percent) of whites said they favored outlawing discrimination in home sales (i.e., whites refusing to sell to blacks). By 2008, over two thirds (69 percent) of whites favored such an antidiscrimination law. Nor are such changes in racial attitudes limited to questions of public policy; they are also reflected in whites' attitudes toward African Americans. In 1977, one quarter of white Americans said that the reason that African Americans have "worse jobs, income, and housing than white people" is that they have "less in-born ability to learn." That percentage had fallen to 9 percent by 2008.[59] Similarly, white Americans have become less likely to agree that whites should be allowed to segregate themselves, less likely to say that "blacks should not push themselves where they are not wanted," and less likely to say that blacks do not have the willpower to rise out of poverty. And, lest one think that such survey questions have no real-world grounding, there has also been a decline in the proportion of Americans who say they would not vote for a black presidential candidate—a trend validated with the election of Barack Obama in 2008.

If racism is diminishing overall, however, that would not necessarily mean that it is falling equally among Americans at all levels of religiosity. The claim that religiosity fosters racism would lead us to expect that religious whites would be slower to adapt to a diverse America. In fact, however, Americans who are more religious or less religious displayed precisely the same liberalizing in racial attitudes over the four decades.

But, you may ask, even with a common downward trend, are religious Americans more likely to express racist views than their less religious counterparts? No. To the contrary, when we account for our standard bundle of demographic control variables—i.e., the other factors that might explain differences in racial attitudes—we find that, among whites, religiosity has no relationship to attitudes on race.[60]

As we have repeatedly noted throughout this book, there are often important differences between intensity of religious commitment and the specific flavor of one's religion. This leads us to ask: Do different religious traditions show different trends in their racial attitudes? No. Over time, we see the same trends among evangelicals, mainline Protestants, Catholics, and people with no religion (the four largest groups for which we have reliable data over time). No matter the specific racial attitude in question, all four of these groups show declines in racism. Figure 9.22 provides an illustrative example: support for anti-miscegenation laws among whites. Note that this figure, like Figures 9.23 and 9.24, accounts for a host of confounding factors (like living in the South, education level, and age)

Figure 9.22

OPPOSITION TO INTERRACIAL MARRIAGE DECLINES
(whites only, with standard demographic characteristics held constant)

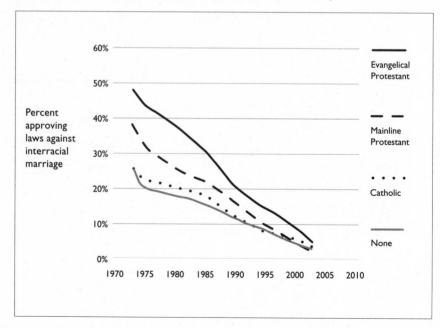

SOURCE: GENERAL SOCIAL SURVEY; DATA LOESS-SMOOTHED.

in order to isolate the differences that can be attributed to religious tradition. First, it is striking to see that, notwithstanding that the Supreme Court outlawed anti-miscegenation laws in 1967,[61] in 1973 nearly half of all white evangelical Protestants favored laws against interracial marriage. Mainline Protestants, Catholics, and nones were far less likely to favor a legal prohibition on black–white marriages. In the ensuing years, however, all four groups have converged to where they all nearly totally oppose such laws.

In Figure 9.23 we see a similar story for the view that blacks are genetically inferior to whites ("have less in-born ability to learn"). In 1977, religious nones were far more averse to this view than members of the three major religious traditions. But all four groups have now converged in their rejection of this form of racism.

This is not to say, though, that we never observe differences in racial attitudes across religious traditions. In general, white evangelicals are the least likely to endorse government policy to ameliorate

Figure 9.23

ANTI-BLACK RACISM DECLINES
(whites only, with standard demographic characteristics held constant)

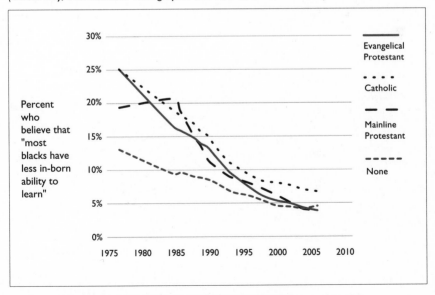

SOURCE: GENERAL SOCIAL SURVEY; DATA LOESS-SMOOTHED.

the effects of racial prejudice. Since the early 1970s evangelicals have been more likely to say that they would vote for a law that "says a homeowner can decide for himself whom to sell his house to, even if he prefers not to sell to Blacks or African Americans" [62] vs. a law "that says that a homeowner cannot refuse to sell to someone because of their race or color." Across all four of the largest religious traditions, Figure 9.24 shows a sharp decline in support for a law that would permit racial discrimination in real estate sales. However, unlike attitudes toward interracial marriage and racial genetic differences, here we do not find complete convergence. Evangelicals remain modestly more likely to favor giving white homeowners the option of not selling their homes to African Americans.

At first blush, there may appear to be an inconsistency in the results we report. On the one hand, evangelical megachurches have relatively high rates of congregational diversity, and yet evangelicals are no less—and perhaps even more—racist than members of other

Figure 9.24

SUPPORT FOR DISCRIMINATION IN HOUSING DECLINES
(whites only, with standard demographic characteristics held constant)

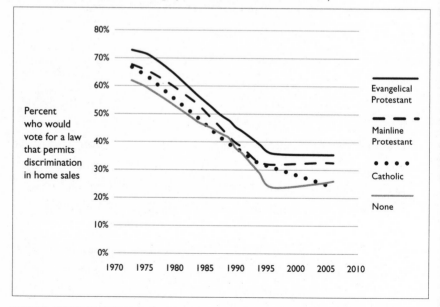

SOURCE: GENERAL SOCIAL SURVEY; DATA LOESS-SMOOTHED.

religious traditions. Actually, though, there is no discrepancy. First, recall that the overall proportion of evangelicals who attend a mega-church is relatively small. Most evangelicals, like most members of all religious traditions, worship in congregations that are racially homogeneous.

Second, even if diverse congregations were the norm among evangelicals, we do not actually know that attending church with, and even being friends with, African Americans leads evangelicals to undergo a change in their attitudes about racial disparities. Indeed, there is reason to think that they would not. Michael Emerson and Christian Smith convincingly argue that evangelicals have a deeply held individualistic belief system that prevents them from considering systemic explanations—and remedies—for racial discrimination.[63] This explanation is consistent with the observation that when compared to seculars, mainline Protestants, and Catholics, evangelicals are less likely to support legal action to address the effects of racism, like laws against discrimination in housing laws. They are also less likely to believe that African Americans are denied equal educational opportunity.[64]

Third, we also note that not all evangelicals are alike, as there are significant differences in racial attitudes within the evangelical population. No matter how racism is measured, it is most pronounced among white evangelicals concentrated in the rural and small-town South. This is perhaps not surprising, especially given the legacy of the apartheid practiced in the Jim Crow South. But it is still discouraging. However, we can find encouragement in the fact that other evangelicals—and members of other religious traditions too—have adapted to ethno-racial diversity. Like the adaptation to changing gender roles described in the previous chapter, most religious Americans have conformed to the broader societal norms endorsing racial tolerance.

To "adapt" and "conform" are passive verbs, chosen because, in general, religion has not served a prophetic role and *promoted* greater racial equality. Religious Americans are following the trend, not setting it. Obviously, there are exceptions, as many religious leaders—

both black and white—have issued stirring, indeed prophetic, calls for racial unity. Nonetheless, religious Americans have not been in the forefront of racially tolerant attitudes. Admittedly, some indicators of racial attitudes veer into legitimate policy debates over what should be done about racism, and thus their interpretation is ambiguous. But other indicators, like the question about whether blacks have "less in-born ability to learn," reflect outright bigotry. Even on these unambiguous measures of racism, white Americans of the major religious traditions have been catching up to their secular counterparts—following, not leading.

CONCLUSION

The United States is a nation that combines high religiosity with high—and rising—ethno-racial diversity. That religiosity and ethnicity would go together is no coincidence, as religion has often been a means to reinforce an ethnic heritage and vice versa. This mutual reinforcement was Will Herberg's insight. Writing in the 1950s, he saw the religious boom of his day as an expression of ethnic identity. Over fifty years later, we still see evidence of Herberg's America. Today, Black Protestants provide the most compelling example of how race and religion correspond. In most black churches, race permeates worship, sermons, music, iconography, programming, social action, and even political activity. Jews are another group in which ethnicity overlaps with religion, and like Black Protestants also have a relatively high level of political activity within their congregations. For African Americans and Jews, their politics is often connected to their ethnicity, which means that their politics is also reflected in their religion. Consequently, Black Protestants and Jews are two of the most politically homogeneous religious groups in America. Their churches and synagogues thus often serve as loci for political activity, as the congregants share much common political ground.

While for Black Protestants and Jews race/ethnicity and religion remain fused, in other denominations a once strong ethnic element has largely faded. This vestigial ethnicity is often found in mainline Protestant churches, like Mount Olivet Lutheran in Minneapolis. Given that the ethnic dimension of their religion has largely evaporated, it is not surprising that of all the religious traditions in America, mainline Protestants report the weakest sense of ethnic identity. Because of the connection between ethnic identity and religious retention, mainline Protestants nowadays have a low rate of sticking with the religion of their childhood.

Like mainline Protestants, "Anglo" Catholics have a similarly low rate of retention and a fading ethnic identity as well. Yet many Catholic parishes are in the midst of a fascinating demographic transformation as Latinos increasingly fill the pews. As a consequence, when taken as a whole Catholic parishes are among the most diverse congregations in America. They are not equally diverse, however, as Anglos, Latinos, and other racial groups mix to varying degrees in Catholic parishes—some are highly diverse, some not at all. But this is only the beginning of the transformation. Looking to the future, the steady growth and high retention of Latinos in the wake of "Anglo" Catholics' declining numbers will result in a larger and larger Latino presence in the American Catholic Church. For many Catholics 11:00 on Sunday morning is likely to be their *most* ethnically integrated hour. Only time will tell whether it will remain so, or whether Latino and "Anglo" Catholics will increasingly congregate in separate parishes.

Evangelicals present another case altogether, as one type of evangelical congregation stands out as especially diverse: the megachurch. Many Americans who attend megachurches worship in some of the most ethnically and racially diverse congregations in America—like Catholics, 11:00 on Sunday morning is not so segregated for them.

Historian Nathan Hatch describes evangelical Protestantism as containing a fundamental paradox between "its egalitarian character and its racism." [65] From the 1700s to the 1900s, racism won out. First came separate seating arrangements, then separate congregations and even denominations, such that we now speak of white and black evangelicalism as separate traditions. With the recent rise in diversity within megachurches, however, some evangelicals seem to have tilted—at least a little—toward the egalitarian side of their tradition.

It is not easy to overcome the cultural, linguistic, and economic obstacles that stand in the way of interracial social relationships. Diverse congregations do not ensure racial and ethnic harmony. While there is a correlation between attending a diverse congregation and having a friend of another race, that does not tell us about the depth of those relationships nor whether those relationships change racial attitudes. Examples abound of congregations whose efforts at fostering connections across racial lines have been difficult, even tense.[66] But, precisely because religion has historically pulled people of different races and ethnicities apart, we have highlighted these two examples of religious organizations that bring people with diverse backgrounds together. Given that multiracial organizations are rare in contemporary American society, that fact alone is worth noting.

We close by returning to the question with which we began: How has the nation's growing diversity affected American religion? In one important respect, we have seen a lot of constancy amid the change. Religion and ethnicity continue to have a symbiotic relationship. Ethnic minorities, whether immigrants or not, frequently turn to religion. Even among whites, ethnic and religious identities often go together.

But change has occurred. Americans of all religions and all levels of religiosity have become more racially tolerant. While religious Americans have not led racial liberalization—and once lagged behind their secular counterparts—recent years have brought convergence in racial attitudes among Americans of different levels of religiosity and across different religious traditions. Nonetheless, modest but important differences remain across religious traditions on racial questions. Most significantly, evangelicals are less likely to perceive systemic causes of racism, and thus less likely to endorse systemic efforts to ameliorate its consequences.

In summing up our findings on how American religion has

responded to growing ethno-racial diversity, we note the similarities with its response to the expansion of women's rights—adaptation to both kinds of broad social change. And, at the personal level there is a similarity to its response to growing income inequality. Within some religious traditions, congregational diversity fosters bridging across racial lines, just as it can lead to connections across class lines. However, the response to increasing racial diversity resembles the reaction to income inequality in another, less positive, way. Just as religious Americans have not been in the vanguard of concern over income equality, they have not led the way in racial tolerance. Social connections across class and racial lines do not necessarily inspire action to increase social justice.

CHAPTER 10

VIGNETTES:
HOW RELIGION AND
POLITICS INTERTWINE

*This chapter highlights congregations from three religious tradi-
tions, each of which illustrates a different way that religion and politics can intertwine. The pastor of Living Word Christian Center,
an evangelical megachurch in Minneapolis, makes his conservative
political views known in church, although not without controversy.
At Beth Emet, a synagogue in suburban Chicago, shared liberal views
are widely discussed and taken for granted by congregants and clergy
alike. By contrast, in an LDS (Mormon) congregation in suburban
Salt Lake City, overt politics at church is rare, but religious influence
on the political views of church members is powerful, though subtle.*

"MORE THAN JUST A CHURCH"

"I got saved after reading a passage from Luke in an e-mail," explains
Sherry Williamson as she stands at the entranceway to the sanctuary
at Living Word Christian Center, the largest church in Minnesota.
Sherry is a tall blond woman dressed in a black skirt, a blue satin
blouse, and gold jewelry, and is a member of the Ambassador Ministry, the small army of volunteer greeters that welcome churchgoers
on their way to worship. A relative of Sherry's is a born again Christian, and would often forward her e-mails containing biblical mes-

sages. One scripture finally spoke to her, and Sherry decided to join an online Bible study. Eventually, she "accepted Christ" and started searching for a place to worship—she "tried a lot of other churches" before settling on Living Word. Attempting to explain what ultimately drew her in, Sherry says, "You just feel it, you know. Walking in the doors is like walking through the gates of heaven. I don't know where I'd be without it."

Tucked away in an industrial warehouse district in the Minneapolis suburb of Brooklyn Park, Living Word Christian Center is a nondenominational congregation that bills itself as "more than just a church." Occupying a former mattress factory transformed by $12 million in renovations, Living Word boasts adult, teen, and children's worship, hundreds of small group fellowships and Bible studies, a café, a bookstore, and a wedding chapel—all under one roof. Churchgoers enter the boxy, nondescript building to find two seemingly endless corridors stretching out to the left and right, and a lavish, airy atrium filled with plush furniture, oriental rugs, and gleaming chandeliers. Glossy promotional displays line the walls, and continuous-loop DVD presentations portray the church as a place to belong, grow, and serve—advertising it as "Positive. Powerful. Practical. Definitely *not* church as usual."

"Welcome! Enjoy the service," Sherry says to a young couple as she hands them a copy of the church's eight-page weekly bulletin, a voter guide, and a pamphlet advertising the church's upcoming event "A Night to Honor Israel." The praise music has already begun in the expansive auditorium that is Living Word's main sanctuary—its padded, fold-down seats clustered around a raised stage and three overhanging JumboTrons. A white cross and the words "Jesus Is Lord" are projected on the back wall of the set, which is decorated with mock pillars and potted plastic trees and shrubs. Here Mac Hammond and his wife, Lynne, the church's founders, offer three worship services each weekend, and address their large audience watching on television and online.

Dottie Jensen, a well-dressed woman in her seventies with white-blond hair, blue eye shadow, and frosted pink lipstick, can often be

found in the front section of the sanctuary during services. Dottie claims the distinction of having been "the first member of this
church," and says that many years before Living Word was founded,
she sensed the need in Minnesota for a truly Bible-based evangelical
church. She "prayed for a pastor" to be sent to start one, and "had a
vision of a map of Georgia," where James McBryde Hammond was
born. She says she saw Pastor Mac as a young man and understood
that he would spend his life in worldly pursuits before responding to
the call of ministry. So when the Hammonds came to Minnesota and
started Living Word, Dottie and other charismatic Christians like her
were ready and waiting.[1]

"Now bow your heads for a moment," Pastor Hammond
instructs his congregation at the beginning of his Saturday evening
sermon. "Lord, we want to thank you for this opportunity to hear
from heaven tonight," he prays, head bowed, hands spread apart.
"And we believe that's exactly what we're going to be hearing. Not
something that some man has thought up or put together. We exercise our faith for divinely inspired utterance and the anointing that
destroys every yoke of bondage, in Jesus' name. Amen."

Anointed and Called

Mac Hammond is an attractive trimly built white man in his sixties with a piercing but personable style. Dressing in expensive suits
tailored to make him look taller, he strikes the profile of a successful
businessman, and has a charming good ol' boy manner. He speaks
with a deep, commanding voice softened by a breathy intonation
and a genteel Southern drawl, and while he paces the stage deliberately and confidently during sermons, he is often reading from a
TelePrompTer. The pastor generally avoids private interviews, surrounding himself with a tight-knit loyal staff. Hammond entered
the business of congregation building after a stint in the Air Force
and an unsuccessful career in the cargo industry. When Mac and
Lynne moved to Minneapolis in 1978, they searched for a church
to join but ended up starting their own Bible study group instead,
which quickly grew to 150 people. Two years later they founded Liv-

ing Word. The first service, held in a hotel conference room, drew twelve people. After six months, attendance had increased to thirty and Mac decided to "listen to the Lord" and quit his failed business pursuits to dedicate himself to the ministry.

By responding to God's call in spite of his lack of education, Hammond explains, he was merely following the biblical pattern for ministry. Citing Ephesians 4:11 in the New Testament as his text, he believes the office of pastor is "supernatural" and that "Jesus assigns these talents to the anointed." The pastoral staff at Living Word comes largely from a secular background, and includes former executives of major corporations such as McDonald's and Northwest Airlines. These associate pastors are ordained by Hammond without formal training so long as they are "grounded in the Word," a characteristic Hammond is able to discern, he says, because he is "grounded in the Word to know." He firmly believes that starting Living Word was a calling from above, and that "everything has been by the hand of God," a belief that many of his congregants share.

Though it bills itself as "practical" and "contemporary," Living Word lacks much of the informality and theological flexibility of other, more seeker-sensitive megachurches. Though his message is contextualized with everyday examples and life lessons, Hammond's sermons mine the scriptures for meaning and expound his personal interpretations of doctrine and prophecy. His preaching is conservative and frequently hard-hitting, often focusing on themes of obedience, sin, and deliverance. "Early on I felt that the Lord had pressed me that the one thing that always had to be in place was clear, concise, in-depth teaching of the Word as it relates to the principles of people's daily lives," says Hammond, explaining his style of preaching. "You can do some things that are entertaining, a passing novelty that will draw a crowd for a season. . . . But the [churches] that have had solid stable growth always center around a good pulpit— the ministry of the Word."

Hammond cites Kenneth Hagin and Kenneth Copeland, leaders of the charismatic movement Word of Faith as his mentors, and certain Pentecostal practices such as faith healing figure prominently into the official doctrines of Living Word. Pastor Mac asserts that strict biblical literalism is the source of everything Living Word espouses: "It is real easy to be selective in your believing. But you can't do that and be pursuing something called Christianity," he preaches. "The Bible is the only definition we have of God and our relationship to him. You have got to accept it in its entirety. Otherwise you are creating a God that is just intellectually comfortable, and maybe *that* is why you haven't seen the power of God in your life."

At a Wednesday night membership class—day three in the five-day series—Pastor Hammond discusses church doctrine, which includes "baptism by the Holy Spirit" as evidenced by "speaking in tongues." Experiencing this spiritual watershed is a requirement for joining the church. Dressed in a turtleneck and an elongated sports coat, Pastor Mac wears a lapel mike and addresses a group of some one hundred potential new members who have gathered in the sanctuary. He becomes animated as he talks about the plan that God has for each individual, but teaches that "He does not reveal it" in one's "natural language." The Holy Ghost teaches us, he says, and "when you are praying in tongues you are speaking about this 'eye-popping destiny' that He has for you." "Amen," says a member of the church's Prayer Ministry, seated in the front row.

"Eliminate any question in your mind. The Bible says if you want to receive you *will* receive," declares Pastor Hammond, as he prepares his charges for a transformative experience. "But here is the rub, it is not just going to usher forth from your mouth. You are a free moral agent. The Holy Ghost does not hijack your vocal cords to make you speak! You must make an utterance. You *must* make a sound. . . . And you have to trust the Holy Ghost to shape that sound into a meaningful prayer language," he explains. "This can feel a little awkward, I can tell you," he adds, recounting his own first experience and how "stupid" he felt as he said "ah, ah, ah" and thought, "This is the baptism of the Holy Ghost?" Hammond's self-deprecation seems to put the crowd at ease. "Don't worry about how you sound. Edification will come as you practice. If you get your mind on the Lord, the flow comes."

Pastor Hammond then invites those who wish to be baptized by the Holy Spirit to approach the altar, and explains that he will lay his hands on each person and begin speaking in tongues so that each new member can join in, one by one. "Don't say anything in English," he instructs, "but don't be silent. I don't care if you copy me. It's a kick-start. I know I am praying in the Spirit. And the Spirit will come to you." About seventy-five people of various ages and ethnicities come forward and line up tentatively along the railing. Hammond goes from one to the next and, staying only a moment, rests his hands on each person's shoulders, offering a quick blessing in English. He then begins speaking in unintelligible syllables. "That's it! Let it keep coming. Keep praying. You've got it," he says a moment later, as he moves to the next person. The prayer ministers stand behind the pastor, stepping in to assist the tongues-speakers as he moves on. An usher walks behind the row of earnest supplicants, his arms outstretched, offering to catch anyone who might fall backward as they are overcome by the Spirit of the Lord.

"People ask what kind of church we are," Hammond says, "and I have settled on, 'We are not a denomination, we are an evangelical, Spirit-filled church.'" Living Word's resistance to denominational affiliation stems from the pastor's belief that independence is "the most scriptural form of church government." He explains that throughout the Bible there is a consistent pattern of God placing one person in the position of authority over a group of believers, and this is the organizational model that Living Word follows. "My preference is not to be part of a denomination," Pastor Mac explains, "because the rigidity is really something that inhibits the local church from really growing—doing what it can to increase— because the decisions are made *for* the pastor, not *by* the pastor, who is the representative anointed by God." Conversely, independent governance "places the pulpit at the center of the decision-making matters" and puts sole leadership responsibility in the hands of the pastor. Hammond puts it this way to new members: "I am the one who is responsible. I am anointed to do this. I'm called to set the direction of the ministry."

"It's All Financially Driven"

Much of Living Word's ministry is centered on helping congregants achieve success as Christians. The idea that "God wants you to be a winner in every area of life"—one of the church's signature catchphrases—is preached regularly and fleshed out in a glossy, twenty-page magazine called *Winner's Way*, published by Mac Hammond Ministries, the nonprofit distributor of the Hammonds' numerous media enterprises. The stated purpose of *Winner's Way* is to expound "Bible principles that will enhance your spiritual growth and help you to win at work, win in relationships, and win in the financial arena." An underlying theme in Hammond's theology and ministry is the belief that God rewards his followers and wants them to obtain as much wealth and influence as possible, which some critics call the "Prosperity Gospel." Though Hammond tends to eschew that rendering of his beliefs, the message that wealth is both a tool for wielding righteous influence and a reward for righteous living emanates clearly from his pulpit.

In a 2006 sermon Pastor Mac preached that "you can never have too much money" to a chorus of cheers from the nearly 1,500 attendees. According to the Hammonds, "God's highest and best is that your whole life becomes a reflection of His abundant provision." In many sermons Pastor Hammond urges his hearers to defeat negative thinking and expect the Lord's blessings. One Sunday he taught that "true Christianity" is consistency and diligence in maintaining high expectations. "God is in the Blessings Business. God is in the Rewards Business," he assured his flock, promising that consistent efforts to achieve "Holy Ghost marks" through righteous living will invite God's blessing of "unlimited resources."

Though he describes his congregation as "very generous," and the church's 2006 income was $33 million, Pastor Mac also feels that financial concerns are a "major frustration." "Every year I feel challenged to generate enough enthusiasm for the finances that we need to do the things we want. Finances are always a limitation," he says. "I hate to seem ungrateful but there always seems to be so much more you would like to be able to do. It is all financially driven." Despite concerns that the church's funds often run short of his vision, Pastor Hammond and his wife are each handsomely compensated for their work at Living Word, a fact that brought him under IRS scrutiny in 2008. And while Hammond maintains that all salaries are within IRS guidelines for a nonprofit, the church has been accused of providing him ethically questionable loans and other sweetheart deals. Regardless of the validity of the claims, the Hammonds are doing exceptionally well—they own two Florida condos worth more than $3 million, two homes in Minnesota, a Lexus, a Porsche, three boats, and a plane.[2] Yet, Hammond is quick to point out, they are also the largest single donors to the church, having given back some $2.5 million over the years. In defense of his generous paycheck Pastor Hammond frequently quotes the New Testament passage 1 Timothy 5:17 about "elders" being "doubly honored," which he interprets to mean that God's anointed are to be "doubly compensated." Those that "keep their clergy poor, keep their ministry poor," he says.

Generating Influence

God has blessed the Hammonds not only financially but also in "souls won," a figure that is reported weekly in the service bulletin. Over its twenty-eight-year history, Pastor Hammond says, Living Word has "enjoyed strong, consistent growth," and now claims some nine thousand "active participants," over thirty ministries, and a staff of four hundred. It runs an eight-hundred-student K–12 Christian school, which is incorporated into the church complex, as are Maranatha College, providing higher education with "an uncompromising Christian environment," and Living Free Recovery Services, a state-licensed outpatient treatment facility for chemical dependency. Living Word has also sprouted several satellite ministries, including the Compassion Center, a social service outreach to inner-city residents, and Club 3 Degrees, "a cutting-edge Christian music club" in downtown Minneapolis that is smoke- and alcohol-free, and whose purpose is "to present the Gospel in a relevant and accessible way for people who wouldn't necessarily step foot inside a church."

Living Word's efforts to enlarge its boundaries are not limited to the unchurched, however. Hammond and his staff have managed to draw together a congregation of believers that is remarkably diverse—racially, ethnically, and socioeconomically. While churches are historically some of the most segregated institutions in America, that is not true of Living Word. Though all but two of the pastors are white, at an average worship service as many as 20 percent of the congregation are nonwhite and, according to internal surveys, new member classes draw between 12 and 17 percent foreign-born attendees. Pastor Tim Burt recalls that "up until five years ago it was unpleasantly white at Living Word," a fact that he "hated" but didn't know how to change. What finally propelled the diversification of Living Word were the efforts of Daniel Gutiérrez, a Peruvian whose parents had joined the church in 1980.

Gutiérrez became a pastor in 2003, and right away noticed lots of "head scratching" about the lack of racial diversity in the congregation, but little action. "Blacks would come to one or two services and then leave," recounts Pastor Daniel, who, as a son of immigrants, was particularly attuned to minority groups. He noted that Brooklyn Park was home to the second largest Liberian population in America—an accessible immigrant group because of their native English. Searching for a point of entry into the community, Gutiérrez finally found it in new member Veronica Urey, who approached him about holding a gathering for Africans in 2001. He gladly offered his home for an informal lunch, and so many people signed up that Gutiérrez appealed to Tim Burt for a larger space. Pastor Burt offered to hold the event at the church, all expenses paid, and in 2002 Living Word held its first African Celebration, which drew nearly a hundred people. The next year 220 attended.

Daniel and Tim both say that the philosophy they used in reaching out to Africans is the same one they have employed in expanding their small groups program: Creating community is about building relationships and groups around affinity. Once a critical mass of Liberians developed, word of mouth became the most effective form of evangelism among nonwhites. "African immigrants know that they are welcomed here," Pastor Burt asserts. Living Word has since offered a luncheon for "people who have an affection for things Spanish," and while attracting Latinos has been less successful, "you have to start somewhere," says Burt. Living Word has also extended itself to Russian and Hmong immigrants, offering busing for their children to attend the Christian Academy, and providing translation headsets at worship. The resultant diversity at the church seems a source of pride for Pastor Burt. "By the grace of God we have done some things right and have had the courage to go down this path," he says.

Living Word's ever-expanding reach is no accident, Pastor Hammond explains, and has been part of his vision from very early in his ministry. Hammond believes that to please God a church must continue to grow: "God is not in a small church" because small churches are merely "religious bless-me clubs," he says. To his mind, the role of the church is to reach beyond its walls, bringing God's message into the community, the nation, and the world. The continued expansion of Living Word and its related ministries, therefore, "is all about generating influence." "To influence a community you have to grow large to have enough of a voice, to have an impact," Hammond explains. "The more visibility you have, the more people you have identifying with your organization and coming to church here . . . then the more voices you have to influence the community."

"Who Is Right and Who Is Wrong"

"You know, I have some strong opinions about the church and politics," says Pastor Hammond, referring to one important domain in which Living Word seeks to exercise its influence. "I do not believe—even though it has become a clichéd and much popularized term—that there is, at least in our founding documents, an intent for church and state to be separated in the way that it has been perceived by our courts in the last fifty years." Citing examples such as "prayer in public schools" and "the Ten Commandments in the courthouse," Hammond laments the fact that "the rise of secular humanism" is "pushing God out of every civic arena imaginable." Pastor Mac believes that the only way to "change the direction the country is going in" is "not being timid in going back into the political arena." "So I preach very actively around election time the need for Christians to be responsible not only as Americans but *as Christians* and to be involved in the political process. Within the parameters of the law I intend to do everything I can do. . . . I am not trying to promote a particular candidate or party, I am saying this," he says, with emotion: "There are some people whose views are more closely aligned with the values we hold dear than other people. We need to be proactive enough to determine who those folks are. And *those* are the people we should vote for."

On October 18, 2008, just two weeks before the nation chose a new president, Pastor Hammond, who will be away for the next two Sundays on his annual elk-hunting trip, takes the opportunity to say a few words about the upcoming election. "Say 'I'm gonna vote,'" he begins, to which his congregation mumbles in response. "Say it *louder*," he coaxes good-naturedly, and the audience obeys. "Okay. Now, as we've pointed out, you vote in line with the *Word*, and what *it* has to say about the basic issues of morality, Amen?" Hammond goes on to educate his hearers about the "standard of morality" the Lord has set up through the Bible, highlighting traditional marriage as an example. "The right to life is one of the most basic of moral issues, and the government should *not* be legislating against these morals," he adds emphatically. "C'mon now!" comes a shout of approval from the congregation. "Any law which encourages or is supportive of the taking of life is wrong," the pastor goes on, which invites a few more shouted "Amens" and a "Yes, that's true!"

"Now we're not going to politicize this process in the church," Pastor Hammond pauses to clarify. "Voting is your personal choice, and you have a responsibility to the Lord, not to any party." He then calls attention to the voter guides distributed at the door and available at the information desk in the atrium. The two-page "non-partisan guide . . . on various issues of concern to the electorate" is published by an organization called Priests for Life, and compares the stands of Barack Obama and John McCain on twelve "key issues," seven of which are life issues such as *Roe v Wade*, "Partial Birth Abortion," "Human Cloning," and "Terri Schiavo." The church also distributes similar guides produced by the Minnesota Family Council, whose stated mission is "to defend and strengthen the families of Minnesota by upholding Judeo-Christian principles in the public arena." The stances promoted in this eight-page leaflet include "defining marriage as the union of a man and a woman," limiting public funding for and increasing legal restrictions on abortion, and curtailing "special employment and legal protections for homosexuals." Hammond encourages each member to use the guides to figure out "who is right and who is wrong where the moral standards of the Lord are concerned," and to "vote accordingly." "*Vote accordingly,*" he repeats, emphatically. With his pre-sermon political commentary approaching the ten-minute mark, Hammond wraps up by drawing a distinction between "social issues" like "welfare, immigration, free trade, and foreign policy," and "moral issues," which are things spoken to by the Ten Commandments. "Forget the social issues! Your vote is in line with the moral issues," he directs, to a chorus of applause and "Amens." "Now I'm glad you agree with that," Hammond says with a grin. "I'm Mac Hammond and I approve this message," he kids, to an eruption of laughter and cheers from his flock.

Though influencing the secular world is high on his list of priorities, Pastor Hammond treads more lightly than he used to when it comes to political issues—after a major firestorm erupted in 2006 surrounding his alleged endorsement of Michele Bachmann, then a candidate for U.S. Congress. A born again Christian with a single-minded opposition to gay marriage, Bachmann was invited by Pastor Hammond to "share her testimony" at three services held just two weeks before election day, and her appearance was advertised at Living Word for weeks in advance. Taking a revivalist tone, Bachmann urged her hearers to "be hot for the Lord and not lukewarm."

"When we are on fire for Jesus we can change the world in His name!" she declared. Bachmann went on to explain that her passion for serving Jesus Christ had shaped her life and inspired her run for office. Before announcing her candidacy, she and her husband first fasted for three days, all the while imploring, "Lord, is this what you want? Is this your will?" On the afternoon of the second day, Bachmann testified to Hammond's congregation, the Lord "made that calling sure." Just in case the Almighty's endorsement wasn't enough, Pastor Mac took the opportunity during the first service to add his support: "We can't publicly endorse as a church—and would not—any candidate," he said, "but I can tell you *personally* that I'm going to vote for Michele Bachmann." His congregation responded with a roar of satisfied laughter.

Bachmann explained to the congregation that her run for Congress was one of the top three races in the nation, the outcome of which could directly affect "defeating radical Islam," "the future of the family," and "the future of freedom." "Suit up, sign up," she said. "It will change you and it will change this world." Despite Bachmann's highly controversial history of organizing "pray-ins" at the state capitol and participating in a prayer circle around the desk of an openly gay state senator, Hammond boldly championed her cause. "It is important, I said *important*, that we put men and women of God in office in our government, Amen!" he declared as Bachmann closed her remarks. "I don't want any more letters about how church and politics don't mix. If that's your opinion then you need to get saved, because the Bible makes it clear that we are to have an effect on the world in which we live, *Amen*." "Glory to God," Hammond concluded.

It wasn't long before clips of the Bachmann services began appearing on YouTube, watchdog groups started crying foul, and a local journalist revealed that Hammond actually couldn't "personally" vote for Bachmann, because he didn't live in her district. The pastor publicly backpedaled, and his associates feared he had finally crossed the line. Yet two years after the media firestorm that culminated in an IRS inquiry into Living Word's compliance with nonprofit tax guidelines, Hammond remains vocal about the role of religion in the public square, and has taken to joking about all the attention his brash statements have drawn. "I guess I'm just dumb enough to take the Word at face value," he says.

Whether in the form of distributing voter guides, inviting politicians as guest preachers, or preaching about "values" from the pulpit—politicking within the walls of the church is only one way Living Word tries to help its congregants "connect the dots" between the gospel and the political issues of the day. The church also frequently promotes conservative political events happening in the community. On October 3, 2006, Focus on the Family, an evangelical organization founded by James Dobson, organized a "Rally for Family Action" near the Minnesota state capitol. Working toward its goal "to protect and promote the definitions of traditional family and *family values*," the organization's appearance in Minnesota was motivated by a contentious battle over gay marriage in the state. Living Word advertised the event in its publications, through church e-mail lists, and over the pulpit, and added to the rally's one thousand attendees by busing children from the church school to the capitol as an after-school activity.

And though Hammond teaches his congregation that such things as foreign policy should take a back seat to "moral issues," his commitment to a literal interpretation of the Bible has led him to join a national network of churches called Christians United for Israel (CUFI), an organization started by Texas evangelist John Hagee. While a major stated objective of Christians United for Israel is the persuading of the fellow faithful to validate the Jewish people's claim on salvation, they are also motivated by the more concrete goal of, as Hammond puts it, "impressing our government with the popular desire of the American people" to support the state of Israel. The activism undertaken by the organization includes petitions, regular meetings with elected officials, and an annual summit in Washington that has drawn as many as four thousand attendees. Each year Living Word also hosts a "Night to Honor Israel," a public event held in the sanctuary that draws a larger crowd than any other gathering at the church. Through song, dance, and fiery preaching, the two thousand attendees are urged to ally themselves with the state and people of Israel, and to support public officials who do the same.

"On the Right Track"

Despite Living Word Christian Center's obvious popularity, Mac Hammond's often bold politicization of the pulpit seems to leave some of his congregants self-conscious in the face of the criticism he has drawn. Many dismiss out of hand the idea that the church significantly affects their political leanings. "I vote as I see fit as a Christian," says one church member. Another admits that "the church helps me think more deeply about social and political issues" but quickly and emphatically adds that he is "not overly influenced" by Hammond's preaching. But notwithstanding their attempts to quell outsiders' disapproval, congregants at Living Word frequently say that they are "thrilled" with Pastor Mac and appreciate a preacher who doesn't apologize for the fact that, as one woman puts it, "the Bible says what it means and means what it says." Besides, she adds, "the Bible says that if you do the right thing you'll be persecuted. You can take that as a sign that you're on the right track." Indeed, Pastor Hammond often defends his uncompromising beliefs and controversial actions with a similar air of defiance: "I say what I want to say, and I don't give a rip whether people stay or go."

COMMUNITY SABBATH

Exiting the Edens Expressway and heading east on Dempster Street through Skokie, Illinois, offers visitors a quick tour of Jewish life in Chicago's near-northern suburbs. Bialy shops and kosher bakeries stand out among the nail salons and convenience stores that dot the landscape, and a remarkable number of synagogues line the street— some in storefronts, some in more traditional sanctuaries, and one in a cubelike former bank building. Though difficult to distinguish from the outside, the temples house congregations widely varied in their beliefs and worship styles—from Ultraorthodox to Reconstructionist, to a Messianic group claiming Jesus as the promised Jewish Messiah.

At 9:00 on a crisp Saturday morning, small groups of men and boys walk down the busy street to Sabbath worship—some dressed in prayer shawls and yarmulkes, and others wearing the black suits and wide-brimmed hats indicative of Hasidism. Further down the road in Evanston—where the strip malls give way to well-maintained homes and tree-lined blocks—a handful of cars turn into a small parking lot, as men and women dressed in jeans, shorts, and sandals make their way into services at Beth Emet The Free Synagogue, home to the largest Reform congregation in the Skokie-Evanston area.

Beth Emet fills a long block and consists of a two-story school building and an A-framed sanctuary with a manicured lawn, a small terrace, and an arched wooden doorway. The building's white stone exterior and modest, functional architecture blend in easily with the surrounding residential area. Though the building is more obviously a house of worship than the rented commercial spaces of smaller temples down the road, no signage on the west side of Beth Emet identifies it as a synagogue, which, according to one longtime congregant, was a condition of the property's zoning agreement and stands as a relic of Evanston's anti-Semitic past.

On their way to the lay-led *Kahal* service, this morning's attendees enter the main hallway of the Beth Emet school, which is lined with old photos of the synagogue's confirmation classes on one side, and brightly colored finger paintings and kid-sized coat racks on the other. A ramped hallway containing a lending library and a tiny gift shop adjoins the school building to the temple, and opens into a foyer where the *kiddush* (a ceremonial blessing of wine and *challah* bread) and *Shabbat Oneg* (a Sabbath wine and cheese reception) are held after Friday night services. The 340-seat sanctuary abuts a large carpeted room used as a congregational overflow, a hall for functions and parties, and a dining room for the synagogue's weekly soup kitchen. Though the corridors are quiet this Sabbath morning, during the high holidays of Rosh Hashanah and Yom Kippur an additional nine hundred chairs must be set up in the overflow to accommodate the crowds.

"Do we have a volunteer to lead us in the *Ashrei?*" asks Naomi Weiss, an enthusiastic young woman with an acoustic guitar strapped over the blue prayer shawl on her shoulders. Naomi serves as cantor at the 9:30 service, for which about twenty people—mostly adults—have now gathered. *Kahal Shabbat,* meaning "Community Sabbath," takes place in the Weiner Room, a more intimate, multipurpose space in the synagogue's basement, and is one of two Saturday services at Beth Emet, both of which are lay-led. Congregants slowly trickle in, finding seats among the 120 maroon vinyl chairs that surround a wide wooden podium, set up in front of a wall of windows that look out onto a small courtyard. Lined with bulletin boards and storage cabinets, the long room is sparsely decorated and its brick walls and linoleum floors give it an institutional feel that is slowly warmed by the hugs and choruses of *"Shabbat shalom"* that fill the space as the group continues to gather. At the back of the room stands a tall cabinet adorned with golden Hebrew characters, which serves as an ark containing the Torah scrolls, an important part of the liturgy for Sabbath morning worship.

A young teenager volunteers to offer the first prayer. *"Ashrei yoshvei veitecha, od y'hal'lucha selah,"* she begins, hesitatingly chanting the Hebrew that is transliterated in the orange paperback prayer book she holds. "Happy are they who dwell in Your house; they will ever praise You," reads the translation. *"Ashrei ha-am she'ka'cha lo, ashrei haam she-Adonai Elohav,"* comes the next line, accompanied by Naomi's guitar. "Happy is the people whose portion is this, whose God is Adonai," comes the response from the small group of worshippers, who intone the familiar prayer's staccato lilt.

The various portions of the Sabbath liturgy such as readings, blessings, and Torah interpretation—called "honors"—have been apportioned by sign-up on a clipboard that Naomi refers to as the service unfolds. As the *Ashrei* concludes a middle-aged man wearing *tallit* and *kipah* (prayer shawl and yarmulke) comes forward to introduce the prayer for Sukkot, the harvest holiday being celebrated this week. "This is an Orthodox perspective, so take from it what you will," he says, before reading an interpretation of the prayer. About halfway through, he stops. "The rest is a little Messianic, so we'll just skip that. We've got our redemption rather than our redeemer," he concludes, to muffled chuckles from the congregation, now numbering about sixty-five.

Seeing itself as an intellectualized and enlightened version of an ancient religion, the Reform movement of Judaism began in Germany and sought to modernize the faith and bring it into harmony with a secular lifestyle. First codified in 1885, the tenets of Reform Judaism emphasized individualism and rational interpretation of the Torah, made observance of customs and laws a matter of personal choice, and rejected rituals in favor of more "Protestantized" worship. Practices such as covering one's head during services, walking to synagogue on *Shabbat*, and keeping *kashrut* (dietary restrictions) were seen by Reform Jews as relics of an ancient and foreign culture, and went largely by the wayside as the denomination took shape.

Early American Reform Jews also parted ways with Orthodoxy by refusing to see themselves as a people living in exile from Israel, and eschewing the movement calling for the reestablishment of the political state of Israel—often referred to as Zionism.[3] They viewed America as their home and Judaism as their chosen religion rather than a definitive identity. Now the largest Jewish denomination in the United States, Reform has continued to evolve as Jews have become increasingly assimilated into American culture. The founding impulse to set aside peculiar practices seen as underscoring ethnic separateness has waned, and some of the faith's tradition and ritual—such as praying and singing in Hebrew—have consequently found their way back into Reform Jewish life. Though the denomination retains its nonnormative teachings about the observance of laws, it is not uncommon to see today's Reform Jews lighting *Shabbat* candles at home or keeping *kashrut*. After the Holocaust and the establishment of the state of Israel in 1948, Reform Judaism also began to return to the idea of global Jewish solidarity and—however slowly—to officially add Zionist language to its denominational platform.

"We're All in This to Make Jews"

In the late 1940s, David Polish, Beth Emet's founding rabbi, was head of a large Reform synagogue in Chicago. An ardent Zionist, Polish was ahead of his time, and his outspoken views on Israel set him at odds with his congregation, who one day locked him out of the synagogue in protest. Along with forty like-minded families in Evanston, Polish soon started Beth Emet, a new Reform congregation with a Zionist orientation. In keeping with the bold spirit of its founding, the fledgling congregation chose a location on the corner of Dempster and Ridge, two main thoroughfares, as a defiant protest against the anti-Semitism of the neighborhood. Originally meeting in an old mansion house on the corner of the lot they purchased, the congregants built an adjoining school, which was used for religious education and "life cycle events," such as *Bar* and *Bat Mitzvahs* and weddings. Despite the resistance from its neighbors, the congregation quickly grew to six hundred families. In the early 1960s construction of a modern synagogue began, and the first *Shabbat* service in the new sanctuary was held on April 3, 1964.

At 7:00 on Monday night the Beth Emet New Member Integration Committee has gathered at Barbara and Larry Adelman's home to brainstorm ways the synagogue can do a better job of attracting and keeping new congregants. Beth Emet currently claims some 840 "members," which—because synagogues generally count membership by household—represents well over two thousand individuals. However, according to Bob Cutler, vice president of the congregation, creating meaningful connections with members is one of Beth Emet's "very great challenges." Only about 10 percent of families "are involved on any regular basis here at the synagogue," he says, meaning they "attend a service, participate in an activity, belong to a committee, or have some personal connection." "Reform is the largest denomination in America, but the affiliation rate is down," explains Peter Knobel, senior rabbi at Beth Emet since 1980. "My sense is that synagogue attendance is also down. We're scrambling to understand how to build community," he says, and the New Member Integration Committee—recently revived after a long hiatus—is an important part of that effort.

Barbara brings out plates filled with cookies and biscotti, and Dave Werner, a younger man and a Beth Emet member of just two years, sits tentatively in his chair, sipping a glass of iced tea. "There are so many social groups, sometimes people just don't know where to start," Larry says, reflecting on the many people he has seen come and go over his thirty-six-year membership at the synagogue. Because weekly worship tends not to be a focus for Reform Jews, most Beth Emet members stay connected largely through an extensive menu of nonworship activities, such as the early childhood program, which includes a drop-in playgroup, a weekday nursery school, a Sunday school, and a summer camp. Beth Emet also runs a religious school for older children and youth, educating them in Hebrew and preparing them for the coming-of-age ceremony called *Bar/Bat Mitzvah*, as well as a youth group whose main focus is social. For adults the synagogue offers extensive educational opportunities. The fall term at Beth Emet includes twenty-three classes covering topics as varied as Torah Chanting Basics, A History of Zionism, Traditions in the Kitchen, and Yoga for You. Social functions such as coffee hours, *Shabbat Oneg*, and dinners around holidays are also a major part of the synagogue's programming, as well as more casual gatherings at in-home supper clubs, called *Chugim*.

"One of the reasons you throw programming at people is that you hope something sticks," Rabbi Knobel explains. Yet all of these programs come at a price. As is common for synagogues, membership at Beth Emet is defined by the payment of dues, which amount to some $3,000 per family per year. New members pay a discounted rate of $750 for the first year, which gives the synagogue a chance to convince them to stay. The dues at Beth Emet, which Bekki Harris Kaplan, the synagogue's executive director, describes as "quite excessive," are one of the major things the committee identifies as an impediment to keeping new members active. When faced with paying higher dues than at any other synagogue in the area, "What will make them come back the second year?" Larry wonders.

Sitting at the head of the Adelmans' table, Bekki thumbs through a stack of printed pages spread over the lace tablecloth in front of her. "The Bergers may come back," she says, circling on the membership roster the names of families she knows have stopped attending. "They're synagogue shopping." "This is worse than the divorce rate," jokes Abe Haas, taking a handful of almonds from a bowl in the center of the table. "The Halberstams have resigned, but they still buy high holiday tickets," Bekki continues. The group throws out various ideas for helping new members integrate into the Beth Emet community more easily, including having a scavenger hunt at the synagogue to help people become familiar with the building, hosting a coffee reception at the rabbi's home, and establishing a mentoring system ("such a nice idea, but people are *so* busy," Barbara interjects). One of the things the committee already does is offer a "welcome basket" to new families that includes *Shabbat* candles, a *tzedaka* box (a piggybank for charity), a gift certificate to a kosher bakery, and a bottle of kosher wine. "We used to deliver them personally," says Rosemary Klein, another committee member, "but it was a hassle." "In an ideal world, every new member would receive a home visit," adds Barbara, but this idea is shrugged off as impossible. "Talk about intimidating," says Dave.

Beth Emet employs roughly eighty staff members and relies on a volunteer board, presidency, and executive committee to oversee the myriad activities that take place at the synagogue in a given week. Lay leadership is generally drawn from the core ten percent of members who attend regularly, and whom Rabbi Knobel refers to as "the usual suspects." "We are highly programmed at Beth Emet," Knobel says, "which is true of most congregations our size or larger." However, the "constantly increasing" level of activity at the synagogue brings with it several drawbacks, including "a lack of focus" and what Knobel calls "a consumer mentality." Rather than expecting to volunteer and contribute to the synagogue's programs, members are more likely to join with, as Bob Cutler describes it, "an expectation that things will be provided for them." Bekki Harris Kaplan agrees. "People's relationship with the synagogue is changing," she explains. "It used to be—when I was a kid and in my parents' generation— you joined a synagogue because that's what [was] expected of you as Jews and you supported the community," she says. Yet this pro-social attitude has been replaced largely by "an expectation of entitlement," laments Cutler, placing a growing burden on Beth Emet's professional staff. "There's a lot more competition than there was ten years ago," Harris Kaplan adds. At one time Beth Emet was the only Reform synagogue in Evanston, but "newer congregations have sort of come into their own now, and we're all quite different," she says, a fact that increases the pressure to attract and keep new members. However, drawing congregants away from a synagogue down the road is never the goal, she is quick to clarify. "Bottom line, we're all in this to make Jews."

The Free Synagogue

Though considerable effort is put toward the program offerings at Beth Emet, many adult members say that what ultimately convinced them to join was something other than the choirs, committees, and activities. A vital part of the synagogue's founding philosophy, and an obvious result of the circumstances that birthed the congregation, is the concept of the "free pulpit." Beth Emet The Free Synagogue officially places no restrictions—ideological or otherwise—upon the rabbinate or individual members. As one long-time congregant describes it, the concept of a "free pulpit" means that "the rabbi is free to have his opinions and to speak what he wants to say. And that goes for anybody else in the synagogue too." This radical openness has created a vigorous intellectual life at Beth Emet, which is what most congregants cite as their primary reason for membership. According to Cantor Erin Frankel, "the baseline level of knowledge of Judaism [at Beth Emet] is far above other congregations. There is a commitment to that intellectual tradition that was started by the founding rabbi. This is a congregation who wants to *know*, and we're looking for people who want to teach us." Seth Lisbon, a member of three years, says that for him the collective yearning for knowledge is the most exciting aspect of life at Beth Emet. "It's smart. It's a learning community," he says.

At an adult study class offered after the Saturday morning service for Yom Kippur, Rabbi Knobel gave a lecture to nearly one hundred congregants on the roots of Reform. He emphasized the movement's embrace of the philosophy of Immanuel Kant, and preached "a God who demands ethics and doesn't care about ritual." For Reform Jews, Rabbi Knobel taught, "the autonomy of the individual" is central, as is the idea that "ethics should be imposed by one's own reasoning rather than by tradition." Earlier in the day, Associate Rabbi Andrea London's remarks during worship had centered on the findings of experimental psychologists about the importance of listening and having a "growth mind-set." "We had very secular messages at all our services over the holidays," she says, "and people loved it."

Such intellectualized discourse is popular at Beth Emet largely because more "religious" ideas about faith and spirituality fail to resonate with most of the synagogue's members, who describe their personal experience of Judaism as tending toward secularism. Margaret Loftis, a convert to Judaism who is one of Beth Emet's most active members, is a self-described atheist. Evie Greenberg, a venerated elder member of the congregation and its longtime president, echoes Margaret's views. "I have to tell you that blind faith is not something that I can talk very comfortably about because I don't have that," she says. "My intense commitment to Judaism is based probably on the intellectual aspect of it. I mean, I like the fact that you can read Torah one year and find something in it and read it the next year and find more." Alexis Rosenbaum, a middle-aged mother of three who grew up at Beth Emet, stopped attending for many years, and then returned when she had children, characterizes her belief in God as "the connection we have between ourselves and other people." She sees prayer as "an intellectual exercise."

While spiritual practices such as prayer, ritual, and mysticism do play a larger role in more conservative Jewish denominations,

Rabbi London feels that this "struggle" with "everyday faith" is not unique to the Reform experience. "Judaism has always had a tension between the intellect and the spirit and how those work together, but it's very difficult to try to talk about that in any denominational sense," she says. And while London suspects that many of her congregants do have some kind of faith in God, "they don't feel like they can talk about it," she says. Evie Greenberg agrees, stating that in her long experience at Beth Emet, personal beliefs aren't generally discussed. "Even in my *Chug* I wouldn't presume to say what anyone believes," she says, referring to the social circle she has belonged to for some forty years, which contains some of her closest friends.

"Jews have a hard time talking theology—it just does not come naturally at all," Rabbi London explains. "For example, there's a Catholic church that we do some interfaith programs with. I was teaching a class with the priest and we decided to do a session on the pivotal story of our faith, so he did Resurrection, and I did revelation of Torah. . . . So the priest and I asked that the tables talk amongst themselves. So we said, 'Catholics, how does Resurrection play out in your life? How is that important to you?' and, 'Jews, how does revelation personally relate to your life?' And I thought that the Jews were going to crawl under the table and run away. It was like, 'personally? What do you mean *personally*?' . . . So one of the tables gets up at the end of the session to share: 'Well, we didn't really talk about how revelation is personally important for us. We talked about how there are fifty-four Torah portions and we read them on an annual cycle.' It was *such* a Jewish response, which was, 'We know all the details, and we can give you all the facts and figures, but don't tell me that it's supposed to *move* me,'" Rabbi London says, bemusedly. "And it *does* move people," she adds, emphatically. "They just can't articulate it; that's the interesting thing. Considering how educated and intelligent Jews are, they have a really hard time articulating this stuff."

"Deed, Not Creed"

Many congregants at Beth Emet who express ambivalence about faith, or a level of discomfort about spirituality, explain their commitment to the Jewish religion as a function of behavior, rather than belief. As one older woman put it, "Being a Jew is not only a thing of faith, it's also a thing of doing. And it's more important for me to do than to believe." Debbie Gerston adds that rather than "sitting down and thinking all day" about her faith, she prefers to be active. "I'm more of a doer," she says. And as to her faith in God, she admits, "I don't know that I'll ever really think that through." Rabbi London shares her congregants' focus on doing. "As we say about Judaism, we're a religion of deed, not creed," she explains. "Exodus says when Moses gives the Torah to the people, the people say . . . 'We will do, and then we will listen.' The understanding being that through the *doing* we come to know God. Not the other way around."

For more Orthodox Jews, "doing" takes the form of careful adherence to law and tradition, which doesn't have much of a place in the Reform denomination. So what, exactly, does the rabbinate at Beth Emet aim to persuade its membership to do? "That which I feel like I'm compelled and obligated to move people to *do*," Rabbi London explains, "is to really reach out and to make the world a better place. I feel like that is a place where I have some responsibility to push. I don't feel like I have a responsibility to push people to light *Shabbat* candles. I think it's really powerful to light *Shabbat* candles—it's made a huge difference in my life and I'll share that with people, but if I got everyone in the congregation to light *Shabbat* candles, you know, I didn't really do much. If I got everybody in this congregation to give ten hours of community service because they felt compelled by their religious tradition to do so, I'd feel like I had done a lot."

Repair the World

"*Tikkun olam*. That's kind of a mantra of the Reform movement," Bob Cutler explains, referring to a Hebrew phrase meaning "repair the world." "One of our missions, so to speak—as a movement, and as a people—is that we should assume a role of trying to better the world, trying to help other people," he says. Though articulating a personal faith is complex and often difficult for many members of the Beth Emet community, describing a felt mandate to be active in solving the problems of society comes almost effortlessly. "I believe that we have responsibilities toward each other, toward the universe," Evie Greenberg emphatically states. "Reform Judaism— probably more than any other denomination—tells us that we need to be responsible for others around us, that we need to have an impact, and I think that Judaism does give us that foundation of being respectful of others, of caring, and of treating this earth properly so that it's going to be here for other generations," says Bekki Harris Kaplan. "It's a movement that is deeply committed to what we call 'Prophetic Judaism,' which in a Christian context would be called 'the Social Gospel,'" Rabbi Knobel adds.

Since its founding, Beth Emet has had a "strong tradition" of activism and community outreach, and Rabbi London says that what first attracted her to the synagogue was "its reputation for being very forward-thinking, intellectual, and progressive; *and* dynamic—really engaged in the outside world, and really doing things for their community." Active in the civil rights movement from very early on, Beth Emet members traveled to Selma, Alabama, with Rabbi David Polish, and hosted Martin Luther King at the synagogue in 1959. Beth Emet also opened the first soup kitchen in Evanston, which is run entirely by congregant volunteers. The majority of active members have served in the soup kitchen numerous times, and the program is so popular that shifts are booked several months in advance.

Indeed, the activities of Beth Emet's Social Action Committee are some of the synagogue's most successful undertakings. Debbie Gerston, a former chair of the committee, rattles off a long list of its campaigns to address a wide range of social and political issues. Early in its existence, the committee participated in a successful lobbying effort to ban handguns in Evanston. They then saw a need for affordable housing, and raised funds to purchase and renovate twenty-four apartments, which they rent to the community at below market rates. The housing project was such a success that the congregation purchased an additional ten units, and at the request of the city began training other nonprofit groups to do the same. Beth

Emet has also volunteered itself as a sanctuary congregation for refugees fleeing El Salvador and Vietnam, and collectively "took in two families, got them stabilized, and got them jobs in the area," Gerston recounts. The congregation also has a volunteer team that works on environmental sustainability both within Beth Emet and in the wider community.

The most recent undertaking of the Social Action Committee has been a synagogue-wide program called Just Congregations. Developed by the Union for Reform Judaism to help synagogues engage in local activism, the program employs Saul Alinsky's model of grassroots organizing, which gets congregants in conversation with one another, helps them identify common concerns, and then encourages them to turn those concerns into advocacy projects. Gerston, now Beth Emet's Just Congregations chair, anticipates that public education, at-risk youth, and funding for elder care—problems taken on by nearby congregations that have already employed the organizing tool—might be some of the issues Beth Emet will choose to get involved in. In addition, of course, to the blood drives, food drives, interfaith exchanges, peace activism, and private voluntarism the congregation already carries out regularly. According to Gerston, all of these social action projects "have always had rabbinical support," but have come largely at the urging of the membership, many of whom feel the synagogue could do even more.

Almost everyone in the congregation finds the synagogue's extensive outreach to be a source of pride. "Being a member of Beth Emet has allowed me to live out my sense of Jewish identity by working on social justice issues with talented and committed people," says one congregant. For many, activism is even more important than worship. "We talk about the importance of worship, and we truly believe it, but for most people, that is not their expression of Judaism," explains Cantor Frankel. "That's why they talk about social action, that's why they talk about Israel, about *Tikkun olam*. These are Reform Judaism's major themes," she says. "The Social Action Committee, the Environment Committee, the soup kitchen . . . those are tangible ways of expressing *Tikkun olam*," Bob Cutler explains. "That comes from religion, but it also becomes social in a way. We have social action because we consider it to be a religious mandate."

"Preaching to the Choir"

"Beth Emet is a moral force," says one new member, "it's not just about words and preaching." Yet words and preaching also have their place at this cerebral synagogue, and the clergy at Beth Emet seldom miss a chance to mingle political issues with religious messages. "There's a politicization in everything we do," explains the executive director. "We try to teach people to be responsible human beings," she says, and the issues discussed openly in worship and study classes range from "soldiers in Iraq to stem cell research." Indeed, because of the thin conception of God and theology but robust sense of collective conscience at Beth Emet, political involvement serves as an important mode of religious expression for synagogue members. For most, the pervasive presence of political discussion, therefore, is taken as a matter of course. "This is part of what I see my Judaism as being—as a way of reflecting what's happening in the world around me," one member says. "How do I understand what's going on around me? How do the people here help me unpack that? How does my Judaism inform the political issues of the day?" These are the kinds of questions she, and many of her fellow congregants, expect to hear addressed from the pulpit—and at Beth Emet, they routinely do.

At 8:15 on a dark Friday evening in September, hundreds of families dressed in formal attire gather for the second of two services to celebrate the eve of Yom Kippur, Day of Atonement, the most solemn and important of Jewish holidays. Those who live close enough to walk to synagogue do so, avoiding the lines of cars waiting to be directed by off-duty police officers into spots on the streets and in the jammed parking lot. A line has formed in the nursery school hallway, and Bekki Harris Kaplan, a tall lively woman dressed in a black skirted suit and pearls, breezes to and fro grasping a walkie-talkie, and pauses briefly to help two middle-aged women distribute tickets at the card table that has been set up to block the entrance to the synagogue. "Finkelstein . . . D, E, F . . . there you are!" says one of the women, handing a white envelope to an elderly couple. "*Shabbat shalom*," responds the man, whose black sateen yarmulke stands up, tentlike, on his balding head. He leads his wife past the table and down the hall into the nearly full sanctuary.

The sanctuary is a low-lit carpeted hall filled with nine long rows of padded, auditorium-style seats clustered around a raised platform called the *bimah*. A large abstract painting in deep, dramatic colors with an overlaid Hebrew inscription hangs above six large Torah scrolls resting in a cabinet veiled in sheer fabric. At the front of the *bimah* stands a table topped with crisp, cream-colored linens, six blue candles, and a *shofar*, or ram's horn, the blowing of which on Saturday afternoon will conclude the two-day holiday of fasting and repentance. Men and women stand up in the rows, greeting one another warmly as late-coming families search for seats before resignedly settling into the rows of folding chairs set up in the overflow.

As the service begins, Cantor Erin Frankel stands behind a wooden podium adorned with an elaborate bouquet of white lilies, and intones the opening strains of the Kol Nidre, a hauntingly beautiful prayer sung in operatically styled Aramaic, accompanied by a professional cellist and choir. A series of liturgical prayers and blessings is then chanted in Hebrew, some of the more familiar of which are sung with vigor by the entire congregation, others by only a handful of voices. Rabbi Knobel's wife lights the six blue candles, and the Torah is then ceremoniously removed from the ark, after which Rabbi London leads the congregation in its annual plea for absolution: "May all the people of Israel be forgiven, including all the strangers who live in their midst, for all the people are in fault," the congregation repeats three times. Rabbi Knobel—a short, self-assured man wearing glasses, a close-cropped beard, and a white robe with a gold-embroidered stole—then takes his place at the podium.

"Yom Kippur is a day that encourages the recognition of flaws, both in persons, and in a nation," he begins, "and we need a national accounting of our behavior. Without such an evaluation we stand little chance of making progress." Relating the Torah story of David and Bathsheba, Rabbi Knobel praises the prophet Nathan's courage for confronting David in his guilt—"thou art the man"—and for "speaking truth to power." He then goes on to deliver a scathing, twenty-minute sermon on the failed role America has played in the Israeli-Palestinian peace process, and the immorality of the war in Iraq—"this generation's Vietnam." "Issues of war and peace are not merely political issues, but issues of religious values. Our tradition mandates wars of self-defense, and rejects wars that are to gain territory or power . . . [and] there is a failure on the part of the religious community, especially the Jewish community—in spite of resolutions passed by our national bodies against war—to actively inspire us to protest the war." Going on to invoke nearly every hot-button issue of the day including abortion, immigration, and "xenophobia," Rabbi Knobel leaves his congregants with the injunction to "consider how this great superpower will use its resources to help bring about a safer, more just and compassionate world."

Part of what makes overtly political messages common at Beth Emet—even on the holiest of holidays—is what many congregants identify as an implicitly shared worldview among Reform Jews. According to Bob Cutler, "The religion per se doesn't proselytize a certain political perspective. It's just that Jews, because of their history—long, collective, communal history—have developed a general outlook toward politics that tends to be clearly more liberal or progressive." "The politics is talked about, but it's in a way like preaching to the choir," he adds. Some members of Beth Emet feel this shared politics is generated by religious teachings, while others put the relationship the other way around. Seth Lisbon says that "when trying to decide a political issue," he will "look at it from my understanding of the Torah." Evie Greenberg agrees: "I don't get [liberal politics] out of a vacuum—I get it from someplace very concrete: the Torah and the rabbinic interpretation." Cantor Frankel, on the other hand, feels that more often, political opinions are formed first, and then cast in a religious light. "We as liberal Jews look for things in Judaism to back up what we already feel," she says. For Bob

Cutler, the shared politics of Beth Emet members comes from a mix of religious teaching and cultural transmission. "There clearly is in our worship, in our prayers, in our liturgy, our texts, and so on, all of these messages about the human condition, war, all of those sort of things. And that sort of permeates the whole consciousness of the Jewish people."

A Beautiful Tradition

When you ask members of Beth Emet why they are involved in their religion, Rabbi London says, "Most will not say 'because I have this deep faith in God.' Most people will say 'it's a beautiful tradition,' or 'the ancient messages are powerful because of the important lessons about our lives that we learn,' or 'it's a strong community.' That's the kind of thing that people will say." Indeed, many members of Beth Emet The Free Synagogue express that being a part of something greater than themselves is central to their identity as Jews, and is something that keeps them active in a synagogue even when their understanding of Hebrew liturgy, their observance of law, and even their faith in God have fallen away. "There's a common element among Jews," says Bob Cutler, "that if I was attending a Jewish worship service in another community . . . and even in a synagogue of a different denomination, I would feel an instant affinity with . . . not only the service, but with the people in attendance. Almost as if we've shared somehow, in some indefinable way, a common background. Even though we may have very different views on faith, observance—everything. We've shared a collective experience even though we've never met." One man in attendance at the Yom Kippur service, who says he comes to Beth Emet only a few times a year, echoes Cutler's feeling. He says he enjoys "reciting the same prayers and singing the same melodies my grandfather sang." "There is something powerful in knowing that thousands, even millions of other people throughout the world are doing the same thing at the same time," he adds. Even Beth Emet's handful of converts— a rarity in Judaism—seem drawn to the sense of community across space and time that is often referred to as Jewish "peoplehood." One woman says of her conversion that as she learned about Judaism, she "became conscious of a wish to belong to the Jewish people—and to join them in their effort to repair the world."

SACRAMENT MEETING

Twenty minutes south of Salt Lake City, Sandy, Utah, straddles State Street, the east–west dividing line of what locals call the Valley. Driving north on 90th South, visitors encounter a small faded sign proclaiming Sandy to be the "23rd Most Livable and 26th Safest City in the U.S.A." With its monstrous shopping malls and traffic-filled roads, Sandy is by every appearance a typical Western suburb. Tucked away off a main thoroughfare, the one-time center of this now sprawling city has fallen on hard times. Consisting mostly of small older homes clustered around a dilapidated Main Street, historic Sandy is, according to one lifelong resident, "socioeconomically depressed," and stands in stark contrast to the countless modern subdivisions that radiate out from it in every direction.

At 1:00 on Sunday afternoon, the large parking lot that wraps around the Sandy West Stake Center of the Church of Jesus Christ of Latter-day Saints is nearly full. The Pioneer Ward—one of some 197 Mormon congregations in Sandy alone—is gathering for "sacrament meeting," as large families and young couples file into the nondescript, one-story brick building, passing a sign that reads "Visitors Welcome" on their way inside. With very few architectural cues identifying it as a house of worship, this Mormon church is typical of the hundreds like it that dot the Wasatch front. A subtle metal steeple adorns the chapel's roof, and looms over the church's manicured landscaping, complete with a close-cropped lawn and three deliberate-looking trees encased in concrete planters. Inside, the building's decor is equally plain: stock blue carpeting, white cinder block walls, and hallways lined with storage cabinets and numbered doors that lead to various small classrooms and administrative offices.

Just outside the sanctuary a large painting of a resurrected Christ hangs next to a floral-patterned couch, but inside the chapel not a single religious image adorns the spare but orderly space. With lofted, wood-paneled ceilings and long windows covered in sheer white curtains, the chapel has an airy but functional feel. "We have one item of ward business to take care of today," says Bishop Jeff Lovell, the lay ministerial leader of the Pioneer Ward, as the opening hymn concludes and the last of about 120 worshippers take their seats. Bishop Lovell lists the names and addresses of families that have moved "into the ward boundaries," and asks them to stand so the congregation can get to know them. "Please join me in welcoming these new members by the raise of the right hand," Lovell says, to which the entire congregation responds instinctively.

The worldwide Latter-day Saints, or LDS, church is a highly organized, centrally governed institution with a strong sense of collective identity. The First Presidency of the Church, consisting of a Prophet and his two counselors, stands at its head, along with a Quorum of Twelve Apostles and eight Quorums of the Seventy, comprised of men who serve as "special witnesses of Jesus Christ," and administer the church's programs in different areas of the world. Rather than choosing a place of worship that is to their liking, Mormon churchgoers are assigned to congregations—called "wards"—based on the location of their homes, a practice that is widely adhered to because of the nearly uniform worship experience across congregations. A cluster of wards comprises a "stake," which meets together a few times a year. Wards tend to be limited in size to 300 to 500 members, with new boundaries being drawn and new wards created by stake leaders when attendance exceeds that range.

"Our opening hymn will be 'There Is a Green Hill Far Away,' after which the sacrament will be administered by the Aaronic priesthood," says Bishop Lovell, an unassuming family man dressed in a dark suit and a blue striped tie. He takes his seat in a padded chair behind the podium as the organist plays a slow, ponderous introduction to a hymn commemorating the crucifixion of Christ. A rotund white-haired man in a sweater and dress slacks adjusts a music stand on the left side of the large raised platform at the front of the chapel, and leads the congregation in a melody drawn from the green hymnals scattered throughout the pew backs.

The Pioneer Ward is one of three congregations that share space in the Sandy West Stake Center, and because of the high concentration of Mormons in the area, its boundaries take in only about twenty square blocks, but include some 425 members. The ward struggles to keep members attending, however, and Bishop Lovell estimates that only about 30 percent participate in worship and other activities. "We kind of have the core group of families that have been here for a while or that will be here for a while, and then we have a number of rental homes or apartments in the area, so we see a lot of people come and go," he explains. And because of the predetermined boundary system, the resultant ward community is fairly diverse, with doctors and university professors worshipping side by side with factory laborers, students, and the unemployed.

Five men approach a wooden altarlike table to the right of the stand and remove a white tablecloth to reveal several trays filled with tiny plastic water cups and bite-sized pieces of white bread on small silver platters. "O God, the Eternal Father, we ask thee in the name of thy Son, Jesus Christ, to bless and sanctify this bread to the souls of all those who partake of it, that they may eat in remembrance of the body of thy Son," a sixteen-year-old boy behind the table says into a microphone, beginning a blessing on the bread and water, the only ritualized aspect of this morning's service. The sacrament is then distributed, row by row, to the seated congregation by a handful of men ranging in age from twelve to fifty. Two young girls in pink and yellow cotton dresses play quietly in the pews, as the cooing of babies and the occasional outbursts of toddlers are hushed by parents trying to maintain the quiet reverence that has fallen over the room.

After several minutes in which the congregation sits silently— some with bowed heads, some reading from leather-bound volumes of scripture—the first "speaker" takes to the podium, which is lowered slightly by Bishop Lovell to accommodate her. "I've been asked to speak today on self-reliance," says Sister Hannah Thompson, a young woman of about twenty-five with long blond hair whose voice wavers ever so slightly with nervousness. She asks the congregation to open the Doctrine and Covenants—a book in the Mormon scriptural canon—to "section 107 verse 100 which reads: 'He that is *slothful* shall not be counted *worthy* to stand, and he that learns not his duty and shows himself not approved shall not be counted worthy to stand. Even so. Amen.'" "This scripture teaches us the value of work," Hannah says, going on to state that individuals must "ask Heavenly Father for help" in becoming self-reliant. "I know this gospel is true, and I've learned that for myself through faith and hope and prayer," she adds at the close of her seven-minute discourse. "In the name of Jesus Christ, Amen," she concludes. "Amen," the entire congregation responds, affirmingly.

Following Hannah's "talk," an older man in a suit stands and addresses the same topic, holding Christ up as "an example of self-mastery." The hour-long meeting then concludes with a hymn entitled "When Faith Endures," and an impromptu benediction is offered by a thirty-something man who carries his young daughter with him up to the podium and cradles her in his arms as he bows his head, asking "Father in Heaven" to bless those who could not be present at the worship meeting, and for help in "applying what we have learned here throughout the week." The organist then begins a short postlude as the congregants greet each other in the pews, laughing and offering hugs and hellos. Slowly, the group makes its way out of the chapel and down the hall to their various classrooms for the remaining two hours of their weekly worship meetings.

"I Know This Church Is True"

The Church of Jesus Christ of Latter-day Saints began in 1820 when a fourteen-year-old farm boy named Joseph Smith Jr. claimed to have seen a vision of God the Father and Jesus Christ in a grove of trees near his home in upstate New York. Joseph Smith taught that he was a prophet called by God to form a new Christian church in which the authority to administer "saving ordinances" such as baptism—having been taken away from mankind because of apostasy—would be restored. Smith also asserted that he had been led to unearth and translate a divinely preserved record of God's dealings with the ancient peoples of the Americas, which he published as The Book of Mormon in 1830. Along with the Bible, this book is considered by Smith's followers to be scripture, and is the source of the church's most common nickname.

In a tiny farmhouse in 1830, a small group consisting of Joseph's friends and family, as well as a few individuals who believed him, gathered to formally and legally establish the church, which steadily gained members, especially among immigrants from the British Isles. Driven from place to place by persecutors, the early "saints" eventually settled in the Salt Lake Valley, and Utah remains the cultural and administrative hub of Mormonism, now a global church some 13.5 million strong. One of the fastest growing religions in America, the church's success at winning converts owes largely to its strongly evangelical spirit. There are currently over 52,000 "proselyting" Mormon missionaries serving throughout the world, joining the ranks of some one million that the church has sent out to proclaim the gospel since its founding.

To Mormons, "proclaiming the gospel" means more than telling Joseph Smith's story. A central feature of Mormon theology is "the plan of salvation," which teaches about souls existing before coming to earth, mortal life as a testing ground for faith and obedience, Christ's mission to pay the price for sins, and "eternal progression"— the potential individuals have to become godlike as they learn, grow, and journey through immortality. Mormons also believe that since the death of Joseph Smith, God has continued to "call" authorized successors who communicate with Him on behalf of the church. The "prophet on the earth today" is eighty-two-year-old Thomas S. Monson, who lives in Salt Lake City and functions as both the spiritual leader and administrative president of the LDS church.

Theology seems to be the central rallying point for members of the Pioneer Ward, and belief in the unique features of Mormon doctrine is essentially a litmus test for joining the church through baptism, which is taken to be an enduring commitment. "For me, theology is very important," says Jonas Stephenson, a lifelong Mormon and Pioneer Ward member. "I know that much better meetings could be generated than the meetings I go to on Sunday. . . . But I don't go to church because I think it's the best thing going on a Sunday morning. I go to church because I know that that's where I should be, and it's the place that will get me closest to God." Lesli, Jonas's wife, agrees. "The busier life gets, dragging two little kids to church for three hours is really hard. And it would be so easy to just start staying home on Sunday," she says. "But I know it's something that I need in my life, I know it's something my kids need in their life, and it's not just a feel-good experience—it's important. We believe it's important for our salvation."

The Stephensons explain that members born into the church as well as potential converts are instructed repeatedly to seek a "personal testimony" of Mormon doctrine by praying and asking God if it is true. Lesli has taken that challenge and feels her prayers have been answered. "The reason I'm a member of the church is, number one, because I know it's true, and I like having that truth in my life," she says. Karley Michaels, an adult convert to the church, agrees. "It brought a lot of light where before there had been a lot of darkness," she says, adding, "It feeds my soul." Donna Berger, a member of the Mormon church since childhood, explains her commitment to the faith this way: "I guess part of it is that it's all I've ever known, but I do have a testimony, I do believe that the church is true. I've gotten answers to prayers, I've had lots of good feelings about things, and I just have a sense of knowing that what I'm doing is right." Donna has had periods of "inactivity" in her life, during which she has not participated in worship, but says she has never doubted the church's teachings. "I've never really even thought to go to another religion," she says.

"A Sacrifice for Everybody"

In congregations such as the Pioneer Ward, members' commitment is far greater than a theological one, however. Because Mormon congregations employ no professional ministers, all worship, instruction, activities, and pastoral ministry are conducted on a volunteer basis by members. Positions in the church are referred to as "callings," and the majority of callings within a ward are pre-designated according to the bureaucratic organization of the church. The Pioneer Ward has an activities committee, a chorister, a Sunday school teacher, and a Young Women's leader, to name a few— as does every other ward worldwide. Bishop Lovell says that part of his job is to invite individual members to fill specific positions, the idea being that each member should have some particular role in the ward. Callings are meant not only to make the congregation function, he explains, but also to foster commitment, growth, and service among the membership. As to how it is decided who will fill what role, Gloria Kittridge, who serves as one of three leaders of the Relief Society, the Pioneer Ward's women's group, says "the church's answer would be that it's divine revelation, and that the Lord knows, and I do believe that. To say that you can't lobby the bishop to get out of a calling or to get into one is not 100 percent true, but I do think that the Lord has some say in what goes on." Callings are not necessarily tailored to an individual's qualifications, Kittridge adds, and a church member could hold dozens of different positions throughout a lifetime.

Jeff Lovell, a thirty-one-year-old with a bachelor's degree and no training in ministry or theology, has been serving voluntarily as bishop for three years, a calling that is generally held for about five. "I didn't feel like it was something I could say no to," he says. "It was very overwhelming at first, just the idea of doing what I have to do as a husband and a father with small children there's a lot of work already. . . . But it's gotten quite a bit better as I've gotten more comfortable with the responsibilities, and as I've gotten a better idea of what I'm doing." Bishop Lovell says he spends about fifteen to twenty hours a week on the ward, and that it "would certainly take more if I had it to give." And making this commitment has come at a personal cost: "There are certain things that get sacrificed," Lovell says, explaining that he started an MBA program just before being asked to serve as bishop three and a half years ago, but had to leave the program because of the calling. "I haven't gotten back to that yet. I think I will, but for the time being that's on hold."

The amount of time members spend performing their callings in the Pioneer Ward varies widely. Karley Michaels, who serves in the ward Relief Society presidency, says she gives ten hours or more per week; Naomi Felton, the ward Young Women's president, estimates she serves between one and six hours per week; and Lesli Stephenson, who functions as a Relief Society teacher, a Compassionate Service coordinator, and the ward playgroup coordinator, says she averages just two hours a week of service. "No one serving in our congregation receives any sort of financial compensation for their work," says Bishop Lovell. "It makes it difficult to serve sometimes in a leadership position because it's not what you're doing for a living, it's what you're trying to get done in the spare time you have." As to whether members ever decline to serve in a particular calling, Gloria Kittridge explains, "If you're called to a position, it's kind of the unspoken rule that you say yes. People do say no, but it's kind of like, it's a sacrifice for everybody. . . . The whole church functions by people being called to things they don't want to do, and they later find out, 'that was so rewarding, I'm really glad I did that.'"

This unspoken rule about giving service to the church means that the Pioneer Ward is almost never lacking in volunteers. Bishop Lovell says that it's easy to get help whenever he needs it. "We have great members here in the ward—we have good people in leadership positions here who are willing to do the work, and I have good counselors who are willing to do what is asked of them." Not only are ward members willing to perform in callings, however, they are also accustomed to providing service outside their designated job. During Sunday meetings, sign-up sheets are distributed throughout the congregation for things like bringing food to a ward activity and offering to provide a meal to the missionaries assigned to work within the ward boundaries. These sign-up sheets usually fill up with names without much urging on the part of the leadership, and the organizer of one ward activity says he quickly "maxed out" on volunteers to help put it on. According to Gloria, one reason ward members are eager to help is "because they've been a recipient [of volunteer service]. When they ever call me to take a meal to someone that's just had a baby, I wouldn't even hesitate to do it because I know how nice it is to have that service."

Giving Their Lives Over to God

Around 6:00 on Monday evening the Roberts family is preparing for Family Home Evening, a program created by Mormon church leaders in 1915 in order to encourage parents and children to set aside time to spend together, in hopes of strengthening the family relationships Mormons consider to be sacred. Known to members as FHE, the practice is a central feature of Mormon culture, and usually involves staying in on Monday nights and taking time to "pray and sing together, read the scriptures, teach the gospel to one another, and participate in other activities that . . . build family unity."[4]

The Roberts' tiny brick home sits on a small corner lot with a green lawn, and its red door opens into an enclosed porch that houses a jumble of strollers, balls, rain boots, bikes, and Big Wheels. Inside, Lizzy bustles about the kitchen in a homemade tie-dyed apron, setting the dinner table in the sparsely furnished but tidy front room, the walls of which bear dozens of family photographs and a large painting of Jesus. Lizzy and Steve Roberts are in their late twenties and the parents of three children—Riley, Amber, and Michelle.

Lizzy hurriedly chops tomatoes and rolls out pizza dough as she mixes up crepe batter for dessert. A soft-spoken but obviously well-educated woman who grew up in Utah, Lizzy spent most of her single years in New York City attempting to launch her career as a children's book illustrator. Marrying Steve shortly after returning to Utah, she continued to illustrate as she raised both Riley and Amber, but says she gave up trying to have a career when Michelle came along. "It was just too much with three—and with trying to do my calling," she says, referring to the fact that she serves in the stake Young Women's presidency, a regional leadership and training body overseeing various ward-level youth programs for teenaged girls. Church service is evidently a priority for both Lizzy and Steve, who serves as the ward executive secretary, a sort of special assistant to the bishop.

"That must be Des," Lizzy says, heading to the front door to answer the bell, chasing after her children who are screaming excitedly. Returning to the kitchen, she's followed by a young African American man dressed in fatigues and knee-high, Goth-style boots. His hair is braided into purple strands that extend beyond his shoulders, and on his fingernails he wears a coat of chipping jet black polish. Des comes over to the Roberts' house once or twice a week, and they seem to have taken him under their wing since he moved into the Pioneer Ward about a year ago. Lizzy greets him casually, asking him how he's been. He washes his hands and joins in the dinner preparations, adding sauce and toppings to the pizzas. Des became a Mormon in 1991 at the age of eighteen, after a long process of conversion that began with seeing a commercial for the LDS church on TV. He says he was impressed early on by how nice the church members he met were to him. Years later, he still recalls attending a conference for youth before his baptism, and it being the first time in his life he felt entirely unaware of his race. He moved to Utah, he explains, to escape the "small-mindedness" and prejudice he experienced elsewhere.

Steve comes home from work at about 6:30, and the family gathers around a large wooden table for dinner. Steve offers Des his chair, and himself sits on a bench pulled up to one side of the table. "Heavenly Father, we thank thee for this food, and ask that it will strengthen our bodies," Riley says, offering a blessing on the spread. They talk about Des's latest job prospects, and how he's doing after having been laid off from a software company. After dinner concludes and the plates are cleared away, Lizzy packs up some extra pizza for Des to take home. Steve and Lizzy then gather the kids around a small upright piano in the front room to sing an "opening song" for Family Home Evening. Des stands to one side with his hands in his pockets, a bemused smile on his face. As Riley climbs up on the piano bench and Michelle adds a few staccato notes to her mom's accompaniment, they sing two children's songs. "*Scrip*ture power, keeps me safe from sin! *Scri*pture power is the pow-wer to win . . . !" The kids take turns getting tossed in the air by their dad during the chorus, squealing with delight for one more verse and one more turn. After the song, everyone moves to the couches in the living room and after a few minutes of gentle urging by her mother, Amber folds her arms on her chest and squints her eyes closed as she says a short and somewhat incomprehensible prayer. Steve then attempts to teach the kids a simple lesson on the importance of the Sabbath day, and tells a biblical story about what Jesus did on the Sabbath. "What does 'Sabbath' mean, Riley?" "What are some of the things we do on Sundays, Amber?" Between hanging over the back of the couch and searching for treasures between the cushions, the kids talk about going to church, visiting cousins, and taking walks on Sundays, and Riley points out that going to the store or to a movie are things they try to avoid. The lesson is over almost as quickly as it began, but Steve has managed to engage the kids for a few minutes at least before they start bouncing around the room again.

Other Mormons too stress the importance of religion in their lives. Asked how much a part of her life church membership is, Gloria Kittridge says it is "definitely a huge part." "Especially now staying home [as a mother], I would say it's even more a part of my life than I ever thought it would be." Gloria's weekly church commitments include daily scripture study and family prayer twice a day, plus three hours of church on Sundays, Family Home Evening on Mondays, and a playgroup for young mothers on Wednesdays. Teenagers attend a weekly activity on Tuesdays. In addition, the women's organization holds a meeting called Enrichment once or twice a month, plus each organization in the ward will put on a family activity once a quarter. Ward members are also asked to make home visits to two or three other members once each month in programs called Visiting Teaching (for women) and Home Teaching (for men). On top of these obligations, members are expected to perform the duties associated with their calling(s), as well as to pay 10 percent of their income to the church in tithing. Having outlined the litany of obligations her ward membership entails, Gloria concludes that to her "it doesn't seem like it [is a big-time commitment]. It's just part of your life," she concludes cheerfully.

"We don't consider it demanding—we would *never* say that it's demanding," explains Joe Bennet, a retiree who raised his family in the Pioneer Ward. "We're just united with people that share the same values and same focus and so you just end up being involved on many different levels because there's so much there." Joe's daughter-in-law, who is also a member of the ward, agrees. "I would say enriching, rather than demanding." Linda Lewiston, who converted to the church a few years ago, recounts that when she was preparing for baptism a fellow LDS member cautioned her, "This is a hard church to be a member of—a lot's expected of you," to which Linda responded, "Well it should be. If it's real to you then [it's hard]." Now, she says, the church shapes her life every single day. Karley Michaels agrees. She says that due to her conversion, Mormonism now defines her "probably about 100 percent." "I am who I am because of this gospel—because of the changes that I've made in my life by joining this church," she explains. "I think there's a great man in our church who said that men and women who give their lives over to God will soon find out that God can make a lot more of their life than they can alone. And I think that that's where it is for me. I think that's the truth."

"An Awful Lot of Civics"

Despite the huge in-church time commitment required of them, members of the Pioneer Ward are also extensively involved in the community outside their congregation. Betty Hapley serves every year as a volunteer judge at the Utah State Fair and the Stephenson family works on behalf of the Wasatch Marine Aquarium Society. Several women in the ward have served on the PTA—both the current president and the president-elect are ward members, and many other Pioneer Ward mothers help out as classroom assistants at the elementary school. Donna Berger volunteers with the Sandy Historical Society, as well as sitting on the Sandy Suburban Improvement District Committee, an elected board that handles municipal

sewer planning. Ward members also participate in the Neighborhood Watch Committee, the Lions' Club, United Way, and a community choir that sings at nursing homes; and four years ago Janet
Weston started a local community garden that has been very popular amongst her fellow congregants. Ward and stake leadership also
take on the administration of the Boy Scouts program in the community, and in addition to private volunteer work, the congregation
often puts on service activities, such as the community blood drive,
and the pledge drive for Primary Children's Hospital that the youth
group sponsored in a recent month.

Joe Bennet, a recipient of the Noal Bateman Service Award,
given annually to the citizen of Sandy who contributes outstand-
ing civic service, is also a lifelong ward member. He says he sees
"no real trade-off" between volunteerism in the community and the
demands of his religious obligations. "My focus for a lot of years
was in the church, and then I picked up on the city," he says. Tony
Canton, who has held many leadership positions in the ward, does
recognize the tension between where ward members allocate their
time to volunteer, but doesn't consider it a hindrance. "It's an issue,"
he says, "because the LDS church does put a lot of time demands on
the people, so it's a little bit harder to do some of these things . . .
but you do what's important to you."

Tony partially credits church leaders' emphasis on civic involvement for the degree to which Mormons engage in their communities. "There's not a lot of political discussion, but there's an awful lot
of civics that are discussed," he says. "Civics in being patriotic, helping your neighbors, getting involved in the community, getting out
and getting involved even in the political process of the candidate
of your choice. Being involved in things that make our society and
our community better—there's a lot of talk about that," he explains.
"Religious motivation" also plays a part in the ward's outward focus,
says Janet Weston. "Some people who don't have plots [in the community garden] actually have volunteered to help with whatever we
might need because I think they like the idea and, to be frank, one
of the tenets of Christianity is feeding the poor and clothing the

naked, you know, giving like that, and so I think that that resonates with them as well." Indeed, humanitarian assistance is a huge part of the Mormon church's activities worldwide. Some 6,400 "service missionaries"—mostly retired couples—work on building, agricultural, and education projects throughout the world, supplementing the over $1 billion in financial and material support the church has distributed globally since 1985. "I feel an obligation to do my part. I also feel like it's a commandment from God to make a contribution," explains Tony Canton. "I do believe that God wants us to leave the world a better place than we found it."

"Pushed over the Pulpit"

Despite the high levels of civic engagement among the members of the Pioneer Ward, most assert that their public activities are privately motivated, and declare unequivocally that little to no politics finds its way into the life of the congregation. "I have *never* heard *anything* spoken from the pulpit that is political," says Jessica Bennet. Another ward member agrees, stating that politics is simply "not discussed" in church. Such comments seem largely a reflection of the LDS church's official policy of apoliticism on the local level. "Every election season the bishop reads letters [from church leadership] saying 'vote your own conscience.' The church is not to be used for any political campaigning or anything like that. That's strictly forbidden," Gloria Kittridge explains. However, Jonas Stephenson acknowledges that this policy isn't always perfectly adhered to when members take to preaching and teaching. But, he says, "I don't think politics in particular is ever pushed over the pulpit in preference to any other bias that a person has. You get speakers all the time that get up there and we hope that they focus on the doctrines of the church, and the gospel, and Christ, but it happens that a person strays from that and starts preaching certain things that are their personal bias. That happens a little bit with politics, but it's not disproportionate to any other bias that a person might take with them to the pulpit. Most people in the ward can see that for what it is."

Though historically such apoliticism has been definitive of modern Mormons' worship experience, a departure from this norm occurred during the 2008 election season, when the First Presidency of the Church issued a statement to be read by bishops over the pulpit in California wards. In reference to the group behind Proposition 8, the ballot initiative to overturn the California Supreme Court's ruling allowing homosexual marriage, the letter stated, "The Church will participate with this coalition in seeking [the initiative's] passage. Local Church leaders will provide information about how you may become involved in this important cause. We ask that you do all you can to support the proposed constitutional amendment by donating of your means and time to assure that marriage in California is legally defined as being between a man and a woman. Our best efforts are required to preserve the sacred institution of marriage." The move by LDS leaders to draw a clear connection between theology and politics, and then issue a directive to congregants, was exceptional and almost wholly unexpected, according to many Mormons. Because the preservation of the traditional family is a major focus of modern Mormonism, the surprise came not in the church's stance on the issue, but rather how explicit and official that stance became.

"If A, then B"

Though the Mormon population in Utah has formed what is perhaps the strongest conservative voting bloc in the country, most members insist that this phenomenon is not the result of directives from inside the church. In fact, many members of the Pioneer Ward seem to pride themselves on being vocal exceptions to the Republican rule in Mormonism. "It seems that most of the people in the ward that are into politics have ties to the less popular party around here," explains Bishop Lovell, himself a conservative. Tony Canton, who preceded Lovell as bishop and has run for office as a Democrat, agrees: "I would say that our collective political views are probably much different than most LDS congregations. There are a lot of Democrats. Surprisingly there are a lot of intellectuals. A lot of teachers, a lot of professors . . . and I think it is a little more liberal thinking than most LDS congregations." Indeed, the Pioneer Ward contains congregants who are pro-choice and pro–gay marriage, individuals who are active in the Utah Democratic Party, and four elected officials—all of whom are Democrats.

Yet conservative voices still form the clear majority in the congregation, as in the church as a whole. Ward member Mike Bennet is proud to represent a set of political opinions widely held throughout Mormondom, explaining that he takes the Republican view "on abortion, gay marriage—all of that," and adds that he is "absolutely against a large welfare state." "It's all about self-governing, it's about being responsible for one's own actions, for one's own decisions," he says. "Sometimes in a more liberal perspective there's a lot of reliance on government, whereas I think the church teaches a lot about being self-sustaining." Still, Bennet acknowledges that such views—while the norm throughout the church—are not shared by all of his fellow congregants. "There is a big dichotomy in the ward—there's a big political separation in our ward," he says.

But this ideological divide mostly manifests itself as "a bantering of ideas back and forth," as his wife, Jessica, describes it. Bishop Lovell agrees that on the rare occasions when political comments are made in lessons or talks, "it's in jest, primarily." And despite the political divide in the ward, those on opposite ends of the spectrum seem to share meaningful relationships. Joe Bennet, Mike's father and a strong conservative, says "I co-teach a gospel doctrine [Sunday School] class with Luke Hurley, who's probably the most fuzzy-headed liberal you could ever imagine. We are so far apart on the political spectrum—as far as you can possibly get—and yet we've been close friends for forty years. We laugh and joke and get along." Mike agrees. "I'm very conservative," he says, "but Tony [Canton] and I go out to lunch once a week and kind of fight for a while, just because it's fun. We're really great friends, and I think even though there are some pretty diverse opinions in the ward, it doesn't ever get in the way of friendships and faith building and stuff like that."

While in Sandy ward members of different political persuasions have come to trust each other's character through personal association, the stigma that is often associated with liberal politics remains strong throughout the Mormon church, according to the church's liberal congregants. "I just think that [the Pioneer Ward] has always been a Democratic bloc," says Gloria Kittridge, who had a career in Democratic politics before becoming a stay-at-home mom. "A lot of the people that live in this area were raised here and then come back because of that, because they've gone other places and kind of felt out of place." Indeed, political liberals are the odd ones out in a church where more than nine in ten members are Republican, and most wards are homogeneous politically. Even in wards where politics is almost never discussed—formally or informally—the pressure to conform to the norm is palpable, says Gloria. Explaining her feelings of being "out of place" as a Mormon Democrat, she says, "there has been kind of this tension within the church about politics—there's always been kind of this unsaid belief that you can't be a Democrat and a good Mormon."

Naomi Felton, a political independent whose sister works for the Service Employees International Union, says she has felt the same pressure to toe the conservative line on political issues: "My husband's parents have said to me, basically, 'Well, if you believe the doctrine, then you would think this way.' It's almost like, 'if A then B.'" Tony Canton has run into this bias many times in the church, and says that he believes "a lot of people are Republicans because they think that that's what the leadership of the church would like them to be. . . . I have had people say to me that they know I'm a good person, they know I'm a good man, they know I was the bishop, but they have a hard time with me being a Democrat." Canton also believes that many politically liberal Mormons keep their views to themselves simply because "they don't want to be branded as a person who has lower standards and lower morals." Though he clearly rejects that reading of the faith, Canton acknowledges that it's difficult to swim against such a strong cultural tide. And California's Proposition 8—where implicit social pressure has given way to explicit directives from church leadership—has complicated the claim of Mormon Democrats that there is more than enough room in the church for differing points of view.

"Eternal Perspective"

Interestingly, members of the Pioneer Ward on both ends of the ideological spectrum say that their political views are largely a product of their religious beliefs—as are the choices they make about virtually everything they do, day in and day out. As Karley Michaels explains it, "If religion is your whole life, then you're going to vote according to the tenets of your religiosity." Yet Democratic congregants tend to cite Christian values such as equality, compassion, and helping the poor as the source of their politics, while Republicans generally point to principles of self-reliance and personal responsibility, as well as the "moral" issues of abortion and homosexuality. All these ideas have a place in Mormon teachings. Arriving at opposite political conclusions while sharing a fierce loyalty to Mormon theology, culture, and church teachings means that reconciling differences won't come easily for the members of the Pioneer Ward.

Yet despite the church's recent political entanglements, most Mormons continue to believe that politics is merely an appendage to their faith. "On Sunday [politics] doesn't make much difference," says Tony Canton, "and politics are important but it's not nearly as important to me as my friendships." The more central work of the Mormon church, say congregants, is impacting individuals' lives for the better, and helping them "progress spiritually." Asked what sort of influence he thinks Mormonism has in society, Joe Bennet explains that Mormons in the Pioneer Ward and throughout the world "are trying to change the hearts of people, trying to change the way they conduct their own lives, the way they live, the way they love, the way they serve, and in that way changing the structures of families, of societies, of cultures, and working from the bottom up." Naomi Felton says that this "eternal perspective" is her main motivation for devoting her life to the church. "There's a lot [theologically] that I don't understand . . . but I don't need to understand everything because when I live what's being taught, I receive blessings and I feel God in my life, and that's all I need."

CHAPTER 11

RELIGION IN
AMERICAN POLITICS

P erhaps the most visible change in American religion over the
last generation is the role it has come to play in the nation's
politics. Religiosity has partisan overtones now that it did not
have in the past. While there are notable exceptions, the most highly
religious Americans are likely to be Republicans; Democrats predominate among those who are least religious. Among the punditry,
this connection between religiosity and the vote has been given the
unfortunate but alliterative label of the God gap—the gap in question referring to the political differences between people at varying
levels of religiosity.[1] It is thus like the so-called gender gap, the difference in the partisan tendencies of men and women. And, like the
gender gap, the coupling between religiosity and partisanship has
become one of those unquestioned generalizations of American
political life—an election day fault line endlessly discussed by political pundits and shrewdly exploited by political operatives.

This chapter and the next examine the connection between religiosity and politics, but from different perspectives. In this chapter, we deal with the political landscape. What has happened in the
nation's politics to drive a wedge between religious and nonreligious
voters? And what might the political future hold? The next chapter
then shifts the focus from what happens in politics to what happens
in churches (and other places of worship). How do individual parishioners come to connect their religion with their politics?

We will first show that the glue which holds religiosity and partisanship together is the political salience of two issues in particular: abortion and same-sex marriage.[2] Attitudes on both are tightly connected to religiosity—which is not a new development. The new part is that they have become politically salient, as the Democratic and Republican parties have taken opposing positions on both abortion and homosexual rights. As the parties have moved apart on these issues, religious and nonreligious voters have moved apart also. But, we suggest, should attitudes on these issues change, the religious divide in politics would likely also change. For while attitudes on same-sex marriage are moving sharply in a liberal direction, those on abortion are becoming somewhat more conservative—with both shifts most pronounced among young people.

Because of its longevity as a shaper of the partisan landscape, changes in abortion attitudes are especially portentous. Abortion has long been a wedge pulling more religious and less religious voters apart from one another. However, if unease with abortion becomes relatively common even among secular voters and comfort with gays relatively common even among religious voters, religiosity could cease to be a source of political division. If so, we could be headed toward a period of political "creative destruction," an opening for political entrepreneurs to forge new coalitions.

RELIGIOSITY AND PARTY PREFERENCE

We begin by confirming the conventional wisdom: Religious and nonreligious voters differ dramatically in their partisan preferences. While the extent and endurance of the religious divide between the parties easily can be exaggerated, as a broad generalization it is accurate to say that religiosity and support for the Republican Party are bound together. While there are many ways to make this point, it is instructive to focus on the frequency of saying grace[3] as a good tracer of religiosity. The more often you say grace, the more likely you are to find a home in the Republican Party, and the less likely you are to identify with the Democrats. Being a political independent,[4] though, is unrelated to grace saying. Indeed, few things about a person correspond as tightly to partisanship as grace saying. We stress that the connection between grace and the GOP is not a fluky result owing to the fact that grace saying is somehow an idiosyncratic measure of religiosity. No matter the yardstick of religious devotion or practice, the story comes out the same. See Figure 11.1. When using our more complete index of religiosity (which does not actually include saying grace as one of its components), the picture looks virtually identical: The highly religious are far more likely to be Republicans than Democrats, those who are low on our religiosity scale largely favor Democrats over the GOP, and religiosity has no bearing on partisan independence. Even when we account statistically for other things that often go along with religiosity—such as marital status, age, region of the country—the connection between religiosity and partisanship remains.[5]

A focus on the broad contours of the religious divide between the parties can obscure as well as reveal. While it is generally the case that a higher level of religious devotion predicts greater support for the Republicans, the connection between religiosity and partisan preference varies in important ways—both across religious traditions and over time. Consider, first, the fact that highly religious members of different traditions vary widely in their Republicanness. Roughly 70 percent of highly religious evangelical Protestants and Mormons identify as Republicans, with highly religious mainline Protestants right behind at 62 percent.[6] However, only half as many highly religious Catholics describe themselves as Republican (35 percent).[7] And, as we saw in Chapter 9, Black Protestants are arguably the most highly religious group in America—including the most frequent grace sayers—and yet are also the least likely to identify as Republicans (merely 14 percent of highly religious Black Protestants do so). In Figure 11.1, the percentage of Republicans among the most frequent grace sayers and/or highly religious would be considerably higher if we were to exclude African Americans. It is highly religious evangelicals, mainline Protestants, and Mormons who

AMERICAN GRACE

Figure 11.1

THE "GRACE GAP": FREQUENCY OF SAYING GRACE PREDICTS PARTY IDENTIFICATION

(with standard demographic characteristics held constant)

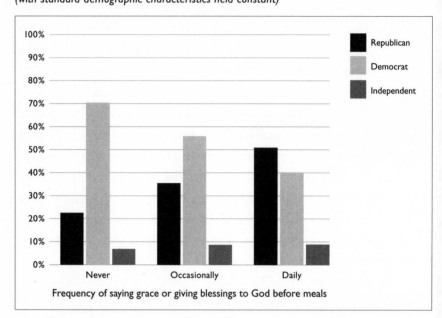

Frequency of saying grace or giving blessings to God before meals

THE "GOD GAP": STRENGTH OF RELIGIOSITY PREDICTS PARTY IDENTIFICATION

(with standard demographic characteristics held constant)

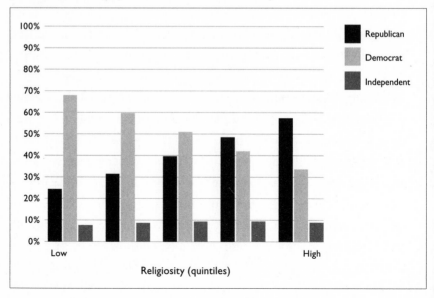

Religiosity (quintiles)

SOURCE: FAITH MATTERS SURVEY, 2006.

are the most likely to be Republicans. Indeed, the fact that highly religious Mormons are also the most overwhelmingly Republican underscores the unusual composition of the Mormon congregation we highlighted in Chapter 10, where we found a critical mass of Democrats. Our Mormon vignette reinforces the fact that even among the most heavily Republican religious group in the country there is still some degree of political diversity, as 20 percent of highly religious Mormons identify as Democrats.

We stress, therefore, that even though we focus most of our attention on how religiosity shapes the partisan landscape, the reader should remember that a tendency is not a certainty. While highly religious Americans tend to be Republicans, that is not an iron law; likewise, while Americans with little or no religion in their lives have an even stronger tendency to be Democrats, there are exceptions.

THE RELIGIOUS DIVIDE OVER TIME

The religious divide between the parties has become well entrenched. However, its emergence was not predestined. For while the political differences between the religious and nonreligious run deep, they are not necessarily permanent. Nor are they a constant, as the religiosity-partisanship connection has varied over time. The General Social Survey is the most convincing source of data to examine the connection between religiosity and partisanship. Figure 11.2, therefore, displays the relationship between the frequency with which someone attends religious services and their party identification, while also accounting for a bundle of other demographic characteristics that might plausibly explain any connection between them.[8] A positive number means that more church attendance predicts a higher likelihood of identifying as a Republican— the higher the number, the greater the relationship. As we see in the figure, the Republicans had a modest advantage among churchgoers in the early 1970s, which likely was fallout from the George McGovern campaign of 1972. McGovern's campaign embodied the initial shock described in Chapter 4 and helped trigger the first after-

Figure 11.2

THE LINK BETWEEN RELIGIOUS ATTENDANCE AND
PARTY IDENTIFICATION HAS VARIED OVER TIME (GENERAL SOCIAL SURVEY)
(whites only, with standard demographic characteristics held constant)

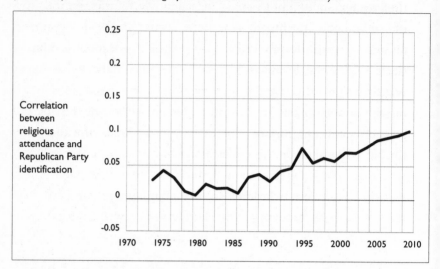

THE LINK BETWEEN RELIGIOUS ATTENDANCE AND PARTY
IDENTIFICATION HAS VARIED OVER TIME (NATIONAL ELECTION STUDIES)
(whites only, with standard demographic characteristics held constant)

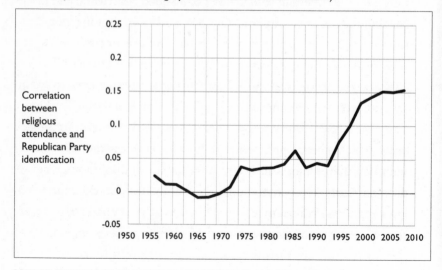

SOURCE: GENERAL SOCIAL SURVEY AND NATIONAL ELECTION STUDIES.

shock. McGovern was famously labeled the candidate of "abortion, amnesty [for draft evaders], and acid." He was also supported by an unusually secular group of activist supporters, which only added to the wariness of religious voters.[9] In the mid-1970s, though, the modest "religiosity advantage" that Republicans had over Democrats disappeared with Jimmy Carter's successful presidential campaign. Carter cultivated an image of being morally upright and was outwardly religious, being the first presidential candidate to describe himself as born again. Then, beginning in the 1980s, the Republicans gained an advantage among highly religious voters, which has continued to grow since. We can take a slightly longer historical view with the National Election Studies, which date back to 1952. Again, we see that there was little to no religious divide in partisanship in the 1950s and 1960s, with a pattern similar to the GSS from the 1970s to the present. The presidential vote affirms the trends in partisanship. In 1952 in the midst of the post-war religious boom, Republican Dwight Eisenhower received exactly the same percentage of support (59 percent) among Americans who attended religious services frequently and among those who never attended. Compare that to 2008, when there was a 22 percentage point difference in support for John McCain between those who attended religious services at least weekly (61 percent) and those who never attended (39 percent).[10]

In other words, the connection between religiosity and partisanship has varied over time, and has grown considerably since the mid-1980s.[11] Indeed, American history teaches us that religion is neither exclusively left nor right, progressive nor conservative. Instead, religion of different sorts has been associated with political causes of different sorts. On some issues, notably those related to race, religion has been invoked to justify both sides of the debate. In the nineteenth century, religion animated advocates of both abolition and slavery. No one put the point better than Abraham Lincoln, who, in his second inaugural address, referred to the two sides of the Civil War by noting that "both read the same Bible and pray to the same God, and each invokes His aid against the other."[12] Lincoln's words, however, obscure an important point about the way religion relates to politics, since they imply a symmetry between the religious justifications of pro- and antislavery advocates. Actually, white Southerners would have been pro-slavery without religion; while white Northerners likely would have been antislavery only because of religion. Likewise during the civil rights era, while the civil rights movement relied substantially on black churches as sources of both organization and inspiration and also found allies in many Northern mainline Protestant churches, some segregationists also found a religious rationale for their beliefs.

Beyond race, throughout America's history other issues have had an explicitly religious impulse, whether it was the drive in the early 1800s to stop the delivery of mail on Sunday, or the campaign for Prohibition, or the broader Progressive movement. Given the close association of religion and American patriotism, opinions motivated by nationalism are often given a religious inflection. The American Revolution had religious impulses. So did anticommunism in the Cold War era, and so does support for the Iraq and Afghan wars today. Religion, however, has also inspired the political left—from pacifists to antiapartheid advocates to the movement to provide sanctuary for undocumented workers.

What is unusual about the current period, then, is not that religion matters in American politics. In a highly religious nation like the United States, we should not be surprised that religion and politics would intertwine. Nor is it unusual that religion has come to matter in the specific domain of presidential politics. For example, John F. Kennedy in 1960—and before him, Al Smith in 1928—faced a stained glass ceiling, as many Protestant voters were wary of a Catholic president. What makes the current period unusual is that church-attending evangelicals and Catholics (and other religious groups too) have found common political cause. We call this the "coalition of the religious." Given that not all religious traditions are equally likely to identify with the Republicans—and Black Protestants barely do at all—it is more accurately labeled the coalition of *most* of the religious. At the same time, the growing ranks of (most) nonreligious voters are also allied, but on the opposite end of the political spectrum.

THE POLITICAL GENERATION GAP

The creation of a new coalition of the religious represents a major change in the foundation of the American political system. But will this be an enduring feature of American politics? The answer lies partly in the process by which the coalition emerged. There are two different but potentially complementary ways in which a partisan shift of this magnitude can occur. The first is change among individual voters, such as when a frequent churchgoer switches from identifying as a Democrat to a Republican. To the extent this occurred, it would suggest that the current divide could disappear rather rapidly as those individuals switch again. Or the shift could occur because of generational replacement, which is much more gradual but also more enduring. That is, as an older generation whose partisan allegiances reflect the coalitions of a previous political era die off, they are replaced by political newcomers who came of age in a period of new political alliances. As the younger generation replaces the older, the new alliances supplant the existing political coalitions.

The evidence suggests both a large generational shift in the connection between religiosity and partisanship and a more modest change among individual voters. The generational differences can be seen in our analysis of the Faith Matters surveys, as the God gap is widest among people under the age of thirty-five, growing progressively weaker among voters in ever older generational cohorts, with the weakest relationship of all observed for those sixty-five and older. Such a pattern is consistent with generational replacement, as the differences could reflect the different eras in which each generation entered the electorate. Older voters formed their political loyalties at a time when there was little or no relationship between religiosity and partisanship, and so their initial partisan orientation was not associated with their level of religious involvement.[13] Younger voters, however, have known only a political system in which religiosity and partisanship are closely aligned.

While suggestive, data from one period of time cannot determine definitively whether the differences we see are owing to generational replacement or simply to maturation as people move through the life cycle. More convincing evidence is found when we track the connection between religiosity and partisanship by interviewing the same people, and their children, over time. By doing so, we can follow changes within the same individuals over time, as well as across generations.

Studies that follow intergenerational trends over time are rare, but fortunately one has been conducted since the mid-1960s, precisely the period of time in which we are interested. In the Youth-Parent Socialization Study, a nationally representative sample of high school seniors and their parents was interviewed in 1965. Researchers reinterviewed both generations in 1973 and again in 1982. In 1997, they returned again to the second generation and then also interviewed the children of the second generation (post-boomers). The resulting data provide an unrivaled opportunity to trace intergenerational trends, including the connections between religiosity and partisanship.

As seen in Figure 11.3, in 1965 we find a modest connection between frequency of worship attendance and voters' party identification. Frequent attenders were slightly more likely to be Republicans. Not surprisingly, the parents and their adolescent children (generations 1 and 2) show almost exactly the same correlation. We can see the generational differences emerge when comparing generations 1 and 2 over time, as by 1973 the baby boomers display a very different relationship between religiosity and partisanship than their parents. In 1973, when those of generation 2 were in their mid-twenties and just reaching political maturity, they show no connection between church attendance and party identification. Among their parents, however, the modest connection observed in 1965 held steady. By 1982, the story changes. The modest relation-

Figure 11.3

THE RELIGIOUS DIVIDE HAS GROWN AMONG BABY BOOMERS, BUT IS WIDEST AMONG THEIR CHILDREN

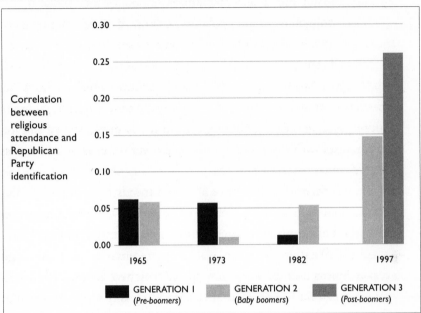

SOURCE: YOUTH-PARENT SOCIALIZATION STUDY.

ship between religiosity and partisanship observed in 1965 and 1973 had disappeared among the older generation, but had reappeared among their children, the boomers.

The changes from the mid-1960s to the early 1980s were small. The real change occurred between 1982 and 1997. In that period, the link between religiosity and partisanship grew substantially among baby boomers; the strength of the connection between religious attendance and party affiliation among the second generation was almost three times as strong as in 1982. Since these are interviews with the same people at different points in time, we can be confident that the emergence of the religiosity divide has entailed some individual-level change, as churchgoing and partisanship have come into alignment. In the words of M. Kent Jennings and Laura Stoker, two political scientists who have done a thorough analysis of these same data:

As gen[eration] 2 moved through adolescence to middle age,
they were much more responsive than their elders to the emerging cultural conflicts infusing American politics, and ended up
much more likely to hold political positions that reflected their
religious preferences and levels of commitment.[14]

While individual change is part of the story, the comparison between
generations 2 and 3—the baby boomers and their post-boomer
children—suggests that generational replacement has played an even
more significant role in the appearance of the connection between
religiosity and partisanship. The post-boomers have nearly twice the
correlation between attendance at religious services and party affiliation as their parents. The strength of the tie between religiosity and
party affiliation among this generation is all the more striking when
we consider that, in 1997, the post-boomers were roughly the same
average age as their parents were in 1973—when their parents' generation evinced no connection between religiosity and partisanship.

In sum, data from this long-running panel study suggest that the
current religious divide has cracked open because of both generational replacement and, to a lesser degree, individual change. The
strong generational component of the God gap's emergence suggests that it will likely endure—while the smaller individual-level
calibration between church and party reminds us that changes in
political alignments can, and do, happen. As we saw in Chapter 5,
this calibration process can even be observed over a single year. And
while political allegiances are sometimes calibrated to be in tune
with one's religion, in our current political environment we also see
evidence that people calibrate their religious involvement to align
with their politics. In any given year, these are small changes but,
cumulatively, they add up.

This process of generational replacement is typical of change
in the partisan landscape. In spite of the usual election year hype
about this or that voting bloc swinging dramatically from one party
to another, changes generally occur through a process more akin to

plate tectonics than earthquakes—steadily over a period of time, not suddenly. Once parties' brand labels take hold among the electorate they do not disappear overnight. Individuals' own partisanship is often a form of self-identity, and is long-standing. This is why we can speak of people being Republicans or Democrats, almost as though party label is a demographic category. Fundamental change in the partisan configuration of the electorate requires large blocs of voters to move from one party to another, and this is far more likely to happen among voters coming of political age than those who have had a long-term partisan affiliation.

Today's religious divide opened up in a gradual process; should it close, that too is likely to be a gradual process.

COUNTRY CLUB VS. SUNDAY SCHOOL REPUBLICANS

In discussing changes in the partisan landscape, it is important that we take a moment to correct a widely held misconception about the Republicans' coalition of the religious. Many pundits speak as though today's Republican Party is split between two opposing factions, defined by what those Republicans do on Sunday mornings.[15] There are those Republicans who spend Sunday mornings on the links—the affluent country club wing of the party. Then, allegedly, there is the downscale Sunday school wing of the party, who spend their Sunday mornings in the pews. Since religion, it is often said, is a salve for the poor, these two wings are thought to inhabit different worlds. If true, this would significantly dampen the electoral significance of the God gap, since it would mean that the two wings of the Republican coalition could easily rupture.

Really, though, the two wings are largely one and the same. Many of those country clubbers are the Sunday schoolers. In our 2006 Faith Matters survey, we divided people into four mutually exclusive categories defined by their level of education and frequency of church attendance. People are either frequent or infrequent church attenders, and have either high or low education (as a reliable marker of socioeconomic status), thus creating four mutually exclusive categories:

1. More than a high school education / Attend church monthly or more
2. A high school education or less / Attend church monthly or more
3. More than a high school education / Attend church less than monthly
4. A high school education or less / Attend church less than monthly

Of these four groups, the highest percentage of Republicans is found among people who attend church frequently *and* have high education.[16] Furthermore, as shown in Figure 11.4, since the 1970s, Republicans have seen gains among college-educated churchgoers—voters with one foot in the country club wing and another in the Sunday School wing of the party.[17]

These Republican gains among college-educated churchgoers go hand in hand with the fact that class and religion have become mutually reinforcing. As detailed in Chapter 8, religion is not only for the poor. Recall that Americans with high socioeconomic status are no less likely to attend religious services as those with low socioeconomic status. In fact, over roughly the last thirty years, it is the working class who have become less likely to attend church relative to the upper class. An increasing skew in the socioeconomic status of churchgoers has accompanied the increasing Republicanness of high-socioeconomic-status churchgoers. So, relative to the working class, college grads are more likely to be church attenders, and those church-attending college grads are increasingly likely to be Republicans. Importantly, these changes are not driven solely by the political transformation of the South, which was once monolithically Democratic but is now a far more Republican region (in presidential elections, overwhelmingly so). When we examine the

Figure 11.4

COLLEGE-EDUCATED CHURCHGOERS ARE MOST LIKELY
TO BE REPUBLICANS (WHITES ONLY)

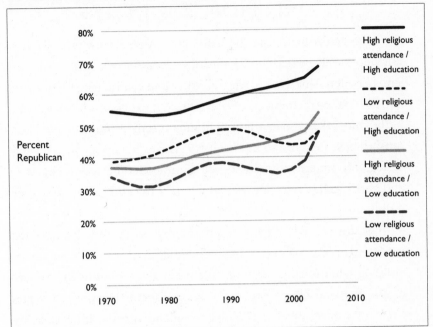

SOURCE: NATIONAL ELECTION STUDIES; DATA LOESS-SMOOTHED.

same trends in education, church attendance, and party identification but leave Southerners out of the picture, the results are nearly
identical.

The political implications of the country club–Sunday school
fusion are profound, as it explains how the GOP succeeds by simultaneously advocating both social and economic conservatism. If a
high level of religiosity were coupled with economic desperation,
the Republicans would have to say very different things to the two
wings of the party. As long as those college grads are in the pews, the
Republicans can preach a single sermon that blends social conservatism with economic policies favored by the educated class. As a matter of fact, political scientist Larry Bartels shows that cultural issues
like abortion and same-sex marriage have the greatest impact on the
votes cast by upper-class voters.[18]

ABORTION AND HOMOSEXUALITY: THE GLUE THAT HOLDS THE COALITION TOGETHER

We have determined that the God gap is neither new, nor fleeting, nor necessarily permanent. Nor does it conflict with the class division between America's parties, another foundational element in the nation's political chemistry. What, though, explains why, beginning in the mid-1980s and continuing to the present, religiosity and partisanship have become so intertwined? Any explanation must be able to account not only for why we see a connection between religiosity and partisanship now, but also why that connection appeared when it did.

The answer, we suggest, lies in the issues that have brought the coalition of the religious together. Politics is always a matter of building coalitions. Coalitions, in turn, come together in reaction to the political issues that are salient. Successful politicians, parties, and movements frame issues in such a way that otherwise disparate groups see themselves as allies in a cause. Coalitions come together around issues, but those issues have to come from somewhere. Because the United States has an extremely porous political system, there are many points of entry for issue entrepreneurs. Political scientist John Kingdon evokes a fitting metaphor when he describes the "policy primeval soup" found in Washington.[19] It is survival of the fittest, and the issues that win—those that rise from the soup to become the big issues voters care about—are often the issues that can bring new groups together, or even create a shared identity among people who previously had little in common.

Given the strength of the religiosity-partisanship connection, one could be forgiven for thinking that religiosity, like one's party preference, shapes opinions on a wide range of issues. This is not so. Instead, religiosity has a tight connection to attitudes regarding abortion and gay marriage, and a more modest correlation—or none at all—to issues that do not pertain to sex and the family. The coalition of the religious has come together around a small bundle of issues.

We base that conclusion on a statistical analysis which accounts for the impact of other personal characteristics that might plausibly be related to the positions people take on the issues of the day (using our standard bundle of demographic controls). By controlling for these other factors, we can be sure that religiosity is not standing in for another factor (like gender or living in the South) that is itself related to religiosity. Religion is only one of myriad factors that affect where people stand on public issues, although the specific factors vary depending on the issue. For some, race matters. For others, gender matters. For still others, economic background matters. And so we account for these many other influences on people's political opinions.

While we cannot claim to have examined every issue imaginable, the 2006 Faith Matters survey did include a wide array, including:

Death penalty

Foreign aid

Immigration

U.S. intervention in world affairs

Protecting civil liberties vs. safety from terrorism

Government efforts to close income gaps between rich and poor

Same-sex marriage

Abortion

As shown in Figure 11.5, the issues fall into three categories: those for which religiosity matters a lot, for which it matters less, and for which it does not matter at all.[20] Of all the issues included in the 2006 Faith Matters survey, only two unequivocally fall into the category where religiosity matters a lot: abortion and same-sex marriage.

Figure 11.5

RELIGIOSITY AND POLITICAL ATTITUDES
(with standard demographic controls held constant)

For attitudes on abortion and same-sex marriage, religiosity matters a lot

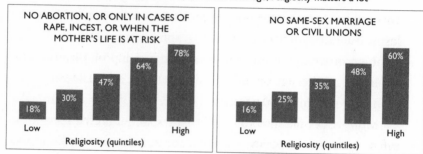

For other issues, it matters less

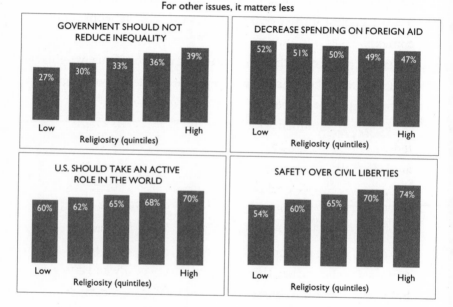

For still other issues, it does not matter at all

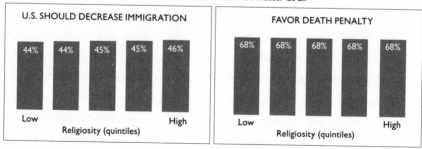

SOURCE: FAITH MATTERS SURVEY, 2006.

Holding everything else steady, when we move from the bottom of the religiosity index to the top, the percentage of Americans who oppose abortion in all but cases of rape, incest, and endangerment of the mother's life rises from about 18 percent to 78 percent—an enormous 60 percentage point gain. We observe a similar, if slightly less substantial, connection between religiosity and attitudes toward same-sex marriage: From the bottom to the top of the religiosity index, the percentage opposing same-sex unions rises 44 percentage points (16 percent to 60 percent).

More issues fall into the "a lot less" category: civil liberties vs. safety, government policy to close income gaps, interventionist foreign policy, and spending on foreign aid. Of these issues, religiosity has the biggest impact on safety vs. civil liberties, with the others trailing behind. Intriguingly, in the "not at all" group we find attitudes on both the death penalty and immigration. Once we account for the myriad other factors that affect public opinion, religiosity has no bearing on where people stand on either one.

Religiosity's influence on public opinion thus has a narrow scope. It does not matter at all for some issues, matters only a little for most, and matters a lot for only two. Abortion and same-sex marriage are the glue holding the coalition of the religious together.

The connection between religiosity and these sex and family issues is necessary to explain the religious divide between the parties, but it is not sufficient. For while the tie between religiosity and partisanship has varied, the link between religiosity and attitudes on both abortion and same-sex marriage has been constant. Since at least 1972, the first year of the General Social Survey, and almost certainly much longer, frequency of religious attendance has consistently been a strong predictor of opposition to abortion and disapproval of homosexuality.[21] (We shall see below, however, that religiosity is becoming less closely associated with attitudes on abortion, at least among young voters.)

So what did change? The answer is that, beginning in the 1980s, sex and family issues—which had long been aligned with religiosity—also became aligned with positions taken by America's two major political parties. As a result, religiosity and partisanship came into alignment.

This alignment occurred because of a change in the political choices offered to voters. If the political choices placed before Americans are uncorrelated with religion, then any political decisions that might be affected by religion are moot. Consequently, for religion to affect the choices voters make, the candidates on the ballot must have contrasting positions on the issues shaped by religion.

To see why the two criteria work in tandem, pretend that you have taken a side in the cola wars and are a partisan of Pepsi rather than Coke. Accordingly, when given a choice of restaurants that are otherwise equal you would prefer one that serves Pepsi. Imagine that we conducted a study in which we tried to predict the restaurants that you frequent. You would expect us to find a correlation between your preference for Pepsi and your preferred restaurants— you are more likely to eat in Pepsi-serving restaurants. From that study, we would conclude that there is a relationship between the brand of soda you like and where you eat. Now, suppose that we ran the same study, but this time all the restaurants in the city serve only Coke. We would no longer find a correlation between soda preference and restaurant choice, as it would appear that whether you like Coke or Pepsi has no bearing on your decision of where to eat. However, the absence of a correlation only reflects the absence of choices. Politics works the same way. Unless candidates in an election differ on an issue—that is, offer voters a choice—that issue cannot be a factor affecting how people vote. It seems obvious, but the changing choices offered to voters are too rarely acknowledged as the explanation for the emergence of the strong relationship between religiosity and the vote.[22]

CHOICES

We have seen that prior to the 1970s whether one went to church had little to do with party preference.[23] Subjects like abortion and homosexuality were not to be uttered in polite company, let alone included in a political platform. Then, American society, and thus politics, underwent a dramatic change. The new divisions within American politics are succinctly captured in the slogan popularized by the women's movement: The personal is the political. Owing to the social tumult of the Sixties, politics came to be defined by a new set of issues that were very personal indeed, including abortion. As we described in Chapter 4, the long Sixties were a shock to American society, the effects of which are still being felt. Then came the first aftershock, which reverberated through American religion, as theologically conservative—largely evangelical—religion was revitalized. This first aftershock also rippled through American politics, causing new cleavages and alliances within the electorate. The coalition of the religious began to come together, and the political movement known as the Religious Right was born.[24]

The many activists who comprise the Religious Right movement, particularly the evangelicals who stand at the center of the movement, are animated by an array of issues: school prayer, pornography, creationism, public displays of religious symbols and monuments, and even a concern for global human rights.[25] However, the specialized issues that motivate small numbers of activists do not necessarily trigger a tectonic shift in the foundations of the parties' coalitions. As political scientist Geoffrey Layman puts it, "Only those issues that capture the sustained attention of the mass public and change its perceptions of and feelings about the parties are capable of creating long-term partisan change."[26] Most of the issues that mobilize activists, who almost by definition have opinions and interests outside the mainstream, do not matter much to "regular" people, the vast majority of whom do not make politics a priority. Few issues spur deep-seated change in the partisan makeup of the general population. Those that do often touch an emotional chord. Civil rights is one example, given the visceral reaction many Americans have to race.[27] Abortion is another.

Why does abortion have such political potency? At the risk of profound understatement, we note that abortion symbolizes more than merely an obstetrical procedure. For people on both sides of the issue, abortion is a highly symbolic issue that touches a raw nerve. In describing the reaction to the Supreme Court's landmark abortion decision, *Roe v. Wade*, political scientist David Leege and his colleagues write that "Religious traditionalists reacted so strongly against the decision because it seemed to threaten and devalue the unique quality that set women, as bearers of children, apart from men."[28] Based on her comprehensive study of abortion activists on both sides of the issue, sociologist Kristin Luker goes even further and describes how, to them, abortion is a referendum on the totality of one's moral worldview:

> The pro-life world view, notwithstanding the occasional atheist or agnostic attached to it, is at the core one that centers around God. . . . [T]he pro-choice world view is not centered around a Divine Being, but rather around a belief in the highest abilities of human beings. For them, reason—the human capacity to use intelligence, rather than faith, to understand and alter the environment—is at the core of their world.[29]

To be pro-life typically, then, indicates more than one's position on abortion. Abortion stands in for a bundle of beliefs that, grouped together, can be called moral traditionalism. Luker was studying activists, that rare breed who have a passion for politics and whose opinions are the most strident. Within the general public, the link between attitudes on abortion and a moral worldview is admittedly weaker, but still easily detected. People with pro-life attitudes are not only more religious when compared to those on the pro-choice side, they are far more likely to disapprove of premarital sex, to believe that it is best if women do not work outside the home, and to say that children should be taught obedience over self-reliance. No matter the measure, pro-life advocates come out as more morally traditional. While we are not suggesting that abortion sits as the prime mover of all sex and family attitudes—among such a cluster of closely related opinions, trying to single out one is undoubtedly a fool's errand—we simply note that abortion is inextricably bound up with moral traditionalism across the board, and has become a potent symbol for a morally traditionalist worldview.

Remember, though, that a political issue can only divide the electorate when voters are presented with a choice on that particular issue. In the case of abortion, the Democratic and Republican parties did not diverge sharply on the issue until the 1980s. In 1976, the Republican platform was more or less neutral on abortion. By 1980 it unequivocally endorsed a constitutional amendment to ban abortion, language that has been preserved ever since. Meanwhile, as described by political scientist Christina Wolbrecht, 1980 was "the first time the Democratic party firmly established itself as pro-choice and expressed its opposition to the curtailment of federal funding for abortions."[30] Beginning in the 1980s, voters had a choice on abortion. The battle lines had been drawn.

Let us be clear about why we draw attention to the parties' national platforms. While few voters read or pay any attention whatsoever to them, they nonetheless reflect the priorities of the activists, donors, and candidates of the party—those who establish the party's brand label in the minds of rank and file voters. Increasingly, abortion was becoming a line of demarcation between Republicans and Democrats. Candidates, especially presidential candidates, learned that they had to toe their party's line on abortion in order to win over the ardent activists. The process is self-reinforcing. Activists and partisans come to learn that "good Republicans" are pro-life (and, likewise, "good Democrats" are pro-choice). As a result, a strong position on abortion feeds on itself—pro-lifers are attracted to the Republican Party, while Republican partisans come to be pro-life. Political scientists Clyde Wilcox and Barbara Norrander describe this process succinctly:

> As party elites moved apart on abortion, voters gradually picked up their signals. Strong partisans for whom abortion was not salient changed their attitudes on abortion to fit cues coming

from party leaders, and those for whom abortion was very salient changed their partisanship to match their attitudes.[31]

The changes occurring in the parties were accompanied by an increasing emphasis on abortion in the nation's churches. However, just as the parties did not react immediately to Roe v. Wade, so too was there a delayed reaction to the decision in at least some religious circles. When the Supreme Court decided Roe v. Wade, opinion about abortion was in flux. While Catholic leaders were decidedly against it, opinion within evangelical circles was unsettled. In 1971, just two years prior to Roe, the Southern Baptist Convention even approved a resolution that called for the legalization of abortion in some circumstances.[32] Following Roe, it took a few years for evangelical leaders to embrace the pro-life cause as fully as their Catholic counterparts. By the late 1970s, though, evangelical opposition to abortion hardened, setting the stage for the coalition of the religious to come together. The old interreligious tensions manifested in Kennedy's 1960 presidential race were forgotten. These former antagonists found that what united them was greater than what divided them.

As the effects of the parties' divergence on abortion rippled through the electorate, attitudes on abortion came to be highly correlated with partisanship. Figure 11.6 shows this clearly, again using data from the General Social Survey (which has used the same measure of abortion attitudes since 1972).[33] As before, even when accounting for the same array of demographic controls, we see that abortion became strongly associated with party identification in the mid- to late 1980s, precisely the time at which the God gap—the link between church attendance and partisanship—also appeared. Since the mid-1980s, the growing linkage between opinion on abortion and partisanship parallels the increasing connection between church attendance and party identification.[34] Today religiosity, abortion, and partisanship form an interlocking triumvirate, but this has not always been the case. When abortion was emerging as a major issue during the 1970s, Democrats were somewhat more likely to oppose

Figure 11.6

ATTITUDES AGAINST ABORTION AND HOMOSEXUALITY HAVE BECOME
MORE STRONGLY CONNECTED TO REPUBLICAN PARTY IDENTIFICATION
(whites only, with standard demographic characteristics held constant)

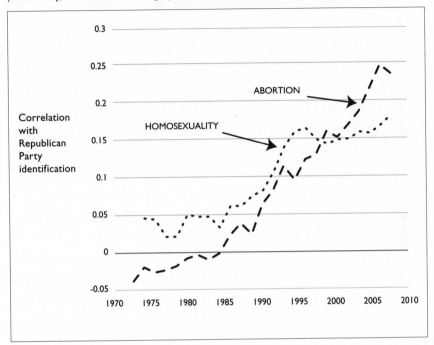

SOURCE: GENERAL SOCIAL SURVEY.

abortion than Republicans, because, in that period, Catholics were overwhelmingly Democratic and pro-life. It was not until the Democratic and Republican parties took distinctive stands on abortion in the 1980s that the issue became a predictor of party sympathies.

The rise of abortion as a dominant dividing line between the parties can easily leave the wrong impression about the nature of public opinion on abortion. Abortion's link to partisanship does not mean that Americans are grouped in either an ardently pro-choice or pro-life camp, with few holding a moderate position. To the contrary, most Americans are in the moderate middle on abortion, as they are on most issues. In the words of political scientists Morris Fiorina, Samuel Abrams, and Jeremy Pope:

The evidence is clear that the broad American public is not polarized on the specifics of the abortion issue. They believe that abortion should be legal but that it is reasonable to regulate it in various ways. They are "pro-choice, buts." [35]

Most people's views on abortion lies in between the two poles of the issue—few Americans endorse a hard-line position banning all abortion and few believe in unfettered abortion on demand. Still, Americans do disagree on just where to draw the line on regulating abortion, and even those moderate differences are enough to divide Republicans from Democrats. Even if few people occupy the extremes of the spectrum of opinion on abortion, it is still the case that those who are more willing to limit abortion (even if they do not want to ban it outright) are more likely to identify as Republicans, while those who are more willing to permit abortion (even if they do not endorse abortion under all circumstances) are more likely to be Democrats. If anything, the relatively modest differences on abortion in the aggregate make its salience as a political issue all the more remarkable. It also suggests that even seemingly small shifts in abortion attitudes can have significant political implications—and, we will show, such a shift appears to be underway.

Recall, though, that abortion is not the only sex and family issue with a strong connection to religiosity. Attitudes toward homosexual rights and same-sex marriage specifically are tightly connected, too. Figure 11.6 also shows the connection between religiosity and attitudes toward homosexuality,[36] which, like opinion on abortion, began to be more strongly associated with Republican Party affiliation in the mid-1980s (although, unlike abortion, its relationship to partisanship has leveled off over the last decade or so).

Given that religiosity and attitudes on sex and family issues are tightly linked, it is not surprising that a majority of Americans who say that religion is very important when they make political decisions also see abortion and same-sex marriage as very important issues to them personally. In contrast, people who say that they do not draw on religion when making political decisions are far less likely to ascribe as much significance to either abortion or same-sex marriage.[37] Those at the poles of these issues place more importance on them than do people with opinions in the middle, and abortion and same-sex marriage opponents place far more importance on these issues than do supporters (see Figures 11.7 and 11.8). Eighty-one percent of people who say that abortion should never be permitted say that it is a very important matter, compared to 39 percent of those who say abortion should always be available as an option; 49 percent of those who oppose same-sex marriage say it is very important, compared to 28 percent of those who favor it. In other words, opponents of abortion and same-sex marriage place a higher priority on sex and family issues than do Americans who favor abortion rights and legal recognition for same-sex relationships.

Figure 11.7

THOSE WHO OPPOSE ABORTION PLACE MORE IMPORTANCE ON THE ISSUE THAN THOSE WHO FAVOR IT

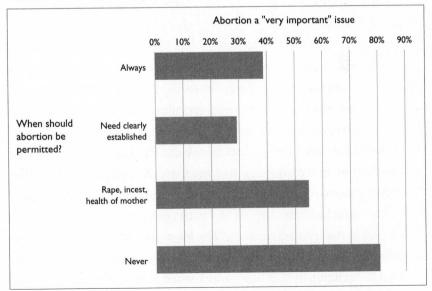

SOURCE: FAITH MATTERS SURVEY, 2007.

Figure 11.8

THOSE WHO OPPOSE SAME-SEX MARRIAGE PLACE MORE IMPORTANCE ON
THE ISSUE THAN THOSE WHO FAVOR IT

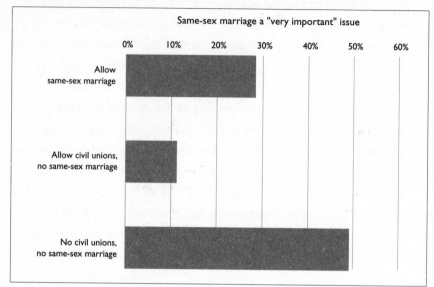

SOURCE: FAITH MATTERS SURVEY, 2007.

A CASE STUDY:
SAME-SEX MARRIAGE IN 2004

The issue of same-sex marriage provides a compelling example of how sex and family issues have been deployed in electoral politics. In 2004, thirteen states held referenda on whether to write a ban on same-sex marriages into their state constitutions, eleven of which were held simultaneously with the presidential election.[38] While the issue of same-sex marriage had been around for years, with referenda held in various other states (including California in 2000), only in the months leading up to the 2004 presidential election did the subject become headline news. The Supreme Judicial Court of Massachusetts had made such marriages legal in that state, and other jurisdictions, including San Francisco, also began granting legally ambiguous recognition to same-sex nuptials.

With these actions, the gauntlet was dropped. The Bush campaign saw an opportunity to energize the Republicans' social conservative base, evangelicals in particular, which GOP chief strategist Karl Rove had publicly identified as a priority of the Bush reelection effort.[39] In states with a same-sex marriage initiative on the ballot, campaign communications targeted to social conservatives emphasized the president's support for "traditional marriage."

Meanwhile, the campaign of John Kerry was boxed in. Characteristically, it was difficult to pin down Kerry's position on same-sex marriage. Officially, he was against it, yet he endorsed civil unions. However, he had been one of only fourteen senators to vote against the federal Defense of Marriage Act (which stipulated that no state could be compelled to recognize same-sex marriages), and had opposed a federal constitutional amendment against gay marriage.[40]

Kerry's difficulty with the issue of same-sex marriage is indicative of the more general troubles such social issues have caused the Democrats in recent years, and why the Republicans are widely seen as the religion-friendly party. A comparison of the direct mail used by the two campaigns in Ohio where, arguably, the presidential election was decided, makes the point. One of the most prevalent pieces of mail sent by the Republican National Committee has an idyllic photo of a church, with text that says "Republicans Believe in America. We are the ONLY party that defends life . . . and protects the unborn from partial birth abortion. We are the ONLY party you can trust to defend traditional marriage . . . one man, one woman" (see Figure 11.9A). With such a flyer, the Republicans' religion-friendly brand is reinforced, while the voter is subtly reminded of the upcoming referendum on same-sex marriage. Bush was hoping to benefit from vote by association. Energized social conservatives would come to the polls to cast a vote against same-sex marriage and, while there, also cast a ballot for him. The evidence shows that this is precisely what happened.[41]

Of the ten most widely distributed pieces of direct mail used in Ohio that mentioned gay marriage, all but one came from the Bush campaign or its allied organizations. The one exception speaks volumes about how sex and family issues have stymied the Democrats,

Figure 11.9A

REPUBLICANS BELIEVE IN AMERICA

We are the ONLY party that defends life...and **protects the unborn** from partial birth abortion.

We are the ONLY party you can trust to defend traditional marriage...**one man, one woman.**

We are the ONLY party that consistently supports **lower taxes for all Americans** – strengthening working families in Ohio.

We are the only party that consistently supports keeping the phrase "Under God" in the Pledge of Allegiance.

If you believe in these values, then we would ask for your vote for our Republican team.

Vote Republican On November 2.

no doubt reflecting the fact that their strategists know that opponents of same-sex marriage care more about the issue than its supporters. The one flyer in the top ten that encouraged a vote against the proposition (and thus in favor of gay marriage) is a Democratic mailer that mentions the referendum obliquely. It contains a sample ballot that shows a "yes" vote for the Kerry/Edwards ticket in large print, and a "no" vote for Proposition 1 in tiny print. Nowhere does it mention that Proposition 1 concerns same-sex marriage (see Figure 11.9B).[42]

Our point is not that sex and family issues are front and center in every election. In fact, even in 2004, same-sex marriage was not the primary issue for most voters. Rather, our point is that over the last generation sex and family issues have become one part of the Republican agenda—in some elections they play a larger role, in others their role is smaller. What is significant is that they play a role at

Figure 11.9B

FRONT

BACK

all, since there was a time in American politics when they did not. Their emergence on the political agenda presented voters with new choices, which were closely related to their level of religiosity.

The Republicans' embrace of moral traditionalism—as well as the explicit use of religious symbolism and language while doing so—has enabled the GOP to cultivate a brand label as the party friendly to religion. In the 2007 Faith Matters survey, we asked our respondents whether they think that each party is friendly, neutral, or unfriendly to religion.[43] Since we wanted to gauge how voters perceive each party's degree of "friendliness" to religion on its own and not relative to the other party, we asked about the Republicans and Democrats separately. It was thus possible for respondents to say that both parties were equally friendly, or unfriendly, to religion. As shown in Figure 11.10, the Republican Party is clearly viewed as the party that is friendliest to religion. Furthermore, this perception does not vary between those who attend church more often, or less so.

Figure 11.10

AMERICANS SEE THE REPUBLICAN PARTY AS FRIENDLY TO RELIGION, DEMOCRATS AS NEUTRAL

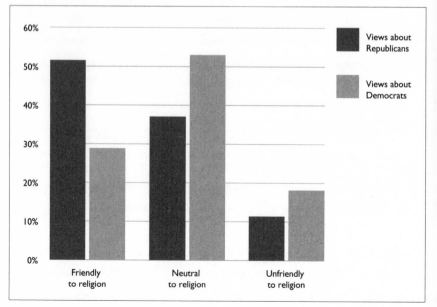

SOURCE: FAITH MATTERS SURVEY, 2007.

In keeping with our theme that religion and the Republican Party are not inextricably linked, a close reading of the data suggests that the Democrats need not despair of ever winning back religious voters. With their emphasis on moral traditionalism, the Republicans have succeeded in convincing a majority of Americans that they are friendly to religion, but this does not mean that most voters reflexively perceive the Democrats to be *un*friendly to religion. Only one in five of the population describes Democrats this way, compared to half the population who see the party as neutral toward religion. Democrats who lament the Republicans' "religious advantage" should find hope in the fact that only a small percentage of the population says that the Democrats are antireligious. Democrats' efforts to counteract the GOP's religion-friendly brand would be much more difficult if voters saw the party as hostile rather than simply neutral to religion.

The Republicans' religion-friendly image has not only had consequences for politics, but also for the American religious landscape. The party's image has contributed to the second aftershock described in Chapter 4, whereby a growing number of younger Americans have come to equate religion with "Republican," and react by turning away from religion. Furthermore, given the unpopularity of the Religious Right as a political movement, it is not clear that being identified as the party friendliest to religion will, in the long run, necessarily be good for the Republican Party.

ARE THE TIMES A-CHANGIN'?

We have seen how the sex and family issues of abortion and gay marriage are the glue that holds the coalition of the religious together. By implication, then, if abortion and gay marriage were not on the political agenda, religious and secular Americans would be much closer to finding common political ground. Indeed, this was the situation in American politics before these sex and family issues came to the fore. We make this point because these two sex and family issues may be on their way to losing their political potency. There are no guarantees in any prognostication, especially about politics, but there is evidence suggesting that change may be coming.

Homosexuality: Increasing Acceptance

We turn first to the changing opinions on homosexuality, and gay marriage specifically. Just as there has been a liberalization of attitudes regarding the propriety of women working outside the home, so is there a similar trend on the acceptance of homosexuality, and the idea of legal recognition for homosexual unions. In 1988, before gay marriage had erupted as an issue of national prominence, the General Social Survey asked a representative sample of Americans whether "homosexual couples should have the right to marry one another." At that time, only 12 percent of Americans agreed that homosexuals should be permitted to marry. By 2006, after the issue had simmered for years, that figure had risen to 35 percent. In 2008, it rose again to 39 percent. In our 2006 Faith Matters survey we find 34 percent in support of gay marriage. However, we also find another 30 percent who support a middle way, civil unions for homosexual couples.

Given generational differences in views toward gay marriage, acceptance of homosexual nuptials will likely keep growing. Young people are increasingly likely to approve of gay marriage, as the generation gap is getting wider. As seen in Figure 11.11, back in 1988, there were only small generational differences in approval of same-sex marriage; overall support for the idea was very low. Fifteen percent of young Americans (born after 1965) favored marriage for same-sex couples, compared to 13 percent among the baby boomers (born between 1945 and 1965), and 9 percent among Americans born before 1945. By 2008, half of young Americans expressed support for same-sex marriage—this is 17 percentage points higher than the baby boomers, and 28 points higher than Americans born before 1945. We even see a rise in support for gay marriage after 2004, the year in which same-sex marriage came to the fore. From 2004 to 2008, overall support for gay marriage rose by roughly 8 percentage points. It would be tempting to extrapolate from the shift between

Figure 11.11

AMERICANS OF ALL AGES HAVE BECOME MORE ACCEPTING OF
SAME-SEX MARRIAGE, BUT YOUNG PEOPLE MOST OF ALL

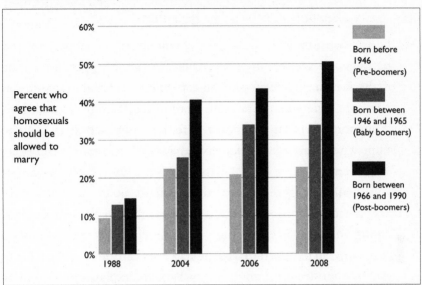

SOURCE: GENERAL SOCIAL SURVEY.

2004 and 2008 and predict that support for gay marriage will grow by
2 percentage points per year. If that were true, gay marriage would
soon become highly popular. As with mutual funds, however, in public opinion past performance is no guarantee of future returns. Opinion change on gay marriage likely accelerated in the wake of 2004,
as this was a time in which gay marriage was very much in the news,
which would be expected to maximize the flux in public opinion.
Whether the trend will continue with the same trajectory remains to
be seen. Nonetheless, it seems highly likely that liberalization on attitudes toward same-sex marriage will continue, as younger Americans have a generally more accepting attitude toward homosexuality.
For example, in 2008 while two thirds of the over-sixty-fives believe
that homosexual acts are "always wrong," that opinion is shared by
only 46 percent of 18–34-year-olds (with 35–49- and 50–64-year-olds
falling in between).

Over the last generation, attitudes to homosexuality (discussed here) and attitudes to gender roles (discussed in Chapter 8) have traced parallel paths. Both working mothers and gay marriage have won increasing acceptance among both religious and secular Americans, though the level of acceptance of both remains lower among the religious. Indeed, the impact of religiosity on support for gay marriage is actually starker now than two decades ago—a function of the fact that twenty years ago, virtually everyone opposed gay marriage. Today, the generations differ from each other in their level of support such that the most religious post-boomer is as likely to support gay marriage (32 percent) as the least religious pre-boomer (32 percent).

When put together, all of this evidence points to one unmistakable trend: Homosexuality is increasingly acceptable, especially among young people. Among young people, religiosity still drives up opposition to gay marriage, but does so starting at a much lower level of opposition. Undoubtedly, part of the explanation for young people's acceptance of same-sex marriage is that they have become politically and socially aware during a period in which homosexuality has been increasingly featured positively in the popular media. Gay characters are common in TV programs and movies and many prominent gay celebrities project an image of respectability.

Pop culture, though, is not the whole story, as there is another overriding explanation for young people's acceptance of homosexuality and same-sex marriage. Young people are also the least religious age group. Since religiosity is such a strong predictor of attitudes toward same-sex marriage, and homosexuality more generally, it comes as no surprise that the most secular cohort of the population is the most accepting of gay marriage.

Based on the inexorable process of generational replacement, we would thus also expect gay marriage to become increasingly acceptable as time passes. As young people become a larger portion of the population, overall approval of homosexuality, including but not limited to gay marriage, will rise. If and when that happens, homosexuality will become less attractive as a wedge issue in politics and will likely cease to be a potent issue at all.

Predicting change based on what appear to be generational differences in opinion must be done cautiously, since we do not know whether the liberalizing trends toward homosexuality will persist. Perhaps the acceptance of homosexuality reflects a period effect—a change that characterizes only a single period of time. If past trends hold, today's young people will likely become more religious as they settle down, marry, and have children. Maybe this rise in their religiosity will result in less support for gay marriage.

Or perhaps not. For one thing, it seems likely that young people's average religiosity will never rise to the level of that of their parents or grandparents, thus constraining their opposition to same-sex marriage. We suspect that the change in attitudes toward homosexuality, and gay marriage particularly, is a deep-seated and enduring shift. The rising acceptance of homosexuality across the population follows the same pattern as opinion toward women's rights (see Chapter 8). Just as there are differences in Americans' opinions on whether a woman's place is in the home, we suspect that gay marriage will not become universally acceptable. When opinions are closely related to religiosity and are thus an extension of a person's moral worldview, they are unlikely to undergo a wholesale change. So while we expect to see a generally liberalizing trend on gay marriage, we also expect to see approval of gay marriage eventually reach a limit. The highly religious will continue to criticize working women and they are likely also to remain opposed to gay marriage. But if that position is held only by a shrinking minority within the population, it cannot continue to be an effective political rallying cry for very long.

Obviously, widespread acceptance has yet to come, as voters continue to reject same-sex marriage at the polls. Generational replacement is a glacially slow process (not to mention that young people are the least likely to vote). Nor is this to say that we expect gay marriage to be universally adopted across the United States, as groups with intensely held opinions and the ability to mobilize politically—like opponents of gay marriage—can often hold sway. Because states vary in their average religiosity, and thus opposition to gay marriage, some states are far more likely than others to resist the drive toward marriage for homosexual couples. Again, we can draw a parallel with the struggle over women's rights. Owing to pockets of intense opposition in key states, much of which came from religious groups, the Equal Rights Amendment was never ratified.[44] Yet in the years since its defeat, support for women's rights has continued to rise.

Abortion: Increasing Ambivalence

We also see evidence that abortion's political potency may weaken, but for the opposite reason that gay marriage will likely diminish in significance. As with gay marriage, the opinions of young people differ from those of their elders. Instead of being more liberal, however, they are somewhat more conservative. It would not be accurate to describe the post–baby boomer generation as ardently pro-life, as few endorse a total ban on abortion, but they are more willing than their parents to place restrictions on abortion. In fact, their attitudes on abortion more closely resemble the opinions of their grandparents. Since this increase in opposition to, or at least unease with, abortion appears in multiple sources of data, we are confident that it is not an idiosyncratic quirk in one survey.

The best source of data over time on attitudes toward abortion is the General Social Survey. Beginning in 1972, the General Social Survey has asked an extremely detailed question about whether respondents would approve of abortion in a wide-ranging series of situations:

If there is a strong chance of serious defect in the baby.

If the woman is married and does not want any more children.

If the woman's own health is seriously endangered by the pregnancy.

If the family has a very low income and cannot afford any more children.

If the woman became pregnant as a result of rape.

If the woman is not married and does not want to marry the man.[45]

We can thus combine the responses into an index, charted in Figure 11.12, that ranges from 0 to 6—from approval of abortion under no circumstances to approval in all of them, with plenty of options in between. Since this same set of questions has been asked in the General Social Survey since 1972, we can trace opinion on abortion over nearly four decades. When viewed in the aggregate, opinion on abortion has remained largely stable.[46] However, there have been some slight peaks and valleys. The most compelling explanation for the ups and downs in support for abortion is that they correspond to the way abortion was framed by opinion leaders in each time period. When, in the 1970s, support for abortion was framed as upholding women's autonomy, attitudes toward abortion warmed. In the mid-1980s, opponents of abortion advocated popular ideas such as parental consent laws, and abortion support dropped slightly. Support for abortion then rose again when, in the late 1980s through early 1990s,

Figure 11.12

YOUNG PEOPLE ARE MORE AMBIVALENT ABOUT ABORTION THAN THEIR PARENTS' GENERATION

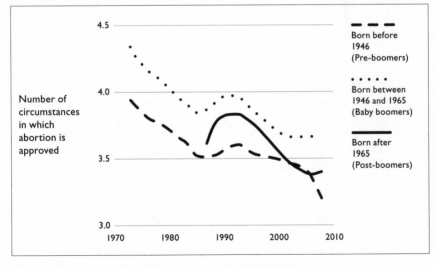

SOURCE: GENERAL SOCIAL SURVEY; DATA LOESS-SMOOTHED.

there was a real possibility that the Supreme Court would overturn *Roe v. Wade*, which would enable states to ban abortion altogether. The last decade or so, however, has seen support for abortion drop—modestly—again.[47]

Our interest is less in the ebbs and flows of overall abortion opinion, and more in the differences across generations. Before we turn to what we find, recall what we saw regarding attitudes on gay marriage. Young people support gay marriage far more than their elders, which is entirely consistent with their low average level of religiosity. Accordingly, we should expect to find that young people are also the most likely to support abortion. In fact, however, people born after 1965 are less pro-choice than their baby boomer parents.

The reluctance to support abortion among young people is especially noteworthy because it goes against the grain on other social trends. The trend has been toward greater cultural liberalism, with young people in the vanguard. Abortion stands as an outlier. Compared to other generations, the post-boomer generation is more likely to identify as Democrats, to describe themselves as having a liberal political philosophy, and as noted in Chapter 4, to support the legalization of marijuana. Nor do young people have more traditional views on other matters related to sex and sexuality. Clyde Wilcox notes that today's young people are more liberal than their elders on nearly every other indicator of sexual attitudes:

> They are far less likely to believe that premarital sex, sex among younger teens, and sexual activity among gays and lesbians is always wrong. . . . [T]he youngest cohort is most liberal on distributing birth control information to young people without parent's permission and on the availability of pornography. They are also more likely to report having seen an X-rated movie recently.[48]

In short, young people are the most sexually permissive generation. Even though liberal sexual attitudes generally correspond with a pro-choice perspective on abortion, they defy that trend. They are an odd combination of liberal on sex but relatively conservative on abortion.

We stress that it is not accurate to describe post-boomers as ardently pro-life. On average, they are willing to support abortion in at least three circumstances,[49] which is a far cry from opposing all abortions. Nor is there a gaping chasm in the abortion attitudes of young people and their parents; the difference is modest—but statistically significant. Furthermore, there has been a slight uptick in approval of abortion among young people in the last few years, suggesting that they might be on a pro-choice trajectory and in years to come may converge with their parents' generation.

Nonetheless, the discrepancy between where we would expect young people's opinion on abortion to be—based on their relatively high levels of secularism—and where it is cries out for an explanation. We can better comprehend the abortion attitudes of the young by parsing the circumstances under which they would permit it. Recall that the General Social Survey asks people whether they approve of abortion in six different situations. Three of them are related to either the physical or mental health of the mother: a serious defect in the baby, the woman's own health is endangered, or a pregnancy resulting from rape. The other three can be described as social or economic reasons: a woman is married and does not want more children, the family cannot afford more children, or an unmarried woman does not want to marry the father.

Whether a hypothetical abortion is for health or social/economic reasons, we see a similar drop-off in support, especially among the post-boomers. When we look just at approval of abortion for health reasons, the post-boomers converge with their grandparents, and even great-grandparents. That is, the baby boomers are a little more likely to support abortion for health-related reasons than either their parents' or their children's generations. The baby boom generation diverges even further from the others on abortion for social/economic reasons. And while recent years have seen a slight uptick in support for this justification for abortion among the post-boomers, they still remain below their parents' generation.

While the cultural barometric pressure is pushing support for gay marriage upward, it appears to have been pressing downward on approval of abortion. Why? There are many plausible explanations. As is often the case when explaining social change, multiple factors are likely working in concert. Recall our earlier mention of how abortion opinion appears to shift, slightly, as the terms of the public debate over abortion shift. Such a perspective can help us make sense of the growing reluctance to endorse elective abortion. In the aftermath of *Roe v. Wade* (decided in 1973), antiabortion advocates pushed for a repeal of the decision and a total ban on abortion, while supporters of abortion rights stressed the dangers of the back-alley abortions that were in living memory. In such a climate, there was little room for nuance. As *Roe* endured and became entrenched, the debate changed. Opponents of abortion increasingly adopted an incremental approach by not focusing on achieving a full-fledged ban on all abortions. Instead, they have centered their attention on advocating abortion restrictions like requiring parental notification for minors, ending intact dilation and extraction (aka partial birth) abortions, requiring pre-abortion counseling, and ending federal funding for groups that provide abortions.

These actions have largely succeeded because while a majority of Americans think abortion should be legal in some circumstances, the majority does not think it should be legal in all circumstances. As Bill Clinton famously put it, abortion "should be safe, legal, and rare"—satisfying the pro-choice movement (safe and legal) while also appealing to abortion moderates (rare). More recently, an example from the 2008 presidential campaign nicely illustrates where the center currently lies on abortion. Both Barack Obama and John McCain were asked by Rick Warren during a forum held at his Saddleback church when they believed "a baby gets human rights." McCain, a longtime opponent of abortion, did not hesitate to answer in black-and-white terms: "at the moment of conception." Obama's response allowed for more shades of gray. With palpable hesitation, Obama spoke at length about the moral gravity of abortion, and the difficulties the issue poses. McCain won applause from the assembled audience, while Obama was met by silence. Following the event, he was panned by social conservatives for saying that determining when life begins is "above my pay grade." While Obama's answer, and his nuanced perspective on abortion more generally, was unpopular among the audience for this event—congregants of an evangelical megachurch—it is closer to the mainstream of American opinion than McCain's position.

It is important to draw a distinction between the old debate over the legality of abortion and the new one over which restrictions should be placed on abortion. A debate over restrictions, without the serious threat that abortion would be banned outright, is a far cry from a debate over whether abortion should ever be permitted. In the current environment, political space has opened up for ambivalence toward abortion, particularly abortion for economic and social reasons, without advocating an absolute ban. Likewise, in this environment one can be pro-choice without defending abortion in all circumstances. Just as post-boomers have only known a world where women commonly work outside the home and where homosexuality is increasingly accepted, so also have they only known a world with the new debate over abortion. Today's young people have also grown up in an era with widespread acceptance and availability of birth control. If contraception is easy to obtain, unplanned pregnancies can appear less like a tragic mistake and more like the consequence of sexual irresponsibility.[50] Pregnancy, in such a view, is the consequence of not taking responsibility for being sexually active and, therefore, abortion means avoiding consequences. The mantra of taking responsibility and owning up to consequences is a powerful political idea, as it applies to issues such as welfare reform, standardized testing, and strictness on crime. While there can always be debate over individual cases, the meaning of "unplanned" changes when birth control is readily available. No one would say that a rape victim should "take responsibility" for not having used birth control, and contraception is irrelevant to cases where delivery puts the mother's life at risk. In both hypothetical situations, young people are as likely as their elders to agree that abortion should be permitted.

We propose still another hypothesis for young people's unease with abortion that, we concede, remains a plausible hunch rather than a tested proposition—the prevalence of in utero ultrasound images. It has become a rite of passage during pregnancy for a woman to have ultrasound photos taken of her developing fetus; often, the expectant mother can even bring home a video of her ultrasound. While we admittedly do not have hard data to test this hypothesis, we strongly suspect that the antiabortion movement has benefited from the improvement in ultrasound quality. When pro-life advocates show films of aborted bloody fetuses, many react with queasiness rather than sympathy. However, ultrasound photos pasted into scrapbooks and passed along by e-mail are a different story. Both of us have had many friends and relatives display ultrasound photos, and never once has an expectant mother used the impersonal word "fetus" to describe what we are seeing. Ultrasounds are pictures of their baby-to-be. Similarly, other improvements in medical technology have likely weakened support for abortion. Operations are performed in utero, while premature babies are increasingly able to survive outside the womb. Like the social ritual of passing around the ultrasound photos, these developments subtly reinforce the strongest argument made by pro-life advocates—the fetus is a not-yet-born baby.

As clear as the data might be, sometimes popular culture can speak even more clearly. A good illustration of young people's increasing uneasiness with abortion is the Oscar-winning movie *Juno*. In the movie, Juno is a wisecracking, irreverent, oddball teen who becomes pregnant after having sex, just once, with her boyfriend. Initially, she casually decides to have an abortion. "I would like to procure a hasty abortion," she says cheekily when calling to make an appointment with an abortion clinic. In spite of her nonchalance, she cannot go through with it. The turning point comes when she meets up with a classmate protesting outside the clinic, who tells her that the baby already has fingernails. "It has finger-nails?" Juno exclaims with surprise. That detail sticks in her mind, and she ends up leaving the seedy abortion clinic without having undergone the procedure.

As with most issues related to abortion, there is a heated debate over *Juno*'s message, specifically over whether it can be accurately characterized as a pro-life movie. We have no interest in enter-ing that debate, although we will note that the disagreement over the movie's message does serve to highlight the potency of abor-tion in the current political climate. To be pro-choice does not pre-clude uneasiness with abortion. We mention the movie because the character of Juno neatly embodies young people's unease with abortion. Members of the Juno Generation are hardly fervent pro-life supporters, but neither do they favor abortion in all circum-stances.

At the risk of trying to wring too much meaning out of a single movie, we observe that *Juno* reflects another trend we see in the data. The character of Juno perfectly personifies the growing secularism of young people that we have chronicled in this book. At no point in the film does she offer a religious reason for choosing not to abort her pregnancy.

To bring us back to the data, we offer some important caveats about the Juno Generation. First, the subtleties in the abortion atti-tudes of young people do not mean that they are ripe for political mobilization for strict restrictions on abortion, or for the pro-life cause in general. Recent ballot initiatives in California and South Dakota, both of which would have made abortions more difficult to obtain, found little support among young voters.[51] In both cases, voters under thirty were the most likely to vote against the initiatives and thus against restricting access to abortion. This is a voting bloc that may be uncomfortable with abortion, at least for some reasons, but has not embraced the pro-life political movement.

The nuance in the attitudes of young people toward abortion is also revealed when we compare how they respond to different ways of asking about abortion. The detailed questions asked in the General Social Survey are sufficiently subtle to detect young people's ambivalence about abortion. When given coarser options, young people don't always display such generational differences. However, even when the abortion opinions of young people look just like the opinions of older generations, this is surprising because we would have many reasons—particularly their low religiosity—to expect them to show a high degree of support for abortion.

CONCLUSION

We began by affirming that the oft-discussed God gap in American politics is real. The Republicans have forged a coalition of the religious—although with exceptions, notably Black Protestants. Over roughly the last three decades, sex and family issues like abortion and same-sex marriage have brought this religious-political coalition together. The coalition will likely hold when sex and family issues are at stake in an election, and as long as the Republicans maintain their religion-friendly image. However, should sex and family issues recede in political significance, religion—or religiosity—will gradually cease to be such a salient political division. The data suggest that abortion and gay marriage may recede as political issues.

There has been a liberalizing trend on same-sex marriage, with younger Americans far more accepting of homosexuality generally, and same-sex unions specifically, than their elders.[52] On abortion, though, we see evidence of a conservative tilt among young people, even though they are also the most secular age group in the population (because of the Juno Generation—secular young people who are nonetheless uncomfortable with abortion).

Each of these trends has a different implication for the future of American politics. The trend on homosexual rights is likely to follow the same pattern as attitudes toward women's rights. Religiosity will remain a predictor of more conservative attitudes, but the floor for those attitudes will keep moving higher and higher. Recall that, in 2008, the most religious young person is just as likely to support gay marriage as the most secular member of his or her grandparents' generation. As the floor rises, opposition to homosexuality, like opposition to women's rights, will cease to be politically viable.

The trend on attitudes toward abortion among young people likely has a different, but no less portentous, implication. First, acceptance of abortion and same-sex marriage differ in that they are moving in opposite directions. For that reason, it would seem less likely that these issues would continue to share the same political platform. And since today's young people will constitute an ever greater share of the future electorate, continuation of this trend would lead aggregate opinion on abortion to shift modestly in a pro-life direction.

Secondly, and more subtly, abortion attitudes appear to have a weakening connection to religiosity among the rising generation. Since it was the tie between abortion and religiosity that brought the coalition of the religious together, any loosening of the abortion-religiosity connection has the potential to pull it apart. This would not necessarily mean that abortion ceases to be contentious, only that the debate over abortion is less likely to be waged along religious lines.

If we are reading the tea leaves right, these trends would not mean the immediate breakup of the coalition of the religious. Nor would they mean the immediate demise of the Religious Right as a political movement, as we are reminded that past rumors of the death of the Religious Right have been greatly exaggerated.[53] Instead, we expect the Republicans' image as the religion-friendly party to endure, as images outlast issues. But party images can change. Adding to the potential for change, more and more Democratic candidates have begun using religious rhetoric and symbolism in an effort to neutralize the Republican advantage among churchgoers.[54] In the short term, these efforts have had little effect, especially with the most religious voters, but over time they might lead to a change in whether the Republicans continue to be identified as the most religion-friendly party.

If sex and family issues fade from the political agenda and the Democrats successfully counterbalance the Republicans' association with religion—admittedly, two big ifs—it is tempting to predict that religion would cease to matter much in American politics. History, however, suggests that religion would still matter, just differently than it does now. Does that sound outside the realm of possibility? If so, consider the following:

- If we described a politician as a fundamentalist Christian, a staunch believer in the literalism of the Bible, and a fierce critic of evolution, which party would you assume he represents?
- How about a politician who was a champion of the poor and a forceful voice against America's involvement in war? Which party label would you think he carries?

It turns out that this is the same politician—three-time Democratic presidential candidate and former secretary of state William Jennings Bryan. No politician in American history better exemplifies the ideological malleability in the connections that can be drawn between religion and politics. For example, Bryan's strident opposition to evolution, grounded as it was in his belief that the Bible should be read literally, was closely tied to his concern for the poor, which also sprang from his belief in the Bible. Bryan was concerned that evolution would justify policies that presumed social Darwinism, whereby the poor were thought to be society's weakest members and thus deserving of their lot in life. Social Darwinists believed that only the fittest—the richest—deserved to flourish, and therefore opposed government action to help the poor. When viewed in this light, Bryan's famous prosecution of John Scopes in the Monkey Trial of 1925 is more complex than simply a knee-jerk rejection of science. While his skepticism toward evolution would presumably resonate among today's social conservatives, his advocacy of wealth redistribution would win the support of today's political progressives. Likewise, Bryan's pacifism, also drawn from his reading of the Bible, would likely endear him to many of today's secular leftists.

Still another example from Bryan's career even better exemplifies the fluidity with which political issues can be framed in religious terms. In 1896, Bryan stood before the Democratic convention and delivered a spellbinding speech for the ages, bringing the delegates to their feet and winning himself the party's presidential nomination. His speech called for an overhaul of the nation's monetary policy. Specifically, Bryan advocated the free coinage of silver, which would have dramatically loosened America's money supply, thus helping borrowers and hurting the monied class. In doing so, he explicitly linked the nation's reliance on the gold standard to the crucifixion of Christ. "You shall not press down upon the brow of labor this crown of thorns, you shall not crucify mankind upon a cross of gold." In his magisterial biography of Bryan, Michael Kazin writes of Bryan's final flourish as he concluded:

> Bryan stunned the crowd with an inspired gesture of melodrama. He stepped back from the podium, pulled his hands away from his brow, and extended them straight out from his body—and held the Christlike pose for perhaps five seconds.[55]

If framing monetary policy in terms of the most sacred image in Christianity seems strange to modern ears, that is precisely our point. Connections between religion and politics do not just happen, but instead must be consciously crafted by opinion leaders.

Given the dynamism of American religion, we should not be surprised that over time the ways in which it intersects with politics change. Going all the way back to the election of 1800, Thomas Jefferson's opponents accused him of being an atheist intent on confiscating the Bibles of New England housewives.[56] Later in the 1800s, there were sharp divisions between the liturgical (Episcopalians, Lutherans, Catholics) and pietistic (Baptists, Methodists) religions. As Catholic immigration swelled, tensions between Catholics and Protestants rose, fanned by Al Smith's candidacy in 1928 but then largely extinguished by Kennedy in 1960. The demise of Catholic–Protestant conflict brought us a new source of religious division between the religious and the secular. Sex and family issues have now united a historically unique coalition of (most of) the religious but, we suggest, should the salience of those issues diminish, the coalition would likely unravel slowly. If so, we would not expect religion to cease to be a significant factor in American politics.

The particular constellation of religion and politics in contemporary America is the product of a particular set of historical contingencies—the shock and aftershocks that realigned the world of morality and religion and the strategic decisions of party leaders about how to respond to that new cleavage. History teaches us that if the current God gap were to fade, we should expect religion and politics to align in new ways, as political entrepreneurs work to construct new coalitions.[57] The change will be in *how* religion affects our politics, not *whether* it does.

CHAPTER 12

ECHO CHAMBERS: POLITICS WITHIN CONGREGATIONS

T he previous chapter told the story of religiosity's emergence as a political fault line. Or at least it told half the story of religiosity and partisan politics, as it focused on the strategies pursued by parties, candidates, and strategists. You might say that it explains how there came to be so much church in our politics.[1] What, though, about politics in church? This chapter thus tells the other half of the story, as it addresses what happens, and does not happen, within America's houses of worship to create a link between religiosity and partisanship.[2]

The answer, it turns out, is subtle. First, we will show that there is little overt politicking over America's pulpits and, to the extent it happens, it is more common on the political left than the right. Nor is there much political mobilization through church channels. Political appeals are far more likely to come through friends, family, neighbors, and even co-workers than from fellow parishioners. In short, there is little politics in church.

The chapter then turns to explaining that what occurs at church can have political significance nonetheless, even if it is more subtle than blatant politicking. There may not be much politics *in* church, but much that has political relevance happens *through* church. First, we will see that the teachings within a religious community can res-

419

onate politically, even if they are not overtly partisan. Those teachings then reverberate within the echo chambers of the friendship networks formed within religious communities, where their political relevance is reinforced. Those echoes resonate loudest—and thus matter most—for those who integrate their religion with their politics.

POLITICS AT CHURCH

Our first point is that explicit political appeals by clergy are relatively rare. That point can perhaps be best made with reference to Pastor Mac Hammond of the Living Word Christian Center, to whom you were introduced in Chapter 10. Recall that in October of 2006, he triggered a controversy when Michele Bachmann, a Republican congressional candidate, spoke in his church. After she spoke, Hammond expressed his support for her. His precise words leave ambiguous the question of whether his words constitute an endorsement, since he explicitly said "We can't publicly endorse as a church and would not for any candidate." His personal enthusiasm for her, however, was unambiguous: "I can tell you personally that I'm going to vote for Michele Bachmann."

Our objective in highlighting this story is not to offer a legal opinion on the question of whether Hammond stepped across the admittedly blurry line that separates permissible and impermissible political commentary from clergy. Rather, we seek to learn from this incident. On the one hand, Hammond's words may confirm the suspicions of many about the role of religion in America's churches, especially those that are evangelical. Here we have an evangelical pastor speaking approvingly about a Republican candidate during a church service. Business as usual, no? If so, though, why would this incident cause such a ruckus and end up as front-page news?

One reason that Hammond's words met with such disapprobation is that, in general, Americans overwhelmingly disapprove of political persuasion by religious leaders. In the Faith Matters surveys we asked our respondents whether they feel "it is perfectly proper for religious leaders to try to persuade people how to vote." The answer came through loud and clear: Overwhelmingly, Americans do *not* think clergy should be in the business of political persuasion. Eighty percent of Americans disagree that religious leaders should try to sway people to vote one way or another. Opposition to clergy members' political mobilization is both deep and broad, and it does not vary much by religious tradition either. Seventy-five percent of evangelicals, 80 percent of Catholics, and 85 percent of mainline Protestants all share the same opinion. Intriguingly, even 76 percent of Black Protestants and 77 percent of Jews—the two religious traditions where, as we will show, faith-based political mobilization is most common—object to political persuasion by religious leaders. Even Mac Hammond has referred to hearing complaints about his politicking from his own church members. During Michele Bachmann's controversial appearance at his church, Hammond told his congregants to stop sending him letters saying that "church and politics don't mix." In other words, even within what appears to be a highly politicized congregation, parishioners still resist blatant politicking from the pastor.

In a religious environment defined by choice, these results are highly suggestive that clergy are not generally in the politicking business. If this many Americans disapprove so strongly of explicit political appeals in the abstract, then clergy who engage in politics risk censure from their members. Even worse, in a competitive religious market they risk an exodus of members. Most people come to church to hear about God, not Caesar. Too much talk of Caesar risks driving them away.

But this inference does not mean that clergy necessarily avoid politics over the pulpit. After all, Americans might object to political persuasion by clergy *because* they have experienced it and decided it is not to their liking. And even if they do not like it, this may not be enough to cause them to leave their chosen congregation. Perhaps we have made too much of the controversy around Mac Hammond, and his words in support of a Republican congressional candidate were not an aberration after all. If true, we should find that politicking over the pulpit is a common occurrence, especially in the evangelical churches whose members form the base of the Republican Party.

We wanted to know both the frequency and volume of over-the-pulpit political appeals, and so we asked the four out of five Americans who have a regular place of worship:

- How frequently social or political issues are discussed from the pulpit.
- Whether their congregation ever organizes demonstrations or marches.
- Whether their congregation ever sponsors voter registration drives or distributes voter guides.

We pause here to note that the business of asking about political activity, especially in an ostensibly nonpolitical environment such as a religious congregation, is fraught with ambiguity over what counts as political. We have chosen to rely on the self-reports of individual churchgoers, which means that we do not know what precisely they have in mind when they indicate, for example, that they have frequently heard sermons on "social or political" issues. Do they mean sermons on the virtues of one political party over another? On abortion? On the scriptural injunction to love one another? We confess that we do not know (although below we will present data on what people do hear at church). It is important to note, however, that we deliberately cast a wide net in capturing activity that might be perceived as political or anything close to political. Thus, we did not just ask about having heard a political sermon, but whether "*social or political* issues are discussed from the pulpit." And we did not ask about demonstrations or marches for a partisan cause, but without specifying a cause asked whether one's congregation organizes *any* such activity.

While self-reports are not the only method to learn what happens inside a place of worship, no other method is necessarily superior or would eliminate ambiguity. For example, another way of determining the frequency of politically tinged sermons would be to observe the sermons themselves. Imagine that we sent observers to the hundreds of thousands of religious services attended by our respondents over, say, a year's time, in order to record when political activity takes place. Even such a massive effort would not clear up the uncertainty over what constitutes political information over the pulpit, as we would still have to determine what counts as political to the people in the pews. And to do so, the most useful information would come from the parishioners themselves. Did they perceive a given sermon to be on a political or social issue? Which brings us back to self-reports of individual churchgoers. Precisely because politics is in the eye of the beholder, we leave it to the beholders to tell us when they perceive political activity at their place of worship. What counts as political is whatever our respondents tell us counts.

We stress that explicit political mobilization of the sort captured in these questions does not exhaust the ways in which politics or politically relevant messages can circulate within a religious congregation—a topic we discuss at length below. Here, though, our focus is on overt politicking.

We made sure that we asked about a variety of potential political activities, since past research has shown that different religious traditions have distinctive repertoires of political mobilization.[3] The 2006 Faith Matters survey confirms that certain forms of political activity are more common in some religious traditions than others. For example, if you went to worship at a black church or Jewish synagogue you would be more likely to hear politics discussed from the pulpit than in an evangelical, mainline, Catholic or, especially, Mormon church (see Figure 12.1).

No matter where you went to worship, though, politics from the pulpit would still be relatively rare. The data are unmistakable—there are differences across the religious traditions but few religious traditions have all that much politicking. As the example of Bethel AME shows (see Chapter 7), politics blends easily with worship in the Black Church, but fewer than half of Black Protestants report hearing a politically tinged sermon at least once a month, while just

Figure 12.1

POLITICAL ACTIVITY AT CHURCH IS RELATIVELY RARE AND VARIES
ACROSS RELIGIOUS TRADITIONS

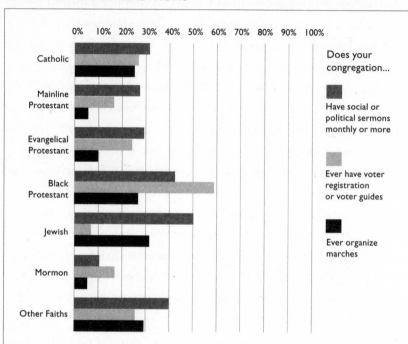

SOURCE: FAITH MATTERS SURVEY, 2006.

shy of 60 percent report that their congregation ever has voter registration drives or distributes voter guides. In evangelical churches,
politics is better described as a sideshow than as the main attraction. Only 24 percent of evangelicals report that their congregation
ever has voter registration or distributes voter guides—even though
voter guides are often described as the primary tactic of the Religious Right movement.[4]

Because the image of the highly politicized church, especially
among evangelicals, is entrenched in the folklore of contemporary
politics, some readers may doubt our conclusion that there is indeed
little politics at church. To assuage those concerns, we have looked
hard to see if we have missed the real story. Our confidence in these
findings is increased by, first, the fact that our results are consistent
with those of other scholars working with totally different data, col-

lected at different times.[5] Consider the words of Mark Chaves, one of the nation's leading sociologists of religion, who has conducted his own study of political activity in America's congregations and arrived at the same conclusion as ours. "Public attention notwithstanding, politics is not an arena in which most congregations actively participate. Politics remains, for most congregations, a peripheral activity."[6]

We then wondered if our measures of political activity were missing what was actually happening on the ground—perhaps there are other forms of political activity flying below our radar and the radar of social scientists more generally. This is where the congregations featured in our vignettes are particularly valuable, as they have given us an opportunity to observe the goings-on in many different religious communities around the United States. The vignettes confirm the results from our national survey, as we observed very little politics coming over the pulpits. There are notable exceptions, particularly Bethel AME in Baltimore and Beth Emet in Evanston, but we knew they were politically active congregations when we chose them.

While the data and our own observations indicate little politics over the pulpit, we did wonder whether the story would be different during an election campaign. Just as Christmas sermons are reserved for December, it is plausible that political sermons are limited to every second November. While it was not feasible to conduct an entirely new survey during an election campaign, we did return to a number of our congregations in the weeks preceding the 2006 congressional election to see whether that highly competitive contest spurred a greater degree of political mobilization than we had earlier observed. Still, we found very little politicking.

Admittedly, the congregations in our vignettes are not a random sample of all churches in America, so perhaps we were simply seeing an unrepresentative slice of American religion. But that seems unlikely given the evidence from our 2007 follow-up survey, where we reinterviewed the same people as in the summer of 2006. We found no evidence of increased political activity in the wake of the November 2006 elections. In fact, there was a modest drop-off in the frequency of social or political sermons (from 30 percent monthly to 22 percent). Between 2006 and 2007, nearly identical percentages of the population reported either voter registration or voter guides at their place of worship.[7] Similarly, the 2000 National Election Study— the leading academic survey of the American electorate—found that during the 2000 presidential campaign only 5 percent of churchgoers reported hearing their clergy endorse a candidate. Probably owing to such a low incidence, the National Election Studies have not asked that question since 2000. But we find further convergence with the Pew Research Center, which in 2000 found that 6 percent of voters who attend church regularly said their "clergy or other religious groups" encouraged them to vote a particular way. This figure rose to 11 percent in 2004. That figure is striking, as even in a year when church-based mobilization was a hot topic, only about one in ten churchgoers reported explicit political direction from religious leaders and/or groups. In 2008, that proportion dropped slightly to 8 percent.[8] In churches attended by white evangelicals, that percentage is only 5 percent. Perhaps surprisingly in light of the attention given to political activity within evangelical churches, a higher proportion, 15 percent, of Catholics reported political encouragement from either their clergy or religious organizations. Still, 15 percent is a relatively small share of America's Catholic population.

FAITH-BASED POLITICS ON THE LEFT

In weaving these different strands of data together, we find compelling evidence that Mac Hammond's words on behalf of a congressional candidate are atypical. In general, politicking at church is unusual. Also unusual is the fact that Pastor Hammond is a man of the right, not the left. In spite of all the attention paid to church-based mobilization on behalf of conservative candidates and causes, churchgoing liberals are actually more likely to report political activity at church than are conservatives. As shown in Figure 12.2, 27 percent of "very conservative" churchgoers report that social and

Figure 12.2

LIBERALS GET MORE POLITICS AT CHURCH THAN CONSERVATIVES

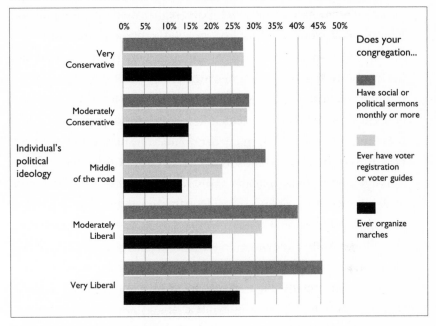

SOURCE: FAITH MATTERS SURVEY, 2006.

political issues are discussed from the pulpit at least once a month, compared to 45 percent of "very liberal" churchgoers.[9]

African Americans are overwhelmingly liberal and attend the most politicized churches, and so one might hypothesize that what we observe as politics in liberals' churches is really politics in the Black Church. It turns out, however, that when we look only at white churchgoers, the results do not change. White liberals are still more likely to report political activity at church than conservatives.

Nor can our results be explained away as liberals reporting conservative politicking in their churches. One could plausibly hypothesize that liberals are sensitized to conservative political activity, which passes unnoticed by conservatives in the very same churches. By this reasoning, liberals in conservative-leaning congregations are dismayed to hear sermons that sound political to them but not to the conservatives sitting next to them in the pews. If this were the explanation for the politics in liberals' churches, we should then expect that the people most likely to report politicking at church are liberal islands in a sea of conservatives. In fact, the opposite is true. The people who are most likely to report political activity at church are liberals who attend a politically homogeneous congregation.[10]

For someone whose view of political activity in churches has been informed only by the era of the Religious Right, these results might seem surprising. Isn't it the right, not the left, that draws on churches to mobilize its political troops? A longer historical view, however, reminds us that many denominations have long been catalysts for political action on socially progressive, left-leaning causes. Surveys of religious leaders have found that, even today, liberal clergy bring more politics to their churches than do conservative pastors.[11] We have only surveys of the parishioners, not their clergy, but still the same pattern emerges. Liberal parishioners echo liberal clergy in reporting more politics over their pulpits.

Since self-described liberals are highly active politically, more so than self-described conservatives, we should not be surprised that they would choose to attend politically active churches. However, while the political activity reported by liberals serves the important purpose of reminding us that religion need not only be a conservative force in politics, neither should we be misled into overstating the political clout of the religious left. Liberal churchgoers represent a small fraction of the American population. To see what we mean, first remember the low overall level of church-based mobilization, even in congregations attended by liberals. Also, keep in mind that there are very few churchgoing liberals. By far, most churchgoers (like most Americans) describe themselves as moderately conservative or middle-of-the-road. All told, liberal churchgoers who attend politically active congregations equal about 2 percent of the population.[12] With such a tiny fraction of the population, liberal churchgoers represent a niche, not a mass, market.

The elevated rate of political activity in liberals' churches demonstrates that religion can be employed across the range of the political spectrum, not just in the African American tradition. But an undue focus on the relatively small number of churchgoing liberals who are regularly exposed to political mobilization would serve only as a distraction from what should be the headline: In most of America's houses of worship, there is little politicking over the pulpit. The evidence converges on the inescapable conclusion that Americans have neither much demand for, nor supply of, political activity in their houses of worship. When they go to church, they are much more likely to hear about God than Caesar, and that is the way they like it. Certainly, there are some clergy who regularly intermingle politics with their religion—often loudly, even flamboyantly (Pat Robertson for example). However, they are the exceptions. Mac Hammond's comments about Michele Bachmann were such an exception.

We can learn from the exceptions. Because politicking over the pulpit is unusual within conservative-leaning congregations, those rare cases can be especially effectual. With fervent believers, a pre-existing organizational structure in place, and tight social networks, congregations in conservative traditions such as evangelicalism and Mormonism are dry kindling for political mobilization. The right issue can serve as a match, igniting their political activity. Examples abound, but same-sex marriage has recently exemplified this sort of rapid, intense political mobilization of churchgoers.

In 2008, conservative churches and especially the Mormon church actively campaigned in favor of California's Proposition 8 that banned gay marriage. Given the media attention paid to church-based political mobilization, the casual observer might have the mistaken impression that such campaigns are common. To the contrary, it is the uncommonness of such mobilization that draws attention and makes the mobilization effective. Just as frequent fires consume the kindling, so can frequent political appeals burn out the people in the pews. We suspect that, for all the political activity in churches attended by left-leaning parishioners, each individual appeal has minimal effect.

POLITICKING AMONG
THE PARISHIONERS

Besides overt politicking from the pulpit there are other channels through which churches might affect how people vote. After all, since churches risk losing their tax-exempt status for engaging in express advocacy on behalf of a partisan cause (but not advocating for or against nonpartisan ballot initiatives), perhaps we should not be surprised by the infrequency of politicking over the pulpit. It could be that the politicking happens among the parishioners. For example, one might be personally approached by a co-parishioner advocating for a candidate or party, the most effective form of political mobilization.[13] To see whether personalized political contact among congregants explains the religious divide, our 2006 survey asked whether, in the last few years, anyone the respondents knew personally had encouraged them to vote one way or another. If so, we asked how they knew the person (or people) who had approached them. Were they family, friends, co-workers, neighbors, or someone they knew through their church?[14]

Church is the least common channel for political mobilization, as seen in Figure 12.3. Only 9 percent of Americans say that they have been contacted by someone they know through their church to vote a certain way, compared to 30 percent who say that they were approached by a friend and 22 percent by a family member. Even co-workers (15 percent) beat out fellow church members.

Neither does the story change much when we look only at people who attend church frequently (nearly every week or more). As expected, a higher percentage of frequent church attenders say that they have been contacted by a co-parishioner than Americans in general, but that figure is still only 17 percent. Since church attenders have more social connections all around, they are also more likely to be contacted by friends, family, neighbors, and co-workers, and so church remains in last place.[15] When we focus squarely on evangelicals, we do not find that they have an unusually high level of personal political contact from fellow church members. Only 15 percent

Figure 12.3

POLITICAL MOBILIZATION IS LEAST COMMON THROUGH CHURCH

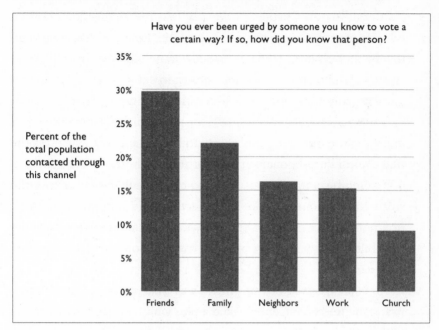

Have you ever been urged by someone you know to vote a certain way? If so, how did you know that person?

Percent of the total population contacted through this channel

SOURCE: FAITH MATTERS SURVEY, 2006.

of evangelical Protestants say that they have been on the receiving end of such a political pitch. And 20 percent of churchgoing political conservatives (many of whom, of course, are evangelicals) report a church-based political appeal, little higher than the 16 percent of churchgoing liberals.

SERMONS

If someone who knew nothing of contemporary American politics were to read only to this point in this chapter, he or she would undoubtedly conclude that religion has little to do with politics. Furthermore, he would likely think that to the extent religion does exert an influence, it is on the left and not the right. Certainly, most political observers today would not describe the connection between religion and politics this way. Religion matters deeply and religious voters tend to populate the right, not the left, of the political spectrum.

Recall that in Chapter 11 we saw that the connection between religiosity and partisanship is owing to the issues that feature prominently on the nation's political agenda. Issues differ in that religiosity shapes opinions for a few—specifically, issues such as abortion and gay marriage—but not for all issues. Accordingly, when one or both of America's parties emphasize issues for which religion matters a lot, we can expect religious voters to favor the party that takes the side of moral traditionalism on abortion and homosexual rights.

To focus on the parties only, however, would miss much of the story. Churches matter too. Even if overt politicking over the pulpit or among fellow church members is rare, this does not preclude the possibility that politically relevant information circulates through congregations.

In 2006, the year of our initial Faith Matters survey, the nonpartisan Pew Research Center asked a nationally representative sample of Americans about the sermons they hear at their place of worship. Specifically, they were asked if they ever heard sermons on an array of topics, from hunger and poverty to abortion to the environment.[16] Far and away the most common topic is hunger and poverty; 91 percent of churchgoers report hearing sermons on the subject. Virtually every churchgoer in America has at some point heard a sermon relating to hunger and the poor. This near-uniformity is consistent with our findings, detailed in Chapter 13, about the philanthropic activities of religious people. And while discussions of poverty could have a partisan cast, we suspect that most do not, based on the observation that religiosity has a very weak correlation with people's attitudes on whether the government should reduce income inequality (see Chapter 11).

In contrast to the ostensibly nonpartisan topics of hunger and poverty, the next most commonly cited sermon subject definitely has partisan overtones, namely abortion. Nearly 60 percent of churchgoers report hearing about abortion at church, a smaller percentage than the 91 percent who have heard sermons about poverty, but still a healthy majority. Among Catholics, 78 percent report having heard a sermon on abortion, while 62 percent of evangelicals have. In contrast, only 37 percent of mainline Protestants recall hearing an abortion sermon.[17] About half of all churchgoers (48 percent) have heard a sermon on "laws regarding homosexuality," the other sex and family issue that figures prominently on the contemporary political agenda.[18] Interestingly, it is among Mormons (68 percent) and Black Protestants (61 percent) where sermons on laws regarding homosexuality are most common, even though they share virtually no other common political ground.[19]

We are struck by the fact that nearly three in five churchgoers report having ever heard a sermon on abortion, the issue that does more than any other to shape the current partisan landscape. This, however, does not mean that sermons on abortion are necessarily frequent. Indeed they must not be, given the relatively low percentage of churchgoers who report hearing a sermon on "social and political issues" at least monthly (as it is difficult to see how a sermon on abortion would not be considered social or political). Yet they are likely frequent enough to have political relevance.

Are sermons on a topic such as abortion appropriately labeled "political"? The answer goes back to our earlier point about the ambiguity of the term. At the very least, a sermon that takes a position on abortion has political relevance, whatever the motivation of the pastor delivering it. Furthermore, there is no doubt that some religious leaders with a political orientation deliberately give sermons on politically salient subjects in accordance with the electoral calendar, even if they do not make any direct appeals to vote one way or another. There are clergy on both the left and right who have no problem helping their flocks make a connection between religion and politics.

These data on sermons only scratch the surface of the many ways that subjects with political relevance circulate within a given religious community. For example, organizations like Focus on the Family have print publications, Web sites, and media broadcasts that speak to issues with a religious grounding (including, but not limited to, abortion) that also map onto the current political agenda. In short, sermons are only one source of politically relevant information to which many churchgoers are exposed.

SORTING

The prevalence of choice in American religion helps explain why the circulation of politically relevant information is so potent. As shown in Chapter 5, we have good reason to believe that some Americans make choices about religion based on their politics. Thus we need not assume that people pick a church, and their friends at church, as political blank slates—that religion always drives people's politics. Politics can also drive the choice of religion, as evidenced by the two aftershocks described in Chapter 4. The politicization of religion has triggered a negative reaction among some, mostly young, Americans. They have pulled away from religion precisely because they perceive it as an extension of partisan politics with which they do not agree. They see religion tied up with conservative politics, and their aversion to the latter has led them to reject the former. Likewise, we have seen how, over time, political conservatives become more religious—the same sorting process, but in reverse.

Furthermore, just as instruction from the pulpit need not be explicitly political to have political implications, neither does the influence of politics on religious choice need to be overt. Indeed, one could choose a religion or a church simply on the basis of other factors that are themselves related to one's partisan preferences. For example, perhaps you prefer a church that reinforces traditional gender roles (like Our Savior Lutheran, highlighted in Chapter 7). This in turn would likely mean a congregation with more Republicans than Democrats. A notable example of how ostensibly nonpolitical criteria for selecting a congregation can have political implications can be seen among our Faith Matters respondents. Not surprisingly, the small minority of people who chose their congregation because of their political or social views are more likely to report that their congregation is politically homogeneous. However, there is nearly as tight a connection between choosing a congregation because of the liturgy or style of worship and the proportion of one's fellow congregants who share the same political outlook.[20]

Politics can also shape religious choice in the sense of who joins, who stays, and who leaves a given faith. The classic example is Catholics who became disaffected when the Vatican affirmed its stance against birth control in 1968—those who stayed undoubtedly differed politically from those who left.[21] Even within a given religion, choice continues to operate as people choose a specific congregation in which to worship and, within that congregation, to associate with some people rather than others. The very fluidity of American religion facilitates political sorting, even if the people sorting themselves are not explicitly guided by their politics in the choices they make.

As we described earlier, in the first aftershock moral traditionalists were either flocking to or staying in church, while moral liberals were emptying out of the pews. Even though private morality, notably one's view on premarital sex, was a greater driver of the surge in conservatively tinged religion than abortion or homosexuality, we saw in Chapter 11 that moral traditionalism is defined by a cluster of issues. People who have moral qualms about premarital sex are also likely to be pro-life on abortion. While Americans were not necessarily consciously sorting themselves into, and out of, churches on the basis of issues with political salience (like abortion), their sorting nonetheless brought politically like-minded people together.

ECHO CHAMBERS

While religious messages, whether delivered over the pulpit or through some other means, play an important role in the tale of the God gap, there is more to the story. Abortion and homosexuality are not the primary issues spoken of from the pulpit and, at any rate, it is not clear how much impact a sermon alone might have. Most people are not very attentive to politics. We cannot take for granted that everyone intuitively knows how religion and politics are "supposed to" align.

People often glean political information from interaction with friends, family, and neighbors. This sort of information sometimes comes through explicit conversations about political topics, but can also be learned from more subtle signals—the joke passed along via e-mail here, an offhand comment there. Accordingly, people whose social networks are rooted in a religious congregation or community are more likely to receive religiously infused signals about many areas of interest, politics included. This is especially true in light of how sorting enables politically like-minded churchgoers to find one another, even if they are not consciously looking for political congruence when selecting a place to worship.

We are not alone in suggesting that, in general, the people we associate with heavily influence our politics,[22] nor are we the first to suggest that religious social networks influence the ways in which individuals piece together their politics and their religion. One major study of political attitudes held by members of twenty-one congregations within a single metropolitan area concluded that the "theological climate" within a church, the opinions held by one's fellow parishioners, correlates more strongly with one's political ideology than do one's own religious beliefs.[23]

In the 2006 Faith Matters data, we also find that religious social networks matter as a source of influence on politics. When we use a measure that reflects the density of social networks formed through one's place of worship, it ranks next to our measure of religiosity in its impact on one's party identification.[24] Religious socializing "explains" roughly half of the connection between religiosity and partisanship. Or, put another way, religious social networks are an important channel for the connections people make between their religion and their politics.

We can see still further evidence of friends at church as a means through which religion and politics come together. Religiosity has a stronger connection to partisanship among people who have a high degree of religious socializing. In fact, among people who have few social connections within their congregation, religiosity and partisanship are only weakly linked. But among those who have an extensive religious social network, religiosity and partisanship are tightly bound (as always, these conclusions are drawn from a statistical model that also accounts for our "usual suspects" of other demographic factors known to influence partisanship).[25] Among people who have very few or no social connections at church, personal religiosity barely affects the likelihood of identifying as a Republican. Yet among those who have a dense religious social network, religiosity is tightly connected to Republican affiliation.

In interpreting these results, one might reasonably ask whether there really are many Americans with high personal religiosity who do not also have a dense religious social network; likewise, are there really irreligious people with a religiocentric web of friends? In both cases, the answer is yes. As you would expect, the correlation between the two is high, but it is far from perfect.[26] More to the point, many people who are highly religious in personal terms have relatively few social connections in their congregation. Likewise, many people have many friendships through a place of worship but are not highly religious (Beth Emet Synagogue provides some examples).

Religious social networks matter as much as they do, we posit, because they serve as echo chambers. Social interaction among like-minded co-religionists reinforces and even hardens one's beliefs, even if the process is subtle. Many of those beliefs will have no political relevance. But in some cases events (or party strategists) make those beliefs politically salient, as with sex and family issues like abortion or same-sex marriage. When they do, being embedded within a social network where common opinions are shared on such issues will only heighten their salience. From there, it is a short step to identifying with the party that takes the same positions on those issues that you do. Even that step is likely helped along by the presence of a few politicos among that network of friends. Exposure to political ideas from people with whom you know you share other values—

which for co-religionists is true almost by definition—is likely to lead you to adopt their politics too.

INDIVIDUALS

We have seen how politically relevant information can be injected into religious social networks and how the echo chambers of religious social networks cause such information to reverberate. The connection between religiosity and partisanship is strongest for those for whom the echoes are loudest. There is, however, one more step to solving the puzzle posed by the God gap. In order for religion to have any bearing on politics, individual voters must believe that religion ought to be taken into account when they make political decisions. In politics, as in many other areas, the salience of religion varies. Religion permeates the lives of some Americans more than others. Forty-four percent of Americans talk about religion weekly or more; 33 percent say that they prefer to purchase services or products from someone who shares their religious beliefs; 31 percent read religious books roughly weekly or more; and 26 percent report that they have abstained from food, drink, or tobacco for religious reasons. It would follow, therefore, that religion also affects how some Americans vote, and that those who draw on religion for their politics are more likely to favor the Republican Party.

This is precisely what we find. The more that religion guides Americans' politics, the more likely they are to be Republicans. And this is not simply because people who say that religion shapes their politics are more personally religious. If you take two people with the same demographic characteristics who have an equal degree of personal religiosity—they attend church with the same frequency, have the same strength of belief in God, and so forth—the one who says religion is more likely to influence his or her political decisions is more likely to be a Republican.

Do we find the importance of connecting religion and politics only because the Republican Party has so successfully created a religion-friendly brand label that to be a Republican means making a link between one's religion and one's politics? There is almost certainly some of that going on, but the case of the Black Protestants suggests that this is not the only explanation. Black Protestants are among the most likely to say that they use their religion when making political decisions and yet they are the most monolithically Democratic religious group in America.

The link individuals make between their politics and their religion is also not driven by exposure to overt politicking at church. In fact, as shown in Figure 12.4, Republicans are least common among members of those religious traditions where politicking is most common. Jews and Black Protestants have the most politicking and the fewest Republicans. Mormons and evangelicals have the least politicking and the most Republicans.

The same religious traditions whose members say that they draw on religion when making political decisions are also more likely to say that religion influences other decisions in their lives on nonpolitical matters like career, family, and health. The link individuals make between their religion and their politics results because religions vary in the degree to which they stress the integration of religious faith into all aspects of life, not because of overt politicking at church.[27] The significance of making a personal connection between religion and politics is, as noted in Chapter 11, only amplified by the fact that people who make such connections are also the most likely to place a priority on the sex and family issues of abortion and same-sex marriage.

Relying on religion for political decisions and having dense religious social networks typically go together. This makes sense, as we would expect that people who integrate religion into their politics would also integrate religion into their lives in other ways, including their social relationships. In fact, the echo chamber effect is amplified among people who say that their religion affects their politics. The most heavily Republican portion of the churchgoing population is people who rely on religion when making political decisions *and* are

Figure 12.4

RELIGIOUS TRADITIONS IN WHICH **INDIVIDUALS** CONNECT FAITH AND POLITICS HAVE MORE REPUBLICANS (EXCEPT FOR BLACK PROTESTANTS)

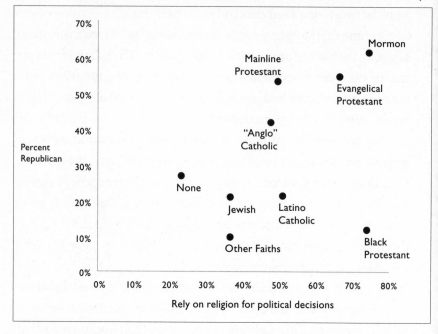

RELIGIOUS TRADITIONS WITH MORE POLITICAL ACTIVITY **AT CHURCH** HAVE FEWER REPUBLICANS

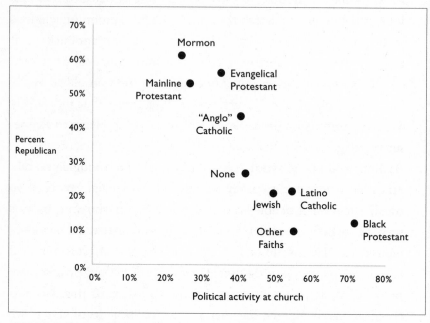

SOURCE: FAITH MATTERS SURVEY, 2006.

embedded in a dense religious social network, not the people who hear the most politics in church.[28]

Black Protestants appear to present an anomaly, but they actually provide further evidence for how religion is translated into politics. Black Protestants rank high both in the degree to which religion informs their politics and in the density of their social networks, and are the most politically monolithic of America's major religious traditions. Within many African American religious networks, however, it is not pro-Republican but pro-Democratic messages that echo.

Although we have focused here on how religious social networks can serve as political echo chambers, this reverberation effect is not limited to networks formed by co-religionists. Political messages can echo in any network of like-minded people, whether based on occupation, group membership, or some other characteristic. The co-workers with whom you go for lunch or the other members of your softball team can also circulate politically relevant information.[29] However, although we are all embedded in multiple networks, not all networks are equal. We suspect that when religion is the common thread that has woven a network together, the political information that circulates carries more moral weight—and is thus more persuasive—than networks formed through other means.

SUMMING UP

We conclude this discussion of how religion affects politics by returning to the hullabaloo that resulted from the appearance of Michele Bachmann at Living Word. It is a telling statement about contemporary politics that it was Pastor Hammond's words that generated so much attention, and not the words of Michele Bachmann. No one seemed to think it unusual that a Republican candidate for Congress would be speaking at an evangelical church, describing how God had called her to run for office. Bachmann is exhibit A that while there may not be much politics in church (the message of this chapter), there is a lot of church in our politics (the message of this previous chapter). Her advocacy of morally traditionalist positions on sex and family issues, coupled with her open embrace of religion on the stump, exemplifies how the Republicans have assembled their coalition of the religious. Over the last generation there have been scores of Michele Bachmanns running for office at all levels of government from the state house to the White House.

In expressing his support for a Republican candidate, Mac Hammond did what many assume evangelical pastors do all the time. But as we have seen, politics from the pulpit is actually unusual. Nor is it common for fellow churchgoers to invite each other to get politically involved. There is simply not much overt politics at church.

Yet this hardly means that nothing of political import happens at church. Although explicit electoral politicking is relatively rare within America's houses of worship, politically relevant information is still communicated over the pulpit and among the parishioners. Politically relevant information, mostly subtle but occasionally overt, reverberates through the social networks formed in and through one's place of worship. The salience of this information is amplified by the political like-mindedness of people who share a given faith. That political congruence, in turn, is owing to the switching, mixing, and matching in American religion. People sort themselves—whether consciously or not—into congregations with politically simpático members, through a self-reinforcing process. The more one kind of person predominates within a given congregation, the more that others who perceive themselves as similar will feel comfortable there (and those who see themselves as different will feel uncomfortable, to the point of leaving). This type of interpersonal sorting even takes place within congregations, as people are likely to gravitate toward friends who are akin to them, in ways including but not limited to their politics.

All of this sorting makes many religious social networks into political echo chambers. When faced with political parties that diverge on issues with religious relevance, it is these echoes—more than any explicit politicking—that matter on election day.

CHAPTER 13

RELIGION AND
GOOD NEIGHBORLINESS

I n the previous two chapters we have examined the linkages between religion and partisan political behavior, noting how those linkages have tightened over the last several decades. We also examined the role of religious social networks in transmitting subtle political messages. In this chapter our focus widens from politics in a partisan sense to civic life more broadly—not how does religion influence our politics, but how does it influence the life of our communities?

Are religious Americans nicer neighbors and better citizens than secular Americans? In his famous Farewell Address, George Washington argued that "of all the dispositions and habits which lead to political prosperity, religion and morality are indispensable supports." Alexis de Tocqueville, the famous French visitor to America four decades later, also thought that democracy in America rested in part on Americans' unusual religiosity.[1]

But is that true today? To be sure, religious folks have sat through hundreds of sermons admonishing them to "love thy neighbor as thyself" and to "do unto others as you would have them do unto you." On the other hand, in many parts of the world religion is linked to intolerance, violence, and mayhem—not to civic good manners. As the seventeenth-century French philosopher Blaise Pascal said, reflecting on the religious wars in his era, "Men never do evil so completely and cheerfully as when they do it from religious conviction."

More recently, Christopher Hitchens succinctly summarizes the civic case against religion: "Religion poisons everything." [2] What does the evidence in contemporary America show? [3]

In this chapter we discover, first, that religious Americans are, in fact, more generous neighbors and more conscientious citizens than their secular counterparts. On the other hand, they are also less tolerant of dissent than secular Americans, an important civic deficiency. Nevertheless, for the most part, the evidence we review suggests that religiously observant Americans are more civic and in some respects simply "nicer."

Next we examine why that is so. Although many devoutly religious people might explain their own civic virtues as manifestations of God's will, we shall discover evidence that theology is not the core explanation for what we shall call the "religious edge" in good citizenship and neighborliness. Rather, communities of faith seem more important than faith itself. Those same religiously based social networks that (as we saw in the previous chapter) convey partisan cues also turn out to be crucial in transmitting civic norms and habits. But before we explore why religious people seem nicer neighbors, what's the evidence that they actually are?

RELIGIOUS AMERICANS ARE MORE GENEROUS

Generosity can be measured most simply by measuring gifts of time and money. We begin with volunteering and then turn to philanthropic giving.

Americans as a whole are generous in volunteering. The most conservative national estimates (from the Census Bureau) suggest that more than one quarter of all Americans volunteer every year, contributing on average roughly 2.5 hours per week. [4] Of all volunteering reflected in the Census Bureau surveys, just over one third (36 percent) is for religious organizations. Our 2006 Faith Matters survey, like many other surveys, suggests even higher rates of volunteerism, for 27 percent of Americans told us they had volunteered for a religious group, while 37 percent to 47 percent told us they had volunteered for at least one nonreligious group.[5]

To be sure, much volunteering by religious people is directed at religious causes, and nonreligious people volunteer very little for such causes. Perhaps, we might conjecture, Americans who volunteer are "specialists," with some of us volunteering for religious causes and others focusing instead on secular causes. Since there are only twenty-four hours in anyone's day, perhaps religious volunteering and nonreligious volunteering are mutually exclusive alternatives.

In fact, however, volunteering for religious groups and volunteering for secular groups turn out to be positively correlated. Of all people who volunteered for a religious group, 91 percent also volunteered for at least one secular group, whereas of those who did not volunteer for a religious group, 69 percent say they did not volunteer for any secular group either. Those of us who volunteer for religious groups are two or three times as likely to volunteer for secular groups as well, compared to those of us who don't volunteer for religious groups. Americans, it seems, mostly choose between volunteering and not volunteering, not between religious and secular volunteering.

It is not surprising in the slightest that churchgoers have a higher rate of religious volunteering than nonchurchgoers. Nonchurchgoers rarely turn up as church ushers. Moreover, a larger share of the volunteering of religious people is for religious organizations, and in that sense religious engagement tends to channel volunteering to religious organizations.[6] However, religion boosts total volunteering so substantially that in addition to their higher rate of religious volunteering, regular churchgoers are also much more likely to volunteer for secular causes. Though religion channels volunteering toward religious institutions, that religious volunteering does not crowd out secular volunteering. Figure 13.1 illustrates that in our 2006 Faith Matters survey religious people are more likely to volunteer for secular organizations, as well as for religious ones.

In the Giving and Volunteering surveys sponsored by the Independent Sector from 1988 to 2001, holding demographic factors

Figure 13.1

RELIGIOSITY PREDICTS BOTH SECULAR AND RELIGIOUS VOLUNTEERING

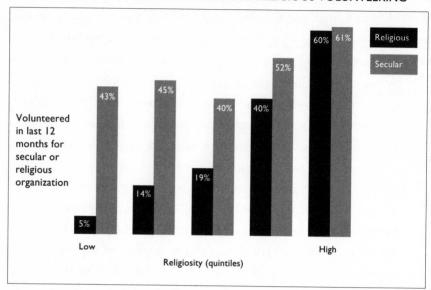

SOURCE: FAITH MATTERS SURVEY, 2006.

constant, 45 percent of weekly churchgoers report nonreligious volunteering (in addition to whatever religious volunteering they do), as compared to 26 percent of nonchurchgoers. Compared to a typical once-a-year churchgoer, the average weekly churchgoer volunteers an extra 10.5 hours a month for religious causes and an extra 6.4 hours a month for secular causes. Since these figures hold constant other demographic predictors of volunteering, the differences in secular volunteering attributable to religiosity are truly remarkable.

As Table 13.1 shows, among secular types of volunteering this religious edge is especially marked for service to poor, elderly, and young people, but (controlling, as always, for other demographic predictors of volunteering) church attendance is a significant predictor for all types of volunteering except for arts and cultural organizations.[7] In round numbers, regular churchgoers are more than twice as likely to volunteer to help the needy, compared to demographically matched Americans who rarely, if ever, attend church.

le 13.1

*E OF VOLUNTEERING BY RELIGIOSITY

h standard demographic and ideological characteristics held constant)

ʌain of volunteering	Attend church at least weekly	Attend church rarely or never
igious group or house of worship	51%	4%
p poor or elderly	40%	15%
ool or youth programs	36%	15%
ʌghborhood or civic group	26%	13%
ɪlth care or particular diseases	21%	13%
s or cultural organizations	9%	6%

'RCE: FAITH MATTERS SURVEY, 2006.

Let us now turn to a material measure of neighborliness—philanthropic generosity. Virtually all major religions exhort their followers to give generously to good causes, and the evidence is overwhelming that religious Americans mostly follow that injunction.[8] "Some people contribute money for a wide variety of causes while others don't," we noted to the Americans we surveyed. "During the past 12 months, did you or your household happen to give any money to any charitable or religious cause?" If the answer was "yes," we then asked how much (in round numbers) they had contributed to (a) all religious causes (including their own congregation) and (b) all nonreligious charities, organizations, or causes.

Our survey confirmed the well-known fact that Americans are, as individuals, a generous people.[9] Eighty percent of our respondents claimed to have made some philanthropic contribution in the previous year.[10] Average annual giving, pulled up by more generous giving at the upper end of the scale, was more than $1,800. However, these aggregate numbers mask a sharp difference between religious Americans and secular Americans.

Of the most secular fifth of our sample, nearly one third (32 percent) acknowledged that they had made no charitable contributions at all in the last year, whereas of the most religious fifth barely one in twenty (6 percent) was that stingy. Moreover, the average annual donations by religious Americans to charitable causes are vastly larger than the average donations by secular Americans. The most secular fifth of our sample reported an average of about $1,000 in total annual household charitable contributions, as compared to more than $3,000 for the most religious fifth. Measuring charitable giving as a fraction of annual income, the average person in the most religious fifth of Americans is more than four times as generous as his or her counterpart in the least religious fifth, roughly 7 percent vs. roughly 1.5 percent.

Once again, one might imagine that religious and nonreligious giving are alternatives, with some specializing in religious giving and others specializing in nonreligious giving. In fact, however, just as with volunteering, giving to religious causes and giving to nonreligious causes are strongly positively correlated. Of all givers to religious causes, 88 percent also gave to secular causes. Of people who gave nothing to religious causes, 60 percent also gave nothing to secular causes. If we focus on giving as a fraction of income, 70 percent of above-average givers to religious causes are also above-average givers to secular causes, while 67 percent of below-average givers to religious causes are below-average givers to secular causes.[11] In short, while a few of us confine our giving either to religious causes or to secular causes, most of us either give to both or give to neither.

It is hardly surprising that churchgoers put more money into the offering plate than nonchurchgoers, but they also give generously to secular causes. Regular churchgoers are more likely to give to secular causes than nonchurchgoers, and highly religious people give a larger fraction of their income to secular causes than do most secular people. Recall from Chapter 1 that religious observance is highest among older Americans, black Americans, women, and Southerners, and that, if anything, religious Americans are slightly poorer on average than secular Americans. Given those characteristics, it is even more striking that religious Americans give more generously than secular Americans, both to religious and to secular causes.[12] (See Figure 13.2.[13])

Even more than in the case of volunteering, religious involvement channels giving toward religious institutions, so the effect of religious involvement on religious giving is very powerful.

Figure 13.2

RELIGIOSITY ENCOURAGES GIVING AS A PERCENT OF INCOME

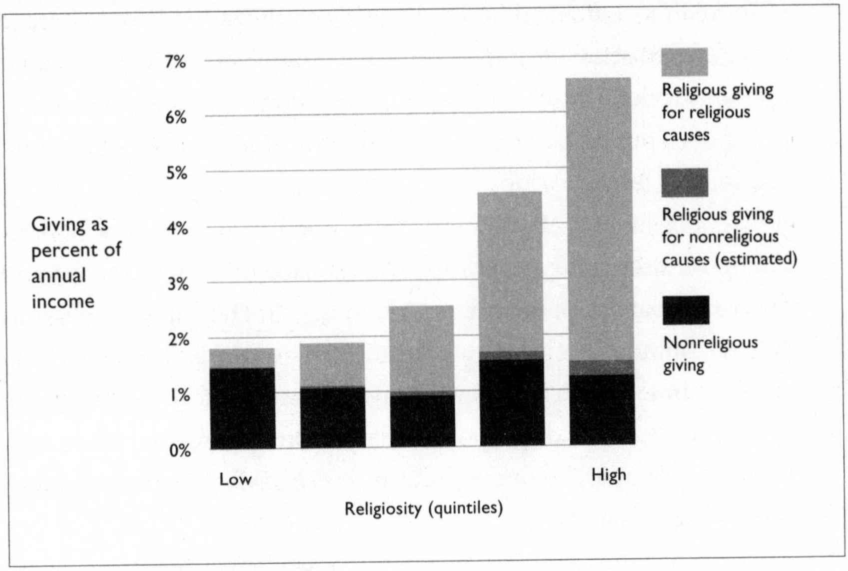

SOURCE: FAITH MATTERS SURVEY, 2006.

On the other hand, religious engagement increases total generosity so strongly that heavy religious giving does not crowd out giving to secular causes, but instead accompanies it, so that religious people give more to both religious and nonreligious causes.[14]

It is the balance between the boosting effect (total contribution) and the channeling effect (religious or secular) of religion that determines religion's contribution to secular causes in both time and treasure. Relative to channeling, the boosting effect of religiosity is greater for volunteering than for giving. In fact, a detailed analysis of the Giving and Volunteering surveys shows that while religiosity has a significant positive effect on secular giving, it has an even greater positive effect on secular volunteering. Conversely, the channeling effect of religiosity is greater for giving than for volunteering. Consequently, the religious edge is less for secular giving than for secular volunteering.

Apart from religion, what exactly do religious Americans give more for? The short answer is "almost everything," but especially for organizations that aid young people and the needy. The national Giving and Volunteering surveys from 1988 to 2001 asked about giving to more than a dozen different types of organizations (listed here in order of frequency of gifts): "informal" (family and friends); health; human services; youth; education; environment; work-based; political; arts; "public benefit" (a mélange of civil rights, community action, and service clubs); foundations; adult recreation; international; and "other." For almost every one of these specific secular sectors, churchgoing Americans are significantly more likely to give financial support than secular Americans.[15] The biggest religious edge is found for giving to educational, youth, and international causes.[16] In short, virtually every part of the American philanthropic spectrum benefits disproportionately from giving by religiously observant men and women, but this is especially true for organizations serving the needy.

The effect of religiosity on giving to secular causes is significant. Other things being equal, the likelihood that an American who never attends church will give money to the American Cancer Society, the Boy or Girl Scouts, a local art museum, or some other secular organization is 60 percent, whereas the likelihood of a similar secular contribution from a comparable person who attends church weekly is 81 percent.[17]

Later in this chapter we shall show that religious people are unusually active in civic life. Is it possible that they are generous in giving and volunteering merely because they are joiners, rather than because they are religious? Two types of evidence argue against the former interpretation.

First, we asked our respondents about their involvement in six categories of secular organizations—parent, youth, or school groups; hobby, sports, or leisure groups; service, social welfare, or fraternal organizations; professional or trade associations; neighborhood, ethnic, or political organizations; and support groups for particular diseases or addictions. Even when we hold such associational membership constant, we find that the religious edge in secular giving and volunteering remains significant. That is, comparing two people who are equally engaged in secular community life, the one who attends church more often is more likely to give and volunteer for secular causes (as well as, of course, for religious causes). In other words, religious people are generous not merely because they are joiners, though that is part of the reason.

Second, religiosity also predicts many sorts of informal altruism, entirely outside organizational contexts. The Panel Study of American Religion and Ethnicity (PS-ARE) in 2006 found that (compared to nonreligious Americans) churchgoers were significantly more likely to say that they give money to "strangers," and the Giving and Volunteering surveys found that churchgoers are more likely to provide financial aid to family and friends.[18]

In 2004 and 2006 the General Social Survey asked Americans about fifteen possible good deeds they might have performed in the previous twelve months, ranging from helping someone find a job to donating blood to looking after a neighbor's plants to letting a stranger cut in line. Not all of these good deeds are associated with greater religiosity, but most are, even when we hold age, gender, race, and education constant. Frequent churchgoers are more likely to:

- Give money to a charity
- Do volunteer work for a charity
- Give money to a homeless person
- Give excess change back to a shop clerk
- Donate blood
- Help someone outside their own household with housework
- Spend time with someone who is "a bit down"
- Allow a stranger to cut in front of them
- Offer a seat to a stranger
- Help someone find a job

Five other types of good deeds are not correlated with religiosity, one way or the other:

- Look after a plant or pet of others while away
- Carry a stranger's belongings
- Give directions to a stranger
- Let someone borrow an item of some value
- Lend money to another person

That said, not a single one of these fifteen types of good deeds is more common among secular Americans than among religious Americans.

Correlation does not prove causation. As we have noted in Chapter 1, religious people differ from nonreligious people in many ways besides religiosity. They are, on average, older, more likely to be female, Southern, and African American, for example. So we tested all our claims about the effects of religiosity on giving by holding constant many other demographic factors, as well as political ideology. *Every significant generalization in this chapter remains accurate when we control simultaneously for gender, education, income, race, region, homeownership, length of residence, marital and parental status, ideology, and age.* In that sense, the correlation between religiosity and giving is not simply spurious. Whether there might be some other unmeasured personal characteristic—perhaps some "niceness gene"—that makes some people both more religious and more generous, or whether religiosity itself actually causes generosity, is a more complicated question to which we return later in this chapter.

Does this generosity vary across different religious traditions? "Yes, but not much" is the answer. As we have seen in Chapter 1 (Figure 1.3), adherents to some religious traditions are more ardently religious than others, but once we take those differences in religious observance into account, differences in generosity among religious traditions are modest. Compared to equally observant adherents of other traditions, mainline Protestants are slightly more likely to volunteer for both religious and secular causes than we might expect, given their rather modest levels of religious observance. Mormons are strikingly more active in giving and volunteering of all sorts, even taking into account their high levels of religious observance. Catholics are slightly less generous to both religious and secular causes, and evangelical Protestants are slightly more generous to religious causes and slightly less generous to secular causes.[19] Keep in mind that since evangelicals are more observant than adherents to most other denominations, their absolute level of generosity is higher for both religious and secular causes; it is only when we exclude that effect of observance that evangelicals seem less generous to secular causes.

If we were most interested in ranking the generosity of various religious traditions, we should look at the absolute differences among them, without adjusting for different levels of observance. But here we are interested in exploring the underlying origins of generosity, so we set the importance of religiosity per se aside for the moment in order to see whether any differences among religious traditions remain. As we have seen, those purely denominational differences are modest, compared to the basic effect of religiosity itself. The main message about volunteering and giving is that how much religion seems to matter more than which religion.[20] The primary predictor of generosity is the strength of one's religious commitment, regardless of one's religious tradition.[21] Indeed, even among those Americans who claim to be affiliated with no religious tradition at all, those who attend church occasionally are more generous than those who never do. How religious someone is counts much more than which religion he or she belongs to.

To summarize what we have learned so far, some Americans are more generous than others. Rather than choosing between religious and nonreligious causes, they volunteer and give more generously to both. In particular, religiously observant Americans are more generous with time and treasure than demographically similar secular Americans. This is true for secular causes (especially help to the needy, the elderly, and young people) as well as for purely religious causes. It is true even for most random acts of kindness. The link is essentially the same regardless of the particular religion or denomination within which one worships, so that the relevant factor is how much one is engaged with religion, not which religion. And the pattern is so robust that evidence of it can be found in virtually every major national survey of American religious and social behavior.[22] Any way you slice it, religious people are simply more generous.

RELIGIOUS AMERICANS ARE MORE CIVICALLY ACTIVE

So far we have seen that religious Americans are more generous— not just within their own religious community, but also in the wider community where they live. We now turn to a wide range of evidence that they are more active in that wider community. In fact, religious Americans are up to twice as active civically as secular Americans.

Education is typically the most powerful correlate of virtually all forms of community activism, partly because education itself fosters cognitive, civic, and organizational skills and partly because education is a good proxy for social status and economic advantage. Yet, holding constant our standard array of other demographic and ideological factors, the civic difference between Americans who attend church nearly every week and those who rarely do so is roughly equivalent to two full years of education. With the partial exception of socioeconomic status, religiosity is, by far, the strongest and most consistent predictor of a wide range of measures of civic involvement.

With all our standard statistical controls, religious Americans are more likely than nonreligious Americans to:

- *Belong to community organizations*, especially youth-serving organizations (e.g., the Scouts), health-related organizations (e.g., the Red Cross), arts and leisure associations (e.g., reading groups, bowling leagues), neighborhood and civic associations, fraternal and service organizations (e.g., Rotary), and even professional and labor groups. All in all, Americans in the most religious fifth of the population belong to 34 percent more organizations than Americans in the most secular fifth. The most religious fifth of the population reported that they had (on average) attended nearly six club meetings in the previous year, as compared to three such meetings for the most secular fifth of the population.

- *Energize community problem solving.* Of the most religious fifth of the population, 29 percent said they had served as "an officer or committee member" of some organization, compared to 14 percent for the most secular fifth of the population.[23] We probed our respondents' civic commitment with two separate questions: "In the last year have you worked together with others to solve a community problem?" and "In the last year have you worked on a community project?" Of the most religious fifth of the population, 36 percent said "yes" to the first question, and 34 percent said "yes" to the second. Of the most secular fifth of the population, 23 percent said "yes" to the first, and 24 percent said "yes" to the second.

- *Take part in local civic and political life*, including everything from local elections to town meetings to political demonstrations. Americans in the most religious fifth of the population report that last year they attended an average of six public meetings at which local affairs were discussed, compared to an average of two such meetings for the most secular fifth of the population. Of the most religious Americans, 56 percent report that they "vote in all or most local elections," compared to 46 percent of the most secular Americans. (Interestingly, people at both poles of the religious spectrum are more likely to vote than people in the center, so this pattern is U-shaped, but the U is lopsided, since turnout is higher among the highly and moderately religious than among the highly and moderately secular.)

- *Press for local social or political reform.* Religious Americans are not mere stalwarts of the status quo. On the contrary, religious Americans are disproportionately represented among local reform activists. Controlling as always for our standard list of background characteristics, including political ideology, 20 percent of religious Americans say that they are a member of some organization that "took any local action for social or political reform in the last twelve months," as contrasted with 11 percent of secular Americans. Fewer than 10 percent of all Americans report that in the previous year they "took part in protest marches or demonstrations," but religious Americans are significantly more likely to have done so than secular Americans. And lest the reader think that these religious activists are primarily pro-life advocates or zealots for other conservative political causes, all this activism is actually more common among religiously involved liberals than among religiously involved conservatives.[24]

Taken together, these measures of civic engagement are remarkably wide-ranging. Some (like public meetings or Scout leadership) are more common among thirty-somethings, whereas others (like voting or Rotary membership) are more characteristic of older Americans. Some (like community projects) are likely to be nonpartisan, while others (like protest marches) are likely to be highly partisan. And yet all show a remarkably consistent contrast between religious and secular Americans.[25] The differences are illustrated in Figure 13.3. Keep in mind that this chart adjusts for other background factors known to influence civic engagement, so in effect the chart compares demographically and ideologically comparable people who differ primarily in their religiosity.[26] The same basic pattern—more civic engagement among religiously observant men and women—repeats itself within each major religious tradition separately, though the pattern is more robust and consistent among mainline Protestants, Black Protestants, and Catholics than among evangelical Protestants. Once again, how much religion matters more than which religion.[27]

It is important to recognize that the religious edge in civic engagement is not linked or limited to the Religious Right. Indeed, for many measures of civic engagement, such as club membership, organizational leadership, and (as we have seen) local reform activities, religiosity matters more for self-described liberals than for self-described conservatives. That is, the difference in activism between a religious liberal and a secular liberal is even greater than the compa-

Figure 13.3

CIVIC ENGAGEMENT AND RELIGIOSITY
(with standard demographic and ideological characteristics held constant)

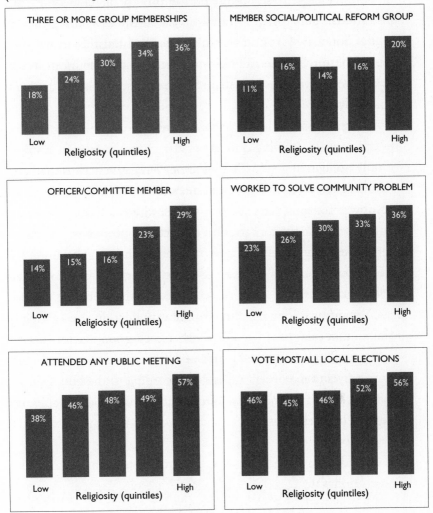

SOURCE: FAITH MATTERS SURVEY, 2006.

rable difference between a religious conservative and a secular conservative.

In a bestselling book Arthur Brooks recently argued that "religious conservatives" are more generous than other Americans, but that argument turns out to be only half right. It is certainly true that religious Americans are more generous and more active in civic life, and it is also true that conservatives tend to be more religious. However, it is their religiosity and not their political ideology that produces the generosity. To praise conservatism as a more generous political ideology is to commit an elementary statistical mistake, for the correlation between ideology and generosity is spurious. It is to give conservative icons like Adam Smith or Edmund Burke credit for God's work.[28]

In fact, across all the surveys we have explored, holding religiosity constant (by looking only at regular churchgoers, for example, or only nonchurchgoers), liberals are never less generous than conservatives and are, by some measures, better neighbors than conservatives. Liberals, for example, work more often on community projects, cooperate more to solve community problems, and volunteer more often to help the sick, the needy, and neighborhood and civic groups, whereas on none of our measures of generosity and civic engagement are conservatives more active. Holding religiosity constant, ideology has little significant effect on total giving or total volunteering, nor on any of the fifteen good deeds discussed earlier, but liberals assuredly give and volunteer more for nonreligious causes than conservatives do. According to the best available evidence, the "civic good guys" are more often religious liberals, not religious conservatives.

RELIGIOUS AMERICANS ARE MORE TRUSTING AND (PERHAPS) MORE TRUSTWORTHY

So far we've seen that religious people rank higher on such civic virtues as giving, volunteering, and civic engagement. Are they also more trustworthy in civic terms? Measuring trust and honesty is trickier, so we used several indirect approaches.

First, we posed six issues of personal ethics to our respondents in the Faith Matters 2006 survey—premarital sex, pornography, divorce, homosexuality, gambling, and concealing income from tax authorities. As Table 13.2 shows (with all standard controls), religious people are more likely to condemn every one of the six behaviors as "always wrong." It is not surprising that religious people are strongly committed to conventional morality on the five issues of family and sexual morality and gambling. More surprising, however, was their response to the one item on our list that dealt with "civic morality"—concealing income from tax authorities. Of all six of these morally debated behaviors, tax evasion is by far the most widely condemned by Americans of all stripes, from the purely secular to the deeply devout. Moreover, religious Americans are significantly more likely to condemn tax evasion than secular Americans. In fact, religious Americans are even more unified in condemning tax cheating than they are in condemning homosexuality or premarital sex.[29]

We cannot infer from Table 13.2 that religious Americans are, in fact, less likely to be tax cheats. Even saints can be sinners, and as many studies have shown, divorce, premarital sex, and so forth are not significantly lower among religious Americans than among secular Americans.[30] Rather, our interpretation is that religious Americans are readier to condemn all violations of conventional morality, including civic morality.

Our second indirect approach to evaluating civic honesty comes

le 13.2

URCH ATTENDANCE AND ETHICAL JUDGMENTS

th standard demographic and ideological characteristics held constant)

	Attend church at least weekly	Attend church rarely or never
	BEHAVIOR IS "ALWAYS WRONG"	
vorce	16%	7%
:ending movies [with] violence,)rofanity, or sexuality	36%	12%
ımbling	38%	16%
:ual relations before marriage	57%	12%
ımosexual acts	77%	31%
ıncealing income from tax authorities	79%	68%

from a series of questions about trust in various groups. Strikingly, it turns out that the average American has more trust in "people who are deeply religious" than in "people who are not religious." Unsurprisingly, religious people are more likely to trust the "deeply religious" than are people who are themselves nonreligious. However, most Americans, whatever their own degree of religiosity, seem to have a trust bias in favor of religious people (see Figure 13.4). Even people who themselves attend church only once or twice a year say that they trust "deeply religious" people slightly more than they trust "people who are not religious."[31] We have no direct evidence that religious people actually are more trustworthy than nonreligious people, but most Americans think they are.

Perhaps because they spend time with trustworthy people, or perhaps because their faith encourages them to look on the brighter side of things, religious people themselves are more trusting of just about everybody than are secular people. Religious Americans

Figure 13.4

MOST AMERICANS TRUST RELIGIOUS PEOPLE MORE THAN
NONRELIGIOUS PEOPLE

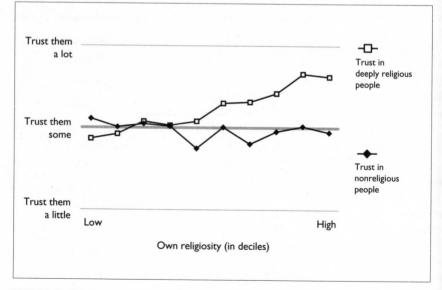

SOURCE: FAITH MATTERS SURVEY, 2006.

express significantly more trust than secular Americans do in shop clerks, neighbors, co-workers, people of their own ethnicity, people of other ethnicities, and even strangers.[32] In short, religious people are both more trusting of virtually everyone else and (in the eyes of others) more trustworthy themselves.

CORRELATION OR CAUSATION?

By many different measures religiously observant Americans are better neighbors and better citizens than secular Americans—they are more generous with their time and money, especially in help-ing the needy, and they are more active in community life. Although the pews contain more conservatives than liberals, their political ideology is largely irrelevant to their neighborliness, as are denomi-national differences. On the other side of the democratic ledger, as we shall see later in this chapter, religious people are less sensitive to the civil liberties of their fellow citizens. In pulling together what we learn in this chapter, it is important to keep in mind that we've been talking about matters of degree. Not all religious people are "nice," and not all secular people are tolerant!

Despite these qualifications, the pervasive robust correlation between religion and good neighborliness demands explanation. "Correlation does not prove causation" is one of the first maxims of statistics, and it is apt here. To be sure, every generalization in this chapter rests on comprehensive statistical controls for demographic or ideological factors that might have produced a spurious corre-lation. Nonetheless, nonexperimental research cannot exclude the potential effects of self-selection, that is, the possibility that some unsuspected factor (perhaps even something genetic) induces both religiosity and neighborliness, producing a spurious correlation, so that simply forcing people to attend church more often would not make them more neighborly.

For better or worse, random-assignment experimental studies—of the sort used to assess the efficacy of medicines, for example—are out of the question here. Even if we could ethically force someone to "take religion once a month," it would be difficult to find a placebo for the control group. One partial though imperfect approach to this problem is to observe the same people over time, looking to see whether when they become more religious (or less religious), they also become better neighbors (or worse) in terms of our measures. As noted in previous chapters and as described in Appendix 2, we used this approach to explore issues of causation by reinterviewing our original 2006 Faith Matters respondents a year later.

This method is not conclusive, especially since one year is a short time in which to observe change in such stable habits as churchgoing and giving or volunteering or voting. Nevertheless, the results from this study are generally consistent with the idea that greater religiosity tends to produce increased giving, volunteering, and civic engagement, while apostasy tends to lower those same measures.[33] Although most people did not change their level of religious observance between 2006 and 2007, some did, and those changes (up or down) were associated with corresponding changes in generosity and community involvement. That fact does not "prove" that religious change "caused" civic change, since both could have been induced by some other change (like getting married or having children, for example, although by controlling for marital and parental status, our analysis rules out those specific examples). The panel study, by allowing us to examine change at the individual level, does, however, make it less plausible to suppose that some enduring personal trait, such as genetic niceness or generic activism, explains the correlation.

Another way to explore issues of causation in social behavior is to investigate *how* a supposed cause (like religiosity) might influence its supposed effect (like greater generosity or civic engagement). Why, in short, are religious people better neighbors? It is to this important question that we now turn.

WHY ARE RELIGIOUS AMERICANS BETTER NEIGHBORS: VALUES AND BELIEFS?

We begin with the possibility that the "secret ingredient" in religiosity has something to do with the beliefs and values of religious people. Every religion represented in contemporary America venerates some version of the Golden Rule—do unto others as you would have them do unto you. In a story that informs all the Abrahamic religions, after Cain had murdered his brother, Abel, God asked Cain where his brother was. "I know not," replied Cain insouciantly. "Am I my brother's keeper?" Cain's query has come to symbolize our reluctance to accept responsibility for our fellows' well-being, and the religious significance of the story is precisely that we must accept that responsibility. Might the explanation for the good neighborliness of religious Americans be as simple as this—that the lessons imparted in hundreds of parables and sermons and homilies over the years have had the effect of fostering altruistic norms and values among the observant? Some of what we are trying to explain might be called altruistic behavior—giving, volunteering, and so forth, but in this section we explore whether the intermediary link between religiosity and such behavior could be altruistic values.

Finding valid survey measures of altruistic values is not simple, since few of us proclaim our selfishness, no matter how selfish we might be. Drawing on extensive previous work by other researchers, however, we posed to our respondents several questions often used to measure altruism and its close cousin, empathy:

1. The following statements ask about your thoughts and feelings in various situations. For each item indicate whether it describes you always, generally, sometimes, rarely, or never.
   - I am quite touched by things that I see happen.
   - Other people's misfortunes do not disturb me a great deal.

2. Agree-disagree (strongly or only somewhat)
   • Personally assisting people in trouble is very important
   to me.
   • These days people need to look after themselves and not
   overly worry about others.

Religious Americans, it turns out, score significantly higher on this
index of empathy and altruistic values. (Figure 13.5 illustrates the
contrast.) Holding other variables constant, among the most secular
fifth of Americans, 48 percent agree that people need to look after
themselves, but among the most religious fifth of the population,
only 26 percent agree. Conversely, among the most secular fifth, only
20 percent say that they are "always" touched by things they see happen, as contrasted with 32 percent of the most religious fifth.[34]

   In fact, among a long list of demographic and ideological
characteristics—education, age, income, gender, race, and so forth—
religion is the strongest predictor of altruism in this sense. In turn,

Figure 13.5

RELIGIOUS PEOPLE EXPRESS MORE ALTRUISTIC VALUES
(with standard demographic and ideological characteristics held constant)

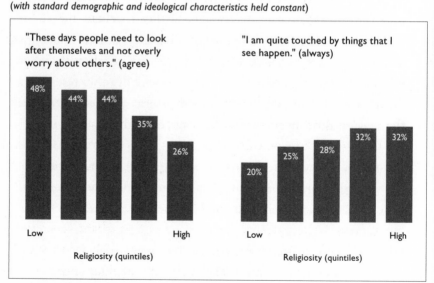

SOURCE: FAITH MATTERS SURVEY, 2006.

altruistic values predict secular giving and volunteering, working on community projects, and other measures of good neighborliness, even with other factors held constant. Thus, one reason why religious people are "do-gooders" seems to be that they are more empathetic and altruistic in outlook than secular Americans. On the other hand, people with altruistic values are not necessarily more engaged in civic life (group membership, public meetings, voting, and so on). So we must seek other explanations for the religious edge on civic activism.

Measuring altruistic values (and the opposite—selfishness) is a delicate art, but precisely the same conclusion—that greater altruism helps explain part of the good neighborliness of religious people—is confirmed in the Giving and Volunteering surveys, as well as in the General Social Survey and the PS-ARE survey. The precise measures of altruistic values and generous neighborliness differ from survey to survey.[35] Nevertheless, the core message from these four independent survey archives is always the same—religiously observant people are less likely to espouse selfish values, and that difference in values helps, in part, explain the religious edge in generosity.

On the other hand, selflessness cannot be the entire explanation, since even comparing two people with identical profiles on the altruism-empathy scale, the one who attends church more regularly is systematically a better neighbor. In round numbers, measurable differences in altruistic values seem to account for no more than 25 percent of the religious edge on generosity and even less of the edge on civic engagement.

Religious beliefs and feelings encompass much more than merely the Golden Rule: beliefs about God, the afterlife, heaven, and hell, the Bible, God's love and God's judgment, the requirements for salvation and eternal life, the fate of this world and the hope of the next, and many more. Table 13.3 lists some of the many theological beliefs and religious commitments that we probed in our Faith Matters surveys.[36] These twenty-five questions elicit vibrant, fundamental convictions for many Americans, but as we shall see they turn out to be utterly irrelevant to explaining the religious edge in good neighborliness.

Table 13.3

MEASURES OF THEOLOGICAL BELIEF AND RELIGIOUS COMMITMENT

Are you absolutely sure, somewhat sure, not quite sure, not at all sure, or are you sure you do no believe in God?

...in life after death?

...in heaven?

...in hell?

Do you believe the world is soon coming to an end, or not?

Have you ever personally experienced the presence of God, or not?

How often do you personally feel God's love in your life?

How often do you personally feel God's judgment in your life?

How important is your religion to your sense of who you are?

How important is religion in your daily life?

How important is religion to you in making decisions regarding your career, family, or health?

How important is religion to you in making decisions on political issues?

Would you call yourself a strong believer in your religion or not a very strong believer?

Do you consider yourself very spiritual, moderately spiritual, slightly spiritual, or not spiritual at all?

How often do you read holy scriptures?

How often do you say grace or give blessings to God before meals?

How often do you pray outside of religious services?

We will all be called before God to answer for our sins. (agree/disagree)

Morality is a personal matter and society should not force everyone to follow one standard. (agree/disagree)

Which comes closer to your views: There are absolutely clear guidelines of what is good and ev OR there can never be absolutely clear guidelines of what is good and evil.

Which comes closest to describing your feelings about holy scripture: Scripture is the actual word of God and is to be taken literally, word for word; OR Scripture is the inspired word of God but not everything in it should be taken literally, word for word; OR Scripture is an ancien book of fables, legends, history, and moral precepts recorded by men?

Which comes closer to your views: Right and wrong should be based on God's laws OR right and wrong should be based on the views of society?

Which comes closest to your views: One religion is true and others are not OR there are basic truths in many religions OR there is very little truth in any religion?

Which comes closer to your views: The path to salvation comes through our actions or deeds OR the path to salvation lies in our beliefs or faith?

Which of the following statements comes closest to your views on the origin and development of human beings: Human beings have developed over millions of years from less advanced form of life, but God guided this process; OR Human beings have developed over millions of years from less advanced forms of life, but God had no part in this process; OR God created human beings pretty much in their present form at one time within the last 10,000 years or so?

SOURCE: FAITH MATTERS SURVEY, 2006.

By comparing what people told us in 2006 and again in 2007, we were able to establish that most Americans have reasonably firm and consistent views on these issues, even on topics that seem esoteric to less religious people, such as "salvation through faith" versus "salvation through deeds." That issue was at the heart of Europe's religious wars of the sixteenth and seventeenth centuries, but we did not expect that nearly half a millennium later in a more secular age most Americans would have stable views on such seemingly arcane theological issues. But they do.

So most religious Americans have firm theological commitments that they believe may determine their eternal fate. It is therefore entirely reasonable to expect that those commitments might be part of the explanation for the distinctive social behavior of religious Americans. In fact, however, we can find no effect whatsoever of those theological views on the religious edge in good neighborliness. Certainly, each of these twenty-five different measures is in itself correlated with religiosity (as measured by church attendance, for example). However, controlling for frequency of church attendance, not one of them is correlated with the measures of good neighborliness that we discussed earlier in this chapter. It is tempting to think that religious people are better neighbors because of their fear of God or their hope of salvation or their reading of the Good Word, but we find no evidence for those conjectures.

Once we know how observant a person is in terms of church attendance, nothing that we can discover about the content of her religious faith adds anything to our understanding or prediction of her good neighborliness—nothing about her views about the Bible or life after death or evolution or eschatology, or her personal experience of God, or the kind of God she believes in, or the importance of religion in her life or in her personal or political decisions, or her views about morality or salvation or evolution or Judgment Day or the Rapture, or her habits of saying grace or reading scripture.[37]

In sum, just as (once we control for frequency of church attendance) different denominations or religious traditions don't differ in good neighborliness, theology and piety and sacraments and devotion also don't seem to matter at all. This conclusion is further strengthened by the fact that once we take into account a person's current level of church attendance, good neighborliness is not at all affected by childhood religious education or religious family background. Whether or not you went to Sunday School as a child seems to have no direct effect on your current civic behavior or your current generosity. What counts is not how well you learned the catechism or the Golden Rule as a child, but how involved you are nowadays in religious networks, as marked (for example) by churchgoing.

One aspect of community connectedness does turn out to be correlated with theology: trust. We saw earlier that religious people are generally more trusting than secular people, but it turns out that fundamentalist religious views (such as the belief that the Bible is literally true in every word, or that the end of the world is at hand) are *negatively* associated with social trust. That is, comparing two people who attend church equally often, the one with more fundamentalist views is less trusting. On the other hand, comparing two people with equally fundamentalist (or equally nonfundamentalist) views, the one who attends church more often is more trusting (see Figure 13.6).[38]

In short, beliefs and belonging point in opposite directions here. Fundamentalist religious convictions are associated with low trust, but adjusting for that theological effect, active participation in a religious community, even a fundamentalist one, is associated with high trust. One instructive way to see this intriguing correlation between theological views and trust in other people draws on two questions about religious experience in our 2006 Faith Matters survey: "How often do you feel God's love in your life?" and "How often do you feel God's judgment in your life?"

Answers to the two questions are, not surprisingly, correlated; religious people more frequently report divine experiences of all sorts. The daunting image of God as stern judge of our failings is common to all Abrahamic faiths. Every Rosh Hashanah, for example, even liberal Jews recite "Let us proclaim the sacred power of

Figure 13.6

SOCIAL TRUST INCREASES WITH RELIGIOUS ATTENDANCE,
BUT DECREASES WITH FUNDAMENTALISM

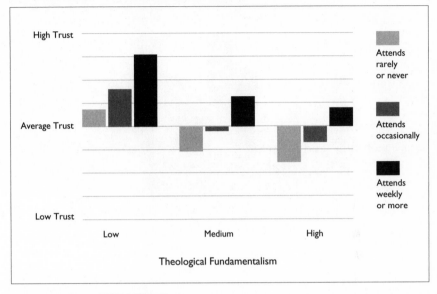

SOURCE: FAITH MATTERS SURVEY, 2006.

this day; it is awesome and full of dread. Now the divine Judge looks
upon our deeds, and determines our destiny." Conversely, all faiths
in America, even the most conservative, include a vision of God as
loving parent, always ready to accept the penitent sinner.

Nevertheless, Americans differ in the nature of their everyday
experience of the divine as judgmental or loving, and those differences turn out to be relevant to their expectations about other people.[39] Experiencing a loving God is associated with high trust in one's
fellow mortals, whereas experiencing a judgmental God is associated with low trust in other people. The highest level of social trust
is expressed by people who "very often" experience God's love, but
"never" experience God's judgment. At the other pole, Americans
who are least trusting of their neighbors are those who experience
God's judgment more often than God's love (see Figure 13.7).[40] Religious liberals more often experience a loving God, and they are
among the most socially trusting of Americans, whereas religious

Figure 13.7

SOCIAL TRUST AND GOD'S NATURE

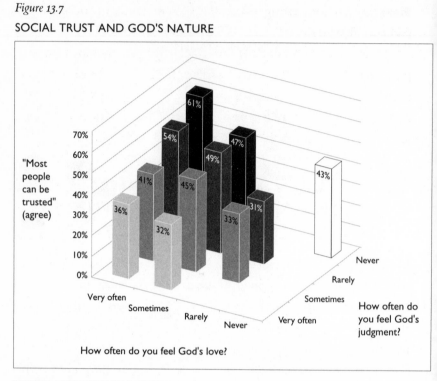

SOURCE: FAITH MATTERS SURVEY, 2006.

conservatives more often experience a judgmental God, and they are among the least trusting of Americans, especially if they are not observant. For highly observant fundamentalist Americans, their theology inclines them toward skepticism about human nature, but their frequent church attendance somehow moves them to a more optimistic view.

Identifying cause and effect between social trust and experience of God may be a fool's errand, but the correlation seems perfectly intelligible. We seem to have consistent expectations about other people's behavior and God's behavior. If God loves us, then we love and trust others, but if God sternly judges us, then we sternly judge and distrust others. Social relations in America may be eased by the fact that most Americans find God more likely to comfort than to afflict. Sixty-two percent told us that they feel God's love "very often," but only 39 percent said the same about God's judgment. Such a comforting, avuncular God encourages social comity and confidence.

Thus, we can occasionally find trace effects of theology on people's civic behavior. But even in this case church attendance itself seems to contain the secret ingredient in explaining why religious people are better, more trusting friends and neighbors. So what is it about going to church that matters?

WHY ARE RELIGIOUS AMERICANS BETTER NEIGHBORS: SOCIAL NETWORKS?

Mobilization or exhortations by clergy seem not to be a major factor in explaining good neighborliness. Parishioners in congregations where political and social issues are frequently discussed by the clergy are no more likely to be better neighbors or civic activists than parishioners in other congregations. The Giving and Volunteering surveys of the 1990s included detailed questions about who had asked you to give or volunteer and for what. Being asked by clergy turns out to help explain who gives or volunteers for religious causes, but seems to have no bearing at all on nonreligious generosity and civic engagement. You're likely to drop more in the offering plate or to serve as church usher if your pastor asks you, but he seems to have little or no impact at all on how you treat your neighbor or whether you give to the United Way.

How about the effect of social networks—that is, the other people you meet at church functions? Here we must distinguish between having many friends and having many friends at church. People who have more friends in general are much more likely than social isolates to give, volunteer, and take part in civic life. In that sense, friends in general have a powerful effect on civic involvement, partly because friends are likely to ask. However, while religious people do have more friends overall than nonreligious people, this difference in general sociability is much too small to explain the substantial religious edge on generosity, neighborliness, and civic engagement.[41]

But friends at church—that is, religiously focused social networks—are an entirely different matter. Having close friends at church, discussing religion frequently with your family and friends, and taking part in small groups at church are extremely powerful predictors of the entire range of generosity, good neighborliness, and civic engagement discussed in this chapter—and not just of religious good works.

So important are these religiously based social networks that they alone account for most of the apparent effects of church attendance. With comprehensive demographic and ideological controls, including density of generic social networks (number of close friends and of confidants), as well as general religiosity, our index of religious social networks (number of close friends in your congregation, participation in small groups in your congregation, and frequency of talking about religion with family and friends) is virtually the most powerful predictor of every measure of good neighborliness discussed in this chapter, no less robust a predictor than education, the universal predictor. When we include this index of religious social networks in the analysis, religiosity becomes entirely insignificant as a predictor of virtually all measures of good neighborliness that we examined: volunteering for secular causes, giving to secular causes, membership in civic groups, working on a community project, collaborating on community problems, working for social reform, attending club meetings, serving as an organizational leader, voting in local elections, and attending public meetings. In virtually every case, although generic friendship ties are a significant predictor, religious social networks are a stronger, more robust predictor.[42]

In other words, devout people who sit alone in the pews are not much more neighborly than people who don't go to church at all. The real impact of religiosity on niceness or good neighborliness, it seems, comes through chatting with friends after service or joining a Bible study group, not from listening to the sermon or fervently believing in God.

In fact, the statistics suggest that even an atheist who happened to become involved in the social life of a congregation (perhaps through a spouse) is much more likely to volunteer in a soup kitchen than the most fervent believer who prays alone. It is religious belonging that matters for neighborliness, not religious believing. In addition, that same belonging nonbeliever is likely to be a better neighbor than a comparable nonbeliever who never enters church. What statistical analysis shows is not that religiosity has no effect on good neighborliness, but that its impact comes almost entirely through religious social networks.

Lest this distinction be thought nonsensical, we need to reemphasize the imperfect correlation in America between believing and belonging. It is true that most people who belong also believe, and most people who don't believe don't belong. But of all Americans who attend church about once a month, nearly one in twenty is not sure that she believes in God. Conversely, more than one in every five Americans who say they are "absolutely sure" about believing in God virtually never attend church. And the evidence, both from our own surveys and from our analysis of other surveys, is unequivocal—when it comes to the religious edge in good neighborliness, it is belonging that matters, not believing.

Keep in mind that these religious friendships are powerful in predicting not merely religious good works, but also secular good works—not merely kindness to fellow congregants, but also kindness to neighbors and strangers. Religious friendships are highly important in predicting good citizenship, even after we take into account that (1) people with more friends at church tend to have more friends in general and (2) friends in general predict good citizenship. And religious friendships are even more powerful predictors of good neighborliness than friendships in general, so that religious ties seem to be a kind of supercharged friendship.[43]

We summarize some relevant evidence from our 2006 Faith Matters survey in Figure 13.8. In round numbers, people with many religiously based social connections are two or three times more likely to be civically engaged and generous, even to purely secular causes, than people with few such ties, regardless of how devout and observant they themselves are. Keep in mind that Figure 13.8 controls

Figure 13.8

RELIGIOUSLY BASED SOCIAL NETWORKS FOSTER CIVIC ENGAGEMENT
(*with standard demographic and ideological characteristics **and church attendance and sociability** held constant*)

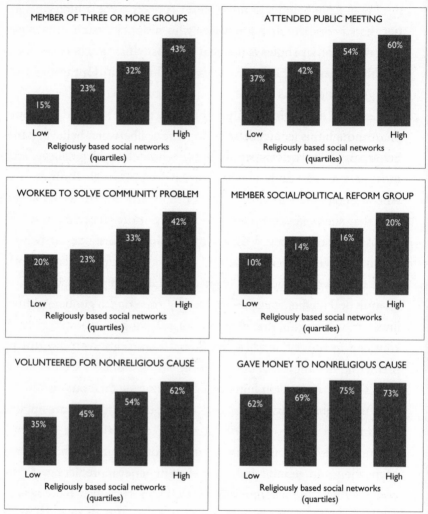

for all standard demographic and ideological factors, as well as for church attendance and general sociability. In effect, it compares people with identical backgrounds, identical records of church attendance, and identical overall numbers of friends and confidants. So having religious friends is more important than simply having friends and being religious yourself. It is in this sense that religious networks are synergistic or supercharged in their effect on neighborliness.

Religiously based social ties seem crucial to explaining the link between religiosity and good neighborliness. Spending time with other religious people will make you a better neighbor, even if you're not terribly pious yourself. Conversely, bowling in a league may move you in the right direction, but not nearly so effectively as bowling in a church league.

Although this verdict that friends at church are the magic ingredient that makes religious people better neighbors is surprisingly clear in our own 2006 Faith Matters survey, we sought to confirm it in all the other national surveys we could find that had asked about religious social networks.[44] In the 2006 PS-ARE survey the fraction of one's closest friends who are actively involved in one's own religious congregation is a powerful predictor of giving, volunteering, civic engagement, and other good deeds, even controlling for demographic and ideological background factors, for the number of one's close friends, and for one's church attendance. For example, Americans whose closest friends are all religiously involved are 50 percent more likely to help neighbors or strangers (financially or otherwise), compared to Americans none of whose closest friends are religiously involved, even holding their own frequency of church attendance constant.

In the 1996 and 1999 Giving and Volunteering surveys, general socializing with family, friends, and neighbors is not a significant contributor to the religious edge in secular giving and volunteering, while socializing with friends from a person's church or synagogue has a very powerful effect. Being asked by clergy to give or to volunteer does not affect generosity to secular causes, though as we have seen it does affect generosity to religious causes. Being asked by friends from church, by contrast, raises both religious and secular giving and volunteering. In other words, compared to nonreligious people, people involved in religious networks behave more generously, in part because they are asked more often by the people they meet in those religious networks to give and volunteer for secular causes, as well as for religious causes.[45]

Good neighborliness (by all our measures) and involvement in religiously based social networks are, in short, highly correlated in every survey we have examined, even when we hold constant everything from demographic and ideological factors to general religiosity and general sociability. In no major national survey have we found evidence that specific religious beliefs predict good neighborliness, once we control for religious social ties. In every major national survey we have found that religious social ties predict good neighborliness, controlling for religious beliefs. That kind of robust correlation is uncommon in the social sciences.

But is this correlation causal? As we noted earlier, without true random assignment experiments (forcing some people to have religiously based friendships and others not to have such friendships), it is impossible to prove that the link is causal.

However, once again we can gain some leverage on this question by examining how our Faith Matters respondents changed between 2006 and 2007. Even more strongly than in the case of church attendance, the evidence on the impact of religiously based social networks suggests that the link may well be causal. Controlling for all standard background factors—in effect, matching respondents as closely as possible, even on their general sociability and general religiosity—we find that people who became more closely involved with religious networks between 2006 and 2007 became better citizens and more generous neighbors. They volunteered more, they gave more to secular causes, they went to more public meetings, they were more likely to vote in local elections and more likely to pitch in on some community project. Conversely, those people whose ties to religious social networks slackened somewhat over this year reduced their civic involvement in all these ways. Gaining (or losing) friends in general did not have any effect on good neighborliness, and becoming more (or less) religious personally did not seem to matter, but gaining (or losing) religious friends did. That fact alone does not prove that the link is causal, but it does increase the plausibility that it is.[46]

One important reason for this striking pattern is that (as we saw earlier) religiously engaged people are also more likely to be engaged in civic life outside of their religious circles. The person you know from your prayer group is likely to be active in the PTA as well, and thus you are more likely to be asked to bake cookies for the PTA social simply because you know her through church. In short, the people you meet at church are not only church people, but are also generous, engaged citizens of the wider community. So religiously based social networks lead people not just inward to the church but outward to that wider secular community, in terms of giving, volunteering, and participating in civic life. This is the civic equivalent of the echo chamber effect that in the previous chapter we found to be so important in amplifying the political effects of religion.

Religiously based social networks are powerful predictors of nonreligious involvement for other reasons as well. We suspect that religiously based ties are morally freighted in a way that most secular ties are not, so that pleas for good works (giving, volunteering, joining a reform movement, serving as a leader in some civic organization, and so forth) seem more appropriate and weightier than comparable requests from a co-worker or someone you know from the gym. The latter may be more likely to invite you to a Red Sox game, but less likely to urge you to contribute to the Jimmy Fund to support cancer treatment for kids.

Moreover, since (as we know from our earlier discussion) religious people individually tend to be more altruistic, it seems likely that connecting with such people tends to evoke peer pressure for you to do good deeds as well. Hanging out with gym rats is likely to increase your concern about fitness, and in the same way hanging out with religious do-gooders is likely to increase your own motivation to do good. Although we lack systematic information about exactly what is discussed in these religious networks, it is possible that religious friends are more likely to raise moral issues, principles, and obligations than friends from a nonreligious context and thus to heighten your own attentiveness to such concerns. The small groups that we visited in religious congregations across the country offered vivid examples of this dynamic. Whether or not these speculations are accurate, the central point is this: Religiously rooted social networks in America have a powerful effect in encouraging neighborliness and civic engagement.

Perhaps close, morally intense, but nonreligious social networks could have a similarly powerful effect. So-called intentional communities, such as the communes of the 1960s, are often founded on the assumption that they might. We cannot exclude that possibility, because we have not found a significant number of such groups nationwide to study. While we cannot deny that secular equivalents of religiously based social networks might exist, we are confident that in America today religious institutions represent by far the most common site of such communities.

If religiously based social networks (having friends at church, belonging to small groups at church, talking about religion with family and friends) are so powerful, what in turn explains involvement in those networks? Our own evidence can take us only a short way toward answering that question. Not surprisingly, people who have dense religiously based personal networks are much more religiously observant and generally more sociable than those with sparse or nonexistent religious networks. They are not distinguished by their education or income or politics or gender or age or the size of their town.[47] They are much more likely to have fundamentalist religious convictions. They report more religious homogeneity among their five closest friends, but also more religious diversity among their wider circle of friends, so it is wrong to think of Americans with dense religious networks as necessarily living in a religiously monochromatic world.[48]

Specifically, having good friends in your religious congregation is best predicted by how religious you are, how old you are, and how long you've been in your congregation. In round numbers, people who've just joined a congregation report two close friends at church. On average, it takes two more years to add a third close friend, ten more years to add a fourth, and another ten years to add a fifth. It takes time to make good friends, even in church! On the other hand, involvement in congregational small groups (another of our measures of religious social networks) is higher among newcomers to large congregations. Such small groups seem to be a starter kit for building informal ties within a congregation, just as we found in our congregational vignettes.

RELIGIOUS AMERICANS ARE LESS TOLERANT OF DISSENT

The evidence we have reviewed thus far suggests that religion encourages good neighborliness and good citizenship, primarily through the powerful influence of religiously inflected social networks. On one important criterion for democratic citizenship, however, religious Americans earn a distinctly less favorable grade—tolerance of civil liberties and political dissent. We now explore what might be called the darker side of religion's link to citizenship.[49] We begin by assessing overall support for civil liberties in today's America, and then turn to religion's role.

Americans, religious and secular alike, are reasonably tolerant of difference and dissent. "It's a free country, after all," Americans steeped in the Bill of Rights are inclined to say. In our surveys we sought to pressure-test this commitment as hard as we could. We asked, "A book that most people disapprove of should be kept out of my local public library—do you agree or disagree? How strongly?" Even more provocatively, we posed the issue of whether "People have a perfect right to give a speech defending Osama bin Laden or al Qaeda." As Table 13.4 shows, most Americans rejected censorship, even in these two cases. However, in the midst of the War on Terror they were understandably less steadfast in defending free speech for those who might be labeled apologists for terrorism. (Because the two questions were intentionally phrased in opposite directions to diffuse response bias, the bold numbers in Table 13.4 represent the pro–civil liberty responses.) Despite the War on Terror and memo-

Table 13.4
SUPPORT FOR CIVIL LIBERTIES

	Speech defending Osama bin Laden is okay	Censor unpopular book
Agree strongly	**30%**	12%
Agree	**27%**	12%
Disagree	8%	**23%**
Disagree strongly	35%	**54%**
	100%	100%

SOURCE: FAITH MATTERS SURVEY, 2006.

ries of 9/11, more than half of all Americans endorse the right to defend terrorists publicly, and more than three quarters reject popular censorship of libraries. In fact, support for civil liberties, at least in these two cases, is stronger in America than in Great Britain, home of the Magna Carta.[50]

Moreover, Americans have become steadily more tolerant of virtually all forms of dissent over the last several decades. Repeatedly since 1972 the General Social Survey has asked three questions about each of five target groups.

> There are always some people whose ideas are considered bad or dangerous by other people.
> 1. If such a person wanted to make a speech in your (city/town/community), should he be allowed to speak, or not?
> 2. Should such a person be allowed to teach in a college or university, or not?
> 3. If some people in your community suggested that a book he wrote be taken out of your public library, would you favor removing this book, or not?

The five target groups that have appeared consistently on this survey since the mid-1970s are:

1. "somebody who is against all churches and religion"
2. "a person who believes that blacks are genetically inferior"
3. "a man who admits he is a Communist"

4. "a person who advocates doing away with elections and letting the military run the country"

5. "a man who admits that he is a homosexual"

Responses to this set of fifteen questions allow us to track trends in
attitudes toward dissent for a range of unpopular groups. Of course,
the five groups are unpopular with different segments of the population, which is precisely why together they provide a useful seismograph of tolerance in America. And this seismograph traces an
unambiguous picture, for on every single one of the fifteen questions tolerance increases significantly over these thirty-six years.[51]
Figure 13.9 summarizes the trends for each of the five groups (aver-
aging responses to speeches, teaching, and books in each case). The
increase in tolerance is greater in some cases (e.g., homosexuality)
than in other cases (e.g., racism), but the basic trend toward greater
civic tolerance is clear. (Figure 13.9 does not reveal it, but most of
that upward shift is due to generational succession, as older, less tol-

Figure 13.9

GROWTH OF CIVIC TOLERANCE IN U.S. (1972–2008)

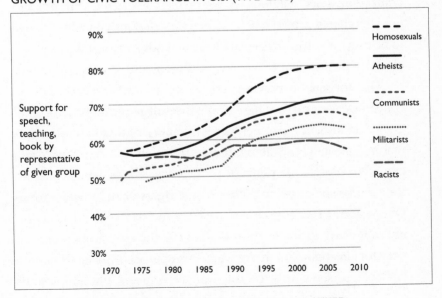

SOURCE: GENERAL SOCIAL SURVEY, 1972–2008; DATA LOESS-SMOOTHED.

erant cohorts born early in the twentieth century were replaced in the population by their more tolerant children and grandchildren.)

Thus, the good news is that Americans are increasingly tolerant of difference and dissent. The bad news (at least from the point of view of religion) is that religious Americans are systematically less tolerant than secular Americans.

That fundamental correlation between religiosity and intolerance has been confirmed in dozens of studies over the last half century. It is true even with many other background factors held constant—age, race, region, education, income, gender, political ideology, homeownership, marital and parental status, and general civic engagement.[52]

Many studies, beginning in the 1950s and including our Faith Matters surveys in 2006 and 2007, have found that the more a person is involved in civic activity, the more supportive he is of civil liberties. For example, in our 2006 Faith Matters survey, members of fraternal organizations or of neighborhood associations are more likely than nonmembers to support the right of others to defend al Qaeda, with or without controls for standard demographic factors. Religious organizations are the most notable exception to that generalization, since religious engagement is associated with less support for civil liberties. The tendency for religiously involved people to be more involved in secular civic life tends to mitigate (but also to obscure) the fact that religiosity itself is correlated with intolerance.

The correlation between religiosity and intolerance has been confirmed with many different measures of religiosity and of intolerance. In measuring intolerance it is important to ask "intolerant of whom?" Generally speaking, those on the left tend to be more concerned to protect the rights of progressive groups, while conservatives tend to be more protective of the rights of right-wing groups. One way of getting around that fact is to ask a respondent first to indicate which group he most dislikes and then to ask about his support for the rights of that group; this approach is called "content controlled." Even with careful content controls, political scientist

James Gibson has found that religious people are less tolerant of their opponents' rights than are secular people.[53]

Our own queries about Osama bin Laden and unpopular books showed that even with regard to such widely disfavored targets, secular Americans offer somewhat firmer support for civil liberties.[54] Once again, our analysis essentially compares demographically and ideologically matched churchgoers and nonchurchgoers. Of nonchurchgoers, 88 percent opposed library censorship, compared to 73 percent of regular churchgoers; and 62 percent of nonchurchgoers supported the free speech rights of Osama bin Laden's defenders, compared to 56 percent of regular churchgoers. The glass here is half full: Even among religious Americans, majorities defend civil liberties for despised causes, but those majorities are significantly slimmer than among secular Americans.

Even more compelling evidence comes from the same battery of fifteen items from the General Social Survey that we have already discussed, because in every single case church attendance is strongly associated with lower support for civil liberties. This pattern is hardly surprising in the case of "avowed homosexuals" and "somebody who is against all churches and religion," for tolerance of those groups is a tougher test for religiously devout people than for secular people. But it is more striking that the same pattern—secular people more tolerant—recurs on questions about racists and militarists, who are probably more disliked by secular people than by religious people and who therefore pose tougher tests for those who are secular.

This pattern persists even with ideology and demography held constant. Comparing, say, two demographically matched young college-educated liberal women (or comparing two demographically matched older less educated conservative men), the one who seldom attends church is likely to be more supportive of the civil liberties of racists, militarists, and so forth than is her more religiously observant counterpart. In other words, the greater tolerance of dissent among seculars is not merely a side effect of political ideology.

Unchurched conservatives are more tolerant of difference and dissent than devout conservatives, and churchgoing liberals are less tolerant than secular liberals.[55]

Another illustration of this asymmetry in support for civil liberties—secular people supportive of the rights of their "opponents," religious people less supportive of the rights of their "opponents"—comes from a pair of questions that we posed in our Faith Matters survey in 2007. We asked whether our respondents agreed or disagreed with each of the following assertions:[56]

- An atheist should be allowed to teach in the public schools.
- A religious fundamentalist should be allowed to teach in the public schools.

Our first important discovery is that even on these intentionally provocative issues, a large majority of all Americans defend diversity and civil liberties. Of all Americans, 72 percent support the rights of atheists to teach in public schools, 74 percent support the rights of fundamentalists to teach in public schools, and 60 percent support the rights of both groups of teachers. At least in this sense most American communities are not riven by culture wars about the private religiosity of public school teachers.

However, the attitudes of religious and secular Americans to the two types of teachers are asymmetrical, as Figure 13.10 shows. Opposition to atheists as teachers is heavily concentrated among highly religious people, whereas opposition to fundamentalists as teachers is less concentrated among secular Americans. Religiously observant Americans strongly dislike atheists, and 43 percent of them want to keep atheists out of the classroom. Secular Americans dislike fundamentalists equally strongly—two researchers in this area refer to antifundamentalism as "a prejudice for the thinking classes"—but only 26 percent of them would forbid fundamentalists from teaching.[57]

In short, much evidence suggests that religious Americans are less stout defenders of civil liberties than secular Americans, and in

Figure 13.10

OPPOSITION TO ATHEIST TEACHERS IS CLOSELY TIED TO RELIGIOSITY, BUT OPPOSITION TO FUNDAMENTALIST TEACHERS IS LESS TIED TO SECULARISM

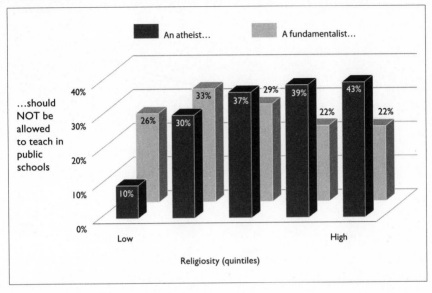

SOURCE: FAITH MATTERS SURVEY, 2007.

that sense, though religious Americans may be more conscientious citizens, they are less enthusiastic than the average American about defending the civil liberties of their opponents.

Intolerance is a variable, not a constant, in American history. We have already seen evidence (Figure 13.9) that over the last three decades Americans as a whole have become more tolerant in civic terms. In fact, the two targets toward which tolerance has increased most rapidly—homosexuals and "somebody who is against all churches and religion"—are the very targets most anathema to religious Americans. One might have supposed that the trends represented in Figure 13.9 represent the drowning out of the views of religious Americans by a swelling chorus of secular voices, but that is not the case. On the contrary, this growth of tolerance for the rights of gays and antireligious viewpoints has actually been slightly greater among religious Americans than among secular Americans.

Figures 13.11 and 13.12 display the trends in support for the civil

AMERICAN GRACE

Figure 13.11

SUPPORT FOR CIVIL LIBERTIES OF OPPONENT OF RELIGION, BY FREQUENCY OF CHURCH ATTENDANCE

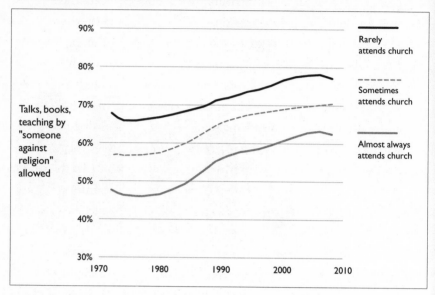

SOURCE: GENERAL SOCIAL SURVEY, 1972–2008; DATA LOESS-SMOOTHED.

Figure 13.12

SUPPORT FOR CIVIL LIBERTIES OF HOMOSEXUALS, BY FREQUENCY OF CHURCH ATTENDANCE

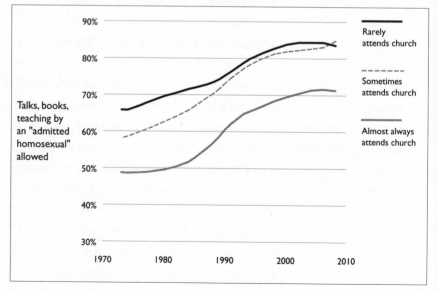

SOURCE: GENERAL SOCIAL SURVEY, 1972–2008; DATA LOESS-SMOOTHED.

liberties of antireligious and pro-gay advocates between 1972 and 2008 by religious and secular Americans. In both cases religiously observant Americans started out much more skeptical of free expression for their cultural adversaries, and in both cases they remain less tolerant today. On the other hand, in both cases the gap between the views of religious and secular Americans has significantly narrowed.[58] It is not that religious Americans have suddenly made their peace with homosexuality or anticlericalism—far from it. But more and more religious Americans seem to be saying "I disagree deeply with what you advocate, but I respect your right to advocate it."

Further analysis (presented in Figure 13.13) shows that this change is driven almost entirely by generational succession among religious Americans. All their lives religious Americans born in the early part of the twentieth century remained skeptical about free expression on behalf of causes they found ungodly. However, younger generations who are as devout as their parents and grandparents—that is, younger people who attend church regularly, believe deeply in the tenets of their faith, and practice its rituals—are more reluctant than those who sat in the same pews a generation ago to deny their ideological and cultural opponents the right to express themselves. In round numbers, as Figure 13.13 shows, about two thirds of churchgoers who came of age before 1945 rejected free expression for antireligious views, whereas about two thirds of churchgoers who came of age after 1965 tolerate such views.

Something about American history over the last century led younger religious cohorts to adopt a "live and let live" attitude to cultural differences. So the dark side of religion's civic impact has become slightly less dark in recent decades, but the shadow remains. A substantial gap persists between religious Americans and secular Americans in their support for civil liberties, even among the youngest cohort. What is it about religion that accounts for greater intolerance among religious people, both now and in the past?

Religious tradition or denomination seems to play a very small role. Evidence both from our Faith Matters surveys and from the General Social Survey shows that within every religious tradition

Figure 13.13

AMONG REGULAR CHURCHGOERS YOUNGER GENERATIONS ARE MORE
TOLERANT OF ANTIRELIGIOUS EXPRESSION THAN OLDER GENERATIONS

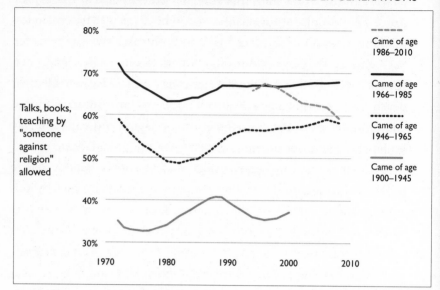

SOURCE: GENERAL SOCIAL SURVEY, 1972–2008; DATA LOESS-SMOOTHED.

(even including people who claim to have no religious affiliation at all) frequent church attendance is associated with less tolerance across the board.[59] Once again, the civic consequences of religion, at least in today's America, seem to depend much more on how much religion, not which religion.

Many explanations have been suggested for the greater intolerance of more religiously observant people—that they are more likely to see the world in "we/they" or Manichaean terms, for example, or that moral absolutism—a clear distinction between right and wrong—is incompatible with the skeptical outlook that is said to undergird civic tolerance. Despite looking, we find no evidence in our own surveys to support either of those theories, but we do find one bit of evidence for a third theory. Religious people, it is sometimes said, have a respect for authority that makes them readier to shun dissent—what Kenneth Wald, Stephen Mockabee, and others have called "'authority-mindedness'—an ideological commitment that values authoritativeness and obedience."[60] Mockabee observed, "child-rearing questions do a good job of identifying the extent to which individuals are authority-minded."[61] So we asked our respondents one simple question about childrearing: "Which is more important for a child to be taught: obedience or self-reliance?"[62]

Figure 13.14 shows the striking results—religious people emphasize obedience, secular people emphasize self-reliance.[63] In turn, authority-mindedness is sufficiently related to our questions about Osama bin Laden and unpopular books that, statistically, it helps explain the greater intolerance of religious Americans. In short, one reason that religious people are readier to suppress dissent seems to be that they are particularly concerned to safeguard authority.[64]

Figure 13.14

RELIGIOUS AMERICANS ARE MORE CONCERNED ABOUT RESPECT FOR AUTHORITY

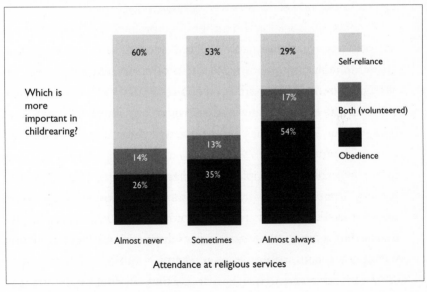

SOURCE: FAITH MATTERS SURVEY, 2006.

ARE RELIGIOUS AMERICANS ALSO HAPPIER, AND IF SO, WHY?

So far in this chapter we've explored how religion affects neighborliness and citizenship, as well as how it affects tolerance. Before closing, it will be instructive to explore what seems a very different question: How does religion affect one's own happiness? Psychologists, economists, and other social scientists in recent decades have begun to grapple with a fundamental issue previously left to parsons and philosophers: What makes life satisfying? This new field of research—loosely termed "happiness studies"—has come to some crisp conclusions.

First, it is surprisingly easy to measure happiness or life satisfaction just by asking us how satisfied we are with our lives. The responses we give to simple survey questions turn out to be consistent with what others say about us and with various physiological measures of body chemistry and brain activity.[65]

Second, the social and demographic predictors of happiness or life satisfaction are reasonably well understood, and those predictors are reasonably uniform around the world.[66] Healthier people, for example, are happier than sick people. Money can buy happiness, especially if you are really impoverished, but above a certain level (roughly the level reached by the average American a few decades ago), more money doesn't buy much more happiness. Personal ties matter a lot. Married people are consistently happier than single people, and good friends matter more than material possessions. Social isolation and depression are strongly correlated. Other social factors that seem to have some impact on happiness and life satisfaction include race, age, and employment status.

Third, many researchers have found that religious people are happier.[67] Indeed, a common finding is that religiosity is among the closest correlates of life satisfaction, at least as strong as income. Why that might be true remains a matter of some controversy (like almost everything else about religion). However, to our surprise, the linkage between religion and life satisfaction seems to be virtually identical in form to the linkage between religion and good neighborliness:

- As with good neighborliness, the correlation between religiosity and life satisfaction is powerful and robust.[68] It remains strong even when we hold constant the same long list of other factors that might have made the correlation spurious. Other things being equal, the difference in happiness between a nonchurchgoer and a weekly churchgoer is slightly larger than the difference between someone who earns $10,000 a year and his demographic twin who earns $100,000 a year.

- As with good neighborliness, religious people are more satisfied with their lives mostly because they build religious social networks, thus reinforcing a strong sense of religious identity. A person who attends church regularly but has no close friends there is actually unhappier than her demographic twin who doesn't attend church at all.

- As with good neighborliness, religious friends remain very important, even when we compare people with equal numbers of friends overall, and in that sense religious friendship seems supercharged. Moreover, as with good neighborliness, the effects of religious social networks do not depend on maintaining a religiously homogeneous social environment; on the contrary, people whose closest friends are all from the same religion are, other things being equal, less happy than those whose friends are diverse.

- As with good neighborliness, theological and denominational differences appear to have virtually nothing to do with the linkage between life satisfaction and religiosity.

- As with good neighborliness, comparing changes in religiosity and in life satisfaction in our 2006 and 2007 interviews suggests that the correlation may be causal. People who become more religious become happier.

- In short, as with good neighborliness, the religious edge in life satisfaction has less to do with faith itself than with communities of faith. For happiness as for neighborliness, praying together seems to be better than either bowling together or praying alone.

CONCLUSION

Was Tocqueville right that religion contributes to American democracy? The evidence suggests that with one important exception he was. Religious Americans are generally better neighbors and more active citizens, though they are less staunch supporters of civil liberties than secular Americans. Moreover, religious Americans are more satisfied with their lives. As we have seen, however, theology and piety have very little to do with this religious edge in neighborliness and happiness. Instead it is religion's network of morally freighted personal connections, coupled with an inclination toward altruism, that explains both the good neighborliness and the life satisfaction of religious Americans.

CHAPTER 14

CHAPTER 14

A House Divided?

There is a good reason that your mother told you never to discuss religion in polite company. Religion, or the lack thereof, informs and shapes people's deep-seated values, their worldviews. Disagreements over religion are often disagreements over fundamentals: the immovable object of one person's beliefs meeting the irresistible force of another's. On the world stage, both history and current events are rife with examples where irreconcilable religious beliefs have led to bloodshed. Here in the United States, recent years have seen the sharpest points of disagreement between religious believers—of nearly all stripes—and those who denounce religious belief of all types.[1]

The bestseller lists are full of books highly critical of religion, countered by pundits whose heated rhetoric decries a public square made "naked" by the absence of religion.[2] Yet the fault line between those who are religious and those who are not hardly exhausts the ways in which religion can be divisive. The increasing volume of a newly emergent secularism, even atheism, has not supplanted the venerable tensions among religions. For example, being so closely bound up with ethnicity (see Chapter 9), religion has the potential to dovetail with, and aggravate, racial and ethnic tensions. And even when ethnicity is removed from the equation, theological disputes can lead to interreligious tension. Should scripture be read literally? Is man inherently sinful? Does salvation rest on God's grace alone, or are good works necessary too?

While religion is potentially divisive everywhere, the United

493

493

States would appear to be a tinderbox for a religious conflagration. Many individual Americans are highly religious while, as a nation, America is religiously diverse—a potentially explosive combination. The nation's history is marred by tragic examples of this potential for religious conflict becoming reality, with violent results. In the contemporary United States religious differences rarely lead to bloodshed. Still, it remains the case that disagreements over religion can touch a raw nerve.

This chapter and the next explore the divisiveness of religion in contemporary America. Is America a house divided against itself? This chapter includes evidence that, on its own, may suggest that Americans are riven by religion. On some matters, there is a gaping chasm between those who are highly religious and those who are highly secular. Furthermore, there are tensions between members of some religious traditions—we will show that while some religions receive high approbation, others are met with suspicion. Yet notwithstanding these tensions, in the next chapter you will also see that religious conflict in today's America is muted. Even with the nation's religious diversity and Americans' high level of religiosity, interreligious relations exhibit more comity than conflict. Indeed, rather than a wedge pushing Americans apart, public expressions of religion often serve to pull them together. Because it is the only world they know, many Americans may not fully realize that this state of affairs presents a puzzle. Neither (a) high religious devotion but little religious diversity nor (b) low devotion but high diversity would present the same risk of conflict. To be high in both devotion *and* diversity, however, is a potentially volatile mixture. It means that people who are religious mix with other people who are equally religious in intensity, but believe in other faiths. One might think that this is a recipe for religious disharmony, and that America would be coming apart at its religious seams. And yet it is not.

The next chapter, and thus the whole book, culminates by offering an answer to the puzzle of America's religious pluralism. To foreshadow the conclusion, we offer new evidence that the high degree of religious acceptance within the United States is tied to Americans' high level of interreligious association, or "bridging," whereby most of us live by, are friends with, or are even married to people of other faiths. As Americans build bridges across religious divides in different domains of their lives, they become more likely to accept those with different beliefs. The religious churn that characterizes American society leads to a lot of interreligious mixing within our neighborhoods, friendships, and families. Consequently, America is graced with the peaceful coexistence of both religious diversity and devotion.

RELIGIOUS DIVISIONS

While our general theme is that religious tensions in the United States are muted, we begin with evidence reminding us that religion is, or at least can be, a source of division. To be divided is largely a matter of perception, and by that standard America is a religiously divided nation. When in the 2006 Faith Matters survey we asked Americans whether "America is divided along religious lines," 72 percent agreed. Nearly half (46 percent) even said they strongly agreed that America is riven by religion. So by this standard ours appears to be a house divided against itself.

Perhaps we should not be surprised that Americans perceive a religious divide, especially in light of the contemporary political environment. As we saw in Chapter 11, there are significant partisan differences between religious and secular Americans. Another striking example of a divide between highly religious and highly secular[3] Americans is their differing opinions on religion's role in society. Should right and wrong be based on God's laws? On this question, the most secular and the most religious Americans have diametrically opposing views. As shown in Figure 14.1, among the most secular tenth of Americans, only 9 percent believe that the laws of God should determine what is right and wrong, in contrast to the nearly unanimous support (97 percent) among the most religious tenth of the population. Throughout this chapter we will make repeated references to these two categories—Americans in the top and bottom

10 percent of religiosity. We do so because, as you will see, these two slices of the population are highly distinctive.[4]

However sharp the apparent division between religious and secular Americans on whether God's laws should define right and wrong, simply comparing people at the two extremes of religiosity—the most and the least—obscures the real story. It would be like examining the distribution of temperatures across the country by looking only at Death Valley, California, and Nome, Alaska. In reality most Americans, even those who are not particularly religious, endorse a moral code based on the laws of God. Among even the moderately religious (specifically, people in the middle of our religiosity index), God's laws receive wide (85 percent) support. Highly secular Americans are the outliers in their belief that God's laws should not determine right and wrong.

We see the same basic pattern, also in Figure 14.1, when peo-

Figure 14.1

MOST AMERICANS SEE A ROLE FOR RELIGION IN AMERICAN SOCIETY

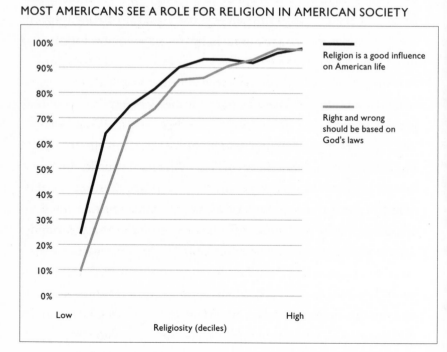

SOURCE: FAITH MATTERS SURVEY, 2006.

ple are asked for their assessment of whether religion's influence has been good or bad for American life. While only about a quarter (24 percent) of the most secular tenth agree that religion has had a positive influence on American life, that figure jumps to two thirds for the next to most secular Americans.[5] It climbs even higher, to 90 percent, for Americans with moderate religiosity, topping out at 98 percent for those at the high end of the religiosity scale.[6]

If you were to put a highly secular and a highly religious American together in the same room, they would likely disagree sharply on the degree of influence religion should have. However, that highly religious person would likely find consensus with anyone who has a modicum of religious belief. Most Americans welcome the influence of religion, at least in the abstract, while only a small and highly secularized segment of the population is decidedly unwelcoming. When it comes to the question of religion's role in society America's house may be divided, but not into two equal parts.

It is not surprising that highly secular Americans doubt religion's value for society, but it is surprising that those with moderately low levels of personal religiosity see a positive public role for religion. What, though, about other aspects of one's worldview, particularly those that do not pertain so explicitly to religion? Almost counterintuitively, personal religiosity has a stronger connection to some opinions that do not involve religion per se than on whether religion plays a positive role in society. For example, in Chapter 13 we saw that religiosity is tightly associated with a core belief that goes to the heart of our most intimate associations: how children should be raised. Just as the language of good and evil strikes a chord with religious Americans, so does a childrearing philosophy centered on obedience. Based on these differences in childrearing philosophy, we expect that a peek at the bookshelves of highly religious Americans would show them to have parenting books by disciplinarian James Dobson; secular Americans seem more likely to have Benjamin Spock's *Baby and Child Care,* which emphasizes children's self-discovery over discipline. In light of the earlier discussion (in Chapter 11) of the religious divisions in American politics, it is worth noting

that attitudes toward childrearing appear to have political implications.[7] Take a further look at those bookshelves, and you are likely to
find that parents who prioritize teaching obedience to their children
also read books by political conservatives, including Dobson, while
those who admire Dr. Spock's approach hold political views on the
left, much like the political leanings of Spock himself.

Religiosity is also related to one of the most fundamental questions of all, namely whether there are "absolutely clear guidelines"
regarding good and evil. Overall, 58 percent of Americans said that
there are such guidelines—a majority, but not an overwhelming one.
However, Figure 14.2 reveals how the belief in good and evil rises
steadily with personal religiosity, from 25 percent among the most
secular tenth, to 56 percent among those of moderate religiosity, to
86 percent among the most highly religious. When political leaders

Figure 14.2

RELIGIOUS AND SECULAR AMERICANS DIFFER ON WHETHER
THERE ARE CLEAR GUIDELINES OF GOOD AND EVIL

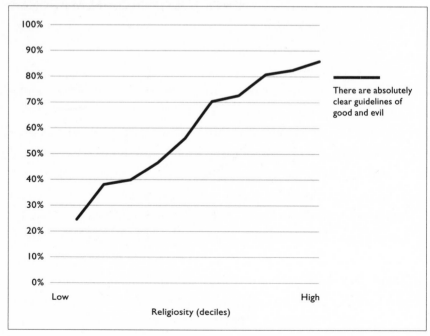

SOURCE: FAITH MATTERS SURVEY, 2006.

speak of evil—whether an empire or an axis—they are speaking to a divided public. Such language resonates with nearly all highly religious Americans, about half of the moderately religious, and few of the least religious.

We see further evidence of religion's potential divisiveness when we turn to the perceptions religious and secular Americans have of each other. As evident in our 2006 Faith Matters survey, each sees the other as both intolerant and selfish, but their own kind as tolerant and unselfish. Figure 14.3 makes clear that the rise in the perception that nonreligious people are intolerant tracks personal religiosity almost perfectly. One in five (20 percent) of the most secular tenth believe that nonreligious people are intolerant, growing markedly among those at the top end of the religiosity scale to about three in five (although note that perceptions bounce around a little among Americans in the top few deciles of religiosity). The picture is reversed for the assessment of whether religious people are intoler-

Figure 14.3

RELIGIOUS AND SECULAR AMERICANS SEE EACH OTHER AS INTOLERANT

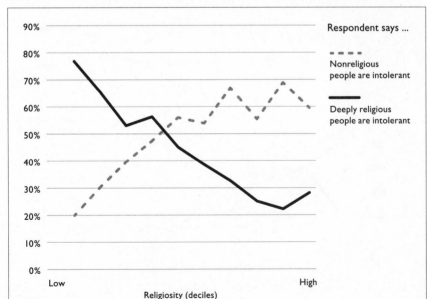

SOURCE: FAITH MATTERS SURVEY, 2006.

ant: The highly religious say "no" (72 percent) while the highly secular say "yes" (77 percent). Moderately religious Americans nearly split their vote—56 percent believe that the nonreligious are intolerant, while 45 percent say the same about the deeply religious. Neither are these differing perceptions limited to tolerance. Highly religious Americans see their secular counterparts as selfish; to the contrary, those who are highly secular describe deeply religious people as selfish. (See Figure 14.4.) These mirror images, we should note, are all the more striking given that respondents were asked separately about people who are "deeply religious" and "nonreligious," and about selfishness and tolerance. There was no reason that perceiving, say, deeply religious people as selfish meant that the nonreligious had to be labeled unselfish. Nor was there a logical connection between selfishness and intolerance.

We pause to note that religious Americans are correct to describe their own kind as unselfish; as Chapter 13 details, people with higher

Figure 14.4

RELIGIOUS AND SECULAR AMERICANS SEE EACH OTHER AS SELFISH

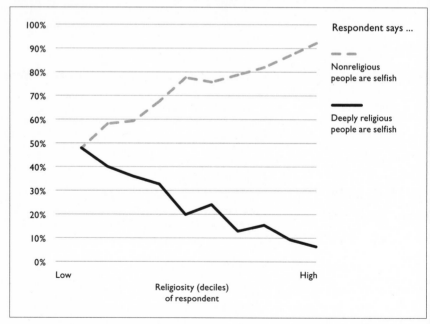

SOURCE: FAITH MATTERS SURVEY, 2006.

religiosity give more of their money and time to charity. Likewise, as we have also seen, secular people are equally correct to describe people like themselves as tolerant. Of course, this also means that the highly religious are incorrect to describe their type as tolerant, and those who are secular incorrectly label the religion-less as self-less. On this test, each side gets only half credit. More importantly, given the sharply contrasting views they have of the other side, is it any wonder that nearly three quarters of Americans see the nation as divided along religious lines?

INTERRELIGIOUS TENSIONS

The divide between secular and religious Americans resembles the God gap in voting, in which the highly religious are more likely to vote Republican and the highly secular vote Democratic. You will recall from Chapter 11 that, while religion's relevance to politics is nothing new, the God gap as we know it today is. In the past, politics was shaped by distinctions drawn between religions—Catholics vs. Protestant, liturgical vs. pietistic. Today, however, the most salient political divide is between religious and secular. The coalition of the religious includes voters of many faiths and stands in counter-point to voters with moderate religious involvement or none at all. Importantly, however, this restructuring of American religion does not mean that political differences among members of different religious traditions have been effaced. As with politics, so it is with religious divisions more broadly. Religious vs. secular is not the only significant societal fault line; differences among religious traditions can also serve as a pressure point. While a sense of embattlement with secular Americans may cause different religious traditions to pull together, tensions among religious traditions still exist.

While we have emphasized the coalition of the religious in national politics, this does not mean that all interreligious friction has been smoothed away. Such friction was evident in the presidential campaign of Mitt Romney, who is a member of the Church of Jesus Christ of Latter-day Saints—a Mormon. In 2008, about the same percentage of Americans told pollsters they would not vote for a Mormon presidential candidate as has said the same about a Catholic candidate in 1960. Interestingly, this percentage remained virtually unchanged from when Gallup asked about Mormons in 1967, when Mitt Romney's father, George (also a Mormon), was running for president.[8] Even more devastating for Romney's prospects in the Republican primaries, evangelicals were particularly hostile to Romney's candidacy, precisely the group he most needed to win over. While some (but by no means all) high-profile evangelicals endorsed him, rank and file evangelical voters remained suspicious.[9] Take, for example, a Harris Poll that used a methodology known to gauge voters' feelings on sensitive issues in early 2008. Among evangelicals, 54 percent said that they would be bothered by a Mormon president, compared to 18 percent of nonevangelicals.[10]

That evangelicals view Mormons so negatively demonstrates that, the coalition of the religious notwithstanding, theological differences between religious groups can still cause friction. In the case of evangelicals and Mormons, they have a lot in common. Both are highly religious groups with consonant opinions on social issues. In the words of legal scholar Noah Feldman, "Mormons share nearly all the conservative commitments so beloved of evangelicals."[11] And yet, evangelicals are reluctant to vote for a Mormon presidential candidate. The explanation centers on evangelicals' unease with many Mormon religious beliefs, as Mormonism is often labeled a "cult" within evangelical circles. Relevant also is the fact that Mormonism and evangelicalism are both proselytizing faiths, and thus are often in head-to-head competition for converts.[12]

Romney's inability to gain evangelicals' support is merely one illustration of religious tensions that endure among Americans. We can also take a more systematic look at patterns of affinity and hostility among religious traditions with a type of question known as a "feeling thermometer." In the 2006 Faith Matters survey respondents were asked to rate members of various groups, including a series of religious groups. A feeling thermometer consists of asking respondents to indicate how warm they feel toward different social groups (or people, or institutions, or whatever) on a scale of 0 to 100. A zero means that the respondent feels as cold as possible, 50 indicates a neutral feeling, and 100 is as warm as possible. Thus, higher numbers mean greater warmth, or greater affinity. This simple question turns out to be an effective way of gauging the gut-level feeling people have toward different groups—in this case, members of various religious traditions.

Feeling thermometers reveal three different kinds of information. First, we can see how members of different religious groups rate their co-religionists—a test of "groupness." Second, they show how members of different religious traditions are viewed by the rest of the population. Third, we can examine patterns of interreligious affinity and hostility. Which religions get along, and which are in tension with one another?[13]

In discussing these results, it is important to note that the mean thermometer rating for all religious groups is 55 degrees. Thus, any thermometer score below 55 means that that group is viewed more negatively than the average. A score below 50 degrees, the neutral point, means that the group in question is viewed really negatively.

As shown in Figure 14.5, no religious group in America feels warmer toward their own group than Mormons. In fact, Mormons feel warmer toward fellow Mormons than Black Protestants feel toward fellow African Americans. Jews are just behind Mormons, followed by Black Protestants and Catholics (who each give their own kind identical ratings). Mainline Protestants, evangelicals, and people with no religion all have less regard for their own group.[14]

We find it no coincidence that Black Protestants and Jews have a similar degree of warmth toward fellow blacks and Jews. These are obviously two groups that have faced antagonism, and as detailed in Chapter 9, are quintessential examples of overlap between religion and ethnicity. We would thus expect them to stick together, if only owing to a sense of embattlement. Given the fading ethnic dimension of Catholicism, at least among "Anglo" Catholics, their group favorability rating is somewhat surprising. It suggests that there is a pan-ethnic sense of Catholic identity.

Figure 14.5

RELIGIOUS GROUPS VARY IN HOW THEY FEEL ABOUT
THEIR OWN GROUP

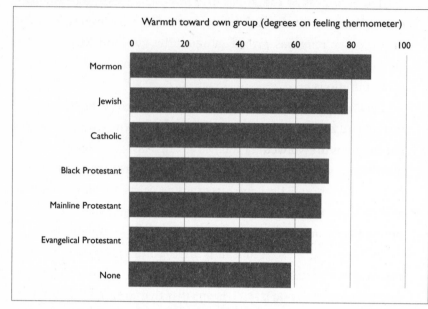

SOURCE: FAITH MATTERS SURVEY, 2006.

Mormons' in-group attachment is perhaps more surprising. Mormonism, as a relative newcomer on the religious scene and an ambitiously proselytizing faith, is not ethnically rooted. We suggest instead that Mormons cohere because they are a religious group that resembles an ethnicity—one based on belief, not blood. Mormonism, in fact, is sometimes referred to as an ethnicity because of Mormons' shared history, legacy of persecution, mass migration, and geographic concentration.[15]

It comes as no surprise that mainline Protestants do not have a stronger sense of in-group attachment, given that "mainline Protestantism" is a blurry social category. While we did prompt respondents with examples of denominations within mainline Protestantism,[16] for many Americans it is simply not a salient category—even for those who are in it. Similarly, a highly subjective classification like "people who are not religious" has a fuzzy definition. The fact that evangelicals also do not have, relatively speaking, a high degree of warmth toward fellow evangelicals also suggests that evangelicalism is not clearly defined in the minds of evangelicals.

The fuzziness of categories like the nonreligious, mainline, and evangelical Protestants only underscores the clear boundaries that define other religious groups. Catholics, Jews, and Mormons are all demarcated clearly—you know if you are one, and you know if someone else is one.

Having examined how members of different religious groups feel toward their own kind, we turn next to how members of different religions are viewed by their fellow Americans. Figure 14.6 displays how Americans rate a range of religious traditions, from large groups like Catholics to much smaller ones like Muslims. Because, as we have seen, people tend to approve of people like themselves, these thermometer scores exclude members of the referent group—

Figure 14.6

AMERICANS FEEL WARMEST TOWARD JEWS, MAINLINE PROTESTANTS, AND CATHOLICS (SCORES REFLECT HOW EVERYONE ELSE FEELS ABOUT EACH GROUP; SIZE OF CIRCLE REPRESENTS THAT GROUP'S SHARE OF THE POPULATION)

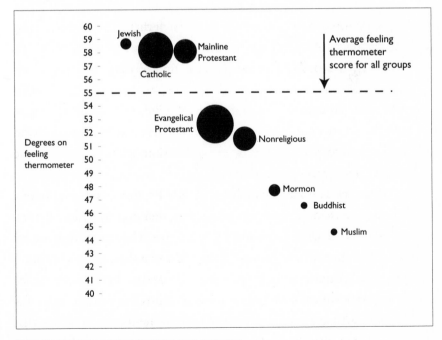

SOURCE: FAITH MATTERS SURVEY, 2006 AND 2007.

e.g., the score for Catholics only includes results for non-Catholics, and thus represents how Catholics are perceived by the rest of the population. Also, note that the size of the circle represents that group's relative share of the U.S. population. Catholics are the largest, Muslims and Buddhists the smallest.

Jews, mainline Protestants, and Catholics all rise to the top, receiving similarly positive assessments.[17] This is to be expected for mainline Protestants, as their very label suggests that they epitomize the mainstream of American religion. It is perhaps a little surprising for Catholics, given the history of anti-Catholicism in America.[18] And, for some readers, it is perhaps most surprising for Jews, given the past intensity of anti-Semitism both in the United States and abroad. We note, however, that we are not alone in finding positive regard for Jews. Awareness of the Holocaust led public expressions of anti-Semitism to drop dramatically in the twenty years following 1945. Since then, anti-Semitism has continued to fall through generational replacement—younger people are less likely to harbor anti-Semitic views than older generations. In October of 2009, the Anti-Defamation League published the results of a study that found "anti-Semitic attitudes equal to the lowest level in all the years of taking the pulse of the American attitudes toward Jews."[19] Of course, we cannot rule out the possibility that our respondents actually harbor negative feelings about Jews and Catholics. Perhaps they cloaked their anti-Semitism and/or anti-Catholicism out of a desire to appear socially acceptable. However, if such social desirability bias obscures any latent anti-Catholicism or anti-Semitism, it only makes the coolness expressed toward other religious groups all the more notable.

Evangelicals and "people who are not religious" are next in line, with rankings below Jews, mainline Protestants, and Catholics. They are both above the neutral point of 50 degrees, but below the overall mean (55 degrees). In relative terms, therefore, these are two moderately unpopular groups. Note that we chose to gauge reactions to nonreligious people rather than a more loaded term like "atheists," of whom there are very few in the United States. While very few of our respondents will know someone who is an avowed atheist, odds are high that many (probably most) will have friends, neighbors, and family who are simply not religious.[20]

Three groups stand out for their unpopularity—Mormons, Buddhists, and Muslims. All three are below the overall mean and also below the neutral point of 50 degrees. The relatively small size of each group is undoubtedly one factor contributing to its low rating, but that can hardly be the whole story. Jews are also a small share of the population and yet receive the highest thermometer scores. The public images of Mormons and Muslims are undoubtedly affected by negative media portrayals of fringe elements in both groups, whether it is fundamentalist polygamists or jihadists. Negative media portrayals do not appear to be the whole story, though, as Buddhists do not get the same negative media attention as Mormons and Muslims. We suspect, therefore, there is something else about Muslims, Buddhists, and Mormons that makes them unpopular, and that apparently lessens any social stigma resulting from openly expressing discomfort with them.[21] These three groups do not have a place in what has come to be called America's Judeo-Christian framework. To recall the tripartite division described by Will Herberg in the 1950s (see Chapter 9), they are neither Protestants nor Catholics nor Jews.

These overall assessments of different religious groups confirm that all religious groups are not viewed with equal favor. While we have, thus far, painted a picture with broad brushstrokes, we can add still more detail by examining how members of each religious tradition rate the others. How do members of group X feel about group Y? In doing so, it is possible to construct a social map that shows which groups feel an affinity toward each other, and which feel a relative coldness. Put more bluntly, we can see who likes, and dislikes, whom. Table 14.1 displays the results; each cell represents the average feeling thermometer score members of group X gave group Y. For example, in the top row we see that evangelical Protestants give Catholics a score of 58 degrees. This means that, as a group, evangelicals rated Catholics 8 degrees above the neutral point of 50 degrees, and 3 degrees above the overall mean of 55: a positive

Table 14.1

WHICH RELIGIOUS GROUP IS WARM, OR COLD, TO WHOM?

Average Feeling Thermometer Scores (0–100)

		THE GROUPS RECEIVING THE RATINGS						
		Evangelical Protestants	Mainline Protestants	Catholics	Jews	Not religious[23]	Mormons	Muslims	Buddhists
THE GROUPS GIVING THE RATINGS	Evangelical Protestants	**66**	64	58	61	50	46	41	41
	Mainline Protestants	58	**69**	63	62	54	51	46	46
	Catholics	54	56	**72**	56	50	50	44	48
	Jews	46	59	64	**79**	64	54	45	64
	Not religious[24]	46	52	53	57	**59**	45	46	55
	Mormons	63	64	67	63	61	**87**	56	54
	Black Protestants	60	55	58	57	47	45	47	36

SOURCE: FAITH MATTERS SURVEY, 2007.

HOW TO READ THIS TABLE: GROUPS THAT WERE RATED ARE ARRAYED HORIZONTALLY (COLUMNS), THE GROUPS DOING THE RATING RUN VERTICALLY (ROWS). SO, FOR EXAMPLE, TO SEE HOW EVANGELICALS VIEW CATHOLICS, LOOK ON THE LEFT FOR "EVANGELICAL PROTESTANTS," AND THEN FIND THE COLUMN MARKED "CATHOLICS." EVANGELICALS' RATING OF CATHOLICS IS 58 DEGREES. BOLDFACED CELLS ARE HOW THAT GROUP RATES ITS OWN MEMBERS.

rating. In contrast, evangelicals gave Mormons a highly negative rating: an average thermometer score of 46 degrees, 4 degrees below the neutral point, and 9 degrees below the mean.

At this level of detail, some highlights stand out:

- Almost everyone likes mainline Protestants and Jews.
- Almost everyone likes Catholics, more than Catholics like everyone else.
- Evangelicals like almost everyone else more than they are liked in return.
- Catholics and evangelicals rate each other warmly. (This is striking given the past animosities between these two groups.)
- Mormons like everyone else, while almost everyone else dislikes Mormons. Jews are the exception, as they give Mormons a net positive rating (suggesting that there is a perceived commonality, given that they are both minority religions).
- Almost everyone dislikes Muslims and Buddhists[22] more than any other group. Jews, however, are quite warm toward Buddhists, while cool toward Muslims.

Regrettably, we are unable to report on the ratings Muslims or Buddhists give to other groups, because there are too few of either group in the national population for us to generate a large enough sample for reliable estimates.[25] That is, Muslims and Buddhists are accurately represented in the Faith Matters surveys—as they should be, given that we interviewed a random cross section of America—but even a survey with over three thousand respondents contains too few of either group to enable us to break them out as distinct categories (see Chapter 1 for more on this point).

We concede that the abstract nature of a feeling thermometer score makes it difficult to evaluate how meaningful these differences are. To put the results in some perspective, we can compare the ratings of religious groups to groups of other types. Politics makes for a good comparison, given that it is the other subject your mother told you never to discuss in polite company. When we look at the ratings liberals give conservatives and conservatives give liberals, it turns out that political ideology engenders stronger reactions than religion. People who describe themselves as "very liberal" are cooler toward conservatives (36), and "very conservative" respondents are, in turn, cooler toward liberals (38) than any religious group is toward another.[26] Keep these thermometer scores of conservatives and liberals in mind during any discussion of interreligious tension—the potential for political conflict seems greater than for conflict over religion. We offer this observation as a first indication that religious tensions in the contemporary United States are relatively subdued.

The abstract nature of feeling thermometer scores also means that we do not have a direct indication of how, or whether, expressing coolness in the artificial setting of a public opinion survey translates into behavior. Accordingly, we should not infer that negative ratings necessarily mean acts of overt hostility toward any group, whether political or religious. The 2006 Faith Matters survey, however, did ask about a concrete indicator of interreligious animosity—disparaging comments heard about one's religion. From this question, we find that expressions of religious hostility in personal interactions do occur, but not with great frequency. Specifically, the question asks: "In your day-to-day life, have people ever made negative remarks about your religious beliefs?" As to whether this happens a lot or a little, the results are a matter of interpretation. A minuscule proportion, only 6 percent, of the American population say that they have often heard negative comments about their religion, while another 23 percent say this has happened "occasionally." Nearly half (46 percent) indicate they have never heard a negative remark directed toward their religion. Is this a lot or a little? For those who are subjected to such comments, it undoubtedly seems a lot. On the other hand, though, almost one half of Americans have never heard a negative comment regarding their religion. In light of the nation's combination of religious diversity and devotion, it seems to us that this is a surprisingly high percentage of Americans who have never had a critical comment made about their religion. The absence of religious negativity seems even more remarkable in light of the feeling thermometer ratings, which reveal the tepid reception some religions receive.

Because of those feeling thermometer scores, we would expect to find that members of some groups are more likely than others to hear negative comments about their religion. The nonreligious, one of the groups with a negative rating, report receiving critical comments only rarely. Only 24 percent of Americans who report not having a religious tradition say that they often or occasionally hear negative remarks about their religious beliefs or, in this case, presumably their lack thereof.[27] While for the nonaffiliated—almost by definition—religiosity is not likely to be a distinguishing characteristic, it is likely to be more noticeable for evangelicals. But only about a third of evangelicals report hearing such remarks often or occasionally. In contrast, 60 percent of Mormons report hearing disparaging remarks about their religious beliefs either often or occasionally (consistent with their negative feeling thermometer ratings).[28]

Do Muslims and Buddhists, two groups with even lower thermometer ratings than Mormons, also receive higher ratings with an increase in religious bridging? Because, as noted, our sample has too few Muslims or Buddhists to isolate a reliable analysis of their experience specifically, we instead report on the larger grouping with the label of "Other faiths"—which includes Muslims and Buddhists, as well as Hindus, Sikhs, and others. Members of this group are about as likely to report unflattering remarks about their religion as are Mormons.

Jews are a different story. Even though they top the feeling thermometer scores, they are nonetheless one of the groups most likely to report being exposed to critical comments about their religion— less than Mormons, but more than evangelicals. Thirty-eight percent of Jews say that they often or occasionally hear such remarks (about the same as "Other faiths").[29]

Religious tension can be exposed during interactions on a personal scale, as in face-to-face conversations. Yet this is not the only way in which negativity toward one religious group or another can show itself. Presidential politics—where the stakes are perceived to be high and tempers flare—also reveals the unease with which certain religious groups are viewed. Candidates from any of the negatively rated groups face hurdles convincing voters that they are like them. Thus, as we have noted, Republican presidential candidate Mitt Romney, a practicing Mormon, had to quell concerns about his religion during his presidential bid in 2008. Similarly, Barack Obama's supporters repeatedly rebutted the recurring false rumor that he was a Muslim, aware that this misperception risked damaging Obama at the polls. Still another example comes from the 2004 presidential contest, when Democratic presidential candidate Howard Dean worked to dispel concern over his perceived secularism.[30] Notwithstanding that evangelicals are regularly described as the base of the GOP, even candidates with conservative Christian roots often soften or downplay their distinctive religious practices upon entering the public limelight—witness, in 2008, spokespeople for vice presidential nominee Sarah Palin stressing that even though she had attended a Pentecostal church, Palin herself had never spoken in tongues.[31]

For the purpose of gauging religious tension, the personal nature of day-to-day interactions and the impersonality of presidential campaigns stand at opposite ends of a spectrum. In between these two extremes are questions relating to policies and practices on a local scale—public, yes, but with a more limited scope than who sits in the Oval Office. All over the country, there are political skirmishes at the local level that reflect conflicts over religion. One perennial flashpoint for controversy is land use and zoning—whether and where religious groups can build, expand, or renovate their places of worship. Can Orthodox Jews build a large complex, complete with synagogue, community center, and school? Can Mormons build a large temple with an imposing spire? Can Muslims build a mosque, complete with a loudspeaker to call worshippers to prayer?[32] Such scuffles are so common that in 2000 Congress unanimously passed a law specifically to give protection to religious groups in local zoning disputes.[33]

How Americans respond to land use matters involving religious groups depends on the religion in question. According to the 2007 Faith Matters survey, an overwhelming majority of Americans (92 percent) say that the construction of a large Christian church in their community would either not bother them (55 percent) or is something they would welcome (37 percent). This level of acceptance is high even among the most secular tenth of the population (87 percent), although their reaction is far less supportive. Eighty-two percent of the highly secular say that they would merely "not be bothered" by a large Christian church, while just 5 percent would explicitly welcome it.

Because of the near-ubiquity of Christian churches in American communities, we were also interested in reactions to a religious facility that would be unfamiliar to many Americans, and so we asked about the construction of a "large Buddhist temple." Based on the feeling thermometer scores a Buddhist temple is a good gauge of religious tolerance, since Buddhists, on average, receive a negative rating.[34] True tolerance entails acceptance of an unpopular group.[35]

The point of asking about both kinds of religious structures is to distinguish among different reasons for opposing their construction. Some people might oppose both a large Christian church and a large Buddhist temple because they object to the construction of any sizable structure in their neighborhood, whether it be a church, a temple, a restaurant, a store. Or it could be because they have an aversion to religion of any kind. However, opposition to a Buddhist temple but not a Christian church would suggest that the concern lies with Buddhism specifically or perhaps "exotic" (or non-Christian) religions more generally.[36]

For Buddhists who might be planning to build a temple, our results contain good news and bad news. The good news is the high overall support, at least in the abstract, for a Buddhist temple. Three quarters of Americans (76 percent) say they have no problem with the construction of a large Buddhist temple in their neighborhood. The bad news is that only a small number (15 percent) would explicitly welcome it in their midst. Even worse news for the Buddhists is that one in five Americans (20 percent) say that they have no problem with a large Christian church but would object to a Buddhist temple.[37] As shown in Figure 14.7, the greatest opposition to a Buddhist temple comes from the most religious segment of the population, who apparently do not find common cause with this particular religious group. Approval of a Buddhist temple drops precipitously as personal religiosity increases. Highly secular Americans are slightly more likely to accept or embrace a Buddhist temple than a Christian church, but of the most religious Americans, half (50 percent) would object to a Buddhist temple, yet another sign of the civic intolerance that we explored in the previous chapter.[38]

As we look back over the evidence on religious acceptance and tolerance, the verdict is mixed. On the one hand, the highly religious and the highly secular view their own kind as generous and tolerant, and those who fall on the other end of the religiosity spectrum as

Figure 14.7

ALMOST EVERYONE IS OKAY WITH A CHRISTIAN CHURCH IN THEIR NEIGHBORHOOD; HIGHLY RELIGIOUS AMERICANS ARE LESS SURE ABOUT A BUDDHIST TEMPLE

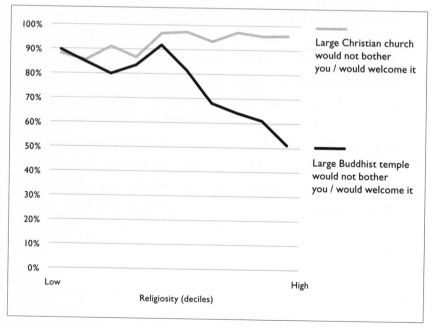

SOURCE: FAITH MATTERS SURVEY, 2007.

selfish and intolerant. Furthermore, some religions elicit a negative reaction from members of certain other religious groups, and still others are viewed coldly by members of nearly every other religious group. Members of some religious groups report that they hear negative comments about their faith on a reasonably frequent basis. And while almost everyone in America would accept a large Christian church in their neighborhood, there is greater ambivalence about a Buddhist temple, especially among the most religious Americans.

NOT SO DIVIDED AFTER ALL

To end the story here might leave the impression that religion is a source of division within America. There are, after all, various pressure points in interreligious relations. However, it is equally important to stress that we keep encountering evidence that religion is not so divisive after all.[39] Americans overwhelmingly agree that religion exerts a positive influence, as only the most secular Americans are clearly uncomfortable with a large role for religion in American society. Furthermore, the coolness with which religious groups view each other does not match the negativity that those on opposite sides of the political spectrum feel toward each other. Overt religious hostility is relatively rare. While religious divisions exist, including some latent interreligious tensions, we should not overstate the capacity of religion to cause tension or division.

In other words, in spite of religion's capacity to sow division, religious conflict in America is muted—a situation made even more puzzling by America's combination of both religious devotion and diversity. The next chapter takes up the puzzle posed by America's religious pluralism.

CHAPTER 15

AMERICA'S GRACE: HOW A TOLERANT NATION BRIDGES ITS RELIGIOUS DIVIDES

T he previous chapter demonstrates that religion can be divisive. For example, 72 percent of Americans say the country is divided along religious lines. That sounds like a lot, and it is. However, the potential for religious conflict can be put in context when we compare Americans' perceptions of religious division to other types of division. The perceived degree of religious divisiveness pales when compared to divisions by race, class, or politics:

- 93 percent of Americans believe America is divided along racial lines
- 96 percent see divisions along economic lines
- 97 percent say the country is divided along political lines[1]

The fact that religion is not nearly so divisive as race, class, or politics is the puzzle this chapter seeks to solve. How can America be both devout and diverse without fracturing along religious lines? To be devout but not diverse would lead to little division (e.g., Poland); likewise if a society is religiously diverse but not devout (e.g., the Netherlands). In the former case, there is little to disagree about. In the latter, there might be much to disagree about but little motivation to do so.

This chapter picks up where the last one left off. Rather than emphasize religion's potential divisiveness, we instead highlight how describing religion as merely "not very divisive" hardly does justice to its role in American public life. For many Americans, religion serves as a sort of civic glue, uniting rather than dividing. Next, we show how most Americans embrace religious diversity— including those who are highly secular and those who are highly religious. We shall also see that many Americans experience religious diversity on a personal scale. Americans typically have friends and family of different faiths, creating their own religiously diverse social networks. The chapter provides new evidence that the diversity embodied within these networks enables the peaceful coexistence of myriad religions in contemporary America. We then go on to demonstrate that most of the American population—save a small but intensely religious segment—are reluctant to assign a unique status to any religion as "true," even their own. A majority of Americans believe that members of other faiths can go to heaven, and this is true even in religions that explicitly teach that salvation is reserved for their own adherents. Finally, we argue that Americans' expansive view of heaven results from their personal experience with people with different religious backgrounds, including their close friends and family. America manages to be both religiously diverse and religiously devout because it is difficult to damn those you know and love.

CIVIL RELIGION

For many Americans, religion—or at least a belief in God—serves to bind the nation together. Embedded in the American psyche is an implicit article of patriotic faith that the nation owes its very existence, and survival, to a God in the heavens. References to deity thus abound during the solemn ceremonial moments of our public life, when the national sense of unity is strongest. When our leaders seek to mobilize, inspire, or console, they invoke God. In arguing that religion serves as a glue holding America's civil society together, sociologist Robert Bellah has described the nation's *civil* religion, which stands apart from the beliefs of any particular sect, denomination, or religious tradition. In his words, "the civil religion was able to build up without any bitter struggle with the church powerful symbols of national solidarity and to mobilize deep levels of personal motivation for the attainment of national goals."[2] Civil religion has no partisan overtones. Thus, Jefferson (Democrat[3]) declared independence with the bold statement that the creator endowed mankind with inalienable rights. Lincoln (Republican) found meaning in the Civil War at Gettysburg by poignantly declaring that America, "under God, shall have a new birth of freedom." Kennedy (Democrat) began his presidency asking for God's blessing and help, "but knowing that here on earth God's work must truly be our own." George W. Bush (Republican) consoled the nation following the September 11 terrorist attacks by saying that he prayed for the comfort of a "power greater than any of us" and citing the 23rd Psalm, "Even though I walk through the valley of the shadow of death, I fear no evil, for You are with me." And lest one think that the growing connection between religiosity and the vote means that civil religion has been supplanted by partisan appeals to religion, such that God is invoked only by Republicans these days, consider the inaugural address of Barack Obama (Democrat). In it, he spoke of "the knowledge that God calls on us to shape an uncertain destiny."

From Jefferson to Obama, the United States has become far more diverse in religious terms, and yet appeals to God at times of national unity are still de rigueur. America's civil religion endures, notwithstanding the myriad faiths, creeds, denominations, and religious traditions found within the population.[4] The First Amendment to the Constitution says that Congress shall pass no law to curtail the free exercise of religion, but these sparse words do not fully reflect the way in which religious diversity is encoded in America's national DNA. Examples abound. Every Thanksgiving—the major holiday most every religion can agree on—Americans celebrate the arrival of the Pilgrims, recounting the Puritans' desire for refuge from religious persecution. In naming the four essential human freedoms, Franklin Roosevelt included the quintessentially American sense of religious liberty, "the freedom of every person to worship God in his own way."

RELIGIOUS DIVERSITY

The civic role of religion has resulted, in large part, from the unique constitutional status afforded religion. The First Amendment to the U.S. Constitution states that Congress will not endorse, or "establish," a religion. In the immediate wake of the nation's founding this clause did not preclude states from supporting particular denominations by, for example, allowing clergy to be paid out of the public purse. By the early 1800s, all such public subsidies for religion ended and nonestablishment was taken to mean that all levels of government are precluded from providing financial support to any particular religion. Thus, no religion has been established as the official national church. Likewise, the U.S. Constitution also prohibits religious tests for public officials. Today, this may seem like a quaint provision, but at the time of the founding it was a significant issue, given that England had employed the Test Acts to limit public office to members of the Church of England. To borrow language from the marketplace, governments in America have not been picking winners and losers in the religious "economy." Instead, religions have had to fend for themselves in attracting, and retaining, members. Furthermore, the constitutional protection provided to the free exercise of religion has created social space for the public expression of religion. This combination—a government restricted from supporting any particular religion, while individuals are largely unfettered from exercising a wide array of religions—has given American religion its vitality.

No founding father is more closely associated with religious liberty than Thomas Jefferson, whose convictions on the subject were undoubtedly affected by his own unorthodox religious beliefs.[5] Jefferson famously summarized the way many Americans think about religious differences: "It does me no injury for my neighbor to say there are twenty gods, or no god. It neither picks my pocket nor breaks my leg." [6]

Jefferson's sentiment provides a vision of religious tolerance that is essentially a quid pro quo—you let me worship as I please and I will do the same for you. By and large, Americans today hold to Jefferson's philosophy. Eighty-five percent agree that "morality is a personal matter and society should not force everyone to follow one standard." Even among the most religious Americans,[7] half believe that morality is a personal matter. *What abt. basis for claim*

If the Jeffersonian conception of religion as a personal, private matter were the extent of how Americans accommodate religious difference, it would probably suffice for keeping simmering religious tensions from boiling over. However, grudging acceptance of others' religious beliefs would mean only that religious diversity is tolerated, not seen as an intrinsically good state of affairs. It could be that religious believers deign to tolerate other religions purely for self-preservation, calculating that since no single religion has majority status it is best to grant a full measure of liberty to other faiths, to ensure maximum liberty for oneself. That is, it could be that Americans do not really think that religious diversity per se is good, but only the best possible situation under the circumstances.

It could be that way, but it appears not to be. By a wide margin, Americans see the value in religious diversity for its own sake. As we see in Figure 15.1, when asked whether "religious diversity has been good for America," 84 percent agree. Furthermore, the endorsement of religious diversity remains high regardless of Americans' own religiosity. While religious diversity loses a little luster among those with the highest levels of religiosity, they still endorse it overwhelmingly (74 percent of Americans in the top decile of religiosity see the good in religious diversity).

Perhaps, you might think, the widespread endorsement of religious diversity hangs on the normative force of "diversity" as the

Figure 15.1

REGARDLESS OF THEIR LEVEL OF RELIGIOSITY, AMERICANS
VALUE RELIGIOUS DIVERSITY

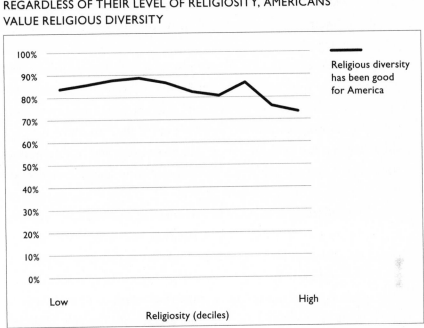

SOURCE: FAITH MATTERS SURVEY, 2006.

buzzword of our time. Who would dare admit that they are uncomfortable with diversity of any sort? In the words of legal scholar Peter Schuck, "diversity is right up there with progress, motherhood, and apple pie."[8] It seems reasonable, therefore, to be suspicious that Americans pay lip service to religious diversity but really harbor suspicions about those of other faiths. After all, we have seen that at least a few religious groups get a chilly reception. What can we really tell about Americans' attitudes regarding religious diversity from abstract questions with little bearing on anyone's daily life? They talk the talk, but do they walk the walk? One answer lies in the religious complexion of our most intimate associations, namely family and friends.

We have already seen, in Chapter 5, that in the most intimate association of all—marriage—Americans are increasingly comfortable with religious diversity.[9] One third of all Americans are married to someone of a different religious tradition, and one half are married to someone who came from a different tradition (the difference being explained by spousal conversions).

However, we do not wish to leave the impression that interreligious marriage is equally fine with everyone. When Americans are asked to project into the future about the potential marriage of a child, we see a measure of ambivalence about marrying outside one's faith. This ambivalence is a perfect illustration of the tension between the religious devotion and diversity that characterizes American society. On the one hand, over two in five Americans say that it is very (22 percent) or somewhat (20 percent) important that their child marry someone of the same religious background. Not surprisingly, it is the most highly religious who place the greatest value on their children marrying someone of the same religion.[10] On the other hand, this still leaves a majority of Americans who say either that it is not important at all (39 percent) or not very important (18 percent) that their children marry within their religion. Interreligious marriage, while not a problem for most Americans, is a concern for some.

We can probe further into Americans' lived experience with religious diversity using a measure that asks about one's neighbors, extended family, and friends. For neighbors and extended family, we asked for a general report—roughly what proportion has the same religious affiliation as you? The results (Figure 15.2) make clear that Americans live in religiously diverse neighborhoods. Only 7 percent say that all of their neighbors share the same religion, and nearly a third report that none do. Not surprisingly, extended families are less diverse than neighborhoods, but even there we find a reasonably high degree of religious heterogeneity. Sixteen percent of Americans indicate that no one in their extended family shares their religion; roughly one in three say that everyone in their extended family does. When it comes to friends, we asked our respondents to be more precise (see Figure 15.3). How many of their five closest friends share their religion? Just under a quarter (24 percent) of Americans say that all of their five closest friends have the same religious affiliation

Figure 15.2

MOST AMERICANS HAVE RELIGIOUSLY DIVERSE FAMILIES AND
NEIGHBORHOODS

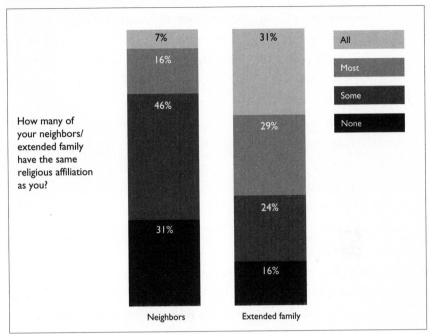

SOURCE: FAITH MATTERS SURVEY, 2006.

that they do, while 17 percent say that none of them do. On average, they told us that 2.6 of their five closest friends are co-religionists.[11]

These numbers all point toward a single conclusion—most Americans are intimately acquainted with people of other faiths. Two out of three have at least one extended family member who is of another religion, while the average American has at least two (technically, 2.4) close friends with a religious affiliation different from theirs. When we ask Americans about religious diversity they speak from personal experience.

The constitutional framework for religion in America does not guarantee this degree of interfaith mingling, mixing, and matching, but it has enabled the religious fluidity that we have described throughout this book. This fluidity, in turn, facilitates interpersonal connections across religious lines. Religious churn means that many

AMERICAN GRACE

Figure 15.3

EVEN AMERICANS' CLOSEST FRIENDS ARE RELIGIOUSLY DIVERSE

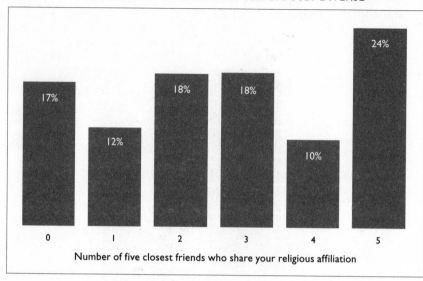

Number of five closest friends who share your religious affiliation

SOURCE: FAITH MATTERS SURVEY, 2006.

Americans change religions, thus introducing family and friends to their new faith. So even if you never change your religion, you almost certainly know someone who has. Such a high state of flux also facilitates the acceptance of religious intermarriage, as it is difficult to maintain bright lines between religions when the boundaries are blurred by frequent switching from one to another.

Some boundaries, however, are blurrier than others. While most Americans have close associations with people of other religions, there are also fascinating differences in the degree to which they experience religious diversity closely. Members of some religious traditions are more likely to have friends, family, and neighbors of different religions than are members of other faiths. We can most easily see these differences by combining all three types of relationships together into a single measure of overall religious homogeneity within one's personal social network.

As displayed in Figure 15.4, Latino Catholics are most likely to score high in religious homogeneity—far higher than any other religious groups. While below Latino Catholics, Black Protestants also

Figure 15.4

MEMBERS OF DIFFERENT RELIGIOUS TRADITIONS DIFFER IN THE
RELIGIOUS HOMOGENEITY OF THEIR FAMILY, FRIENDS, AND NEIGHBORS

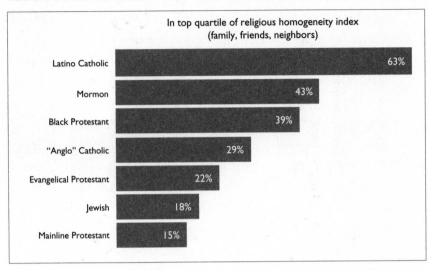

In top quartile of religious homogeneity index
(family, friends, neighbors)

Latino Catholic	63%
Mormon	43%
Black Protestant	39%
"Anglo" Catholic	29%
Evangelical Protestant	22%
Jewish	18%
Mainline Protestant	15%

SOURCE: FAITH MATTERS SURVEY, 2006.

rank high. The high degree of homogeneity is to be expected for
both Latinos and African Americans, as people tend to associate with
others of the same ethno-racial group.[12] Latinos are thus likely to be
friends with other Latinos, and blacks with other blacks. Likewise,
we would expect them to be friends with Latino Catholics and Black
Protestants. The result is that both groups have a high level of religious homogeneity among their family, friends, and neighborhoods.
The especially high degree of homogeneity among Latino Catholics
is likely a reflection of limited integration between Latino and non-
Latino populations within the United States.

Black Protestants are matched by Mormons in their degree of
religious homogeneity. (The gap between the two groups is too
small to be statistically meaningful.) Here we have further evidence
that Mormons resemble an ethnic group. Mormons have an unusually high strength of religious identity, and share a distinctive culture. Furthermore, they are often met with disapprobation from
members of other religions. As a cause, a consequence, or both,

Mormons stick together: They marry each other, live by each other, and associate with one another. Puzzlingly, "Anglo" Catholics also have a relatively high level of religious homogeneity. This might have been expected in the 1950s or earlier, when the church stressed the importance of marrying within the faith and Catholics were concentrated in the ethnic neighborhoods of urban centers. Today, however, Catholics have a high rate of interreligious marriage, and increasingly have left the old neighborhoods in the city to buy a house in the suburbs.[13] When put alongside the relatively high regard Catholics show for fellow Catholics, the relatively high degree of religious homogeneity within their social networks is perhaps less surprising. Both are mutually reinforcing evidence that while the explicitly ethnic dimension of Catholicism has faded—except among Latinos—"Anglo" Catholics nonetheless are somewhat more likely to stick together than are either evangelical or mainline Protestants, or even Jews.

RELIGIOUS BRIDGING

Although differences in levels of religious diversity by religious tradition are interesting and important, one should not miss the forest for the trees. *Most Americans are intimately acquainted with people of other faiths.* This, we argue, is the most important reason that Americans can combine religious devotion and diversity. We call it the "Aunt Susan Principle." We all have an Aunt Susan in our lives, the sort of person who epitomizes what it means to be a saint, but whose religious background is different from our own. Maybe you are Jewish and she is a Methodist. Or perhaps you are Catholic and Aunt Susan is not religious at all. But whatever her religious background (or lack thereof), you know that Aunt Susan is destined for heaven. And if she is going to heaven, what does that say about other people who share her religion or lack of religion? Maybe they can go to heaven too.

To put the Aunt Susan Principle in more technical terms: We are suggesting that having a religiously diverse social network leads to a more positive assessment of specific religious groups, particularly those with low thermometer scores. In offering this hypothesis, we can look beyond our hypothetical Aunt Susan for reasons to think that religiously diverse social networks do indeed have a positive effect on interreligious acceptance. One place to find such a rationale is in the literature on social capital, by which we mean the norms of trust and reciprocity that arise out of our social networks. Some social capital consists of bonding, or interconnections among people with a common background. Other social capital is bridging in nature, and thus connects people of different backgrounds. While both bonding and bridging each serve important purposes, bridging is vital for the smooth functioning of a diverse society. When birds of different feathers flock together, they come to trust one another.[14]

The significance of bridging social capital for building intergroup acceptance is rooted in the venerable theory of social contact. This theory is often loosely described as positing that contact among people of different but salient social groups reduces prejudice. That, however, is not an accurate description of the theory. As articulated in the mid-1950s by Gordon Allport, the theory actually says that four conditions have to hold before contact diminishes prejudice: All parties must have equal status, share common goals, have intergroup cooperation, and have the support of authorities, law, or custom. In the setting of an interreligious friendship, the first and the fourth are clearly met: Most friendships presumably entail equal status, and the sheer frequency of interreligious contact indicates its widespread societal support. The constitutional protections afforded religious liberty contribute further to the normative force behind religious diversity. Furthermore, very few religious traditions actively discourage their members from interacting with those of other faiths; indeed, the evangelistic nature of many American religions means that they encourage making friends with people of different religious backgrounds. It also seems likely that friendships are characterized by the second and third conditions, namely common goals and cooperation. Indeed, in reviewing hundreds of intergroup contact studies, social psychologists Thomas Pettigrew and

Linda Tropp "assumed that friendship requires the operation of conditions that approach Allport's specifications for optimal contact."[15] Their results confirm that intergroup friendships are an example of the socially salutary consequences of contact among people of different social groups. The Pettigrew and Tropp analysis even suggests that intergroup friendships reduce prejudice to a greater extent than other forms of contact, leading Pettigrew to recommend that "potential for friendship" be added as a fifth condition to the social contact theory.[16]

We expect that religious diversity within social networks—religious bridging—will foster greater interreligious acceptance. We find this is indeed the case when you look at who is friends with whom. To pick just one example, there is a positive correlation between, say, having an evangelical friend and rating evangelicals positively. On its own, we concede, such a finding is not terribly persuasive; there is obviously a huge problem in determining what causes what. Do you rate evangelicals positively because you have an evangelical friend, or are you friends with an evangelical because you are warm toward evangelicals? With a survey taken at a single point in time, this is impossible to answer.

Far more convincing is an analysis of who becomes friends with whom. In earlier chapters, we have used the fact that the Faith Matters surveys can measure changes in the same individuals over time to show that politics affects religion (Chapter 5) and that gaining more religious friends increases good neighborliness, civic engagement, and even happiness (Chapter 13). Now we employ the same type of analysis to see whether an increase in religious bridging leads to an increase in interreligious acceptance.[17] While we must caution that such an analysis of panel data does not definitely determine causation—the Holy Grail of any social science analysis—it does provide much stronger evidence for causation than a single-shot survey.[18]

The logic of the analysis is simple. We simply see whether, over the course of a year, gaining a friend of group X means warmer feelings toward group X. Note that we exclude anyone who has adopted the religious label in question, to rule out the possibility that because respondents have converted to a new religion, they simultaneously gained new friends in that same religion and became more positive toward it. For example, anyone who became an evangelical is excluded when we examine the impact of gaining an evangelical friend. Our results, then, cannot be explained by an enthusiasm for a new way of life that both increases the feeling thermometer rating and leads to new friends who share that way of life. Furthermore, we have tested whether having greater warmth toward the group in question in the first wave leads to becoming friends with a member of that group in the second wave. In other words, perhaps you are already warm toward evangelicals and, because of that warmth, end up friends with an evangelical. In those cases where we find a significant impact of gaining a friend within a particular group, we find no evidence that the warmth leads to the friendship rather than the other way around.

Our analysis finds strikingly consistent results, as there are multiple examples of how religious bridging corresponds to a warmer assessment of the group in question. Gaining an evangelical friend means a more positive evaluation of evangelicals; gaining a nonreligious friend means warmer regard for "people who are not religious."[19]

While determining the statistical significance of the increase in warm feelings is straightforward, gauging the substantive importance is less so. Upon gaining an evangelical friend, the thermometer score for evangelicals rises by 7 degrees—more than the gap between the initial average rating for evangelicals and the neutral point of 50 degrees. That seems to us like a substantively important rise. The thermometer score for nonreligious people rises 4 degrees—less, but still noteworthy.

Stepping back from the subjective question of whether a 7 or 4 degree gain is big or small, we acknowledge that feeling thermometers are an abstract, even artificial, indicator. And so when we speak of feelings toward a group as measured by a thermometer, we cannot necessarily conclude that this means that members of these groups will get along. On-the-ground cooperation is much more difficult than saying you feel warm or cold toward one group or another. On the other hand, however, such attempts at cooperation will be smoother if prior opinions about the group are positive rather than negative.

These results for the consequences of religious bridging are compelling evidence that the purported effects of social contact—under the right conditions—are not merely a fuzzy-headed aspiration. Here we have verification that our friends affect how we perceive the religious groups to which our friends belong. (Indeed, the existing research suggests that this phenomenon is not limited to religious groups, but applies to other social categories too, like race, ethnicity, and class.)

In making sense of these results, we must note that someone we have described as a "new friend" may not actually be so new. Instead, it could be that an existing friend has adopted a new religion. Or it could be that the respondent comes to learn of a friend's previously unknown religion. Neither possibility changes the interpretation of the results, nor their importance. Either situation still suggests that knowing someone within a particular religious group means a more positive assessment of that group in general—whether you have known that someone for a long time or not.

A process by which one becomes friends with someone first, and then comes to know their religion second, is an example of a more general process by which people come to like one member of an "outgroup," and then generalize their positive feelings to the group as a whole. First, you become friends with someone without being aware that she is a member of the outgroup. As the friendship develops, her outgroupness becomes salient but by that time you are already friends. From there, it is a short step to concluding that other, perhaps all, members of this particular outgroup are not so bad after all.

Interreligious friendships are a likely candidate for this type of revelation. While there are some exceptions (e.g., Ultraorthodox Jews, Sikhs, Old Order Amish), the religious affiliation of most

Americans is not obvious from outward appearances. In this respect, interreligious contact is qualitatively different from contact with people of different races and, arguably, of different socioeconomic backgrounds. It is therefore likely that in the early stages of many friendships, neither party's religious affiliation is salient. However, given the high rate of religious adherence in the United States, it is also likely that friends become aware of one another's religious affiliation—as suggested by the fact that virtually all respondents to the Faith Matters surveys were able to describe the religion of their five closest friends. From there, it is a small step to recognizing commonality with other members of that friend's religion.

In *America and the Challenges of Religious Diversity*, Robert Wuthnow summarizes a series of in-depth interviews with people who have experienced this inadvertent contact with someone of a different religion. In describing how Americans are exposed to people of different religions, Wuthnow writes:

> [The exposure] occurs because a friend happened to belong to another religion, not because the person was actively engaged on a quest for new spiritual experiences. Often this exposure is involuntary (for example, being dictated by being assigned a roommate of a different religion in college) or focuses less on religion and more on sports, music, and other interests. In many instances, it nevertheless broadens a person's horizons and reinforces the idea that there are valuable things to be learned from other religions.[20]

Call this the My Friend Al Principle, a corollary of the Aunt Susan Principle. You become friends with Al for, say, your shared affinity for beekeeping. As you get to know Al, you learn that in addition to his regard for apiculture, he is also an evangelical Christian. Prior to learning that, you may have been suspicious of evangelicals. But if your pal Al is an avid beekeeper—just like you—and is also an evangelical, then perhaps evangelicals are not so bad after all.

The My Friend Al Principle has a strong intuition behind it.

Indeed, we would have been surprised if gaining a new friend from a particular social group did *not* lead you to reevaluate members of that group more generally. There is a more intriguing possibility, however. Can becoming friends with Al the beekeeping evangelical mean a higher regard for people of still other religious backgrounds? Perhaps upon realizing that you can be friends with Al, a member of a religious group you once viewed with suspicion, you come to reevaluate your perception of other religious groups too. Call this a spillover effect.

To find out if spillover occurs, we can once again turn to comparing the same people at two different times. In this case, we examined whether an increase in the overall religious diversity among one's close friends leads to a more positive assessment of various religious groups. The more religious groups that are represented among your close friends, the more religious bridging within your friendship network. An evangelical with an evangelical friend does not count as bridging; a Catholic with an evangelical friend does count. Compare that same Catholic to another who has an evangelical friend *and* a second friend who is not religious. The friendship network of the second is more religiously diverse than that of the first. With such an index of religious bridging we can again see what happens when change occurs over time.

What happens when someone's friendship network becomes more religiously diverse? Does more bridging lead to a more positive assessment of other religious groups, even those that were not added to the friendship network? In other words, can becoming friends with evangelical Al mean warmer feelings toward Mormons or people without religious faith at all? Is there spillover?[21]

In a word, the answer is "yes." We find convincing evidence in favor of a spillover effect. For example, increased religious bridging leads to greater warmth toward "people who are not religious." The increase is 3 degrees on the feeling thermometer, a modest but nonnegligible gain. We also find that greater religious bridging corresponds to an increase in warmth toward Mormons. An increase of one more religiously bridging friendship leads to an increase in warmth toward Mormons of 2 degrees. Again this is admittedly not a huge gain, but it is a gain nonetheless. The gain is all the more notable because our index of religious diversity does not include Mormons.[22] In other words, bridging to friends of other religions corresponds to positive feelings toward two of the most unpopular religious groups in America: the nonreligious and Mormons.

The waters are muddied when we examine whether an increase in bridging leads to more positive feelings toward Muslims. Recall that one of the categories included in the religious diversity index is someone of a "non-Christian religion," of which Islam is an example. So it is possible that the increase in religious diversity results from adding a Muslim friend; we are unable to be sure that this is a true spillover effect. With that caveat in mind, we note that more religious diversity within an individual's social network has an impact on the perception of Muslims that resembles the increase in warmth toward Mormons—roughly 2 degrees.[23]

As a parallel with our earlier analysis, we also tested for the possibility of reverse causation: whether warmth toward the group at time 1 in question leads to religious bridging at time 2. It does not.

In sum, we have reasonably firm evidence that as people build more religious bridges they become warmer toward people of many different religions, not just those religions represented within their social network. The increases in thermometer ratings are modest, but then the elapsed time between surveys is short. Social networks do not change much over a single year, so it is amazing that we find any effects at all. Based on these short-term results, it seems reasonable to expect that, over time, an increase in interpersonal religious bridging will continue to have a similar effect, smoothing tensions among people of different religions.

Furthermore, if we can see the effects of interreligious friendships, and over only a single year at that, it is also reasonable to assume that interreligious marriages have a far more potent effect. And, as we saw in Chapter 5, the rates of interreligious marriage have increased dramatically over the last century. Rising interreligious marriage almost certainly means rising acceptance for people of other religions, not only among the spouses themselves but also for their extended family members.

These results can also illuminate why, in Chapter 14, we saw that some religious groups are viewed unfavorably, specifically Muslims, Buddhists, and Mormons. While religious bridging appears to foster more acceptance of all religions that may seem exotic or unusual, there is even greater acceptance when a bridge is built to a member of that specific group. Thus, groups viewed coldly are those with which most Americans have little or no personal exposure. Given the small size of their respective populations, this would help to explain why Muslims and Buddhists are viewed in relatively negative terms. And, when we remember that Mormons have a high degree of religious homogeneity within their own familial and social networks, it also helps to explain why they are perceived negatively as well. All three groups are also concentrated in particular parts of the United States, which further limits the prospects for religious bridging and thus greater acceptance. While greater bridging overall is likely, over the long haul, to boost approval of these groups, we would expect their image problem to disappear even more rapidly as more and more Americans count a Buddhist, a Muslim, or a Mormon among their friends and family.

WHO GOES TO HEAVEN?

Americans, we have seen, affirm that religious diversity is a good thing, and confirm that belief with their religiously diverse social networks. Along with the value they place on religious diversity is a widespread belief that there are many paths to heaven. In the Faith Matters surveys we asked "can a person who is not of your faith go to heaven or attain salvation, or not?"[24] A whopping 89 percent of Americans believe that heaven is not reserved for those who share their religious faith. Americans are reluctant to claim that they have a monopoly on truth. Their hesitation to adopt a "members only" perspective on who goes to heaven illuminates their positive attitude toward religious diversity. It is not just that they have adopted Jefferson's minimal standard of avoiding picked pockets and broken legs. Rather, they endorse the legitimacy of others' religious beliefs. Large majorities of even the stricter religious traditions believe in an equal opportunity heaven. Eighty-three percent of evangelicals, for example, say that other religions can bring salvation; eighty-seven percent of Black Protestants believe so (see Figure 15.5).

Wait, a skeptic might reasonably ask, what do people think of when they hear a question about "someone not of your faith"? Are members of the numerically dominant Christian faiths just thinking of other Christians? Are Baptists merely telling us that Methodists can go to heaven too? If so, their belief that other religions lead to heaven would still be meaningful—disputes among Christians have historically been fierce—but would nonetheless mean something other than the belief that even non-Christians have a place in heaven. If Baptists are thinking of Methodists, that is one thing, but if they are thinking of Muslims, that is quite another.

Figure 15.5

AMERICANS OVERWHELMINGLY BELIEVE THAT PEOPLE OF OTHER RELIGIONS CAN GO TO HEAVEN

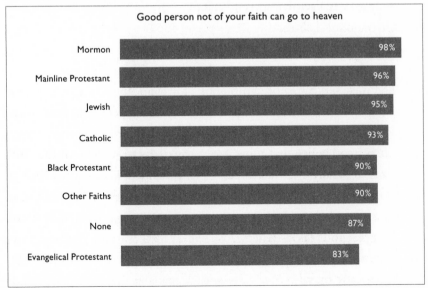

Good person not of your faith can go to heaven

Mormon	98%
Mainline Protestant	96%
Jewish	95%
Catholic	93%
Black Protestant	90%
Other Faiths	90%
None	87%
Evangelical Protestant	83%

SOURCE: FAITH MATTERS SURVEY, 2007.

To determine the limits of Christians' ecumenism, in 2007 we asked a second question of those who said that people of different religions could go to heaven.[25] "Does that include non-Christians or only Christians?" Before we report the results, we pause to note that Christian scripture does not appear to leave much room for doubt on whether non-Christians can be saved. For example, the New Testament records Jesus as saying that "I am the way, the truth, and the life: no man cometh unto the Father, but by me." [26]

Notwithstanding this scriptural injunction (and many more like it), most Americans who belong to Christian faiths told us that they believe non-Christians can go to heaven. Of those who said that people of other faiths could attain salvation, 89 percent of Catholics, 82 percent of mainline Protestants, and 100 percent of Mormons say that salvation extends to non-Christians. The percentages are noticeably lower for Black Protestants and evangelicals, at 69 and 65 percent respectively, but still constitute a clear majority.

We can put the two questions together—can anyone of a different faith go to heaven? Does that include non-Christians?—to determine the overall percentage of members of Christian faiths who believe that non-Christians can go to heaven. As displayed in Figure 15.6, for Mormons it is 98 percent; for Catholics, 83 percent; for mainline Protestants, 79 percent; for Black Protestants, 62 percent; and for evangelicals it is 54 percent. Clearly, Mormons, Catholics, and mainline Protestants all have an expansive view of heaven. The numbers are more ambiguous for evangelicals and Black Protestants. Once more, we have a glass-half-full vs. glass-half-empty conclusion. Glass-half-empty people would point out that these latter two groups are considerably less likely than the other traditions to believe that heaven takes all good people regardless of religion. On the other hand, glass-half-full people would note that, in both groups, a majority see heaven as welcoming non-Christians. Whether the glass is half full or half empty, one cannot deny that a large number of Americans, even in the religious traditions that have historically stressed that theirs is the only way to heaven, instead see

Figure 15.6

EVEN WHEN THOSE OTHER RELIGIONS ARE NOT CHRISTIAN

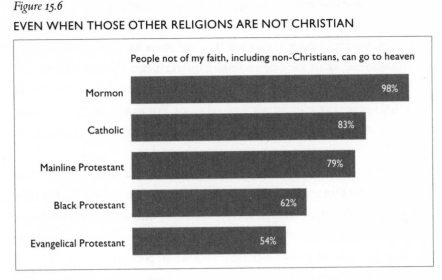

SOURCE: FAITH MATTERS SURVEY, 2007.

many roads to salvation. By any standard, this bodes well for inter-religious relations.

Lest our hypothetical critic be concerned that the Faith Matters surveys have somehow produced idiosyncratic conclusions, other researchers have asked similar questions about Americans' acceptance of faiths other than their own and found similar results. The most comprehensive of these surveys is a recent study by the Pew Forum on Religion & Public Life, which concluded that "most American Christians, including evangelicals, have more than just other Christian denominations in mind when they say that there are many paths to salvation."[27] The Pew results, however, also reveal that, in the eyes of most Christians, not all non-Christian faiths are equally likely to lead to salvation. For example, when asked specifically whether Islam leads to eternal life, only 35 percent of evangelicals agreed.[28] Interestingly, in a rare example of divergence from evangelicals, a much higher percentage—58 percent—of Black Protestants believe that Islam is a path to heaven, perhaps because the number of Black Muslims in America means that many Black

Protestants are personally acquainted with someone of the Islamic faith.[29]

A similar picture is painted by a question asked in the 2007 Pew Religious Landscape Survey, whether one's religion is "the one true faith leading to eternal life." Once again, only a minority of Americans agree. Only about 40 percent of evangelicals and Black Protestants, a little under 20 percent of Catholics, and a little over 10 percent of mainline Protestants believe that theirs is the one true faith.[30]

Still further confirmation of Americans' ecumenism arises from the studies of "Middletown," arguably the most studied city in America. In 1977, all high school students in Middletown (Muncie, Indiana) were asked whether they agreed that "Christianity is the one true religion and all people should be converted to it." Thirty-eight percent agreed—roughly consistent with the more recent data we have reported above. Because this community was the subject of intensive research by sociologists Robert and Helen Lynd in the 1920s and 1930s, it is possible to make comparisons across the decades. The change is dramatic. When the identical question about Christianity was asked of all Middletown high school students in 1924, 94 percent agreed that Christianity is the one true religion. In other words, over fifty years there was a precipitous decline in the belief that Christianity is the one and only true religion. Significantly, this decline in religious chauvinism came not because of diminishing religiosity. To the contrary, by every possible indicator Middletowners were far more religious in the late 1970s than in the 1920s.[31] These data from Middletown also highlight the generational differences in religious tolerance. Young people today are even more accepting of other religions than their parents and grandparents. According to the 2007 Faith Matters survey, nearly nine in ten (87 percent) Christians under age thirty-five believe that non-Christians can go to heaven, compared to 70 percent of people sixty-five and older.

The expansive—if not total—ecumenism of Americans is all the more notable in light of what clergy believe. In many faiths there is a wide gulf between the beliefs of clergy and laity with regard to

who is eligible for heaven. We can say this because of a survey conducted by political scientist Corwin Smidt and his colleagues. They
asked clergy in different Christian denominations whether they
agreed that "there is no way to salvation but through belief in Jesus
Christ."[32] In sharp contrast to the ecumenical views of the American
public, clergy are far more likely to see a single road to heaven. Even
in denominations generally thought to be fairly liberal, a high proportion of clergy endorse belief in Jesus as the sole source of salvation. For example, 63 percent of clergy in the Evangelical Lutheran
Church in America agree that Jesus is the only way (in spite of its
name, the theology of the ELCA puts it in the mainline Protestant
camp). This was also true for 59 percent of United Methodist clergy
and 57 percent of clergy from the Presbyterian Church, USA.

These numbers for mainline Protestants, however, are dwarfed
by those from the clergy in evangelical and Black Protestant denominations. The statement that salvation comes only through Jesus is
endorsed by:

- 100 percent of clergy from the Church of God in Christ, and
  98 percent of leaders in the African Methodist Episcopal Church,
  two historically black denominations.
- 100 percent of clergy from the Presbyterian Church in America
  (not to be confused with the Presbyterian Church, USA), 98 percent
  from the Missouri Synod Lutherans, 98 percent from the Church of
  Christ, 97 percent of Southern Baptist pastors, 96 percent of Christian Reformed leaders, and 92 percent of clergy from nondenominational but evangelical-leaning congregations (i.e., megachurches).

Across this range of Christian denominations we see a disconnect
between the leaders at the pulpits and the people in the pews. Most
Christian clergy see salvation as exclusively Christian, while most
Christians have a more—if not completely—inclusive view of who
will be saved in the hereafter.

The clergy–laity disconnect was made clear to us more vividly than is possible with a dry statistical report on who believes what. Early in our research for this book, one of us (Putnam) spoke about our work to a group of Lutheran theologians from the Missouri Synod, one of the evangelically inclined denominations within Lutheranism (the denomination of Our Savior Lutheran, featured in Chapter 7). They were shocked that such a high percentage of Americans believe that there are many ways to get to heaven. One theologian spoke up firmly that those who believe that are simply *wrong*. And judging from murmurs of approval from the group, he was not alone in his opinion. In an attempt to reconcile this apparent heresy, another member of the audience proposed that, surely, Missouri Synod Lutherans do not take such a casual view toward salvation. What ensued was social science research in real time, as an on-the-spot analysis of the 2006 Faith Matters data stored on Putnam's laptop revealed that 86 percent of Missouri Synod Lutherans said that a good person who is not of their faith could indeed go to heaven. Upon hearing this news, these theologians were stunned into silence. One wanly said that as teachers of the Word, they had failed.

We claim no qualifications to assess the theological implications of believing in a heaven that is not an exclusive club. The sociological implications of our findings are clear, however. A leading, perhaps even the primary, reason that America manages to be both highly religious and highly religiously diverse is that most Americans do not believe that those with a different religious faith are damned. Devotion plus diversity, minus damnation, equals comity.

The explanation for the fact that so many Americans appear to disregard the theology of their religions rests in the religious bridging within their personal social networks. If you are highly religious, your Aunt Susan and your pal Al both produce a form of cognitive dissonance. You know you are supposed to believe that only people who believe as you do will enter heaven. However, Susan and Al are both the salt of the earth, and so surely heaven has a place for them. Most Americans, it appears, resolve this discrepancy in favor of believing that Susan and Al can go to heaven after all.

WHO IS A GOOD AMERICAN?

Asking about eligibility for heaven is an important indicator of how Americans view the eternal prospects of those who believe differently than they do, which in turn sheds light on the level of religious tolerance in America. What, though, about tolerance of the irreligious? And what if we ask not about the hereafter, but the here and now? Do Americans think that being religious is a prerequisite for being a "good American"?

There are many reasons to think that they do. Americans have long merged patriotism and religion, as evidenced by the vestigial examples of religious symbolism at many moments of nationalistic ceremony. Examples of America's civil religion, discussed above, only reinforce the symbiosis between God and country. Since the 1950s, the Pledge of Allegiance has contained the words "under God." Similarly, this was the decade when "In God We Trust" was inscribed on American coins and currency. And, as noted in Chapter 1, it was in the 1950s that public monuments with the Ten Commandments were placed all around the country. During this period of conflict with an expansionist and officially atheist Soviet Union, these public expressions of religion reminded Americans that theirs was a godly nation facing a godless foe. More recently, in the immediate wake of the September 11, 2001, terrorist attacks, members of Congress from both parties linked arms on the steps of the Capitol and sang not the National Anthem but "God Bless America."

Even though religion and patriotism seemingly fit hand in glove, the 2006 Faith Matters survey reveals that Americans are nonetheless willing to include people who are not religious in their conception of an upstanding citizen. Eighty-seven percent of Americans agree that people "without a religious faith" can be "good Americans." So, in spite of Americans' own high degree of religiosity, and the enduring legacy of America's civil religion, the nonreligious are welcomed as full members of the national community. Interestingly, this is nearly the same percentage of Americans (89 percent) who believe that people of a different faith can go to heaven.

We see a further parallel between religious tolerance and the acceptance of the nonreligious as full Americans. If interreligious relations are enhanced by religious bridging, it seems reasonable to think that religious bridging would also lead people to accept the patriotic bona fides of people without religious faith. In other words, just as we found that an increase in religious bridging corresponds to warmer feelings toward religious outgroups, we might expect more bridging to lead to the full acceptance of an outgroup—those without a religion—into the national community. This is a high bar to clear, since so many of our respondents had already told us that even the non-religious could be good Americans. Just as a helium-filled balloon cannot ascend any higher than the ceiling, so is there a ceiling expanding on the acceptance of the non-religious as good citizens.

Although a high percentage of Americans already see secularists as patriots, this percentage climbs higher with more religious bridging. That is, when we use the same test we described above—testing the impact of increasing religious diversity among one's friends over roughly a one-year time span—we see that more bridging means a small but statistically significant increase in the likelihood of agreeing that religious faith is not essential to good Americanness. (See Appendix 2 for methodological details.)

This finding suggests that interreligious contact can lead to a redefined social boundary. Rather than being dismissed as unpatriotic, people without a religious faith are instead viewed as full-fledged members of the national community. In other words, having a religiously diverse group of friends seems to lead to widening the circle of "we." E pluribus unum.

THE LESS TOLERANT TENTH: A MINORITY OF "TRUE BELIEVERS"

The vast majority of Americans seem entirely comfortable in a religiously pluralist world, but several indicators point to a small minority (roughly one in ten of all adults) who are "true believers." As we have seen, 11 percent of believers say that people of other faiths cannot reach heaven. Similarly, as Figure 15.7 shows, approximately 13 percent of all adults say that "one religion is true and others are not."[33] It is worth looking more closely at this group, especially since they seem to represent the worst fears of secular Americans. In many respects those Americans who say there is only "one true religion" are distinctive, even compared to highly religious evangelicals. (Table 15.1 summarizes the statistical evidence.)[34]

First, even in an America that is more religiously observant than any other advanced nation, this group of true believers is yet more intensely religious. They are, virtually without exception, absolutely sure about God's existence. Religion is fundamental to their personal identity and daily life. They are twice as likely as other Americans to attend church every week (many of them more than once). And because they are passionate about their faith, they are much more active in personal evangelism, sharply dissenting from the more common view among other Americans that in terms of religion "everyone should leave everyone else alone."

Figure 15.7
FEW AMERICANS ARE "TRUE BELIEVERS"

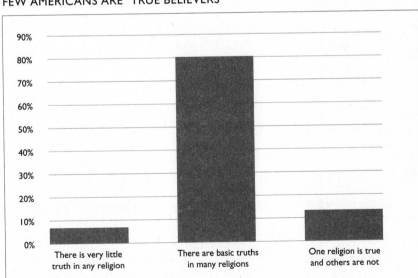

SOURCE: FAITH MATTERS SURVEY, 2006.

Table 15.1

WHO ARE THE MINORITY OF "TRUE BELIEVERS" IN THE AMERICAN RELIGIOUS LANDSCAPE?

	One true religion?	
	Yes	No
Highly religious (even compared to other Americans)		
Religion is "very important" to my sense of who I am	83%	44%
Attend church every week	60%	32%
Absolutely sure I believe in God	96%	77%
Okay to try to convert other people (vs. "everyone should leave everyone else alone")	71%	39%
Have tried to convert someone	54%	22%
Highly deferential to religious authority		
There are absolutely clear guidelines of what is good and evil	88%	54%
It's better to follow leaders and teachings of religion rather than one's own conscience	54%	20%
Scripture is actual word of God and is to be taken literally	63%	29%
"Absolutely sure" belief in hell	71%	46%
Avoiding sin in everyday life decisions is "extremely important"	47%	23%
The world is soon coming to an end	63%	34%
It is more important for a child to be taught obedience than self-reliance	69%	39%
Very conservative, especially on moral issues		
Premarital sex is always morally wrong	72%	29%
Make abortion illegal even in case of rape/incest	34%	12%
Gambling is always morally wrong	55%	25%
Oppose both gay marriage and civil unions	60%	31%
Self-described "conservative"	70%	41%
Somewhat less comfortable with religious pluralism		
Religion is a private matter that should be kept out of public debates over social and political issues	45%	73%
Morality is a personal matter, and society should not force everyone to follow one standard	54%	69%
Religious diversity has been good for America	70%	86%
My values are "very" threatened in America today	34%	20%
Trust "deeply religious people" more than "nonreligious people"	42%	25%
A book that most people disapprove of should be kept out of my local public library	44%	23%
Live in religiously homogeneous environment with fewer Aunt Susans and pal Als		
Spouse currently in same religious tradition as me	83%	66%
All five closest friends in same religion as me	38%	21%
All members of extended family in same religion as me	39%	29%
"Very important" that my children marry someone of my own faith	60%	16%

SOURCE: FAITH MATTERS SURVEY, 2006.

Second, compared to most Americans they have a very clear, religiously derived sense of good and evil. Whereas 80 percent of other Americans say they follow their own conscience in matters of right and wrong, more than half of the "true believers" give precedence instead to religious leaders and teachings. They are roughly twice as likely as other Americans to be strict biblical literalists, to be certain about the reality of hell, to anticipate Judgment Day anytime now, and be wary of sin and evil in everyday life. Not surprisingly, they think that obedience, rather than self-reliance, is the cardinal virtue to be imparted to children. They are, in short, moral absolutists.

Third, religious true believers in America today are deeply conservative, especially on moral issues, above all on questions of sexual morality. They wholeheartedly condemn premarital sex and homosexuality, at a time when most other Americans are coming to terms with those two sexual revolutions. They overwhelmingly oppose abortion, one third favoring a legal ban even in the case of rape and incest. They are more than twice as likely as other Americans to condemn gambling as "always morally wrong." It is hardly surprising that most true believers describe themselves as "conservative," 32 percent as "very conservative," compared to only 10 percent of other Americans who say they are "very conservative."

Fourth, true believers are (compared to other Americans) somewhat less comfortable with religious pluralism and with the idea that religion and morality are primarily private and personal matters. They are less convinced that religious diversity is a good thing, and probably for that reason they are more bothered by an alien religion, even one as mild-mannered as Buddhism. (True believers are half again as likely to object to the construction of a Buddhist temple in their community, 33 percent to 21 percent for other Americans.) They feel that their own values are especially threatened by the modern world, and they are somewhat readier to rid library collections of unpopular books. They are slightly less trusting of other people, drawing an especially sharp distinction between deeply religious people (whom they trust) and nonreligious people (whom they don't). To be sure, even these true believers have been visibly influenced by the American tradition of religious and civil toleration, and on all these indicators a substantial number join the national consensus in favor of pluralism and tolerance, but that consensus is narrower among this less tolerant tenth of the population.

Finally and most significantly, these true believers live in more religiously monochromatic social environments. They are less likely to have married outside their faith, and they are much more insistent than other Americans that their children remain inside that faith. (If it is, as they believe, the one true faith, that is hardly surprising.) They are less likely than other Americans to have ties of kinship or friendship outside their own faith. In short, true believers are much less likely to have an Aunt Susan or pal Al to perturb their unquestioning faith.

The vast majority of Americans belong to religions (above all, Christianity) that claim unique status as the one true religion. Most of us recite creeds that embody that claim. From a sociological point of view, however, what is remarkable is how few of us really are "true believers" in this sense. For these few Americans, religious faith is serious enough to suggest fanaticism, and Figure 15.8 shows how

Figure 15.8

ONE TRUE RELIGION?

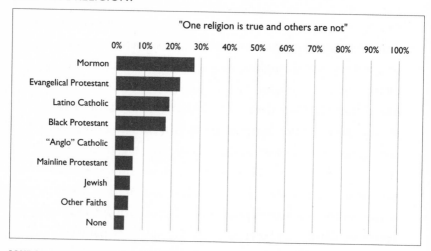

SOURCE: FAITH MATTERS SURVEY, 2006.

they are distributed among our major religious traditions. Unsurprisingly, perhaps, they are somewhat more common among religious traditions (especially the Mormon and evangelical traditions, both black and white) that are more sectlike, using nomenclature introduced by Max Weber and recently revived by Laurence Iannaccone, Roger Finke, and Rodney Stark, among other scholars.[35] Otherwise, in their age, gender, education, region, and other demographic traits, true believers seem a perfect mirror of America. Moreover, the incidence of true believers seems to be highly stable over time, since the responses represented in Figure 15.8 are virtually identical to responses to the same question in the General Social Surveys of 1988 and 2008. This hard-core, deeply moralistic less tolerant tenth of the population gives us a glimpse of what a highly religious America might look like without Aunt Susan and my pal Al.

In today's America, however, true believers constitute only a small fraction of the faithful in every religious tradition. More specifically, while a majority (52 percent) of true believers as identified here are evangelicals, the great majority (75 percent) of evangelicals are not true believers. "Faith without fanaticism" accurately describes most Americans.

CONSEQUENCES OF BRIDGING

Multiple strands of evidence point in the same direction. When Americans associate with people of religions other than their own—or people with no religion at all—they become more accepting of other religions. Religious intermarriage is perhaps the most profound example. Over the course of the last century, there has been a steady rise in the frequency of marriage across religious lines, which we argue is closely tied to the widespread ecumenism within the American population. Husbands and wives are presumably willing to believe that the other can go to heaven (who would marry someone on their way to hell?), even if they have different religions. However, this first-order effect is not the only way that interreligious marriage can affect interreligious relations. Second-order effects rip-ple through an extended family. Even if you and your own spouse do not have different religious backgrounds, most Americans have an Aunt Susan in the family.

Religious bridging is not limited to intermarriage. Interfaith friendship is even more common than marriages across religious boundaries. Most Americans have at least one close friend of another religion, and many have multiple friends of other faiths. Even over a short period of time, we have seen that a small increase in such religious bridging corresponds to warmer feelings toward at least two relatively unpopular religious groups (Mormons and the non-religious). Furthermore, we have seen that religious bridging can expand Americans' sense of who is fully a member of the national community.

Individually, each of these findings and observations might be considered intriguing. Taken together they form a convincing pattern. Interreligious mixing, mingling, and marrying have kept America's religious melting pot from boiling over.

CONCLUSION

This chapter began with a puzzle. How can Americans combine high levels of both religious diversity and devotion? America's religious comity is even more puzzling given the recent state of religious polarization described throughout this book. Recall the story of the shock and two aftershocks that we recounted in Chapter 4. In the wake of the sexually libertine Sixties, conservative religion grew in both size and prominence—including political prominence. And then, in response to that growth and presence in partisan politics, there has been a second backlash in which increasing numbers of Americans, especially young people, have turned away from religion. These seismic events have reverberated throughout American society, and so the moderate religious middle—the once thriving segment of the religious spectrum—has shrunk.

Given this state of affairs, there would appear to be considerable potential for religious tension. As we have seen, religious and secular Americans have differing worldviews, and see each other in starkly different terms. There are also latent tensions between members of some religious traditions—while some religions are viewed negatively across the board. Furthermore, history provides many examples of such tension turning to violence. For example, in 1834 anti-Catholic riots in Charlestown, Massachusetts, destroyed the Ursuline convent; in 1844 there were deadly riots in Philadelphia over rumors that Catholics were going to remove the Bible from the public schools.[36] Nor are Catholics the only group to face such animus. In the face of growing hostilities between Mormons and non-Mormons, in 1838 the governor of Missouri issued an order that all Mormons were to leave his state or be killed. This extermination order actually remained on the books until 1976.[37]

Such examples of religiously inspired violence are tragic, but fortunately they also are rare. America has had sporadic religious riots, but no sustained religious wars. From its founding, America has had religious toleration encoded in its national DNA. In saying this, we must recognize that at the time of the Founding magnanimity toward different religions was contained to various Protestant sects—Catholics, Jews, Muslims, and certainly atheists were not included. Nonetheless, the early years of the republic were informed by John Locke's conception of religious toleration. Locke spoke of the "necessity and advantage" of religious toleration, justifying it as a means of keeping the civil peace. From Locke, it is a small step to Thomas Jefferson's acceptance of different faiths so long as they do not infringe on his freedoms.

Over time, however, that minimal conception of toleration on practical grounds has evolved into an explicit embrace of religious diversity for its own sake. There were bumps in the road along the way, as evidenced by outbreaks of anti-Catholicism, anti-Semitism, anti-Mormonism, and any number of other anti-isms. Eventually, though, the national sentiment moved from grudging acceptance of other faiths to a way station of tacit approval to an outright embrace of religious differences as ecumenism took hold in the mid- to late twentieth century. And even if the religious diversity of today is not completely inclusive, it still is far more expansive than anything imagined by the Founders. Catholics are squarely in the American mainstream, while Jews are the best liked religious group in the country. Religious pluralism is embraced, as shown by the extremely high percentage of Americans who say such diversity is good for the country.

In tracing the evolution and expansion of religious pluralism, we acknowledge the important role of the nation's constitutional infrastructure. The U.S. Constitution's prohibitions on both an established religion—which eventually came to mean any public support for religious entities by government at any level—and religious tests for public office helped to create a flourishing religious ecosphere. In a never-ending process, many different variants of religion emerge, adapt, evolve, and innovate. In America, religion is not static but fluid. Not only are religions changing, but individual Americans themselves frequently undergo religious change—finding religion, dropping out of religion, or switching from one religion to another.

This fluidity has contributed to the steady growth of interreligious mingling and marrying. Geographic segregation by religion has largely ended, while social segregation along religious lines is also mostly a thing of the past. As Americans have come to live by, make friends with, and wed people of other religions, their overlapping social relationships have made it difficult to sustain interreligious hostility. While not every religion escapes hostility, interreligious tensions are far more muted today than in the America of yesterday or in many other nations today.

How has America solved the puzzle of religious pluralism—the coexistence of religious diversity and devotion? And how has it done so in the wake of growing religious polarization? By creating a web of interlocking personal relationships among people of many different faiths.

This is America's grace.

ACKNOWLEDGMENTS

A book of this size and scope could not have been produced without the assistance and support of many colleagues, friends, and family.

Pride of place in accounting for contributions to this project must go to the talented, hardworking researchers who accompanied us on our voyage of discovery. Shaylyn Romney Garrett joined the team early, as a field researcher on many of the field studies that she eventually turned into the vignettes of this book. Shaylyn is graciously personable, extremely conscientious, and highly observant—all essential gifts in a good ethnographer. She writes like an angel, and her name deservedly appears on the title page of this book. She was joined on our extraordinary team of field researchers by Shelby Meyerhoff, Byron Pacheco Miller, and Deborah Talen.

Other able researchers were members of our "moveable feast" research seminar over the five years of this project, analyzing data and reviewing far-flung literatures in sociology, psychology, political science, history, constitutional law, philosophy, theology, and yet more. They included Lydia Bean, Nick Carnes, Jill Goldenziel, Erin Graves, Matt Greenfield, Eitan Hersh, Sarah Hinkfuss, Ridhi Kashyap, James Laurence, Rebecca McCumbers, Shelby Meyerhoff, Byron Pacheco Miller, Nan Ransohoff, Amy Reynolds, and Nate Schwartz. Several colleagues on the project should be singled out because of the depth of their engagement: Valerie Lewis, Chaeyoon Lim, Sean McGraw, Carol Ann McGregor, Matt Pehl, and Danny Schlozman. Our team was notably diverse in the religious orientations of its members, for it included a Catholic priest (along with several lay Catholics), a Unitarian minister, a Muslim, a Quaker, two Mormons, several Jews (Reform to Orthodox), several conservative (and liberal) evangelicals, a few mainline Protestants, and several without religious affiliation. Our discussions were fascinating!

The initial suggestion and generous financial support for our work came from the John Templeton Foundation, as part of their initiative on "spiritual capital." We are grateful to the Foundation's president, Dr. Jack Templeton, Jr., to Dr. Arthur Schwartz, and especially to Kimon Sargent, Vice President for Human Sciences, for their encouragement to explore new scientific perspectives on religion without intellectual impediment. Similarly generous and sensitive support came from the Legatum Institute; we are grateful to its founder, Christopher Chandler, and especially to the Institute's Senior Vice President, Will Inboden.

We thank the leaders and members of the two dozen religious congregations who generously hosted us, often for weeks at a time, who responded graciously to our questions, and who shared their religious convictions, practices, and even doubts with us. The leaders of the congregations appear by name (and by permission) in our vignettes, while pseudonyms provide a measure of privacy to the scores of congregants who helped us understand their faiths. We thank them all for their remarkable hospitality—"remarkable" not least in the fact that virtually no one whom we approached in the course of this research declined to help.

In addition to the congregations described in our vignettes, we benefited from our visits with the following congregations: Church of the Good Shepherd, Acton, Massachusetts; St. George's Church, Maynard, Massachusetts; Christ Church of Hamilton and Wenham, Massachusetts; Mount Olivet Lutheran Church, Minneapolis, Minnesota ; Lakewood Church, Houston, Texas; Holy Family Catholic Community, Inverness, Illinois; Willow Creek Community Church, South Barrington, Illinois; St. Paul of the Cross Catholic Church, Park Ridge, Illinois; St. Odilo Parish, Berwyn, Illinois; Ascension Catholic Church, Oak Park, Illinois; St. Sylvester Parish, Chicago, Illinois; and St. Anthony Parish, Cicero, Illinois.

Mounting an unprecedented national panel survey of religion and civic life with a comprehensive roster of questions and a gratifyingly high response rate required expertise and energy from many people. International Communications Research conducted the surveys, and Melissa Herrmann and David Dutwin demonstrated high professionalism and exceptional skill, generosity, and forbearance in responding to our endless queries. We are also grateful to the dozen scholars who generously helped us design the questionnaire. An interdisciplinary Who's Who of experts on survey research and religion, they are thanked by name in Appendix I. Lara Putnam and Mario Perez helped with the translation of the questionnaire into Spanish.

Academics in some fields are notoriously competitive, so we were deeply appreciative to discover that scholars of religion were exceptionally generous in offering help, even to relative newcomers like us. In addition to the dozen who helped design the questionnaire, sixteen experts devoted several days to reading an initial draft of this book and discussing it in a day-long seminar in Cambridge in January 2010. These colleagues were (as we had hoped) amiably ruthless in discerning "opportunities for improvement" in that draft. While some of the deficiencies they discovered doubtless remain, we are very grateful for their skilled investment in our work. This Eric M. Mindich Symposium was sponsored by Harvard's Institute for Quantitative Social Science (IQSS), and we thank its director, Gary King, for his encouragement throughout the life of this project. (Jeff Blossom, Center for Geographic Analysis, IQSS, provided technical support for the maps in Chapter 9.) Participants in the 2010 Mindich symposium included Christopher Achen, Nancy Ammerman, Larry Bartels, Mark Chaves, Michael O. Emerson, Claudine Gay, John Green, Stephen Macedo, Pippa Norris, Kay Schlozman, Paul Solman, Sidney Verba, David Voas, Christopher Winship, Alan Wolfe, and Robert D. Woodberry. We marvel at the generosity of this all-star team.

We also received constructively critical comments on various sections of the book from Katie Bacon, Peter Cerroni, Susan Crawford, Rose-Marie Klipstein, Virginia Park, Christin Putnam, Lara Putnam, Carol Thompson, Edwenna Werner, and Clyde Wilcox. In May 2009 Michael Cromartie of the Pew Forum on Religion and Public Life invited us to brief some of America's most distinguished journalists and commentators on religion about our findings. It would be inappropriate to name these participants in this setting, but we are grateful to Michael and his colleagues for a lively and productive conversation that enriched this book.

We are acutely conscious of the hundreds of improvements that we owe to these generous colleagues, while we remain responsible for the remaining flaws.

To convert a research project to a book requires expert help. We thank Bob Bender, our editor, and his colleagues at Simon & Schuster, for demonstrating that even in today's turbulent publishing business, the older virtues of respect for language and sensitivity to ideas can endure. Our partnership with Rafe Sagalyn (Putnam's literary agent for more than fifteen years) remains as productive and enjoyable as it has been from the outset. Rafe was creatively involved in every stage of this book from conception to cover design. Working with him continues to be one of the great pleasures of our professional lives.

Our most important partners in this project were the members of the Saguaro team in the Taubman Center for State and Local Government at Harvard's John F. Kennedy School of Government. David Ellwood, Dean of the Kennedy School; John Haigh, Executive Dean; Edward Glaeser, Director of the Taubman Center; and Sandra Garron, Executive Director, facilitated and encouraged our work in many ways. Originally "Saguaro Seminar" referred to a series of meetings of community leaders and scholars to discuss civic renewal in America, but it has come to apply to a range of explorations of social capital and civic engagement, as described in detail at http://www.hks .harvard.edu/saguaro. Members of the Saguaro administrative staff during this project on religion have included Tracy Blanchard, Zoe Clarkwest, Karena Cronin, Kristin Ellard, Shaylyn Romney Garrett, Ami Preisz, Abby Williamson, and particularly Courtney Francik.

The trio at the heart of the Saguaro administrative team must be unsurpassed anywhere in American academic life. Kylie Gibson joined our team as a staff assistant only in 2008, but quickly showed exceptional talent, both intellectual and managerial. In the end she took responsibility for all aspects of the production of this book from reading drafts to correcting proofs. Tom Sander, Executive Director of the Saguaro Seminar, and Louise Kennedy Converse, Deputy Director, have collaborated closely with Putnam for more than fifteen years, and their effectiveness reached new heights during this project. They were centrally involved in raising and managing a multi-million dollar budget. They oversaw our far-flung team of researchers, as well as an endless series of project meetings and conference calls. They debated substantive points of our argument with us, helping us to refine our views. Tom pitched in with initial drafting and statistical analysis, while Louise planned efforts to carry our message to multiple audiences and (as a skilled graphic artist) designed the charts in this book. All three kept a half-dozen other Saguaro balls in the air while we concentrated on finishing this book. *American Grace* simply would not exist without the talent, boundless energy, intellectual commitment, and morale-boosting good fellowship of this trio. We are unable adequately to acknowledge our debt to them.

David Campbell adds:

I am grateful for the helpful advice in the many conversations about this book that I have had with my colleagues at Notre Dame, especially the lunches with my colleagues in Decio Hall: Darren Davis, Geoff Layman, John Griffin, David Nickerson, and Christina Wolbrecht. The food was remarkably mediocre, but the conversation made up for it. (Mostly).

I appreciate also the helpful comments offered during presentations at a Notre Dame political science colloquium, as well as talks given to the Rooney Center research workshop. Eileen Botting, Michael Coppedge, Rodney Hero, Mark Noll, and Dianne Pinderhughes provided insightful observations.

I also benefitted from the support of Notre Dame's College of Arts and Letters, particularly that of current dean John McGreevy and former dean Mark Roche. Mark was especially generous in permitting me to be released from teaching in order to work on *American Grace* at a critical point in the project.

Most importantly, I thank my family for all that they have endured over the years that I have worked on *American Grace*. I am grateful that my daughter, Katie, and son, Soren, continually remind me of what really matters. Most of all, I am deeply grateful to my wife, Kirsten. She truly exemplifies "American grace." Kirsten both lives her faith and contributes to her community—all while building bridges across many different divides. I only write about this stuff; she actually does it. And so it is to Kirsten, Katie, and Soren that I have dedicated this book.

Robert D. Putnam adds:

Princeton's Center for the Study of Democratic Politics hosted my work on this project during 2006–07. I am grateful to those Princeton faculty and students with whom I discussed the research, and especially to Larry Bartels, Director of the Center, and Michele Epstein, Assistant Director, as well as to Chris Achen and Robert Wuthnow, who spent hours expertly guiding me down unfamiliar paths, both methodological and substantive.

Bob Wuthnow and Mark Chaves of Duke are among America's foremost sociologists of religion, as our endnotes show. Each has written compellingly on this subject, yet each has been unselfishly and unfailingly supportive as we explored terrain that they already knew well. Four friends of more than forty years standing—Robert Axelrod, Dennis Thompson, and Bob and Nan Keohane—continued to provide emotional and intellectual encouragement.

Throughout this project I have been generously supported by the University of Manchester (England), where I hold a visiting professorship. I thank Dean Alistair Ulph and Professor Ed Fieldhouse of Manchester for their intellectual encouragement and friendship.

My wife, children, and now grandchildren have been constant companions on all the major research projects of my career. Fortunately that has not changed as we have all matured. Jonathan, Lara, and Christin—all distinguished professionals—critiqued try-outs of the arguments in this book, while loving me despite occasional familial lapses. Rosemary remains the emotional core of my life and the only person with whom I have discussed virtually every page that I have ever written. She knows how grateful I am for a half-century's partnership. Apart from our children, we take greatest pride in our six grandchildren, to whom this book is dedicated.

THE FAITH MATTERS SURVEYS

The bulk of the data in *American Grace* comes from the Faith Matters surveys, original sources of data we designed, implemented, and analyzed. These are among the most thorough surveys of Americans' religious and civic lives ever conducted. As described in Appendix 2, Faith Matters is a two-wave panel study, meaning that we recontacted our original respondents roughly nine months after they were initially interviewed. This second wave has turned out to be critical for our analysis, as a two-wave study offers numerous analytical advantages over a single cross-sectional survey. Furthermore, panel studies on religion are rare. Other than a few technical papers presented to small audiences, primarily of academics, *American Grace* is the debut of findings from the Faith Matters data.

Both waves of the Faith Matters study were generously funded by the John Templeton Foundation. We stress, however, that the Templeton Foundation has played no role in the analysis or interpretation of the data we have collected.

We began the process of designing Faith Matters in July 2005 by holding a one-day meeting at Harvard with an interdisciplinary group of experts on religion and survey research. Our group included Christopher Achen (Princeton University), Willam Galston (Brookings Institution), John C. Green (University of Akron/Pew Forum on Religion & Public Life), Anna Greenberg (Quinlan Rosner Research), Fredrick Harris (Columbia University), Ralph Hood (University of Tennessee, Chattanooga), Jon Krosnick (Stanford University), Martin Marty (University of Chicago), Robert Sampson (Harvard University), Rev. Timothy Scully, C.S.C. (University of Notre Dame), Christian Smith (University of Notre Dame), and Christopher Winship (Harvard University). These experts offered a wealth of advice, for which we are most grateful. (While we attempted to take all of their advice, we alone are responsible for any shortcomings in the study.)

Following that meeting, our research team began writing survey questions, often by drawing on existing data sources. Wherever possible, therefore, Faith Matters has replicated questions asked in other surveys, enabling us to validate our findings with different sources of data. As shown below, we were pleased to find that whenever we have cross-checked results from Faith Matters with other national surveys, we have found that our results largely conform to those of other data sources.

The first wave of Faith Matters was administered in the summer of 2006 by International Communications Research. The first wave survey had a total of 3,108 respondents, all age eighteen or older. Interviews were conducted in both English and Spanish. To ensure the accuracy of our Spanish translation, we had it backward-translated into English again. Respondents were offered $25 for completing the survey, which, on average, took between forty-five minutes and an hour to complete. The survey was conducted by telephone.

When asked if they would like to participate in the survey, respondents were not told that it was a study about religion. Instead, interviewers introduced themselves and said that the survey was being conducted on behalf of researchers at Harvard and Notre Dame, and that it was "on some current events."

The response rate for the survey, calculated according to the criteria established by the American Association for Public Opinion Research, was 53 percent.[1] (For those readers unfamiliar with survey research, that response rate is quite good for a telephone survey.) The data have been weighted by gender, age, race, region, and education according to the March supplement of the 2005 Current Population Survey. The weighting is merely precautionary, however, as it has very little effect on the results.

There is not space here to detail every single question, but we do provide some illustrative comparisons of questions asked in the 2006 Faith Matters (FM) survey which can be cross-validated in other surveys. Table A1.1 displays the comparison between FM 2006 and the 2006 General Social Survey for age, gender, race, having no religious affiliation, religious attendance, and frequency of prayer. Whether we look at weighted or unweighted data, the two surveys produce similar results. One exception is the frequency of attendance at religious services, which is higher in FM 2006 than the General Social Survey. In the GSS, 26.2 percent (weighted) report attending religious services weekly or more, compared to 35.7 percent (weighted) in FM 2006. The FM 2006 data, however, produce an estimate of weekly attendance that is lower than both the 2007 Pew Religious Landscape Survey (39.5 percent, weighted) and the Gallup Poll, which in 2006 reported that 42 percent of Americans attend religious services weekly or more. The Gallup results are "based on an aggregated dataset of 68,031 interviews, conducted by Gallup between January 2004 and March 2006."[2] In other words, FM 2006 falls in the mid-range when comparing across these four datasets—higher than the GSS, but lower than the Pew Religious Landscape Survey and the Gallup Poll.

On other measures related to religiosity, the FM 2006 results match other data sources very closely. Indeed, in virtually every case in which we have found the same question posed in a credi-

le A1.1

MPARING FAITH MATTERS AND THE GENERAL SOCIAL SURVEY

	GSS 2006		Faith Matters 2006	
	unweighted	weighted	unweighted	weighted
(mean)	47.1	45.3	49.7	45.9
1ale	44	46	47	48
cation (mean # of years)	13.3	13.3	13.9	13.3
'hite	73	72	74	69
Io Religion	17	17	15	17
ray several times a day	31	30	28	26
ttend religious service weekly or more	26	26	38	36

Table A1.2

COMPARING FAITH MATTERS AND THE NATIONAL ELECTION STUDY ON ABORTION

	National Election Study 2008 (weighted)	Faith Matt 2006 (weigl
By law, abortion should never be permitted	15	16
The law should permit abortion only in case of rape, incest, or when the woman's life is in danger	27	30
The law should permit abortion for reasons other than rape, incest, or danger to the woman's life, but only after the need for the abortion has been clearly established	18	14
By law, a woman should always be able to obtain an abortion as a matter of personal choice.	40	40

ble national survey in the same period, the Faith Matters results are within a few percentage points of the other survey. For example, FM 2006 and the 2008 National Election Study asked the identical abortion question. The results are nearly the same, as shown in Table A1.2.

We find a similar convergence between FM 2006 and a Gallup Poll question from 2006 on evolution. Both questions used exactly the same wording. (See Table A1.3.)

For the 2007 follow-up survey, our original respondents were sent a letter inviting them to participate a second time, and offering a $15 incentive if they did so. This was a shorter survey, averaging about half the time of the first wave. The second wave had a 62 per-

Table A1.3

COMPARING FAITH MATTERS AND GALLUP ON EVOLUTION[3]

	Gallup Poll 2006	Faith Ma 2006
Human beings have developed over millions of years from less advanced forms of life, but God had no part in this process;	13	12
Human beings have developed over millions of years from less advanced forms of life, but God guided this process	36	38
God created human beings pretty much in their present form at one time within the last 10,000 years or so	46	45
Other/Don't Know	5	5

cent reinterview rate, which is on par with the reinterviewing rates of the General Social Survey and National Election Studies, the two primary omnibus national surveys used by sociologists and political scientists (and funded by the National Science Foundation). Even with a reasonably high response rate, our follow-up survey is slightly less than fully representative of our original sample. Two overlapping groups, the young and the less religious, had a lower than average recontact rate.

Because young people move more often, it is typically harder to track them down in a later panel wave. We suspect that more religious people were slightly more enthusiastic about completing a second survey focused heavily on religion. Our analyses of the second wave have been weighted to account for this potential bias in the second wave. Table A1.4 displays the weighted and unweighted results for an illustrative group of key questions. Note the underrepresentation of both the young and nones in the unweighted data. However, on other measures of religiosity, like religious service attendance, importance of religion, and belief in God the follow-up comes very close to the original survey.

The complete questionnaires for both waves of the Faith Matters survey can be found online at: americangrace.org.

le A1.4

MPARING THE 2006 (ORIGINAL) AND 2007 (PANEL) FAITH MATTERS SURVEYS

	Original sample (2006)		Panel sample (2007)	
	unweighted	*weighted*	*unweighted*	*weighted*
ge	49.7	45.9	52.7	45.4
Male	47	48	44	48
cation (mean # of years)	14.0	13.2	14.2	13.4
White	77	73	83	73
ncome ($1000)	55.6	51.5	57.6	51.9
Married	56	53	59	54
Kids at home	37	41	33	41
No Religion	15	17	14	16
ttend religious service weekly or more	29	28	30	28
ortance of religion (0–3)	1.8	1.8	1.8	1.7
elief in God (0–5)	3.6	3.6	3.6	3.6

DATA ANALYSIS

This appendix touches on two aspects of the data analysis employed in *American Grace:* (1) the specific methods used to analyze the Faith Matters panel; and (2) the method used to translate the statistical results into intuitive metrics.

Panel Data Analysis

In different parts of this book, we make claims that religion influences individual attitudes and behaviors. In Chapter 13, for example, we claim that certain aspects of religiosity make people better neighbors or citizens. In Chapter 15, we discuss how having more bridging friendships (friends of different religions) leads to greater religious tolerance. Making causal claims like these with survey data, however, is daunting. To begin with, religious people may differ from nonreligious people in ways that make them both better neighbors and better citizens. For example, a certain "niceness gene" may engender religiosity and good citizenship. To be sure, the analyses in this book control for many such factors that could contribute to both religiousness and good neighborliness, but it is still possible that factors we failed to observe or measured poorly induced a spurious relationship (correlation) between religiousness and good neighborliness. The causation could also run in the other direction: In the case of bridging friendships and religious tolerance, for example, religious tolerance might produce more bridging friendships rather than the other way around.

The panel design of the Faith Matters surveys offers some important advantages over typical cross-sectional surveys for addressing these challenges. Most important, outcomes (such as good neighborliness) are measured before and after some "intervention" (for instance, change in religiosity), so that adjustments can be made for initial differences in the outcome variable between the people who experienced the intervention and those who did not.[1] Thus by controlling for these baseline differences—in this example, good neighborliness—we can tease out the true effects of increased religiosity. In a sense, panel data allow us to compare two people who were similar both in religiosity and good neighborliness at time 1, but diverged in religiosity over the next year, and see whether the change in religiosity over the period made them also differ in good neighborliness.

Panel data are not a panacea, especially when the two waves of data were collected less than a year apart. The short interval between the Faith Matters survey waves is particularly problematic since religious beliefs and behaviors rarely change significantly over such a short period. This short interval, in fact, makes it harder to detect real causal relations, and thus biases our results in a conservative direction. In addition, with only two waves we cannot fully exclude the possibility of reverse causation. Still, the panel design of the Faith Matters surveys is a great improvement over most previous studies based on purely cross-sectional data. The FM data are particularly valuable because very few panel surveys with a representative national sample have focused on both the civic *and* religious lives of a large, representative sample of Americans.

To fully utilize the panel design of the Faith Matters surveys, we used both change score and analysis of covariance (ANCOVA) models, the two most common methods used to analyze two-wave panel data.[2] The two approaches differ in how they adjust for initial differences in the outcome variable.

The change score model takes the difference in the outcome variable (good neighborliness in our example) between the two waves of the study and examines how it is related to the difference in religiosity over the same period. This model is often estimated using fixed effects. An important advantage of this approach is that it eliminates any time-invariant individual characteristics (for example, genetic factors) so that the estimated effect is less vulnerable to unobserved or poorly measured differences between individual respondents. This model, however, does not rule out a possibility that some change in respondents' lives between wave 1 and wave 2 of the panel may have led to matching changes in both religiosity and good neighborliness.

The ANCOVA model, on the other hand, adjusts for the initial differences in the outcome variable by including the outcome measure (e.g., good neighborliness) at time 1 as a control variable. We can also adjust for the initial difference in religiosity by including the intervention variable (e.g., religiosity) at time 1 as a control variable. Sociologist Paul Allison suggests that this model could be particularly relevant when the outcome at time 1 affects who experiences the intervention and who does not—for example, when good neighborliness at time 1 influences whether one becomes more religious between time 1 and time 2.

As sociologists Stephen Morgan and Christopher Winship point out, the two models make different assumptions about how the outcome variable would have changed had there been no intervention.[3] Unfortunately, testing which assumptions better fit our data is impossible without at least three waves of panel data. Without such data, we focus on whether the two approaches yield similar results. If the results from the two models are consistent, that suggests that our findings are not sensitive to the model's particular assumptions.

In the course of our analyses we estimated many models, to test for the robustness of our conclusions. If changes in the model specification do not significantly alter the results, we can be more confident in that conclusion. Here for reasons of space we offer only two illustrative models from our panel analysis, one predicting good neighborliness from religious social networks and one predicting interfaith tolerance from bridging religious ties.

The first two models in the table below show that the respondent's social networks in his or her congregation predict the frequency of volunteering, regardless of which model we choose. The

ANCOVA model (model 1) controls for the frequency of volunteering and church attendance in 2006 (time 1) along with many other social and demographic characteristics. Still, congregational social networks significantly predict the frequency of volunteering in 2007 (time 2). In model 2, we estimated the same relationship between congregational social networks and the frequency of volunteering using the change score method. This model controls for one time-varying covariate, that is, change in church attendance between 2006 and 2007. Although the size of the coefficient is smaller than in model 1, congregational social networks still significantly predict the frequency of volunteering. The next two models examine the relationship between bridging friendships with evangelical Protestants and the respondent's feeling thermometer score toward evangelical Protestants as a group (how warmly he or she viewed that group). Again, both ANCOVA and change score models yield similar results: Having bridging friendships with evangelicals is positively related to holding warmer thermometer scores toward evangelical Protestants in both models.

Translating Multivariate Statistical Results Into Intuitive Metrics

Throughout *American Grace*, we report and display results derived from multivariate statistical models. As any reader of social science research can attest, such results are typically presented in complex tables of coefficients, of which Table A2.1 is a perfect illustration. To ensure that our findings are interpretable to readers who are not necessarily well-versed in statistical methods, we have translated them into more intuitive metrics. Typically, we report the percentage of people who have done something or who hold a particular attitude. For example, in Chapter 11 we display Figure 11.5, which shows the relationship between religiosity and various political attitudes. Here we display the graph for abortion attitudes contained in that figure as an illustration of how we have generated the results we display throughout the book. Each bar represents the percent-

A2.1

PARING ANCOVA AND CHANGE-SCORE MODELS

	(1)+ Frequency of volunteering in 2007	(2)† Frequency of volunteering (2007–2006)	(3)+ Feeling thermometer toward evangelicals in 2007	(4)† Feeling thermometer toward evangelicals (2007–2006)
ency of volunteering per year in)06 (logged)	0.546‡ (0.020)			
ch attendance in 2006	0.002 (0.001)			
regational social networks in 2006	0.239** (0.073)			
ch attendance (2007–2006)		0.004* (0.002)		
ber of friends in 2006		0.156* (0.074)	-0.198 (0.159)	
iosity index in 2006			6.136*** (0.598)	
ng thermometer toward evangelical 2006			0.388*** (0.023)	
ing friendship with evangelicals			4.062*** (1.173)	
ber of friends (2007–2006)				1.252*** (1.204)
iosity (2007–2006)				1.179*** (1.784)
ing friendship with evangelical 2007–2006)				6.850*** (1.524)
tant	-0.041 (0.251)	1.487‡ (0.058)	35.805*** (4.356)	45.322*** (2.785)
ber of group		1914		1909
ber of observations	1737	2800	1533	2905
uared	0.405	0.006	0.382	0.025

ESE MODELS WERE ESTIMATED WITH ALL OF THE STANDARD CONTROL VARIABLES. THE RESULTS THE CONTROL VARIABLES HAVE BEEN OMITTED.

ESE MODELS WERE ESTIMATED WITH THE FIXED-EFFECTS METHOD.

$.05$, ** p <0.01, *** p <0.001

age of people in that "quintile of religiosity"—intuitively, the slice of the population with that level of religiosity—who oppose abortion. In generating that percentage, we have held constant an array of demographic variables. More technically, we have estimated a statistical model using the ordered logit estimator with the following controls: age, gender, living in the South, education, marital status, having children, ethnicity (Latino), and race (African American). We then used CLARIFY, a statistical routine developed by Gary King,

Figure 11.5

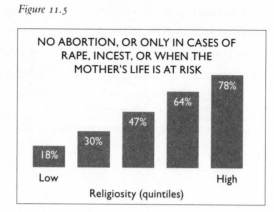

NO ABORTION, OR ONLY IN CASES OF
RAPE, INCEST, OR WHEN THE
MOTHER'S LIFE IS AT RISK

78%

64%

47%

30%

18%

Low   High

Religiosity (quintiles)

Michael Tomz, and Jason Wittenberg, to translate the coefficient for religiosity into the predicted probability of a respondent selecting each of the possible response options. In doing so, we set the control variables to their mean values. CLARIFY uses statistical simulation (often called "Monte Carlo" simulation) to generate predicted values from a statistical model using any of the standard estimators: linear regression, logistic regression, ordered logit, etc.

The creators of CLARIFY have described it in more technical terms:

> CLARIFY uses stochastic simulation techniques to help research- ers interpret and present their statistical results. It uses whatever statistical model you have chosen and as such changes no statisti- cal assumptions. As a first step, the program draws simulations of the main and ancillary parameters from their asymptotic sam- pling distribution, in most cases a multivariate normal with mean equal to the vector of parameter estimates and variance equal to the variance-covariance matrix of estimates.[4]

The program draws a set of simulated parameters (we have used the program's default of 1,000 simulations). The CLARIFY user then sets the explanatory variables to the appropriate value and generates a predicted value for the dependent variable—a far more intuitive outcome than reporting a coefficient. A further advantage of using CLARIFY in this way is that the predicted values are estimated with a measure of uncertainty, as it produces confidence intervals for the values. These are essentially a "margin of error," which have enabled us to see when two values are different enough from one another that they would only have occurred by chance in 5 (or fewer) trials out of 100.

NOTES

1. RELIGIOUS POLARIZATION AND PLURALISM IN AMERICA

1. See the Supreme Court case *Van Orden v. Perry*, 545 U.S. 677 (2005).

2. Philip E. Converse, "Religion and Politics: The 1960 Election," in *Elections and the Political Order*, ed. Philip E. Converse, Warren E. Miller, Donald E. Stokes, and Angus Campbell (New York: John Wiley & Sons, 1966), 123.

3. Sam Harris, *The End of Faith: Religion, Terror, and the Future of Reason*, 1st ed. (New York: W. W. Norton, 2004); Christopher Hitchens, *God Is Not Great* (New York: Twelve Hachette Book Group, 2007); Stephen L. Carter, *The Culture of Disbelief: How American Law and Politics Trivialize Religious Devotion* (New York: Basic Books, 1993); Richard John Neuhaus, *The Naked Public Square: Religion and Democracy in America*, 2nd ed. (Grand Rapids: William B. Eerdmans, 1997).

4. James Davison Hunter, *Culture Wars: The Struggle to Define America* (New York: Basic Books, 1991).

5. The statistics in this and the following two paragraphs all come from the Faith Matters surveys, described in detail below.

6. See, however, research on the accuracy of reporting church attendance, which suggests that we should take these self-reports with a grain of salt: C. Kirk Hadaway, Penny Long Marler, and Mark Chaves, "What the Polls Don't Show: A Closer Look at U.S. Church Attendance," *American Sociological Review* 58, no. 6 (1993); Robert D. Woodberry, "When Surveys Lie and People Tell the Truth: How Surveys Oversample Church Attenders," *American Sociological Review* 63, no. 1 (1998); Tom W. Smith, "A Review of Church Attendance Measures," *American Sociological Review* 32, no. 1 (1998); and Mark Chaves, *Continuity and Change in American Religion*, Chapter 1 (forthcoming 2011).

7. These results all come from the 2005–2007 World Values Survey.

8. The British figures come from a replication of the Faith Matters surveys (described below) that we have conducted in the U.K.

9. The precise wording of the question is:

> We'd like to ask about various ways in which some people practice religion, whether or not they belong to a particular congregation. The first/next item

is say grace or give blessings to God before meals. Do you do this several times a day, roughly once a day, a few times a week, roughly once a week, occasionally, or never?

Other items in the list include reading scripture, tuning into religious programs on TV or radio, and praying outside of religious services. The order of the items was randomized for each respondent.

10. See Appendix 1 for details about the two Faith Matters surveys.

11. Mark A. Noll, *American Evangelical Christianity: An Introduction* (Malden, MA: Blackwell, 2001), 10.

12. Christian Smith, *American Evangelicalism: Embattled and Thriving* (Chicago: University of Chicago Press, 1998), 5.

13. Some analysts use the term "conservative Christians" to refer to this group, but this terminology risks conflating theology and political ideology. See, for example, Andrew M. Greeley and Michael Hout, *The Truth About Conservative Christians: What They Think and What They Believe* (Chicago: University of Chicago Press, 2006).

14. Brian Steensland et al., "The Measure of American Religion: Toward Improving the State of the Art," *Social Forces* 79, no. 1 (2000).

15. We are grateful to John Green for his extraordinary generosity in assisting us in classifying Protestant denominations as either evangelical or mainline.

16. In the Faith Matters surveys nondenominational Christians look like denominational evangelicals on virtually every variable. This same pattern is found in the General Social Survey after the 1980s, though prior to the 1980s the then much smaller group of nondenominational Christians had looked like liberal Protestants. Since nondenominational Christians as a group now seem indistinguishable from denominational evangelicals, we have assigned all nondenominational Christians to the evangelical tradition. We have not made this assignment on the basis of the beliefs or behavior of individual respondents, so as not to conflate belonging with the other dimensions of religiosity. If we had used, say, a type of religious behavior (church attendance, for instance) to pick out individual evangelicals, then we would not be able to compare evangelicals' church attendance to that of other religious traditions.

The following denominations are coded as evangelical: Assembly/ Assemblies of God, Evangelical/Born Again, Brethren (or the Brethren Church), Christian Missionary Alliance, Christian Reformed Church, Church (or Churches) of Christ, Church of the Brethren, Church of the Nazarene, Four Square Gospel, Free Methodist Church, Grace Brethren Church, Holiness, Missouri Synod Lutheran, Wisconsin Synod Lutheran, Nazarene, Pentecostal, Plymouth Brethren, Salvation Army/ American Rescue Workers, Southern Baptist, Wesleyan, Free Church,

Nondenominational-Independent Evangelical, Independent Baptist, Non-denominational/Independent Baptist, Missionary Baptist, National Baptist, First Baptist, General Baptist, Free Will Baptist, Primitive Baptist, other Baptist (not further specified), Free Methodist, Christian Methodist Episcopal/Methodist Episcopal, other Methodist, Presbyterian Church in America (Evangelical Presbyterian), other Presbyterian, Evangelical (not further specified), Born Again/Bible/Gospel/Missionary, Evangelical Free Church/Free Church, Evangelical Covenant Church, Evangelical, "Just Christian" (nondenominational), "I am just a Christian," Church of God (not further specified), Church of God/Anderson, Indiana, Church of God/Cleveland, Tennessee, Church of God, Christian Missionary Alliance, Pentecostal Church of God, Pentecostal Holiness Church, United Pentecostal, Pentecostal (not further specified), interdenominational or community church, Nondenominational Christian/Baptist/Protestant, Seventh-Day Adventist, Mennonite.

17. Kenneth D. Wald and Allison Calhoun-Brown, *Religion and Politics in the United States* (Lanham, MD: Rowman & Littlefield, 2007), 30.

18. The following denominations are coded as mainline Protestant: American Baptist Churches in USA, Congregationalist, Disciples of Christ, Evangelical Lutheran Church in America, Reformed Church in America, United Church of Christ, United Methodist Church, United Presbyterian Church, Lutheran (not further specified), Methodist (not further specified), Presbyterian Church USA/United Presbyterian Church, Interfaith or Ecumenical Protestant Church.

19. For our purposes, we define a Black Protestant as any African American who identifies as any kind of Protestant. We have not limited Black Protestants to those who attend a historically black denomination, owing to the fact that predominantly African American congregations are found within many Protestant denominations. For example, the emphatically black Chicago church attended by Barack Obama and led by Rev. Jeremiah Wright is affiliated with the United Church of Christ, not a denomination typically associated with Black Protestantism. Indeed, it is classified as within the mainline Protestant tradition. We also experimented with defining Black Protestants as African Americans who attend a congregation that is composed predominantly of African Americans (which is possible because we asked respondents to report on the racial composition of their congregation). As noted in Chapter 9, when we do so the distinctiveness of Black Protestants is only more pronounced. However, for the sake of using the simplest possible classification system, we have opted to classify Black Protestants as "Protestants who are black."

20. Technically, Mormons are members of the Church of Jesus Christ of Latter-day Saints.

21. Owing to the large number of respondents in our Faith Matters survey, we have enough Jewish and Mormon respondents for reliable analysis. Their relatively small share, however, means that we are not able to make further distinctions within these two traditions. Thus, for example, we are unable to differentiate between Orthodox and Reform Jews.

22. For instance, the 2006 Faith Matters survey has thirteen Muslim respondents, which is too few for statistical comparisons.

23. "None" has become the standard term used by sociologists of religion when referring to people with no religious affiliation. For an early use of the term, see Glenn M. Vernon, "The Religious 'Nones': A Neglected Category," *Journal for the Scientific Study of Religion* 7, no. 2 (1968).

24. Mark Chaves, *Continuity and Change in American Religion*, Chapter 2.

25. The six measures are:

   • How important is religion in your daily life? Is it extremely important, very important, somewhat important, or not at all important?

   • We'd like to know how important various things are to your sense of who you are. When you think about yourself, how important is your religion to your sense of who you are—very important, moderately important, slightly important, or not at all important?

   • Would you call yourself a strong believer in your religion or not a very strong believer in your religion? [Strong, not very strong, somewhat strong, no religion]

   • How often do you attend religious services? [Several times a week, every week, nearly every week, 2–3 times a month, about once a month, several times a year, about once or twice a year, less than once a year, never]

   • We'd like to ask about various ways in which some people practice religion, whether or not they belong to a particular congregation. The next item is prayer outside of religious services. Do you do this several times a day, roughly once a day, a few times a week, roughly once a week, occasionally, or never?

   • We're going to ask you about various things that some people believe in and others don't. The first item is [God]. Are you absolutely sure you believe in God, somewhat sure, not quite sure, not at all sure, or are you sure you do not believe in God? [Other items in this question included heaven, hell, life after death, and horoscopes; the order of items was randomized.]

   For statistical mavens, here are the results of the factor analysis.

   Factor loadings:

Importance of religion	0.86
Religion is important to sense of self	0.82
Strong believer in religion	0.79

Religious attendance	0.74
Frequency of prayer	0.75
Belief in God	0.72
Eigenvalue	2.57

26. In addition to a general sample of the British population, our Faith Matters survey in the U.K. also included an oversample of the British Muslim population.

27. The two camps come closer to consensus on a middle way, as 39 percent of less religious Americans endorse the view that evolution has been guided by God, compared to 21 percent of the most religious segment of the population.

28. Fifty-nine percent of the most religious, 7 percent of the least.

29. Roughly 75 percent of both groups say they ate out in the last seven days, while 13 percent of each attended a sporting event during that same period of time.

30. Both groups report watching roughly three hours of TV per day.

31.

	Top 20% of religiosity	Bottom 20% of religiosity
More spending on crime	69%	60%
More spending on border	52%	64%
More spending on the poor	66%	56%

SOURCE: FAITH MATTERS SURVEY, 2006.

32. The gender differences are as follows, with the specific percentage point difference in parentheses:

Spiritual person (10)

Experienced presence of God (9)

God's laws (12)

God created world (10)

Good and evil (9)

World will end soon (9)

Scripture is literal (7)

Everyone will answer for sins (6)

Read scripture daily (9)

Talk about religion daily (9)

Read religious books daily (6)

33. Figure 1.5 displays the relative religiosity in each state according to the Pew Research Center's Religious Landscape Survey. This survey has a much larger number of respondents than Faith Matters, and thus produces

more reliable estimates for the states. Even then, it groups the following pairs of states together, treating them as one unit: Connecticut and Rhode Island; Montana and Wyoming; North and South Dakota. It also combines Maryland and Washington, D.C. The Religious Landscape Survey includes items that are very similar to those asked in Faith Matters, although we are unable to replicate our religiosity index precisely. The religiosity index we report thus includes:

> % in state who are absolutely certain that there is a God
> % who say that religion is very important in their lives
> % who attend religious services weekly
> % who pray at least once daily

Across the eight major Census regions the Faith Matters religiosity index is highly correlated with this Pew index: 0.98.

34. We highlight this percentage because serving in a leadership position within a congregation is an example of how churches build civic skills, like knowing how to organize a meeting or give a speech. Congregations are often an incubator for such skills, especially among people who do not have the opportunity to develop them through their education or workplace. In this way, congregations can serve as a bridge to other forms of civic involvement. See Sidney Verba, Kay Lehman Schlozman, and Henry E. Brady, *Voice and Equality: Civic Voluntarism in American Politics* (Cambridge: Harvard University Press, 1995).

35. In this case, "churchgoer" simply means someone who reports having a congregation where they at least occasionally attend services. We use the term "church" here and elsewhere as a necessary shorthand to mean all places of worship; this avoids the clunky phrasing of "church, synagogue, temple, mosque." We mean no offense by our use of the term.

36. Catholicism is obviously another major religious tradition that is organized into congregations. However, historically the Catholic parish has differed from the typical Protestant congregation in that Catholics were expected to attend the parish within whose boundaries they lived, while membership in Protestant congregations is a matter of choice, not place. That said, however, a Catholic parish typically provides the same services as a Protestant congregation.

37. R. Stephen Warner, "The Place of Congregation in the Contemporary American Religious Configuration," in *American Congregations: New Perspectives in the Study of Congregations*, Volume 2, ed. James P. Wind and James M. Lewis (Chicago: University of Chicago Press, 1994), 54–100.

38. Alan Wolfe, *The Transformation of American Religion: How We Actually Live Our Faith* (New York: Free Press, 2003), 228.

39. R. F. Spencer, "Social Structure of a Contemporary Japanese-American Buddhist Church," *Social Forces* 26, no. 3 (1948): 281, 288.

40. All the congregational leaders we contacted consented to have their congregation included in our study. We are grateful for their cooperation. Unless otherwise indicated, any factual information reported about a given congregation comes from our own observations or those interviews.

2. VIGNETTES: THE OLD AND THE NEW

1. The Episcopal Church in the United States of America is a "Province" of the Anglican Communion, a worldwide organization of churches considered to be in full communion with the Church of England. Because of its membership in this association, and because its historical and doctrinal roots lie with the Church of England, the term "Anglican" is often used interchangeably with "Episcopal" and "Episcopalian."

2. In a July 2009 interview, Fr. Tony Buquor noted that since the writing of this section Trinity Concord has experienced "a slight increase in average Sunday attendance" due to an influx of younger families, "many" of whom are "former Roman Catholics." Between 2003 and 2009 Church School attendance tripled due to that same influx. Fr. Buquor also notes that parish life has rallied on some fronts: Trinity Concord's outreach relationship with an inner-city parish has been revitalized; and the handicrafts group, which currently gathers biweekly, recently held an informational meeting designed to attract new members, and drew twenty intergenerational attendees.

3. A frequent way in which parish size was described by both the clergy and laity interviewed here is through a framework developed by the Alban Institute, an ecumenical think tank that studies congregational life. This typology includes the pastoral parish, community parish, program parish, and corporate parish. Often congregations will use this language in describing the nature of their church, and their goals for growth.

4. "Promise and Paradox: A Parish Profile of Trinity Church in the City of Boston 2005" (Boston: Trinity Church, 2005), H1.

5. Ibid., 3.

6. Ibid., B4.

7. Peter Drucker, as quoted by Krista Tippet, "Rick and Kay Warren at Saddleback," American Public Media, *Speaking of Faith*, August 21, 2008, interview. <http://speakingoffaith.publicradio.org/programs/2008/warren/transcript.shtml> (accessed June 10, 2010).

8. Warren, Rick. *The Purpose Driven Church: Growth Without Compromising Your Message and Mission.* Grand Rapids: Zondervan, 1995, 56.

9. "Rick and Kay Warren at Saddleback." American Public Media, *Speaking*

of Faith, August 21, 2008, interview. <http://speakingoffaith.publicradio .org/programs/2008/warren/transcript.shtml> (accessed June 10, 2010).

3. RELIGIOSITY IN AMERICA: THE HISTORICAL BACKDROP

1. For excellent treatments of this period, see Robert Wuthnow, *The Restructuring of American Religion* (Princeton: Princeton University Press, 1988); Alan Wolfe, *The Transformation of American Religion: How We Actually Live Our Faith* (New York: Free Press, 2003); Patrick Allitt, *Religion in America Since 1945: A History*, Columbia Histories of Modern American Life (New York: Columbia University Press, 2003); Sydney E. Ahlstrom, *A Religious History of the American People* (New Haven: Yale University Press, 1972); Andrew M. Greeley, *Religious Change in America* (Cambridge: Harvard University Press, 1989); Wade Clark Roof and William McKinney, *American Mainline Religion: Its Changing Shape and Future* (New Brunswick: Rutgers University Press, 1987); and Claude S. Fischer and Michael Hout, *Century of Difference: How America Changed in the Last One Hundred Years* (New York: Russell Sage Foundation, 2006), Chapter 8.

2. Roger Finke and Rodney Stark, *The Churching of America, 1776–1990: Winners and Losers in Our Religious Economy* (New Brunswick: Rutgers University Press, 1992); E. Brooks Holifield, "Towards a History of American Congregations," in *American Congregations*, ed. James P. Wind and James W. Lewis (Chicago: University of Chicago Press, 1998), 23–53; C. Kirk Hadaway, Penny Long Marler, and Mark Chaves, "What the Polls Don't Show: A Closer Look at U.S. Church Attendance," *American Sociological Review* 58, no. 6 (1993); Michael Hout and Andrew M. Greeley, "The Center Doesn't Hold: Church Attendance in the United States, 1940–1984," *American Sociological Review* 52, no. 3 (1987); and Greeley, *Religious Change in America*.

3. Lincoln Barnett, "God and the American People," *Ladies' Home Journal* (November 1948): 230.

4. Gallup Poll Reports. The Gallup membership figures have showed signs of uneven decline since the 1970s, and over the last decade the figure had fallen to 63 percent in 2009.

5. Gallup Poll reports; for 1948 only, Barnett, "God and the American People"; Mark Chaves and Shawna L. Anderson, "Continuity and Change in American Religion, 1972–2008," in *Social Trends in the United States, 1972–2008: Evidence from the General Social Survey*, ed. Peter Marsden (Princeton: Princeton University Press, forthcoming).

6. Wuthnow, *The Restructuring of American Religion*, 5–6.

7. Scott M. Meyers, "An Interactive Model of Religiosity Inheritance: The Importance of Family Context," *American Sociological Review* 61, no. 5 (1996); Darren E. Sherkat, "Counterculture or Continuity? Competing

Influences on Baby Boomers' Religious Orientations and Participation," *Social Forces* 76, no. 3 (1998); Michele Dillon and Paul Wink, *In the Course of a Lifetime: Tracing Religious Belief, Practice, and Change* (Berkeley: University of California Press, 2007).

8. Strictly speaking, whether society changes as a result of life cycle change depends on the relative size of various birth cohorts, but for the moment we can leave that qualification aside by assuming a constant birth rate.

9. Figure 3.1 is based on the General Social Survey, 1972–2008. Essentially the same patterns appear in the entirely independent National Election Studies archives, 1952–2008, which gives us reasonable confidence that the patterns are robust.

10. Throughout this book, we often employ a method to smooth out the trendlines displayed in the figures. Invariably, surveys produce "noise" in any given year—random perturbations that cause a trendline to bounce up and down. The trends are clearest, therefore, when we cancel out the noise, just as an audio recording is clearest when static is canceled out. The specific "noise-canceling" method we have employed is called LOESS smoothing. In technical language, LOESS fits a regression line for each year using that year's data point and the data surrounding it. The smoothed value, therefore, is the value that regression line takes at that particular year. In other words, it is similar to a weighted average, since the smoothed values are based on multiple years of data. The more nearby data points that are taken into account, the smoother the line. Conversely, for trends with only a small number of data points, the smoothing will be incomplete (and thus, not very smooth). We express our gratitude to Valerie Lewis for her expertise in smoothing, and all her hard work in generating these figures. For more details, see: William S. Cleveland, "Robust Locally Weighted Regression and Smoothing Scatterplots," *Journal of the American Statistical Association* 74, no. 368 (1979): 829–36. The choppiness evident in the first years for the cohorts born in the 1970s and 1980s reflects the small sample size as these cohorts began to enter adulthood, as well as our related statistical inability to "smooth" those lines.

11. For methodological discussions of how age, period, and cohort effects can be analyzed, see Philip E. Converse, *The Dynamics of Party Support: Cohort-Analyzing Party Identification* (Beverly Hills: Sage Publications, 1976); Glenn Firebaugh, "Methods for Estimating Cohort Replacement Effects," in *Sociological Methodology 1990*, ed. Clifford Clogg (Oxford: Basil Blackwell, 1990), 243–62; and Norval D. Glenn, *Cohort Analysis*, 2nd ed. (Thousand Oaks: Sage Publications, 2005). Because of a mathematical indeterminacy, for the most part we must rely on external assumptions about plausibility and parsimony in making such calculations, although recently advanced

statistical techniques are being developed for these issues; see Yang Yang et al., "The Intrinsic Estimator for Age-Period-Cohort Analysis: What It Is and How to Use It," *American Journal of Sociology* 113, no. 6 (2008).

12. For a virtually identical summary judgment about trends in attendance at religious services, see Chaves and Anderson, "Continuity and Change in American Religion, 1972–2008." See also Stanley Presser and Mark Chaves, "Is Religious Service Attendance Declining?" *Journal for the Scientific Study of Religion* 46, no. 3 (2007).

13. Gallup Poll data on membership in a church or synagogue mimics this long, slow decline in religious commitment, falling (somewhat unevenly) from 76 percent in 1947 to 73 percent in 1965, 71 percent in 1976, 69 percent in 1990, 68 percent in 2000, and 63 percent in 2009. The trend seems to have accelerated since 2000. We suspect that this trend too is mostly attributable to generational processes of cohort replacement, but since the Gallup data on year of birth are not publicly available, we cannot confirm that suspicion.

14. College-bound youth over this period constitute roughly one half of young people, and in many ways they are unrepresentative of all young people. However, according to the General Social Survey, 1972–2008, religious attendance declined slightly more rapidly among non-college-educated young people (18–29) than among their college-educated peers. Thus, the trend in Figure 3.3 probably understates the overall generational decline.

15. Using surveys repeated at a small sample of colleges between 1920 and 1970, Dean Hoge observed declining levels from 1920 to the late 1930s, an increase through the early 1950s, and then a rapid decline to 1969. Dean R. Hoge, *Commitment on Campus: Changes in Religion and Values over Five Decades* (Philadelphia: Westminster, 1974).

16. These responses mirror what we know from other evidence—bigger intergenerational drops among Catholics, mainline Protestants, and Jews, smaller drops among evangelical and Black Protestants, biggest in the Northeast, slightest in the South. To be sure, we are comparing religious attendance at a time in the lives of the parents' generation when that generation had children at home with the respondents' own attendance now, but the declines shown in Figure 3.4 cannot be explained by the modest increase in religious attendance (one more church service per year) that is associated with the fact of having children at home. Among respondents who now have children at home (and are thus at the same stage of life as their parents were when they were growing up), 46 percent say that they attend church less now than their parents did then, exactly the same as for the sample as a whole.

17. On the history of this period, see Ahlstrom, *A Religious History of the American People* and Wuthnow, *The Restructuring of American Religion*, 53–53. On

the negative effect of the world wars on religion in the U.K., see Robert Currie, Alan D. Gilbert, and Lee Horsley, *Churches and Churchgoers: Patterns of Church Growth in the British Isles Since 1700* (Oxford: Clarendon Press, 1977).

18. S. Presser and L. Stinson, "Data Collection Mode and Social Desirability Bias in Self-Reported Religious Attendance," *American Sociological Review* 63, no. 1 (1998); Hadaway, Marler, and Chaves, "What the Polls Don't Show."

19. Systematic evidence on trends in church attendance in the 1940s and 1950s, especially among blacks, is extremely limited. The Gallup raw data are unavailable for analysis, so we have to rely on published Gallup figures. Thus, for detailed breakdowns by gender, race, education, and race, we are limited to the National Election Studies, beginning in 1952. The NES survey reports slightly lower average weekly church attendance than the Gallup Poll, but basically tracks the Gallup cohort patterns shown in Figure 3.6. Our systematic knowledge of black religiosity nationwide in those years is therefore limited to the 100–150 black respondents in each biennial NES survey. With all their weaknesses, those data suggest that as early as 1952 (and probably before that) black churchgoing was relatively high (upward of 50 percent weekly), and that it began to slip from that elevated level in the late 1950s. Blacks contributed more than their share to the high *levels* of churchgoing in the 1950s, but they seem to have contributed less than their share to the *growth* of churchgoing.

20. This is precisely the same cohort praised as the "Greatest Generation" by Tom Brokaw in *The Greatest Generation* (New York: Random House, 1998), and as "the long civic generation" in Robert D. Putnam, *Bowling Alone: The Collapse and Revival of American Community* (New York: Simon & Schuster, 2000). Within this cohort it was the college men whose rate of church attendance rose most sharply. According to the National Election Studies archives, weekly churchgoing among college-educated white men almost doubled in little more than a decade between 1952 and 1964 from about 29 percent to about 53 percent. The comparable increases among women and less educated men were somewhat smaller.

21. Ahlstrom, *A Religious History of the American People*, 952.

22. Allitt, *Religion in America Since 1945*, 33.

23. Ahlstrom, *A Religious History of the American People*, 953; our inflation adjustment. See also Wuthnow, *The Restructuring of American Religion*, 27.

24. Robert Wuthnow, "Recent Pattern of Secularization: A Problem of Generations?" *American Sociological Review* 41, no. 5 (1976); Wuthnow, *The Restructuring of American Religion*, 17.

25. "By 1950, the number of students enrolled in Protestant and Jewish seminaries was about double the prewar figure, while at Catholic seminaries

it was up by 30 percent." Wuthnow, *The Restructuring of American Religion*, 37.

26. George Gallup and D. Michael Lindsay, *Surveying the Religious Landscape: Trends in U.S. Beliefs* (Harrisburg: Morehouse, 1999), 7, 19.

27. Barnett, "God and the American People," 231.

28. Putnam, *Bowling Alone.*

29. George Gallup and Jim Castelli, *The People's Religion: American Faith in the 90's* (New York: Macmillan, 1989), 9.

30. Robert N. Bellah, "Civil Religion in America," *Daedalus* 96, no. 1 (1967).

31. Ahlstrom, *A Religious History of the American People*, 951.

32. Ibid., 954–55.

33. Ibid., 954.

34. Allitt, *Religion in America Since 1945*, 31.

35. Maurice Isserman and Michael Kazin, *America Divided: The Civil War of the 1960s*, 3rd ed. (New York: Oxford University Press, 2008), 251.

36. Wuthnow, *The Restructuring of American Religion*, 138–45. Ahlstrom, *A Religious History of the American People*, 747–48, 957–59; Martin E. Marty, *Modern American Religion*, Volume 3: *Under God, Indivisible, 1941–1960* (Chicago: University of Chicago Press, 1986); George M. Marsden, *Fundamentalism and American Culture*, 2nd ed. (New York: Oxford University Press, 2006).

37. Uta Andrea Balbier, "Billy Graham's Crusades in the 1950s: Neo-Evangelicalism Between Civil Religion, Media, and Consumerism," *Bulletin of the German Historical Institute* (Spring 2009), 71–80.

38. Will Herberg, *Protestant—Catholic—Jew: An Essay in American Religious Sociology* (Garden City: Doubleday, 1955); Gerhard Lenski, *The Religious Factor: A Sociological Study of Religion's Impact on Politics, Economics, and Family Life* (New York: Doubleday, 1961), esp. 327. That two classic accounts of contemporary American religion would prove so quickly and fundamentally wrong is a cautionary reminder to the authors of this book of the need for modesty.

39. Wuthnow, *The Restructuring of American Religion*, 71–172.

4. RELIGIOSITY IN AMERICA: SHOCK AND TWO AFTERSHOCKS

1. Sydney E. Ahlstrom, *A Religious History of the American People* (New Haven: Yale University Press, 1972), 1080–81.

2. David J. Harding and Christopher Jencks, "Changing Attitudes Toward Premarital Sex: Cohort, Period, and Aging Effects," *Public Opinion Quarterly* 67, no. 2 (2003).

3. Judith Treas, "How Cohorts, Education, and Ideology Shaped a New Sexual Revolution on American Attitudes Toward Nonmarital Sex, 1972–1998," *Sociological Perspectives* 45, no. 3 (2002).

4. Attitudes toward extramarital sex remained much more conservative than attitudes toward premarital sex, and moved in a generally more conservative direction over the rest of the century. Attitudes toward homosexuality remained conservative until the 1990s, when rapid liberalization occurred, as we discuss toward the end of this chapter.

5. Changes in views on sexual issues were especially dramatic among Catholics. Between 1963 and 1974, the fraction of all Catholics (not just the young) saying that premarital sex is always wrong fell from 74 percent to 35 percent, that remarriage after divorce is always wrong from 52 percent to 17 percent, and that contraception is always wrong from 56 percent to 17 percent. Andrew M. Greeley, *The Catholic Revolution: New Wine, Old Wineskins, and the Second Vatican Council* (Berkeley: University of California Press, 2004), 39.

6. Maurice Isserman and Michael Kazin, *America Divided: The Civil War of the 1980s*, 3rd ed. (New York: Oxford University Press, 2008), 249.

7. Gallup Poll reports and General Social Survey, 1972–2008.

8. Robert Wuthnow, *The Restructuring of American Religion* (Princeton: Princeton University Press, 1988), 145.

9. George Gallup and Jim Castelli, *The People's Religion: American Faith in the 90's* (New York: Macmillan, 1989), 12; Ahlstrom, *A Religious History of the American People*, 1086; Wuthnow, *The Restructuring of American Religion*, 159.

10. Gallup and Castelli, *The People's Religion*, 12. See also Ahlstrom, *A Religious History of the American People*, 1017. Father Andrew Greeley, in his *Religious Change in America* (Cambridge: Harvard University Press, 1989), 47–50, provides evidence that the birth control edict itself accounted for most, if not all, of the decline in Catholic observance.

11. According to the Gallup Poll reports, between 1957 and 1973 average weekly church attendance fell from 74 percent to 55 percent among Catholics and from 44 percent to 37 percent among Protestants. Among people under thirty attendance fell between the 1950s and the 1970s from 40 percent to 30 percent among Protestants, and from 73 percent to 35 percent among Catholics. See http://www.gallup.com/poll/117382/Church-Going-Among-Catholics-Slides-Tie-Protestants.aspx (accessed June 10, 2010). Even in our 2006 Faith Matters survey, nearly half a century later, the boomer generation constituted a disproportionate share of all ex-Catholics (a large group that itself constituted at least a third of all Americans who had been raised as Catholics).

12. Isserman and Kazin, *America Divided*, 258.

13. For a largely sympathetic account of religious innovations of the 1960s, see Robert S. Ellwood, *The Sixties Spiritual Awakening: American Religion Moving from Modern to Postmodern* (New Brunswick: Rutgers University

Press, 1994). See also Robert Wuthnow, *After Heaven: Spirituality in America Since the 1950s* (Berkeley: University of California Press, 1998).

14. Robert N. Bellah et al., *Habits of the Heart: Individualism and Commitment in American Life* (Berkeley: University of California Press, 1985), 221.

15. Amanda Porterfield, *The Transformation of American Religion: The Story of a Late-Twentieth-Century Awakening* (New York: Oxford University Press, 2001), 18.

16. Wuthnow, *The Restructuring of American Religion*, 12, 144–52, 173–214; Isserman and Kazin, *America Divided*, 254.

17. All data in this paragraph have been compiled from Gallup Poll Reports.

18. Figure 3.6 is based on Gallup Poll archives, but the same pattern appears in the National Election Studies data, which show a drop in weekly or near-weekly church attendance from 47 percent in 1956 to 34 percent in 1966 among Americans aged twenty-five to thirty-four.

19. In the National Election Studies data, weekly or near-weekly church attendance among all blacks fell from 50 percent in the 1950s to 43 percent in the 1960s and 35 percent in the 1970s, a drop roughly three times as large as the comparable drop among whites in those same decades. The decline in black churchgoing from the 1950s to the 1970s was essentially identical among men and women and among Northerners and Southerners, but it was almost entirely concentrated among blacks under thirty. Similarly, the Gallup Poll reports show essentially no black–white difference in religious attendance from the mid-1960s until the late 1970s, when blacks resumed their traditional edge in religiosity. If these data are accurate, it is startling that in the very years of the black civil rights movement, led in large part by young black churchmen, young blacks were deserting church in even greater numbers than were their white counterparts. As a historical matter, this issue deserves greater attention.

20. National Election Studies data. See also the evidence in Figure 4.2 from the annual American Freshman survey.

21. General Social Survey. Precisely the same pattern appears in the National Election Studies, using a slightly different measure of church attendance: When the boomers' parents had been in their thirties, 45 percent of them attended church weekly or near-weekly. When the boomers were in their thirties, only 30 percent did so.

22. The fraction of Americans who said religion was losing influence rose from 14 percent in 1957 to 31 percent in 1962 and 70 percent by 1969–1979. Gallup Poll reports, Gallup and Castelli, *The People's Religion*, 10; George Gallup and D. Michael Lindsay, *Surveying the Religious Landscape: Trends in U.S. Beliefs* (Harrisburg: Morehouse, 1999), 7.

23. Gallup and Castelli, *The People's Religion*, 11.

24. According to the General Social Survey, people who had at least some col-

lege education remained a minority of the population aged eighteen to twenty-nine until the 1990s.

25. Dean R. Hoge, Cynthia L. Luna, and David K. Miller, "Trends in College Students' Values Between 1952 and 1979: A Return of the Fifties?" *Sociology of Education* 54, no. 4 (1981). Comparable surveys of Marquette University students in 1961, 1971, and 1982 show precisely the same pattern: Students in this Midwestern Catholic college in 1961 were very conservative on religious, social, and sexual issues. A decade later their counterparts were surprisingly more liberal on virtually all dimensions; Weekly attendance at Mass, for example, had fallen from 95 percent to less than 50 percent. After another decade virtually all these trends were reversed, with the exception of issues of sexual morality. David O. Moberg and Dean R. Hoge, "Catholic College Students' Religion and Moral Attitudes," *Review of Religious Research* 28, no. 2 (1986).

26. Our generalization about the changing meaning of "nondenominational" is based on our extensive examination of the religious views and behavior of this category in the General Social Survey, 1973–2008. Another group of GSS respondents says that they belong to no denomination, but rarely attend church. They share none of the religious characteristics of evangelicals, so we follow the standard practice and exclude these non-church attending nondenominational Christians from the category of evangelicals. In contrast, in the Faith Matters data we do include these nondenominational Christians in the evangelical category. See note 16, Chapter 1, for further explanation. In this part of our work we exclude the GSS data from 1972 because of some unexplained anomalies in the sample for that year. Including 1972 would seem to strengthen the rise of the evangelicals, but like other scholars, we lack confidence in the reliability of that year's evidence. We have basically relied on the recoding of the GSS denominational data into the standard "religious tradition" format compiled at http://www.iu.edu/~soc/pdf/RELTRADsyntax_3versions.pdf (accessed June 10, 2010). For the 1973–1983 period the GSS failed to gather sufficiently detailed information on denominational affiliations, however, so for a few anomalous denominations, such as Missouri Synod Lutherans, we have adjusted the raw data to make the GSS evidence consistent over time.

27. Much evidence from our Faith Matters surveys confirms that on many different issues, both sociopolitical (e.g., abortion) and religious (e.g., importance of religion in their personal lives), evangelicals and nones are polar opposites. We use the word "extremes" in this descriptive sense, with no implication that either pole is "extremist" in any pejorative sense.

28. Because until very recently the General Social Survey and the National Election Studies interviewed only English speakers, their historical evi-

dence missed most of the growing numbers of Latino immigrants and thus underestimated the Catholic fraction of the population. We have adjusted Figures 4.4, 4.5, and 4.6 to take this problem into account, basing our estimates of Latino Catholics on our own Faith Matters surveys, conducted in Spanish as well as English.

29. Michael Hout and Andrew M. Greeley, "The Center Doesn't Hold: Church Attendance in the United States, 1940–1984," *American Sociological Review* 52, no. 3 (1987); Greeley, *Religious Change in America*, 43–45.

30. Strictly speaking, we allocate people to pews on the basis of the religious identification of the people, not on the basis of what pews they are actually sitting in. Examined in detail, that is not always accurate, since people occasionally attend services in denominations other than the one that they claim as their own. See *Many Americans Mix Multiple Faiths* (Pew Forum on Religion & Public Life, December 2009). As a guide to national trends in attendance, however, this is a reasonable shortcut. The tiny slice of nones shown as attending church in Figures 4.5 and 4.6 reflects the fact that a modest fraction of nones nevertheless attend church.

31. Figures 4.5 and 4.6 imply weekly attendance figures of roughly 40 percent, consistent with most national survey reports. As we have noted earlier, most researchers believe that these figures exaggerate actual attendance, but we know of no evidence that this constant exaggeration significantly impairs the comparisons across time or across religious traditions that are our focus here.

32. Greeley, *Religious Change in America*, 83.

33. The scholarship on the rise of evangelicals and the Religious Right has become enormous, and we make no effort here to summarize that literature. Important landmarks are James Davison Hunter, *American Evangelicalism: Conservative Religion and the Quandary of Modernity* (New Brunswick: Rutgers University Press, 1983); Christian Smith, *American Evangelicalism: Embattled and Thriving* (Chicago: University of Chicago Press, 1998); George M. Marsden, *Fundamentalism and American Culture*, 2nd ed. (New York: Oxford University Press, 2006); Andrew M. Greeley and Michael Hout, *The Truth About Conservative Christians: What They Think and What They Believe* (Chicago: University of Chicago Press, 2006).

34. Michael Hout, Andrew Greeley, and Melissa J. Wilde, "The Demographic Imperative in Religious Change in the United States," *The American Journal of Sociology* 107, no. 2 (2001); Greeley and Hout, *The Truth About Conservative Christians*; Michael Hout and Claude S. Fischer, "Why More Americans Have No Religious Preference: Politics and Generations," *American Sociological Review* 67 (April 2002). Hout and his colleagues focus on the evangelical share of Protestants, not the evangelical share of Americans, but the logic of their argument applies to our question as well.

35. According to the General Social Survey, converts as a fraction of all current evangelicals rose from roughly 25 percent in the 1970s to roughly 37 percent in the 2000s. Both the GSS and our 2006 Faith Matters survey converge on our estimate of one third of current evangelicals as converts, even though the surveys use somewhat different measures of religious background and contemporary religious affiliation. Exactly how many evangelicals are converts depends in part on how we categorize families of origin that were mixed and how we categorize nondenominational churches, but no matter what standard of comparison we use—converts to a given tradition as a fraction of all converts, converts to a given tradition as a fraction of all people currently in that tradition, or converts to a given tradition as a fraction of all potential converts to that tradition—evangelical converts were more numerous than converts to all other religious traditions combined (except "none") after the 1970s.

36. In the 1960s Rodney Stark, Charles Y. Glock, and University of California Survey Research Center, *American Piety: The Nature of Religious Commitment* (Berkeley: University of California Press, 1968) found much switching from conservative (evangelical) to liberal (mainline) Protestantism, associated with upward social mobility, but by the 1980s Wade Clark Roof and William McKinney, *American Mainline Religion: Its Changing Shape and Future* (New Brunswick: Rutgers University Press, 1987) concluded that such switching had declined since the 1960s. Stark and Glock found in a nationwide survey in the mid-1960s that "denominational changes among American Protestants follow a pattern of movement to churches with more liberal, modernized theologies and away from churches that are still foursquare for traditional orthodoxy. . . . If our data are reliable, it would appear that members of the conservative bodies are slowly draining away" (latter quote at p. 203). Two decades later, by contrast Roof and McKinney concluded that "all evidence points to less upward switching, or conservative-to-liberal transfer of religious membership, now than in the past. . . . Conservative Protestants show net gains from switching today, in contrast to their earlier losses; they are losing proportionately fewer to other faiths today because of their greater attraction and appeal in the religious marketplace" (Roof and McKinney, p. 175). More generally, on the rising educational and class levels among evangelicals, see Rebekah Peeples Massengil, "Educational Attainment and Cohort Change Among Conservative Protestants," *Journal for the Scientific Study of Religion* 47, no. 4 (2008); Kraig Beyerlein, "Specifying the Impact of Conservative Protestantism on Educational Attainment," *Journal for the Scientific Study of Religion* 43, no. 4 (2004); Ralph E. Pyle, "Trends in Religious Stratification: Have Religious Group Socioeconomic Distinctions Declined in Recent Decades?" *Sociology of Religion* 67, no. 1 (2006); and Christian Smith and Robert Faris,

"Socioeconomic Inequality in the American Religious System: An Update and Assessment," *Journal for the Scientific Study of Religion* 44, no. 1 (2005). Some analysts argue that the increased loyalty of upwardly mobile evangelicals in the 1970s and 1980s can be explained by the higher social status of evangelicalism, whereas others argue that whatever it was that drew nonevangelicals to evangelicalism—moral outrage, in our view—might also explain the increased loyalty of those raised as evangelicals. We have no decisive proof on this issue one way or the other. Some have suggested that the greater loyalty of evangelical offspring might have been due to more thorough religious education among evangelicals, but in the 2006 Faith Matters survey respondents raised as evangelicals are only faintly more likely to report regular religious education as children (73 percent) than respondents raised as Catholics or mainline Protestants (70 percent). The frequency of religious education is slightly lower among more recent cohorts, but that decline is essentially identical for evangelicals, Catholics, and mainline Protestants.

37. Change driven by differences in birth rates between religious traditions must show up between successive birth cohorts, not within the adult lifetime of individuals. In fact, however, an age-period-cohort analysis of the GSS suggests that most of the increase in evangelicals' share of the population between the early 1970s and the early 1990s was within-cohort change, not between-cohort change.

38. The term "born again" gained currency after 1976, when candidate Jimmy Carter proclaimed that he was "born again." We have found no consistent evidence on trends in the frequency of born again experiences. Gallup Poll data are inconsistent and combine "born-again" and "evangelical" in a single question, making it impossible to distinguish the two, but suggesting a rise from about 35 percent in 1975 to about 42 percent in 1996. The General Social Survey began asking about this topic in 1988, and those data offer no evidence at all that the born again experience has become more common, either in the trend between 1988 and 2008 or in generational differences visible in those years. Two thirds of evangelicals describe themselves as "born again," as do one third of nonevangelicals. The decline in biblical literalism among evangelicals is apparent even when we exclude nondenominational evangelicals from our analysis.

39. David A. Roozen and C. Kirk Hadaway, *Church and Denominational Growth* (Nashville: Abingdon, 1993); Rodney Stark and Roger Finke, *Acts of Faith: Explaining the Human Side of Religion* (Berkeley: University of California Press, 2000); Robert Wuthnow, *Sharing the Journey: Support Groups and America's New Quest for Community* (New York: Free Press, 1996).

40. Interview with Rev. Pat Brennan, priest at Holy Family Catholic Community, September 26, 2007.

41. I Corinthians 14:8.

42. Greeley and Hout, *The Truth About Conservative Christians*, 11–39; Joseph B. Tamney, *The Resilience of Conservative Religion: The Case of Popular, Conservative Protestant Congregations* (Cambridge: Cambridge University Press, 2002).

43. D. Michael Lindsey, *Faith in the Halls of Power: How Evangelicals Joined the American Elite* (New York: Oxford University Press, 2007).

44. See also W. Bradford Wilcox, *Soft Patriarchs, New Men: How Christianity Shapes Fathers and Husbands* (Chicago: University of Chicago Press, 2004).

45. Our conclusions here are based on a multivariate analysis of religious identification (evangelical) among white General Social Survey respondents (1973–1991), including controls for gender, education, region, marital status, year of birth, and religious family background, as well as views on school prayer, homosexuality, pornography, premarital sex, feminism, and abortion. Catherine Bolzendahl and Clem Brooks, "Polarization, Secularization, or Differences as Usual? The Denominational Cleavages in U.S. Social Attitudes Since the 1970s," *Sociological Quarterly* 46, no. 1 (2005): 47–48, find significant differences between evangelicals and adherents to other religious traditions in terms of attitudes on gender roles, abortion, and various issues of sexual morality, but that only on premarital sex and abortion did these differences grow after 1970, as evangelicals became more conservative, compared to other religious traditions.

46. For the evidence on presidential preferences in 1980 and 1988, see Gallup and Castelli, *The People's Religion*, 19. Our 2007 Faith Matters survey asked people's feelings about various political and religious groups, using a 0–100 feeling thermometer, where 50 is neutral. Both "evangelical Protestants" (55) and "conservatives" (53) were rated, on average, much more favorably than "the Christian Right" (45), suggesting that this mix of religion and politics had produced a toxic synergy.

47. Louis Bolce and Gerald De Maio, "Religious Outlook, Culture War, Politics and Antipathy Toward Christian Fundamentalists," *Public Opinion Quarterly* 63, no. 1 (1999): 29–61; Gallup and Castelli, *The People's Religion*, 19.

48. Mark Chaves, *Continuity and Change in American Religion*, Chapter 7 (forthcoming, 2011).

49. David Kinnaman and Gabe Lyons, *Unchristian: What a New Generation Really Thinks About Christianity—And Why It Matters* (Grand Rapids: Baker, 2007). Clyde Wilcox and Carin Robinson, *Onward Christian Soldiers*, 4th ed. (Boulder: Westview, 2010), Chapter 2, report that in recent years, organizations of the Religious Right such as Focus on the Family have had serious difficulty in recruiting young members. These groups have found in focus group research that this youth resistance is rooted in young people's

objections to linking religion and politics, and especially to the combative political strategy pursued by the Religious Right.

50. Though there was some attention to religious nones as early as 1968 (Glenn M. Vernon, "The Religious 'Nones': A Neglected Category," *Journal for the Scientific Study of Religion* 7, no. 2 [1968]), they were a small segment of the population at that time. The first major work on the sharp rise in nones in the 1990s was Michael Hout and Claude S. Fischer, "Why More Americans Have No Religious Preference," 165–90.

51. The specific rate of nones depends a bit on how we pose the question, but less than one might think. No matter what wording a survey uses, virtually every long-term survey archive shows a sharp rise in nones beginning in roughly 1990–92 and heavily concentrated among younger people. For some unknown reason the upturn did not appear in the Gallup Poll surveys until about a decade later, but it is unmistakable there as well.

52. Technically speaking, Hout and Fischer estimate that "more than half" of the recent increase in nones is generationally based and about one third reflect a rise of nones among all generations after 1990. Michael Hout and Claude S. Fischer, "The Politics of Religious Identity in the United States, 1974–2008," Paper Presented at the 2009 Annual Meeting of the American Sociological Association, San Francisco, August 7–11, 2009.

53. The ratio of those who wanted organized religion to have more influence to those who wanted it to have less influence also shifted against religion over this period, from 30:22 in 2001 to 24:34 in 2008, according to http://www.gallup.com/poll/1690/religion.aspx (accessed June 10, 2010).

54. Smith and Snell find that 26 percent of their sample of young adults aged eighteen to twenty-three in 2008 can be classified as "Disengaged" from religion as they attend religious services less than a few times a year and identify themselves as not religious. Christian Smith and Patricia Snell, *Souls in Transition: The Religious and Spiritual Lives of Emerging Adults* (New York: Oxford University Press, 2009).

55. Hout and Fischer, "Why More Americans Have No Religious Preference"; Hout and Fischer, "The Politics of Religious Identity in the United States, 1974–2008"; Barry A. Kosmin and Ariela Keysar, "American Nones: The Profile of the No Religion Population: A Report Based on the American Religious Identification Survey 2008" (Hartford: Trinity College, 2009); Joseph O. Baker and Buster G. Smith, "The Nones: Social Characteristics of the Religiously Unaffiliated," *Social Forces* 87, no. 3 (2009).

56. As we report in the next chapter, our panel survey revealed a high degree of instability among nones. One third of those who disclaim all religious affiliation this year will report some affiliation next year, and their departure will be offset by people who claimed a religious affiliation this year, but next year will report none. At the same time, the other reli-

gious beliefs and behaviors of these switchers change very little between the two years, so they are not really converts. We call them "liminals," since they seem to stand at the edge of some religious tradition, unsure whether to identify with that tradition or not. "Liminal nones" account for much of the anomalous religiosity of nones. Stable nones, that is, people who report in both years that they have no religious affiliation, are, in fact, much less religious in their beliefs and values than liminals, though few of them are self-described atheists or agnostics. Stable nones are more common in younger cohorts, which is consistent with the hypothesis that they (and not the liminals) account for most of the post-1990 rise in nones, though more research will be required to confirm this hypothesis. See Chaeyoon Lim, Carol Ann MacGregor, and Robert D. Putnam, "Secular and Liminal: Discovering Heterogeneity Among Religious Nones," *Journal for the Scientific Study of Religion* 49, no. 4 (2010).

57. Hout and Fischer, "The Politics of Religious Identity in the United States, 1974–2008." *Faith in Flux: Changes in Religious Affiliation in the US* (Pew Forum on Religion & Public Life, April 27, 2009), at http://pewforum.org/docs/?DocID=409 (accessed June 10, 2010). Robert Wuthnow, *After the Baby Boomers: How Twenty- and Thirty-Somethings Are Shaping the Future of American Religion* (Princeton: Princeton University Press, 2007), argues that nearly all the decline in church attendance and the rise in nones among young adults is attributable to delays in marriage. The post-boomer generation has simply postponed religion because its members have postponed marriage. We have carefully analyzed all the available evidence, particularly the General Social Survey, and controlling for marriage and childbearing does not reduce the observed rise in nones.

58. Hout and Fischer, "The Politics of Religious Identity in the United States, 1974–2008." We largely follow the influential Hout-Fischer interpretation of the rise of the nones, except that while they emphasize political ideology as the source of the antireligious backlash, we also consider moral and social beliefs part of the mix.

59. Treas, "How Cohorts, Education, and Ideology Shaped a New Sexual Revolution on American Attitudes Toward Nonmarital Sex, 1972–1998"; Clyde Wilcox and Barbara Norrander, "Of Moods and Morals: The Dynamics of Opinion on Abortion and Gay Rights," in *Understanding Public Opinion*, 2nd ed., ed. Barbara Norrander and Clyde Wilcox (Washington, D.C.: Congressional Quarterly Press, 2002), 121–48.

60. The specific questions used in Figure 4.15 are "marijuana should be legalized" and "it is important to have laws prohibiting homosexual relationships."

61. Our conclusions here are based on a multivariate analysis of religious identification ("none") among GSS (2000–2008) respondents born in the 1980s,

including controls for gender, education, region, marital status, race, and religious background, as well as views on premarital sex, school prayer, homosexuality, marijuana, and abortion.

62. As we explain in Appendix 2, panel surveys like ours, while not providing conclusive evidence of the direction of causation, do offer stronger evidence than mere correlation in a single survey.

63. *Faith in Flux: Changes in Religious Affiliation in the US* (Pew Forum on Religion & Public Life, April 27, 2009) at http://pewforum.org/docs/?DocID=409 (accessed June 10, 2010).

5. SWITCHING, MATCHING, AND MIXING

1. Exodus 3:15. The expression "from generation to generation" appears many times in both the Hebrew Bible and the New Testament in reference to the commandment to pass on religious commitments intergenerationally.

2. "Virtually the same reply" means, for example, "several times a year" and "once or twice a year"; or "every week" and "nearly every week."

3. For purposes of this comparison, we collapsed responses on both questions to a comparable 7-point scale. The stability for most questions on religion in our Faith Matters surveys is higher than for most questions on political and social topics, even for virtually identical questions, such as "How often do you talk about religion [about politics] with family and friends?"

4. Of our Faith Matters respondents who were nones in 2006, but would tell us they were something in 2007, 20 percent told us in 2006 that they had attended church in the previous week. Of those who were somethings in 2006, but nones in 2007, 23 percent told us that they had attended church in the previous week. For consistent somethings, the figure was 52 percent, and for consistent nones, the figure was 5 percent. In other words, regardless of which religious identity the liminal nones claimed at a given moment, they were consistently midway between true somethings and true nones in their religious observance. Their nominal affiliation changed, but their behavior did not. When we asked respondents in 2007 whether they had experienced any change in their religious beliefs or practices in the previous year, only 8 percent of the former nones (now something) said they had become more religious, and of the 2007 nones who had been something in 2006, only 3 percent said they had become less religious.

5. For more on liminality, see Victor Witter Turner and Edith L. B. Turner, *Image and Pilgrimage in Christian Culture: Anthropological Perspectives* (New York: Columbia University Press, 1978). For a more detailed and technical presentation on religious liminals, see Chaeyoon Lim, Carol Ann

MacGregor, and Robert D. Putnam, "Secular and Liminal: Discovering Heterogeneity Among Religious Nones," *Journal for the Scientific Study of Religion* 49, no. 4 (2010).

6. *Many Americans Mix Multiple Faiths* (Pew Forum on Religion & Public Life, December 2009).

7. Other important studies of religious retention and switching include Darren E. Sherkat, "Tracking the Restructuring of American Religion: Religious Affiliation and Patterns of Religious Mobility, 1973–1998," *Social Forces* 79, no. 4 (2001); Scott M. Meyers, "An Interactive Model of Religiosity Inheritance: The Importance of Family Context," *American Sociological Review* 61, no. 5 (1996); C. Kirk Hadaway and Penny Long Marler, "All in the Family: Religious Mobility in America," *Review of Religious Research* 35, no. 2 (1993); Dean R. Hoge, Gregory H. Petrillo, and Ella I. Smith, "Transmission of Religious and Social Values from Parents to Teenage Children," *Journal of Marriage and Family* 44, no. 3 (1982); Claude S. Fischer and Michael Hout, *Century of Difference: How America Changed in the Last One Hundred Years* (New York: Russell Sage Foundation, 2006): 197–202.

8. Three different survey archives give essentially identical results for retention rates in 2006–2008, despite somewhat different operational measures: GSS: 71 percent; Pew: 72 percent; Faith Matters: 73 percent.

9. This is a useful place to note the complexities of measuring retention rates for the children of mixed marriages. In such cases one could make a case for assigning the family to the father's religion, to the mother's religion, to the religion within which the respondent says he or she was raised, or simply leaving such cases out of the analysis. Generally speaking, in mixed marriages mothers are slightly more likely to have a religious affiliation than fathers, and the child's adult affiliation is more likely to match the mother's affiliation than the father's, so we generally use mother's religion as the baseline in the case of mixed marriages. Nevertheless, virtually all our conclusions in this book are robust in the sense that they remain valid however those ambiguities are resolved, although in a few cases our precise numerical conclusions might be slightly different, depending on how we categorized parental religion. Note too that while the General Social Survey asks about the religion within which the respondent was raised, our Faith Matters surveys asked [separately] about the father's and mother's religion. While those two approaches generally coincide, they produce slightly different estimates of retention. There is some slippage between parental religion (even when both parents are in the same religion) and the religion in which one was raised, since some parents decide not to raise their children in their own religion. Finally, we should note that all such questions depend on honest, accurate recall of religious affiliations of some decades earlier. Given the fuzziness even of current reli-

gious affiliations, it is not surprising that recall of parental affiliations is also fuzzy. That said, our 2006–2007 Faith Matters Panel Survey found a reasonably high test-retest reliability of descriptions of parental religion. Nearly 80 percent of parents were assigned to the same religious tradition both times, and the vast majority of exceptions were exactly analogous to the liminals we discovered among our respondents themselves—that is, parents who were described as a "something" in one wave of the panel survey and as a "none" in the other wave. It seems likely these are cases in which the parental affiliation with a given religious tradition was, in fact, genuinely ambiguous. ("If Dad said he was a Catholic, but never went to Mass and hated the church, was he really a Catholic?")

10. As a technical matter, because of how "Black Protestant" is operationally defined in our analyses as described in Chapter 1, any black person who is a Protestant is classified in that category. This step, though practically unavoidable, inevitably underestimates the number of converts among blacks. Another special difficulty is that until very recently the GSS excluded Spanish-speaking respondents. For that reason, in this chapter we often focus specifically on switching and lapsing among whites only.

11. For whites only the figures are roughly 22 percent and roughly 31 percent. Most religious switching occurs before the age of thirty, but to the extent that switching also occurs later in life, these comparisons tend to understate the long-term rise in switching, since the cohorts born late in the twentieth century have had less time to switch than those born earlier.

12. Even the General Social Survey has too few people from other religious traditions to be able to calculate reliable estimates of switching across different birth cohorts. We limit our analysis to white respondents because of the special difficulties in calculating switching rates for blacks, the poor representation of Spanish speakers in the GSS, and the small number of Asian Americans. (Since we, like other researchers, define "Black Protestant" as any African American who is a Protestant, switches among Protestant denominations, however distinct they might be, are ignored in this classification scheme.) For an examination of switching behavior among African Americans, see Darren E. Sherkat, "African-American Religious Affiliation in the Late 20th Century: Cohort Variations and Patterns of Switching, 1973–1998," *Journal for the Scientific Study of Religion* 41, no. 3 (2002). For an examination of switching between Jewish denominations, see Bernard Lazerwitz, "Denominational Retention and Switching Among American Jews," *Journal for the Scientific Study of Religion* 34, no. 4 (1995); and Benjamin T. Phillips and Shaul Kelner, "Reconceptualizing Religious Change: Ethno-Apostasy and Change in Religion Among American Jews," *Sociology of Religion* 67, no. 4 (2006).

13. C. Kirk Hadaway and Wade Clark Roof, "Those Who Stay Religious

'Nones' and Those Who Don't: A Research Note," *Journal for the Scientific Study of Religion* 18, no. 2 (1979).

14. As discussed in Chapter 4, although youth in recent years are delaying marriage and parenthood, two life circumstances typically associated with greater religious observance, that is at best a minor part of the story of the recent rise in nonaffiliation among more recent cohorts.

15. For an excellent case study of this process, see Richard Alba and Robert Orsi, "Passages in Piety: Generational Transitions and the Social and Religious Incorporation of Italian Americans," in *Immigration and Religion in America,* ed. Richard Alba, Albert J. Raboteau, and Josh DeWind (New York: New York University Press, 2009). For a general history of American Catholicism, see Jay P. Dolan, *The American Catholic Experience: A History from Colonial Times to the Present* (Notre Dame: University of Notre Dame Press, 1992).

16. On apostasy among Catholics, see Dean R. Hoge, "Why Catholics Drop Out," in *Falling from the Faith: Causes and Consequences of Religious Apostasy,* ed. David G. Bromley (Newbury Park, CA: Sage, 1988), 81–99.

17. Depending on exactly how parental affiliation is defined in the case of mixed marriages, in our 2006 Faith Matters survey roughly 43 percent of the offspring of "Anglo" Catholic parents no longer identify as Catholics, compared to roughly 22 percent of the offspring of Latino Catholics.

18. For a more in-depth look at mainline Protestants, see Wade Clark Roof and William McKinney, *American Mainline Religion: Its Changing Shape and Future* (New Brunswick: Rutgers University Press, 1987).

19. On religious socialization more generally, see Robert Wuthnow, *Growing Up Religious: Christians and Jews and Their Journeys of Faith* (Boston: Beacon, 1999).

20. Of all respondents in our 2006 Faith Matters survey, two thirds said that as children they had attended Sunday School or other religious education classes "very often," and of them, 24 percent had subsequently left their family's religious tradition, compared to 34 percent of those who said that they had "rarely" or "never" attended religious education classes as children.

21. Meyers, "An Interactive Model of Religiosity Inheritance."

22. Ruth 1:16.

23. Unfortunately, the General Social Survey has not asked about spouse's original religion since 1994, so we are unable to carry this analysis beyond that year.

24. In the 2006 Faith Matters survey the correlation between religiosity and ideological self-placement (on a 5-point liberal–conservative scale) is .29 among nonswitchers and .42 among switchers. The comparable correlations between religiosity and party identification are .12 among non-

switchers and .25 among switchers. In the GSS 1972–2008 survey archive the correlation between church attendance and ideological self-placement is .15 among nonswitchers and .26 among switchers, and the comparable correlations between church attendance and party identification are .04 among nonswitchers and .11 among switchers.

25. This analysis is based on the General Social Survey.

26. This generalization is true whether we measure political ideology by party identification or by views on issues like abortion or gay marriage, and it is true whether we measure religiosity by church attendance, by frequency of prayer, by strength of religious commitment, or by religious identification (e.g., nones vs. evangelicals). Using a much longer panel that is centered on the baby boomers, M. Kent Jennings and Laura Stoker, "Changing Relationships Between Religion and Politics: A Longitudinal, Multigeneration Analysis" (Paper presented at the annual meeting of the International Society of Political Psychology, Portland, Oregon, 2007), find a different result—namely, indirect evidence that religious preferences have causal priority. Further research will be necessary to resolve this discrepancy.

27. As of our 2006 Faith Matters survey, ex-Catholics outnumbered Catholic converts by four to one: the identical estimate emerged from the large survey conducted in 2007 by the Pew Forum on Religion & Public Life, *U.S. Religious Landscape Survey* (2008): 26.

28. R. Laurence Moore, *Selling God: American Religion in the Marketplace of Culture* (New York: Oxford University Press, 1994). Generally speaking, in an industry facing a market in which brand loyalty fell for exogeneous reasons, many economists would predict that firms would increase their marketing activities and seek to differentiate their products in order to appeal to specific niches of the market.

29. For similar estimates of current intermarriage rates, see the Pew Forum on Religion & Public Life, *U.S. Religious Landscape Survey Religious Affiliation: Diverse and Dynamic* (February 2008), pp. 34–35, available at http://religions.pewforum.org/pdf/report-religious-landscape-study-full.pdf (accessed June 10, 2010). This study reports "that 27% of married people are in religiously mixed marriages. If marriages between people of different Protestant denominational families are included, the number of married people in religiously mixed marriages is nearly four-in-ten (37%)." Other important studies of religious intermarriage include Allan L. McCutcheon, "Denominations and Religious Intermarriage: Trends Among White Americans in the Twentieth Century," *Review of Religious Research* 29, no. 3 (1988); Matthijs Kalmijn, "Shifting Boundaries: Trends in Religious and Educational Homogamy," *American Sociological Review* 56, no. 6 (1991); Evelyn L. Lehrer, "Religious Intermarriage in the United

States: Determinants and Trends," *Social Science Research* 27, no. 3 (1998); Darren E. Sherkat, "Religious Intermarriage in the United States: Trends, Patterns, and Predictors," *Social Science Research* 33, no. 4 (2004).

30. Available data of the intermarriage rate in Northern Ireland are slightly inconsistent, but roughly 10 percent seems the most reasonable estimate. See Valerie Morgan et al., *Mixed Marriages in Northern Ireland* (Coleraine: University of Ulster, 1996); Wanda Wigfall-Williams and Gillian Robinson, "A World Apart: Mixed Marriage in Northern Ireland," *Northern Ireland Life and Times Survey Research Update,* No. 8 (2001); and subsequent updates from the Northern Ireland Life and Times Survey.

31. The information on past intermarriage rates is gathered by looking backward through the marital experience of GSS respondents who were actually interviewed in the years after 1972. Marriages that did not survive are thus undercounted, and this fact artificially lowers the apparent intermarriage rate, since divorce is more likely, statistically speaking, in mixed marriages. However, if we restrict our analysis only to respondents who have never been divorced, we find precisely the same long-term trend toward more frequent intermarriage in more recent marriage cohorts. In short, the pattern in Figure 5.4 is unlikely to be attributable to selection bias, though the exact *level* of intermarriage may be slightly underestimated in the historical data. More detailed analysis of these data and of our 2006 Faith Matters survey hints that the increase in intermarriage may have slowed slightly in the last decade or so, but the evidence is still too thin to be sure.

32. Figure 5.4 is calculated on the basis of a version of our standard measure of religious tradition—slightly adapted to fit the available evidence. As Sherkat, "Religious Intermarriage in the United States," notes, our ability to estimate intermarriage rates over the last decade or so is limited because the GSS last asked about spouse's religion of origin in 1994.

33. The only major compositional change over this century was the decline in the fraction of mainline Protestants nationwide, so simply by chance more mainline Protestants would find nonmainline partners. Increasing exogamy among mainline Protestants reflects this pool effect, but that accounts for only part of the total increase in exogamy, as can be seen in Figure 5.9. See also Matthijs Kalmijn, "Intermarriage and Homogamy: Causes, Patterns, Trends," *Annual Review of Sociology* 24 (1998); and Kalmijn, "Shifting Boundaries."

34. Data analyzed from World Values Survey Web site. The fact that any given cohort did not change much between 1982 and 1990 suggests, though it does not prove, that life cycle and period effects were relatively unimportant on this measure of interfaith openness.

35. On religious intermarriage earlier in American history, see Anne C. Rose,

Beloved Strangers: Interfaith Families in Nineteenth-Century America (Cambridge: Harvard University Press, 2001) and Peter J. Thuesen, "Review: Children of the Religious Enlightenment: The Question of Interfaith Marriage in Nineteenth-Century America," *Reviews in American History* 31, no. 1 (2003).

36. Mark Chaves and Shawna L. Anderson, "Continuity and Change in American Religion, 1972–2008," in *Social Trends in the United States, 1972–2008: Evidence from the General Social Survey*, ed. Peter Marsden (Princeton: Princeton University Press, forthcoming). Mark Chaves, *Continuity and Change in American Religion*, Chapter 2 (forthcoming, 2011).

37. Robert Wuthnow, *The Restructuring of American Religion* (Princeton: Princeton University Press, 1988), 97. Because intermarriage was historically slightly higher among better educated groups, part of the growth in intermarriage might be explained statistically by the growth in educational levels during the twentieth century, but education is a small part of the story. Intermarriage has actually increased more rapidly among the less educated, virtually closing the gap with more educated Americans.

38. Peter Michael Blau and Joseph E. Schwartz, *Crosscutting Social Circles: Testing a Macrostructural Theory of Intergroup Relations* (New Brunswick: Transaction, 1997).

39. In Figures 5.7 and 5.8 we distinguish Latino from non-Latino (or "Anglo") Catholics because the ethnic minority status of Latinos has a distinctive effect on both norms and behavior regarding religious intermarriage. Latino Catholics are distinctively less open to intermarriage, probably because the assimilation process of these new immigrants has only just begun.

40. The same patterns appear in both the General Social Survey and our 2006 Faith Matters survey. All this is even truer of nonmarital partnerships— more intermarriage and less convergent conversion. The sample sizes for Mormons and Jews are small (N = 33–35), but the patterns are so distinctive that the results are worth noting.

41. In Figure 5.8, "currently interfaith" means that the spouses are currently in different religious traditions, and "originally interfaith" means that the spouses were originally in different religious traditions. Calculating intermarriage rates is technically complicated, especially since the Faith Matters surveys gathered data only on the respondent's religion of origin, not the spouse's religion of origin. However, since we know the conversion rate of the respondents, we can adjust the figures to take account of conversion by either spouse. The figures for "originally interfaith" are thus estimates, accurate to within 1–2 percent. The difference between the two bars in each pair reflects, roughly speaking, the results of convergent conversion by one or both of the spouses. Note that the pairs of bars are

defined in terms of the parents' religion, not the current religion of the respondent. So, for example, the figure implies that 25 percent of the children of Jews are currently in interfaith marriages, not that 25 percent of Jews today are in interfaith marriages. When the family of origin was itself mixed, we count the mother's religion as the religion of origin, since our work and previous work agree that in such cases the mother's religion is more likely to be inherited.

42. We have confirmed the following generalizations in detailed analysis of the Faith Matters surveys and (where the data are available) the General Social Survey. Generally speaking, the patterns apply *both* to actual intermarriage rates and to attitudes toward intermarriage.

6. INNOVATIONS IN RELIGION

1. We thank Matthew Pehl for introducing us to the chapel car. For more information, see Francis C. Kelley, *The Story of Extension* (Chicago: Extension Press, 1922); Wilma Rugh Taylor, *Gospel Tracks Through Texas: The Mission of the Chapel Car "Good Will"* (College Station: Texas A&M Press, 2005).

2. We thank Nick Carnes for his participant observation of LifeChurch.

3. Alan Wolfe, *The Transformation of American Religion: How We Actually Live Our Faith* (New York: Free Press, 2003), 126.

4. Roger Finke, Avery M. Guest, and Rodney Stark, "Mobilizing Local Religious Markets," *American Sociological Review* 61, no. 1 (1996), 203–18; Roger Finke and Laurence R. Iannaccone, "Supply-Side Explanations for Religious Change," *The ANNALS of the American Academy of Political and Social Science* 527 (1993), 27–39; Roger Finke and Rodney Stark, "Religious Economies and Sacred Canopies: Religious Mobilization in American Cities, 1906," *American Sociological Review* 53, no. 1 (1988), 41–49; Laurence R. Iannaccone, "Introduction to the Economics of Religion," *Journal of Economic Literature* 36, no. 3 (1998), 1465–95; R. Stephen Warner, "Work in Progress Toward a New Paradigm for the Sociological Study of Religion in the United States," *American Journal of Sociology* 98, no. 5 (1993), 1044–93.

5. For more on George Whitefield, see Frank Lambert, "Pedlar in Divinity: George Whitefield and the Great Awakening, 1737–1745," *Journal of American History* 77, no. 3 (1990), 812–37. For more on Dwight Moody, see Bruce J. Evensen, *God's Man for the Gilded Age: D. L. Moody and the Rise of Modern Mass Evangelism* (New York: Oxford University Press, 2003). For more on Billy Graham, see Mark A. Noll, *American Evangelical Christianity: An Introduction* (Malden, MA: Blackwell, 2001).

6. Scott Thumma, Dave Travis, and Leadership Network (Dallas, Texas), *Beyond Megachurch Myths: What We Can Learn from America's Largest Churches*, 1st ed. (San Francisco: Jossey-Bass, 2007).

7. We express our gratitude to Frs. Sean McGraw and Gary S. Chamberland for their assistance in clarifying the reforms of Vatican II.

8. Mark Chaves, *Ordaining Women: Culture and Conflict in Religious Organizations* (Cambridge: Harvard University Press, 1997).

9. Roger Finke, "Innovative Returns to Tradition: Using Core Teachings as the Foundation for Innovative Accommodation," *Journal for the Scientific Study of Religion* 43, no. 1 (2004), 19–34; Lynn Davidman, *Tradition in a Rootless World: Women Turn to Orthodox Judaism* (Berkeley: University of California Press, 1991).

10. Mark Chaves, *Congregations in America* (Cambridge: Harvard University Press, 2004), 155.

11. Although, interestingly, the congregational death rate is very low; see Shawna L. Anderson et al., "Dearly Departed: How Often Do Congregations Close?" *Journal for the Scientific Study of Religion* 47, no. 2 (2008), 321–28.

12. The figure of one quarter undoubtedly understates the full proportion of Americans who have ever shopped for a congregation for a reason other than a move, since it does not include people who have at other times in their life searched for a new congregation for other reasons.

13. Robert Wuthnow, *After Heaven: Spirituality in America Since the 1950s* (Berkeley: University of California Press, 1998).

14. Gerald Gamm, *Urban Exodus: Why the Jews Left Boston and Catholics Stayed* (Cambridge: Harvard University Press, 1999).

15. Robert Wuthnow, *After the Baby Boomers: How Twenty- and Thirty-Somethings Are Shaping the Future of American Religion* (Princeton: Princeton University Press, 2007).

16. Interestingly, that percentage remains essentially the same when we exclude people who moved to a new community (operationalized as moving to a new county).

17. When people who move to a new community are included, this rises to 18 percent.

18. Being married means that someone is roughly 4 percentage points more likely to report switching congregations, while owning a home means a 7 percentage point drop in the likelihood of switching (holding everything else in the model constant at its mean value).

19. In a model that holds all of the other variables constant at their means, we estimate that 15 percent of people who are not at all satisfied with their current congregation switched to a new one, compared to 11 percent of those who are slightly satisfied, 8 percent of those who are moderately satisfied, and 6 percent of those who are very satisfied. *Ceteris paribus,* people with no friends in a congregation are 7 percentage points more likely to switch congregations than someone with more than ten friends.

20. Michael Hout and Claude S. Fischer, "Why More Americans Have No Religious Preference: Politics and Generations," *American Sociological Review* 67, no. 2 (2002), 165–90.

21. The transcript of the event can be found at http://pewforum.org/events/?EventID=221 (accessed December 14, 2009).

22. Peter Steinfels, "In Rejecting a Church's Ad, Two Networks Provide Fodder for a Different Debate," *New York Times,* December 18, 2004.

23. Dan Kimball, *The Emerging Church: Vintage Christianity for New Generations* (Grand Rapids: Zondervan, 2003).

24. Wuthnow, *After the Baby Boomers.*

25. Tim Conder, "The Existing Church/Emerging Church Matrix: Collision, Credibility, Missional Collaboration, and Generative Friendship," in *An Emergent Manifesto of Hope,* ed. Doug Pagitt and Tony Jones (Grand Rapids: Baker, 2007), 97–108.

26. Kimball, *The Emerging Church,* Preface.

7. VIGNETTES: ETHNICITY, GENDER, AND RELIGION

1. For more information on the nuances of LCMS teachings about Closed Communion, see http://www.lcms.org/pages/internal.asp?NavID=422 (accessed June 10, 2010).

2. In the charged debate over abortion, both sides accuse the other of co-opting a misleading label. Because there is no neutral language on this issue, we have opted to use the labels each side has chosen for itself: pro-life (for those who oppose abortion) and pro-choice (for those who support a woman's right to have an abortion).

3. Charles E. Lincoln and Lawrence H. Mamiya, *The Black Church in the African American Experience* (Durham: Duke University Press, 1990), 14.

4. W. E. B. Du Bois, *The Philadelphia Negro* (New York: Lippincott, 1899), 266.

8. THE WOMEN'S REVOLUTION,
THE RISE OF INEQUALITY, AND RELIGION

1. R. Laurence Moore, *Selling God: American Religion in the Marketplace of Culture* (New York: Oxford University Press, 1994), 275.

2. "Bush Tells Group He Sees a 'Third Awakening,'" *Washington Post,* September 13, 2006.

3. We thank participants of the Mindich symposium held to discuss an earlier draft of this book at Harvard University in January 2010 for encouraging us to treat these issues at some length.

4. One minor exception: Jewish women are, on average, slightly less likely to attend religious services than Jewish men, but they are much more likely to pray daily, to say that religion is important in their daily lives, and to be active in their congregation.

5. Our basic conclusions about the adaption of religious Americans to the gender revolution echo the classic work of Sally K. Gallagher and Christian Smith, "Symbolic Traditionalism and Pragmatic Egalitarianism: Contemporary Evangelicals, Families, and Gender," *Gender & Society* 13, no. 2 (1999), 211–33.

6. Sara M. Evans, *Born for Liberty: A History of Women in America* (New York: Free Press, 1989), notes that many poor nonwhites were forced to enter the workforce earlier than whites. On the employment history of nonwhite women, see also Teresa L. Amott and Julie A. Matthaei, *Race, Gender, and Work: A Multi-Cultural Economic History of Women in the United States*, rev. ed. (Boston: South End, 1996), and Francine D. Blau, Marianne A. Ferber, and Anne E. Winkler, *The Economics of Women, Men, and Work*, 5th ed. (Upper Saddle River, NJ: Pearson/Prentice Hall, 2006), 129–31. Data on labor force participation by gender are available from the Bureau of Labor Statistics Current Population Survey, for the information cited here, see http://www.bls.gov/cps/cpsaat2.pdf (accessed June 10, 2010).

7. Barbara F. Reskin and Patricia A. Roos, *Job Queues, Gender Queues: Explaining Women's Inroads into Male Occupations* (Philadelphia: Temple University Press, 1990).

8. White women working full-time, year-round earned 60.5 percent of full-time, year-round men's earnings in 1980 and this rose to 73.9 percent by 2000. Among twenty-five- to thirty-four-year-olds with four years of college, women's wages were 73.9 percent in 1980 and had risen to 83.3 percent by 1995. See Current Population Survey, Outgoing Rotation Groups. See also Claudia Goldin, "A Pollution Theory of Discrimination: Male and Female Differences in Occupations and Earnings," in *National Bureau of Economic Research Working Paper* Series, no. 8985 (2002).

9. Women spend eight more hours a week on average on housework and an extra hour a day on child care. See Suzanne Bianchi and Lynne Casper, "American Families," *Population Bulletin* 55, no. 4 (2000), 1–48; see also Table 9. American Time Use Survey, http://www.bls.gov/news.release/atus.t09.htm (accessed June 10, 2010).

10. For example, women went from 4.9 percent of lawyers in 1970 to 27.6 percent of lawyers in 2003 and from 9.7 percent of physicians and surgeons in 1970 to 29.9 percent in 2003. Blau, Ferber, and Winkler, *The Economics of Women, Men, and Work*, Chapter 5, p. 143. On religious leadership roles for women, see Mark Chaves, Shawna Anderson, and Jason Byasee, "American Congregations at the Beginning of the 21st Century," in *National Congregations Study* (Durham: Duke University, 2009), 5.

11. Claudia Goldin and Lawrence Katz, "The Power of the Pill: Oral Contraceptives and Women's Career and Marriage Decisions," *Journal of Political Economy* 110, no. 4 (2002), 730–70; Blau, Ferber, and Winkler, *The Econom-*

ics of Women, Men, and Work; Evans, *Born for Liberty: A History of Women in America;* Stephanie Coontz, *The Way We Really Are: Coming to Terms with America's Changing Families* (New York: Basic Books, 1997); Stephanie Coontz and Nancy MacLean, "Postwar Women's History: The 'Second Wave' or the End of the Family Wage," in *A Companion to Post-1945 America,* ed. Jean-Christophe Agnew and Roy Rosenzweig (New York: Wiley-Blackwell, 2006).

12. The relevant passage from the Southern Baptist Convention's (1998) *Baptist Faith and Message* reads: "The husband and wife are of equal worth before God, since both are created in God's image. The marriage relationship models the way God relates to His people. A husband is to love his wife as Christ loved the church. He has the God-given responsibility to provide for, to protect, and to lead his family. A wife is to submit herself graciously to the servant leadership of her husband even as the church willingly submits to the headship of Christ. She, being in the image of God as is her husband and thus equal to him, has the God-given responsibility to respect her husband and to serve as his helper in managing the household and nurturing the next generation." See R. Marie Griffith, *God's Daughters: Evangelical Women and the Power of Submission* (Berkeley: University of California Press, 1997); Sally K. Gallagher, *Evangelical Identity and Gendered Family Life* (New Brunswick: Rutgers University Press, 2003); Sally K. Gallagher, "Where Are the Antifeminist Evangelicals?: Evangelical Identity, Subcultural Location, and Attitudes Toward Feminism," *Gender & Society* 18, no. 4 (2004), 451–72; and Susan M. Shaw, "Gracious Submission: Southern Baptist Fundamentalists and Women," *National Women's Studies Association Journal* 20, no. 1 (2008), 51–77.

13. The Our Savior Lutheran vignette hints at the complexities regarding women and feminism in church. Even in this highly traditional church where women are expected to be silent, lack the right to vote, and are described as men's "helpmates," many women congregants work outside the home, some in high-level professional positions, a fact that seems incongruous with their second-class status in church. While some women in OSL are unhappy with their exclusion from church governance, few seem to vote with their feet and leave.

14. The Mormon church does not have a professional clergy, but male lay leaders fill all posts in the congregational and church hierarchy.

15. St. Paul said that women must not exercise authority over men, but must "be silent" (1 Timothy 2:12) and "Wives, submit yourselves unto your own husbands, as unto the Lord. For the husband is the head of the wife, even as Christ is the head of the church: and he is the savior of the body. Therefore as the church is subject unto Christ, so let the wives be to their own husbands in every thing" (Ephesians 5:22–24). See also 1 Peter 3:1–6.

16. All figures in this paragraph are from the General Social Survey. Our comparisons are between women who regularly attend church and those who almost never do.

17. Because the age composition of various religious groups changed substantially during these decades, and because women's participation in the labor force is correlated with age, Figure 8.1 (as well as Figure 8.2) controls for age composition. The estimates for each year are computed by regressing labor force participation on birth cohort and church attendance and the resulting annual estimates are then LOESS-smoothed. Measures of full-time work, part-time work, and labor force participation all tell broadly the same story.

18. Data from the General Social Survey.

19. The wording of the questions in Figure 8.2 is as follows:

> 8.2a: Do you approve or disapprove of a married woman earning money in business or industry if she has a husband capable of supporting her? (Disapprove)
>
> 8.2b: It is much better for everyone involved if the man is the achiever outside the home and the woman takes care of the home and family. (Agree)
>
> 8.2c: It is more important for a wife to help her husband's career than to have one herself. (Agree)
>
> 8.2d: A working mother can establish just as warm and secure a relationship with her children as a mother who does not work. (Disagree)
>
> 8.2e: Women should take care of running their homes and leave running the country up to men. (Agree)
>
> 8.2f: If your party nominated a woman for President, would you vote for her if she were qualified for the job? (No)

20. According to the General Social Survey, in 1977, 11 percent of all American women said that premarital sex was always or almost always wrong, but disagreed that "it is much better for everyone involved if the man is the achiever outside the home and the woman takes care of the home and family." By 2006–2008 that fraction (progressive on gender, but conservative on sex) had increased to 17 percent of all American women, and 43 percent of that group were evangelicals, compared to 24 percent of all women. The fraction of all evangelical women who fell in this category (progressive on gender, conservative on sex) rose steadily from 8 percent in 1977 to 28 percent in 2006–2008.

21. Mark Chaves, *Ordaining Women: Culture and Conflict in Religious Organizations* (Cambridge: Harvard University Press, 1997); see especially pp. 14–37, 182–83.

22. The U.S. Department of Labor reported in 2004 that women made up 13.9

percent of clergy in 2003 as reported in Blau, Ferber, and Winkler, *The Economics of Women, Men, and Work,* 142.

23. Chaves, Anderson, and Byasee, "American Congregations at the Beginning of the 21st Century," 5.

24. The 1986 General Social Survey question was "Do you favor or oppose women as pastors, ministers, priests, or rabbis in your own faith or denomination?" (or for Catholics, [Do you agree or disagree that] "it would be a good thing if women were allowed to be ordained as priests?") Because in that year the GSS was not conducted in Spanish, the results for Latino Catholics are unreliable. The 2006 Faith Matters question was Agree/Disagree: "Women should be allowed to be priests or clergy in my house of worship."

25. We constructed an index of fundamentalist beliefs based on these five issues in the Faith Matters survey in 2006. The top decile of this scale accounts for 27 percent of all evangelical Protestants. In this paragraph we compare the views of that most fundamentalist quarter of all evangelicals with the views of the other three quarters of evangelicals. Our index of fundamentalist beliefs is composed of the following five items; the fundamentalist choice in each case is shown in italics:

   • Which of these statements comes closest to describing your feelings about holy scripture: *Scripture is the actual word of God and is to be taken literally, word for word*; OR Scripture is the inspired word of God but not everything in it should be taken literally, word for word; OR Scripture is an ancient book of fables, legends, history, and moral precepts recorded by men?

   • Do you believe *the world is soon coming to an end*, or not?

   • Some people believe that the path to salvation comes through our actions or deeds and others believe that *the path to salvation lies in our beliefs or faith*. Which comes closer to your views?

   • I'd like to ask your views about how life on earth unfolded. Which of the following statements comes closest to your views on the origin and development of human beings? Human beings have developed over millions of years from less advanced forms of life, but God guided this process; OR Human beings have developed over millions of years from less advanced forms of life, but God had no part in this process OR *God created human beings pretty much in their present form at one time within the last 10,000 years or so.*

   • Which of the following statements comes closest to your views: *One religion is true and others are not* OR There are basic truths in many religions OR There is very little truth in any religion.

26. Claude S. Fischer and Greggor Mattson, "Is America Fragmenting?" *Annual Review of Sociology* 35, no. 1 (2009): 437.

27. Peter Gottschalk and Sheldon Danziger, "Inequality of Wage Rates, Earn-

ings and Family Income in the United States, 1975–2002," *Review of Income and Wealth* 51, no. 2 (2005), 231–54; Thomas Piketty and Emmanuel Saez, "Income Inequality in the United States, 1913–1998," *The Quarterly Journal of Economics* 118, no. 1 (2003), 1–39; Kathryn M. Neckerman and Florencia Torche, "Inequality: Causes and Consequences," *Annual Review of Sociology* 33 (2007), 335–57; Bruce Western, Deirdre Bloome, and Christine Percheski, "Inequality Among American Families with Children, 1975 to 2005," *American Sociological Review* 73, no. 6 (2008), 903–20; and Wojciech Kopczuk, Emmanuel Saez, and Jae Song, "Earnings Inequality and Mobility in the United States: Evidence from Social Security Data Since 1937," *Quarterly Journal of Economics* 125, no. 1 (2010), 91–128.

28. Claudia Goldin and Lawrence Katz, "Decreasing (and Then Increasing) Inequality in America: A Tale of Two Half-Centuries," in *The Causes and Consequences of Increasing Inequality*, ed. Finis Welch (Chicago: University of Chicago Press, 2001), 37–82.

29. Douglas S. Massey et al., "The Geography of Inequality in the United States, 1950–2000 [with Comments]," *Brookings-Wharton Papers on Urban Affairs* (2003): 29. On growing residential segregation by social class, see also Claude S. Fischer et al., "Distinguishing the Geographic Levels and Social Dimensions of U.S. Metropolitan Segregation, 1960–2000," *Demography* 41, no. 1 (2004), 37–59, especially p. 49; Paul A. Jargowsky, "Take the Money and Run: Economic Segregation in U.S. Metropolitan Areas," *American Sociological Review* 61, no. 6 (1996), 984–98; and Paul A. Jargowsky, "The Reconcentration of Poverty," paper presented at the 31st Annual Research Conference of the Association for Public Policy Analysis and Management, Washington, D.C. November 7, 2009.

30. Christine R. Schwartz and Robert D. Mare, "Trends in Educational Assortative Marriage from 1940 to 2003," *Demography* 42, no. 4 (2005), 621–46. See also Matthijs Kalmijn, "Shifting Boundaries: Trends in Religious and Educational Homogamy," *American Sociological Review* 56, no. 6 (1991), 786–800; and Matthijs Kalmijn, "Intermarriage and Homogamy: Causes, Patterns, Trends," *Annual Review of Sociology* 24 (1998), 395–421.

31. Theda Skocpol, *Diminished Democracy: From Membership to Management in American Civic Life* (Norman: University of Oklahoma Press, 2003), Chapters 4 and 5; Michael Kremer and Eric Maskin, "Wage Inequality and Segregation by Skill" in *National Bureau of Economic Research Working Paper Series*, no. 5718 (1996).

32. Gordon S. Wood, "Religion and the American Revolution," in *New Directions in American Religious History*, ed. Harry Stout and D. G. Hart (New York: Oxford University Press, 1997), 173–205. See also Nathan O. Hatch, *The Democratization of American Christianity* (New Haven: Yale University Press, 1989).

33. Hatch, *The Democratization of American Christianity*, p. 14; Timothy Law-
    rence Smith, *Revivalism and Social Reform in Mid-Nineteenth-Century America*
    (New York: Abingdon, 1957), 60, 92; Leigh Eric Schmidt, *Holy Fairs: Scot-
    tish Communions and American Revivals in the Early Modern Period* (Prince-
    ton: Princeton University Press, 1989), 104; William Gerald McLoughlin,
    *Revivals, Awakenings, and Reform: An Essay on Religion and Social Change in
    America, 1607–1977* (Chicago: University of Chicago Press, 1978). For the
    contrary view, of the Second Great Awakening as a movement aimed at
    social control, not social reform, see Paul E. Johnson, *A Shopkeeper's Millen-
    nium: Society and Revivals in Rochester, New York, 1815–1837*, 1st rev. ed. (New
    York: Hill & Wang, 2004).

34. McLoughlin, *Revivals, Awakenings, and Reform*; Robert William Fogel, *The
    Fourth Great Awakening and the Future of Egalitarianism* (Chicago: University
    of Chicago Press, 2000).

35. Herbert G. Gutman, "Protestantism and the American Labor Movement:
    The Christian Spirit in the Gilded Age," *The American Historical Review* 72,
    no. 1 (1966), 74–101; Ken Fones-Wolf, *Trade Union Gospel: Christianity and
    Labor in Industrial Philadelphia, 1865–1915*, American Civilization (Philadel-
    phia: Temple University Press, 1989); Leslie Woodcock Tentler, "Present
    at the Creation: Working-Class Catholics in the United States," in *Amer-
    ican Exceptionalism?: U.S. Working-Class Formation in an International Con-
    text*, ed. Rick Halpern and Jonathan Morris (New York: St. Martin's, 1997),
    134–57.

36. Allen D. Hertzke, "Evangelicals, Populists, and the Great Reversal: Prot-
    estant Civil Society and Economic Concern" (Cambridge: Conference on
    the Politics of Economic Inequality in the Twentieth Century, Kennedy
    School of Government, Harvard University, 1996).

37. Charles Monroe Sheldon, *In His Steps: "What Would Jesus Do?"* rev. ed.
    (New York: H. M. Caldwell, 1899), 11–12.

38. Hertzke, "Evangelicals, Populists, and the Great Reversal," p. 6.

39. Ibid. and David O. Moberg, *The Great Reversal: Evangelism and Social Con-
    cern*, rev. ed. (Philadelphia: Lippincott, 1977).

40. We do not emphasize here a topic of much concern to previous students
    of class and religion, namely, class differences among religious denomina-
    tions and traditions. The earliest work on this topic, H. Richard Niebuhr,
    The Social Sources of Denominationalism (New York: Henry Holt, 1929),
    distinguished between "sects" (especially evangelical Protestants) and
    "churches" (especially mainline Protestants). Members of "sects" were
    lower in class origin than members of "churches." Over time, however,
    denominations (like Catholics, Methodists, and Mormons) tended to move
    upscale, even as upwardly mobile individuals switched to higher-status
    denominations. That linkage between class and denomination became

blurred in the second half of the twentieth century, as religious traditions tended to converge in class terms, and ideological differences became more important than class differences. See Wade Clark Roof and William McKinney, *American Mainline Religion: Its Changing Shape and Future* (New Brunswick: Rutgers University Press, 1987) and Jerry Z. Park and Samuel H. Reimer, "Revisiting the Social Sources of American Christianity, 1972–1998," *Journal for the Scientific Study of Religion* 41, no. 4 (2002), 733–46. Recent work, however, suggests that class rankings among specific denominations remain significant and may have stabilized. See Christian Smith and Robert Faris, "Socioeconomic Inequality in the American Religious System: An Update and Assessment," *Journal for the Scientific Study of Religion* 44, no. 1 (2005), 95–104.

41. Roof and McKinney, *American Mainline Religion*, 115.
42. The same generational pattern toward increasing class bias in church attendance appears in the General Social Survey, the National Educational Studies, and in the Roper Political and Social Trends archive, with either education (relative or absolute) or income as a measure of socioeconomic status, though more clearly with education. Attendance measures differ from archive to archive, but the trends by education are very similar. The growth of the class gap is sharper for men than for women, and if anything, sharper among blacks than among whites and among evangelical Protestants than among other traditions. If all races are analyzed together, this trend is masked, because nonwhites are poorer, less educated, and more religious, but the growing class gap appears in each race, considered separately. See also Park and Reimer, "Revisiting the Social Sources of American Christianity, 1972–1998."
43. For an alternative view on social class and secularization, see Pippa Norris and Ronald Inglehart, *Sacred and Secular: Religion and Politics Worldwide* (New York: Cambridge University Press, 2004). The correlation between religiosity and social class depends in part on whether we measure public and behavioral religiosity (such as church attendance or congregational involvement) or private and psychological religiosity (such as private prayer or the self-described "importance of religion"). Generally speaking, socioeconomic status is positively correlated with public religiosity, but negatively correlated with private religiosity, though in neither case is the relationship very strong. See Philip Schwadel, "Poor Teenager's Religion," *Sociology of Religion* 69, no. 2 (2008): 125–49, and the works cited there.
44. We borrow this image from E. E. Schattschneider, *The Semi-Sovereign People: A Realist's View of Democracy in America* (New York: Holt, Rinehart & Winston, 1960), p. 35.
45. For earlier work on this topic, focused on upward bridging to elected officials, corporation executives, scientists, and the wealthy, see Robert

Wuthnow, "Religious Involvement and Status-Bridging Social Capital," *Journal for the Scientific Study of Religion* 41, no. 4 (2002), 669–84. Wuthnow finds that with comprehensive statistical controls—except for general sociability—upward bridging is more common among members of religious congregations than among other Americans.

46. Evidence that evangelical congregations are more diverse in terms of the income and education of members comes from the National Congregations Study, 1998. Evidence that evangelical congregations have denser social ties among members comes from many surveys, including our 2006 Faith Matters survey. Mark Chaves has suggested to us that the downward class bridging characteristic of evangelicals might also be a remnant of their personal upward social mobility, a plausible hypothesis, but not one we can test with the available evidence.

47. We have confirmed our essential generalizations about cross-class bridging and religiosity in our 2006 Faith Matters survey, the 2000 Social Capital Community Benchmark Survey, and the Panel Study of American Religion and Ethnicity (PS-ARE), 1st Wave (2006), the only three national surveys of which we are aware that measure downward bridging. The patterns are not identical in all three surveys, especially as regards the mechanism that links religiosity with downward bridging, but the basic pattern is found in all three. This replication of our key finding is all the more convincing because the specific measures of bridging differ somewhat from survey to survey. For example, the Faith Matters surveys asked about "a close friend [who is] a manual worker," the Benchmark Survey about "a personal friend [who] has been on welfare" and "a personal friend [who] is a manual worker," and the PS-ARE survey about "talking with someone on welfare." The PS-ARE survey does not include a measure of number of friends in general, so we were unable to control for general sociability in our analysis of those data. For more information about the Panel Study of American Religion and Ethnicity, directed by Michael O. Emerson and David Sikkink, see Michael O. Emerson, David Sikkink, and Adele D. James, "The Panel Study on American Religion and Ethnicity: Background, Methods, and Selected Results," *Journal for the Scientific Study of Religion* 49, no. 1 (2009), 162–71. We are very grateful to Professors Emerson and Sikkink for generously allowing us access to this valuable data archive.

48. Figure 8.6 does not control for party identification, since party choice might well be an effect, rather than a cause, of these policy views. However, even with controls for party, religiosity continues to have a modest but significant impact on the views in Figure 8.6.

The actual survey questions include: (1) Some people say that one of the big problems in this country is that not everyone has an equal chance, whereas others say that the social and economic differences among people in this country are justified. Which comes closer to your views?; (2) Some people think government should take a bigger role in helping the poor, whereas others think individuals and private charities should play a bigger role. Which comes closer to your views?; (3) Would you like to see the federal government spending for aid to poor people increased, decreased, or kept the same?; (4) Some people think that the government in Washington ought to reduce the income differences between the rich and poor, perhaps by raising the taxes of wealthy families or by giving income assistance to the poor. Others think that the government should not concern itself with reducing this income difference between the rich and poor. Which comes closer to your views?

49. Although evangelicals in some contexts are said to have a distinctively individualist approach to public policy, in this case evangelicals are no more likely to favor private charity over public action than mainline Protestants or white Catholics. Compare Christian Smith, *American Evangelicalism: Embattled and Thriving* (Chicago: University of Chicago Press, 1998), Chapter 7.

50. Hertzke, "Evangelicals, Populists, and the Great Reversal," 6.

9. DIVERSITY, ETHNICITY, AND RELIGION

1. For a summary of the Census Bureau's projections, see http://www.census.gov/Press-Release/www/releases/archives/population/012496.html (accessed March 4, 2010).

2. Oscar Handlin, *The Uprooted: The Epic Story of the Great Migrations That Made the American People* (New York: Grosset & Dunlap, 1951), 117. For data on immigration, see 2010 Statistical Abstract: Historical Statistics (Washington, D.C.: U.S. Census Bureau, 2010), http://www.census.gov/compendia/statab/hist_stats.html (accessed June 13, 2010).

3. Martin Marty, "Ethnicity: The Skeleton of Religion in America," *Church History* 41, no. 1 (1972), 5–21.

4. Will Herberg, *Protestant—Catholic—Jew: An Essay in American Religious Sociology* (Garden City: Doubleday, 1955), 40.

5. In the General Social Survey (2006–2008), 30 percent of first-generation immigrants report attending religious services weekly, compared to 25 percent in the second generation, and 32 percent in the third generation. In the Panel Study on American Religion and Ethnicity, 41 percent of the first generation attend services weekly, compared to 30 percent of the second generation, and 41 percent of the third generation. Note that while the overall level of attendance varies between these two studies the intergenerational pattern is identical.

6. See Charles Hirschman, "The Role of Religion in the Origins and Adapta-

tions of Immigrant Groups in the United States," *International Migration Review* 38, no. 3 (2004), 1206–33; Helen Rose Ebaugh and Janet Saltzman Chafetz, *Religion and the New Immigrants: Continuities and Adaptations in Immigrant Congregations* (Walnut Creek, CA: AltaMira, 2000); R. Stephen Warner and Judith G. Wittner, eds., *Gatherings in Diaspora: Religious Communities and the New Immigration* (Philadelphia: Temple University Press, 1998); and Won Moo Hurh and Kwang Chung Kim, *Korean Immigrants in the United States: A Structural Analysis of Ethnic Confinement and Adhesive Adaptation* (Rutherford, NJ: Fairleigh Dickinson University, 1984).

7. We have opted to use "Latino," rather than "Hispanic." For most purposes, the terms are interchangeable.

8. More technically, the proportion of people with Dutch ancestry explains 80 percent of the variance in the percentage of Christian Reform adherents within a county. Explained variance refers to how much of the change, or variance, in something we wish to explain (call it Y) can be attributed to one or more predictors in a statistical model. If the predictors in question had no relationship to Y, then the explained variance would be zero. If they could perfectly predict Y, then the explained variance would be 100 percent.

9. Imagine that all counties were arrayed in a long list, from those with the highest proportion of Lutherans at the top to those with the lowest proportion at the bottom. These maps display the counties as divided into four equal segments: those in the top 25 percent, the next lowest 25 percent, and so forth (i.e., quartiles). Note that the proportion of Lutherans it takes to be in the top 25 percent for the Lutheran map will be different from the proportion of German Americans in the counties at the top of the German American map. In other words, these maps do not indicate the absolute proportion of any group within a county. Instead, they show the distribution of each group around the country.

10. Paul Perl, Jennifer Greely, and Mark M. Gray, "What Proportion of Adult Hispanics Are Catholic? A Review of Survey Data and Methodology," *Journal for the Scientific Study of Religion* 45, no. 3 (2006), 419–36.

11. Interestingly, the percentage of people with Irish heritage in a county has a very weak statistical relationship to the percentage of Catholics.

12. Jay P. Dolan, ed. *The American Catholic Parish: A History from 1850 to the Present*, Volume 1: *Northeast, Southeast, South Central* (Mahwah: Paulist Press, 1987); Jay P. Dolan, ed. *The American Catholic Parish: A History from 1850 to the Present*, Volume 2: *Pacific States, Intermountain West, Midwest* (Mahwah: Paulist Press, 1987).

13. The question specifically asked: "We'd like to know how important various things are to your sense of who you are. When you think about yourself, how important is your [occupation/ethnic or racial background/religion]

to your sense of who you are—very important, moderately important, slightly important, or not at all important?" The ordering of occupation/ethnic or racial background/religion was randomized for each respondent.

14. Note that responses to these two questions could correspond because of "response set," or the habitual response to similar-sounding questions. However, we are reassured that this relationship is not only owing to response set, because strength of racial identity is also related to many other measures of religiosity even when, as shown later in this chapter, we also control for demographic characteristics.

15. Hart M. Nelsen, Raytha L. Yokley, and Anne Kusener Nelsen, *The Black Church in America* (New York: Basic Books, 1971); C. Eric Lincoln and Lawrence H. Mamiya, *The Black Church in the African American Experience* (Durham: Duke University Press, 1990); Andrew Billingsley, *Mighty like a River: The Black Church and Social Reform* (New York: Oxford University Press, 1999).

16. Andrew M. Greeley and Michael Hout, *The Truth About Conservative Christians: What They Think and What They Believe* (Chicago: University of Chicago Press, 2006), 70.

17. Mary E. Patillo-McCoy, *Black Picket Fences: Privilege and Peril Among the Black Middle Class* (Chicago: University of Chicago Press, 1999).

18. Nathan O. Hatch, *The Democratization of American Christianity* (New Haven: Yale University Press, 1989), 103.

19. Michael O. Emerson and Christian Smith, *Divided by Faith: Evangelical Religion and the Problem of Race in America* (Oxford: Oxford University Press, 2000), 26, 34.

20. Gunnar Myrdal, *An American Dilemma: The Negro Problem and Modern Democracy* (New York: Harper & Brothers, 1944), 938, 942.

21. Mary Patillo-McCoy, "Church Culture as a Strategy of Action in the Black Community," *American Sociological Review* 63, no. 6 (1998), 767–84.

22. Seventy-four percent of Black Protestants say that religion is somewhat or very important when they make political decisions, compared to 67 percent of evangelicals and 49 percent of mainline Protestants. (Only Mormons rank near Black Protestants, also at 74 percent.) Thirty-two percent of Black Protestants say that they have participated in social or political action with fellow church members. In this case, mainline Protestants are next, at 25 percent, while only 20 percent of evangelicals say that they have done this.

23. See Allison Calhoun-Brown, "Upon This Rock: The Black Church, Nonviolence, and the Civil Rights Movement," *PS: Political Science & Politics* 33, no. 2 (2000), 168–74; Larry L. Hunt and Janet G. Hunt, "Black Religion as BOTH Opiate and Inspiration of Civil Rights Militance: Putting Marx's Data to the Test," *Social Forces* 56, no. 1 (1977), 1–14; Aldon D. Morris, *The*

Origins of the Civil Rights Movement: Black Communities Organizing for Change (New York: Free Press, 1984); Aldon D. Morris, "The Black Church in the Civil Rights Movement: The SCLC as the Decentralized Radical Arm of the Black Church," in *Disruptive Religion: The Force of Faith in Social Movement Activism*, ed. Christian Smith (New York: Routledge, 1996), 29–46; and Hart M. Nelsen and Anne Kusener Nelsen, *Black Church in the Sixties* (Lexington: University Press of Kentucky, 1975). However, for evidence to the contrary see Gary T. Marx, "Religion: Opiate or Inspiration of Civil Rights Militancy Among Negroes?" *American Sociological Review* 32, no. 1 (1967), 64–72.

24. See John Dollard, *Caste and Class in a Southern Town,* 2nd ed. (New York: Harper, 1949); Myrdal, *An American Dilemma;* Edward Franklin Frazier and C. Eric Lincoln, *The Negro Church in America* (New York: Schocken, 1974); and Ralph J. Bunche, *The Political Status of the Negro in the Age of FDR* (Chicago: University of Chicago Press, 1973).

25. Frederick C. Harris, *Something Within: Religion in African-American Political Activism* (New York: Oxford University Press, 1999), 65.

26. Sandra L. Barnes, "Black Church Culture and Community Action," *Social Forces* 84, no. 2 (2005), 967–94.

27. The 2004 numbers come from the 2006 wave of the Faith Matters survey, while the numbers for 2006 come from the 2007 wave of Faith Matters. The 2008 figures are from the 2008 National Election Study.

28. Greeley and Hout, *The Truth About Conservative Christians,* 70.

29. Two thirds of blacks say that their race or ethnicity is very important to their sense of who they are, as do 43 percent of Latinos. That compares to 26 percent of Asian Americans, and 19 percent of whites.

30. 1.5 percent of Latinos are mainline Protestants.

31. These results are derived from a statistical model that accounts for religious homogeneity among family, friends, and neighbors, age, gender, living in the South, education level, being married, having children at home, and race. All control variables were set to their means.

32. This specific quote comes from a speech King gave at Western Michigan University in 1963, although he said it often. See http://www.wmich.edu/library/archives/mlk/q-a.html (accessed March 6, 2010). Even though this phrase was popularized by Martin Luther King, its provenance is less clear. Michael Emerson, a leading expert on race and religion, writes that "This quip, or some version of it, is said so often that it seems many people have become numb to it. I have never been able to verify who first said it. Some say Martin Luther King; others attribute it to people much before his time": Michael O. Emerson with Rodney M. Woo, *People of the Dream: Multiracial Congregations in the United States* (Princeton: Princeton University Press, 2006), 5.

33. Ibid., 35.
34. Ibid., 85.
35. In examining respondents' reports on their congregational diversity between 2006 and 2007, we discovered that 155 people had reported in 2006 that within their congregation "about a quarter or less" had the same race or ethnicity, but then reported "about three quarters" in 2007. These people had not changed their congregation in the span of the year or less between the two surveys. Since such a rapid demographic change is highly unlikely, we instead assume that they misunderstood the question. Most likely, when they reported "about a quarter or less" share of their same race/ethnicity, they thought we were asking about the proportion with a *different* racial or ethnic background. To correct for this assumed error, we have recoded these people using the less diverse of their two responses. We note that this is a conservative adjustment, since it deflates the percentage of people reporting that theirs is a diverse congregation. When we run our analysis with the unadjusted measure, however, our conclusions do not change.
36. Richard Nadeau, Richard G. Niemi, and Jeffrey Levine, "Innumeracy About Minority Populations," *Public Opinion Quarterly* 57, no. 3 (1993); Lee Sigelman and Richard G. Niemi, "Innumeracy About Minority Populations: African Americans and Whites Compared," *Public Opinion Quarterly* 65, no. 1 (2001).
37. Based on our analysis of the National Congregations Study.
38. Ihsan Bagby, Paul M. Perl, and Bryan T. Froehle, "The Mosque in America: A National Portrait" (Washington, D.C.: Council on American-Islamic Relations, 2001).
39. Based on our discussion above of the distinctiveness of Black Protestants, the reader may wonder about the 13 percent of the people we classify as Black Protestants who do not attend racially homogeneous congregations. If we limit our analysis to Black Protestants who attend a racially homogeneous congregation, the distinctiveness of Black Protestants is even more pronounced.
40. The model includes the entire age range of our respondents (that is, age is modeled as a continuous variable), but we illustrate its impact by comparing someone at age twenty to someone at age seventy.
41. Ethno-racial heterogeneity is measured using an index that reflects the racial categories used by the U.S. Census Bureau. The more evenly distributed the groups, the more diverse the county. Using a measure of diversity at the level of the census tract produces nearly identical results.
42. Our measure of congregation size benefits from the repeated interviews we conducted a year after the original Faith Matters survey. When we look only at people who report that they did not switch congregations

in the preceding year, we find that many people who give extremely high estimates of their congregation's size in one year report a much lower number in the other year. Since the differences cannot be because they changed congregations, and it is extremely unlikely that a congregation would grow or shrink by a factor of 10 or 20 in a single year, the differences are best explained by the fact that many people are bad at estimating large numbers. Accordingly, we cap our measure of congregational size at five thousand, which likely has the effect of slightly diminishing any impact we find for congregational size.

43. Results from a logistic regression model, with attending a diverse congregation (three fourths or less are of the same race or ethnicity as the respondent) as the dependent variable. The increases in probability are derived from the model, holding everything else constant at its mean value.

44. For results that are similar to these (although with a different conceptualization of evangelical congregations), see Joseph Yi, *God and Karate on the South Side: Bridging Differences, Building American Communities* (Lanham, MD: Lexington, 2009).

45. William V. D'Antonio, *Laity, American and Catholic: Transforming the Church* (Kansas City: Sheed & Ward, 1996); Helen Rose Ebaugh, Jennifer O'Brien, and Janet Saltzman Chafetz, "The Social Ecology of Residential Patterns and Membership in Immigrant Churches," *Journal for the Scientific Study of Religion* 39, no. 1 (2000), 107–16; Eugene C. Kennedy, *Tomorrow's Catholics, Yesterday's Church: The Two Cultures of American Catholicism*, 1st ed. (New York: Harper & Row, 1988).

46. Throughout this discussion, we use the term "Anglo" Catholics to refer to Catholics who are not Latinos. This group is predominantly, but not entirely, white. The term should not be confused with the Anglo-Catholic wing of Episcopalianism. Within the Catholic community, it is common to hear "Anglo" as the term to describe non-Latinos.

47. Jay P. Dolan, *The Immigrant Church: New York's Irish and German Catholics, 1815–1865* (Baltimore: Johns Hopkins University Press, 1975); Jay P. Dolan, *In Search of an American Catholicism: A History of Religion and Culture in Tension* (New York: Oxford University Press, 2002).

48. This number includes parishes that used a mix of both English and another language.

49. Joseph J. Casino, "From Sanctuary to Involvement: A History of the Catholic Parish in the Northeast," in *The American Catholic Parish: A History from 1850 to the Present,* vol. 1, ed. Jay P. Dolan (Mahwah: Paulist Press, 1987), 7–116.

50. Dolan, ed. *The American Catholic Parish*, Volume 1 and Volume 2.

51. Edmund M. Dunne, *The Church and the Immigrant*, in *Catholic Builders of the Nation: A Symposium on the Catholic Contribution to the Civilization of the*

United States, Vol. II, ed. C. E. McGuire (Boston: Continental, 1923), 4–7. Note the use of the word "races" to refer to groups that today would be called ethnicities: Poles, Italians, Slovaks, etc.

52. For findings similar to ours (although with much greater detail), see the report by the Pew Research Center: *Changing Faiths: Latinos and the Transformation of American Religion,* http://pewresearch.org/pubs/461/religion-hispanic-latino (accessed December 13, 2009).

53. As mentioned in Chapter 5, roughly one third of Catholics have shopped for a congregation. In that chapter we note that this is relatively high given the geography-based assignment to parishes, but it is still one of the lowest rates of congregation shopping among America's major religious traditions. The only group with a similarly low rate of congregation shopping as Catholics is Mormons, who also use a geography-based system of assigning a place of worship.

54. Michael O. Emerson, "Managing Racial Diversity: A Movement Toward Multiracial Congregations" (paper presented at the New Politics of Religious Communities: Managing Diversity and Inequality, American Sociological Association, August 10, 2009), 10.

55. Mark Chaves, *Continuity and Change in American Religion,* Chapter 6 (forthcoming, 2011).

56. As has been the case throughout our discussion of congregational diversity, we are indebted to the work of Michael Emerson. See Chapter 4 of *People of the Dream* for broadly consistent findings about the correlates of attending a racially diverse congregation.

57. Results derived from a logistic regression model that controls for religious tradition, education, living in an urban and suburban area ("rural" is the omitted category), region of the country, gender, race, age, racial heterogeneity of the respondent's county, and level of congregational involvement. All control variables were set to their means.

58. Deborah L. Hall, David C. Matz, and Wendy Wood, "Why Don't We Practice What We Preach? A Meta-Analytic Review of Religious Racism," *Personality and Social Psychology Review* 14, no. 1 (2010), 126–39. Note that this article is based on a meta-analysis of psychological studies that employ very different measures of religiosity than those employed throughout this book, and so it is difficult to weigh their findings against ours.

59. The reason we report different starting and ending points for these trends is that the General Social Survey has not asked all these questions every year.

60. For others who have found consistent findings, see Victor J. Hinojosa and Lynne M. Jackson, "Religion and the Paradox of Racial Inequality Attitudes," *Journal for the Scientific Study of Religion* 43, no. 2 (2004), 229–38; R. Khari Brown, "Denominational Differences in Support for Race-Based

Policies Among White, Black, Hispanic, and Asian Americans," *Journal for the Scientific Study of Religion* 48, no. 3 (2009), 604–15.

61. *Loving v. Virginia* U.S. 1 (1967).

62. In earlier years, the term "Negroes" was used.

63. Emerson and Smith, *Divided by Faith*.

64. Specifically, the question on educational opportunity in the General Social Survey asks whether African Americans have "worse jobs, income, and housing than white people" because "most African Americans don't have the chance for education that it takes to rise out of poverty."

65. Hatch, *The Democratization of American Christianity*, 106.

66. Paul Lichterman, Prudence L. Carter, and Michele Lamont, "Race-Bridging for Christ? Conservative Christians and Black-White Relations in Community Life," in *Evangelicals and Democracy in America:* Volume 1, *Religion and Society*, ed. Steven Brint and Jean Reith Schroedel (New York: Russell Sage, 2009), 187–220.

10. VIGNETTES: HOW RELIGION AND POLITICS INTERTWINE

1. In this context, a "charismatic" Christian refers to someone who believes that particular spiritual gifts described in the New Testament are present today. Those include speaking in tongues and faith-healing.

2. "Watchdog Group: Church Violated Federal Tax Law," *Star Tribune* (Minneapolis), February 9, 2007; "The Kingdom and the Power of Mac Hammond," *Star Tribune* (Minneapolis), February 11, 2007.

3. Historically, the term "Zionism" has referred to the political movement calling for the reestablishment of the state of Israel, viewed by some Jews as a divinely promised homeland for the "exiled" Jewish people throughout the world. Since the establishment of the state in 1948, the term "Zionism" has come to mean the continued belief in the worldwide "peoplehood" of Jews, the collective desire and responsibility to support the state of Israel as their physical and spiritual homeland.

4. The Church of Jesus Christ of Latter-day Saints. "What Is Family Home Evening?," October 8, 2009, http://www.lds.org/hf/display/0,16783,4224-1,00.html (accessed June 10, 2010).

11. RELIGION IN AMERICAN POLITICS

1. For just a few of many examples of the term "God gap," see Amy Sullivan, "The Origins of the God Gap," *Time*, July 12, 2007; Peter Steinfels, "In Politics, the 'God Gap' Overshadows Other Differences," *New York Times*, December 9, 2006; Dan Gilgoff, "Barna Survey: The God Gap in American Politics Alive and Well," *U.S. News & World Report*, March 31, 2009; and Hanna Rosin, "Closing the God Gap," *The Atlantic*, January/February 2007. For the most up-to-date treatment of the God gap, see Corwin

Smidt et al., *The Disappearing God Gap? Religion in the 2008 Presidential Election* (New York: Oxford University Press, 2010).

2. Throughout this chapter, we use the terms "same-sex marriage" and "gay marriage" interchangeably.

3. The question is worded: "We'd like to ask about various ways in which some people practice religion, whether or not they belong to a particular congregation. The next item is 'Say grace or give blessings to God before meals.' Do you do this several times a day, roughly once a day, a few times a week, roughly once a week, occasionally, occasionally, or never?" Note that the question includes both "grace" (generally, a Christian term) and "give blessings to God before meals," which applies to many faiths. For ease of exposition, we will refer to saying grace.

4. Political independents are those known as "pure" independents, as they do not acknowledge even leaning toward one party or the other.

5. Figures control for age, gender, living in the South, education, marital status, having children, ethnicity (Latino), and race (African American). All control variables have been set to their means. The estimator is ordered logistic regression.

6. By "highly religious" we mean those who score in the top third of our religiosity index.

7. When we look only at "Anglo" Catholics, the percentage of Republicans among the most highly religious is only slightly higher (41.5 percent).

8. It is not possible to replicate our full religiosity index in the General Social Survey, so we use frequency of worship attendance as our measure of religious commitment.

9. Geoffrey Layman, *The Great Divide: Religious and Cultural Conflict in American Party Politics* (New York: Columbia University Press, 2001).

10. Based on our analysis of the 1952 and 2008 National Election Studies.

11. Figures control for education, age, gender, marital status, and living in the South. Results are a three-period moving average of standardized beta coefficients. Party identification is measured using the standard 7-point scale that ranges from Strong Democrat, Weak Democrat, Independent but leaning Democrat, Pure Independent, Independent but leaning Republican, Weak Republican, and Strong Republican. Frequency of church attendance is measured differently in the two studies, and has changed over the course of the National Election Studies. Between 1952 and 1968, the NES church attendance item had the following response options: Never/No religion, Seldom, Often, Regularly. Beginning in 1970, they changed to Never/No religion, Few times per year, Once or twice a month, Almost every week, Every week. Thus, comparisons before and after 1970 should be made cautiously. In the General Social Survey, frequency of church attendance is measured with the following categories: Never, Less than

once a year, Once a year, Several times a year, Once a month, 2–3 times a month, Nearly every week, Every week, More than once a week. This scale has remained the same since 1972. Owing to the distinctive relationship between religiosity and partisanship and African Americans, they have been omitted from the analysis.

12. Ronald C. White, *Lincoln's Greatest Speech: The Second Inaugural* (New York: Simon & Schuster, 2006).

13. For more evidence of a generational replacement explanation for the God gap, see David E. Campbell, "The Young and the Realigning: A Test of the Socialization Theory of Realignment," *Public Opinion Quarterly* 66, no. 2 (2002), 209–34.

14. M. Kent Jennings and Laura Stoker, "Changing Relationships Between Religion and Politics: A Longitudinal, Multi-Generation Analysis" (Paper presented at the annual meeting of the International Society of Political Psychology, July 4–7, 2007), 22.

15. Thomas Frank, *What's the Matter with Kansas? How Conservatives Won the Heart of America* (New York: Metropolitan, 2004).

16. Note that Figure 11.4 does not include African Americans.

17. Some readers may question whether a college education can truly be considered an indication of high socioeconomic status, given rising levels of education in the American population. In results not shown, we have accounted for "education inflation" by constructing a measure of relative educational attainment (years of education divided by the average education in the population in that same year). The results are unchanged from Figure 11.4.

18. Larry M. Bartels, *Unequal Democracy: The Political Economy of the New Gilded Age* (Princeton: Princeton University Press, 2008). Larry M. Bartels, "What's the Matter with *What's the Matter with Kansas?*" *Quarterly Journal of Political Science* 1, no. 2 (2006), 201–26.

19. John W. Kingdon, *Agendas, Alternatives, and Public Policies*, 2nd ed. (New York: HarperCollins, 1995).

20. Figures control for age, gender, living in the South, education, marital status, having children, ethnicity (Latino), and race (African American). All control variables have been set to their means. The estimator is ordered or binary logistic regression, depending on the dependent variable.

21. As indicated in note 8 above, we are unable to replicate our religiosity index in the General Social Survey, so we rely on frequency of religious service attendance as a measure of religiosity. We have no reason to think that these results would be substantively different if we did have the religiosity index over this period of time.

22. For a more thorough discussion of this point, see Morris P. Fiorina, Samuel J. Abrams, and Jeremy C. Pope, *Culture War? The Myth of a Polarized*

America, 2nd ed. (New York: Pearson Longman, 2006). Fiorina and his colleagues deserve full credit for convincingly making this argument.

23. John C. Green, *The Faith Factor: How Religion Influences American Elections* (Westport: Praeger, 2007).

24. The cluster of people and organizations that comprise the movement we are describing is also often called the Christian Right (or, alternatively, the New Christian Right). We believe, however, that Religious Right is a slightly better description, since our focus is on the rising significance of religiosity.

25. Allen Hertzke, *Freeing God's Children: The Unlikely Alliance for Global Human Rights* (Lanham, MD: Rowman & Littlefield, 2004).

26. Layman, *The Great Divide*, 207.

27. Edward G. Carmines and James A. Stimson, *Issue Evolution: Race and the Transformation of American Politics* (Princeton: Princeton University Press, 1989).

28. David C. Leege, et al., *The Politics of Cultural Differences: Social Change and Voter Mobilization Strategies in the Post–New Deal Period* (Princeton: Princeton University Press, 2002), 124.

29. Kristin Luker, *Abortion and the Politics of Motherhood* (Berkeley: University of California Press, 1984), 186, 188.

30. Christina Wolbrecht, *The Politics of Women's Rights: Parties, Positions, and Change* (Princeton: Princeton University Press, 2000), 47.

31. Clyde Wilcox and Barbara Norrander, "Of Moods and Morals: The Dynamics of Opinion on Abortion and Gay Rights," in *Understanding Public Opinion*, 2nd ed., ed. Barbara Norrander and Clyde Wilcox (Washington, D.C.: Congressional Quarterly Press, 2002), 124–48. See also Greg D. Adams, "Abortion: Evidence of an Issue Evolution," *American Journal of Political Science* 41, no. 3 (1997).

32. Mark Oppenheimer, *Knocking on Heaven's Door: American Religion in the Age of Counterculture* (New Haven: Yale University Press, 2003).

33. Figures control for education, age, gender, marital status, and living in the South. African Americans are excluded. Results are standardized beta coefficients, and are smoothed with a three-period moving average.

34. Data from the National Election Studies show a similar trend. However, the National Election Studies changed its abortion question in 1980, so comparisons before and after that date should be made with caution. The parallel trends in the NES and General Social Survey are all the more striking given that they ask different questions about abortion. One cannot attribute the growth in the abortion–party identification connection to an idiosyncrasy of the way a particular abortion item is worded.

35. Fiorina, Abrams, and Pope, *Culture War? The Myth of a Polarized America*, 92.

36. Note that the indicator we use is a question that asks whether the respondent believes that "sexual relations between two adults of the same sex" are always wrong, almost always wrong, wrong only sometimes, or not wrong at all. This is different from, though related to, asking about the legal recognition of same-sex relationships. One could logically believe that homosexual activity is morally wrong, but that homosexual relationships still deserve legal protection, or vice versa.

37. Seventy-one percent of 2006 Faith Matters respondents who say that religion is important for their political decisions also say that abortion is an issue of personal importance to them, compared to 38 percent of people for whom religion plays no role in their political decision making. Fifty-five percent of those for whom religion informs their politics indicate that same-sex marriage is an important issue, compared to 19 percent of those who have no religious influence in their politics. Note that we do not see such a tight connection between using religion when making political decisions and the importance of other issues, like immigration and the Iraq War. While people who say religion is very important to their politics are modestly more likely to say that either the Iraq War or immigration is an important issue, there is no difference between those who say that religion is not important versus somewhat important. And even the difference between those who say religion is not important and those who say it is very important pales in comparison to the size of the differences for abortion and same-sex marriage.

38. Louisiana and Missouri held their referenda during the first round of a run-off and a primary election, respectively.

39. American Enterprise Institute, "The Bush Presidency: Transition and Transformation" (transcript prepared from a tape recording) (available at www.aei.org2001, accessed June 10, 2010).

40. Associated Press, "Kerry Signed Letter Backing Gay Marriage," *USA Today*, February 11, 2004; Robin Toner, "Democrats Join Fray on Marriage," *New York Times*, February 26, 2004.

41. David E. Campbell and J. Quin Monson, "The Case of Bush's Re-Election: Did Gay Marriage Do It?," in *A Matter of Faith: Religion in the 2004 Presidential Election*, ed. David E. Campbell (Washington, D.C.: Brookings Institution Press, 2007), 120–41; David E. Campbell and J. Quin Monson, "The Religion Card: Gay Marriage and the 2004 Election," *Public Opinion Quarterly* 72, no. 3 (2008), 399–419.

42. The images of these direct mail flyers were collected by researchers at Brigham Young University's Center for the Study of Elections and Democ-

racy, in their 2004 Campaign Communications Survey. We are especially grateful to Quin Monson for his assistance with these images.

43. This question is frequently asked by the Pew Forum on Religion & Public Life.

44. Jane J. Mansbridge, *Why We Lost the ERA* (Chicago: University of Chicago Press, 1986).

45. Since 1977, the GSS has also asked included a seventh item on the list: "The woman wants it for any reason." Since this item is not available for every year, we do not include it in our figures. However, adding it (and starting the time series at 1977) makes no difference in our substantive conclusions.

46. Fiorina, Abrams, and Pope, *Culture War? The Myth of a Polarized America.*

47. Clyde Wilcox and Patrick Carry, "The Puzzling Case of the Abortion Attitudes of the Millennial Generation," in *Understanding Public Opinion*, 3rd ed., ed. Barbara Norrander and Clyde Wilcox (Washington, D.C.: Congressional Quarterly Press, 2009), 123–44.

48. Ibid., 6. The one exception is disapproval of extramarital affairs, as young people are slightly more likely to say that extramarital sex is always wrong than other age groups. We speculate that this could be the fallout of rising divorce rates. This is the generation that has seen divorce become increasingly common, and as a reaction is inclined to disapprove of a leading cause of divorce. Or it could be because of a more romanticized notion of marriage among young people.

49. Technically, in 3.6 circumstances.

50. We are indebted to Clyde Wilcox for his insights on the turn against approval of abortion among young people. Many of the ideas discussed in this section came up in conversations with Clyde, and are also found in the chapter he and Patrick Carry have written on the abortion attitudes of the millennial generation. He also deserves credit for coining the term "Juno Generation," which will be discussed later in this chapter.

51. This observation is made by Wilcox and Carry. "In California, Proposition 4 would have amended the state constitution to require parental notification on abortion, although the measure allowed many exceptions. The Millennial Generation voted against this relatively mild abortion measure by nearly two to one and was the most solidly opposed of any cohort. South Dakota Initiative 11 would have banned abortions, except to protect the health and life of the mother and in cases of rape or incest in which the pregnancy was less than twenty weeks. All age groups opposed this more severe restriction, but once again opposition was strongest among those under thirty." Wilcox and Carry, "The Puzzling Case of the Abortion Attitudes of the Millennial Generation," 140–41.

52. Robert Andersen and Tina Fetner, "Cohort Differences in Tolerance of

Homosexuality: Attitudinal Change in Canada and the United States, 1981–2000," *Public Opinion Quarterly* 72, no. 2 (2008), 311–30; Norrander and Wilcox, "Of Moods and Morals."

53. Clyde Wilcox and Carin Larson, *Onward Christian Soldiers? The Religious Right in American Politics*, 3rd ed. (Boulder: Westview, 2006).

54. Amy Sullivan, *The Party Faithful: How and Why Democrats Are Closing the God Gap* (New York: Scribner, 2008).

55. Michael Kazin, *A Godly Hero: The Life of William Jennings Bryan* (New York: Alfred A. Knopf, 2006), 61.

56. Daniel L. Driesbach, "Thomas Jefferson, a Mammoth Cheese, and the 'Wall of Separation Between Church and State,'" in *Religion and the New Republic: Faith in the Founding of America*, ed. James H. Hutson (Lanham, MD: Rowman & Littlefield, 2000), 65–114.

57. E. J. Dionne, *Souled Out: Reclaiming Faith and Politics After the Religious Right* (Princeton: Princeton University Press, 2008).

12. ECHO CHAMBERS: POLITICS WITHIN CONGREGATIONS

1. We use the term "church" as shorthand to refer to all houses of worship.

2. For a detailed discussion of how political information circulates in churches, see Paul Djupe and Christopher Gilbert, *The Political Influence of Churches* (New York: Cambridge University Press, 2009).

3. Sociologist Mark Chaves, for example, has shown that white evangelical Protestant churches specialize in distributing voter guides, black churches are the most likely to conduct voter registration guides, while Catholic parishes organize more demonstrations and marches than other congregations: Mark Chaves, *Congregations in America* (Cambridge: Harvard University Press, 2004). Likewise, there are differences in political activity within the different branches of Protestantism: James L. Guth et al., *The Bully Pulpit: The Politics of Protestant Clergy* (Lawrence: University of Kansas Press, 1997).

4. Clyde Wilcox and Carin Larson, *Onward Christian Soldiers? The Religious Right in American Politics*, 3rd ed. (Boulder: Westview, 2006).

5. Chaves, *Congregations in America*; John C. Green, *The Faith Factor: How Religion Influences American Elections* (Westport: Praeger, 2007); Sidney Verba, Kay Lehman Schlozman, and Henry E. Brady, *Voice and Equality: Civic Voluntarism in American Politics* (Cambridge: Harvard University Press, 1995); Clyde Wilcox and Lee Sigelman, "Political Mobilization in the Pews: Religious Continuity and Electoral Turnout," *Social Science Quarterly* 82, no. 3 (2001), 524–35.

6. Chaves, *Congregations in America*, 95.

7. In 2006, 27 percent reported voter guides/voter registration at church, compared to 27.5 percent in 2007—a statistically insignificant difference.

8. Pew Research Center for the People and the Press, "High Marks for the Campaign, a High Bar for Obama" (Washington, D.C., 2008).

9. Likewise for other forms of congregational activism. Twenty-six percent of very liberal Americans say that their congregation organizes marches and demonstrations, compared to 16 percent of those who are very conservative. Thirty-six percent of the very liberal attend congregations that sponsor voter registration drives or distribute voter guides, while 27 percent of people who are very conservative say the same.

10. Sixty-four percent of those who are "very liberal" and who say that "all or almost all" of their congregation share their political outlook report at least one political activity in church, compared to 46 percent of those who are "very conservative."

11. Corwin E. Smidt, "This World Is Not My Home? Patterns of Clerical Involvement in Politics over Time," in *Pulpit and Politics: Clergy in American Politics at the Advent of the Millennium*, ed. Corwin E. Smidt (Waco: Baylor University Press, 2004), 301–22.

12. Seventy-nine percent of the population has a congregation, 7 percent of whom say they have a "very liberal" ideology—that's a total of 5.5 percent. But only 40 percent of that sliver report hearing monthly political sermons (5.5 x 40 percent = 2.2 percent).

13. Verba, Schlozman, and Brady, *Voice and Equality*; Donald P. Green and Alan S. Gerber, *Get Out the Vote! How to Increase Voter Turnout* (Washington, D.C.: Brookings Institution Press, 2004); Steven J. Rosenstone and John Mark Hansen, *Mobilization, Participation, and Democracy in America* (New York: Macmillan, 1993).

14. The responses were not mutually exclusive of one another, so respondents could choose more than one option.

15. Fellow churchgoers comes in behind co-workers when we limit the analysis to people who are employed.

16. The Pew question asked whether you have ever heard a sermon on each topic, whereas the Faith Matters surveys asked about all sermons on social and political topics, but the results are quite consistent. Among the Pew items, five topics seem inherently political: the situation in Iraq, laws about homosexuality, laws about immigration, the death penalty, and stem cell research. The sixth topic—abortion—is likely to be considered political in nature as well. Twenty-nine percent report never hearing a sermon on those first five topics. When you add abortion to the list, the proportion drops to 22 percent. By comparison, 26 percent of respondents to the 2006 Faith Matters survey say that they never hear sermons on social or political issues (without any specific content mentioned)—right in between 22 and 29 percent.

17. Fifty-six percent of Black Protestants, 50 percent of Jews, and 46 percent of Mormons report having heard a sermon an abortion.

18. Rounding out the other issues: 49 percent of all churchgoers have heard a sermon on the situation in Iraq, 45 percent on the environment, 29 percent on the death penalty, 24 percent on stem cell research, 18 percent on immigration law, and 7 percent on evolution.

19. Fifty-four percent of evangelicals, 44 percent of Catholics, 36 percent of mainline Protestants, and 31 percent of Jews report hearing a sermon on laws pertaining to homosexuals.

20. Specifically, 13 percent of those who say that their political or social views were not important in choosing their current congregation report that all or almost all of their congregation share the same political views. That rises to 35 percent among those who say that political or social views were a very important criterion in selecting the church they attend. When we compare those who say the liturgy or style of worship was unimportant vs. very important, the percentage reporting political homogeneity within their congregation rises from 9 percent to 24 percent.

21. Andrew M. Greeley, *Religious Change in America* (Cambridge: Harvard University Press, 1989).

22. For a small sample of the vast research into the political influence of social networks, see Bernard R. Berelson, Paul Lazarsfeld, and William N. McPhee, *Voting: A Study of Opinion Formation in a Presidential Election* (Chicago: University of Chicago Press, 1954); Robert Huckfeldt, Eric Plutzer, and John Sprague, "Alternative Contexts of Political Behavior: Churches, Neighborhoods, and Individuals," *Journal of Politics* 55, no. 2 (1993), 365–81; Robert Huckfeldt and John Sprague, *Citizens, Politics, and Social Communication: Information and Influence in an Election Campaign* (New York: Cambridge University Press, 1995); David Knoke, *Political Networks: The Structural Perspective* (New York: Cambridge University Press, 1990); Paul F. Lazarsfeld, Bernard Berelson, and Hazel Gaudet, *The People's Choice: How the Voter Makes Up His Mind in a Presidential Campaign*, 2nd ed. (New York: Columbia University Press, 1948); and Robert D. Putnam, "Political Attitudes and the Local Community," *American Political Science Review* 60, no. 3 (September 1966), 640–54.

23. Kenneth D. Wald, Dennis E. Owen, and Samuel S. Hill, "Churches as Political Communities," *American Political Science Review* 82, no. 2 (1988): 541.

24. The measure of religious social networks consists of (a) the number of close friends within one's congregation; (b) the frequency of participation in prayer and other small groups; (c) the frequency of talking about religion with family and friends. These items have been combined in a fac-

tor score. The statistical model on which this statement is based includes whites only, and also controls for ideology.

25. Owing to the distinctive partisanship of African Americans, they are omitted from this analysis.

26. The correlation coefficient for the Religiosity Index and the Religious Social Network Index is 0.67 (significant at the 0.001 level).

27. Note that accepting this statement does not necessarily mean that religious teachings cause people to more fully integrate religion into their lives. The same observation would be made if people selected a religion on the basis of how much it stresses total integration between religion and other domains.

28. For those with a statistical background: This statement is based on a statistical model that includes the standard group of demographic variables, and has an interaction term for "rely on religion for politics" and "religious social networks." The interaction term, which is statistically significant, shows that the two factors work together to move people toward the Republican end of the partisan spectrum (in a model that also includes the main effects for both component terms of the interaction). The dependent variable is a 3-point scale for party identification, with strong, weak, and leaning partisans coded together. The estimator is ordered logistic regression.

29. Diana C. Mutz, *Hearing the Other Side: Deliberative Versus Participatory Democracy* (New York: Cambridge University Press, 2002).

13. RELIGION AND GOOD NEIGHBORLINESS

1. George Washington, "Farewell Address," (1796): http://avalon.law.yale .edu/18th_century/washing.asp (accessed June 16, 2010); Alexis de Tocqueville, trans. Arthur Goldhammer, *Democracy in America* (New York: Library of America, 2004). See especially Volume 2, Part 1, Chapter 5, "How Religion Uses Democratic Instincts in the United States."

2. Blaise Pascal, trans. W. F. Trotter, *Pensées* (Mineola, NY: Dover, 2003), 265; Christopher Hitchens, *God Is Not Great: How Religion Poisons Everything* (New York: Twelve Hachette Book Group, 2007), 15–36.

3. For another extensive analysis of this question that reaches broadly similar conclusions to our own, see Corwin Smidt et al., *Pews, Prayers, and Participation: Religion and Civic Responsibility in America* (Washington, D.C.: Georgetown University Press, 2008).

4. http://www.volunteeringinamerica.gov/national (accessed June 10, 2010). The questions for this estimate are these: "This month, we are interested in volunteer activities, that is, activities for which people are not paid, except perhaps expenses. We only want you to include volunteer activities that you did through or for an organization, even if you only did them

once in a while. Since September 1 of last year, have you done any volunteer activities through or for an organization?" [If no]: "Sometimes people don't think of activities they do infrequently or activities they do for children's schools or youth organizations as volunteer activities. Since September 1 of last year, have you done any of these types of volunteer activities?" Respondents were considered volunteers if they answered "yes" to either of these questions. Such volunteers were then asked about the number and type of organizations for which they volunteered and total hours spent volunteering.

5. In our 2006 Faith Matters survey we asked all respondents, "Some people volunteer, others don't. Did you happen to volunteer in the past 12 months? By volunteering, I mean any unpaid work you've done to help people besides your family and friends or people you work with." If the response was "yes," we asked how often they had volunteered in the last 12 months, and we asked specifically about volunteering for "a religious group or house of worship." Of all respondents who said they had volunteered at all, we asked one half (randomly selected) whether or not they had volunteered for each of the following five types of nonreligious causes: "health care or fighting particular diseases," "school or youth programs," "any organization to help the poor or elderly," "any arts or cultural organizations," and "any neighborhood or civic group." We asked the other half of the sample simply whether or not they had volunteered for "any nonreligious group or organization." We suspect that in our surveys, as in all such surveys, some people are inclined to modestly exaggerate their own generosity, so all the estimates we give may be slightly high. Moreover, the more one probes about different sorts of volunteering, the higher the total estimate. In our case the single-probe version produced an estimate of 37 percent for nonreligious volunteering, but the five-probe version generated an estimate of 47 percent for nonreligious volunteering. Nonetheless, the 2006 Faith Matters estimates are broadly consistent with results from other studies. The comparable figures from the Giving and Volunteering surveys, sponsored in 1988–2001 by the Independent Sector, are 24 percent for religious organizations and 36 percent for nonreligious organizations. Using a single probe, PS-ARE found a rate of 29 percent and the GSS a rate of 46 percent for all types of volunteering combined, whereas the Pew surveys probed for six different types of volunteering, yielding a total volunteering rate of 70 percent. For more information about the Panel Study of American Religion and Ethnicity (PS-ARE) see Michael O. Emerson, David Sikkink, and Adele D. James, "The Panel Study on American Religion and Ethnicity: Background, Methods, and Selected Results," *Journal for the Scientific Study of Religion* 49, no. 1 (2009), 162–71.

6. David E. Campbell and Steven J. Yonish, "Religion and Volunteering in

America," in *Religion as Social Capital: Producing the Common Good,* ed. Corwin Smidt (Waco: Baylor University Press, 2003), 87–106.

7. All religious edge differences are statistically significant at the .01 level or better. Comparable analyses of the Social Capital Community Benchmark Survey (2000) and of the Giving and Volunteering surveys (1988–2001) produce results virtually identical to those in Table 13.1.

8. For further evidence of the link between religiosity and philanthropy, see Roger J. Nemeth and Donald A. Luidens, "The Religious Basis of Charitable Giving in America: A Social Capital Perspective," in *Religion as Social Capital: Producing the Common Good,* ed. Corwin Smidt (Waco: Baylor University Press, 2003), 107–20; Robert Wuthnow and Virginia A. Hodgkinson, *Faith and Philanthropy in America* (San Francisco: Josey Bass, 1990); Mark D. Regnerus, Christian Smith, and David Sikkink, "Who Gives to the Poor? The Influence of Religious Tradition and Political Location on the Personal Generosity of Americans Toward the Poor," *Journal for the Scientific Study of Religion* 37, no. 3 (1999), 481–93; Peter Dobkin Hall, "Religion, Philanthropy and Civic Engagement in Twentieth Century America," in *Gifts of Money and Time: The Role of Charity in America's Communities,* ed. Arthur C. Brooks (Lanham, MD: Rowman & Littlefield, 2005), 159–84; and Mark Wilhelm, Patrick Rooney, and Eugene Tempel, "Changes in Religious Giving Reflect Changes in Involvement: Life-Cycle and Cross-Cohort Evidence on Religious Giving, Secular Giving, and Attendance" (Center on Philanthropy, Indiana University, Bloomington, 2005).

9. All the generalizations that follow are based on extensive analysis of our 2006 Faith Matters national survey. Unless otherwise noted, we have also confirmed them, comprehensively and in detail, by parallel analyses of the Social Capital Community Benchmark Survey (2000), the Giving and Volunteering surveys sponsored by the Independent Sector, 1988–2001, the 2006 Panel Study on American Religion and Ethnicity of Rice University, and the Pew Religion and Public Life surveys, 2001–2007. Replicating our analysis across many different data archives helps to assure that our conclusions do not rest on the methodological peculiarities of any single study, nor on any single measure of religiosity, civic engagement, or generosity.

10. A similar question in the General Social Survey in 2002 and 2004 found a giving rate of 78 percent. Comparable data from the annual Independent Sector Giving and Volunteering surveys, 1988–2001, suggested a slightly lower rate of giving at roughly 70 percent, though the giving rate in those surveys varied substantially from year to year, depending on slight changes in question wording and sequence.

11. The first comparison in this paragraph comes from the Giving and Volunteering 1988–2001 survey archive, the second from the Faith Matters

2006 survey. Results from these two independent sources are virtually identical.

12. Our estimates of the effects of religion on nonreligious giving are designed to be conservative. First, while most religious donations go to purely religious purposes, like clerical salaries and church buildings, about 5 percent of the money put into the offering plate goes to nonreligious causes—aid to the homeless, Third World health care, and the like; see Mark Chaves and Sharon L. Miller, *Financing American Religion* (Walnut Creek, CA: AltaMira Press, 1999). Second, there is some ambiguity about giving to religiously affiliated charities, like Catholic Charities or United Jewish Appeal: Are they religious or nonreligious? To the extent that our respondents report such contributions as "religious," rather than "nonreligious," our discussion here underestimates the role of religious people in supporting nonreligious causes.

13. Figure 13.2 is based on the 2006 Faith Matters survey. Precisely the same pattern appears in the Giving and Volunteering 1988–2001 survey archive. That the same pattern appears in two different survey archives in different periods, using different operational measures of philanthropy and religiosity, strengthens our confidence that the pattern is robust.

14. The logistic regression analysis that underlies our analysis of religiosity and giving holds constant income, financial worry, age, years of education, region (South), marital and parental status, gender, race, and year of survey. The data in the text come from the Giving and Volunteering data archive, but exactly the same pattern appears in the 2006 Faith Matters survey. The odds of a person contributing to a religious institution rise by 6 percent for each additional week they attend church annually, and the odds of their contributing to a secular institution rise 0.6 percent for each additional week they attend church annually.

15. The only sectors for which donations are not associated with church attendance are "environmental" and "public benefit" causes.

16. For evidence of widespread involvement in religious youth groups, see Christian Smith and Melinda Lundquist Denton, *Soul Searching: The Religious and Spiritual Lives of American Teenagers* (New York: Oxford University Press, 2005). For further evidence of the role of religion in international causes, see Robert Wuthnow and Valerie A. Lewis, "Religion and Foreign Policy Altruism: Evidence from a National Survey of Church Members," *Journal for the Scientific Study of Religion* 47, no. 1 (2008), 191–209.

17. These figures from our 2006 Faith Matters survey hold standard demographic factors constant at the sample means. The comparable figures from the Giving and Volunteering surveys are 55 percent and 65 percent.

18. The PS-ARE survey also asked about giving money to close family, to

friends, and to neighbors, and that sort of informal financial help was not significantly enhanced by religiosity, though in the same survey "helping" and "giving advice" to family, friends, and neighbors were positively correlated with religiosity.

19. In the Giving and Volunteering surveys 1988–2001, Catholic giving to religious causes appears to be slightly below that of other denominations, but none of the other religious traditions are significantly distinctive. Examining both the Giving and Volunteering surveys of the 1990s and the Faith Matters survey of 2006, there is some evidence that moderate evangelicals have become more inclined to secular giving over time while continuing to be generous in their religious giving. All of these generalizations about denominational differences are true with standard demographic characteristics held constant. These findings are also largely consistent with Dean R. Hoge et al., "Giving in Five Denominations," in *Financing American Religion,* ed. Mark Chaves and Sharon L. Miller (Walnut Creek, CA: AltaMira Press, 1999), 3–10.

20. The generalizations of this paragraph are drawn from our Faith Matters survey, but are essentially consistent with comparable results from the Giving and Volunteering and PS-ARE surveys. The Giving and Volunteering surveys do, however, suggest that the channeling effect—the tendency of increasing religiosity to concentrate total giving or total volunteering relatively more heavily on religious causes, as total giving or volunteering rises—is greatest among evangelical Protestants, and is nonexistent among Catholics and Black Protestants. Others too have found evidence that evangelicals concentrate on giving and volunteering within their group: Robert Wuthnow, "Mobilizing Civic Engagement: The Changing Impact of Religious Involvement," in *Civic Engagement in American Democracy,* ed. Theda Skocpol and Morris Fiorina (Washington, D.C.: Brookings Institution Press/Russell Sage Foundation, 1999), 331–63; Philip Schwadel, "Individual, Congregational, and Denominational Effects on Church Members' Civic Participation," *Journal for the Scientific Study of Religion* 44, no. 2 (2005), 159–71; Campbell and Yonish, "Religion and Volunteering in America"; Franklyn C. Niles and James Clawson, "Small Group Involvement and Civic Engagement in America" (paper presented at the Annual Meeting of the American Political Science Association, Boston, August 29–September 1, 2002).

21. For statistical mavens, we find in the Faith Matters surveys, the Giving and Volunteering archive, and the PS-ARE data that church attendance is a powerful predictor of both religious and secular giving, that the correlation is stronger for religious than for secular giving, that there are only very modest differences in the intercepts across the religious traditions,

and that there are no significant interaction effects between religious tradition and church attendance in their effect on giving.

22. The linkage between religiosity and helping appears to be a global phenomenon; Gallup finds links on all continents between religiosity, giving, volunteering, and helping strangers. See Brett Pelham and Steve
Crabtree, "Worldwide Highly Religious More Likely to Help Others,"
Gallup, http://www.gallup.com/poll/111013/Worldwide-Highly-Religious
-More-Likely-Help-Others.aspx (accessed June 10, 2010). Social psycholo-
gist Daniel Batson and his colleagues report evidence that religious people
tend to exaggerate their good deeds more than other people. Thus our
estimates of the size of the effect in this chapter may be somewhat exaggerated, but the effects we report are so substantial and pervasive that they
are unlikely to be spurious: C. Daniel Batson, Patricia Schoenrade, and
W. Larry Ventis, *Religion and the Individual: A Social-Psychological Perspective*, rev. ed. (New York: Oxford University Press, 1993), Chapters 9 and 10.

23. We cannot be certain how many of these organizational posts reported
by religious Americans are, in fact, in religious organizations. In addition,
highly religious Americans reported that they had "chaired a meeting or
given a speech" an average of seven times in the previous year, compared
to an average of four times for the most secular Americans. Most of the
leadership activities that religious Americans report took place within religiously affiliated groups, but they are also represented in leadership in secular organizations. A third of the most religious fifth of the population
report having chaired a meeting or given a speech in the previous year,
which testifies to the remarkable role of religious organizations in providing opportunities to learn civic skills. See Sidney Verba, Kay Lehman
Schlozman, and Henry E. Brady, *Voice and Equality: Civic Voluntarism in
American Politics* (Cambridge: Harvard University Press, 1995).

24. Our initial interviews were done at the time of the 2006 demonstrations
on behalf of immigrant rights, a liberal cause, and we suspect our survey picked up the importance of religious organizational infrastructure
for that movement.

25. Independent confirmation for this correlation between religiosity and
civic engagement comes from the General Social Survey, 1972–2008 and
the PS-ARE survey in 2006. In the GSS, controlling for standard predictors of civic engagement, church attendance is a highly significant predictor of frequency of associational membership, frequency of seeing
neighbors, and voting in local and presidential elections. In the PS-ARE
survey, controlling for standard predictors of civic engagement, church
attendance is a highly significant predictor of voting, attending a public
meeting or a political rally, and working for (or giving money to) a party

or candidate, as well as many forms of giving money, advice, and personal help.

26. Figure 13.3 shows the logistic regression between our index of religiosity and various measures of civic engagement, with all control variables held at their mean values; the controls include age, race, education, income, gender, marital and family status, homeownership, years in community, and ideological self-placement. The measures of civic engagement are based on these six questions: (1) "I'm going to read a list of various groups and organizations. Just answer 'yes' if you have been involved in the past twelve months with this kind of group: (a) a hobby, sports, arts, music, or other leisure activity group; (b) a service, social welfare, or fraternal organization; (c) a youth, parent, or school support organization; (d) a professional, trade, farm, or business association; (e) a neighborhood, ethnic, or political association; and/or (f) a support group or self-help program for people with specific illnesses, disabilities, or addictions, or their families." (2) "Have you served as an officer or committee member of any organization in the past 12 months?" (3) "About how many times in the past 12 months have you attended any public meeting?" (4) "Did any of the groups that you are involved with take any local action for social or political reform in the past 12 months?" (5) "Have you worked together with someone or some group to solve a problem in the community where you live in the past 12 months?" (6) "Some people vote in local elections, others don't. Thinking about recent local elections, have you voted in all of them, most of them, some of them, rarely, or never?"

27. Similarly, the religiosity–civic engagement links found in the PS-ARE survey are essentially identical across the various religious traditions, except that mainline Protestants seem more involved in political activities than other religious traditions.

28. Arthur C. Brooks, *Who Cares: The Surprising Truth About Who Is Charitable, Who Isn't and Why It Matters for America* (New York: Basic Books, 2006): "Political conservatives are, on average, more personally charitable than liberals" (p. 11). But that is fundamentally misleading, *even in the very surveys on which Brooks relies.* Statistically speaking, the partial correlation between conservative ideology and various measures of generosity and good citizenship, controlling for religiosity as well as other standard demographic factors, is never significantly positive and sometimes significantly negative. This is true in our Faith Matters surveys, in the PS-ARE survey, and even in the Benchmark 2000 survey used by Brooks himself. We have been unable to find *any* national survey that shows a positive effect of political conservatism on compassion, holding religiosity constant. Brooks clearly understands the necessity of appropriate statistical controls in other contexts, and he concedes in passing (pp. 46–50) that controlling for religion, con-

servatives are *not* more generous, but the book's central claim, as the book jacket says, is that "conservatives really are more compassionate and more generous than liberals."

29. For cross-national evidence from forty countries that religiosity boosts "tax morale," that is, a moral commitment that tax cheating is wrong, see Benno Torgler, "The Importance of Faith: Tax Morale and Religiosity," *Journal of Economic Behavior & Organization* 61, no. 1 (2006), 81–109. The order in which the six ethical issues in the 2006 Faith Matters survey were posed was varied randomly from respondent to respondent, and the results for tax evasion were exactly the same, whether that item happened to be asked first or last. Thus, the responses to that issue seem unaffected by the context of other questions about personal morality.

30. For a more detailed examination of religion and marital and sexual behavior, see Vaughn R. A. Call and Tim B. Heaton, "Religious Influence on Marital Stability," *Journal for the Scientific Study of Religion* 36, no. 3 (1997), 382–92; and Mark Regnerus, *Forbidden Fruit: Sex and Religion in the Lives of American Teenagers* (New York: Oxford University Press, 2007).

31. We combine here people who say "once or twice a year" and those who say "less than once a year," excluding those who say "never."

32. This generalization is based on the 2000 Social Capital Community Benchmark Survey. Controlling for all standard demographic and ideological factors, church attendance is a statistically significant predictor of trust in each of the listed groups—neighbors, shop clerks, "most people," and so forth. This broad pattern is fully confirmed in the 2006 Faith Matters and General Social Survey (1972–2008) archives. In this section, we consider trust and distrust in other people, in neighbors, shop clerks, and the like, but we leave aside trust or distrust specifically about other religious groups. Questions about how much Catholics trust Protestants or how much secular people trust evangelicals, for example, are treated in Chapter 14 as part of our discussion of culture wars and religious cleavages in American society.

33. On measuring altruistic values, see Tom W. Smith, "Altruism in Contemporary America: A Report from the National Altruism Study." GSS Topical Report No. 34 (National Opinion Research Center/University of Chicago: June 2003). http://publicdata.norc.org:41000/gss/DOCUMENTS/REPORTS/TopicalReports/TR.34.pdf (accessed July 14, 2010).

34. All these figures hold other demographic and ideological variables constant at their sample averages.

35. Our General Social Survey analysis was based on the same four questions used in the Faith Matters surveys. The indicators of selfishness we used in the Giving and Volunteering analysis were: Agree/disagree: (1) "We all have the right to concern ourselves with our own goals first and fore-

most, rather than with the problems of other people"; (2) "Most people with serious problems brought these problems on themselves"; (3) "I often become more irritated than sympathetic when I see someone crying"; and (4) "Individuals can do little to alleviate suffering in the world." The only useful measure of altruistic values in the PS-ARE survey was: Agree/disagree: "The most important thing in life is my own happiness."

36. The sequence of questions in Table 13.3 is not the same as in the actual survey. Instead, related questions were scattered throughout the questionnaire to minimize the effect that any single answer might have on related questions. Of course, respondents realized that the broad topic of the interview was religion and civic life, but we sought to minimize contextual effects on specific questions. The questionnaire is available at americangrace.org.

37. Saying grace and frequency of prayer are the only measures on this list that seem to have any linkage at all to good neighborliness, for we find some evidence in our own surveys, in the General Social Survey, and in the PS-ARE survey that (controlling for church attendance) praying frequently is associated with private acts of kindness, though not with participation in organized volunteering or philanthropy or other forms of civic engagement.

38. Our measure of trust here is a factor score index that combines responses to two questions: (1) "Generally speaking, would you say that most people can be trusted or that you can't be too careful in dealing with people?" and (2) "Would you say that most of the time people try to be helpful or that they are mostly just looking out for themselves?" As always, the pattern in Figure 13.6 is true, even with standard demographic controls. It is fully confirmed in both our 2006 Faith Matters survey and in the General Social Survey (1972–2008). For other work in this vein, see Joseph R. Daniels and Marc Van der Ruhr, "Trust in Others: Does Religion Matter?," *Review of Social Economy* (forthcoming).

39. See also Paul Froese and Christopher Bader, *One Nation Under Four Gods: How Our Diverse Views of God Are Shaping America* (New York: Oxford University Press, forthcoming).

40. The entirely empty cells in Figure 13.7 are categories for which we had too few respondents to calculate a reliable index of social trust. In other words, very few Americans said they sometimes experienced God's judgment, but never experienced God's love. People who never feel either God's judgment or God's love are mostly secular in outlook, so their experience of God is largely irrelevant to their social trust; that cell is therefore shown in distinctive shading in Figure 13.7.

41. We have confirmed this generalization independently in the PS-ARE survey, the Giving and Volunteering surveys, and our own Faith Matters sur-

veys. The finding is based on slightly differently worded questions in each case, which only strengthens the finding's persuasiveness, but generally speaking, the surveys ask people how many "friends" or "close friends" they have.

42. Our core finding of the importance of religious social networks is independently confirmed in the PS-ARE survey and the Giving and Volunteering surveys.

43. There have been few studies that look explicitly at religious social networks. For a notable exception see Brian D. McKenzie, "Religious Social Networks, Indirect Mobilization, and African American Political Participation," *Political Research Quarterly* 57, no. 4 (2004), 621–32.

44. We are not the only scholars to note the unusual power of religiously based social networks to foster civic engagement. Robyn L. Driskell, Larry Lyon, and Elizabeth Embry, "Civic Engagement and Religious Activities: Examining the Influence of Religious Tradition and Participation," *Sociological Spectrum* 28, no. 5 (2008), 578–601; Niles and Clawson, "Small Group Involvement and Civic Engagement in America"; Ziad Munson, *The Making of Pro-Life Activists: How Social Movement Mobilization Works* (Chicago: University of Chicago Press, 2008).

45. These conclusions from the Giving and Volunteering surveys are based on extensive multivariate analysis with full controls for background demographic and ideological factors. This analysis suggests that at very high levels of engagement in religious networks (and thus very high levels of total giving and volunteering), the channeling effect (toward religious giving and volunteering) may actually begin to depress nonreligious giving and volunteering, but for the most part religious networks increase the likelihood of nonreligious giving and volunteering.

46. See Appendix 2 for a summary of our panel methodology and what it can and cannot prove.

47. Religious networks seem to be slightly denser in the South, sparser in the Northeast, and sparser among whites.

48. We asked two sets of questions about the religious affiliations of friends: (1) "Thinking about your 5 closest friends, how many of them have the same religious affiliation as you?" and (2) After asking how many "close friends" the respondent had, we asked whether any among them was (a) evangelical Protestant, (b) mainline Protestant, (c) Jewish, Muslim, or some other non-Christian religion, (d) Catholic, and (e) not religious. People with denser religious social networks tended to cite a higher fraction response to the first question, but also to cite friends from a higher number of religions other than their own in response to the second set of questions.

49. For another example of the limitations of religious social capital, see Paul

Lichterman, *Elusive Togetherness: Church Groups Trying to Bridge America's Divisions* (Princeton: Princeton University Press, 2005). Lichterman finds that religious groups tend to be involved in many civic activities, but when interfaith groups try to work together for a good civic cause they lack the ability to bridge religious difference.

50. In our U.S. Faith Matters surveys in both 2006 and 2007, 57 percent of all Americans agreed that "people have a perfect right to give a speech defending Osama bin Laden or al Qaeda," but in a comparable Faith Matters survey in the United Kingdom in 2008, only 32 percent agreed with that statement. In the 2006 U.S. survey, 77 percent disagreed with the view that "a book that most people disapprove of should be kept out of my local public library," compared to 54 percent of British respondents in the 2008 survey.

51. This trend toward greater tolerance is least marked (though still statistically significant) in the case of speeches, teachers, and books that argue that "blacks are genetically inferior," but since racism itself has become so delegitimized over these decades, increasing tolerance toward those who express it is even more striking.

52. Most studies have found that tolerance is higher among better educated people, younger generations, civically involved people, liberals, and less religious people, though obviously there are exceptions. See Samuel Andrew Stouffer, *Communism, Conformity, and Civil Liberties* (Garden City: Doubleday, 1955); Herbert McClosky and Alida Brill-Scheuer, *Dimensions of Tolerance: What Americans Believe About Civil Liberties* (New York: Russell Sage Foundation, 1983); James L. Gibson and Richard D. Bingham, "On the Conceptualization and Measurement of Political Tolerance," *The American Political Science Review* 76, no. 3 (1982), 603–20; James L. Gibson, "Enigmas of Intolerance: Fifty Years After Stouffer's *Communism, Conformity, and Civil Liberties*," *Perspectives on Politics* 4, no. 1 (2006), 21–34; Aubyn S. Fulton, Richard L. Gorsuch, and Elizabeth A. Maynard, "Religious Orientation, Antihomosexual Sentiment, and Fundamentalism Among Christians," *Journal for the Scientific Study of Religion* 38, no. 1 (1999), 14–22; Vyacheslav Karpov, "Religiosity and Tolerance in the United States and Poland," *Journal for the Scientific Study of Religion* 41, no. 2 (2002), 267–88; and Sam Reimer and Jerry Z. Park, "Tolerant (In)Civility? A Longitudinal Analysis of White Conservative Protestants' Willingness to Grant Civil Liberties," *Journal for the Scientific Study of Religion* 40, no. 4 (2001), 735–45.

53. James L. Gibson, "The Political Consequences of Religiosity: Does Religion Always Cause Political Intolerance," in *Religion and Politics in America*, ed. Alan Wolfe and Ira Katznelson (New York and Princeton: Russell Sage and Princeton University Press, forthcoming).

54. Belatedly, we realized that some of our religious respondents were prob-

ably thinking about pornography when responding to our question about unpopular books, which may help explain in part the contrast on that item.

55. The generalizations in this paragraph rest on analyses of both the General Social Survey and our 2006 Faith Matters survey.

56. The two questions were part of a longer list of agree-disagree items, which were presented in random order. Thus, these two were rarely presented back to back.

57. Louis Bolce and Gerald De Maio, "Religious Outlook, Culture War, Politics and Antipathy Toward Christian Fundamentalists," *Public Opinion Quarterly* 63, no. 1 (1999), 29–61; Louis Bolce and Gerald De Maio, "A Prejudice for Thinking Classes: Media Exposure, Political Sophistication, and the Anti-Christian Fundamentalist," *American Politics Research* 36, no. 1 (2008), 155–85. In the 2008 National Election survey, people who said they had no religious affiliation rated "Christians" 64 (more favorable than average) on a 100-point feeling thermometer, but rated "fundamentalist Christians" 43 (less favorable than average). Admittedly, on some "Establishment Clause" constitutional issues, like silent prayer in schools, secularists would be described as "intolerant" by people at the religious end of the spectrum.

58. Reimer and Park, "Tolerant (In)Civility? A Longitudinal Analysis of White Conservative Protestants' Willingness to Grant Civil Liberties," analyzing the same data through 1998, did not find a significant narrowing of the gap between religious and secular Americans. However, cohort succession moves at the same slow, steady pace as life, birth, and death. Thus, the passage of ten years since their research has made the narrowing of the gap more apparent. The gaps in tolerance in Figures 13.11 and 13.12 between those who rarely or never attend church and those who always or almost always attend church narrowed significantly between 1972 and 2008.

59. Reimer and Park, "Tolerant (In)Civility? A Longitudinal Analysis of White Conservative Protestants' Willingness to Grant Civil Liberties," did find in the General Social Survey that even holding church attendance constant, people affiliated with conservative Protestant denominations were even less tolerant than adherents to other religious traditions. On the other hand, in our Faith Matters surveys we can find no evidence that any religious tradition is distinctively more or less tolerant, once we control for religious observance in general.

60. Stephen T. Mockabee, "A Question of Authority: Religion and Cultural Conflict in the 2004 Election," *Political Behavior* 29, no. 2 (2007), 221–48; Kenneth D. Wald, Dennis E. Owen, and Samuel S. Hill, "Habits of the Mind: The Problem of Authority in the New Christian Right," in *Religion and Political Behavior in the United States*, ed. T. G. Jelen (New York: Praeger, 1989), 93–108. These authors make a clear distinction, which we share,

between respect for authority and an "authoritarian personality." "Rather than a defective personality trait, authority-mindedness is understood to be 'an intentionally adopted' worldview that 'self-consciously values authority.'" Mockabee, "A Question of Authority: Religion and Cultural Conflict in the 2004 Election," 225, quoting Dennis E. Owen, Kenneth D. Wald, and Samuel S. Hill, "Authoritarian or Authority-Minded? The Cognitive Commitments of Fundamentalists and the Christian Right," *Religion and American Culture* 1, no. 1 (1991), 73–100.

61. Mockabee, "A Question of Authority," 226.

62. There is a long tradition of asking this question in social research on religiosity. See, for example, W. Bradford Wilcox, "Conservative Protestant Childrearing: Authoritarian or Authoritative?," *American Sociological Review* 63, no. 6 (1998), 796–809; Duane F. Alwin, "Religion and Parental Child-Rearing Orientations: Evidence of a Catholic-Protestant Convergence," *American Journal of Sociology* 92, no. 2 (1986), 412–40; and Gerhard Lenski, *The Religious Factor: A Sociological Study of Religion's Impact on Politics, Economics, and Family Life* (New York: Doubleday, 1961).

63. An emphasis on self-reliance is also predicted by education, liberal political ideology, and race (white), but religiosity remains the most powerful single predictor of this measure, even when other demographic factors are controlled.

64. Mockabee, "A Question of Authority: Religion and Cultural Conflict in the 2004 Election," shows that (controlling for many demographic factors, as well as measures of religious affiliation, religiosity, and fundamentalism) the childrearing measure as a proxy for authority-mindedness predicts attitudes toward gays, feminists, fundamentalists, Muslims, abortion, and the death penalty, as well as political ideology, patriotism, and military strength.

65. Frank M. Andrews and Stephen Bassett Withey, *Social Indicators of Well-Being: Americans' Perceptions of Life Quality* (New York: Plenum, 1976); Ed Diener et al., "Subjective Wellbeing: Three Decades of Progress," *Psychological Bulletin* 125, no. 2 (1999), 276–302; Daniel Kahneman and Alan B. Krueger, "Developments in the Measurement of Subjective Well-Being," *Journal of Economic Perspectives* 20, no. 1 (2006), 3–24. A more technical discussion would need to make subtle distinctions among different species of subjective well-being. In general, self-ratings of "happiness" seem to reflect short-term, situational moods, whereas self-ratings of "life satisfaction" seem to measure longer-term, more stable evaluations, but both produce broadly consistent results.

66. See John F. Helliwell and Robert D. Putnam, "The Social Context of Well-being," *Philosophical Transactions of the Royal Society* 359, no. 1449 (2004), 1435–46; Richard Layard, *Happiness: Lessons from a New Science* (London:

Penguin, 2006); Bruno S. Frey, *Happiness: A Revolution in Economics* (Cambridge: MIT Press, 2008). Roughly half of the observed variation in life satisfaction appears to reflect genetic and personality factors.

67. Christopher G. Ellison, "Religious Involvement and Subjective Well-Being," *Journal of Health and Social Behavior* 32, no. 1 (1991), 80–99; Christopher G. Ellison, David A. Gay, and Thomas A. Glass, "Does Religious Commitment Contribute to Individual Life Satisfaction," *Social Forces* 68, no. 1 (1989), 100–23; Abbott L. Ferriss, "Religion and the Quality of Life," *Journal of Happiness Studies* 3, no. 3 (2002), 199–215.

68. Our measure of life satisfaction asked people how satisfied they were with their lives on a 10-point scale from "extremely satisfied" to "extremely dissatisfied." Numerous studies have shown that responses to this question correspond well with external reports on respondents and with observed behavior: Andrews and Withey, *Social Indicators of Well-Being;* Diener et al., "Subjective Wellbeing; N. Donovan and D. Halpern, "Life Satisfaction: The State of Knowledge and Implications for Government," ed. Strategy Unit of the Cabinet Office (London, 2002); John F. Helliwell, "How's Life? Combining Individual and National Variables to Explain Subjective Well-Being," *National Bureau of Economic Research Working Paper Series,* No. 9065, 2002. Published as John F. Helliwell, "How's Life? Combining Individual and National Variables to Explain Subjective Well-Being," *Economic Modelling* 20, no. 2 (2003), 331–60; Frey, *Happiness;* Kahneman and Krueger, "Developments in the Measurement of Subjective Well-Being." For a detailed presentation of our analysis, see Chaeyoon Lim and Robert D. Putnam, "Religion, Social Networks, and Subjective Well-Being" *American Sociological Review* 75, no. 5 (2010).

14. A HOUSE DIVIDED?

1. James Davison Hunter, *Culture Wars: The Struggle to Define America* (New York: Basic Books, 1991); Robert Wuthnow, *The Restructuring of American Religion* (Princeton: Princeton University Press, 1988).

2. Sam Harris, *The End of Faith: Religion, Terror, and the Future of Reason,* 1st ed. (New York: W. W. Norton, 2004); Christopher Hitchens, *God Is Not Great: How Religion Poisons Everything* (New York: Twelve Hachette Book Group, 2007); Stephen L. Carter, *The Culture of Disbelief: How American Law and Politics Trivialize Religious Devotion* (New York: Basic Books, 1993); Richard John Neuhaus, *The Naked Public Square: Religion and Democracy in America,* 2nd ed. (Grand Rapids: William B. Eerdmans, 1997).

3. Throughout this chapter, we will refer to highly religious and highly secular people. By "highly religious," we mean people who rank in the top decile of the religiosity index discussed in Chapter 1, while "highly secular" means those in the bottom decile. Moderates are in the fifth decile.

4. This is a different comparison than the quintile (top and bottom fifths) that we used in Chapter 1. The reason is that the top and bottom tenths (technically, the top and bottom deciles) are the most distinctive swaths of the population.

5. More technically, those in the second decile of religiosity.

6. The assessment of whether religion has had a positive or negative influence is based on the following two questions: (a) whether respondents thought that the influence of religion on American life was increasing or decreasing, and then (b) whether the trend they identified in (a) is a good or bad thing. People who said that religion's influence is increasing and that is good, or who said that it is decreasing and that is bad, were classified as believing that religion has had a positive influence. The mirror image categories were combined to identify people who believe that religion's influence has been negative.

7. George Lakoff, *Moral Politics: How Liberals and Conservatives Think*, 2nd ed. (Chicago: University of Chicago Press, 2002); Stephen T. Mockabee, "A Question of Authority: Religion and Cultural Conflict in the 2004 Election," *Political Behavior* 29, no. 2 (2007), 221–48; David C. Barker and James D. Tinnick III, "Competing Visions of Parental Roles and Ideological Constraint," *American Political Science Review* 100, no. 2 (2006), 249–63.

8. Jeffrey M. Jones, "Some Americans Reluctant to Vote for Mormon, 72-Year-Old Presidential Candidates: Strong Support for Black, Women, Catholic Candidates" Gallup News Service, http://www.gallup.com/poll, 2007 (accessed March 7, 2010).

9. Some of the leaders in evangelical circles who endorsed Romney include Richard Land of the Southern Baptist Convention; John Willke, founder and past president of the National Right to Life Committee; Paul Weyrich, co-founder of the Moral Majority; Randy Tate, a former head of the Christian Coalition; Robert Wolgemuth, former chairman of the Evangelical Christian Publishers Association; Robert Taylor, a dean at Bob Jones University. And while James Dobson never endorsed Romney, he did offer supportive words on his behalf.

10. The method in question is known as a list experiment. For a full description of this method, and a more detailed treatment of the results, see J. Quin Monson and Scott Riding, "Social Equality Norms for Race, Gender, and Religion in the American Public During the 2008 Presidential Primaries" (paper presented at the Transformative Election of 2008 Conference, Ohio State University, October 1–4, 2009). For other academic studies of voters' reactions to Mormons, see David E. Campbell, J. Quin Monson, and John C. Green, "Framing Faith: How Voters Responded to Candidates' Religions in the 2008 Presidential Campaign" (paper presented at the Annual Meeting of the American Political Science Association, Toronto, Septem-

ber 3–6, 2009); Monika McDermott, "Establishing Mormon Stereotypes and Their Effects on Mitt Romney's 2008 Presidential Run" (paper presented at the annual meeting of the Midwest Political Science Association Meeting, Chicago, April 2–5, 2009); and Brett V. Benson, Jennifer L. Merolla, and John G. Geer, "Two Steps Forward, One Step Back? Bias in the 2008 Presidential Election" (n.d.).

11. Noah Feldman, "What Is It About Mormonism?" *New York Times Magazine*, January 6, 2008.

12. For more on this point, see Benson, Merolla, and Geer, "Two Steps Forward, One Step Back? Bias in the 2008 Presidential Election."

13. In other analyses we have accounted for the fact that different people give either warmer or colder ratings across the board, by adjusting each feeling thermometer score to the overall average of scores given by that person. To accommodate the fact that respondents have different baselines—some cluster all their ratings at the top of the scale, others at the bottom—we have calculated a global average of all the ratings given by each respondent, and then examine whether his or her thermometer score for the group in question exceeds or falls below that global average. In so doing, we account for individual-level differences in thermometer ratings, and can thus keep our eye on the relative scores each respondent gives. With a few exceptions (that are noted) the results using relative warmth are identical to those using the absolute thermometer scores. Since the latter are easier to interpret, that is where we focus our attention.

14. We did not ask people to rate Black Protestants as a group. Figure 14.5 shows Black Protestants' average rating of African Americans.

15. Stephan Thernstrom, *Harvard Encyclopedia of American Ethnic Groups* (Cambridge: Belknap, 1980).

16. When asked about mainline Protestants, respondents were given "Methodists or Lutherans" as examples.

17. The evaluation for Buddhists comes from the 2007 Faith Matters survey because we only asked about Buddhists in 2007. We report the evaluations of the other groups in the 2006 Faith Matters survey, although the results would be substantively identical if we used 2007 instead.

18. The degree to which anti-Catholicism persists in American society is a matter of controversy. Philip Jenkins, *The New Anti-Catholicism: The Last Acceptable Prejudice* (Oxford: Oxford University Press, 2003).

19. The quotation appears in a news release from the Anti-Defamation League, available at http://www.adl.org/PresRele/ASUS_12/5633_12.htm (accessed February 27, 2010). For the entire report, see http://www.adl.org/Anti_semitism/poll_as_2009/default.asp (accessed June 10, 2010).

20. For example, in the 2008 National Election Study "atheists" received an average feeling thermometer score of 41 degrees.

21. Robert Wuthnow, *America and the Challenges of Religious Diversity* (Princeton: Princeton University Press, 2005).

22. For more on how Muslims are perceived in America, and why, see Ozan Kerem Kalkan, Geoffrey C. Layman, and Eric M. Uslaner, "Bands of Others? Attitudes Toward Muslims in Contemporary American Society," *Journal of Politics* 71, no. 3 (2009), 847–62.

23. Respondents were asked to rate "people who are not religious."

24. Defined as having no religious affiliation.

25. The 2006 Faith Matters survey has thirteen self-identified Muslims and twenty-three Buddhists.

26. The single lowest rating among religious groups is the rating evangelicals give to Muslims (41 degrees).

27. There is no way of knowing whether people with no religion report comments on their irreligiosity as negativity toward their "religious" beliefs. It could also be that the nonreligious say that they never receive comments, good or bad, about their nonexistent religious beliefs.

28. Thirteen percent of Mormons say that they often hear disparaging remarks about their religion.

29. Twelve percent of Jews indicate that they "often" hear negative remarks about their religion.

30. Franklin Foer, "Beyond Belief: Howard Dean's Religion Problem," *The New Republic*, December 29, 2003/January 5, 2004/January 12, 2004.

31. See, for example, http://www.cnn.com/2008/POLITICS/09/08/palin.pastor/index.html (accessed December 13, 2009).

32. Samuel G. Freedman, *Jew vs. Jew: The Struggle for the Soul of American Jewry* (New York: Simon & Schuster, 2000); Marci Hamilton, *God vs. the Gavel: Religion and the Rule of Law* (New York: Cambridge University Press, 2005).

33. The Religious Land Use and Institutionalized Persons Act (RLUIPA).

34. To ensure that the order of the questions did not inflate the approval or disapproval of either a Buddhist temple or Christian church, respondents were randomly assigned to be asked about one or the other first.

35. Wendy Cadge, *Heartwood: The First Generation of Theravada Buddhism in America* (Chicago: University of Chicago Press, 2004).

36. Wuthnow, *America and the Challenges of Religious Diversity.*

37. Negligible percentages are okay with a Buddhist temple but not a Christian church (3 percent) or object to both (5 percent).

38. There are also interesting distinctions between the religious traditions, even when we also account for our set of demographic variables and attitudes toward the construction of a Christian church—which controls away any antidevelopment or antireligion sentiment. Compared to mainline Protestants, Black Protestants and evangelicals are less likely to approve

of a Buddhist temple, while Catholics and Jews are slightly more likely. "Other faiths," which include Buddhists, are considerably more likely, as are Mormons (who often face opposition to the construction of their temples). Note that the results for Catholics and Jews are only on the cusp of the conventional standard for statistical significance (p = 0.10 and p = 0.13 respectively).

39. Alan Wolfe, *One Nation, After All: What Middle-Class Americans Really Think About God, Country, Family, Racism, Welfare, Immigration, Homosexuality, Work, the Right, the Left, and Each Other* (New York: Penguin, 1998).

15. AMERICA'S GRACE: HOW A TOLERANT NATION BRIDGES ITS RELIGIOUS DIVIDES

1. These figures are all from the 2006 Faith Matters survey.
2. Robert Bellah, "Civil Religion in America," *Daedalus* 134, no. 4 (2005): 50.
3. Technically, Jefferson was a Democratic-Republican, the forerunner of the modern Democratic Party.
4. Robert Wuthnow, "Religious Diversity in a 'Christian Nation': American Identity and American Democracy," in *Democracy and the New Religious Pluralism*, ed. Thomas Banchoff (New York: Oxford University Press, 2007), 151–70.
5. Vincent Phillip Munoz, *God and the Founders: Madison, Washington, and Jefferson* (New York: Cambridge University Press, 2009).
6. Thomas Jefferson, "Notes on Virginia," in *A Wall of Separation? Debating the Public Role of Religion*, ed. Mary C. Segers and Ted G. Jelen (Lanham, MD: Rowman & Littlefield, 1998), 127.
7. Meaning those in the top decile of religiosity.
8. Peter H. Schuck, *Diversity in America: Keeping Government at a Safe Distance* (Cambridge: Belknap, 2003), 12.
9. Evelyn L. Lehrer, "Religious Intermarriage in the United States: Determinants and Trends," *Social Science Research* 27, no. 3 (1998), 245–63.
10. Of people in the top decile of religiosity, 61 percent say it is very important that their child marry within the faith, while another 21 percent say it is somewhat important.
11. It is reasonable to ask whether estimates of religious heterogeneity within a friendship network are likely to be accurate. The literature on political heterogeneity within social networks suggests that people tend to overestimate the degree of political congruence among their friends: Robert Huckfeldt and John Sprague, *Citizens, Politics, and Social Communication: Information and Influence in an Election Campaign* (New York: Cambridge University Press, 1995). We suspect that religion is a lot like politics, in that neither affiliation is immediately apparent. However, our interest below is in examining what happens when religious diversity within a social net-

work *increases*. As long as the misreporting of religious diversity remains constant between the two waves of the Faith Matters study, it will not affect our interpretation of change. It would be like a bathroom scale that always adds five pounds to your weight. Such a scale would be inaccurate, but could still indicate whether you have gained weight.

12. Tom W. Smith, "Measuring Inter-Racial Friendships," *Social Science Research* 31, no. 4 (2002), 576–93.

13. Andrew M. Greeley, *The Church and the Suburbs* (New York: Sheed & Ward, 1959).

14. For a detailed discussion of social capital, see Robert D. Putnam, *Bowling Alone: The Collapse and Revival of American Community* (New York: Simon & Schuster, 2000).

15. Thomas F. Pettigrew and Linda R. Tropp, "Does Intergroup Contact Reduce Prejudice? Recent Meta-Analytic Findings," in *Reducing Prejudice and Discrimination*, ed. Stuart Oskamp (Mahwah: Lawrence Erlbaum, 2000), 93–114.

16. Thomas F. Pettigrew, "Intergroup Contact Theory," *Annual Review of Psychology* 49 (1998).

17. See Appendix 2 for a detailed discussion of the analysis of panel data.

18. For those interested in the statistical details, the results reported here are from a fixed effects model, which holds constant any time-invariant characteristics for each respondent, and thus only reflects change within each respondent, and not differences between respondents. There is no need to control for demographic variables, since they do not change over the course of the panel. Each model, however, does control for two potentially confounding factors that can change in a year's time. The first is the number of close friends reported by the respondent, to separate the impact of increased religious bridging from a general increase in sociability. The second is the respondent's level of religiosity, to ensure that religious bridging is not confounded with either an upswing or a downturn in intensity of religious commitment.

19. We do not find that there is a statistically significant increase in warmth toward Catholics and mainline Protestants upon adding a Catholic or mainline Protestant friend. In both cases, there is a positive relationship, but we cannot rule out that it is because of chance. Recall, however, that both Catholics and mainline Protestants start out with a relatively high thermometer rating. When using the relative thermometer score, we find a small but statistically significant rise in warmth toward Catholics. However, we also find that greater pre-existing warmth toward Catholics at time 1 predicts gaining a Catholic friend at time 2, which calls the direction of causality into question. Given these complications in interpreting the results for Catho-

lics, it is safest to say that we do not have convincing evidence that gaining a Catholic friend leads to greater warmth toward Catholics.

20. Robert Wuthnow, *America and the Challenges of Religious Diversity* (Princeton: Princeton University Press, 2005), 139.

21. In testing for a spillover effect, we excluded anyone who gained a friend of the group in question. For example, when looking at attitudes toward evangelicals we exclude those people who had gained an evangelical friend, or who became an evangelical themselves. In other words, we are isolating what happens to your attitudes toward group X when you add a friend of group Y. Any results we find cannot be because you are, or became, a member of group X, nor because you became friends with someone in group X.

22. Since we did not ask specifically about whether our respondents are friends with a Mormon, we are unable to tell whether our respondents gained a Mormon friend in the year between the two waves of the survey.

23. Note, however, that the results for Muslims are tentative because we do not find a statistically significant increase in warmth toward Muslims when we employ relative, rather than absolute, thermometer scores. The direction of the relationship is the same, namely positive, but with relative scores we cannot rule out the possibility that the increase was due to chance.

24. We asked this question in both the 2006 and 2007 Faith Matters surveys, and the results are virtually identical. The follow-up question about whether non-Christians can go to heaven, however, was only asked in the 2007 survey. For consistency's sake, we report the results from the 2007 survey in both Figures 15.5 and 15.6.

25. This question was asked in the 2007 follow-up survey.

26. John 14:6.

27. The report can be found at http://pewforum.org/docs/?DocID=380#1 (accessed December 13, 2009).

28. Evangelicals are also unsure about the eternal prospects for Hindus, Buddhists, atheists, and "people with no religious faith"—no more than 35 percent of evangelicals believe that any of these faiths (or the lack thereof) can lead to eternal life. In general, Black Protestants are modestly more likely than evangelicals to believe that these specific groups of non-Christians can achieve eternal life, while mainline Protestants and Catholics are much more likely to believe this.

29. For more on this point, see Darren W. Davis, *Negative Liberty: Public Opinion and the Terrorist Attacks on America* (New York: Russell Sage, 2007), 210–11.

30. Mormons are the most likely to believe that theirs is the one true faith.

Recall from above that they are also the most likely to believe that even people who are not of their faith will go to heaven. This apparent discrepancy can be explained by the distinctive Mormon practice of posthumous baptism. Mormons believe that people can be baptized into the Mormon faith on behalf of their ancestors, thus giving them an opportunity to obtain salvation. Therefore, Mormons believe that theirs is the one true faith while simultaneously believing that people not of their faith can go to heaven (because they can be baptized posthumously).

31. Theodore Caplow, Howard M. Bahr, and Bruce A. Chadwick, "Piety in Middletown," *Society* 18, no. 2 (1981), 34–37.

32. Corwin Smidt, ed., *Pulpit and Politics: Clergy in American Politics at the Advent of the Millennium* (Waco: Baylor University Press, 2004).

33. Only people who in response to an earlier question said that they believe in life after death were asked the question about who goes to heaven (89 percent of the American population). Of those, 1 percent said that they do not believe in heaven or salvation. We asked everyone about whether there is truth in one or many religions, but we also allowed respondents to indicate that "there is very little truth in any religion"—6.7 percent chose that option. Interestingly, this is lower than the percentage that does not claim a religious affiliation for themselves. Responses to these two questions are reasonably, but not perfectly, correlated (r = .30). We use the question about "one true religion" for identifying true believers, rather than the question about heaven, because the former made sense to nearly everyone.

34. Table 15.1 represents only the bivariate relationship between "true believer" and various other traits. In every case, however, that correlation remains strong and highly significant, even with controls for identification with the evangelical Protestant tradition.

35. In *The Churching of America, 1776–1990: Winners and Losers in Our Religious Economy,* (New Brunswick: Rutgers University Press, 1992), Roger Finke and Rodney Stark distinguish between "churches" and "sects" as follows: "Churches are religious bodies in a relatively low state of tension with their environments. Sects are religious bodies in a relatively high state of tension with their environments" (p. 41). See also Laurence R. Iannaccone, "A Formal Model of Church and Sect," *American Journal of Sociology* 94, Supplement (1998), 5241–68.

36. Jay P. Dolan, *In Search of an American Catholicism: A History of Religion and Culture in Tension* (New York: Oxford University Press, 2002); Noah Feldman, *Divided by God: America's Church-State Problem—And What We Should Do About It* (New York: Farrar, Straus & Giroux, 2005).

37. Richard Neitzel Holzapfel and T. Jeffrey Cottle, *Old Mormon Kirtland and Missouri* (Santa Ana, CA: Fieldbrook, 1991).

APPENDIX 1: THE FAITH MATTERS SURVEYS

1. This is according to AAPOR's RR3 formula.
2. http://www.gallup.com/poll/22579/Church-Attendance-Lowest-New-England-Highest-South.aspx (accessed May 19, 2010).
3. The Gallup Poll results are taken from an online article by Gallup, Inc. The article reports only integers, not decimals. See http://www.gallup.com/poll27847/Majority-Republicans-Doubt-Theory-Evolution.aspx (accessed May 19, 2010).

APPENDIX 2: PANEL DATA ANALYSIS

1. Stephen L. Morgan and Christopher Winship, *Counterfactuals and Causal Inference: Methods and Principles for Social Research* (New York: Cambridge University Press, 2007).
2. Paul Allison, "Change Scores as Dependent Variables in Regression Analysis," in *Sociological Methodology 1990*, ed. Clifford Clogg (Oxford: Basil Blackwell, 1990), 93–114; Charles N. Halaby, "Panel Models in Sociological Research: Theory into Practice," *Annual Review of Sociology* 30 (2004), 507–44; Morgan and Winship, *Counterfactuals and Causal Inference.*
3. Morgan and Winship, *Counterfactuals and Causal Inference.*
4. "What CLARIFY Does," available online at http://gking.harvard.edu/clarify/docs/node1.html [accessed May 19, 2010]. See also Gary King, Michael Tomz, and Jason Wittenberg. "Making the Most of Statistical Analyses: Improving Interpretation and Presentation." *American Journal of Political Science* 44, no. 2 (2000), 347–61; Michael Tomz, Jason Wittenberg, and Gary King. CLARIFY: Software for Interpreting and Presenting Statistical Results. Version 2.1. Stanford University, University of Wisconsin, and Harvard University. January 5, 2003. Available at http://gking.harvard.edu.

INDEX

Page numbers in *italics* refer to figures.